What were Hank Aaron's lucky fours?

How many people visited Expo '74?

What is "unconscious racism"?

Where is the black gold rush?

Where are the new cultural centers?

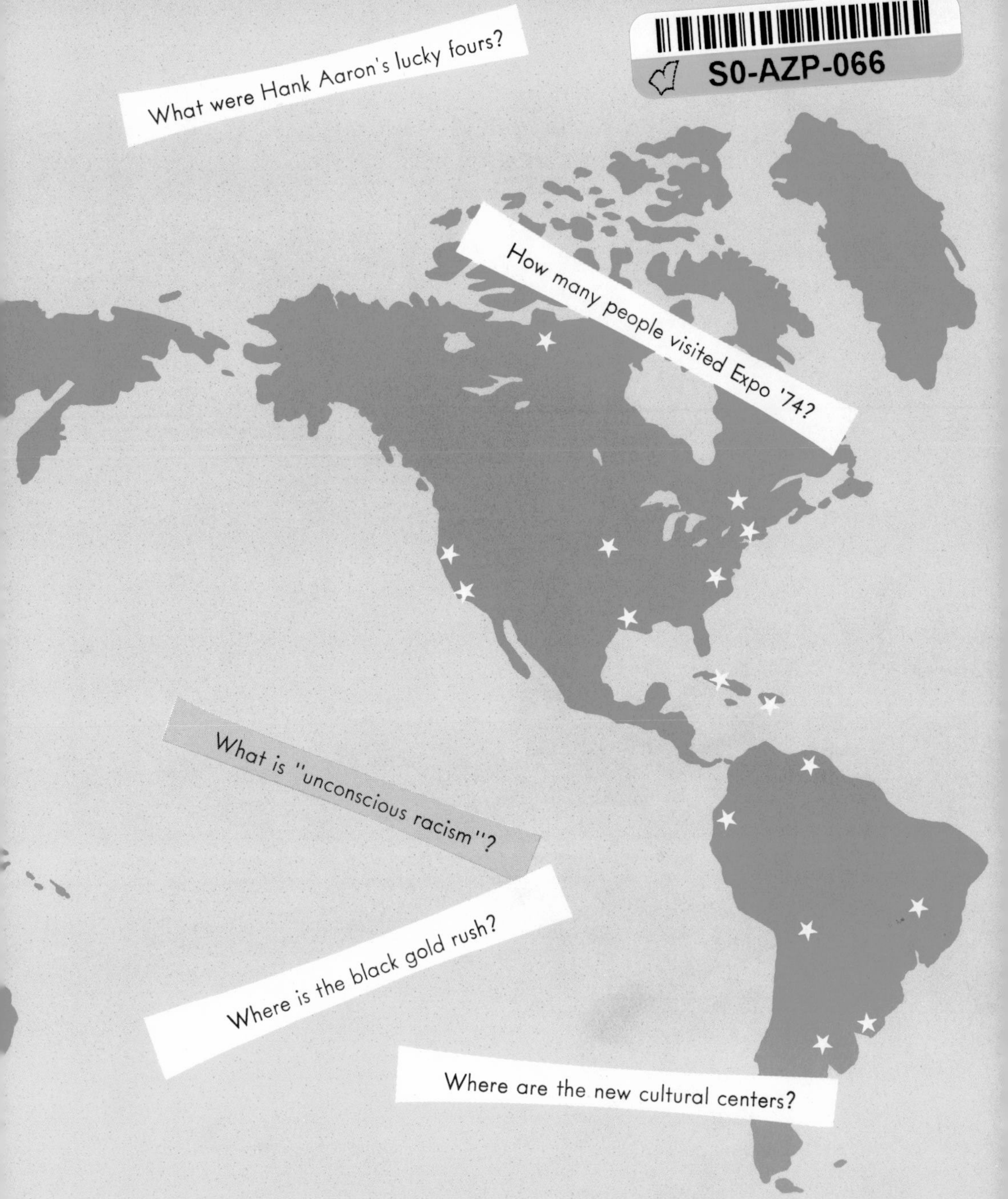

Between the covers of your year book you will find the answers to these and many other questions. You will also discover articles on the events, trends, and personalities of 1974—which taken altogether, made this different from all other years.

1975

WORLD TOPICS YEAR BOOK

Editor in Chief . . . DON LAWSON
B.A., Litt. D., Cornell College

Year Book Editor . . . MARILYN ROBB TRIER
B.A., University of Chicago; Arts Consultant,
Tangley Oaks Educational Center

Production Director . . . CROSBY J. LISKE
Graduate, Art Institute of Chicago

Advised and assisted by the Consultants and
the Editorial and Research Staffs of the
TANGLEY OAKS EDUCATIONAL CENTER

TANGLEY OAKS EDUCATIONAL CENTER • LAKE BLUFF, ILLINOIS

THE AMERICAN FARM, traditionally a basis of the country's strength, is becoming the bread basket of the world. In 1974 the United States was the world's major exporter not only of wheat and feed grains, but of rice as well, controlling a larger share of the earth's exportable supplies of grain than the Middle East controlled of world oil exports. On this Wisconsin farm Holsteins graze in a pasture surrounded by fields of corn and oats and stacks of hay.

1975 WORLD TOPICS YEAR BOOK

The Board of Educators

Tangley Oaks Educational Center, Lake Bluff, Illinois, U.S.A.

Library of Congress Catalog Card Number: 56-31513
International Standard Book Number 0-87566-011-8

Made in the United States of America

Foreword

Year of Reckoning

The year of the first double-digit inflation in peacetime, the year of Watergate reckoning, the year of the first presidential resignation in American history, was also a campaign year. Two concerns dominated the election, anxiety about the economy and political morality.

There was an upheaval of resentment against the lawlessness of the Nixon White House. The Watergate scandal gave rise to what analysts called the "politics of full disclosure" and the "politics of character."

There was an upheaval of resentment against extreme disorder in the economy — inflation, unemployment, rising taxes — and against those who were blamed for bringing this disorder to pass.

The voters imposed the predicted penalty on the Republican party, and it remained to be seen whether the 94th Congress with its Democratic majority could, in the words of Senate Democratic leader Mike Mansfield, "get together and work cooperatively" with Republican President Gerald Ford.

Your Key to History

Your year book presents the complex march of history at your fingertips. With its thorough index you can find the information you are seeking in a moment. Its numerous photographs tell the story of the year in a way that words cannot equal. Each illustration is indexed so that you can find it easily.

The Calendar of the Year

The *Calendar* which appears at the front of each year book records each day's headline events. In the articles that constitute the main portion of the book these events are woven into perspective, insofar as this is possible so close to the events. Some of the subjects treated demand a longer view. For them we must go back into the recent past to trace the development of the forces at work, with the aim of presenting a balanced view. Refer also to your encyclopedia for useful background information on the year's developments.

Your Family History

Just as you turn to your year book to learn what the world was doing, you consult it also to recall what your family did in the past year. Too often we forget family events. We believe that your family is entitled to its own historical record, compiled year by year. A special section of the year book is set aside as a record of *Our Family's History for the Year*.

The Publishers

Calendar of 1974 Events

JANUARY						
S	M	T	W	T	F	S
		1	2	3	4	5
6	7	8	9	10	11	12
13	14	15	16	17	18	19
20	21	22	23	24	25	26
27	28	29	30	31		

6. The United States returned to daylight saving time in an effort to reduce winter consumption of fuel.

11. Japan announced a mandatory energy saving program requiring industry to reduce its use of fuel by 5 to 15 percent.

12. Pres. Habib Bourguiba of Tunisia and Colonel Muammar el Qaddafi of Libya agreed on union of their countries.

13. The Miami Dolphins defeated the Minnesota Vikings in the Super Bowl.

17. Israel and Egypt reached

FARM CHILDREN lead an ecologically better life than their city cousins. The life-style of farming plus the world food shortage, U.S. farm productivity, and the likelihood of continued high grain and produce prices were luring Americans into agriculture in 1974. The U.S. Census Bureau reported that more people were migrating back to farms than left and that percentagewise there were more young people working farms than during the 1950s.

an agreement on the separation of their military forces along the Suez Canal.

19. France set the franc free for a period of six months, breaking the Common Market monetary agreement.

21. The Ninety-second Congress began its second session.

FEBRUARY

S	M	T	W	T	F	S
					1	2
3	4	5	6	7	8	9
10	11	12	13	14	15	16
17	18	19	20	21	22	23
24	25	26	27	28		

4. British coal miners voted to strike by an 81 percent margin.

Pres. Nixon sent Congress his $304.4 billion budget for the 1974-75 fiscal year.

5. Pope Paul VI sent eighty-one-year-old Jozsef Cardinal Mindszenty of Hungary, now in exile in Austria, into retirement.

Patricia Hearst, a granddaughter of William Randolph Hearst, was abducted in Berkeley, Calif.

7. Prime Minister Edward Heath of Great Britain dissolved Parliament and called a general election for February 28.

The Symbionese Liberation Army announced it was responsible for the kidnapping of Patricia Hearst.

8. The three Skylab astronauts returned to earth after eighty-four days in orbit, the longest manned space flight to date.

9. British coal miners went on strike.

11. A thirteen-nation energy conference opened in Washington, D.C.

12. Aleksandr Solzhenitsyn, the dissident Soviet writer, was arrested in his Moscow apartment by a team of Soviet police agents.

The Symbionese Liberation Army in Berkeley, Calif., asked Randolph Hearst, the newspaper executive, for more than $230 million in free food for the poor in return for the release of his kidnapped daughter, Patricia.

13. The U.S.S.R. stripped Aleksandr Solzhenitsyn of his Soviet citizenship and exiled him to West Germany.

17. A soldier landed a stolen Army helicopter on the south lawn of the White House and was immediately captured.

The U.S. Treasury announced Secret Service agents would no longer protect former Vice-President Spiro Agnew.

19. William Simon, federal energy administrator, ordered emergency allocations of 84 million gallons of gasoline to twenty states.

The Senate Watergate committee decided not to hold further public hearings.

A Democrat, Richard Vanderveen, won Vice-President Gerald Ford's vacated congressional seat in Michigan.

20. Foreign Ministers from twenty-four American and Caribbean nations met in Mexico City.

The last Israeli soldiers evacuated Egyptian territory on the west bank of the Suez Canal seized during the October War, meeting the deadline set by the disengagement treaty.

Kidnappers abducted J. Reginald Murphy, editor of the *Atlanta* (Ga.) *Constitution.*

22. Pakistan recognized Bangladesh in a sudden move preceding the opening in Lahore of a major conference of Moslem nations.

The Atlanta Constitution announced that $700,000 in ransom money had been delivered to the "American Revolutionary Army" that kidnapped J. Reginald Murphy, the paper's editorial writer.

The Hearst Corporation offered to contribute another $4 million in free food for the needy if the Symbionese Liberation Army releases Patricia Hearst unharmed.

23. Police in Atlanta, Ga., recovered almost $700,000 in ransom after arresting and charging an ex-convict and his wife with the kidnapping of J. Reginald Murphy who was released February 22.

Federal energy chief William Simon announced a two cents per gallon increase

THE U.S. CORN CROP was cut by drought and early frosts to an estimated 16 percent below 1973 production. Although supplies of good quality corn and other grains were expected to meet domestic and commercial export needs, grain reductions curtailed U.S. food aid to a hungry world.

in the price of gasoline sold by independent retail dealers, effective March 1.

25. Herbert Kalmbach, Pres. Nixon's personal lawyer, pleaded guilty to allegations he had promised an ambassador a better assignment for a $100,000 campaign contribution.

27. Lieutenant William Calley, Jr., was released on $1,000 bond pending an appeal of his conviction for murdering twenty-two Vietnamese civilians at My Lai.

28. The British voted to choose 635 members of the House of Commons.

MARCH						
S	M	T	W	T	F	S
					1	2
3	4	5	6	7	8	9
10	11	12	13	14	15	16
17	18	19	20	21	22	23
24/31	25	26	27	28	29	30

1. A federal grand jury indicted seven former members of Pres. Nixon's administration or of his 1972 reelection campaign on charges of covering up the Watergate scandal.

3. A Turkish jumbo jet crashed after take-off from Paris, killing all 344 persons aboard in the worst air disaster in history.

4. Harold Wilson, Labor party leader, became British prime minister, the first in forty-five years whose cabinet lacked a majority in the House of Commons.

6. British coal miners ended their strike after the government agreed to a 35 percent pay raise.

7. An unprecedented general strike began in Ethiopia.

John D. Ehrlichman and Charles W. Colson were indicted for their alleged part in the 1971 break-in at the office of Dr. Lewis Fielding, Daniel Ellsberg's former psychiatrist.

11. The state of emergency in Great Britain, declared on November 13, was formally ended by Prime Minister Harold Wilson.

13. Arab oil ministers agreed to end the embargo against oil shipments to the United States.

18. The Arab oil countries, except Libya and Syria, ended their oil embargo against the United States.

19. Senator James Buckley of New York, who had staunchly supported Pres. Nixon, became the first conservative Republican in Congress to call on the president to resign.

25. Leonid Brezhnev, U.S.S.R. Communist party leader, began a crucial three-day discussion with U.S. Secretary of State Henry Kissinger in the Kremlin.

29. The White House agreed to surrender all the materials subpoenaed by special Watergate prosecutor Leon Jaworski.

A federal grand jury in Cleveland, Ohio, indicted a member of the National Guard and eight former members on charges of violating the civil rights of four Kent University students who were shot to death and of nine others who were wounded in a campus demonstration on May 4, 1970.

30. Secretary of State Henry Kissinger married Nancy Maginnes, a former aide to Nelson Rockefeller, in Arlington, Va.

APRIL						
S	M	T	W	T	F	S
	1	2	3	4	5	6
7	8	9	10	11	12	13
14	15	16	17	18	19	20
21	22	23	24	25	26	27
28	29	30				

2. Pres. Georges Pompidou of France died at the age of sixty-two.

1974 CALENDAR

The ***QE 2,*** crippled and adrift off Bermuda, prepared for the transfer of her 1,630 passengers to a Norwegian cruise ship racing to a rendezvous in mid-ocean.

3. Alain Poher, the Centrist president of the French Senate, was officially proclaimed the acting president of France.

Pres. Nixon announced he would pay $432,787.13 in back taxes plus interest after Congressional investigators and the Internal Revenue Service concluded the president had underpaid his taxes.

4. India asked the United States to resume foreign aid.

Hank Aaron hit the 714th home run of his baseball career, tying Babe Ruth's record.

9. India, Pakistan, and Bangladesh signed an agreement to repatriate Pakistani prisoners of war, and Bangladesh dropped the war-crimes trial planned for the prisoners.

10. Premier Golda Meir of Israel announced her resignation.

11. The House Judiciary Committee issued a subpoena ordering Pres. Nixon to turn over all tapes and documents previously requested: the first subpoena ever served a president by a House committee.

W. A. Boyle, former president of the United Mineworkers of America, was convicted on three counts of first-degree murder in the slaying of Joseph Yablonski, a union rival.

14. Israeli and Syrian forces fought their biggest battle since the October War atop Mount Hermon.

15. The army of Niger seized power, overthrowing the government of President Hamani Diori who had ruled since the country's independence from France in 1960.

17. William Simon was named by Pres. Nixon to succeed George Shultz as secretary of the treasury.

18. A subpoena commanding Pres. Nixon to give the Watergate prosecutor tape recordings and other records was served on the White House.

19. Syria and Israel fought their first air battle since the October War over the Golan Heights.

21. Colombia held its first presidential election in over twenty years.

22. Yitzhak Rabin, commander of Israel's armies in the 1967 war with the Arabs, won the Labor party's nomination to succeed Golda Meir.

25. Army officers seized control of the Portuguese government, ousting Premier Marcello Gaetano.

28. John Mitchell and Maurice Stans were acquitted in New York of all charges in their criminal conspiracy case.

MAY

S	M	T	W	T	F	S
			1	2	3	4
5	6	7	8	9	10	11
12	13	14	15	16	17	18
19	20	21	22	23	24	25
26	27	28	29	30	31	

6. Chancellor Willy Brandt of West Germany resigned in the wake of a spy scandal.

7. Finance Minister Helmut Schmidt was chosen to replace Willy Brandt as chancellor of West Germany.

8. Prime Minister Pierre Elliott Trudeau's government toppled when the Canadian House of Commons rejected his budget.

9. The House Judiciary Committee formally began its inquiry into the conduct of the president of the United States.

14. General Antonio de Spinola took office as president of Portugal.

15. Walter Scheel was elected president of West Germany.

16. Helmut Schmidt was sworn in as West German chancellor.

17. Terrorist bombs in the Irish Republic killed twenty-five during Dublin's rush hour.

18. India became the sixth nation to explode a nuclear device.

19. The Labor party government of Australia headed by Gough Whitlam remained in office after a narrow victory in a mid-term election.

Valery Giscard d'Estaing won the French presidential election by a slender margin.

24. Leon Jaworski, Watergate special prosecutor, appealed directly to the Supreme Court in an effort to subpoena sixty-four presidential office conversations, asking the court to decide whether the claim of executive privilege can block the prosecutor's access to evidence.

28. In Northern Ireland, the coalition government of moderate Protestants and Roman Catholics collapsed. brought down by the general strike of Protestant extremists.

29. Israel and Syria agreed on an accord to separate their forces on the Golan Heights.

30. The House Judiciary Committee formally notified Pres. Nixon that his defiance of committee subpoenas "might constitute a ground for impeachment."

JUNE

S	M	T	W	T	F	S
						1
2	3	4	5	6	7	8
9	10	11	12	13	14	15
16	17	18	19	20	21	22
23/30	24	25	26	27	28	29

2. Bhutan crowned eighteen-year-old King Jigme Singhi Wangchuk.

3. Yitzhak Rabin became Israel's fifth premier after his coalition government won par-

A WATCHFUL MOTHER HEN supervises her chicks while the rooster stands in the background. In the U.S. poultry industry about 2.9 billion broilers are raised annually, but higher feed costs resulted in a reduction in poultry output in the fourth quarter of 1974.

OPEN CONTAINERS of nuts, seeds, and spices are part of the stock in this grocery store in Isfahan, Iran. Between one-fifth and one-third of the world's food production is rendered unfit for human consumption by spoilage because many persons fear harmful effects from chemical food preservation.

liamentary approval by a narrow margin.

Charles Colson, who had been one of Pres. Nixon's closest aides, pleaded guilty to attempting to obstruct justice in the 1971 trial of Dr. Daniel Ellsberg.

8. A military and economic agreement was signed by the United States and Saudi Arabia.

9. Pres. Nixon began a nine-day trip to the Middle East, marking the first time a U.S. president has toured Arab countries while in office.

11. Secretary of State Henry Kissinger threatened to resign unless he was cleared of "illegal or shady activity."

14. Pres. Nixon and President Anwar Sadat of Egypt signed a sweeping declaration of friendship and cooperation between the two formerly hostile countries.

16. President Hafez al-Assad of Syria and Pres. Nixon announced in Damascus the restoration of diplomatic relations between their countries, broken off since the Arab-Israeli war of 1967.

17. China conducted a relatively large nuclear test in the northwest part of the country.

23. Rudolf Kirchschläger was elected president of Austria.

26. Pres. Nixon and other leaders of the North Atlantic alliance (NATO) signed a new declaration intended to end bickering among the members.

27. France and Iran signed a massive ten-year, $4 billion development agreement.

29. Leonid Brezhnev of the U.S.S.R. and Pres. Nixon signed a ten-year economic agreement in Moscow.

A landslide that covered a highway section near Bogotá, Colombia, killed an estimated 200 persons.

30. Mrs. Martin Luther King, Sr., sixty-nine-year-old mother of the slain civil rights leader, was shot to death by a young black man as she played the organ in Atlanta's Ebenezer Baptist Church, where her husband is pastor.

JULY

S	M	T	W	T	F	S
	1	2	3	4	5	6
7	8	9	10	11	12	13
14	15	16	17	18	19	20
21	22	23	24	25	26	27
28	29	30	31			

1. Pres. Juan Perón of Argentina died in Buenos Aires; his wife, Vice-President Isabel Peron assumed the presidency, becoming the first woman chief of state in Argentina.

7. West Germany won the World Cup soccer championship.

11. The House Judiciary Committee made public the evidence it has received in its impeachment inquiry into Pres. Nixon's role in Watergate.

12. John Ehrlichman, former domestic affairs advisor to Pres. Nixon, and three other defendants were found guilty of conspiring to violate the civil rights of Dr. Daniel Ellsberg's former psychiatrist.

15. Cypriot troops led by Greek officers overthrew the government of Cyprus, ousting President Makarios.

17. A time bomb exploded in Britain's Tower of London, killing more than forty tourists.

19. Generalissimo Francisco Franco, gravely ill, delegated his powers as ruler of Spain to his designated successor, Prince Juan Carlos de Borbon.

20. Turkey struck Cyprus with powerful land, sea, and

THE 1974 APPLE CROP cost 20 percent more to grow. Washington was the nation's largest apple-producing state; New York was a close second with a 19 million-bushel apple crop.

THE U.S. GRAIN on this Japanese barge is part of the 6 million tons of feed grain and 3 million tons of soybeans that Japan buys from U.S. farmers. American agriculture depends on foreign markets for three-fourths of all farm sales of wheat, half of the farmers' soybean sales, and a third of their corn sales.

air forces, vowing to topple the Greek-oriented government that deposed President Makarios.

22. A cease-fire was agreed upon in Cyprus.

23. Greece's military rulers announced they were turning the nation back to civilian rule.

24. The U.S. Supreme Court ruled Pres. Nixon must provide potential evidence for the criminal trial of his former associates.

Constantine Caramanlis, new civilian premier of Greece, announced the release of all political prisoners.

27. The House Judiciary Committee voted 27-11 to impeach Pres. Nixon for obstruction of justice.

29. John Connally, Democratic governor of Texas from 1963 to 1969 and Republican secretary of the treasury under Pres. Nixon, was indicted by a Watergate jury on five counts dealing with bribery, perjury, and conspiracy to obstruct justice.

30. Greece and Turkey reached agreement on a new Cyprus cease-fire.

The House Judiciary Committee voted to charge Pres. Nixon with a third article of impeachment for unconstitutionally defying its subpoenas.

AUGUST

S	M	T	W	T	F	S
				1	2	3
4	5	6	7	8	9	10
11	12	13	14	15	16	17
18	19	20	21	22	23	24
25	26	27	28	29	30	31

2. The EPA (Environmental Protection Agency) ordered production of the most widely used pesticides in the United States – aldrin and dieldrin–stopped on the ground that their use provides an "imminent danger" to public health.

5. Pres. Nixon admitted publicly that six days after the Watergate burglary he had ordered a halt to the investigation of the break-in for political as well as national security reasons, and he released transcripts of three June 23, 1972, conversations.

6. Pres. Nixon told his cabinet he would not resign, but would remain in office while the presidential impeachment process ran its course.

The Senate Foreign Relations Committee unanimously cleared Secretary of State Henry Kissinger of allegations of wiretapping from 1969 to 1971.

8. Pres. Nixon in an address to the nation said he would resign the presidency at noon on August 9.

9. Gerald Ford assumed the presidency of the United States at 11:35 A.M. and took the oath of office at 12:03 P.M.

12. All eight members of a team of Soviet women mountain-climbers died as they tried to conquer Lenin Peak in the Pamirs: it was one of the world's worst mountain-

FARM LAND PRICES skyrocketed when soybean, wheat, and corn prices began to soar. Net farm income has risen more than 60 percent since 1972.

eering disasters.

14. Turkish forces began heavy air and ground attacks on Cyprus.

16. Turkey's invasion force completed the division of Cyprus into two areas and declared a cease-fire.

19. Rodger Davies, U.S. ambassador to Cyprus, was killed when a bullet penetrated the U.S. Embassy in Nicosia.

Pres. Ford announced he would grant limited amnesty to the 50,000 Vietnam war draft evaders and deserters.

20. Nelson Rockefeller, sixty-six-year-old former governor of New York, was nominated as vice-president by Pres. Ford.

SEPTEMBER						
S	M	T	W	T	F	S
1	2	3	4	5	6	7
8	9	10	11	12	13	14
15	16	17	18	19	20	21
22	23	24	25	26	27	28
29	30					

4. Pres. Ford named George Bush U.S. envoy to China, replacing him as chairman of the Republican National Committee with Mrs. Mary Louise Smith.

8. Pres. Ford granted former Pres. Nixon an unconditional pardon for any federal crimes he may have committed during his term in office.

12. Emperor Haile Selassie who ruled Ethiopia for fifty-eight years, was deposed peacefully by the military.

16. Pres. Ford offered conditional amnesty to Vietnam War draft evaders and deserters who agree to work for up to two years in public service jobs.

General Alexander Haig, Jr., White House chief of staff, was appointed by Pres. Ford to be supreme allied commander in Europe.

19. Former Pres. Nixon was subpoenaed by Watergate prosecutor Leon Jaworski to appear at the Watergate cover-up trial.

20. Greek Cypriot and Turkish Cypriot leaders agreed to a general release of all prisoners of war.

21. A hurricane swept Honduras, driving 50,000 from their homes.

23. Senator Edward Kennedy removed himself from presidential candidacy.

Former Pres. Nixon was admitted to a California hospital for treatment of phlebitis.

25. Former Lieutenant William Calley, Jr., was released from prison when his My Lai murder conviction was overturned by a U.S. district judge who cited "massive pretrial publicity."

28. Betty Ford, wife of the U.S. president, underwent surgery for breast cancer.

30. President Antonio de Spinola of Portugal resigned and was replaced by General Francisco de Costa Gomes, chief of the defense staff.

OCTOBER						
S	M	T	W	T	F	S
		1	2	3	4	5
6	7	8	9	10	11	12
13	14	15	16	17	18	19
20	21	22	23	24	25	26
27	28	29	30	31		

1. The Watergate cover-up trial opened before Federal Judge John J. Sirica in Washington, D.C.

10. Great Britain's Labor party was returned to power in the general elections with a bare three-seat majority.

12. Leon Jaworski, saying that the work of the Watergate special prosecutor was largely finished, announced he would retire on October 25.

14. Pres. Ford vetoed Congress's controversial spending authority bill that would stop U.S. military aid to Turkey.

17. Congress approved a compromise measure to continue military aid to Turkey until December 10, provided Turkey does not send U.S. arms to Cyprus.

Pres. Ford appeared before a Congressional panel to explain his unconditional pardon of former Pres. Nixon.

Margaretta Rockefeller, wife of vice-presidential nominee Nelson Rockefeller, underwent a breast cancer operation.

18. Vice-presidential designate Nelson Rockefeller disclosed that as a result of an Internal Revenue Service audit of his federal income and gift taxes for the last five years, he must pay an additional $820,718 in income taxes and an additional $83,000 in gift taxes.

21. Pres. Ford met with President Luis Echeverria in Mexico.

23. The Greek Government arrested and exiled former President George Papadopoulos.

26. Four armed prisoners raided the chapel of Scheveningen penitentiary, the Hague, Netherlands, during Mass and took twenty-six hostages.

Henry S. Ruth became the third special Watergate prosecutor.

29. John C. Sawhill was replaced as federal energy administrator by Andrew E.

1974 CALENDAR

Gibson, a former assistant secretary of commerce.

Former Pres. Nixon underwent urgent surgery to prevent a blood clot in his leg from moving to his lungs.

NOVEMBER						
S	M	T	W	T	F	S
					1	2
3	4	5	6	7	8	9
10	11	12	13	14	15	16
17	18	19	20	21	22	23
24	25	26	27	28	29	30

1. Pres. Ford visited hospitalized former Pres. Nixon in Long Beach, Calif.

5. Democrats won additional congressional seats in the national U.S. election.

8. Eight former Ohio National Guardsmen were acquitted of violating the rights of students at a demonstration at Kent State University in Ohio on May 4, 1970, in which four students were killed and nine wounded.

9. A federal judge in Columbus, Ga., released on bond William Calley, Jr., who had been convicted by an army court-martial of murdering twenty-two persons at My Lai, South Vietnam.

10. A national coal strike began.

12. The U.N. General Assembly voted 91-22 to suspend South Africa's participation in the assembly's current session, an unprecedented decision in U.N. history.

Pres. Ford withdrew the name of Andrew Gibson as federal energy administrator, following disclosure of Gibson's lucrative severance contract with an oil transporting company earlier.

13. Yasir Arafat, head of the Palestine Liberation Organization, spoke at the United Nations.

16. The World Food Conference ended in Rome, Italy.

17. Prime Minister Constantine Caramanlis won an overwhelming victory in Greece's first democratic election in more than a decade.

18. Pres. Ford began a state visit to Japan.

20. A Lufthansa airliner crashed shortly after take-off from Nairobi, Kenya, killing fifty-nine in the first fatal crash of a 747 jumbo jet.

21. Pres. Ford flew to Seoul, South Korea, for a one-day visit.

22. The U.N. General Assembly approved a resolution giving the Palestine Liberation Organization observer status at the United Nations.

Representative Morris K. Udall of Arizona became the first Democrat to declare officially his candidacy for the presidency in 1976.

25. Premier Kakuei Tanaka of Japan, besieged with an alleged financial scandal, announced his resignation.

28. Brigadier General Tafari Banti was elected by the military junta of Ethiopia to succeed Chief of State General Aman Michael Andam who was killed while resisting arrest.

29. A court-appointed panel of three physicians told Federal Judge John Sirica that former Pres. Nixon would not be physically able to testify at the Watergate cover-up trial before February 6 and would be unable to testify by deposition before January 6.

FRUITS AND VEGETABLES represent not only food calories, but fuel energy calories as well in the present era of energy-intensive agriculture. American farms consume more than a calorie of fuel energy for every food calorie produced and by the time that food calorie is on the table, roughly another five fuel calories have been spent processing, transporting, storing, and preparing the food. The whole process accounts for almost 12 percent of U.S. energy use and the amount is climbing by about 3.3 percent a year.

CATTLE were charged with being the villains of the world food picture in 1974, accused of munching precious grain that should be eaten directly by the world's hungry. A beef cow eats seven pounds of grain to produce one pound of beef while being fattened in the feedlot.

DECEMBER

S	M	T	W	T	F	S
1	2	3	4	5	6	7
8	9	10	11	12	13	14
15	16	17	18	19	20	21
22	23	24	25	26	27	28
29	30	31				

1. All ninety-three persons aboard died in a TWA 727 jetliner crash near Upperville, Va.

2. Takeo Miki was chosen by the Diet to succeed Kakuei Tanaka as premier of Japan.

4. The United Mine Workers ended the coal strike.

5. Federal Judge John Sirica ruled that former Pres. Nixon need not testify in any way at the Watergate cover-up trial.

8. Greece voted two to one to become a republic and eliminate the monarchy.

10. The Senate voted 90 to 7 to approve the nomination of Nelson A. Rockefeller as vice-president.

11. Prime Minister Ian Smith of Rhodesia announced a cease-fire in hostilities with black nationalists on the northern border and the release of all detained black Rhodesian leaders.

12. Governor Jimmy Carter of Georgia, a Democrat, became the second person to announce his candidacy for president.

Elizabeth Ann Bayley Seton became the first American-born saint by Pope Paul VI's decree.

14. Pres. Ford arrived at Fort-de-France, Martinique, to talk with President Valéry Giscard d'Estaing.

15. General Alexander Haig, Jr., assumed supreme command of Allied forces in Europe.

19. Nelson Rockefeller was confirmed as forty-first vice-president of the United States.

20. The Ninety-Third Congress adjourned.

23. Pres. Ford ordered William Colby, director of the Central Intelligence Agency (CIA), to report on allegations of CIA spying on U.S. citizens.

24. A leak from a refinery on Japan's scenic Inland Sea became the nation's biggest oil spill, stretching eighty miles by twenty miles.

25. A cyclone devastated Darwin, Australia.

29. A severe earthquake destroyed Patan, Pakistan.

30. Gold went on sale in the United States at midnight.

HENRY AARON
by
ART DUNN, Editor

Sunday Sports Section
Chicago Tribune

The New Champ. Baseball has a new home run champion — Henry Louis Aaron.

George Herman (Babe) Ruth held the game's loftiest title for thirty-nine years, and many assumed it was his for all time. Then along came Aaron to depose the Babe on April 8 by driving a fastball through the Georgia rain, his 715th career home run during an incomparable twenty-one-year career.

A low-key, quietly religious man, Aaron approached Ruth's glamor record as he had spent most of his playing days —without his just recognition. "During much of his career," a columnist wrote, "people looked through Aaron and saw Mickey Mantle and Willie Mays."

After an injury cut short his rookie season in 1954 with thirteen home runs, Aaron never hit fewer than twenty (in 1974) in the ensuing twenty seasons. His high yield was but forty-seven, and he won just three National League titles and tied for a fourth in 1963. In comparison, Ruth's high number was sixty, and he took ten American League crowns outright and tied for two more.

Consistency and relative freedom from injury, coupled with consummate power, paid off for Aaron, though after his twentieth season with the Milwaukee/Atlanta Braves, "Oh Henry" needed just one home run to tie Ruth and two to become the game's premier long-ball hitter.

The Historic Feat. The end was anything but quiet and free of fanfare. Before the final assault, Aaron received hate letters from bigots who apparently could not stand the thought of a Negro gaining baseball's most revered record.

HANK AARON holds up the ball that broke Babe Ruth's home-run record.

Then the opportunistic Braves' management decided to hold Aaron out of the season-opening series in Cincinnati so he could tie and pass Ruth before Atlanta fans, who did not exhibit much interest before or after the historic feat.

Baseball Commissioner Bowie Kuhn overruled Atlanta Board Chairman William Bartholomay and ordered Manager Eddie Mathews, a former teammate of Aaron's, to have Henry in the starting lineup in at least two of the three games, provided he was healthy.

Aaron proved he was in fine shape—mentally and physically. On his first swing of the 1974 season, April 4, Aaron bombed a fastball from Cincinnati's Jack Billingham and sent it soaring over the left field wall. It was Aaron's ninety-sixth career home run off the Reds, more than he has hit against any other team.

Ironically, both Aaron and Ruth wore Braves' uniforms when they struck Number 714. Ruth, also forty but badly out of shape, connected three times in Pittsburgh during his final major league game as a member of the Boston Braves.

Aaron sat out the second game in Cincinnati, but played the following day, again at Kuhn's insistence, and went hitless. The stage thus was set for April 8, Atlanta's home opener against the Los Angeles Dodgers.

The furor around Aaron now was intense and at least one offer was made to pay $25,000 for the 715th home run ball. Through it all, Aaron remained outwardly calm. His only apparent concession to the pressure was an occasional cigarette in the dugout runway.

Monday, April 8, was a rainy night in Georgia as a national television audience and 53,775 onlookers waited impatiently for the big swing. Aaron did not keep them waiting long. He was walked the first time up without taking the bat off his shoulder.

In the fourth inning, with the rain pelting the field, pitcher Al Downing fell behind Aaron and tried to sneak a high fastball past him. It was like trying to get a filet mignon past a starving man's fork. Henry uncorked his thirty-four-ounce bat with his buggy-whip wrists and sailed Downing's serve into the Braves' bull pen in left. Pitcher Tom House caught it and almost beat Aaron to home plate to present the ball to his teammate.

"I'm thankful to God it's over," said Aaron in his characteristically soft-spoken manner to the assembled multitude that included his parents, four children, and second wife, Billye.

Early Playing. Henry Louis Aaron was born February 5, 1934, in Mobile, Ala., the third of eight children of Estella and Herbert Aaron, a construction worker. Babe Ruth was thirty-nine and had hit 686 home runs when Aaron was born. Fifteen months later the Bambino would retire, and thirteen years hence Jackie Robinson was to break major league baseball's color barrier.

Aaron's formal baseball training began with the Mobile Black Bears in 1951 as a shortstop. The following year he left his native Alabama to barnstorm with the Indianapolis Clowns, from whom the Braves purchased his contract for $10,000.

Boston, a year away from moving to Milwaukee, sent Aaron to Eau Claire, Wis., in the Northern League where he was voted best rookie. In 1953, Aaron, now a second baseman for Jacksonville, Fla., led the South Atlantic League in runs batted in and was named the league's most valuable player. He hit a modest twenty-two home runs.

The Braves. Two years in the minors were enough to convince the Braves that Aaron was ready. When Bobby Thomson suffered a broken ankle, Aaron was inserted in left field. The youngster batted .280 and slammed those thirteen home runs before he fractured his ankle in early September. That sliding fracture was the only serious injury of his career.

Aaron appeared in twenty-two all-star games (for three years in the early 1960s, there were two all-star games a year) and finished with an undistinguished .197 batting average. He did not make an extra base hit in the midsummer classic until 1971 when he homered in Tiger Stadium.

But in his two appearances in the World Series, Aaron was every bit a superstar.

His eleventh inning home run against St. Louis clinched Milwaukee's first pennant in 1957. The blow was Aaron's 109th round tripper and, he wrote in his autobiography, "My shiningest hour." It put him into the World Series against New York and gave him his first look at Yankee Stadium ("The House that Ruth Built") at age twenty-three.

"If you're playing in a World Series and your spine doesn't tingle some that first day you walk out of the clubhouse, you're dead and don't know it," said Aaron years later.

The awestruck kid was not intimidated at the plate. He rattled out eleven hits, three of them home runs, drove in seven runs, hit for twenty-two total bases, and batted .393. All this while playing errorless ball in center field because regular Billy Bruton was injured. The Braves won the series in seven games.

New York gained a measure of revenge in 1958 by winning in seven games. Aaron again feasted on Yankee pitching by averaging .333 to conclude his series log with a .364 mark.

The Braves had one more chance for the series when they won the Western Division title in 1969. But that was the year of the Miracle Mets, who eliminated

HISTORIC BOX SCORE

LOS ANGELES	ab	r	h	bi	ATLANTA	ab	r	h	bi
Lopes 2b	2	1	0	0	Garr rf	3	0	0	1
Lacey 2b	1	0	0	0	Lum 1b	5	0	0	0
Buckner lf	3	0	1	0	Evans 3b	4	1	0	0
Wynn cf	4	0	1	2	Aaron lf	3	2	1	2
Ferguson c	4	0	0	0	Office cf	0	0	0	0
Crawford rf	4	1	1	0	Baker cf	2	1	1	0
Cey 3b	4	0	1	1	Johnson 2b	3	1	1	0
Garvey 1b	4	1	1	0	Foster 2b	0	0	0	0
Russell ss	4	0	1	0	Correll c	4	1	0	0
Downing p	1	1	1	0	Robinson ss	0	0	0	0
Marshall p	1	0	0	0	Tepedino ph	0	0	0	1
Joshua p	1	0	0	0	Perez ss	2	1	1	0
Hough p	0	0	0	0	Reed p	2	0	0	0
Mota ph	1	0	0	0	Oates ph	1	0	0	1
					Capra p	0	0	0	0
	34	4	7	3		29	7	4	5

Los Angeles ....003 001 000—4
Atlanta ....010 402 00x—7

E—Buckner, Cey, Russell 2, Lopes, Ferguson. LOB—Los Angeles 5, Atlanta 7. 2b—Baker, Russell. HR—Aaron. S—Garr. SF—Garr.

	IP	H	R	ER	BB	SO
Downing (L 0-1)	3	2	5	2	4	2
Marshall	3	2	2	1	1	1
Hough	2	0	0	0	2	1
Reed (W 1-0)	6	7	4	4	1	4
Capra	3	0	0	0	1	5

Downing pitched to four batters in 4th
WP—Reed.
Time—2:27. Attendance—53,775.

Atlanta though Aaron averaged .357, hit three home runs, and drove in seven runs in the trio of games.

"He played as if he realized it was his last chance (to appear in a World Series), and it was," wrote Furman Bisher, *Atlanta Journal* sports editor.

But it was not to be his last chance in the limelight. In 1973, at age thirty-nine, Aaron slammed forty home runs to move within one of Ruth's record, and suddenly no one was looking through Aaron any more. His booming bat placed him on center stage in the sports world.

The 1974 Season. He finished 1974 with twenty home runs, boosting his career total to 733. At season's end, he was giving serious consideration to another season. "I'm hoping that's not my last home run," he said after his final shot of the campaign.

Aaron was asked after he had gone past Ruth to assess his achievement. "The home run is the Cadillac of baseball records," he responded. "But Babe Ruth will still be regarded as the greatest home run hitter who ever lived. And I expect someone to come along and tag me someday. I'm not trying to make anybody forget Babe Ruth, I just want them to remember Henry Aaron." The man from Mobile surely has accomplished that.

Late in the year Aaron accepted a post as designated hitter for the Milwaukee Brewers.

The Number Four was a conspicuous digit in Henry Aaron's final assault on Babe Ruth's career home run record. First, the double 4s on Aaron's back, a combination he selected in his first spring training—1954—quite by random. The Braves offered Aaron Number Five, but he wanted a double figure instead.

Aaron was forty years old when he slammed his 714th home run, the night of April 4, 1974—4/4/74. The homer heard round the world came off Pitcher Jack Billingham of Cincinnati who wears Number 43.

Four days later, still in the fourth month, Aaron passed Ruth during the fourth inning of the Braves' fourth game of the season.

AARON'S MILESTONES

HOMER	DATE	WHERE	PITCHER
No. 1	April 23, 1954	St. Louis	Vic Raschi
No. 100	Aug. 15, 1957	Cincinnati	Don Gross
No. 200	July 3, 1960	St. Louis	Ron Kline
No. 300	April 19, 1963	New York	Roger Craig
No. 400	April 20, 1966	Philadelphia	Bo Belinsky
No. 500	July 14, 1968	Atlanta	Mike McCormick
No. 600	April 27, 1971	Atlanta	Gaylord Perry
No. 649	June 10, 1972	Philadelphia	Wayne Twitchell
No. 700	July 21, 1973	Atlanta	Ken Brett
No. 709	Sept. 8, 1973	Atlanta	Jack Billingham
No. 713	Sept. 29, 1973	Atlanta	Jerry Reuss
No. 714	April 4, 1974	Cincinnati	Jack Billingham
No. 715	April 8, 1974	Atlanta	Al Downing

No. 649 enabled Aaron to pass Willie Mays in second place on all-time list; No. 709 enabled Aaron to break Babe Ruth's record for most home runs in a league.

Africa

THE TINY SHRINE of Mekane Medhane Alem, tucked away in an enormous cave, is one of 15,000 churches belonging to the Ethiopian Orthodox Church, one of the richest and most powerful of organizations in Ethiopia. In August the church synod issued a document protesting proposed constitutional changes that would disestablish this national church, charging that the reforms would give "leeway to non-Ethiopian and non-African religions," thereby fostering cultural colonialism.

by
ELIZABETH EISELEN
Author, *Africa* (1966)
President, National Council for Geographical Education

The Sahel. Africa 1974 saw a continuation of many problems from 1973. Among them was the triple threat of drought, famine, and starvation in the Sahel—the southern fringe of the Sahara. Following a visit there in January, Secretary General Kurt Waldheim of the United Nations said, "Peoples and countries could disappear from the face of the map if long-range help is not received. I have never been so shaken by what I have seen in all my life."

The Sahel is an overgrazed and overpopulated region. Even the trees have been cut down to provide leaves for the

AFRICA

RELIEF FOOD in famine-stricken Niger was carried atop heads as well as by camel caravans financed by the United Nations into remote areas of the parched country that could not be reached by truck convoys. The United States provided more than half of the nearly 200,000 tons of food, mainly sorghum, that pulled Niger through the drought.

animals to eat. With the sparse grass gone and the trees killed, the desert has been creeping southward at the rate of thirty miles or more a year.

People, too, are moving South, where they become refugees in countries already having trouble caring for their own people. For example, thousands of Tuareg refugees from Mali are seeking aid in Niger. In September, the *New York Times* reported, "The fate of the Malian Tauregs remains in suspense. They are herdsmen who have lost their herds, living on charity in a country that is embarrassed by their presence, and unwilling to return to the control of a government that neglects their needs. The fear that one day Niger will simply push them across the border haunts them."

In two of the countries of the Sahel, Upper Volta and Niger, army coups resulted in changes of government during 1974. Both are among the poorest nations of the world, and the years of drought and famine added to the unrest of the people. In Upper Volta, the army seized power on February 8. President Sangoulé Lamizana stayed on as president, but the prime minister was ousted, the constitution suspended, and the National Assembly dissolved.

Then on April 16 the government of President Hamani Diori of Niger was toppled. Lieutenant Colonel Seyni Kountche declared himself chief of state and head of a supreme military council.

Lack of protein in their diets is leaving many children of the Sahel with permanent brain damage. Malnutrition has left others susceptible to such diseases as measles, diphtheria, and cholera. These spread rapidly in refugee camps. When diphtheria broke out in a camp in Chad, people begged that no drugs be brought in. They said, "Let the diphtheria rage, for starvation is too slow a death."

During the summer, rains broke the

drought in parts of the "famine zone," but people will still need aid for years to come. Under the best of conditions millions of people of the Sahel have only a subsistence living and their span of life is no more than forty years.

Portugal's African Territories. On April 25 a military coup overthrew the government of Portugal, and on May 14 General Antonio de Spínola became head of the government. He was already on record as saying that the African territories were costing Portugal more than they earned so that the Portuguese would gain more financially than they would lose by giving up the territories.

To give up the territories is not easy, for Portuguese explorers discovered Guinea in the fifteen century, and it was in the sixteenth century that Portugal established its first settlements in Angola and Mozambique. However, during 1974 General Spínola announced, "The moment has come for our overseas territories to take their destinies into their own hands. This is the historic moment for which Portugal, the African territories, and the world have been waiting: peace in Portuguese Africa finally achieved in justice and freedom."

Events moved quickly. Guinea-Bissau received its independence in September, although part of the territory had already declared itself independent in 1973. Independence was to come to Mozambique on June 25, 1975, and to Angola in 1976. No one will be surprised if these dates are pushed up.

The success of independence in Angola and Mozambique will depend on cooperation between the black majorities and the white minorities, for few blacks in these countries have been adequately trained to assume governmental and economic responsibilities. Unfortunately, in spite of the promise of independence, clashes are continuing in both countries between black guerrillas and white Portuguese settlers. Samora Machel, the leader of the Front for the Liberation of Mozambique (FRELIMO) says, "We are not going to discuss independence with Portugal because independence is a right, an inalienable right."

Ethiopia. The year opened with perhaps millions of Ethiopians receiving famine relief in northern, eastern, and southern provinces. This was required because of poor harvests in 1973 and conditions in which animals were dying from lack of grass on overgrazed lands.

By February an undercurrent of uneasiness began to appear in the cities, although it seemed unrelated to the famine. In Addis Ababa taxi drivers, teachers, and students began rioting and striking to protest high prices, poor living conditions, and unemployment. Later in February troops siezed control of Asmara, the country's second largest city. The troops said that they did not want to overthrow the government, although many asked for greater participation in the government. They did, however, want enough pay to live. They wanted to close the gap between the conservative nobility, the rich Ethiopian Orthodox church (Coptic Christian), the wealthy private landowners, and the restless young students, intellectuals, and radicals.

This was the start of several months of "creeping revolution." Haile Selàssie, emperor of Ethiopia, Lion of Judah, Elect of God, and King of Kings, remained head of state and the symbol of authority, but the military was taking over. The moderates, however, kept things under control.

After forty-four years as monarch of Africa's oldest independent nation, Haile Selassie was being prodded gently but firmly into granting the army's demands. He made no effort to oppose them and quietly lost the last remnants of power. On September 12, the world's oldest and

AFRICA

longest reigning monarch was deposed, accused of misrule and embezzlement of millions of dollars. His son, the semi-invalid Crown Prince Asfaw Wossen, was designated king, with no power, to succeed his father. However, he stayed in Europe where he has lived for several years. The government was actually in the hands of the Armed Forces Coordinating Committee.

For some weeks it continued to be a peaceful revolution, but on November 23, 60 former cabinet ministers and government officials were executed. Among them was the general who had become Ethiopia's leader after the ouster of Haile Selassie. At least 140 more were still to be tried.

Zaire. One of the most surprising news items to come out of Africa in 1974 was Zaïre's announcement that henceforth Christmas will be celebrated on June 24. That is the date when the country's current constitution was proclaimed and the date on which the nation's currency—the zaïre — was first circulated. The date of Christmas was changed to emphasize that Zaïre was not founded on religious grounds.

It was in Zaïre in October that Muhammad Ali knocked out George Foreman for the heavyweight championship of the world. President Mobutu brought the fight to the capital city of Kinshasa to show the world that Zaïre is a developing nation to be reckoned with. The *Christian Science Monitor* quoted the Voice of Zaïre radio network as saying, "Although most people still mispronounce Zaïre as one syllable instead of two (Zaa-ear), at least more now know that my nation exists and where it is."

Of greater economic importance is the continuing work on the Inga power project and the start on the world's longest power line. The line will extend from Inga to the copper province of Shaba in the Southeast. There a new copper refinery and a huge new copper mine are being developed and will use the power.

Rhodesia. Early in 1974 Rhodesia launched a "Settlers 74" campaign with the goal of a million names of possible immigrants. These people were then mailed pamphlets in which Rhodesia was described as a nation of abundant land, cheap food, golden sunshine, and happy Africans. It said, "You deserve a better life." No mention was made of the increasing attacks by black guerrillas from Zambia and the ever-present tension in a country where 250,000 whites rule more than 5 million blacks.

Some of those who responded found living and working conditions far from ideal. Rhodesia needs workers with technical skills. Instead, those who came often lacked these skills or were retired people looking for a cheap place to live. At the same time, many young men were leaving the country. White immigration in 1974 scarcely exceeded the number of whites who left Rhodesia.

In late July, the party of Prime Minister Ian Smith won a total victory in a general election, but this did nothing to solve the long-term problem of black discontent. The Rhodesian government continues to refuse to share power with blacks except under a plan that would take forty to sixty years for blacks to reach equal representation with whites in parliament.

Meanwhile black guerrilla fighters from Zambia are moving deeper and deeper into Rhodesia, with some activity only fifty miles from Salisbury in 1974. With neighboring Mozambique heading for independence and black rule in 1975, many specialists in African affairs think time is running out for white-minority rule in Rhodesia. Nor is Prime Minister Smith getting any sympathy from white-governed South Africa for his hard stand.

South Africa. Never before have South African whites been as uncomfortably

AFRICA'S ANIMALS draw more tourists to the Dark Continent than any other single feature, but the great African game parks are under such pressure from the increasing human population that some ecologists give them no more than another ten years of effective life. The lands surrounding the Samburu Game Reserve in northern Kenya, where these elephants roam, are no longer uninhabited or even vaguely owned tribal territories but increasingly private properties, defended by people who resent having their farms tramped down by hungry mammoths.

aware of black opinion as in 1974. World opinion against South African governmental policies also showed up late in the year when the United Nations denied South Africa a vote in the current assembly.

In January a pact between a white opposition leader and the chief minister of the Zulus stated:

1. Change must be brought about by peaceful means.
2. All people of all races must have a chance for material and educational advancement.
3. Constitutions, blueprints, and plans for the future should not be made by some of the people for all the rest of the people. An all-race consultative body should be established as soon as possible.
4. A federation seems the best constitutional method of avoiding domination by one group of another.
5. The cultures and separate identities of the various groups must be safeguarded, and a bill of rights must be drawn up to protect individual rights.

The pact concluded, "On the basis of these principles we declare our faith in a South Africa of equal opportunity, happiness, security, and peace for all its people." Liberal whites considered the joint statement a triumph for those who hope for a peaceful future for South Africa, but the government remained opposed to desegregation.

Nevertheless, whether prompted by the pact or simply by concern for others, there were evidences during the year that apartheid was beginning to break down. Johannesburg did away with special hours for blacks in its museums, art galleries, and the zoo. Municipal parks, public benches, and libraries are now free for use by all races. Plans are being made to permit blacks to buy their own homes in African townships.

Wages are rising for many blacks, although they are still below wages for whites. A greater number of skilled jobs are opening for blacks, and a government-backed training program is preparing workers for these jobs. In fact, faced with the pressure for more skilled workers, the government is tending more and more to be color-blind.

Yet the government remains in white hands, and publicly Prime Minister John Vorster says, "I will never allow the sharing of our white sovereignty." In an April election the white voters supported the government, but the liberal opposition party elected six instead of its usual one member to parliament.

Many of the eased restrictions impress the white South Africans more than outsiders. The latter see the cities being rebuilt into modern cities for the whites. The Coloureds, Asians, and Bantu are being located in settlements of their own outside the cities. Thus, while some evidence exists that apartheid is weakening, the segregated living patterns are strengthening.

South Africa's policy toward Namibia (South West Africa) was changing also during 1974. Increasing pressure has been put on South Africa to relinquish its hold on the territory which it has administered since World War I. In September, South Africa informed the United Nations that whites and nonwhites are starting talks on constitutional development in Namibia. Then in November, South Africa said that self-determination for Namibia might occur much sooner than the ten years previously announced.

What all this means only time will tell, but Prime Minister Vorster has said, "If opponents of apartheid will only give this country a chance of about six months, they will be surprised at where South Africa stands." South Africa's foreign minister has said, "It is essential to make adaptations because time is running out." Will the changes and adaptations be evident when the six months are up in 1975?

Libya-Tunisia and Libya-Egypt. On January 12, Libyan Premier Muammar Qaddafi and Tunisian President Habib Ben Ali Bourguiba signed an agreement for merger of the two countries into a new country, the Arab Islamic Republic. It was to have one constitution, one executive and one legislative branch of government, one army, and one flag. The idea of merger astonished most people because President Bourguiba is a moderate and was the first to call for a negotiated settlement with Israel, while Colonel Qaddafi is impulsive and violently anti-Israeli. However, Tunisia has a population surplus and Libya has a worker shortage, and Libyan oil money could strengthen Tunisia's economy.

In less than a week Tunisia had a new foreign minister, Habib Chatti, and the merger was on the way out. He promised that Tunisia would not merge with Libya as long as Morocco and Algeria opposed the merger. Both were highly critical of it and not likely to change their minds soon.

Meanwhile the merger of Libya and Egypt was in trouble. Egypt is now receiving financial support from Saudi Arabia and no longer needs Libya's oil money. Also, Colonel Qaddafi advocates a total Arab war with Israel which Egyptian leaders believe would be a disaster for Egypt. Furthermore, in April, President Anwar Sadat of Egypt accused Colonel Qaddafi of involvement in an attempted revolt at Cairo's military academy. Finally, in September, the never-completed merger of Libya and Egypt was annulled. In its place Egypt and Libya agreed to substitute "good neighborliness" for a formal commitment to unity.

Other Highlights of 1974. In March news came out of Uganda that an attempted army coup against President Idi Amin had failed. Whether true or not, the incident was used as an excuse for the systematic killing of the officers believed involved. These deaths only added to the list of thousands of lives lost in tribal massacres and secret assassinations since President Amin came into power in 1971.

In May, Algeria resumed diplomatic relations with the United States. Relations had been broken off when the United States supported Israel in the 1967 Middle East war.

In June in Sudan the eight Arab guerrillas who had murdered one Belgian and two U.S. diplomats in March, 1973, were sentenced to life imprisonment. President Jaafir al Nemery commuted the sentence to seven years and released the guerrillas to the Palestine Liberation Organization. The United States immediately recalled its ambassador.

In August Spain announced that it had asked the United Nations to organize a referendum on independence to be held in 1975 in Spanish Sahara. King Hussan II of Morocco said, "Morocco will not permit the setting up of an artificial state in the southern part of our country. Any unilateral move by Spain in the Saharan territory will force us to act in defense of our legitimate rights."

In August also, the high schools of Somalia were closed for a year and the

MUD GRANARIES with conical straw roofs provide storage for rice, sorghum, and millet crops for the Dogons on the Bandiagara escarpment in Mali. The Frobenius Institute in Frankfurt, West Germany, is compiling an inventory of the various forms of African mud architecture, an exceptionally important but hitherto ignored branch of African culture. Mud buildings, some of them built in the sixteenth century, can be found in many West African states, but are no longer being constructed.

30,000 students were sent out in teams of ten to live with the nomads. Their objective is to teach the nomads to read and write, and to instruct the women in health care, nutrition, and cooking. The students will also help to conduct Somalia's first national census of people and animals.

Alaska

by
MICHAEL COPE
Internationally Syndicated Columnist

The Oil Bonanza. As wellhead oil prices in the Middle East doubled, then trebled, so the tempo quickened throughout 1974 in America's forty-ninth state, Alaska, as surveyors and construction crews prepared to market the huge oil discovery at Prudhoe Bay where the state's northern coast meets the bleak, mostly frozen Beaufort Sea.

In a world desperately short of energy resources, lonely Alaska—isolated from the rest of the United States by Arctic seas and neighboring Canada—suddenly assumed enormous importance.

Although it was eight years ago the geologists first pinpointed the existence there of some 10 billion barrels of oil, and 26 trillion cubic feet of natural gas as well, getting it to the energy-hungry markets 2,000 miles and more away in the southeast has confronted the planners with unique climatical, sociological, and environmental problems.

But during 1974 work at last began on supply routes for the building of a 789-mile pipeline from Prudhoe Bay, which is nearly 400 miles north of the Arctic Circle, to Valdez at the northern end of Prince William Sound in the Gulf of Alaska on the state's southern coast, where oil will be shipped to American West Coast ports in ocean tankers.

The cost of this engineering feat, biggest-ever in the petroleum industry, is $4.5 billion. The pipeline, designed to carry 2 million barrels a day, which is about 12 percent of the U.S. total oil consumption, is scheduled for completion in late 1977. The initial flow rate will be 600,000 barrels a day.

ALASKA'S FRAGILE BEAUTY is to be protected from damage caused by the trans-Alaska pipeline through environmental rules and regulations which hopefully will prevent the disruption of wildlife migrations and oil spills. This small stream runs clear and cold near Ketchikan, Alaska.

The discovery of Alaskan oil and the desperate need for it has opened up one of the remotest regions in the world. About 8,000 workers joined the construction gangs in a dozen camps dotted along the pipeline's route north of the Yukon River. Even as the long winter nights began, construction crews worked under floodlights to make the final link-up in the 360-mile service road connecting Prudhoe Bay with the Yukon River, an all-weather, gravel-surfaced, two-lane secondary highway which will join the existing Richardson Highway paralleling the pipeline route south from Fairbanks to the Valdez terminal. Seven camps for the construction crews have also been built south of the Yukon, and when pipelaying starts in the spring of 1975 a full work force of 14,000 will be employed.

As winter closed in with its semi-darkness and numbing cold sending the mercury down to 60 below zero (Fahrenheit), John F. Ratterman of the Alyeska Pipeline Service Company, formed by the consortium of eight oil companies to design, construct, and operate the pipeline, announced proudly: "We are about two weeks ahead of schedule."

Environmental Problems. Such a massive engineering project has confronted its designers and builders with equally massive problems. About half of the pipeline will be elevated above the ground; the rest will be buried beneath the ground. But whether above or below, environmental authorities have insisted the disturbed land must be revegetated with sequence planting of annual and perennial grasses.

Even Alaska's half million caribou have been considered, although Dr. Peter

BOATS at the edge of Prudhoe Bay are ice-locked for the duration of the long Arctic winter. Most of Alaska's goods arrive by barge from West Coast ports, and the transportation of pipeline supplies and additional consumer goods ordered by Alaskan merchants to take advantage of the boom are straining Alaska's freight transport capacity. Shipments rose by 25 percent in the first quarter of 1974.

G. Lent of the University of Alaska insists the huge pipeline poses no problems ("man's harassment, particularly aircraft, is the biggest worry"). Nevertheless, the pipeline builders had wildlife experts carry out tests on 110 groups of caribou to determine whether they preferred to pass under or over the pipeline—"but 75 percent balked at either route."

Policing the pipeline construction for the conservationists is the Arctic Environmental Council, formed in 1974 by the Arctic Institute of North America. Robert C. Faylor, director of the Institute's Washington and Alaska offices, stressed: "We are representing the public interest. This is the biggest construction job in the world today and it affects the environment more directly than almost any other province. This is an important test case . . . We're more concerned with developing a model for the future in dealing with environmental issues in the public interest affected by major developmental projects."

Sociological Impact. It is the sociological impact of the Prudhoe Bay discovery and the "Big Pipe" to the south that perhaps has the greatest effect on the forty-ninth state. With 2 million barrels of oil a day eventually flowing out of the Prudhoe Bay area at a wellhead price of $7 a barrel and the state taking 19 percent in taxes and royalties, Alaska's treasury will be boosted by an additional $1 billion a year.

Some of the doubts and concern over this sudden doubling of income were voiced by Dr. Robert B. Weeden, professor of wildlife management at the state university: "People are beginning to talk about 'impact' — chaos and confusion, housing starts, soaring real estate prices, plans for double-shifting in local schools, and crime waves . . . It isn't so much the construction we are worried

PLANE touches down at Point Barrow to load winter supplies for the last leg of the flight to oil-rich Prudhoe Bay.

about; it's the money and what it leads to. There is going to be a terrific call for income, for building unneeded roads to soak up the surplus. We will destroy everything we know, except possibly the weather."

Job Hunters. Just as the prospect of gold attracted fortune-hunters to the Klondike, so the prospect of earning big money on pipeline construction has lured thousands of Americans to their northernmost state. They drove up the old Alaska Highway (built during World War II), 1,500 miles long through Canada, only to find a 12 percent unemployment rate, the highest anywhere in the country, and the Alyeska Pipeline Company firmly committed to hiring Alaskan residents first. "We have had to warn people in every state not to come to Alaska," said the company.

In Anchorage, the state's biggest city which many of the job-seekers head for, social service agencies reported a sharp upsurge in destitute migrants from the forty-eight southern states. There were twice as many applicants for unemployment checks. Each week every food-stamp line included five to ten new families from the south, and the Salvation Army reported a 30 percent increase in the demand for emergency food and housing.

New Capital. With the wealth which will soon flow from the oil deposits, Alaskans voted in 1974 in favor of building themselves a new capital city somewhere in the interior wilderness between Anchorage and Fairbanks. Juneau, the state's present capital on the coast of the southeastern panhandle, inaccessible by road or rail and ringed by mountains, has long been criticized. With a population of only 6,000 it is the nation's smallest state capital. The ballot success was due largely to the efforts of the Capital Relocation Committee which three times since 1960 has forced the same issue to unsuccessful votes. Bitter opposition from a Juneau-based lobby, called Alaskans United, labelled it "a tax-eating capital in the wilderness" and ran a series of television commercials which said of the ballot question, "That's not a choice—that's fiscal insanity."

ALASKAN WORKERS, lured by pipeline wages ranging from $900 a week for unskilled labor to $1,200 a week for skilled jobs, have left such traditional Alaskan industries as king crab fisheries looking for help. Alaska residents had first call on the 6,000-plus pipeline jobs open in the spring. Only those few positions requiring skills not available in Alaska were filled by out-of-state applicants.

Governor William A. Egan at once appointed a panel to recommend three possible sites for the new capital, one of which will be chosen by public ballot. A tentative 1980 completion deadline has been set for what Alaskans are already calling their "permafrost Brasilia," and estimates are that it would cost as much as $500 million.

PIPELINE SUPPLIES such as this stockpile of the Alaska Aggregate Corporation near Anchorage, were purchased locally as much as possible, boosting the state's economy tremendously. The largest construction job ever attempted, the pipeline project was expected to cost at least $6 billion by its scheduled completion date in 1977.

Natural Gas Deposits. But money is not likely to be Alaska's problem in the future, because even if the oil revenues are not enough in themselves, there are multibillions more from the 27 trillion cubic feet of natural gas deposits at Prudhoe Bay.

Exploitation and development plans for this energy are not as advanced as for the oil. Still to be decided is the pipeline route for moving the gas to midwestern and eastern U.S. markets. The most favored is a trans-Canada route proposed by a twenty-seven-company consortium working under the name of Arctic Gas. Its route is southeastward from Prudhoe Bay, through Canada's Mackenzie River delta, then southward to a point near Calgary, Alta. Here the line would fork, with one spur arching eastward through the upper midwest to the Atlantic seaboard, the other branching southwest into California. Cost to the U.S.-Canadian border would be $5.7 billion.

The other proposal is for an 809-mile all-Alaska route, costing $3.5 billion, which would terminate at Sheep Bay, thirty-five miles east of the oil pipeline terminal at Valdez. There it would be liquified and shipped in LNG (liquified natural gas) tankers to West Coast ports where it would be regasified.

Officials in both Washington and Ottawa expect another two years of discussions and proposals before a decision is made. But meanwhile, Arctic Gas has applied to the Canadian government for permission to build its 2,600-mile pipeline through Canada. The advantage of the Arctic Gas plan is that it could tap an additional 7 trillion-cubic-foot natural gas deposit in Canada's Mackenzie delta.

Whatever natural gas route is finally decided, it will surely be fiercely debated, lobbied, and criticized. The Alaska legislature has already passed a joint resolution endorsing the all-Alaska route. Governor Egan said his administration would insist the Prudhoe Bay gas be funneled through the state: "When the fuel crisis hit, Canada arbitrarily abrogated contracts, raised prices, and took advantage of the situation. In thinking about large volumes of gas, the security of the nation requires that it goes through Alaska." At the same time, a powerful group of midwestern congressmen began lobbying the Federal Power Commission for the trans-Canada gas route. Their argument is that a pipeline feeding directly into the Midwest would be more economical and more secure than one built across Alaska requiring the natural gas to be tanked in liquid form to West Coast ports.

But in the long term, the oil and gas discoveries in Alaska are not only a powerful weapon for winning back some of the economic power seized by the Middle East oil nations, but also a means of opening up the forty-ninth state and recording more development in a few years than Alaska has seen in the past century since the United States bought the territory from the Russians.

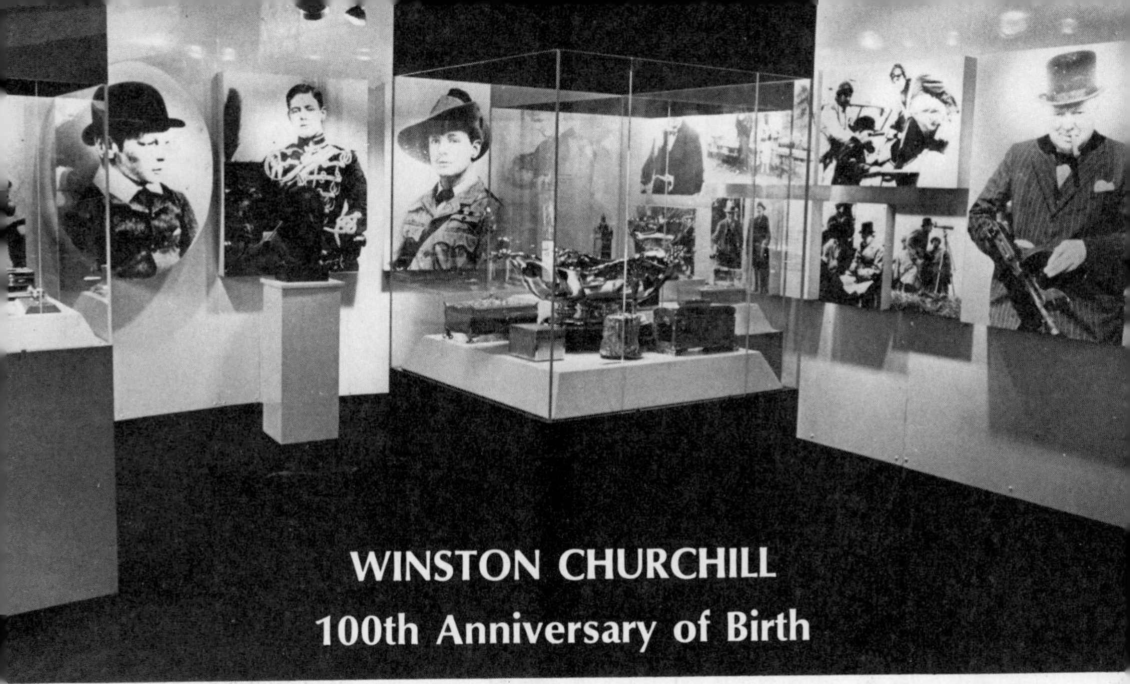

WINSTON CHURCHILL
100th Anniversary of Birth

CHURCHILL PHOTOGRAPHS dominate the display in the museum at Chartwell. Other Churchill exhibitions were set up at Blenheim Palace, his birthplace, and at Somerset House, London, where the largest collection of Churchill memorabilia is assembled.

AS WARTIME LEADER of Great Britain in World War II, Churchill cheers his people on, carrying a steel helmet and gas mask over his shoulder. In December Congress, marking the centennial, passed a resolution which noted that Sir Winston was one of two persons who have been made honorary U.S. citizens. General Lafayette of France was the other.

CHARTWELL, Churchill's country house twenty-five miles south of London, logged over 160,000 visitors during 1974, a year the British government decreed as a twelve-month commemoration of the man who dominates the country's twentieth-century history.

Antiques

MAPLE AND PINE BOXES were made continuously in New England and New York Shaker communities from about 1798 to the 1960s. Part of the Edward Deming Andrews collection, the containers above were in the Shaker exhibition at the Renwick Gallery of the National Collection of Fine Art in Washington, D.C. On the antique market Shaker pieces soared in price in connection with the bicentennial of the founding of the sect: starkly beautiful ladderback chairs reached $200, a sewing desk sold for $3,500, and a pine trestle table went for $2,750.

Collectomania. When the famous Sotheby Parke-Bernet auction house in New York City opened "Heirloom Discovery Week" in March, more than 3,500 antique-conscious Americans swarmed in the first day to get free verbal appraisals of their treasures. In twenty-four hours $1 million worth of silver, quilts, clocks, and other collectibles were appraised.

The U.S. rush to collect antiques is partially sparked by inflation and an unpredictable stock market, partially by growing awareness of the beauty of the old and the fun of antique-collecting as a hobby. The fact that 30 percent of the thousands of dealers across America have been in business for only three years or less attests to its growth.

Collecting antiques is no longer the privilege of the very rich, for collections have expanded to include almost everything from comic magazines to Kewpie dolls. In 1974 depression glass, made in vast quantities between 1920 and 1940, was one of the hottest collecting fields with buys still possible for as little as $2. The thousands of collectors, who support two monthly newspapers *(Depression Glass Daze* and *Depression Glass Ads and Fads)* and fifty depression-glass clubs, were fast pushing prices skyward, however. A ruby-red "American Sweetheart" pattern bowl sold for $750 during the year.

Wildlife Laws and Antiques would seem to be worlds apart, but antiques enthusiasts were made dramatically aware

of conservation regulations when government agents began visiting dealers and confiscating scrimshaw carved from whale bone and teeth and other old pieces made from newly protected animals. The Endangered Species Act which went into effect December 28, 1973, was aimed primarily at halting mass commercial operations responsible for the wholesale slaughter and poaching of animals now threatened with extinction, but it also bars transporting across state lines such antiques as Victorian music boxes embellished with feathered birds, eighteenth-century tortoise shell objects, Art Deco crocodile picture frames and purses, scrimshaw, vintage guns with whalebone rests, and Japanese netsuke, tiny sculptures with whale-ivory toggles.

Unless they can prove the objects were purchased before the law went into effect, violators can have their property seized and be assessed a maximum fine of from $1,000 to $20,000 for each offense. In the case of whale products, conservation organizations point to increased smuggling spurred by soaring prices despite the restrictive laws. Whale teeth were selling for $55 a pound, up from $5 a pound in 1969.

FACING RABBITS, from the fourth quarter of the nineteenth century, is one of eighty American hooked rugs shown at the Museum of American Folk Art in New York City in the fall. The exhibition was so popular it was extended into 1975.

While antique dealers scoffed at the idea of agents attempting to confiscate whalebone corsets and the myriad other old whale products on dealers' shelves, the U.S. Fish and Wildlife Service began an educational television campaign in November to spell out the new federal regulations on consumer goods, antiques, and souvenirs. The object was to stamp out all traffic in goods, old or new, made from endangered species.

Art

THE CONVERSION OF THE MAGDALENE **(1598) by Michelangelo Merisi da Caravaggio, the great master of Italian Baroque art, was purchased from an Argentinean family for $1.1 million and put on display at the Detroit Institute of Arts on January 14. The painting depicts the moment in the life of Mary Magdalene when, in the presence of her sister Martha, she first receives the miraculous revelation of Jesus's message of Divine grace through love.**

REPENTENT MAGDALEN **by Georges de La Tour was purchased by the National Gallery of Art, Washington, D.C., from a French collector for an estimated $8 million and went on view on September 28. Painted between 1639 and 1643, it depicts Mary Magdalen staring into a mirror, indicating introspection. The mirror reflects only a skull, symbol of death. A flickering flame from a hidden candle, symbolizing the temporality of human life, throws haunting shadows on the saint's face and arms.**

CLAUDE MONET shocked the public by painting the interplay of light and shade on everyday subjects, as in this *Lady in a Garden, Saint-Adresse,* now in the Hermitage, Leningrad, U.S.S.R. In an 1874 exhibit by a group of French artists who had broken with the traditions of realism, Monet entered a painting he called *Impression-Sunrise* and the critics derided the show's artists as Impressionists, a label they themselves adopted. On December 13 the Metropolitan Museum of Art in New York City celebrated the 100th anniversary of Impressionism with a monumental exhibition that was scheduled to run through February, 1975.

KAKIEMON ENAMELED PORCELAIN BOWL and cover made in Japan in the mid-seventeenth century was part of a collection of 300 objects of top quality Asian art valued at between $10 and $15 million that John D. Rockefeller, III, gave to the Asia Society during the year.

Automobiles

Supply and Demand. Shaken by the gasoline shortage, auto buyers were demanding small cars in January and February. They wanted them so much they were willing to wait up to two months for delivery.

Manufacturers revved up their small-car production and cut back on medium and luxury models. Eyeing their profit margins, they raised prices on the smaller cars from 15 to 25 percent and loaded the cars with options and luxury "appointments." The plan was to meet the new small-car demand, but make as much money as before.

The customer had other ideas. He looked at the price tags on the 1975 models and either kept his old jalopy or went out to the used-car lot and bought a full-sized car for the same or a lower price. Used-car sales skyrocketed by 70 percent during the year.

The small-car segment slumped in October from its high, a 53.8 percent share of the market, to 46.3 percent, with some subcompacts going from a high of 12.6 percent to 7.2 percent. Because the price spread between the luxury small car and the basic full-size car had become less, standard-size cars and intermediates began to recapture some of the market. Automakers, who had had an oversupply of big cars during the energy crisis, now had an oversupply of small cars.

Under conditions of oversupply and

PORTLAND, ORE., DRIVERS lined up before daybreak on a January Saturday in sometimes futile attempts to get gasoline for the week-end. During the shortage most gas stations closed by noon on Saturdays and were not open at all on Sundays. By May the gasoline shortage had eased throughout the United States but the price per gallon did not come down.

low demand, the free enterprise system prescribes price cuts. With the exception of Ford's $150 decrease on the Pinto, the automobile industry did not take that path. Instead, it appealed to the federal government to stimulate consumer demand and to Congress to postpone establishing pollution and safety standards that would increase prices.

By November, sales of 1975 models were down 38 percent from sales of 1974s a year before when business was already depressed because of the Arab oil embargo. The auto industry had a stockpile of 1.7 million unsold cars. Unemployment in the sector was forecast to reach 20 percent during the 1974-1975 winter. The picture of a suffering Detroit cast gloom over the whole American industrial economy, because car sales are basic to U.S. business. Layoffs outside the auto industry tend to be greater than inside when car sales drop.

The increasingly price-sensitive auto market proved a boon to foreign car sales. With regained price advantage, imported cars sold well in comparison with the sagging fortunes of Detroit's products. By October retail sales of foreign cars had risen 6.33 percent above the 1973 level.

A Safety Puzzle. The only dividend from the 1973-1974 gas shortage was a steep reduction in traffic deaths. Just why the number of traffic fatalities declined at a faster rate than the consumption of gasoline was a puzzle, but the slower, safer speeds resulting from the national 55 mile-per-hour limit seemed to be a major factor.

The National Safety Council said that almost 8,000 fewer people died in traffic accidents during the first eight months of the year than during the same period in 1973, a reduction of 21 percent. From January 1 through May 30 the monthly decline in fatalities averaged almost 25 percent. Yet gasoline consumption during this period fell by only 5 to 15 percent. By late spring and summer driving had become increasingly less safe. In June the number of deaths was 19 percent below the June, 1973, level. The decline in August was only 12 percent.

BUMPER STICKER BOOM

As many as one out of every ten cars rolling down U.S. highways displayed a bumper sticker in 1974. Their messages touched on practically all aspects of life in America and reflected nearly all extremes of political thought.

The advent of pressure-sensitive paper made the bumper sticker possible, and the Texas Memorial Museum in Austin, which boasts a collection of about 10,000, dates its oldest strip to 1948. For about twenty years bumper stickers were primarily used for advertising and promotion — either for business or politics. About five years ago they began to express popular opinions and quickly became the brief modern replacement for the old street-corner soapbox speech.

Flaunting their feelings, Americans flashed the following bumper stickers as they passed in their cars:

America: Love It or Leave It.

Women's Lib: The Oppressed Majority.

Don't Blame Me, I Voted for McGovern.

If You Don't Like Cops, Next Time You're in Trouble, Call a Hippie.

Jail to the Chief.

Live Dangerously: Take a Deep Breath.

Honk if You Love Jesus.

Protect Our President from Liberals and Traitors.

When Guns Are Outlawed, Only Outlaws Will Have Guns.

The World Is Mad.

A CREWMAN whips his air hose out of the way after changing a wheel on Donnie Allison's car in the Daytona 500 at Daytona Beach, Fla. A crowd of 80,000 watched Allison—who had inherited the lead with twenty laps to go when Richard Petty blew a tire—lose his chance to win as he in turn blew a tire in front of the grandstand. Petty won the race for the second time in a row and the fifth time overall.

Auto Racing

by

ART DUNN

Editor, Sunday Sports Section
Chicago Tribune

The Indianapolis 500, which had death, fire, and rain to contend with last year, needed only to overcome a $1 million law suit before the fifty-eighth running of the famed race.

Five car owners sued the Speedway and the U. S. Auto Club (USAC) because they had been denied a chance to qualify. Three days before the green flag dropped, the suit was dismissed.

The race developed into a two-man duel between a pair of Texas veterans, A. J. Foyt of Houston, who won the pole position with a qualifying speed of 191.632 mph, and Johnny Rutherford from Ft. Worth, second fastest qualifier.

USAC had cut the total fuel allotment by 70 gallons to 280 and limited the on-board supply to 40 gallons in an effort to make the 500 a safer trip after fiery crashes last year killed a driver and crewman and critically injured David (Salt) Walther.

The changes apparently worked, because the Indy was raced without serious incident, and drivers were forced to rely more on strategy than on sheer speed.

Foyt led for 175 miles until the gear box in his Coyote broke on the 141st lap, spewing smoke and oil on the paved brickyard.

The thirty-six-year-old Rutherford then guided his Team McLaren Offenhauser to the front, pacing the field for 122 laps, including the final twenty-four. His victory margin was twenty-two seconds over Bobby Unser's time. They were the only two of the starting thirty-three drivers who completed the full 200 laps.

Rutherford, a popular and soft-spoken man who had failed to finish in ten previous Indy starts averaged 158.589 mph. The day following the race he received $245,031.52 from the record Indy purse of $1,015,686.

Billy Vukovich, son of the late two-time Indy winner, Bill, Sr., took third. Gordon Johncock, who won the rain-shortened 1973 500, finished fourth. Walther, running for only the second time since last year's accident, completed 141 laps, good for seventeenth place.

Revson. Indianapolis and Grand Prix driver Peter Revson was killed in March during a practice run for the South African Formula 1 Grand Prix in Kyalami. Revson, thirty-five, won the British Grand Prix and finished second in the 1971 Indy 500 when he was the fastest qualifier.

Grand Prix. Brazil's Emerson Fittipaldi captured the '74 Grand Prix title on the strength of three victories. Richard Petty took the checkered flag in ten NASCAR events to win his fifth stock car championship.

Aviation

TOP BRASS watch a test flight in this prize-winning Military Picture of the Year by John W. Gorman. The B-1 intercontinental bomber, designed to replace the aging B-52 at a cost of $76 million a plane, made its first flight on December 23. It was the second significant test of a military craft in two days: on December 22 France's F-1 Mirage fighter-bomber with a new higher-powered M-53 engine was tested at Istres, France.

THE BLIMP may win over the Wright brothers' aircraft, yet. Lighter-than-air ships enjoyed a brief span of popularity before the rapid development of airplanes and a series of accidents squelched their growth, but the energy crisis revived interest in these craft. The National Aeronautics and Space Administration (NASA) announced plans to do a study of the passenger and cargo efficiency of the dirigible, and the Soviet Union has decided to develop a nuclear-powered dirigible to help open up Siberia.

Baseball

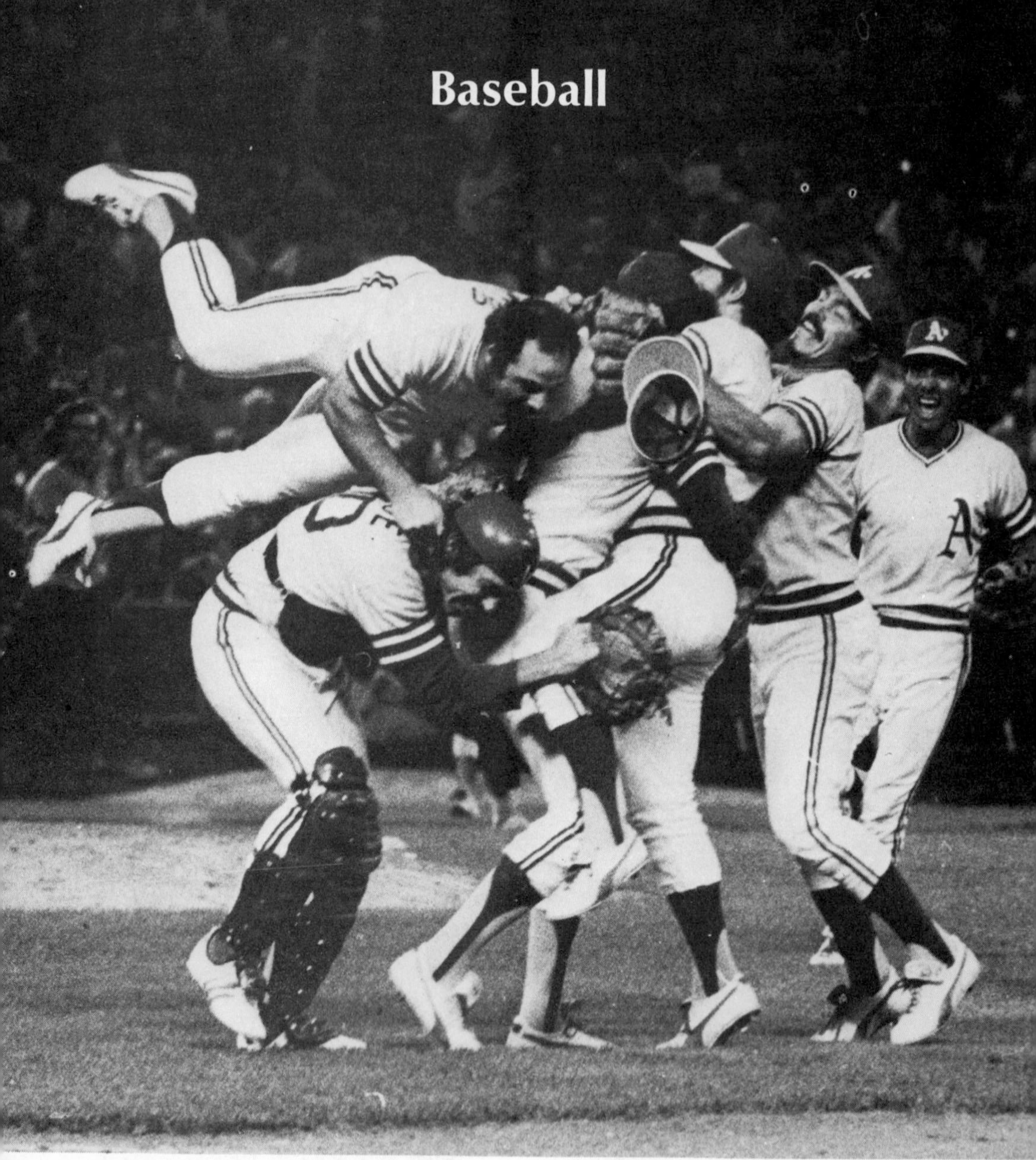

THE JUBILANT OAKLAND A'S form a victory pyramid after winning their third straight World Series on October 17. At top left, Sal Bando jumps atop the pile comprised of, from the left, catcher Ray Fosse, relief pitcher Rollie Fingers, infielder Gene Tenace, infielder Dick Green, and infielder Bert "Campy" Campaneris.

by
STEVE NIDETZ
Sports Department
Chicago Tribune

Records. While Henry Aaron was breaking the most revered baseball record, that of most home runs in a career, fleet-footed St. Louis Cardinal outfielder Lou Brock was chasing another ghost.

Brock, at thirty-five, took off after the

Batting Leaders — .300 Hitters

AMERICAN LEAGUE

	G	AB	R	H	Avg.
Carew, Minnesota	153	599	86	218	.364
Hargrove, Texas	130	414	57	134	.323
Orta, Chicago	138	521	75	166	.316
McRae, Kansas City	147	533	71	166	.308
Piniella, New York	140	518	71	158	.305
Maddox, New York	137	466	75	141	.303
Burroughs, Texas	150	519	84	167	.301
Randle, Texas	152	521	65	157	.301
Yastrzemski, Boston	148	515	93	155	.301
Allen, Chicago	128	462	84	139	.301

NATIONAL LEAGUE

	G	AB	R	H	Avg.
Garr, Atlanta	142	606	87	214	.353
Oliver, Pittsburgh	146	617	96	198	.321
Gross, Houston	155	589	77	185	.314
Buckner, Los Angeles	144	580	83	182	.314
Madlock, Chicago	127	453	65	142	.313
Zisk, Pittsburgh	148	536	75	158	.313
Garvey, Los Angeles	156	642	95	200	.312
R. Smith, St. Louis	143	517	79	160	.309
McBride, St. Louis	150	559	81	173	.309
Brock, St. Louis	154	635	105	194	.306
Montanez, Philadelphia	140	527	55	160	.304
Stargell, Pittsburgh	144	508	90	153	.301
Cash, Philadelphia	157	687	89	206	.300

Pitching Leaders — 20-Game Winners

AMERICAN LEAGUE

	IP	H	BB	SO	W	L	ERA
Hunter, Oakland	318	268	46	143	25	12	2.49
Gaylord Perry, Cleveland	322	230	99	216	21	13	2.51
Jenkins, Texas	328	286	45	225	25	12	2.82
Ryan, California	332	221	202	367	22	16	2.87
Tiant, Boston	311	282	82	176	22	13	2.92
Kaat, Chicago	277	264	63	142	21	13	2.95
Cuellar, Baltimore	269	253	86	106	22	10	3.11
Busby, Kansas City	294	284	92	198	22	14	3.39
Wood, Chicago	320	305	80	169	20	19	3.59

NATIONAL LEAGUE

	IP	H	BB	SO	W	L	ERA
Phil Niekro, Atlanta	302	249	88	195	20	13	2.38
Messersmith, Los Angeles	292	228	93	221	20	6	2.59

season stolen-base record set twelve years ago by the Dodgers' Maury Wills. And Brock, who helped lead the Cardinals to a World Championship when traded to

BASEBALL

St. Louis in 1964, caught and passed the major league record September 10 in St. Louis.

On that night, against Philadelphia, Brock stole two bases to break the record and wound up the season with 118 stolen bases, but, alas, no pennant.

Races. For the first time since divisional play began in 1969, major league baseball came up with four pennant races, three of which went down to the last two days of the season. Only defending world champion Oakland, seeking its third straight title, clinched the American League West crown before the last week. But not before Manager Billy Martin's surprising Texas Rangers gave the A's a run for almost six months.

Los Angeles, in the National League West, and Baltimore, American League East, both clinched on October 1. The Dodgers, who blew a huge lead last year to Cincinnati, this time hung on and wrapped things up with an 8-5 victory over Houston the same day the Reds were eliminated with a 7-1 loss to Atlanta. The Orioles used the same combination of events, beating Detroit 7-6, while second-place New York lost 3-2 to Milwaukee in ten innings, to take the division.

But once again the most excitement was generated in the National League East, where both Pittsburgh and St. Louis battled into their final three games tied for the lead. But when the Pirates won their next two games against the Cubs and the Cardinals split with Montreal, it all came down to that last cold night in Pittsburgh.

The Cubs battled to a 6-4 lead going into the bottom of the ninth. The Cardinals, who were snowed out of their game in Montreal, listened to a telephone-radio hookup in their hotel rooms. With two out, a run home, and Manny Sanguillen on third base, Pirate Bob Robertson was facing Cub pitcher Rick Reuschel with two strikes on him. Reuschel threw, Robertson swung and missed, and it appeared to be over. But the ball bounded away from Cub catcher Steve Swisher, Robertson rambled to first, and Sanguillen scored the tying run. The Pirates, finding salvation, went on to win the game in the tenth inning, and the Cardinals were finished.

Playoffs. The playoffs were brief and to the point. The Dodgers, winning three out of four games, surprised the Pirates with their hitting. The A's, holding Baltimore scoreless for thirty-one straight innings, also took three out of four games.

Dodger pitchers Andy Messersmith, Don Sutton, and Mike Marshall contained the big bats of the Pirate lineup for all but one game. It was the Dodgers, in fact, who pounded out a 12-1 score in the finale.

Oakland had trouble scoring runs against Baltimore, but with Blue Moon Odom, Rollie Fingers, Ken Holtzman, Vida Blue, and Jim "Catfish" Hunter holding off the Orioles, the A's were winners.

World Series. It was to be the first all-California World Series in baseball history. The Western migration that began in 1958 when the Dodgers and Giants left New York City had reached fruition.

And the Oakland A's, seeking to be the first team since the Yankee dynasties of the 50s and 60s to win three straight championships, were in a fighting mood even before the series started.

Fingers and Odom got into a brawl in the Oakland dressing room the day before the series was scheduled to open in Los Angeles. And rumors were heavy that A's manager Al Dark would be replaced after the series, regardless of the outcome.

But that didn't halt Oakland from jumping to a 1-0 lead in the series by edging the favored Dodgers 3-2 in the

BASEBALL

first game. Oakland used a combination of a Reggie Jackson homer, a Burt Campaneris squeeze bunt, and Ron Cey's error to score all the runs they needed. Hunter made a rare relief appearance to save the game for Holtzman.

The Dodgers, however, evened things up in game two behind Sutton and Marshall. Los Angeles won 3-2 when A's pinch-runner Herb Washington, the former Michigan State sprint star, was picked off first base by Marshall in the ninth inning.

Hunter came back to win the third game for the A's, once again by a score of 3-2, as the series shifted to Oakland. Fingers returned from the ranks of the injured to pick up the save.

In the fourth game, which Oakland won 5-2 to take a 3-1 lead, Holtzman helped himself early with a home run off Messersmith. But the Dodgers came back to tie the game in the sixth. Jim Holt, however, later delivered a bases-loaded single to break the tie for the A's. Fingers made his third relief appearance in four games to save the victory for Holtzman.

On October 17 the stage was set for the A's to capture their third straight crown. As both teams battled through six innings tied at 2-2, Marshall entered in the seventh inning as the Oakland fans became more volatile, throwing bottles and cans at Dodger left fielder Bill Buckner and delaying the game.

The delay obviously upset Marshall, who later was voted the Cy Young Award as the best pitcher in the National League. Joe Rudi led off the A's seventh with a towering drive into the left field seats to give Oakland a 3-2 lead.

Fingers came on once again to pitch for the A's in the eighth inning, and Buckner greeted him with a line drive to center field. When Bill North bobbled the ball, Buckner didn't hesitate rounding second and trying for third base.

N. L. STANDINGS
FINAL

EASTERN DIVISION

	W.	L.	Pct.	G.B.
Pittsburgh	88	74	.543	...
St. Louis	86	75	.534	1½
Philadelphia	80	82	.494	8
Montreal	79	82	.491	8½
New York	71	91	.438	17
Chicago	66	96	.407	22

WESTERN DIVISION

	W.	L.	Pct.	G.B.
Los Angeles	102	60	.630	...
Cincinnati	98	64	.605	4
Atlanta	88	74	.543	14
Houston	81	81	.500	21
San Francisco	72	90	.444	30
San Diego	60	102	.370	42

A. L. STANDINGS
FINAL

EASTERN DIVISION

	W.	L.	Pct.	G.B.
Baltimore	91	71	.562	...
New York	89	73	.549	2
Boston	84	78	.519	7
Cleveland	77	85	.475	14
Milwaukee	76	86	.469	15
Detroit	72	90	.444	19

WESTERN DIVISION

	W.	L.	Pct.	G.B.
Oakland	90	72	.556	...
Texas	84	76	.525	5
Minnesota	82	80	.506	8
Chicago	80	80	.500	9
Kansas City	77	85	.475	13
California	68	94	.420	22

What he didn't see, however, was right fielder Jackson retrieving the ball and getting it to second baseman Dick Green, who drilled a perfect strike to third baseman Sal Bando.

When Buckner slid into third, the ball was waiting, Bando applied the tag, and the Dodgers were dead. Fingers picked up his fourth save, an achievement which later won him the Most Valuable Player award.

Two days after the series ended, Dark

MAUREEN GORMAN of the South Trenton (N.J.) Little League shows off her batting prowess and her fielding ability at second base. The Little League, Inc., which regulates play by 2.5 million boys in thirty-one countries, opened enrollment in its program to girls during 1974.

was rehired by owner Charles O. Finley.

While the Dodgers had entered the series talking about a new dynasty, it was Oakland's flamboyant A's, feuding and fighting as usual, who left the series with a dynasty only their owner Finley could break up.

First Black Manager. Baseball broke the management color barrier, twenty-seven years after Jackie Robinson became the first black player. On October 3, 1974, the Cleveland Indians named Frank Robinson to manage the club next season. Robinson, a thirty-nine-year-old native of Beaumont, Texas, was a Most Valuable Player in both major leagues during his nineteen-year career. Robinson said he will continue playing part time with Cleveland as a designated hitter. He replaces Ken Aspromonte.

Catfish Hunter. The baseball establishment received a jolt in mid-December when pitcher Jim (Catfish) Hunter, Oakland's Cy Young Award winner, was declared a free agent by a three-man arbitration panel. Hunter, who won eighty-eight games over the past four seasons, claimed Charles O. Finley did not live up to the terms of his contract when Finley did not make premium payments on the pitcher's insurance contract.

Twenty of the twenty-four major league teams entered into open bargaining for Hunter's services after a ruling by Commissioner Bowie Kuhn. On New Year's Eve, the New York Yankees announced the signing of the twenty-eight-year-old North Carolinian to a multi-year contract worth a reported $3.75 million.

Finley filed suit to overturn the arbitration ruling, but the volatile owner struck out in court. Finley, who was successful last year in keeping former A's manager Dick Williams from bolting to the Yankees, said he would appeal the Oakland Superior Court decision.

Basketball

by
ART DUNN

Editor, Sunday Sports Section
Chicago Tribune

MOSES MALONE, who at nineteen signed a $3 million pro contract with the Utah Stars in August, watches his tap-in fall in the basket for two points during the first period of the Stars' game with the New York Nets at Uniondale, N.Y., in October. It was the former high school star's first official pro game.

College Basketball. Unfortunately for North Carolina State, 1974 will be remembered as the year the University of California at Los Angeles (UCLA) lost, rather than the year of the Wolfpack.

Johnny Wooden's remarkable Bruins, winners of the seventh straight National Collegiate title and nine of the last ten, saw two streaks come to an end. Early in the year, they had stretched their record number of victories to eighty-eight when they faced Notre Dame in South Bend.

The Bruins, led by super center Bill Walton, owned an eleven-point lead with three minutes left, but a tenacious Irish press wiped it out. UCLA, foreshadowing a critical lapse that would surface again in March, wilted under pressure and Dwight (Iceman) Clay's last-second shot from the corner pulled out a 71-70 victory for Notre Dame.

Included in UCLA's streak victims was North Carolina State. The Wolfpack succumbed easily 84-66 at a neutral site late in 1973. It was to be their only defeat of the campaign. The previous season the Wolfpack had gone undefeated, but sat home during the National Collegiate Athletic Association (NCAA) playoffs on probation, the result of successfully recruiting superstar David Thompson.

The two powerhouses marched on toward their anticipated showdown for the title, but the rematch came in the NCAA semifinals at Greensboro, N.C., no neutral site for the Bruins.

As in the game against Notre Dame, UCLA earned sizable leads. But North Carolina State twice came from eleven points back, and one of Thompson's spectacular leaping receptions on a lob pass tied the game 65-65 at the end of regulation.

Each team scored one basket in the first overtime, and State stalled for an unsuccessful last shot. Walton and Keith Wilkes ran off seven straight points in the second overtime before the Wolfpack resorted to a desperation pressure defense.

The defending champions refused to

BASKETBALL

COLLEGE ALL-AMERICANS

1st Team

Bill Walton, UCLA
Keith Wilkes, UCLA
David Thompson, North Carolina State
John Shumate, Notre Dame
Marvin Barnes, Providence

2nd Team

Len Elmore, Maryland
Campy Russell, Michigan
Larry Fogle, Canisius
Bobby Jones, North Carolina
Bill Knight, Pittsburgh

stall, and Thompson climaxed a furious comeback with a bank shot that gave the Wolfpack a 76-75 lead. The winners added four free throws in the final minute for an 80-77 victory. Thompson finished with twenty-eight points. Walton had twenty-nine points and eighteen rebounds, but seven-foot four-inch Tom Burleson prevailed in key plays.

The finals were somewhat anticlimactic as North Carolina State downed Marquette 76-64. The Warriors from Wisconsin had defeated Kansas in the other semi, but State opened a nineteen-point lead early in the second half and stalled the rest of the way.

Indiana schools dominated the other postseason tournaments. Purdue won the National Intercollegiate Tournament (NIT), and Indiana crushed Southern Cal in the first conference runnersup tourney at St. Louis.

Professional Basketball. One old name returned to the pinnacle of the National Basketball Association (NBA) during a year in which six veteran stars retired.

The Boston Celtics, who won eleven championships in the Bill Russell era, captured their first league title since 1969; and Wilt Chamberlain, Jerry West, Oscar Robertson, Dave DeBusschere, Willis Reed, and Jerry Lucas played their last games.

Boston won the Atlantic Division crown—as they had done a year ago—then downed Buffalo in six games in the first round. The Braves, a playoff team for the first time, were paced by Center Bob McAdoo and guard Ernie DiGregorio, the league's rookie of the year. McAdoo, twenty-two, became the youngest player ever to lead the NBA in scoring, with a 30.6 average.

The Celtics' next assignment was New York, and they eliminated the defending champions in five games, losing only the third at home. Milwaukee, meanwhile, was breezing past Los Angeles and Chicago in nine games, one over the minimum.

Neither team could win two games in a row in the see-saw seven-game final, and neither won more than one at home, another rarity. Down 3-2 and playing in Boston Garden, the Bucks pulled a dramatic 102-101 double-overtime triumph

NBA STANDINGS

ATLANTIC DIVISION	W.	L.	PCT.
Boston	56	26	.683
New York	49	33	.598
Buffalo	42	40	.512
Philadelphia	25	57	.305
CENTRAL DIVISION	W.	L.	PCT.
Washington	47	35	.573
Atlanta	35	47	.427
Houston	32	50	.390
Cleveland	29	53	.354
MIDWEST DIVISION	W.	L.	PCT.
Milwaukee	59	23	.720
Chicago	54	28	.659
Detroit	52	30	.634
K.C.-Omaha	33	49	.402
PACIFIC DIVISION	W.	L.	PCT.
Los Angeles	47	35	.573
Golden State	44	38	.537
Seattle	36	46	.439
Phoenix	30	52	.366
Portland	27	55	.329

JOHN HAVLICEK (17) of the Boston Celtics tries to block a pass by Milwaukee Bucks Bob Dandridge in the first quarter of the Bucks-Celtics NBA championship playoffs in April.

when center Kareem Abdul-Jabbar scored his thirty-fourth point on a hook shot with three seconds left. Boston's John Havlicek tallied thirty-six, including nine in the second overtime.

But the Bucks were no match for Havlicek, six-foot nine-inch center Dave Cowens, and guard JoJo White, losing the showdown and the title 102-87. Cowens, held to sixteen points in game six, outscored (28-26) and outrebounded (14-13) seven-foot two-inch Jabbar in the clincher.

Jabbar paced all scorers in the playoffs at 32.2, but the resilient Havlicek was named Most Valuable Player for his tenth playoff series in twelve seasons with Boston.

The New York Nets set an American Basketball Association record by winning the league title in fourteen playoff games, one less than Indiana in 1970. They completed the blitz by downing Utah in five games.

Julius (Dr. J.) Erving paced the storybook Nets by winning his second straight league scoring title with a 27.4 average. The twenty-four-year-old six-foot seven-inch forward triggered the Nets' fast break which eliminated the Stars in the final 111-100. Dr. J. scored twenty points, and rookie Larry Kenon collected twenty-two.

Bermuda Triangle

by
DON LAWSON

Editor in Chief
Tangley Oaks Educational Center

Drawings by George Armstrong

FLIGHT 19 was never heard from again and no trace of the planes found.

"Triangle of Death." The year 1974 was a quiet one in the Bermuda Triangle. Twice during the year private yachts were reported missing in the area, but these reports were later proved erroneous.

However, interest did not slacken in the mysterious "Triangle of Death," as it has sometimes been called. The news media continued to speculate about it, and encyclopedia research departments continued to receive a steady stream of inquiries about the more than one hundred ships and airplanes and more than one thousand lives that have been lost in the triangle since 1945. As a matter of fact, one of the most common requests received by encyclopedia research departments is for information on the Bermuda or Devil's Triangle sea zone.

BERMUDA TRIANGLE

What is the Bermuda Triangle? The Library of Congress reference department states: "It is an area off the Atlantic coast of the United States noted for a high incidence of unexplained losses of ships and aircraft. The apexes of the triangle are generally accepted as Bermuda, Florida, and Puerto Rico."

The National Geographic Society calls the 440,000 square miles of open sea that encompasses the Bermuda Triangle "a twilight zone for ships and planes. Though many ships and planes travel the triangle each day without mishaps,

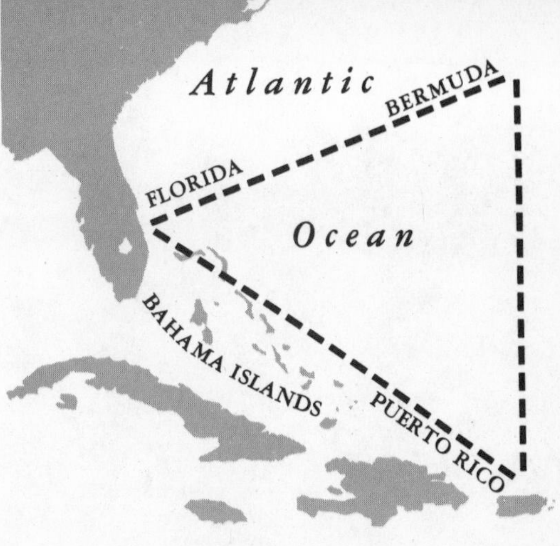

THE BERMUDA TRIANGLE

U.S. NAVY FACT SHEET ON THE LOSS OF FLIGHT 19

"At about 2:10 P.M. on the afternoon of 5 December 1945 Flight 19, consisting of five TBM Avenger Torpedo Bombers, departed from the U.S. Naval Air Station, Fort Lauderdale, Florida, on an authorized advanced overwater navigational training flight. In charge of the flight was a senior qualified flight instructor, piloting one of the planes. The other planes were piloted by qualified pilots with between 350 and 400 hours of flight time of which at least 55 was in TBM type aircraft. The weather over the area covered by the track of the navigational problem consisted of scattered rain showers with a ceiling of 2,500 feet within the showers and unlimited outside the showers, visibility of 6-8 miles in the showers, 10-12 otherwise. Surface winds were 20 knots with gusts to 31 knots. The sea was moderate to rough. The general weather conditions were considered average for training flights of this nature except within showers.

"A radio message intercepted at about 4:00 P.M. was the first indication that Flight 19 was lost. This message, believed to be between the leader on Flight 19 and another pilot in the same flight, indicated that the planes were lost and that they were experiencing malfunction of their compasses. Attempts to establish communications and to reach the troubled flight were in vain. All radio contact was lost before the exact nature of the trouble or the location of the flight could be determined. Indications are that the flight became lost somewhere east of the Florida peninsula and was unable to determine a course to return to their base. However, the evidence is insufficient to determine exactly what did happen. The flight was never heard from again and no trace of the planes found.

"One search aircraft was lost during the operation, a PBM patrol plane which was launched at approximately 7:30 P.M. 5 December 1945, to search for the missing TBM's. This aircraft was never heard from after take-off. No trace of the plane or its crew was ever found."

A COAST GUARD SEAMAN looks at a life-saver and life-jacket from the missing S.S. *Marine Sulphur Queen.*

an unusual number of craft have disappeared there leaving no trace. Neither wreckage nor victims were ever found. Thrusting into the triangle is the western part of the Sargasso Sea, also a legendary twilight zone for mariners."

The Legend of the Bermuda Triangle really began in 1918. The U.S.S. *Cyclops,* a Navy collier carrying a crew of 213 and 67 passengers, set out from Brazil on its way to the United States with a cargo of manganese.

The *Cyclops* called at Barbados, British West Indies, for fuel and provisions. In fair March weather the ship sailed northward into the triangle—and oblivion. A massive search failed to find a single clue.

The disappearance still perplexes the U.S. Navy. Recently, however, a spokesman pointed out a little-known fact, perhaps significant: the *Cyclops* carried a "tough" contingent of court-martialed seamen being returned to the United States for imprisonment.

Vincent Gaddis, in his book *Invisible Horizons,* gives case histories of some twenty other ships and airplanes that have met their silent doom in or near the triangle since World War II.

"Everything Is Wrong." One of the eeriest cases involved five Navy torpedo bombers from the Naval Air Station at Fort Lauderdale, Fla. The bombers soared up into a sunny blue Atlantic sky on December 6, 1945.

Soon, odd messages came from the patrol leader. He radioed in alarm, "Everything is wrong . . . strange. We

THE S.S. *MARINE SULPHUR QUEEN.*

BERMUDA TRIANGLE

can't be sure of any direction. Even the sea doesn't look as it should." Then, silence.

A huge Martin Marine flying boat went to look for the missing bombers. In twenty minutes it, too, vanished without a trace.

In 1963, the American merchant ship *Marine Sulphur Queen,* a fishing boat, and two Air Force tanker jets disappeared.

No common cause — violent air turbulence, heavy seas, meteorites, magnetic storms, water spouts — could seem to account for the occasional loss of both ships and aircraft in the Burmuda Triangle and the utter lack of clues to explain their fate. The International Oceanographic Foundation points out, however, that "the area is noted for strong magnetic anomalies which may result in inaccurate compass readings."

Navy View. The U.S. Navy's official point of view is that the disappearances are a "strange coincidence." It does not believe that any twilight zone exists where supernatural forces gobble up ships and planes. There are others, of course—and especially those men who sail the seven seas and fly above them —who believe otherwise about the unsolved mystery of the Bermuda Triangle. Perhaps the year 1975 will provide an answer.

U.S. NAVY FACT SHEET FOR U.S.S. CYCLOPS

"Prior to the **Cyclops** being assigned to the Naval Overseas Transportation Service, she was operating with the Train of the Atlantic Fleet basing at Hampton Roads, Va. On 9 January 1918 she was detached from this duty and assigned to the Naval Overseas Transportation Service. At this time, she was at Hampton Roads loading a cargo of 9,960 tons of coal. At completion of loading she sailed for Bahia, Brazil, arriving there January 22. She discharged her cargo and sailed on January 25 for Rio de Janeiro, Brazil, arriving there on the 28. There she loaded up a commercial cargo of 10,800 tons of manganese ore and sailed on February 16, via the Barbados for Baltimore, Md., where she was due March 13. She arrived at the Barbados 3 March 1918 for coal and left on March 4. Since her departure there has been no trace of the vessel.

"The disappearance of this ship has been one of the most baffling mysteries in the annals of the Navy, all attempts to locate her having proved unsuccessful. Many theories have been advanced, but none that satisfactorily accounts for her disappearance. There were no enemy submarines in the Western Atlantic at the time, and in December, 1918, every effort was made to obtain information from German sources regarding the disappearance of the vessel. Information was requested from all attachés in Europe with the result that it is definite that neither German U-boats nor German mines came into the question. The only German information on the loss of the **Cyclops** was from American sources which stated that the ship left the Barbados in March, 1918, and has not been heard of since.

"There have been many stories circulated giving supposed clues to the loss of **Cyclops** but all have failed of confirmation."

A DREAM IN HIS EYES **won Kurt Smith of the *Lorain* (Ohio) *Journal* the title of Newspaper Photographer of the Year from the National Press Photographers Association.**

Black America

by
VIRGIL A. CLIFT, Ph.D.
Professor of Education
New York University

Problems of Greatest Concern to the leaders of 23 million black Americans in 1974 were: (1) the economic crisis in the country, and (2) progress in obtaining greater civil rights and equality of opportunity, which had become much more difficult.

The worsening economic recession and inflation which adversely affected employment opportunities caused chaos in many black communities. Advancement in employment opportunities for middle- and upper-income blacks was severely curtailed. Unemployment increased markedly for those in unskilled and semiskilled jobs. Hardest hit were black males between eighteen and twenty-eight years of age in the largest cities. In many ghettos unemployment for this group was as high as 40 percent, whereas national unemployment averaged 5 or 6 percent.

The economic climate also placed a great hardship on the 325,000 black college students. Scholarship aid for them was drastically reduced as colleges and universities faced tighter budgets and economic problems. Foundations and industry made fewer grants for scholarship aid. Part-time and summer employment was lower than it had been at any time in more than two decades.

There was widespread concern on the part of blacks that advances in civil rights were more difficult to obtain. The view was widely held that the U.S. Supreme Court and other branches of

BLACK AMERICA

the federal government were far less supportive of civil and individual rights since the first Nixon administration. For nearly fifty years gains had been made by blacks and other minorities in achieving equality of opportunity by favorable rulings of the U. S. Supreme Court. Appointees to the high court by Nixon shifted the balance to a more conservative posture. The result was that black leadership shifted its strategy in striving to achieve more equitable opportunities; it brought fewer cases into the federal courts because of fear that the high court would rule unfavorably on their cases and thereby negate gains that had been made in civil rights over the past five decades.

Education. The two most controversial problems in education for blacks were busing to achieve integrated education and testing as a means of placing students in programs or as a means for selection and promotion of teachers.

Busing school children to achieve racial integration attracted national attention in 1974 because of violence associated with it in Boston, New York, and other cities. Strong emotions have clouded the issues to the extent that it is appropriate to discuss this issue in its historical context in order to arrive at a better understanding of the problem.

During the two decades following the 1954 U.S. Supreme Court decision *(Brown* v. *Topeka)* outlawing *de jure* segregated education, various means were tried to eliminate segregated schools. The waves of blacks who had migrated to the cities were concentrated in black communities. Schools located in all-black communities became all-black schools. In most communities where the black population reached 50 percent, schools reflected that change, and white parents usually sent their children to private schools or moved from the community to other locations where their children could attend all-white schools or schools with very low black enrollments. This created segregated or racially-imbalanced schools. Thus many schools for blacks were in fact segregated schools, sometimes referred to as *de facto* segregated, as distinguished from *de jure* segregated, the term used for segregation sanctioned by law. Busing became one of the ways used to correct racial imbalance or segregation.

Most legal and educational authorities who have studied the problem agree that racially segregated education imposes hardships on black students. The broader community considers black schools to be inferior. In fact, in quality as judged by academic achievement, students typically perform more poorly in segregated schools. Programs for blacks are frequently less demanding and rigorous because no one expects rigor and high-level achievement. Sociologists use the term "self-fulfilling prophecy" to refer to this phenomenon. People and institutions perform in ways the broader society expects them to perform.

The all-black school was objected to by most blacks also because it relegated those attending these schools to inferior status. It was thought that students would have a double stigma to overcome: that of race and that associated with attending a school regarded by the majority group as inferior. All of this was thought to develop a feeling of inferiority on the part of black students which would damage ego-structure, affect the personality negatively, and result in low levels of aspiration and motivation. Black children were being denied an opportunity to study with peers who were highly motivated; they were in schools with a limited number of desirable role models from the higher socio-economic groups to emulate. For these and other reasons various attempts have been made to correct racial im-

BLACK LIFESTYLE has a character of its own, as exemplified in *Couple* by William Kesler of the *Topeka Capital-Journal*. The picture won first prize in the portrait/personality class of the thirtieth annual Pictures of the Year awards sponsored by the National Press Photographers Association and the University of Missouri's School of Journalism.

balance.

When busing has been used to desegregate schools, it has become one of the most controversial problems to confront communities. Few issues have been known to generate so much emotionalism. In some communities, both North and South, emotions have erupted into rage and violence.

The busing issue became a problem of national significance after the 1968 Supreme Court decision that "free choice" plans were acceptable only if they actually abolished racially segregated schools. It held also that school districts must follow a desegregation plan "which promises realistically to work now." For many communities busing seemed to be the only way of meeting the court mandate.

In August, 1970, Congress passed a $75 million Emergency School Assistance Program Act to assist in school desegregation. The federal courts had been requiring busing in urban areas to remedy racial imbalance. By 1971, after a long series of court cases and controversies in communities, the Supreme Court in *Swann* v. *Charlotte-Mecklenburg Board of Education* decided on a desegregation plan which would require a substantial increase in busing. The court indicated only one limitation to busing: "An objection to the transportation of students may have validity when the time or distance traveled is so great as to risk either the health of children or significantly impinge on educational progress."

Congressional reaction came quickly. Antibusing amendments were added to pending educational legislation. Comprehensive legislation was proposed which would prescribe what desegregation remedies courts could order and would limit greatly the use of busing. Also a proposed Constitutional amendment to prohibit busing received great support.

The Nixon administration changed positions on busing several times between 1970 and 1974. This resulted in more confusion and conflict. The Department of Health, Education, and Welfare appeared to the public to be ambivalent or to shift positions from time to time in providing districts with funds to assist in desegregating schools. When the new Congress convened in 1974, no one knew what the national policy on busing was or what it would be.

Then in July, 1974, the Supreme Court held, in a five-to-four decision in *Milliken* v. *Bradley*, that interdistrict busing between Detroit and its suburbs was not an appropriate remedy for segregated schools in the city. The court maintained that the plaintiffs had not demonstrated that actions of suburban school districts had resulted in segregation, but it did not close the door on all cross-district busing plans. It did place the burden of proof on those who seek to desegregate schools by busing.

History and experience has taught black Americans that it is impossible to have equal opportunities when facilities and institutions are segregated. There has never been an instance where the separate-but-equal doctrine has worked. Since education is of such great significance in the improvement of the quality of life for the individual, most blacks see the desegregation issue as the most compelling one confronting them.

Affirmative Action, Quotas, and Reparation Pay. For the past five years there has been greater emphasis on affirmative action as a means of hiring larger numbers of women and minority people. Most of the original emphasis came from the civil rights movement of the 1960s which resulted in open admissions for minority college students. By 1974 the general concept had been expanded to include quota hiring to ensure that minorities were employed in various industries and institutions in about the proportion they represented in the population. The federal government and the courts had become very active in affirmative action in urging, and in some instances insisting, that employers with government contracts give evidence of unusual effort and success as equal opportunity employers.

Three events during the first of the year were generally regarded as precedents which promised to set a trend in hiring and promoting blacks and other minorities.

(1) In March in Jackson, Miss., Justice Department lawyers helped to negotiate a plan which would give blacks preference in the hiring of state patrolmen. Jackson also agreed to award up to $1,000 each to black employees such as janitors who had never had an opportunity to get better jobs. Further, the city agreed to increase the black work force 40 percent, which was the per-

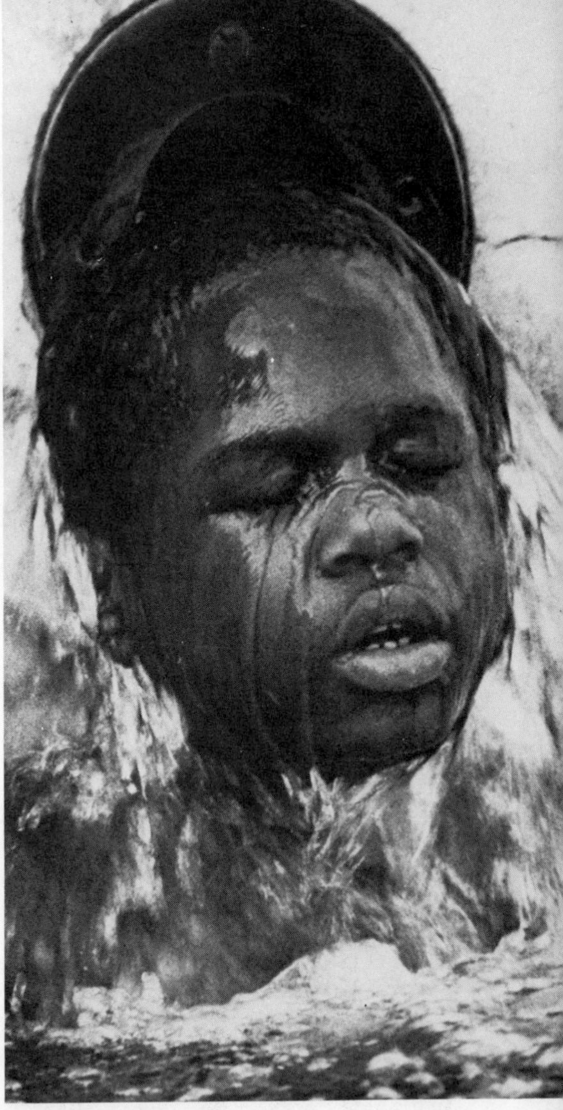

COOLING OFF. This picture by Ronald T. Bennett of Washington, D.C., was the first-place winner in the weather picture contest sponsored by the Outboard Marine Corporation.

BLACK AMERICA

centage of blacks in the population. Outside the South several federal courts had ruled in favor of quota hiring.

(2) Two weeks after the Jackson plan was announced, labor and management in the steel industry announced a voluntary nationwide plan to end race and sex discrimination in hiring, employment, and pay practices. This agreement came after long negotiations with the federal government. The new plan affected nearly 50,000 workers, most of whom were black.

(3) At about the same time the Bell Telephone Company was ordered by a federal court to end all discrimination and to compensate women and minority workers who had been discriminated against.

It was expected that these three events would take on much greater significance when the economic climate of the nation as a whole improved.

GRAY MARBLE HEAD of a black man from the Hellenistic period was purchased by the Brooklyn Museum in New York. Over twenty-two centuries old, the sculpture was described as the finest representation of a Negro of the ancient world known to exist.

Politics. Gains continued to be made in the area of politics. There were more than 3,000 black elected officials in forty-four states and the District of Columbia. This included seventeen congressmen and one U. S. senator. Since 1969, each election saw a 15 percent gain in the number of black officials. Even though the number of black officials continued to increase, their effectiveness in dealing with problems peculiar to blacks was curtailed by the fact that the whole political process had been hampered by Watergate and related problems. Many blacks had become convinced that civic, social, and economic problems of the group would not receive adequate attention so long as major political and economic problems plagued the nation as had been the case in 1974.

More than $2\frac{1}{2}$ million blacks in the South had registered to vote since 1963. Blacks account for about 15 percent of the region's registered voters; they represent 22 percent of the region's population. By 1974 there were about as many black elected officials in the South as in the North.

Governor Melvin Evans of the Virgin Islands became the first black to head the Southern Governors' Conference, once a bastion of resistance to civil rights. Evans succeeded Governor George Wallace of Alabama.

Los Angeles Mayor Thomas Bradley became the first black president of the forty-nine-year-old National League of Cities.

Howard Woodson, the first black speaker of the New Jersey Assembly, completed a two-day stint as governor during the simultaneous absence from the state of the governor and president of the Senate.

Arthur A. Fletcher, Republican party

consultant for minority affairs, said more blacks were running for office on the Republican ticket in 1974 than in any year since Reconstruction.

Blacks elected to the U.S. House of Representatives on November 5 were:

(1)	Yvonne Braithwaite Burke	Los Angeles, Calif.
(2)	Shirley Chisholm	Brooklyn, N.Y.
(3)	William L. Clay	St. Louis, Mo.
(4)	Cardiss W. Collins	Chicago, Ill.
(5)	John Conyers, Jr.	Detroit, Mich.
(6)	Ronald V. Dellums	Berkeley, Calif.
(7)	Charles C. Diggs, Jr.	Detroit, Mich.
(8)	Walter Fauntroy	Washington, D.C.
(9)	Harold Ford	Memphis, Tenn.
(10)	Augustus F. Hawkins	Los Angeles, Calif.
(11)	Ralph Metcalfe	Chicago, Ill.
(12)	Parren J. Mitchell	Baltimore, Md.
(13)	Robert N. C. Nix	Philadephia, Penna.
(14)	Charles Rangle	New York, N. Y.
(15)	Louis Stokes	Cleveland, Ohio
(16)	Barbara Jordan	Houston, Texas
(17)	Andrew Young	Atlanta, Ga.

Of the more than 3,000 black elected officials, the largest number were to be found in Michigan, Alabama, New York, and Mississippi, with from 150 to nearly 200 each. Only six states—Hawaii, Idaho, Montana, North Dakota, South Dakota, and Utah—had no elected black officials.

Honors, Awards, and Special Events. The National Association for the Advancement of Colored People (NAACP) awarded the fifty-ninth Springarn Medal to U. S. District Court Judge Damon J. Keith of the Eastern District of Michigan. The ceremony was presided over by Judge William H. Hastie (retired) of the U. S. Court of Appeals for the Third Circuit, Philadelphia. Judge Hastie, one of the first black federal judges, was a Springarn Medalist thirty-one years ago.

Frank Robinson became the new thirty-nine-year-old manager of the Cleveland Indians, the first black manager in the 105-year history of major league baseball, at a salary of $180,000.

On the sixth anniversary of Dr. Martin Luther King's murder, Hank Aaron asked the executives of the Cincinnati Reds, host team for the first baseball game of the season, to honor Dr. King by calling for a moment of silence among the fans. The executives refused. However, Aaron hit his 714th home run, tying Babe Ruth's record. Later he broke Ruth's record.

In June the mother of the late Martin Luther King, Jr., was murdered during services at the Ebenezer Baptist Church in Atlanta. Her assailant, a black, said he had been ordered by God to kill.

Frank Wills, the black night watchman who summoned police who arrested Watergate burglars, has been unemployed most of the time since that event. The National Urban League granted him a scholarship so that he can improve his skills.

Paul Gibson, Jr., former airline executive, became a deputy mayor of New York City.

Aldrage B. Cooper became the first black mayor of New Brunswick, N. J.

John L. S. Holloman, Jr., became the $65,000-a-year president of New York City's Health and Hospital Department, the largest municipal medical care system in the world.

Earl Hunigan, former executive officer of the Federal Aviation Administration's Southern Region, was named deputy administrator for management at the U. S. Department of Agriculture's Food and Nutrition Service.

Joe Gilliam became the first black quarterback. He played with the Pittsburgh Steelers of the National Football League.

Willie Mays retired from baseball after twenty-two seasons in the major leagues and became a coach with the New York Mets.

Muhammad Ali defeated George Foreman and regained the World's Heavyweight Championship. Ali was stripped of the title seven years earlier when he refused on religious grounds to serve in the armed forces.

Books for Children

by

VIRGINIA HAVILAND

Head, Children's Book Section, Library of Congress; reviewer of children's books, *Horn Book Magazine;* author of *Children and Literature* (1973), editor of *Favorite Fairy Tales Told in India* (1973), compiler with Margaret N. Coughlin of *Yankee Doodle's Literary Sampler of Prose, Poetry, and Pictures* (1974).

***FAGIN IN HIS CELL,* a George Cruikshank illustration for Charles Dickens's *Oliver Twist,* was part of the show, The Artist as Illustrator of His Age: The World of George Cruikshank, at Princeton University's Harvey S. Firestone Library.**

No Change Yet. In spite of heightening economic ills—inflation, paper shortages, high costs of binding and printing, and the shrinking (both actual and apparent) of book budgets, the some 2,000 new children's books published in 1974 did not represent a significant change in number from the previous year. (The first six months showed an increase.) Announcement of cutbacks will be reflected, however, in the books published in 1975. In the face of this imminent retrenchment, one sees a tendency to eliminate marginal or risky books and to produce a higher proportion of clearly useful nonfiction, since library demands are strong here. The number of lavish, full-color picture books, now often costing six or more dollars for a thirty-two page volume, has diminished, while the success of the paperback, including picture books and originals as well as reprints, has increased. It has been reported that $72 million was spent on paperbacks for classroom use by schools during the school year 1973-74.

Picture-Book and Easy-to-Read Needs have strong attention, in tune with emphasis on early childhood education. Fewer imports of picture books appeared. Costlier printing abroad has erased the advantage of hitherto more economical foreign production, and it has lessened the coproduction arrangements. Economics, however, has not eliminated all elegantly issued American books. Volumes sure to do well, on the strength of their creators' previous successes as well as because of freshness of creativity, such as William Steig's *Farmer Palmer's Wagon Ride* and Uri Shulevitz's *Dawn* (both Farrar, Straus and Giroux) evince lavish attention to optimum aesthetic value.

Poetry. An unusual amount of first-rate poetry and rhymes, both new and traditional, came forth in attractive picture books. Poet Jack Prelutsky added two gay volumes to his output of easy, entertaining rhymes: *Circus,* illustrated by Arnold Lobel, and *The Pack Rat's Day and Other Poems,* illustrated by Margaret Bloy Graham (both, Macmillan). From another genuine poet, Norma Farber, came *Where's Gomer?* (Dutton), an entertaining Noah's ark tale illustrated with humorous nineteenth-century details by William Pène Du Bois, while from N. M. Bodecker came delicious fun with rhymes and pictures in *Let's Marry Said the Cherry and Other Nonsense Verses*, Atheneum/a Margaret K. McElderry Book). In picture-book format, though not limited to or even intended for the young picture-book age, were published lavishly illustrated volumes: *City* (Houghton) by the architect David Macaulay—whose art the year before in *Cathedral* made him an honor winner for the 1974 Caldecott Award—and in full, rich color *Lumberjack* (Houghton) by the Canadian artist William Kurelek.

Fantasy and Nonsense. In this year when nonfiction books seemed to outnumber fiction, some of the most original, creatively conceived stories were fantasy or nonsense, although they were possibly fewer in number than earlier. With the great press success—it was directed to both adult readers and buyers for young people—of *Watership Down* (Macmillan) by English prize-winner Richard Adams, an allegorical hero tale set in a society of rabbits, other fantasy-reading also beyond the expected younger age appeared. Elizabeth Pope's *The Perilous Gard* (Houghton) recreates early England's West Country when belief in the supernatural had daily force and meaning, and its young hero all but loses his life to witchcraft. For younger girls and boys herbal folklore became the core of a backward-in-time fantasy in *Lavender Green Magic* (Crowell) by Andre Norton, who deals with superstitious beliefs of colonial New England.

Nonfiction, as well as fiction, aimed to satisfy omnivorous interests in the occult —looking into the future and calling on the manifold arts of magic: books on palmistry, astrology, hexes, spells, and other mystical manifestations, and black magic. Two such books are scientist Roy Gallant's *Astrology: Sense or Nonsense; Do the Stars Control Your Destiny?* (Doubleday); and Daniel Cohen's *Curses, Hexes, and Spells* (Lippincott). The latter is included in a publisher's series called the Weird and Horrible Library.

Bicentennial Books. With the bicentennial of the American Revolution nearing, the publishing of works related to our earlier political and cultural history became heavier. They ranged from such substantial works as George Sanderlin's *A Hoop to the Barrel: the Making of the American Constitution* (Coward, McCann & Geoghegan), Donald Barr Chidsey's *The World of Samuel Adams* (Nelson), and a number of others, to charmingly illustrated fictionalized vignettes of colonial history for first reading. Among these are Patricia Lee Gauch's *This Time, Tempe Wiek?*, about a colonial girl of legend who used her wits to keep her horse from thieving revolutionary mutineers, and Ferdinand Monjo's *King George's Head Was Made of Lead*, in which a cantankerous statue in New York City views events of the stamp tax—each with pictures by Margot Tomes (Coward, McCann and Geoghegan.)

Americana. An unusual burst of publishing surveyed Americana in arts, crafts, and children's literature. Elinor L. Horwitz's *Mountain People, Mountain Crafts* (Lippincott) presents the distinctive Appalachian way of life and crafts; and Aldren Watson, of Vermont, shows with careful detail in *Country Furniture* (Crowell) related arts also inherited from early settlers. The latter book has an interest chiefly for mature older readers and adults. The picture of literature available to children in eighteenth- and nineteenth-century America is shown by the reprinting of such earlier works as Louisa May Alcott's *An Old-Fashioned Thanksgiving* (Lippincott) and Lydia

Maria Child's *The New England Boy's Song About Thanksgiving,* now titled from its first line, *Over the River and Through the Wood* (Coward, McCann & Geoghegan), with color pictures by Brinton Turkle. An anthology selected from juvenilia in the Rare Book Collection of the Library of Congress, *Yankee Doodle's Literary Sampler of Prose, Poetry, and Pictures* (Crowell), of interest especially to adults, also appeared.

Foreign Lands. Interest was not confined to the United States; the rest of the world received strong publishing emphasis. China invited attention from numerous researchers and travelers, resulting in Gil and Ann Loescher's *The Chinese Way; Life in the People's Republic of China* (Harcourt Brace Jovanovich), Ruth Sidel's *Revolutionary China: People, Politics, and Ping-Pong* (Delacorte), and Jules Archer's *China in the Twentieth Century* (Macmillan). The Third World, particularly Africa, continued to achieve strong publisher attention, both in fiction and nonfiction. Peoples of Africa were presented with authority and interest for young readers in books illustrated with photographic distinction, among them E. Jefferson Murphy's *The Bantu Civilization of Southern Africa* and Aylette Jenness's *Along the Niger River: an African Way of Life* (both, Crowell). For younger readers there appeared *Jambo Means Hello: Swahili Alphabet Book* (Dial) by Muriel Feelings, with drawings by Tom Feelings, a book presenting in distinctive fashion village life in East Africa.

Ethnic Books. Books appealing to minority groups in the United States exhibited an ongoing concern with the interests of blacks, Spanish-speaking groups, and, with notably increasing attention, the American Indian. Indian writers are sought, as have been blacks, but only Virginia Driving Hawk Sneve has had regularity in publishing. Her most recent book is another historical story about the Dakota Indians, *When Thunders Spoke* (Holiday). More nonfiction than fiction was published about the American Indian, with, as in other years, new volumes of folklore—notably Gerald McDermott's adaptation and illustration in brilliant picture book format of *Arrow to the Sun: a Pueblo Indian Tale* (Viking) and John Bierhorst's editing of *Songs of the Chippewa,* with pictures by John Servello (Farrar, Straus and Giroux).

Black writers published have increased in number. Virginia Hamilton offered two outstanding contributions this year: *M.C. Higgins, the Great* (Macmillan)—the story of an engaging boy hero in strip-mining coal country, a picture of problems but without overt message; it won the year's *Boston Globe-Horn Book Magazine* Award — and a biography, *Paul Robeson: the Life and Times of a Free Black Man* (Harper). Another revealing biography is Jesse Jackson's *Make a Joyful Noise Unto the Lord! The Life of Mahalia Jackson, Queen of Gospel Singers* (Crowell) which provides an account of the civil rights movement as this singer contributed to its development.

In another ethnic direction, attention turned to Jewish history in *World of Our Fathers: The Jews of Eastern Europe* (Farrar, Straus and Giroux), by Milton Meltzer, the well-known historian of black history.

Women's Lib. Not an actual minority, but a group also stressing human rights, women received more attention than usual in books for young people. The Crowell "Women of America" series brought its number of volumes up to twenty-two biographies. Victoria Ortiz's *Sojourner Truth* (Lippincott) successfully projects through an ex-slave's life the double issues of abolition and women's rights. So, also, does Elizabeth Gray

BOOKS FOR CHILDREN

Vining's *Mr. Whittier,* in which the poet is shown to have been an ardent supporter of antislavery movements and a friend of Lucy Larcom and other proponents of liberation for women. In a lighter vein, and for a younger audience, is the delightfully humorous story *The Liberation of Clementine Tipton* (Houghton) by Jane Flory, which succeeds as a period story of Philadelphia at the time of the Centennial Exposition of 1876. A social picture of a lively, affluent household (an American "Upstairs-Downstairs" situation) it is, in addition, a characterization of a spirited child whose rebelliousness parallels her new English governess's stand on women's rights.

Problem Probers. Young people are the target readers of thoughtful books reporting present or predicted disorders of the adult world due to overpopulation, excessive pollution, and exhaustion of natural resources. On the latter subject same Dorothy E. and L. A. Shuttlesworth's forceful *Disappearing Energy: Can We End the Crisis?* (Doubleday). Interest in energy production, keeping the environment in balance, and recycling — see, for the very youngest, *The Compost Heap* by Harlow Rockwell (Doubleday) — have led to a profusion of science books on publishing lists. Unusual and highly specialized areas of technology and natural science have been clearly treated for the young in such books as *Shakes, Quakes, and Shifts: Earth Tectonics* by scientist Franklyn M. Branley and *Neurons: Building Blocks of the Brain* by Leonard A. Stevens (both Crowell).

Social and psychological problems or disorders treated in fiction frequently introduced negative aspects of life (once kept out of books for young people) as they affect the individual as well as the group. These fill the contemporary novels designated "young adult" but actually read by many sixth graders — stories dealing with drugs, premarital sex and pregnancy, gangs and crime, loneliness and brutality, with parents and other adults being shown as fallible, or worse. Robert Cormier's *The Chocolate War* (Pantheon) illustrates graphically the torture and tragedy inflicted on an independent-thinking hero by gang dictatorship in a parochial secondary school. All is not negative in such stories, however. On the positive side — and the book named above is, in spite of its dark side, meaningful and perhaps inspiring — are stories in which young people are seen as strong, loyal, and loving. One such example, dealing inexplicitly but realistically with premarital sex, is Mil-

***DUFFY AND THE DEVIL,* a Cornish version of Rumpelstiltskin by Harve and Margot Zemach, received the Caldecott Medal for "the most distinguished American picture book for children."**

dred Lee's poignant *Sycamore Year* (Lothrop, Lee and Shepard).

Public Censorship to force removal of books considered "unsuitable" for consumption by young people became all-too-frequent tests of library and school book selection authority. Controversy erupted over the inclusion of street language, claimed religious blasphemies, and unpatriotic sentiments, as in the Charleston, W. Va., issue of use in the county schools of new readers designed to relate to ethnic groups and today's sophisticated students.

Book Awards stimulated searches for quality in books belonging to a wide range of categories and the awards reveal various contemporary points of view. One emphasis is clearly the importance of excellence in books for the very young. The Irma Simonton Black Award (Bank Street School) in its second year honored two beginner books, recognizing children's own verdicts: Bernice Freschet's *Bear Mouse* (Scribner), a picture book illustrated by Donald Carrick; and Remy Charlip's and Burton Supree's *Harlequin and the Gift of Many Colors* (Parents Press), illustrated by Charlip. The Caldecott Medal of the American Library Association, for the artist of "the most outstanding American picture book" went to Margot Zemach for her illustration of *Duffy and the Devil*, a Cornish version of the folktale "Tom Tit Tot," retold by Harve Zemach. Another picture book citation was the *Boston Globe-Horn Book Magazine* Award to Tom Feelings for his pictures in *Jambo Means Hello*, by Muriel Feelings (Delacorte).

The Children Book Showcase for its third annual competition and exhibition-plus-program of illustrated books chosen by experts for "outstanding graphic merit" selected thirty-one titles of 1973, chiefly books for the picture book age, produced by a variety of techniques and media. This successful venture is sponsored by the Children's Book Council whose membership includes some sixty publishers of children's books.

The highest awards for literature—the coveted Newbery Medal of the American Library Association and the National Book Committee's National Book Award for children's literature—were presented in 1974 for entirely unlike books. The former, chosen by children's librarians, went to Paula Fox for *Slave Dancer* (Bradbury)—the story of a flute-playing boy impressed on a slave ship to "dance" the slaves for exercise on their voyage from Africa. The other, selected by a committee of three critics, was given to Eleanor Cameron for *The Court of the Stone Children* (Dutton), a betwixt-two-worlds fantasy set in a San Francisco museum.

Two awards had purposeful concerns: the Child Study Award, which was voted to Doris Buchanan Smith for *A Taste of Blackberries* (Crowell), a moving story of a small boy's dealing with the death of his best friend; and the Jane Addams Award of the Women's International League for Peace and Freedom which went to Nicholasa Mohr's *Nilda* (Harper), an autobiographical story of poverty in the Puerto Rican area of New York City.

The American Section of the International Board on Books for Young People was involved in the biennial international Hans Christian Andersen Awards—the "Little Nobels." The medal for writing was presented to Maria Gripe of Sweden whose stories, both realistic *(Hugo* and *Josephine)* and fairy-tale *(The Glassblower's Children)*, are published in the United States by Seymour Lawrence. The winner for illustration was Farshid Mesghali of Iran, a few of whose many picture books have been published in the United States by Carolrhoda Books.

Boxing

by

ART DUNN

Editor, Sunday Sports Section
Chicago Tribune

Muhammad Ali, perhaps the most controversial — and best — fighter ever, dramatically won back the heavyweight crown which was nonviolently lifted from him seven years ago for refusing to be drafted.

Ali's eighth round knockout of champion George Foreman earned the once and future champion the adulation of continents and an even split of the record $10 million purse.

The stunning upset was achieved in the predawn hours in Kinshasa, Zaïre, before sixty thousand onlookers in the emerging nation once known as the Belgian Congo and millions who watched on closed-circuit television.

His greatest and richest triumph came exactly fourteen years after Ali (then known as Cassius Clay) won his first professional fight in Louisville. Though his career was marked with bizarre events in and out of the ring, the self-proclaimed "rumble in the jungle" was as dramatic as any.

Facing an undefeated, ferocious puncher six years his junior, Ali was a decided underdog, and was expected to become the forty-first pro victim of Foreman. The odds remained against Ali even after the fight was postponed six weeks when an out-of-shape Foreman suffered a cut above his eye during training in September.

It was a situation not unlike 1964 when the brash youngster floated and stung Sonny Liston to first capture the heavyweight title.

FIGHTING from the ropes, Muhammad Ali became the second man in boxing history to regain the heavyweight championship when he defeated George Foreman at 4 a.m. on October 29 in Kinshasa, Zaire. Speaking of the fight, Ali said, "I didn't dance. I hadn't started dancing yet, when the fight ended. Foreman had no punch. I stayed on the ropes."

BOXING

Throughout the long prefight buildup, Ali promised Foreman and the world that his speed with hands and feet would nullify the champion's power and youth. "We're gonna dance," Ali chanted to anyone who listened.

But when the two men stepped into the ring in Stade du 20 Mai at 4 a.m., Kinshasa time, Ali did not dance or float or shuffle. He retreated to the corner where Foreman wanted him, pressed his back against the ropes, and took all the champion could throw for much of the first seven rounds.

Foreman and even Ali's handlers were shocked at the sudden deviation from his hit-and-run tactics. But while the challenger did not float, he did sting Foreman repeatedly as he lay against the ropes and taunted his adversary to hit him.

Then in the eighth round, with Foreman drained from roundhouse swings at the stationary target, Ali caught the champ with a barrage of short jabs. A straight right sent Foreman spinning in the middle of the ring, where he fell on his back and leaned on his elbows with a dazed look as Referee Zack Clayton counted him out.

"Allah was with me and because of it this man looked like nuthin'," Ali boasted in the postfight interview. "If you believe in Allah nuthin' can hurt you—not even a George Foreman. I told you all I was the greatest. Never again make me an underdog—not until I turn fifty years old."

Trainer Dick Sadler, who had brought Foreman carefully to the top of his profession, tried to explain the smashing defeat of his man who had dispatched Californian Ken Norton in two rounds at Caracas, Venezuela, in March.

"Everything we planned to do—cutting the ring, overpowering Ali, going after him—was designed to put him on the ropes. And there he was. Just exactly where we wanted him. The bird's nest was on the ground. It was time to sit down and eat the feast. But George didn't do it right. He wasn't doing what he was supposed to. Hard combinations. Getting in closer. He wasn't setting him up with his left hand. We *told* him. It didn't register."

Other Title Fights: Middleweight champion Carlos Monzon of Argentina stopped welterweight king Jose Napoles in seven rounds. The victory in Paris was Monzon's ninth successful defense. His Mexican challenger was trying to become the fourth man in history to win the middleweight title while wearing the welterweight crown.

Earlier, Napoles knocked out Hedgemon Lewis of Detroit in the ninth round.

Texan Oscar Alvarado retained the junior middleweight crown by knocking out Ryu Sorimachi in the seventh round in Tokyo.

Antonio Cervantes of Colombia took the junior welterweight title by KOing Victor (Millon) Ortiz in the second round at Cartagena, Colombia.

Roberto Duran of Panama regained the lightweight title with an eleventh-round knockout of Esteban DeJesus, handing him the first loss of his career. Ben Villaflor defended his junior lightweight title twice in 1974, holding Apollo Yoshio to a fifteen-round draw in March and KOing Yasutsune Uyehara.

Korean Soon Hwan Hong won the bantam crown by decisioning South African Arnold Taylor in the loser's home country.

Light heavyweight Bob Foster defended his title once this year, then retired with a 51-7-1 record. He last fought a fifteen-round draw with Jorge Ahumada in Albuquerque. Foster won the title from Dick Tiger in May, 1969. He twice tried for the heavyweight crown, but was knocked out by Ali and Joe Frazier.

by
MICHAEL COPE
Internationally Syndicated Columnist

Canada

PEGGY'S COVE, St. Margaret Bay, Nova Scotia.

Unique among the developed nations of the West, Canada alone continued to register advances on most of its growth indexes during 1974, while the rest of the world reeled under the double onslaught of inflation and recession. It was a year which saw Canada's immense mineral wealth command new respect and interest from other nations.

It was in this climate the country went to the polls in an enforced summer election and returned Prime Minister Pierre Elliot Trudeau's Liberal party with a comfortable majority which enabled the government to get on with the job of exploiting the nation's vast wealth at a crucial time. Internationally, Canada spoke from a position of strength; she sharply warned of looming differences with the United States, and Trudeau himself flew to Europe in the fall to warn the nine nations of the European Economic Community (EEC) that Canada's resources were not up for grabs.

But at home, whatever viewpoint it was seen from, Canada acted only in an expansionary mood. As a noted Montreal economist, Kurt E. Hass, defined it: "For the first time, the Canadian economy has become the envy of the industrial countries of the Western world."

Oil Rich. Much of this envy centered on Canada's rich oil deposits, particularly the Athabasca oil sands 250 miles north of Edmonton, Alta., where there is more oil than in all the Middle East reserves combined. Other oilfields, already in production in Alberta and neighboring Saskatchewan, make Canada the only Western nation exporting oil during these times of desperate energy shortage.

A FREIGHT CAR stands ready for loading in a northern Canadian lumber yard. In searching for national identity, Canadians have become enchanted with the history of their railroads. Pierre Berton's bestselling story of the Canadian Pacific's construction across the continent, published as *The Impossible Dream* in the United States, was made into a $2 million television series by the Canadian Broadcasting Corporation. Its premiere in March was watched by 3.6 million people, not including children, or one adult Canadian out of four.

Because there is no pipeline to carry the prairie oil to eastern Canada, particularly to the dense consumer markets around Montreal and Toronto, Canada still had to import 900,000 barrels a day from the Middle East and Venezuela. The soaring prices demanded for these imports she offset by exporting about the same amount to the American West. The Canadian government levied a $6.40 export tax on each barrel, an action which put Canada in the almost unique position of achieving a zero trade balance on oil supplies.

Canada's economic stability is vested not only in her oil deposits, but also in her mineral resources, particularly base metals, and a rapidly maturing manufacturing sector. Together, these not only effectively insulated Canada from staggering deficits of payments incurred by rising oil prices, but also maintained the nation's growth rate. Gross national product (GNP) figures for 1973 showed a 14.8 percent increase over the previous year, a total of $118.7 billion. Even with the inflation factor removed, real growth still measured 7.1 percent, and all figures contributing to the GNP were up—consumer expenditures by 8.6 percent, investment in plant and equipment by 18 percent, personal income by 14.1 percent, and personal disposable income by 14.2 percent. Trading statistics contributed also. The $15,109 million worth of goods exported during the first six months of 1974 represented an overall 23 percent increase. Still on the upward trend, Canada predicts that within the next five years she will be producing 80 percent more copper, 61 percent more iron ore, 25 percent more lead, 30 percent more nickel, and 55 percent more zinc than she did in 1970. This at a time when the United States anticipates its own production of 68 percent of the metallic minerals required by its industry will fall to 42 percent in the next ten years. If confirmation of Canada's op-

NOVA SCOTIA OXEN wear brass-studded head yokes that are carefully fitted to the horns so that the animals can put the full strength of their massive necks into pulling. In 1974 Nelson Zinck of Nova Scotia won the top trophy in the International Ox Pulling Contest in Cumberland, Maine, when his pair of oxen towed 9,000 pounds of concrete blocks a distance of three feet.

KLONDIKE TRAIL OF '98

THE KLONDIKE GOLD RUSH ANNIVERSARY

Seventy-five years after the rush to find gold along the Klondike River called the vast wild Yukon Territory to the world's attention, gold-crazed prospectors are again scouring the mountain streams of western Canada with pans in their hands. The new rush is triggered by the soaring price of gold, up from the fixed rate of $35 an ounce to $150 an ounce and higher.

For $10 a year a panner in the Klondike can get a renewable lease on a claim which gives him 500 feet of creek frontage and the land stretching back 1,000 feet on each side of the creek. By May, Klondike claims had doubled the number for the entire year of 1973.

It is the history of the gold rush that provides the basis for the second largest industry of the Yukon, tourism. In 1974 more than 300,000 visitors from the "outside," meaning any place not in the Yukon, trooped through Diamond Gertie's Gambling Hall and reveled in the ballads of Robert W. Service, the troubadour of the Klondike Gold Rush.

"There are strange things done
in the midnight sun
By the men who moil for gold."

CANADA

timism was needed, it was reflected in the Bank of Montreal's Business Review: "Looking ahead, the economy is bound to receive a significant stimulus from investments in energy-related projects."

The Election. Politically, the Canadian electorate reacted decisively in July's general election when it returned 141 members of Prime Minister Trudeau's Liberal party to the 264-seat Ottawa Parliament, thus ending twenty-one months of minority government which followed the fall, 1972, election when the Liberals won only 109 seats. The snap election was forced in May when the Conservatives and the socialist New Democratic parties combined to defeat the government on a vote in Parliament. It was a vigorous and serious election campaign, devoid of the charismatic imagery which first swept Trudeau into office in 1968. His casual, almost contemptuous approach to the 1972 election nearly lost him office, a lesson he took to heart. This time he campaigned tirelessly, presenting the Liberals' platform intelligently, logically, and persuasively. The result was a decisive mandate.

The election was politically significant and indicative of the times. It was fought largely on the issue of inflation which had been running at about 10 percent in Canada. Both the right-wing Progressive Conservatives who held 106 seats in the previous Parliament, and the socialist New Democratic party (NDP) which had thirty-one seats, combined to vote against the government's annual budget. This alliance of the political right and left was based on the belief that mandatory, legislated wage and price controls were the only way of halting inflation. Trudeau, to keep his minority government functioning during the previous twenty-one months, had accommodated the left-wing NDP parliamentarians, but he firmly rejected their demand for wage and price controls. Inflation, he insisted, was an international problem which could be overcome only by stimulating the economy and increasing productivity.

Forcing the election was something of a gamble for the New Democratic party which rebounded disastrously. With thirty-one seats in the previous Parliament the socialists—perhaps trying to take a lesson from the success of other left-wing parties in Europe, particularly Great Britain, and in Australia and New Zealand, where socialist governments rule or are partners in coalition administrations—mistakenly believed Canada was on the same threshold of political change. The result was the New Democrats not only lost fifteen of the thirty-one seats they had held before, but the party's leader, lawyer David Lewis, was personally defeated in his Toronto constituency, as was his deputy, John Harney. It was clear many left-leaning Canadians were not prepared to risk wage and price controls and switched their NDP votes to the Liberals, particularly in industrialized Ontario where the Liberals took fifty-five of the eighty-eight seats.

For Robert Stanfield, a remote, high-principled Nova Scotian, it was the third straight defeat for his Progressive Conservative party, which won only 95 of the 264 seats at stake. The result was a net loss of eleven seats. Like his Conservative counterpart in Great Britain, Edward Heath (who has now lost three elections out of four), it must be suspected Stanfield will soon step down from the leadership. Already his successor is being tipped as Peter Lougheed, the premier of Alberta province where the vast deposits of oil have earned him the nickname "Blue-Eyed Oil Sheik of the West." Lougheed delivered all nineteen of Alberta's federal seats to the Conservatives in the election.

For Trudeau it was a remarkable elec-

THE LIGHTHOUSE at Peggy's Cove, one of Nova Scotia's 356 lighthouses and fog alarms, guards the entrance to St. Margaret Bay. To protect this province's natural beauty for Canadians, officials alarmed at the growing numbers of Americans buying vacation tracts began to appropriate U.S.-owned private property in Nova Scotia. Ontario has put a heavy tax on land purchases by nonresidents, and on Prince Edward Island where foreigners control 15 percent of the shoreline, large purchases of land by noncitizens require Cabinet approval.

CANADA

toral win and comeback. Having now won three elections in a row, he is in the same category of political greats as Sir John A. Macdonald, the nation's first federal prime minister who confederated the remaining British North American colonies into a single nation 108 years ago, and Mackenzie King, the unbeatable Liberal prime minister of Canada who ruled for twenty-one years.

The New Cabinet. A month after the election, Trudeau reorganized his cabinet, the biggest change being External Affairs Minister Mitchell Sharp's switching jobs with Allan MacEachen, president of the Canadian Privy Council and government leader in the House of Commons. Sharp, who is sixty-three, had been external affairs minister since the first Trudeau administration in 1968. MacEachen, fifty-three, is a former university professor from Nova Scotia. Another significant change in the post-election ministerial shuffle was the dropping from the cabinet of Senator Paul Martin, a former external affairs minister in the administration of the late Prime Minister Lester Pearson who preceded Trudeau. Senator Martin had been government leader in the Senate, the upper chamber of the two Houses of Parliament. He was later named to head Canada's important diplomatic post in London where the senior representative of a Commonwealth country is titled high commissioner, although he ranks in every respect with an ambassador.

U. S. Relations. Shortly before the election, External Affairs Minister Sharp reported to Parliament on what he termed a "new phase in Canada's relations with the United States." He said: "There are . . . several areas of great importance for both Canada and the United States such as the resource, economic, and environmental sectors, where the formulation and implementation of our respective national policies will not necessarily coincide. Close consultation and mature consideration are necessary to ensure American understanding of policies likely to affect their interests.

"On the one hand, the elaboration of a Canadian energy policy must . . . not only take our own long-term requirements into account but also the consequences of the United States's intention to become self-sufficient by 1980. On the other hand, the Canadian desire to develop mineral resources at its own pace and to encourage further processing in Canada may not entirely accord with the United States's desire for rapid exploitation of known resources, an accelerated program for exploration for unproven resources, and the importation of resources in increasing amounts in their raw form."

While this declaration emphasized "The United States will remain Canada's major economic partner," it warned also "we can expect problems to occur." This was probably the most important policy statement to emerge from Ottawa during the year, and the reason behind it was twofold: growing Canadian nationalism, which has undoubtedly been boosted by Canadian awareness not only of the vast amount of wealth locked up in the nation's resources, but the power and influence that goes with it, and the Canadians' almost passionate desire to reduce their economic dependence on the United States, which is at the root of much of Canada's nationalism. In effect, the Canadians were saying that the days of what had become almost the traditional transborder relationship under which the products of Canada's mines and quarries fed the industrial machines and sophisticated technology of the United States were over. In future, the Canadians were determined to shape and develop their own technological and industrial destiny.

But, as the Canadians saw it, all this

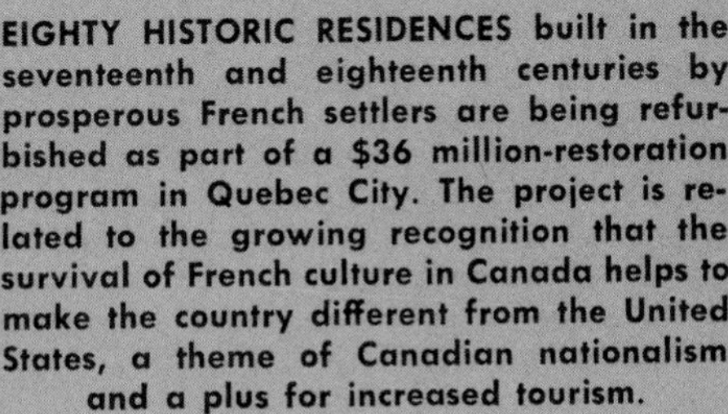

EIGHTY HISTORIC RESIDENCES built in the seventeenth and eighteenth centuries by prosperous French settlers are being refurbished as part of a $36 million-restoration program in Quebec City. The project is related to the growing recognition that the survival of French culture in Canada helps to make the country different from the United States, a theme of Canadian nationalism and a plus for increased tourism.

SEEING THE ST. LOUIS GATE in Quebec City from a carriage driven by a French-speaking coachman appeals to tourists in French Canada. Continuing the French-English linguistic war, the Quebec Assembly in July adopted legislation making French the only official tongue within the province's borders, even though Canada's constitution guarantees the use of both English and French in Quebec's legislature and courts.

was not enough; they also put legislative teeth into their new relationship with a twenty-five-page list of regulations and new working rules to tightly control foreign investment in Canada. The Foreign Investment Review Act not only gave the government a virtual veto of any proposed foreign takeover of a sizeable Canadian company, but also guaranteed the right to review such businesses as are already foreign-controlled, which still amount to more than 50 percent of Canada's industry.

Canada and the EEC. It was essentially the same message which Prime Minister Trudeau took to Europe when he visited France and Belgium in October. At Brussels, the administrative headquarters of the nine-nation European Economic Community, he said: "We are telling the Europeans bilaterally and as a community: You may think you will be able to take all our raw materials out. You ain't. We think it is good for you to be there as we define our policies. If you believe in your destiny as we believe in it, you had better be in there." The bluntness was characteristic of Trudeau, but it affirmed the purpose of his European visit which was to emphasize Canada's separate (from the United States) identity. This, as he saw it, was a necessary prerequisite to securing some sort of loose contractual trade and economic agreement with the EEC. For the most part the European reaction was one of surprise. But, as is so often the case with Trudeau, there was an even deeper hidden meaning. It was the first official visit to France by a Canadian leader since the late President Charles de Gaulle's deliberately inflammatory re-

CANADA

mark to a crowd of French-Canadian separatists in Montreal, in the course of a state visit to Canada in 1967: "Vive le Quebec Libre." At the time, the Canadian government formally requested de Gaulle to leave the country. In Paris, Trudeau was politely received and protocol scrupulously observed; a cautious French reaction to international fence-mending.

Three Important Appointments. The year also saw three important appointments in Canada. The first was the new governor-general, the resident symbolic representative of the Crown and an integral part of the constitutional process. He is Jules Leger, a French-Canadian career diplomat who had represented Canada as ambassador in Mexico, France, and the EEC headquarters in Brussels. He is the son of a rural Quebec storekeeper, and his elder brother, a cardinal in the Roman Catholic church and a former archbishop of Montreal, is a famous missionary in a West African leper colony. The new governor-general took his oath of allegiance to Queen Elizabeth II in the red-carpeted Senate Chamber in Ottawa using the Leger family Bible. And it was perhaps a sign of the new sense of Canadian unity when Prime Minister Trudeau, also a French-Canadian, said: "May I respectfully ask that your first official act be to convey to Her Majesty, the Queen of Canada, a message expressing loyalty of the people."

Another important appointment was that of Mr. Justice Boris Laskin as the new chief justice of Canada (who acts on behalf of the governor-general during the latter's absence). The appointment was a controversial one. Justice Laskin, a former law professor, was one of the most junior of the nine judges who constitute the Supreme Court, although his brilliant dissenting opinions have become judicially famous in Canada. It would seem that Trudeau, also a former law professor, was anxious, as one commentator expressed it, "to shake up this cautious and conservative body," the Supreme Court.

The third appointment of note was that of Mrs. Pauline Emily McGibbon as lieutenant-governor of Ontario, the first woman to hold vice-regal office in Canada. She has had a long and distinguished association with Canadian artistic and educational institutions, and was also the first woman chancellor of the University of Toronto.

Milestones. Another significant first for Canadian women during the year was the acceptance by the 101-year-old Royal Canadian Mounted Police and the sixty-five-year-old Ontario Provincial Police, of women recruits. "They will carry service revolvers, billies and handcuffs, and will receive extra physical training with the emphasis on self-defense," said a police statement.

Another milestone in Canada's development was the October report of Statistics Canada that the population had passed the 22 million mark. Ontario has the largest population of the ten provinces with 7,988,000 and Prince Edward Island the smallest with 115,000 out of a total population of 22,207,000.

In Retrospect, 1974 was an eminently satisfactory year for most Canadians; real growth factors had been maintained at a time when inflation had reached such proportions in other industrialized countries that recession and retrenchment were the only means left with which to combat it. Because of its vast energy and other resources, Canada acquired new stature and importance in the world, and Canadians, with a majority government again firmly in control in Ottawa, displayed a refreshingly new front of unity and purposefulness to the rest of the world, all of which augured well for the future.

Careers

THE INFLATION VACATION found Americans picking resorts closer to home and staying a shorter time. Domestic air travel boomed because many U.S. citizens who in 1973 might have driven long distances flew instead and rented a car upon arrival, scared by gasoline shortages early in 1974. Overseas flights to Europe, on jets such as this 747 unloading at London's Heathrow Airport, showed passenger declines for the first time in the postwar period, a direct result of four trans-Atlantic fare increases since January.

CAREERS IN TRAVEL

by

ROBERT SCOTT MILNE

Independent Travel Writer

Big Business. Travel is a broad field that cuts across many others, so there are many kinds of careers to be had in the travel business.

Travel is very big business. Several U.S. states and many countries of the world derive their primary income from it. Encompassing such varied areas as souvenirs, accommodations, ships, and big passenger aircraft, as well as all kinds of personal services, it engages many people—in the United States, about 10 million.

CAREERS

One of the special inducements to work in the travel industry is the opportunity to travel oneself, either as part of the job, or during vacation time at greatly reduced rates. A high percentage of the jobs in travel are held by women.

Travel Agencies. To operate a travel agency one must have some capital, have experience in the field, and be named as agent for the main associations of carriers. A few years spent working for another travel agent has traditionally constituted the best preparation for becoming an agent. A number of colleges now offer specialization in travel, or — as at Niagara University — in travel, transportation, and tourism. A young person taking such a course would be wise to work for a travel agency or carrier or for a hotel during school vacations, to gain practical experience along with formal training by graduation.

Doing a good job in a travel agency requires that one keep up with a tremendous amount of information about the constantly changing conditions in travel all over the world. Rate schedules are very complex and change with the seasons. New hotels are built and old ones change their names. Ship and air routes vary. So intelligence is required, as well as a pleasant personality for dealing with customers and carriers and hotels.

In the Major Airlines these jobs are more specialized. A ticket agent sells tickets to passengers, determines the fares, fills out the ticket forms, and may weigh baggage and charge for excess weight. Reservation sales agents give information and accept reservations over the telephone only. Being on the telephone all day long can become very tedious. Traffic representatives visit such potential customers as convention managers or club presidents who might charter entire airplanes, in order to build business for the airline.

Stewardesses and stewards attend the flight briefing, check food and beverages and the condition of the cabin, welcome passengers aboard and check their tickets, check seatbelts, give safety information, and serve meals and beverages. On shuttle flights they may sell tickets.

Women fill these jobs on most domestic U.S. lines, but men are employed, usually with women, on many international routes of U.S. and other airlines.

Passenger Shipping Lines have many occupations similar to those of airlines, such as ticket clerks; and a parallel organization of operating personnel. There are not many career opportunities for Americans at present, however, because there are very few U.S. passenger ships in operation, and the European companies in the shipping business generally hire their personnel at home.

Hotels and Motels provide the traveler with bed and board and almost everything else he needs in his daily life away from home; therefore they need workers in a broad spectrum of occupations, most of them concerned with serving the traveler. These service occupations — cleaning rooms, making beds, moving furniture, carrying luggage, operating elevators, preparing food — provide opportunity for persons without education and for immigrants who do not speak the language of the country. A person in one of these jobs may be poorly paid and may have to depend on tips, but such a job gives him a living, and perhaps free meals, while he prepares himself for a better job.

At the top of the scale in hotels, on the other hand, more and more education is being required, and the rewards are increasing commensurately, with managers of major hotels earning over $50,000 per year.

One method of advancement in the

hotel business is to save money, borrow more, and build or buy one's own hotel. In 1970, of 190,000 hotels in the United States, more than 100,000 were operated by owner-managers.

A four-year course in hotel and restaurant administration, along with vacation work in hotels and restaurants, now provides the best entree to a position as assistant manager or management trainee in a hotel, although some of these positions are still being filled by promotion from within the staff. The Hotel School at Cornell University is highly regarded in the United States, and there are several hotel schools in Switzerland that are famous around the world.

The best advancement potential is in chain hotels, since they keep expanding and want to ensure continuity of their operating programs by promoting from within the chain.

Intercity Bus Lines offer jobs as drivers to men who are good at driving, calm under tension, and tactful and courteous with customers. They usually require a high school education and a minimum age of twenty-four. Most bus lines give new drivers from two weeks to three months of instruction. Pay is according to miles driven, usually with a guaranteed minimum. In 1970 the average pay for regular and substitute drivers was $10,800. The U.S. Department of Transportation limits working hours and requires rest periods.

Railroads, like bus, air, and ship lines, use many station agents, clerks, shop workers, communicators, and engineers. Conductors, the railroaders most in contact with the traveling public, reach their job level usually after long service as brakemen (also called flagmen and trainmen). The conductor is captain of the train crew, in charge of everything, and responsible for passengers and freight. He tells the engineer when to start and orders him to stop if the train's safety requires it.

CANOEISTS navigate the Rio Grande River in Big Bend National Park, Texas. Lowered attendance at U.S. national parks farthest from heavily populated areas indicated that fewer people were willing to travel great distances for recreation in 1974.

The great reduction in U.S. railroad service about 1970 left many senior conductors without jobs and willing to fill openings as they became vacant, so the outlook for conductors' jobs, like other railroading jobs, is not good.

On the other hand, there are now a few openings for young women as hostesses on railroads that are trying hard to woo passengers away from the airlines.

Carnivals and Circuses

by
MARCELLO TRUZZI

Head, Department of Sociology
Eastern Michigan University

CLOWNS form the funny bone of the circus. To ensure a good supply, Clown College in Sarasota, Fla., gives clowning applicants eight weeks of free training that includes physical education, yoga, make-up, and personality development (each clown must project a definite personality). Three nights a week the clown students must watch the movies of W.C. Fields and other great comedians.

Confusion. Because both circuses and carnivals are colorful forms of outdoor entertainment and both use tents, the general public often confuses the two. Actually, carnivals and circuses differ greatly and are socially quite distinct forms. Whereas carnivals—emphasizing public participation, especially on rides

CARNIVALS AND CIRCUSES

and in games—are an extension of the medieval fair, the circus is basically a spectator entertainment and is an extension of theater. Carnival personnel seldom overlap with circus workers, and the social and economic structures of the two institutions are different.

Differences. The circus is essentially an international theatrical form with performers traveling extensively around the world. It is a major entertainment institution in many countries, especially in the Soviet Union and several Communist countries where it is run by the state. Though there are circuses in the Far East, their form there, as exemplified by the Peking Circus, is quite different from that found in the West. The carnival, however, is more distinctly American. The recent history of these two forms in America has seen a marked decline in the number of circuses while the carnival has grown steadily more popular. Whereas the "golden age" of the circus in America (1871-1915) saw over one hundred different circuses traversing the United States, there are today only about a dozen shows actively touring. On the other hand, carnivals on the road in 1974 numbered nearly two thousand. Though still the largest circus in the United States, Ringling Brothers, Barnum and Bailey ("The Greatest Show on Earth") — which is actually composed of two largely independent units separately touring the country — is today no longer under canvas and has dispensed with many of its earlier features including the "sideshow" (the display of human curiosities or "freaks"), the "cookhouse" (the eating tent for circus personnel), and the once giant parade through the visited city. At the same time, carnivals have become gigantic enterprises which sometimes even use what were once exclusively circus acts as free displays to attract crowds to the carnivals' own features.

Circus History. The circus has been defined as "a traveling and organized display of animals and skilled performances within one or more circular stages known as rings before an audience encircling these activities." In this form, it is usually considered to have had its origin in England in 1770 under the direction of Philip Astley, commonly called the Father of the Circus. Following the European model, John Bill Ricketts opened the first circus in the United States in 1793. In the early years, the circus was a one-ring affair, and it played in buildings or the open air. In 1830, Aaron Turner took his show out under a round tent, ninety feet in diameter, which was the first such tent ("Big Top") ever used. And in 1881, the Barnum and Bailey Circus introduced three rings under its Big Top. These innovations, coupled with the introduction of the railroad as its carrier (first used in 1853), created what was to become the distinctly American form of the circus that most of us are familiar with in the United States today.

Since 1771, over a thousand circuses and menageries have toured the United States. In the peak year of 1903, at least ninety-eight circuses toured the country. In its heyday, the American circus was an immense organization with hundreds of employees, and the giant circus parade through a city might extend as long as three miles and take five hours to move through the streets.

Because of the problems created by urbanization in modern society — including such things as the current inability to find large lots near the center of the city, interference of the automobile with the holding of parades, and a changing public mentality — the circus is today in a serious state of decline. The few larger shows left are still economically successful, but even these do not approach their previous size.

GRAVITY-DEFYING RIDES that puree, liquefy, grind, and slice the senses are part of the carnivals' traditional attractions.

Carnival History. A rough definition of the modern carnival is that it is a traveling entertainment consisting of rides, games, refreshments, and separated attractions. The American carnival is usually thought of as having emerged from the World's Columbian Exposition in Chicago in 1893. Several concessionaires met to consider the effects of the slim attendance at the exposition, and this resulted in their decision to move the assembled attractions to various cities, at first to existing fairgrounds, but later in the form of a traveling street fair. These small affairs moved about at first by means of horsedrawn wagons, and in 1914 the Smith Greater Shows moved by truck. The railroads are commonly used today by the larger shows, and the Royal American Shows use eight double-length railroad cars to transport over fifty rides and attractions and seven under-canvas shows. It is estimated that in the United States some 85 million people attend carnivals annually.

Circus Personnel. Though the circus includes administrative and other personnel, the performers who provide the spectators with entertainment constitute the central core of the show. Any list of circus acts would have to include such forms as (1) equestrian, (2) trapeze, (3) acrobatic, (4) clowning, (5) bounding, (6) juggling, (7) strength exhibition, (8) trained animal, (9) equilibristic or balancing, (10) thrill, and (11) posing or display. These categories are not mutually exclusive, and many acts combine several of these elements.

The circus has usually had a relatively rigid social order. Administrators, performers, sideshow personnel, band members, concessionaires, and work crew personnel were even formally separated in their eating and living conditions. Most writing about the circus has been highly romanticized and thus has greatly understated the undemocratic aspects of American circus life.

Despite the decline in the size and scope of the circus in America and most of Europe, the quality of circus performance is still very high. Many artistic performance "records" have been set in recent years. Some of these are undoubtedly due to technological improvements (for example, trampolines that bounce a gymnast higher, juggling props that are lighter and precision-made), but it may also be that today's performer has had to be more dedicated, given the smaller market for his talents which makes competition more keen.

In recent years, circus skills have been

CARNIVALS AND CIRCUSES

incorporated into some university and high school physical education programs. Florida State University has produced excellent performers through its program which includes a small touring show. The same is true of the Sailor Circus of Sarasota High School in Sarasota, Fla., which even has its own Big Top. New York University also offers training in many circus skills through its theater program. Most performers in circuses, however, enter their occupations through apprenticeship or family background in the circus. A major exception today is the case of the Clown College started by the Ringling Brothers, Barnum and Bailey Circus to train clowns for its units.

Carnival Personnel. The carnival is generally a far more egalitarian organization than the circus. This partly stems from its very different economic structure. Whereas the circus is normally owned and operated by a single entity, the carnival is usually a temporary coalition of many independent entrepreneurs who contract to join together to work at a location. The carnival thus expands and contracts throughout a season depending upon where it is playing and the size of the lot.

Carnival personnel generally include (1) the show owner (the central operator who contracts with smaller entrepreneurs) and administrative employees, (2) the independent ride, show, and concession owners, (3) the performers, and (4) workers. To some degree, these persons constitute a hierarchy within the carnival, but the social order is not highly rigid as it typically is in the circus. Whereas the circus places great value upon artistic performance, the world of the carnival centers far more upon the daily economic operation of parting customers from their money. This concern often resulted in the past in over-zealous attempts by carnival workers in the form of illegal gambling attractions whose outcomes were secretly under the control of the operator. Such activities are today relatively rare, especially in the larger shows, but such elements in the carnival's past have acted to create a fascinating subculture wherein the "carnie" is viewed as a clever hustler able to take economic advantage of his customer or "mark." In many ways, the world of the carnival is the last outpost for the now marginal extreme proponent of our free enterprise system (with heavy emphasis on the principle of *caveat emptor* or *let the buyer beware*). But just as the world of the customer is seen as an outside society to be manipulated, the world of the carnival is a tightly knit and highly loyal subculture with complex norms.

As with the circus, most carnival personnel who are *regulars* were born into carnival life. With the decline in the circus, many circus personnel have been finding themselves moving into the carnival world, something extremely rare twenty years ago.

Circus and Carnival Language. Because circuses and carnivals constitute tightly knit subcultural environments, they have developed an elaborate argot or specialized slang. Many of the terms used in the circus (for example, the familiar distress cry of "Hey Rube!") can also be found in the carnival. But there are important differences between the institutions even in regard to some common terms (for example, the exhibition of freaks is called a "sideshow" in the circus but that term is used for most attractions of a carnival, and the freak show is called a "ten-in-one"). In general, the argot found in the circus refers simply to special circus conditions, such as props. The carnival, however, has gone much further in developing special terms for things with ordinary names because carnival workers often wish to keep a townsperson who overhears their conversation from understanding its meaning. There is even a special distorting "language" used by carnival workers —they call it "Carnie" but it has been called "Z-Latin" by some others—whereby speech can be made unintelligible to the outsider unfamiliar with its systematic principles of word distortion.

Changing Institutions. Both circuses and carnivals have undergone great social changes since their beginnings. Both institutions were involved with numerous illegal activities in their early years (especially crooked gambling known as "grift"), but as the forms became popular and the shows grew larger, most such practices were eliminated. Most outdoor amusements today are what their personnel call "Sunday School shows" in that illegal practices have been eliminated. Just as circuses largely rid themselves of the "grift" during their golden age, now that carnivals have become a big business, they too have realized that such petty thievery is a poor business practice that needs to be policed if a show wishes to return successfully to a community. Though some small shows still contain elements of the old unscrupulous practices, most shows today are safe for citizens and provide much excellent entertainment for relatively low cost.

THE CAROUSEL whirls a youngster astride a flying wooden horse round and round to the tune of rollicking music at a carnival in Great Monmouth, N.J. When the National Carousel Roundtable, an organization dedicated to the preservation of old merry-go-rounds, held its first meeting early in 1974 at Heritage Plantation in Sandwich, Mass., it attracted more than 190 carousel buffs from the United States and Canada.

In adapting to social conditions, circuses and carnivals continue to change. The modern circus has in many ways reverted to patterns found in its early history (including the revival of the single-ring circus by Hoxie Brothers Circus and emphasis on song and dance in circus productions). New economic patterns are developing as circus acts are brought together to form an *ad hoc* or special circus under local sponsorship and management, and such packaging is developing into circuits reminiscent of early vaudeville. Carnivals are also developing new patterns as some giant shows are emerging under more centralized ownership with greater economic control by a single entity. This expansion in size can be contrasted with the fact that many carnival subunits—and recently some circus acts — are today playing in shopping centers and their parking lots. Whatever future forms they might take, circuses and carnivals will probably continue to operate as long as there are "children of all ages" interested in going to them.

Catholicism

by
THE REVEREND ALBERT O. GRENDLER

Editor, *The Globe*
Sioux City, Iowa

The Bishops' Synod. Perhaps the main religious event in the Catholic church for the entire year of 1974 was the Synod of Bishops meeting in Rome, which opened on September 27 and lasted for over one month.

Theme of the synod was The Evangelization of the Modern World, and more than two hundred top leaders of the Catholic church were in attendance. Delegates representing the United States included three cardinals and two archbishops. They were: Cardinal John Krol, president of the National Conference of Catholic Bishops and spiritual leader of the Catholic church in Philadelphia, Pa.; Cardinal John Carberry, St. Louis, Mo.; Cardinal John Dearden, Detroit, Mich.; Archbishop Joseph Bernardin, Cincinnati, Ohio; and Archbishop John Quinn, Oklahoma City, Okla.

Among the first delegates to address the synod was Cardinal Krol. The cardinal began his address by commenting on the "dismal portrait of youth" as painted by some today. The cardinal admitted that young people are rejecting "traditional structures of government, of society, of the family, and even of the church," but felt they should not be classified as "rebellious, irreligious, or as strangers to Christ."

Cardinal Krol continued by saying that in youth there is genuine receptivity for Christ and his Gospel which the church cannot ignore. He then switched his emphasis to the inactive members of the church and said, "Since they will not

AT ST. PETER'S BASILICA in the Vatican the Roman Catholic Synod of Bishops began a month-long meeting on September 27 to examine the theme, "evangelization in the modern world."

CATHOLICISM

come to us it is the church that must go to them." He suggested two approaches for contact with the inactive: one through the laity and through lay organizations, the second through the mass media of communications.

Cardinal Krol ended his opening address by saying that evangelization needs the laity to be successful and urged greater stress be placed on the role of the laymen in the church.

The role of women was brought into focus by several delegates from European as well as African nations.

Archbishop Bernardin reported the conditions and views of the church in North America, Oceania, Australia, and New Zealand. He said it was as if the churches of these countries were reshaping themselves, going through a state of purification at the price of some confusion. The archbishop also mentioned some reaction to changes and a perplexing ongoing disagreement between parents and educators on how to transmit the faith to the younger generation.

Among some of the remedies needed, Archbishop Bernardin said, were "more concentration on adult formation in faith, more thorough training of religious educators, the realization of the full potential offered by Catholic schools and other educational institutions, and finally the recognition of the need for a new dialogue of the theological and episcopal communities on the church for the welfare of God's people."

The delegation of American hierarchy who attended the synod called it the best one yet. The five American Latin-rite bishops, in a statement reflecting on the synod, said, "Through our participation in the synod we have sought to reflect the experience and insights of the church in the United States with regard to evangelization."

The delegates continued, "The synod has not 'solved' the problems the church faces in evangelization, but simple solutions to complex matters were never anticipated."

In his closing remarks to the synod the pope himself touched the core problem the synod finally found itself facing: "Certainly the breadth and complexity of the theme (evangelization in the modern world) did not allow it to be dealt with exhaustively in a short time."

The synod did make clear that the entire Christian community shares in the responsibility to bring the Gospel to all persons by the witness of Christian living as well as in words.

The Pope. In his Easter message Pope Paul VI urged men to renounce the pleasure-seeking, false "gospel of life," and instead live by the "Gospel of the Cross."

The pope said, "The Gospel of the Cross is the law of duty, service, sorrow, love, and sacrifice and is the wise and true interpretation of human life."

Although the pope was recuperating from a bout with the flu, he celebrated his Easter Mass on the steps of St. Peter's Basilica before a crowd estimated at 250,000 people. Speaking to the crowd in St. Peter's square on the feast of Pentecost, the birthday of the church, the pope asked, "Where has the joy of the Catholic faith gone?" The pope continued by upbraiding Christians who "vegetate in doubt and silly criticism."

In a papal document issued June 13 Pope Paul clarified the church's teaching regarding Mass stipends. The new norms for stipends went into effect July 1. The new norms had little or no effect on practices concerning Masses in the United States, according to the National Conference of Catholic Bishops.

Marian Devotion. Pope Paul VI issued a major document on devotion to the Blessed Virgin Mary entitled *Marialis Cultus.* In an effort to demonstrate the relevance of the Blessed Virgin to mod-

POPE PAUL VI, shown here speaking at the United Nations, is the most traveled pope in Roman Catholic history. In September he toured the three Italian towns associated with St. Thomas Aquinas, a papal pilgrimage last made by Pope Benedict XIII in 1727.

ern times, the pope said, "the restoration, in a dynamic and more informed manner, of the recitation of the rosary and through the intercession of the Blessed Virgin as an approach to Christ is encouraged by all the faithful."

The 17,000-word papal document was released from the Vatican in March.

New Rite for Confession. The Congregation for Divine Worship at the Vatican issued a revised liturgy for the Sacrament of Penance in an effort to express more clearly both the nature and effect of the sacrament.

The revised liturgical rites were outlined in four main chapters. In the New Order of Penance document the chapters were entitled: The Reconciliation of Individual Penitents; The Reconciliation of Many Penitents with Individual Confessions and Absolution; Reconciliation of Many Penitents with General Confession and Absolution, and Various Texts for Use in the Celebration of Reconciliation.

The new directives were not issued to cause any unexpected changes in the communal celebration of the sacrament, but rather to attempt to enrich the celebration of reconciliation.

The traditional Catholic teaching on the Sacrament of Penance is maintained in the new document. Maintaining of individual confessions was firmly established also by the U.S. bishops. However, the new order did allow that implementation of the Sacrament of Penance be left to the respective bishops' conferences.

Children's Masses. The Vatican released guidelines for children's Masses in an attempt to "initiate youth gradually into participation in community Masses." The 3,500-word directory contained certain liturgical ceremonies for children as well as recommended music.

The directory specifies that the general structure of the celebration and certain texts must remain identical in all Masses.

U.S. Catholicism. Archbishop Jean Jadot, apostolic delegate in the United States, at a press conference held in Portland, Ore., discussed the Roman Catholic church in the United States. The papal representative said that since his coming to the United States he has discovered a "very living church" in this country and added that even though he was concerned about polarization in the church he also believed that polarization is "also a sign of life." One of his greatest discoveries, he said, "was to see how very strong and how good the intellectual activity is in the Catholic church here in the United States."

The 1974 International Conference on Charismatic Renewal in the Catholic Church was attended by 25,000 people on the campus of Notre Dame University in South Bend, Ind.

The surprise of the meeting was a healing service conducted during a four-and-one-half-hour service, during which Mrs. Barbara Shelmon, a Catholic nurse and proclaimed healer, emerged as a central figure.

After the claim of several participants that they had been healed, many in attendance left the football stadium "awe-struck" and "breathless," but some non-charismatic observers walked away with questions concerning the entire event.

Cardinal Leo Suenens of Brussels, Belgium, also participated in the meeting.

Membership. According to the *1974 Yearbook of American and Canadian Churches,* Catholic population figures for North America were set at 48,465,438. This represented an increase of only 5,011 over the previous year.

USCC. As early as March the U.S. Catholic Conference (USCC) began urging that amnesty be granted to selective conscientious objectors of the war in Vietnam.

Before a Congressional subcommittee USCC officials pointed out that present U.S. draft laws do not make any provision for conscientious objectors.

Reflecting the position taken by U.S. Catholic bishops in 1968, the USCC urged a provision be made in selective service laws for sincere conscientious objectors to any war.

A booklet entitled *Toward Reconciliation* was published and released by the USCC to aid in participation by the faithful during Holy Year.

Author of the booklet, Father Walter Burghardt, S.J., a professor of Theology at Catholic University, said, "We must learn to cut down on waste and must learn to live with less. By practicing these virtues they will bring us closer to God."

Cardinal Timothy Manning of Los Angeles wrote the foreword to the thirty-seven-page booklet.

The twin themes of the Holy Year as announced by Pope Paul are Renewal and Reconciliation.

In an effort to better coordinate and consolidate several areas of the USCC and the National Council of Catholic Bishops (NCCB) both organizations have undergone a vast reorganization.

A study was started in June, and results of the study were being implemented by late October. The entire thrust of the plan is to better utilize existing departments, to cut costs, and to adjust personnel. Approximately 10 percent of the total working force of three hundred will be dismissed under the reorganization.

Bishop James S. Rausch serves as general secretary for both conferences.

The Exorcist, a movie about a young girl's being possessed by the devil, brought the praise of some; other critics passed the movie off as "so much fairy tale." Many clerical critics claimed the entire movie carried many misconceptions about the actual rites of exorcism.

However, *The Exorcist* did bring greater attention to the existence of evil in our society. As one critic said, "Perhaps for some it is the shock needed to return them to God."

Church's Influence on Strike. A bitter strike developed between the workers and the Farah Company, a firm that manufactures clothing, and was finally ended when company officials agreed to allow unionization of its plants. During the course of the strike the workers gained the sympathy and support of many U.S. bishops across the nation. The twenty-one-month-old strike ended when over one-half of the Farah employees signed union membership cards.

Bishop Sidney Metzger, of El Paso, Tex., a leading supporter of the nationwide boycott-strike, called on those involved in the strike "to put an end to the bitterness, hatred, and mistakes that had occurred in the dispute." Later Bishop Metzger urged support of the company's products.

Population Control. The U.S. Coalition for Life urged a U.S. Senate subcommittee on appropriations for labor and health to stop funding abortions under the Medicaid program or through Aid for Families with Dependent Children. Paul Haring, a spokesman for the Coalition for Life, told the subcommittee members that more than twenty-five states were using federal funds to pay for abortions. Haring urged an amendment be attached to the funding bill which would prohibit abortions from being paid for with federal funds.

Chairman of the subcommittee, Senator Warren Magnuson of Washington, agreed to offer such an amendment but said he would not give it much support.

Father Bernard Haering, a noted German moral theologian, expressed shock when it was learned that babies conceived in test tubes had in several cases been implanted into a woman's womb and later were born alive.

Father Haering called the test-tube fertilizations a form of manipulation of human life. He said experimentation with test-tube fertilization is a field in which science should not act alone without advice from ethical thinkers.

The late Pope Pius XII objected to the practice of artificial insemination in 1949.

The Vatican's delegate to the August U.N. World Population Conference in Bucharest, Hungary, was Father Henri de Riedmatten.

On the eve of the opening of the conference the pope warned a purely statistical approach "could prevail, with grave consequences, if every other aspect of the problem was not taken into account by the conference." Later the Vatican released a statement in opposition to the final position recommended by the conference on the promotion of contraception as a means of controlling world population. The Vatican was the only one of the 136 members to express its opposition to the principal document issued by the conference.

St. Peter's House-Church. One of the most noteworthy archaeological finds was the excavation of St. Peter's home at Capernaum, Israel. The Franciscan Order began their work there in 1921. Digging resumed in 1968 and has brought evidence that the first century dwelling of St. Peter was a place of worship as well as a residence.

Through the painstaking work of piecing together minute bits of plaster and other articles the Franciscans have found early writings on the wall or graffiti with such exclamations as, "have mercy," "Amen," and "Lord Jesus Christ help . . ."

According to experts in the field the find is exceptional since very rarely is a church or house of worship discovered dating prior to the fourth century.

Holy Land Churches. The Holy Father spoke of the necessity to continue the "living witness" of the Christian community in the Holy Land in an apostolic exhortation addressed to the "bishops, clergy and faithful of the world." The pope spoke of the "increased needs of the church in the Holy Land" and also suggested an annual offering be taken up each year in all churches of the world for support of the churches located in the Holy Land.

China

by
WERNER LEVI

Professor of Political Science
University of Hawaii
Author of *International Politics: Foundations of the System* (1974)

The Secrecy surrounding public affairs in China has, once more, made it difficult to know what troubles were brewing within the country. The complaints, accusations, and criticisms appearing in the newspapers and radio and on wall posters indicated clearly that another power struggle was taking place among the ruling cliques. As usual, each faction was trying to enlist mass support, thereby

ON A CHINESE COMMUNE a machine blows wheat into the air to winnow out the grain while workers sweep up the chaff to feed to the pigs. China has more than doubled its production of food grains during the past twenty-five years of Communist rule.

extending their rivalries and splits right to the Chinese people.

Two Power Struggles. Fundamentally, it appeared, two different confrontations were taking place. One was between what might be called the extremist and the conservative wings of the Communist movement; that is to say, between those who wanted to continue the "permanent revolution" at all cost, and those who wanted Chinese politics to calm down so that internal reconstruction and development could proceed undisturbed. The other, less important confrontation was between the centrists and the regionalists, that is, between those wanting to concentrate all power in Peking and those wanting to diffuse it and give the regions more autonomy. There were overlaps and alliances between many factions, each using the other for its own purposes. Thus, some favoring regionalism also were either extremists or conservatives; and the same was true of the centrists. The complexity of the situation was further enhanced by the odd way in which, publicly at least, the power struggle was carried on.

Historic Pseudonyms. Instead of defining their positions and naming names, the factions were using historic situations and figures as pseudonyms, so to speak, in order to characterize contemporary conditions and living personalities. The power struggle was conducted in terms of ancient history and with reference to individuals long dead. This explained why Confucius had suddenly become again a central figure in Chinese politics. The venerated philosopher had now become a "political swindler" and "hypocrit," a "stubborn, cruel, weak, sinister, and cunning" despot, an apologist for the slave-holding aristocracy. The late Marshal Lin Piao was accused of having, among his many sins, worshipped Confucius "like all reactionaries in history." Together with the old sage he was made the symbol of all "ultra-Rightists" and "counterrevolutionary extremists." Like Confucius, Lin and his followers were

CHOU EN-LAI, seventy-six years old, became seriously ill during the second half of 1974.

accused of wanting to return to the old order. They were accused of preaching, like Confucius and Mencius, intellectual and administrative elitism for governing the country and of belittling the value of the masses and the working class. By advocating "restraint and a return to the rites," Lin and his surviving followers were advocating a return to capitalism and the ending of the revolutionary struggle.

By contrast, the first emperor of the Ch'in Dynasty, Ch'in Shih Huang Ti (259-210 B.C.) and the Legalist school, were praised to the public as revolutionaries and liberators of the slaves, destroying the reactionary thoughts of Confucius and Mencius. Their greatest merit was to unify China under the "dictatorship of the newly rising feudal landlord class." This oblique reference to indi-

A CHINESE WOMAN braids garlic plants together before her commune's rabbit hutch. A delegation of American agricultural scientists toured Chinese communes for four weeks and reported in September that the Chinese were well protected against famine. They brought back a large variety of Chinese food plants for further research.

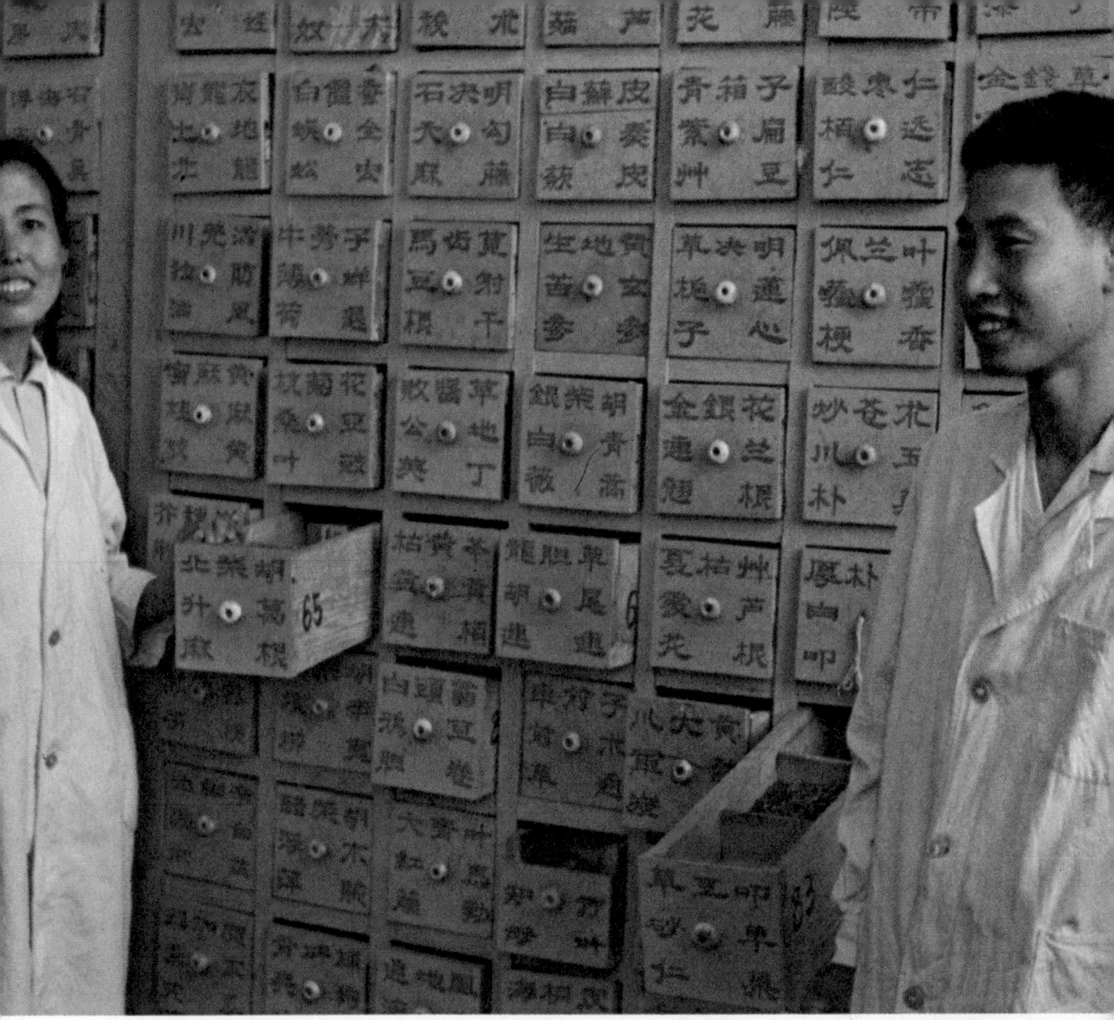

IN THE HOSPITAL at the Lu Gou Chiao Henmin Gungsha (Marco Polo Bridge People's Commune) near Peking, herbs are stored in boxes for use in the ancient folk remedies that have been integrated with twentieth century advances in Chinese medical practice. Since the 1971 relaxation of U.S. trade bans, many of China's best-known pills, powders, and tonics have been imported into America. The U.S. Food and Drug Administration has passed ingredients ranging from ground deer antlers to dried silkworm, but has confiscated several tons of Chinese remedies because their labels make a variety of unproven cure-all claims.

viduals dead for over two thousand years was to indicate clearly the need for the unification of China today—by revolutionary means. For one way in which the great emperor achieved his goal was by burning dissenting books and burying alive dissenting scholars. These were "precisely revolutionary actions" and "revolutionary violence" to defend and maintain the unity of China and destroy the reactionary, slave-owning class.

Strangely enough, poor old Confucius was also used by the moderates to criticize the regime of Mao Tse-tung. The idea of the superior man as ruler of the country, the worship of the "words of the sage" were condemned. It was easy to identify the person of Mao and his sayings in the *Little Red Book* in these condemnations.

All sides in this struggle claimed that they were fighting ideas, not men, with

MIDDLE SCHOOL STUDENTS in Nanking take an exercise break.

CHINESE EDUCATION

by

W. RICHARD STEPHENS

Vice-President for Academic Affairs
Greenville College
Greenville, Ill.

The "liberation," as the Chinese refer to Mao Tse-tung's takeover of mainland China, brought with it a new way of life and education. Especially can the change be observed in the educational relationship of the mother and child. Since the revolution "liberated" women to work outside the home in factories, less than 10 percent of young Chinese mothers are housewives.

While mothers are at work, their children up to three years of age are close by in collectives supervised by neighborhood committees. Nurseries for infants up to eight months are located in the factories, and the working mothers get a half-hour break mornings and afternoons to breast-feed and mother their infants. Sometimes, however, the grandparents care for the children, an old family tradition now disdained by many because the young fear that their children will not learn to value a collective society.

At the age of three and one-half a Chinese child is ready for kindergarten. Teachers emphasize concepts of sharing and concern for others. Much like those in Russian schools, all lessons carry political meanings. School children are organized into groups called Little Red Soldiers, for the purpose of doing work and learning a collective identity. High school students often accompany their teachers to the farms or factories for periods up to several months. There they learn to labor for the consummation of the cultural revolution in the People's Republic of China. These emphases on education reflect the position of Chairman Mao that the future of the republic is in the hands of its children.

IN CHINESE HIGH SCHOOLS the classroom atmosphere is formal. Students raise their hands, wait to be called upon, stand and recite crisply, and sit down promptly.

KINDERGARTENERS sing "In Praise of the Tenth Party Congress."

WHEN BOY MEETS GIRL in China, it is very unusual for them to walk arm in arm as this couple in Shanghai is doing. Even hand-holding in public is rare. Although the legal minimum marriageable age in China is eighteen for women and twenty for men, few Chinese marry that young. The Communist party has stressed that twenty-five and twenty-eight are more suitable ages for matrimony.

these debates. Yet the parallels between the past and the present were so carefully worked out that hardly any doubt could remain as to what and who was meant in today's China. Generally those advocating moderate measures for the building of China, those favoring friendly relations between China and the rest of the world, including the Soviet Union, those trying to cool the revolutionary fervor were the targets of these attacks. They may have included Premier Chou En-lai. Occasional public criticism of cadres, the political workers, for showing "apathy" could be taken as a sign that the general public was confused and that the political leadership in the lower ranks was uncertain either about what the "correct" line might be or which the winning faction would be! In any case the struggle indicated deep concern with the prevailing factionalism in China and especially a possible split once Mao, now eighty-one-years-old, and Chou En-lai, now seventy-six-years-old, would no longer rule the country.

Speculation about the Successors to these two men was a favorite pastime during 1974 among the Chinese themselves and foreign "China watchers." Early in the year, the question seemed to turn mainly around Mao. The problem seemed relatively light because Mao had withdrawn from major activities during the last few years. Power seemed to be in the hands of Chou En-lai, so that only when he became seriously ill during the second half of the year the question of succession became very acute indeed.

Mao let it be known that he was not in favor of a chief of state. Such a position, to him, was purely formal and wasteful. This attitude, incidentally, may explain why the long-promised National People's Congress was not convened, for the choice of a chief of state was one of its functions. There was talk of "collective leadership" mainly for the reason that the many and wide-ranging duties hitherto taken care of by Chou En-lai could hardly be handled any longer by any one man. There was speculation also that Wang Hung-wen might become the leader of China. He had been propelled into prominence in 1973 when, at the age of thirty-eight, he became a member of the Politburo and had been seen frequently at Mao's right side during official functions. But he was an extremist and had many enemies. Moreover, he was young and "half-baked" as some Chinese pointed out. More likely, he was being groomed for a high post in the future rather than already chosen for the country's highest office. Nevertheless, he seemed to be fighting against Vice-Premier Teng Hsiao-ping who seemed to have been chosen by Mao and Chou, perhaps as a "caretaker" premier, and who appeared more often in charge of official business than Wang. Teng, aged seventy, had been recouped by Chou from the oblivion into which the Great Proletarian Cultural Revolution had pushed him. He had many enemies among the Leftist-controlled Politburo. But he had good support among the higher ranks in the army, administration, and the party apparatus, presumably enabling him to emerge victorious in a contest for top leadership and keep the whole country united.

Appeals for Unity. With the jockeying for favorable positions in the expected change of leadership, all sides seemed concerned that political strife should not tear China asunder once again. Everywhere appeals to unity could be heard. The reference to historic figures rather than living individuals may also have been intended to prevent direct, open struggle. Mao was reported to be walking a middle path. He gave the extremists his blessing in their attacks upon Confucius and Lin Piao, for he could hardly be expected to abandon his cherished "permanent revolution." But he was also not in favor of reviving the upheavals of the Great Proletarian Cultural Revolution.

The Role of the Army in all this maneuvering could be considered as symptomatic of the factional strife which seemed to be more a preparation for future decisions than a final settlement of the political contest. The one certain thing was that the military were important in the power struggle and that their own power had been reduced. But it was not as certain which faction benefited from the change. Early in the year, ten of the eleven commanders of the regions were transferred to new posts. This move could be interpreted as the weakening of the military in provincial politics and the continuing restructuring of the party. In line with this interpretation was the argument that diminished independence of the military in the provinces meant a strengthening of the central powers in Peking and their ability to rely more on the generally conservative military leaders in the provinces. At the same time, however, the shifting of the commanders could also be the result of attacks upon them by the extremists who now obtained a freer hand for action in the provinces. Mao may have supported such a change as part of his middle-path strategy. It gave the extremists more freedom in the provinces while at the same time strengthening the more conservative government apparatus under the control of Chou En-lai.

The New Turbulence. There was no doubt that Mao did not want his country to stand still politically. A major article in the *People's Daily* of February 2 was an appeal to stir the masses into motion, to continue the revolution, and to prevent a return to the past. The "mass political struggle to criticize Lin Piao and Confucius" was carried out throughout the country by Workers' Theoretical Study Groups, cadres, Mass Critical Groups, and party committees engaging in criticism and self-criticism. Classes at the universities, which had only just begun after the Cultural Revolution, were stopped again and the students instructed to discuss Confucius critically and to produce wall-posters. Party officials were told not to let declining production interfere with the workers' study groups. The rationale provided for these activities was that "traitors" like Lin Piao and former president Liu Shao-ch'i would arise again and again. The revolutionary struggle could therefore never be ended.

The new turbulence had some similarities to the Cultural Revolution. But, at least during 1974, also significant differences. Few names were named and no enemies identified specifically. The appeals were for mass participation in the class struggle, not for a fight against particular groups. The army remained in the background and its influence was reduced. No organized groups like the Red Guards had appeared to spearhead a new movement, although there were reports of the extremists building an "urban militia" recruited mostly from the 50 million youths disillusioned with the results of the Cultural Revolution. What had apparently brought about the new turbulence was a rapid revival of the "ultra-Left" after its decline following the Cultural Revolution. The moderation and consolidation after the revolution were attacked by the more radical factions and a defense was necessary. The leadership of the extremists: Chiang Ch'ing (Mao's wife), Wang Hung-wen, Chang Ch'un-ch'iao, Yao Wen-yüan, and K'ang Sheng were still concentrated in Shanghai. Their anti-Confucian campaign and anti-Westernism (the banning of Beethoven, Mozart, Schubert, and others from Chinese concert halls) seemed to have Mao's blessing. But whether they would succeed in penetrating Peking remained an unanswered question.

Foreign Affairs. Chou En-lai related the domestic situation to foreign affairs by telling visiting foreign dignitaries that China's contribution to the peoples of the world had so far been rather modest but that now, under the impact of her new enthusiasm, the situation would change. Yet China could hardly be accused of having neglected international politics during the year. Her major goals became quite evident: to become a great power and to develop her economy. Both goals required an active role in world politics. It was also evident that under the guidance of Chou En-lai China would choose the path of moderation to achieve these goals. For, while lip service continued to be paid to the support of "national liberation movements," to the development of a "spirit of proletarian internationalism" throughout the world, and to the defeat of "great power chauvinism," action was designed to expand the range of friendly and profitable relations with other countries.

In Southeast Asia, China's support of insurgents and revolutionaries turned noticeably cool. She reduced her military commitments and gradually disengaged herself politically. At the same time, she

EAGER BUYERS crowd the counter at a Chinese store. This picture is part of a portfolio on the People's Republic of China that won Giorgio Lotti of the Italian magazine, *Epoca*, the World Understanding through Photography award in the thirty-first annual Pictures of the Year competition at the University of Missouri.

expanded official diplomatic relations with several states (Malaysia and the Philippines) and trade relations with several others. Her occupation of the Paracel Islands, involving brief fighting with South Vietnam, and her claim to ownership of the islands as well as to "the natural resources in the sea areas around them" made clear that control over the potential oil resources in the South China Sea motivated her actions. China progressed further with normalizing relations with Japan by signing an air agreement, as a result of which direct flights between Tokyo and Peking were established, but those between Tokyo and Taiwan were interrupted. This was the second major agreement (after a trade pact in January) between the two nations, with agreements on fishing and shipping remaining in the negotiation stage. China was obviously wooing Japan away from the U.S.S.R.

In the Sino-Soviet-USA triangular relationship, China tried to play an influential role, aiming at independence and equality. Her basic attitude toward the two powers was "a plague on both your houses." But it was qualified by China's assumption that, as her delegate to the United Nations put it, the Soviet Union was the more "vicious" of the two. Consequently, the verbal war between the two Communist states and their border incidents proceeded as usual, notwithstanding a Chinese offer to sign a nonaggression treaty with the Soviet Union. Trade between China and the Communist countries did not share in the general rise of China's foreign trade. At the Law of the Sea Conference in Venezuela, China severely attacked the Soviets' "imperialist" position and tried desperately, once again, to identify herself with the Third World on the grounds that, as she had already stated in the United Nations, the Socialist camp no longer existed, and China was not "aligned" with anybody. Although in line with this identification China enthusiastically welcomed the oil policies of the Arab states as "historic pioneering action" in defense of national resources against "imperialist plunder and exploitation," she was also worried about growing Soviet influence in western and, for that matter, southern Asia. These Chinese fears of being encircled by the Soviet Union and her friends conditioned China's policies toward the United States.

In spite of some aggressive language and much criticism—mandatory to make China's wooing of the Third World credible—the detente in Sino-American relations held. There were two good reasons. One was that it was in China's interest to have a strong Western world and a strong American presence in Asia as a counterweight to the Soviet Union. China favored the North Atlantic Treaty Organization (NATO) and American troops in Europe. She was remarkably quiet about American naval activity in the Indian Ocean, and she welcomed close American relations with Iran and Pakistan. The other reason was that the United States could supply the goods China needed for her development. Trade rose from virtual nonexistence in 1971 to about $1.3 billion in 1974 and was expected to reach several billion by 1980. The major American exports were agricultural products (wheat, corn, cotton, and soybeans) and machinery, especially oil-drilling and oil-exploring equipment. The main Chinese exports were tin, hog bristles, cotton fabrics, art objects and raw silk. A problem in this trade was that it was ten to one in favor of the United States. The expectation was that as China developed her industries and particularly her oil resources she could balance this uneven relationship.

Taiwan. American trade with China surpassed China's trade with the Soviet Union, but it was still less than American trade with Taiwan (over $3 billion). The trend was clear, however. The time was foreseeable when mainland China would be a more attractive trade partner than Taiwan. Adding to this her greater political significance, it was not surprising that the "barrier" Taiwan represented to full diplomatic relations between China and the United States was gradually dissolving. The United States maintained diplomatic relations with Taiwan, the only major power to do so, but they became more and more a formality as official and economic relations with the mainland expanded. Joint statements by Peking and Washington referring to one China and one Chinese people indicated that the existence of Taiwan no longer created major difficulties. The Nationalist government, almost completely isolated diplomatically but conducting a flourishing trade with many states, felt it could survive as long as the United States continued material support. But the withdrawal of 3,000 of the 8,000 American troops on Taiwan might have been an indication that such support was dwindling. The State Department made no secret of its hope that the "two China" problem might be solved conveniently by an agreement between the two Chinas in the foreseeable future.

EARLY PENNIES were twice as large as today's cents.

Where Did All the Pennies Go? Businesses complained that they could not get pennies from the banks. Banks complained they could not get enough pennies from the Federal Reserve. The Federal Reserve complained that despite a speedup of production by the Mint (to more than 35 million pennies a day, up from 20 million a day in 1973), it could not meet the demand for pennies, which was double what it had been in 1973.

In the unprecedented penny-pinch the U.S. Treasury promised a special citation "for patriotically responding to the U.S. Mint's June, 1974, appeal" to any citizen returning $25 worth of pennies to his bank. However, businesses, in addition to asking customers for exact change for purchases, began to offer bonuses for the scarce one-centers. For example, at some McDonald's franchises 500 pennies brought a customer a $5 bill and a free quarter-pounder hamburger.

The Piggy Bank Factor. Despite the Mint's assertion that 30 billion pennies should be in circulation, the copper penny had become an endangered specie(s). While some people saw it shrinking in buying power, others saw it as an inflation hedge as the copper it contained rose rapidly in value. Copper, which composes 95 percent of the Lincoln head (the other 5 percent is zinc), shot up in price because of lowered production and heavy industrial use. When a coin's metal value is greater than its currency value, the piggy-bank factor, or widespread hoarding, comes into play.

The U.S. Mint, which had already experienced the piggy-bank factor with Kennedy half-dollars and silver dollars, asked Congress to allow the secretary of the treasury to determine when and whether to permit the Mint to produce pennies of aluminum. A bill, H.R. 11841, was hastily passed by the Senate. The shift in metals would save the taxpayer a substantial $40 million a year because of the lower cost of aluminum, but would cause havoc in vending machines. Testing showed that an aluminum penny would jam the nation's 4 million vend-

WINNERS in the national Bicentennial Coin Design competition were announced in March. From left to right are Seth Huntington's Independence Hall, Dennis R. Williams's Liberty Bell overlapping the moon, and Jack Ahr's colonial drummer. Each artist received $5,000.

ing machines between 5.2 and 9.8 percent of the time because of its light weight.

Unfortunately, this emergency bill helped to stir up a panic market in 1974 copper cents. A myth arose that 1974-S cents (pennies minted in San Francisco) would be a scarce issue and that collectors could not ever hope to obtain uncirculated specimens at face value from their local banks. By July dealers were selling $50 bags of 5,000 ordinary 1974-S pennies for $900.

Director of the Mint Mary Brooks was forced to announce: "We have no intention of changing the present copper cent in this calendar year." She also revealed that 400 million pennies would be produced in 1974 at the San Francisco minting facility, a precise figure which the Mint does not usually disclose. As an additional antispeculation measure 1974-S pennies were accumulated in San Francisco, shipped to Philadelphia and Denver, mixed into bags of cents produced at these facilities, and quietly distributed without announcement to Federal Reserve banks in every part of the country. To further curb penny-savers who hoped to make their fortunes by melting down their coins for the copper, the Treasury made such action a criminal offense.

The Numismatic Price Rocket for collectors' coins continued its spectacular ascent in 1974. In May the all-time high price for a single U.S. coin became $200,000 when a dealer purchased the 1907 Roman numeral "ultra high relief" Saint-Gaudens proof double eagle ($20 gold coin). Only thirteen to sixteen specimens of this coin are known, and some of them, including the coin sold, were reportedly used by President Theodore Roosevelt as presentation pieces. In June an ancient Greek decadrachma brought a bid of $272,000 at an auction in Zurich, Switzerland, a new peak for a single foreign coin. Since European auction houses charge the buyer a 15 percent commission, the total price for the silver coin was $314,000.

Other high auction prices for coins in 1974 included $150,000 for an 1875 proof U.S. $3 gold piece, $110,000 for an 1884 proof double eagle, $60,000 for an 1858 proof half eagle ($5 gold coin), and $50,000 for an 1863 proof quarter eagle ($2.50). An 1877-dated copper pattern striking of a never-issued $50 gold coin was sold for $50,000, a record high price.

At an auction in Geneva, Switzerland, a top price was achieved by a special issue gold coin (called a "shauguldiner") struck in 1511 by Maximilian I, emperor of the Holy Roman Empire, to commemorate his marriage in 1479 to Mary of Burgundy, when it sold for $53,000 against an estimated valuation of $17,300 in the auction catalog.

by

GODFREY SPERLING, JR.

Bureau Chief, *The Christian Science Monitor*

"I HAVE NEVER been one to quit in the face of adversity and I will not be a quitter now. I know what it is I have to fight and I am resolved to do so." This statement by the sixty-five-year-old Arkansas Democrat Wilbur Mills was issued on December 30 when he confessed his erratic behavior in the fall was due to alcoholism but announced he would retain his seat in Congress.

A Power Shift. The upsurge of Congress and congressional power was the governmental highlight of 1974.

Congress, confronted with a president who was flexing his muscles after a record 1972 victory margin, took strong steps in 1974 to cut Richard Nixon down to size. First, it probed and persisted in probing until it forced a corrupt president out of office. Then it put curbs on the president's war-making powers. And it followed this action by enacting reforms on presidential campaigns.

The Ninety-third Congress will be remembered most of all, of course, for the way it dogged Nixon's Watergate footsteps until it finally brought about his resignation.

It was the Senate committee under Senator Sam Ervin that brought much of the Watergate illegality to light. It was during these Senate hearings that John Dean electrified the nation with his accusations against the president — charges which brought Watergate right to the president, himself. This same Senate committee was responsible, too, for discovering the White House tapes—the evidence which later was to show conclusively that the president had been involved in a cover-up and that he had lied to the American people about his involvement in this cover-up.

And it was the House Judiciary Committee under Peter Rodino that evoked a strong, bipartisan vote for presidential impeachment, making that verdict in the House almost certain. Further, this very momentum toward impeachment was causing sentiment in the Senate to shift toward conviction at the moment when the president decided to avoid the vote by stepping down.

This was only the second major congressional impeachment action against a president. The first was a century ago when Andrew Johnson was impeached and came within a vote of being convicted.

The resurgence of Congress, dramatized by the congressional impeachment hearings and the resignation of the president, is being acknowledged by President Gerald Ford in the way he is assiduously

FORMER ASTRONAUT JOHN GLENN leaves the voting booth on November 5. He defeated Cleveland mayor Ralph Perk for the U.S. Senate seat from Ohio.

wooing the congressional leaders of both parties. Some observers say he is doing this because the Democrats control Congress. But it goes beyond that. He sees the power shift and knows that it is likely to be there for a long time to come —whether Democrats or Republicans are in the ascendancy on Capitol Hill.

The Responsibility of Congress. This shift in power toward Congress leaves the legislative branch with a very special responsibility: it must give the nation some measure of leadership, particularly if the president is not leading or shows an inability to lead.

Thus, while Nixon left the nation largely adrift on economic and energy matters in the latter stages of his administration, it was up to the powerful, Democratic-controlled Congress to fill this void. It did not. Instead, it played the role of critic—assailing Nixon programs but not coming up with effective alternatives.

However, Senate Majority Leader Mike Mansfield and Speaker Carl Albert were promising — as the year closed — that the new Congress would be more responsive to the nation's needs. They indicated they would have antirecession and anti-inflation programs of their own very early in the new year.

Vice-Presidential Confirmations. Another significant congressional action in 1974 was the Senate and House confirmation of two vice-presidents, first Gerald Ford and later Ford's appointee, Nelson Rockefeller.

Congress looked hard at Ford's finances and found little to question. But committees in both houses balked for a while in confirming Rockefeller after learning that he had made a large number of gifts to people in public life. Further, Congress was greatly disturbed by the disclosure that Nelson Rockefeller had sponsored the publication of a book about his gubernatorial opponent, Arthur Goldberg, a book that was not exactly complimentary in its thrust.

For a while it appeared that the Rockefeller selection might not go through. But after further hearings the committees determined that Rockefeller was worthy of support for the vice-presidency.

Within days of this confirmation Rockefeller was put to work by the president. Rockefeller was named chairman of a blue-ribbon citizens' committee to look into charges that the Central Intelligence Agency (CIA) has been conducting illegal domestic espionage during the last several years.

Significant Actions by the Ninety-third Congress on the legislative front include the following:

Campaign finance reform was enacted, providing for strictly enforced limits on how much any presidential or congressional candidate can spend and how much any one person can contribute to any candidate. Public funds now will be available for presidential candidates — during both primary and general elections.

CONGRESS

Congress enacted a budget control act which is expected to assure tighter congressional control and oversight of current spending.

A start was made at protecting rights of workers in private pension plans. In a move which could affect some 30 million American workers, Congress set up minimum standards for pensions.

After previous futile efforts to curb presidential war-making, Congress enacted a law forbidding a president to commit U.S. troops to warlike situations for more than two months without express approval of Congress.

A trade bill, granting the president broad authority to lower tariff and non-tariff barriers in return for reductions by foreign nations, was passed in the last few days of the congressional session. One provision of this bill was that the president could not relax trade with the Soviet Union unless the Soviets relaxed their emigration restrictions on Jews.

Congress passed more stringent anti-trust legislation, increasing fines to $1 million for corporations and $100,000 for individuals from the current ceiling of $100,000 for both. The maximum prison penalty was also increased from one to three years.

Congress, in response to a request by the president, reinstated the wage-price council. The council was empowered to monitor wages and prices. It did not give the president power to apply controls.

Congress passed a strip mining bill, providing for federal and state regulation of strip mining for coal and for the reclamation of lands that had been previously stripped and abandoned. The president vetoed the bill because he said it would diminish U.S. energy resources and increase unemployment.

The Congress authorized $2,697,-226,000 in economic and foreign aid for 1975. The bill also authorized a suspension of military aid to Turkey until there was progress toward a military solution in Cyprus. But it authorized the president to delay the cutoff until February 5, 1975.

REPRESENTATIVE AL ULLMAN (D.Ore.) succeeded Wilbur Mills as chairman of the House Ways and Means Committee, which was expanded from twenty-five to thirty-seven members. Mills, who took over the chairmanship in 1958, resigned it on December 10.

Congress voided a White House agreement to turn over the Watergate-related Nixon tapes to former President Nixon. Instead the bill turned the tapes, together with other Watergate-related documents, over to the federal government.

Congress passed a record $82.6 billion defense budget, lopping off $4.4 billion from the president's proposed budget.

Congress repealed the "no-knock" provision which enabled federal agents in some circumstances to enter and search dwellings without first knocking and identifying themselves.

Congress also authorized the first major housing bill since 1968 and the first minimum wage increase since 1967.

Congress approved a six-year, $11.9 billion program to aid mass transit systems.

Crime

RIDIN' HIGH **by David Kryszak of the *Detroit News* won the spot news photography award from the National Headliner Club.**

Who's to Blame? According to Attorney General William B. Saxbe, the federal government spent $3.2 billion in the past six years on crime-fighting programs and for help to local police departments — with what appear to be negative results. While the 1972 report on crime of the Federal Bureau of Investigation (FBI) showed a slight downward trend, the most recent figures tell a different and depressing story: a 6 percent increase in 1973, with the upward surge continuing into 1974. Some changes in the type of offense and in the type of individual involved in criminal activities may be noted.

Juvenile Crime. The age of offenders has been going down. Since children grow up faster today than ever before, they set out on wrong roads earlier in life. The increase in crimes perpetrated by girls is attributed by some to greater family instability and to the greater freedom and aggressiveness of women in the 1970s. Many courts are not staffed to handle these cases adequately. In the past, detention and sentencing has been rare for minor misdeeds, but the authorities are now inclined to bear down harder on girls. Social workers and others involved in criminology say that while boys' crimes tend to be against society, girls' crimes — often robberies to get money for drugs — tend to be against themselves — they "self-destruct."

White-Collar Crime. With ample evidence of crime at the highest official level, it is not surprising that malfeasance is found at lower levels of government. Ralph Nader and others complain of leniency — that white-collar lawbreakers are given the "breaks." (Such was not the case in Chicago, Ill., where half a dozen office-holders were jailed in 1974.) White-collar crime includes illegal campaign contributions, kickbacks and bribe-taking, forgery, auto and other thefts, drug violations, fraud, and embezzlement. The $36,000-a-year bureaucrat in Washington who stole two shirts may have gotten off with a fine. Juries are reluctant to convict a respectable citizen. Saxbe promised that the Justice Department will prosecute rich and poor alike, but equal justice for all often depends on equal legal talent for all.

From Stamps to Bulldozers. Pilfering from shops, drugstores, and supermarkets amounts to a substantial annual loss to merchants — for which the public eventually pays in higher prices. Small establishments cannot afford the well-concealed electronic equipment and two-way mirrors used by most big stores, nor even a store detective. The nice-looking woman shopper who tucks a $10 silk scarf under her coat, the person who lifts a small item from a drugstore shelf, the office worker who purloins stamps and pencils, these constitute a business hazard and a nuisance, but the offenses are not usually worth taking to court. But the waterfront scoundrels who get away with bulldozers and other valuable pieces of cargo in transit are responsible for a billion-dollar drain on the economy. As much as 25 percent of a shipment has been known to disappear en route. In industrial plants thefts range from tools to finished products. Is simple honesty becoming a rarity in our society? Not yet, but . . .

Cracking a System. Computer systems offer a brand-new opportunity to

AN IMPRISONED MAN and a caged bird form a strong design in *Life's Longing*, by prisoner Dieter Voight. It was exhibited in West Germany's Art in Jail show.

a technically trained wrongdoer — one with a high IQ. One successful young businessman gained knowledge of computers by studying IBM manuals; then, posing as a journalist, visited the Western Electric Company, watched demonstrations, and had explanations made for him. Carrying on his investigations at another company, still as the inquiring reporter, he observed on a computer the call number of its order system. Next, on his home telephone he placed orders for equipment; the scheme worked. This enterprising person surrendered to the district attorney, admitting guilt, and was given a short jail sentence. With this experience behind him, he formed a computer security company and held seminars to teach businessmen how to plug holes in their systems.

Cyprus

TURKISH PARATROOPERS hold aloft the Turkish flag after landing north of Nicosia on July 20 during Turkey's invasion of Cyprus.

by
MICHAEL COPE
Internationally Syndicated Columnist

Double Disaster. It will take all the traditional resilience that 3,000 years of mostly violent history have bequeathed to the 600,000 inhabitants of the small (3,572 square miles) island of Cyprus to recover from the double disaster of revolution and invasion which shattered the tranquility of the eastern Mediterranean in 1974.

The trouble began in July when the 10,000-man Cyprus National Guard, led by Greek army officers and supported by the right-wing Pan-Hellenist EOKA-B movement, deposed the Cypriot president Archbishop Makarios, who fled to Great Britain. Government leadership was assumed by the EOKA movement, which since the pre-1960 days of British colonial rule had advocated *Enosis* — constitutional union with mainland Greece. Because of the bitterly opposed ethnic differences between the 482,000 Greek-speaking Christian Cypriots and the 118,000 Turkish-speaking Moslem Cypriots, and notwithstanding the presence of 2,300 U. N. troops and police from seven countries (Britain, Canada, Australia, Finland, Denmark, Sweden, and Austria) who had been keeping an uneasy peace between the two for ten years, the Turkish government in Ankara, fearful the Turk-Cypriots would be subjugated if Cyprus were integrated with Greece, ordered its army to invade. After bitter fighting the Turkish army occupied and consolidated its control over the northern third of Cyprus, and by year's end the only solution in sight was the possibility of creating a new bizonal federal state.

Makarios. Leading up to these disastrous events were months of deteriorating relations between Archbishop Makarios and the ruling Greek junta in Athens. Makarios had grown increasingly concerned at the control and influence the 650 Greek officers had over the National Guard and EOKA-B. The officers launched the revolution when Makarios wrote to General Phaidon Gizikis in Athens, (then the Greek president, but subsequently deposed) and ordered him to withdraw the Greek officers, claiming he had documentary proof they were "... a breeding ground for outlaws and a lair for plotters against the state."

The Coup itself was brief and relatively bloodless, but within a few days 5,000 Turkish troops had landed. Some came by parachute, but the invasion was mainly a seaborne one with beachheads established around the northern resort town of Kyrenia. The Turkish buildup reportedly reached a peak of 8,000 troops. Their advance southward to a point just north of Nicosia, the inland capital, and to the coastal resort of Famagusta in the east, displaced more than 200,000 Cypriots of both communities, many of whom were still living in temporary and badly overcrowded refugee camps as the winter rains began in September.

The consequences of the coup and invasion were more far-reaching than the immediate troubles they brought upon the once idyllic island (where, history has it, Aphrodite the ancient Goddess of Love was spawned from the warm, foaming waters of the Mediterranean). It exposed a weak link in the southeastern flank of the North Atlantic Treaty Organization (NATO). Since Cypriot independence in 1960 the British had maintained two large sovereign bases there — one for strike aircraft, the other for ground troops — occupying ninety square miles. As the occupying Turkish army and the enclaved Greek-Cypriots began hammering out plans for a new federal bizonal state in November, it was suggested a prerequisite would be the evacuation of all foreign troops, including the British forces there, as well as the occupying Turkish army. NATO's other links in that area are Greece and Turkey themselves, whose traditional hostility, polarized over the Cyprus crisis, could effectively cancel each other out of the alliance.

Economic Picture. But it was the destruction and division of Cyprus itself which prompted one correspondent to write: "Returning to the island after only two months is like visiting an old, sick friend slowly fading away." Economically, the coup and invasion can only have a permanent and deeply di-

SAILORS armed with machine guns are common in Cyprus.

ON THIS ROCK, a hundred feet from Cyprus's northern shore, Aphrodite, the Greek goddess of love whom the Romans called Venus, was, according to legend, born of the foam of the sea.

visive effect on what was previously the most prosperous society in that part of the Mediterranean, with a diversified economy based on tourism, citrus fruits, wine exports, and a growing industrial segment, and an average wage of $1,400 a year. The Turkish advance finally halted in September along what was subsequently known as the Attila Line; but the third of the island occupied by the invading Turks contained 70 percent of Cyprus's most productive resources including water, cereal-growing land, and citrus plantations, and much of the meager mineral resources — copper, copper pyrites, and stone and lime. Both Famagusta and Kyrenia, the island's two major tourist centers, were also occupied by the invading Turks.

Andreas Patsalides, an economist trained at Harvard and the London School of Economics in England, who for six years before last summer's troubles served as finance minister in the Makarios administration, estimated the island's vital exports had fallen by as much as 70 percent. Housing and feeding the thousands of refugees alone had made it necessary for Cyprus to seek $141 million in foreign loans; this in itself was an economic disaster for the island nation which only the year before had recorded its first balance-of-payments deficit in several years, a mere $14 million. The biggest loss to the economy was the abrupt cutoff of the tourist flow—which had reached nearly 450,000 persons a year, most of them from Europe—and foreign earnings—which in three years had increased from $19 million in 1970 to $52.2 million. Ten hotels in the popular resort of Famagusta were bombed and strafed by Turkish jets during the fighting, and while Greek-Cypriot negotiators were optimistic the Turks would eventually withdraw from Famagusta (which would allow 50,000 displaced Greek-speaking refugees to return to their homes), it was seen as unlikely the Turks would similarly return Kyrenia which was expected to become the capital of the self-governing Turkish section in any bizonal federal state.

Alternatives. The only alternative would be the establishment of two separate sovereign states on the island. While Ankara was silent on this possible solution, both Greek and Turkish-Cypriots on the island were opposed to it. Dr. Iacovos Aristodou, director-general of the government's planning bureau, said the first essential step was the return of both Greek and Turkish refugees to their original homes. "If the refugees don't go back, I see little economic future for either part of the island. We shall be condemned to eternal underdevelopment and misery. When you split a small economy like Cyprus, neither half can be viable."

DEATHS

CHARLES A. LINDBERGH, who achieved fame by flying alone across the Atlantic in 1927, died on August 26 at 72 on the island of Maui of a malignant tumor of the lymphatic system. He had been living quietly in Hawaii for several years. After receiving medical treatment earlier in the month in New York City he was flown back to Maui to meet death in a lonely cabin facing the sea, sustained by the presence of his wife and son. This epitomized the style of a man who valued his privacy highly and had often found himself thrust into the limelight.

Lindbergh was born in Minnesota, descended from a Swedish family that had settled in that state. His father was a lawyer and a representative in Congress. After a brief stay at the University of Wisconsin, young Lindbergh quit college to enter a commercial aviation school. On completing his studies, he worked for an aircraft company, then was employed as a U.S. airmail pilot. He resigned to devote himself with quiet determination to his dream of flying the Atlantic. Financial backing came from St. Louis to build his "Spirit of St. Louis." When on May 20 he took off from Long Island this modest youth was an unknown, but when he came down at Le Bourget airfield near Paris thirty-three hours and twenty-nine minutes later he had become an international hero. He tolerated the parades and plaudits, refusing all rewards save the $25,000 prize which had been offered. From a captaincy in the Air Force Reserve, he was advanced to the rank of colonel. Lindbergh traveled widely to promote and popularize aviation. Returning to private life, he married Anne Morrow, daughter of the U.S. ambassador to Mexico, and their flights together became a romantic idyll. Deep tragedy befell them in 1932 when their infant son was kidnapped and, after highly publicized negotiations, found dead. With the approach of World War II Lindbergh lost some of his popularity by affiliating with an antiwar organization, America First. Once the country had entered the war, he served in the Air Force, flying fifty combat missions. He served the government as well as commercial companies as aviation consultant. Recently the ecology movement seems to have been a major interest.

CAPTAIN CHARLES A. LINDBERGH poses on a New York airfield with his mother, Mrs. Evangeline Lindbergh, in front of his plane, "Spirit of St. Louis," before embarking on his lone hop across the Atlantic Ocean in May, 1927.

DEATHS

DAVID ALFARO SIQUEIROS, Mexican muralist, died on January 6 in Cuernavaca of cancer, aged 77. He was the lone survivor of the great triumvirate of artists — the others being Diego Rivera and José Clemente Orozco — that drew worldwide attention to Mexican art more than thirty years ago. It was a vigorous, proletarian art of social protest, depicting the struggle of exploited workers for justice and freedom. Siqueiros, a Communist from youth and a lifelong political activist, was often arrested and sometimes jailed for leading demonstrations and organizing unions. Nevertheless the government recognized his talents and subsidized his murals, which may be seen today on the interior and exterior walls of Mexican public buildings, in parks, and in the museums of other countries. Siqueiros became a millionaire from the sale of his easel paintings.

HARRY GOLD, a Communist who was convicted as an atomic spy courier, died in August, 1972, although his death was not generally known until February, 1974. A Swiss-born research chemist, Gold was recruited in 1945 to contact the British physicist Klaus Fuchs, a Soviet agent then working at the Los Alamos laboratory, and to secure from him and transmit to the U.S.S.R. atomic-energy secrets. Gold was a star witness at the trial which resulted in the conviction of Julius and Ethel Rosenberg as spies. Questions have been raised with respect to Gold's confession of guilt and about the validity of the F.B.I.'s evidence against him. He was paroled in 1966, having served fifteen years of a thirty-year sentence.

D. W. BROGAN, emeritus professor of history at Cambridge University, died in Cambridge, England, on January 5, aged 73. The British historian, whose works included ten volumes on the United States, also wrote with authority on modern French history. Sir Denis, who was knighted in 1963, was a popular lecturer and transatlantic radio personality.

WILLIAM F. KNOWLAND, 65, former Republican leader of the U.S. Senate, died on February 23 of a gunshot wound inflicted by himself, near Guerneville, Calif. Knowland entered California politics early, serving in the state senate at the age of twenty-seven. In 1945 he became the youngest member of the U.S. Senate, when he was appointed to fill an unexpired term. After 1958, when he was defeated in his race for the governorship, he devoted himself to state and local issues as publisher of the *Oakland Tribune*. Although he was a liberal on some issues, Knowland was firm in his stand against Communist China and in his advocacy of right-to-work laws.

SOL HUROK, 85, successful impresario, died in New York City on March 5 of a heart attack. For more than sixty years Hurok — whose forte was discovering and promoting talent — had been engaged in introducing to the American public the outstanding orchestras, ballet troupes, opera companies, and individual performing artists of Europe, with special enthusiasm for presenting those from the Soviet Union. Russian-born, Hurok emigrated to the United States at the age of eighteen, and began his long career in 1911, when he persuaded the violinist Efrem Zimbalist to play at a fund-raising affair for the Socialist party. Famous for his unflagging energy as well as for his ability to handle temperamental artists, Hurok remained active to the day of his death.

PETER REVSON, racing driver, was

DEATHS

killed near Johannesburg, South Africa, on March 22, when his car crashed and burst into flames in a practice run for the South Africa Grand Prix. Revson, 35, had survived previous accidents during the fourteen years he participated in racing events. He won the 1971 runner-up award in the Indianapolis 500, and had expected to race in that event in 1974. Although a member of the Revson cosmetic family, Peter Revson was not a direct heir. He attended several colleges but never graduated.

SAMUEL GOLDWYN, producer of many excellent, Oscar-winning films, died at his home in Los Angeles, Calif., on January 31, at the age of 91. The Hollywood tycoon was already a legendary figure due to the dramatic ups and downs of his career, to the high quality of his productions, and to the roster of important names — actors, writers, and directors — associated with his enterprises. Goldwyn's fractured English, "Goldwynisms," — whether authentic or coined by publicity men — became a part of the language, and of the legend.

Born in Warsaw, Samuel Goldfish (who was to change his name later) arrived in this country at the age of thirteen. Ambitious and energetic, he proved his ability as a businessman before marrying the sister of Jesse I. Lasky, with whom he produced a feature-length film, *The Squaw Man.* Following this auspicious start, there came a long list of superior pictures — *Wuthering Heights, The Best Years of Our Lives, The Little Foxes, The Secret Life of Walter Mitty,* and *Arrowsmith.* Goldwyn came out of retirement in 1959 to make his last film, *Porgy and Bess.*

GOLDWYNISMS

"Gentlemen, include me out."

"An oral agreement is not worth the paper it's written on."

"They're always biting the hand that lays the golden egg."

"You've got to take the bull by the teeth."

"I'll tell you in two words — Im Possible."

"Goldwyn pictures griddle the earth."

SAMUEL GOLDWYN

FRANK McGEE, N.B.C. newsman and host of the "Today" television show, died of bone cancer in New York City on April 17, aged 52. McGee won the esteem of colleagues and public by his lucid and forthright presentation of the daily news. Born in Louisiana and schooled in Oklahoma, McGee entered the broadcasting field soon after serving in World War II. Advancing from small stations over the year, in 1971 he assumed the prestigious "Today" position. McGee was the creator of some highly praised documentaries and was the winner of the Peabody Award for his coverage of Pope Paul's visit to the United States.

VINCENT STARRETT, critic, essayist, poet, and newspaper man, died in Chicago, Ill., on January 5, at the age of 87. His early career included service as a war correspondent in Mexico. Starrett, one of the founders of the Baker Street Irregulars, became widely known as an expert on Sherlock Holmes. He wrote *Books and Bipeds* and *Best Loved Books of the Twentieth Century.*

ERRETT CORD, automobile designer and business tycoon, died in Reno, Nev., on January 2, at the age of 79. Famous as the producer of the 1937 avant-garde Cord 810, a luxury car, he had to abandon his creation. It was a machine for which the public was not ready. In later years Cord was successful in many business ventures and became a prominent figure in Nevada politics.

CHARLES E. BOHLEN, 69, U.S. government adviser on Soviet affairs, died in Washington, D.C., of cancer on January 1. Bohlen, trained for the diplomatic service, came to the fore as a translator for President Franklin D. Roosevelt in his conferences with Stalin at Teheran. For more than thirty years he served in succeeding administrations as an expert on the Soviet Union, and was appointed ambassador to that country in 1953. In 1962 President John F. Kennedy made him ambassador to France.

TEX RITTER, singing cowboy, died in Nashville, Tenn., on January 2, aged 67. Ritter's ambition to be a country lawyer was sidetracked when he discovered his talent as an entertainer. His country-western records and his cowboy movies brought him fame and riches. An attempt to enter Tennessee politics as a state senator failed.

GENERAL GEORGE GRIVAS, right-wing leader of the Cypriot underground, died in Limassol, Cyprus, on January 27, aged 75. He came to the fore in 1955 as a leader in the struggle to unite the island, then under British rule, with Greece. When Cyprus achieved independence, Grivas carried on a small guerrilla war against the president, Archbishop Makarios, and opposed his policy of compromise with the Turkish minority.

MORRIS KANTOR, 77, artist and teacher of painting, died in a Nyack, N.Y., hospital on January 31, following a long illness. Born in Russia, Kantor began his art studies soon after he came to the United States at the age of fifteen. Highly regarded as a teacher, he also achieved high rank for his own contribution to the art of painting, and was the winner of several important awards.

JOHN C. GARAND, inventor of the rifle which bears his name, died in a Springfield, Mass., hospital on February 18, aged 86. The Canadian-born Garand displayed his mechanical genius in 1934 when, while an employee at the Springfield Armory, he invented the semiautomatic 30-caliber M-1 rifle. Adopted by the Army in 1936, it was not replaced until 1957. In 1944 Garand was given the government's Medal for Merit, but never received the promised compensation for his invention.

DEATHS

GEORGES J. R. POMPIDOU, eighteenth president of the modern French Republic, died on April 2 in Paris, aged 62. The cause of death was not announced, but it was known that Pompidou had been in failing health. An impressive state funeral in the Cathedral of Notre Dame was attended by the representatives of seventy nations. Pompidou, a native of Auvergne, was no politician. Highly educated and gifted with a brilliant mind, he was a valued officer in the banking house of Rothschild before he became Charles de Gaulle's close associate, mainly as financial adviser. Appointed premier in 1962, he remained discreetly in the shadow of his dynamic, colorful chief. Following de Gaulle's retirement in 1969, Pompidou was elected president, thanks to division among the left-wing parties. Although he was regarded as a good administrator, during his five years in office he showed little initiative in solving his country's serious problems and pursued a policy of somewhat liberalized Gaullism.

GEORGES POMPIDOU

ADOLPH GOTTLIEB, American abstract artist, died of a stroke in New York City on March 4, at the age of 70. Born of parents who had emigrated from Hungary, Gottlieb studied art in New York City and in Paris. A later sojourn in Arizona was to leave a marked influence on his work. He was a founder of the abstract-expressionist movement and disparaged pop art and pop culture. In 1963 Gottlieb won the Grand Prix at the Sao Paulo Bienal.

CHET HUNTLEY, former television newscaster, died of cancer in Bozeman, Mont., on March 21, aged 62. Huntley was born in the Far West to which he had returned after his retirement. His start as a communicator was made on a small radio station in Seattle, Wash. After 1937 he was affiliated with N.B.C., gradually working up to the evening news spot with David Brinkley. The partnership lasted from 1957 to 1970. Recently Huntley had been engaged in organizing a huge recreational complex in Montana, scheduled to be dedicated in March.

BILLY DE WOLFE, a featured performer in motion pictures and on the stage, died in Los Angeles, Calif., of lung cancer on March 5, at the age of 67. Known both as a comedian and as a dancer, he appeared in many musicals, including *The Ziegfeld Follies.* Among his film successes were *Call Me Madam* and *Dixie.*

LOUIS I. KAHN, 73, American architect, died suddenly of a heart attack on March 17 on arriving in New York City from Dacca, Bangladesh. He had gone there to oversee work on government buildings which he had designed. At the time of the death the Estonian-born Kahn was professor of architecture at

DEATHS

the University of Pennsylvania, where he had received his training. Among the famous buildings created by Kahn are the Yale Art Gallery and the Salk Institute in California.

BUD ABBOTT

BUD (WILLIAM A.) ABBOTT, an actor who teamed with Lou Costello for more than two decades in slapstick comedy routines, died of cancer in Woodland Hills, Calif., on April 24. He was 78 years old. Born into show business, Abbott joined Costello after a series of theatrical jobs. The two low-comedy buffoons were popular features on the vaudeville circuit, in motion pictures, and on television, with Abbott as straight man.

BLOSSOM SEELEY, 82, a headliner in vaudeville and burlesque, died in New York City on April 17.

FRED FREED, television producer and writer of prizewinning documentaries, died in New York City on March 31, at 53.

HAL (HAROLD VINCENT) BOYLE, newspaper correspondent in three wars and Pulitzer Prize winner, died in New York City on April 1, aged 63.

DOROTHY FIELDS, 68, member of the Song Writers Hall of Fame and author of lyrics for many Broadway musicals, died in New York City on March 28.

CAPTAIN EDWARD H. MOLYNEUX, British fashion designer whose clothes were worn by social and stage celebrities, died at Monte Carlo, Monaco, on March 22, at the age of 82.

TIM (MILES GILBERT) HORTON, Canadian hockey star and successful businessman, died in an automobile accident in Ontario on February 21, aged 44.

ANNA Q. NILSSON, Swedish-born film actress, died in Hemet, Calif., on February 11, aged 85.

JACK COLE, choreographer of many musicals and teacher of dancing, died in Los Angeles, Calif., on February 17, at the age of 60.

AGNES MOOREHEAD, versatile actress of stage, screen, and television, died in Rochester, Minn., on April 30, aged 67.

GLENN MORRIS, 1936 Olympics decathlon champion and a former film "Tarzan," died on March 31 after a long illness in Palo Alto, Calif., aged 62.

DEATHS

MURRAY CHOTINER, 64, lawyer and close friend of former President Richard Nixon, died in Washington, D.C., on January 30, from injuries received in an automobile accident.

MARGARET LEECH PULITZER, widow of Ralph Pulitzer and winner of two Pulitzer Prizes for her historical works, died in New York City on February 24, aged 80.

JAMES DAUGHERTY, 84, writer, artist, and illustrator of many children's books, died in Boston, Mass., on February 21, aged 84.

LEWIS W. DOUGLAS, former U.S. ambassador to Great Britain, businessman, and rancher, died in Tucson, Ariz., on March 8, aged 79.

KATHARINE CORNELL, an actress whose artistry and charm brought a quality of real distinction to the American theater, died at her home in Vineyard Haven, on the island of Martha's Vineyard, Mass., on June 9. She was 81, and had not acted since the death of her husband and manager, Guthrie McClintic, in 1961. Born in Berlin, Germany, where her father was studying surgery, she was brought up in Buffalo, N.Y. In a family devoted to amateur theatricals, it was natural that she should have chosen a career on the stage. After experience in a stock company, she appeared on Broadway, where her talent was immediately recognized. Her lovely voice and dark beauty won favor even for mediocre plays. For many years, at the head of her own company, she brought fine plays to cities and towns throughout the country. Among her great roles were Elizabeth in *The Barretts of Wimpole Street;* and Candida in George Bernard Shaw's play of that name. Miss Cornell declined to appear in movies or television.

LARRY DOYLE, captain of the New York Giants from 1907 to 1920 and winner of baseball awards, died at Saranac Lake, N.Y., on March 1, aged 87.

EARL W. SUTHERLAND, winner in 1971 of the Nobel Prize in physiology and medicine for his research on hormones, died in Miami, Fla., on March 9, aged 58.

QUINTO MAGANINI, composer, conductor, and head of the American Conservatory at Fontainebleau, France, died in Greenwich, Conn., on March 10, at the age of 77.

LILLIAN RED WING ST. CYR, 90, American Indian actress of *The Squaw Man* and other Western films, died in New York City on March 12.

KATHARINE CORNELL

MIKHAIL TIKHONRAVOV, 73, pioneer in cosmic technology and in the development of the Soviet Union's rocketry and space programs, died in Moscow on March 7.

B. EVERETT JORDAN, 77, former Democratic senator from North Carolina who was defeated in 1972, died in Saxapahaw, N.C., on March 15.

A. RAYMOND KATZ, 78, Hungarian-born artist whose murals and stained glass embellish many synagogues and other houses of worship, died in Miami Beach, Fla., on March 24.

DANIEL F. GERBER, who in 1929 started putting canned strained baby foods on the market, died in Fremont, Mich., on March 18, aged 75.

FRANCOISE ROSAY, French actress who during a sixty-one-year career appeared in American, British, French, and German films, died in Paris on March 28, aged 82.

HOWARD GREER, designer for motion picture stars and later for the general dress trade, died in Los Angeles, Calif., on April 17, at the age of 78.

JOHN HENRY LEWIS, 59, light heavyweight champion boxer from 1935 to 1939, died in Berkeley, Calif., on April 14.

MARCEL PAGNOL, playwright and French film director with an international reputation, died in Paris on April 18, aged 79.

ALEXANDRE DUMAINE, French master chef and proprietor of a famous restaurant at Saulieu, France, died in his native village of Digoin, on April 23, aged 78.

FRANZ JONAS, fourth president of the Austrian Republic and former mayor of Vienna, died in that city on April 23, at the age of 74.

BETTY COMPSON, popular star of silent films and early talkies, died in Glendale, Calif., on April 18, aged 77.

MARGARET CLAPP, former president of Wellesley College and Pulitzer Prize-winner for her biography of John Bigelow, died in Tyringham, Mass., on May 3, aged 64.

SAMUEL WYLIE, Episcopal bishop of Northern Michigan and former dean of the General Theological Seminary in New York City, died while on a visit to that institution on May 6, aged 55.

DEL E. WEBB, former baseball player for the Yankees and founder of a huge construction and real estate business, died in Rochester, Minn., of lung cancer on July 3, at the age of 75.

JOHN CROWE RANSOM, 86, poet and leader of an influential group of Southern writers, died on July 5 in Gambier, Ohio, site of Kenyon College, where he had taught for many years.

WILLIAM H. (RED) FRIESELL, JR., football referee, athlete, and businessman, died in Pittsburgh on July 23, aged 80.

GEORGE KELLY, winner of a Pulitzer Prize for his play *Craig's Wife* and a former vaudeville actor, died in a hospital in Bryn Mawr, Pa., on June 18, aged 87.

SHOLOM SECUNDA, 79, composer and songwriter, famed for his contributions to Jewish music, died in New York City on June 13.

JUAN DOMINGO PERON

JUAN DOMINGO PERON, president of Argentina, died in Buenos Aires on July 1 at the age of 78. The death of this once-powerful and popular leader intensified the country's turbulence. Perón's young wife, elected vice-president in 1973, stepped into the office — the first woman head of state in the Americas. Perón, a military man, rose to prominence after participating in a bloodless coup which overthrew the government in 1943. Reforms to benefit farmers and urban laborers were promised. Gaining control of several government departments, Perón ran for the presidency and was twice elected. With his wife, the late Eva Duarte, who died in 1952, he succeeded in building a strong labor movement and in reducing somewhat the holdings of the great landowners. After running the country highhandedly for nine years, Perón was ousted in 1955, accused of broken promises, the arbitrary use of authority, and the introduction of Fascist concepts. Following an eighteen-year exile in Spain, he came back in 1972, regaining the presidency in 1973. An old man, in failing health, he was unable to cope with the violence and division that plagued the country.

THE DUKE OF GLOUCESTER, uncle of Queen Elizabeth II, whose life was spent in army service and in performing minor royal duties, died at his home in Northhamptonshire on June 18, at the age of 74.

MIGUEL ANGEL ASTURIAS, Guatemalan author and diplomat, winner of the Nobel Prize in literature in 1967 and of the Lenin Peace Prize in 1966, died in Madrid on June 9, aged 74.

DONALD CRISP, 93, acclaimed character actor and Oscar winner for his role in *How Green Was My Valley,* died in Van Nuys, Calif., on May 25.

STEWART ALSOP, political columnist and author of several books on national affairs, died of leukemia in Bethesda, Md., on May 26, at the age of 60.

SIR JAMES CHADWICK, 82, winner of the Nobel Prize in physics in 1935 for his discovery of the neutron — an important step in the development of nuclear energy — died in London on July 24.

DARIUS MILHAUD, innovative French composer and one of the famous "Six," died at his home in Geneva, Switzerland, on June 22, at the age of 82. Born into a prosperous and gifted Jewish family in Aix-en-Provence, Milhaud as a child studied the violin, abandoning it for composition while at the Paris Conservatory. Early works were influenced by a sojourn in Brazil. His prolific creative life was interrupted by World War II during which he taught in an American college.

ALAN DUNN, 73, whose witty cartoons appeared in *The New Yorker* for nearly forty years, died in New York City on May 20.

EARL WARREN

EARL WARREN, who retired as chief justice of the U.S. Supreme Court in 1969, died on July 9 at the age of 83 in a Washington, D.C., hospital. Warren's sixteen-year tenure as chief justice was marked by so many controversial, important, and generally liberal decisions that it came to be known as "Warren's Court." Warren preferred it to be remembered as the "People's Court." During this period the Supreme Court, despite the basic conservatism of most of its members, was transformed into an institution that actively responded to rapid social change. And Warren himself, a Republican, moved with the times: he wrote opinions that outraged the extreme Right to the point of demanding his impeachment.

This strong, friendly, hard-working man with a Scandinavian family background was born in Los Angeles and was familiar with deprivation as a youth. After graduating from the University of California, he attained a law degree and began to practice. Entering politics at the county level, he later served as state attorney. As a public official he had the reputation of being a "law and order" man. He was elected governor of California for three successive terms: the second time he ran on both Republican and Democratic tickets. He was encouraged to seek the Republican nomination for vice-president in 1948 and for president in 1952, in the latter case having no hope of winning against Dwight D. Eisenhower. The following year, however, Eisenhower appointed him chief justice to fill the vacancy in that position. Of the score or more of significant decisions of the Warren court, the following may be mentioned: ending racial segregation laws in the United States, broadly applying the Bill of Rights to the states, forbidding compulsory prayer and Bible reading in the public schools, protecting freedom of choice in the areas of marriage and birth control, and decreeing the reapportionment of state and federal legislative districts with the aim of equalizing the population of each district—a decision in which Warren took especial pride.

MARSHAL GEORGI ZHUKOV, military leader of the U.S.S.R. during World War II, died in Moscow on June 18 at the age of 77. Zhukov, a conscript in the czar's army at the time of the Russian Revolution, defected to join the Red forces and the Communist party. His military genius brought him to the fore in the 1940s, when, after action on many other fronts, he defended Moscow and later Stalingrad from the advancing Germans. Zhukov won the Hero of the Soviet Union award on four occasions.

WAYNE MORSE, U.S. senator from Oregon from 1945 until 1968, died in a hospital in Portland, Ore., on July 22, aged 73. Wisconsin-born, Morse first came into prominence as head of the Oregon University Law School. Elected to the Senate in 1944 as a Republican he later switched parties; but in both he was a pronounced liberal. A long-

DEATHS

winded but witty speaker, he opposed the Vietnam war, fought for civil rights, and in general defended the underdog. He was running for election to the U.S. Senate at the time of his death.

TYREE GLENN, jazz trombonist of the big band era, died at the age of 61 in a New Jersey hospital on May 18.

DAN TOPPING, millionaire sportsman and baseball and football executive, died of emphysema in Miami, Fla., on May 18, aged 61.

LORD PATRICK BLACKETT, 78, outstanding British scientist and Nobel Prize winner in physics in 1948, died in London on July 13.

DAME SIBYL OF SARK, ruler as a benevolent dictator of the Channel island of that name, died there on July 14, aged 90.

PAR LAGERKVIST, 73, Swedish Nobel Prize-winning author, died of a stroke in Stockholm on July 11.

HAJ AMIN EL-HUSSEINI, powerful Arab leader and formerly grand mufti of Jerusalem, died in Beirut, Lebanon, on July 4, aged 80.

VANNEVAR BUSH, scientist and administrative genius, died in Belmont, Mass., on June 28, aged 84. Bush's professional life, during which he served seven presidents as science adviser, was mainly associated with the Massachusetts Institute of Technology. From that base he organized and directed the engineers responsible for the development of the technology and weapons which were vital in winning World War II. Bush published a number of books and received many honors, including the Atomic Pioneers Award.

ADELLE DAVIS, 70, controversial health food advocate and author of popular books on nutrition, died of bone cancer at her home in Palos Verdes Estates, Calif., on May 31.

JOHNNY MACK BROWN, 70, all-American college football star and featured actor in many Western movies of an earlier day, died in Woodland Hills, Calif., on November 14.

CORNELIUS RYAN, 54, author of *The Longest Day* and *A Bridge Too Far*, both dealing with World War II, died of cancer in New York City on November 23.

CYRIL CONNOLLY, 71, British critic and author of novels and books of essays, died in London on November 26.

TUSS McLAUGHRY, former football coach at Brown, Amherst, and Dartmouth, and member of the College Football Hall of Fame, died in Norwich, Conn., on November 26, at the age of 81.

CLIVE BROOK, British actor, well known for his work on the stage, in films, and on television, died on November 17 in London.

ERSKINE CHILDERS, 68, who succeeded Eamon de Valera as Ireland's second Protestant president, died of a heart attack while delivering a speech on November 17.

GEORGE BRUNIS, 74, jazz trombonist, once a member of Ted Lewis's band and leader of Dixieland groups, died in Chicago on November 20.

SAM RICE, outfielder with the Washington Senators and member of the Baseball Hall of Fame, died in Rossmor, Md., on November 13, aged 84.

GEN. CARL SPAATZ

GENERAL CARL A. SPAATZ, recipient of many honors and decorations for his valiant service in World War II, died on July 14 in Walter Reed Hospital, Washington, D.C., at the age of 83. He commanded U.S. strategic bombing in Europe and later in the Pacific. After the war he was appointed first chief of staff of the Air Force when it became a separate branch. A West Pointer, Gen. Spaatz was one of twenty-five Americans to wear the "wings" of the Army's First Aero Squadron.

DAVID OISTRAKH, 65, acclaimed Russian violinist, died on October 24 in Amsterdam, where he was conducting a series of concerts with the Amsterdam Philharmonic Orchestra. Oistrakh was born in Odessa, where, as a Jew, music was one of the few professions open to him. His talent was evident from the age of five, when his father gave him a miniature violin. Fame came quickly after his debut. He was known in the United States through recordings before coming here on tour in 1955. Oistrakh was highly esteemed by his colleagues throughout the world, as well as by his own countrymen. The Soviet Union gave him its highest award, the Stalin Prize.

LOUIS B. RUSSELL, JR., 49, who underwent heart transplant surgery more than six years ago and had survived this operation longer than any other patient, died on November 27 in Richmond, N.Y.

JOSEF KRIPS, 72, Vienna-born conductor of leading symphony orchestras here and abroad, died of lung cancer in Geneva, Switzerland, on October 12.

ROBERT KLEBERG, JR., 78, sportsman, breeder of Santa Gertrudis cattle, and president of the mammoth King Ranch, Inc., in Texas, died of lung cancer in Houston on October 13.

H. L. HUNT, ultraconservative billionaire oilman, died in Dallas, Texas, on November 29, at the age of 85.

JAMES J. BRADDOCK, 69, winner of the world heavyweight boxing championship in 1935 when he defeated Max Baer, died in North Bergen, N.J., on November 29.

VITTORIO DE SICA, 73, Italian film-maker and director of such films as *The Bicycle Thief* and *Shoeshine,* died in Paris on November 13, shortly after the opening there of his last work, *The Voyage.*

EDWARD V. SULLIVAN, sports writer, Broadway columnist, and host of a Sunday evening television show that ran for twenty-three years, died of cancer of the esophagus on October 13 in New York City. Sullivan held newspaper jobs before realizing his talents as a showman. From the fringes of the entertainment world he landed in the big time with the launching in 1948 of the nationally televised "Ed Sullivan

Show." Because of its variety and originality and Sullivan's own unique personality, it successfully held its audience of many millions over the years.

JAY HANNA *(JEROME HERMAN)* "*DIZZY*" DEAN, popular baseball pitcher, died in a Reno, Nev., hospital on July 17, following a heart attack. He was 63 years old. His wife and his brother Paul, also a ball player, were with him at the end. Born in Lucas, Ark., this Ozark farm boy played his way into the big time in his early twenties. While playing with the St. Louis Cardinals from 1932 to 1936, he grew to be a folk-hero for his uncanny pitching skill, his comical antics on the sidelines, and his picturesque mishandling of the English language. During this period Dizzy won 120 of his 150 big league victories. After being sold to the Chicago Cubs, he continued to play even after being handicapped by injuries suffered on the field. When he retired in 1941, his record stood at 150 victories, 83 losses, for a winning percentage of .644, and an earned-run average of 3.03. As a broadcaster of Saturday games on radio and television Dizzy amused both himself and his listeners. In 1953 he was elected to the Baseball Hall of Fame.

LILI DARVAS, Hungarian-born stage and screen actress and widow of playwright Ferenc Molnar, died in New York City on July 22, aged 72.

GEORGE RADCLIFFE, 96, former Democratic senator from Maryland and New Deal supporter, died in Baltimore on July 29.

JACQUELINE SUSANN, author of the bestselling *Valley of the Dolls* and other popular novels, died of cancer in New York City on September 21, aged 53.

ZALMAN SHAZAR, 84, who was president of Israel from 1963 to 1973, died in Jerusalem on October 5.

"DIZZY" DEAN, left, poses with his brother Paul "Daffy" Dean in 1934.

ILONA MASSEY

ILONA MASSEY, a Hungarian film beauty who appeared in television and radio serials and also on Broadway, died August 20 in Bethesda, Md., at the age of 62.

CLIFF ARQUETTE, 68, the Charlie Weaver of television's game show "The Hollywood Squares," died of a heart attack in Los Angeles on September 23, ending a long career in vaudeville, radio, and television.

LUTHER H. HODGES, businessman, ex-governor of North Carolina, and secretary of commerce under President John F. Kennedy, died in Chapel Hill, N.C., on October 7, aged 75.

PAUL G. HOFFMAN, an American statesman of liberal views, administrator of the Marshall Plan and later head of the U.N. development fund, died in New York City on October 8 at the age of 83.

ANNA SEXTON, 45, winner of the Pulitzer Prize for poetry in 1967, died at her home in Weston, Mass., on October 4, a possible suicide.

ROSS PARKER, lyricist and composer of many songs, including "There'll Always be an England," died at his home in England on August 2, at the age of 59.

MOSES SOYER, 74, Russian-born American painter and art teacher, twin brother of the equally distinguished artist Raphael Soyer, died while painting a portrait in his New York City studio on September 3.

HARRY PARTCH, avant-garde composer who based his music on an octave of forty-three intervals and who invented many bizarre musical instruments, died on September 3 in San Diego, Calif., at the age of 73.

ANDRE DUNOYER DE SEGONZAC, famous French naturalist painter, died in Paris on September 17, at the age of 90.

NORMAN KIRK, prime minister and foreign minister of New Zealand, died in Wellington, New Zealand, of a heart attack on August 31, at the age of 51. A man of humble origins, Kirk qualified as an engineer by taking a correspondence course. He rose in the ranks of the Labor party and in 1957 was elected to the one-chamber Parliament. When his party won a majority in the election of 1972, he became prime minister. He worked for the balanced development of the islands, opposed the French nuclear tests in the Pacific, recognized the Communist regime in China, and pulled New Zealand troops out of the Vietnam war.

GENERAL CREIGHTON W. ABRAMS, 59, died on September 4, following surgery for cancer. West Point-trained, Abrams saw heavy action in World War II as a tank commander in the First Armored Division — from the beachhead of Normandy on across Europe to the Rhine. The Abrams name and tactics became legendary, even among the Germans. After the war he served in the Pentagon. He was chief of staff of four combat corps in the Korean War. Abrams ended his military career as commander of U.S. forces in Vietnam, where his aim was to avoid casualties, and back up the Vietnamese and stiffen them to fight their own war.

WALTER BRENNAN

WALTER BRENNAN, 80, Oscar-winning motion picture star and a featured player in the television series "The Real McCoys," died of emphysema in Oxnard, Calif., on September 21.

ALEXANDER P. DE SEVERSKY, inventive genius in the field of aeronautics, died in New York City on August 24, at the age of 80. A flyer in the Czarist air force during World War I, De Seversky came to the United States at the conclusion of that war and during his long life made significant contributions to the development of American strategic air power.

V. K. KRISHNA MENON, ardent agitator for Indian independence and defense minister during Nehru's presidency, when he built up India's military establishment, died in New Delhi on October 6, aged 77.

U THANT

U THANT (Thant had no first name and "U" is a title of respect), third secretary general of the United Nations, died of cancer in New York City on November 25, aged 65. A native of Burma, Thant served two five-year terms in

THE FLAG-DRAPED COFFIN of U Thant lay in state at U.N. headquarters in New York City for twenty-four hours.

office before failing health obliged him to resign. These were years of severe stress, covering the "cold war," the Cuban missile confrontation, the 1967 Arab-Israeli war, and troubles in the Congo, Kashmir, and elsewhere. In several of these crises, Thant showed his ability as a patient and practical negotiator. A Buddhist and a man of rare spiritual gifts, Thant was completely devoted to his difficult tasks. He incurred the wrath of American leaders by his consistent opposition to U.S. military involvement in Southeast Asia.

Born in Pantanaw, Burma, and educated as a teacher in Rangoon, Thant joined his friend of college days, U Nu, in the independence movement. After Burma freed itself of British rule in 1948, he served Prime Minister Nu and his country in many responsible positions. In 1957 he became Burma's chief representative at the United Nations.

BISHOP STEPHEN G. SPOTTSWOOD, retired leader of the African Methodist Episcopal Zion Church in Washington, and board chairman of the National Association for the Advancement of Colored People, died at his home in the capital on December 1, aged 77.

KURT HAHN, innovative German educator who founded the Gordonstoun School in Scotland, attended by Prince Charles and other members of the British royal family, died at his home in Hermannsberg, West Germany, on December 15, aged 88.

STERLING NORTH, literary critic, editor, and author of *Rascal*, died in Morristown, N.J., on December 22, aged 63.

HARRY HOOPER, 87, oldest member of the Baseball Hall of Fame, died on December 17 in Santa Cruz, Calif.

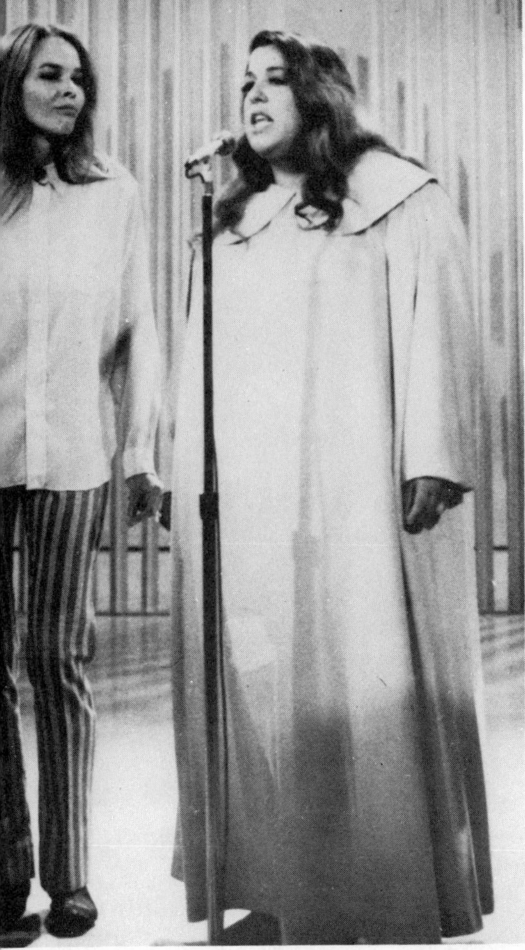

"MAMA" CASS ELLIOTT

"MAMA" CASS ELLIOTT, folk singer and performer in popular rock groups, including the Mamas and the Papas, died suddenly on July 29 in London, where she was preparing to give a concert. A heart attack, brought on by overweight, was the probable cause of death.

WALTER LIPPMANN, analyst of the American political and social scene for more than half a century, died in New York City on December 14, at the age of 85. Lippmann's newspaper columns, his books and magazine articles often served as guidelines to the country's leaders. Nonpartisan, he freely criticized both Democrats and Republicans. Beginning his career as an idealistic near-Socialist, he veered to more conservative views over the years. He believed that Western civilization had suffered a spectacular decline in the twentieth century, due mainly to the failings of the democratic peoples—as instanced by U.S. intervention in Vietnam, which he considered an avoidable catastrophe, one that affronted his faith in reason and common sense.

Lippmann was an only child, born into an affluent German-Jewish family in New York City. At Harvard University, his literary and other talents brought him recognition and opportunity. He became a founder of *The New Republic*, and later an editor of the *New York World* and a columnist for the *New York Herald-Tribune*. Among the books he published over the years were *Public*

WALTER LIPPMANN

JACK BENNY plays duets with two famous accompanists: President Harry S. Truman, left, and Vice-President Richard M. Nixon in 1959.

Opinion and *Drift and Mastery*. Lippmann's important honors included two Pulitzer prizes and the Presidential Medal of Freedom.

ANATOLE LITVAK, 72, Russian-born film director, who worked in both Hollywood and Europe, died in Paris on December 15.

AMY VANDERBILT, 66, syndicated columnist and authority on good manners, plunged to her death from a window in her New York City home on December 27. Author of *Amy Vanderbilt's Complete Book of Etiquette,* she also conducted radio and television programs in this field.

GEORGE H. EARLE III, diplomat and former governor of Pennsylvania, died on December 30 in Bryn Mawr, Pa., aged 84.

JACK BENNY, popular comedian of stage, radio, and television, died of cancer of the pancreas at his home in Beverly Hills, Calif., on December 27, aged 80. Born in Chicago, son of a Russian Jewish immigrant, Benny — by birth Benjamin Kubelsky — was brought up in Waukegan, Ill. He quit school in the ninth grade and went into vaudeville as a violinist, but violin-playing became only a part of his comedy routine as his talent as a funny man developed. Over the years he performed in motion pictures and musicals, on television, and on radio, where he had his own show for twenty-three years. Benny never lost his touch or his timing, and even after retirement continued to make frequent benefit appearances.

HARRY HERSHFIELD, 89, cartoonist, columnist, and creator of comic strips, died in New York City on December 15.

THE ROYAL SHAKESPEARE THEATER at Stratford-on-Avon, England, is home for Britain's prestigious Royal Shakespeare Company. Sir Hugh Willatt, director of the British Arts Council, threatened in November to merge the great repertory group with Britain's National Theater if the council's $45 million budget for theater support was not increased by $12 million for 1975.

The Fabulous Invalid. Under the headline "There Is Now A National Invalid," *Variety*, the show business weekly, declared: "The American legit season of 1973-1974 was in most respects dismaying. Both economically and theatrically it was the worst in many years." It reported that "the combined total gross for both Broadway and the road was $91,797,267, a slump of 9.15 percent below the 1972-1973 period," and a record low for the last nine years. When the season officially closed on June 30, only forty-six plays, musicals, and revues had been presented, down from sixty-three in 1972-1973.

Broadway profits were becoming pipe dreams and it was increasingly difficult to raise money for new shows. Mounting a one-set straight play cost between $150,000 and $175,000, and musicals ran up to $1 million to produce. Only eleven musicals premiered, as contrasted with twenty-one in the 1972-1973 season.

Yet by summer the fabulous invalid was looking better. Audiences kept fourteen shows going, compared with eleven in the summer of 1973. The public paid $10.2 million for tickets, up by almost $1 million from the previous summer. In the fall the Great White Way was ablaze, with all its forty theaters booked.

According to some company managers, the good news happened not in spite of inflation, but because of it. The theater-going public was not traveling at all or was taking shorter U.S. trips rather than going abroad. Its pleasure and leisure money was funneling into the theater.

The Audience. Who comprised the theater-going public? Mostly the rich and the well-educated, according to a survey conducted for the Ford Foundation. In a sampling of 6,000 people in twelve major metropolitan areas of the United States, it was found that only 16 percent had ever attended a live professional play.

FACT. Anxiety over the problems of the theater resulted in the First Annual Congress of Theater (FACT) at Princeton, N.J., June 2-6. The meeting brought together 191 delegates representing diverse aspects of the theater from all sections of the United States.

Delegates from the nonprofit theater did not seem ready to cooperate with what they had labored so long against — Broadway commercialism. After all, although Off Broadway was declining in importance, Off-Off-Broadway was drawing thousands of playgoers to more than 700 productions, and regional theater was figuring increasingly in the process of presenting new plays and playwrights. Of the forty-six shows that opened on Broadway in 1973-1974, twenty-one were first presented by nonprofit theaters. The fastest-growing show business enterprise in the United States was the dinner theater.

Recognizing these trends, Bernard Jacobs, president of the Shubert organ-

BRAZIL'S NATIONAL THEATER in Brasilia, designed by the country's world-famous architect Oscar Niemeyer, will be completed and opened in April, 1976. At FACT, delegates voted unanimously to protest the arrest of two theater companies in Brazil.

ization which owns fifteen of Broadway's theaters and shares with Irving Berlin ownership of a sixteenth, complained that "the profit theater as we know it is dead." He was challenged by producer Richard Barr who said, "Broadway is still the stamp of approval for theater talent." FACT ended with agreement to follow up suggestions and meet again within a year.

by

RICHARD F. STAAR, Ph.D.

Associate Director of the Hoover Institution on War, Revoution and Peace at Stanford University; editor, *1974 Yearbook on International Communist Affairs*, and author, *The Communist Regimes in Eastern Europe* (2nd rev. ed., 1971; 4th printing, 1973)

The Soviet Influence. Unable to generate enough support for a world conference of Communist parties during 1974, the Soviet Union apparently will strive for an all-European meeting as a preliminary step in that direction. *Pravda* reported on September 10 a meeting at Lyons, France, of representatives from six West European Communist groups, including French, Italian, and West German party leaders. Reservations were voiced by Rumanian and Yugoslav spokesmen, who demanded equality and refused to accept any special authority of the U.S.S.R. or criticism of mainland China at a future regional conference.

Yugoslavia reportedly was the target of contingency plan "Polyarka," the Soviet military occupation of that country after the death of eighty-two-year-old Tito. News from Bucharest alleged that Moscow had demanded an extraterritorial corridor across Rumania to link the Ukraine with Bulgaria. *Die Presse* in Vienna reported on September 17 that Russian troops were massing in southern Hungary. That same month allegations surfaced that Czechoslovakia, Hungary, and the U.S.S.R. had supported a secret, anti-Tito group. Establishment of a pro-Soviet government in

IN WARSAW a young couple applying for an apartment is likely to have to wait eight years, according to official statistics. The Polish government has given high priority to building 7 million apartments in housing complexes such as this by the year 1991.

Yugoslavia would provide the U.S.S.R. military with access to the Adriatic and bring about an end to Rumanian independence.

East-West Relations. In the area of East-West relations, negotiations for a mutual and balanced force reduction in Europe resumed on September 24 but remained deadlocked between two proposals. North Atlantic Treaty Organization (NATO) spokesmen had offered a cutback in ground strength to 700,000 men for each side. Warsaw Pact representatives want a 15 percent across-the-board reduction which would leave the U.S.S.R. and Eastern Europe with the same preponderance in ground troops, tanks, and tactical aircraft. However, the thirty-five-nation Conference on Security and Cooperation in Europe did agree to more than half of the coexistence principles, a basis for economic relations, and a preamble to the statement on humanitarian problems. It was hoped that this phase could end before 1975, when a meeting at the highest level would be arranged.

Warsaw Treaty Organization (WTO) defense ministers met at Bucharest in early February. Later that month a WTO command post exercise was held in Rumania, about the same time that Soviet contingency plan "Polyarka" was revealed in Nos. 5 and 6 of the Austrian magazine *Profil.* The source for this information is a defector, former Major General Jan Sejna who had been in charge of the Communist party organization for the defense ministry in Prague. Maneuvers by East European armed forces continued with exercises in Czechoslovakia and East Germany during March. The end of the month, the WTO military council met at Budapest and adopted unannounced recommendations. The most important meeting, however, took place in mid-April at Warsaw where the WTO political-consultative committee brought together all bloc party and government leaders.

The communiqué did not mention China but acknowledged the importance of nonalignment. Special resolutions were adopted on the Middle East, Vietnam, and Chile. No reference appeared concerning extension of the Warsaw Pact which is due to expire after twenty years in May, 1975, unless renewed for another decade. Simultaneous dissolu-

THE FORTIFIED CITY of Dubrovnik on the Adriatic Sea offers a medieval world to the 40 million tourists visiting Yugoslavia. Within its walls fourteen churches and monasteries, a half-dozen galleries, seven museums, and several old "public" buildings are tightly packed between red-roofed limestone houses.

tion of NATO and WTO were offered again, with the proviso that military security throughout Eastern Europe must be maintained. A joint exercise by navies of East Germany, Poland, and the Soviet Union that included amphibious landings took place during September 4-13 in the Baltic Sea.

The Council for Mutual Economic Assistance (CMEA) began the year with announcement of plans for a worldwide communications system "Intersputnik" to transmit television, telephone, and telegraph. Other agreements involve pro-

EAST GERMANY'S TWENTY-FIFTH ANNIVERSARY

A NEW TELEVISION TOWER soars over East Berlin. East German officials now admit that most of their citizens can tune in to West German television, but continually hammer home their *Abrenzung* or "walling off" line, insisting that East Germans will prosper only in a Socialist society with a Socialist culture.

After nearly a quarter century of isolation, East Germany celebrated its diplomatic acceptance by the West together with its twenty-fifth anniversary on October 7. To the United States, which became the last of the victorious Allies of World War II to recognize the German Democratic Republic on September 4, the country is symbolized by the ugly concrete Berlin Wall built in 1961 to prevent East Germans from escaping to the West.

Behind that wall is a prosperous nation of 17 million people who live in the ninth largest industrial country in the world and make more money per capita than the people of any other country in the Soviet bloc.

Despite its name it is no democracy. It is a highly centralized bureaucratic state totally dominated by the Socialist Unity party and allied "forever," its constitution says, to the Soviet Union. A network of economic, military, and political ties links the U.S.S.R. and East Germany. Propaganda signs outside factories all over the country proclaim: "The Soviet Union—source and inspiration of all our achievements."

HELMETED EAST GERMAN SOLDIERS, forty-five tanks, fifty rockets and missiles, and more than one hundred artillery pieces paraded down Karl Marx Allee in East Berlin on October 7 to celebrate the anniversary. This show of military might was condemned by the United States, Great Britain, and France.

SYMBOLS OF THE SOVIET PRESENCE abound in East Berlin. According to U.S. military intelligence, the U.S.S.R. has 533,000 soldiers in military bases in East Germany.

THE POTSDAM DECLARATION which decided the disposition of German territory after World War II was signed in this villa in Potsdam, East Germany. It is now a museum.

duction of nuclear energy, electricity, and textile machinery. For the first time in the twenty-five years of CMEA, the 1974 Soviet economic plan includes a special section on integration with other bloc states.

Yugoslavia (associate member), Hungary, and Czechoslovakia began work on a 500-mile oil pipeline to the Adriatic. A new port will take up to 300,000-ton tankers from the Middle East and North Africa. With the price of Soviet petroleum to increase in 1975 and domestic requirements rising, several East European states are negotiating with Algeria, Egypt, Iraq, and Libya to fill their energy needs.

On this same subject the twenty-eighth CMEA session held at Sofia during June 18-21 agreed to construct a high tension power line and a gas pipeline and to accelerate the nuclear energy program throughout the bloc. It also decided to speed up coordination of the 1976-1980 economic plan and adopted standards for certain commodities. Rumania did not participate in this last agreement nor in the financing or construction of the gas pipeline which will extend from Orenburg, U.S.S.R., to the Soviet western border.

Another problem within CMEA involves payment for imports from the West. Czechoslovakia needed an additional $1 billion during 1974 for such purchases. Hungary intended to pass on to the domestic consumer about 30 percent of the higher prices. East Germany's foreign trade minister announced that his country would scrutinize carefully future trade with the West. On the other hand, almost all East European countries reported bumper harvests due to automation, smaller farm units, and private initiative.

Albania is not a member of CMEA and has charged the U.S.S.R. with using it as an instrument of exploitation. The two countries broke off diplomatic relations in 1961. In general, Albania repeats Chinese verbal attacks against the Soviet Union. It also continues to allow publications and radio broadcasts by a dissident Polish Communist group. Support from most other East European leaders for the Moscow-initiated attempt to organize a world conference of Communist parties has been denounced as anti-Marxist by Albanian leader Enver Hoxha.

In domestic affairs, the thirty-first anniversary of the secret police was celebrated in March. Some 400,000 workers voted in the single-slate trade union elections during May. The following month the constitution was changed to provide for a 250-member legislature. Elections to the national legislature or People's Assembly were held on October 8.

A plenum of the Albanian Workers' party central committee met the end of July and discussed strengthening the defense of the country. One of the former Soviet submarines impounded in 1961 by the Albanians at the port of Valona began operating with a Chinese crew and under the People's Republic of China flag in the fall. Also in late September a report from diplomatic sources indicated that Albania's defense minister Beqir Balluku, suspected of pro-Soviet leanings, had been dismissed.

Bulgaria, the end of March, held a national Communist party conference which discussed higher labor productivity. Abandonment of the promised five-day work week indicated shortcomings in the economy. This was followed in early July by a Politburo shake-up and dismissal of the three youngest candidate members who also lost their other posts. They were replaced with two full and four candidate members, for new totals of twelve and six respectively. In the latter category are the defense and foreign ministers. The ousted individuals received ambassadorships during August.

External policy remained closely coordinated with the Soviet Union. Party leader Todor Zhivkov visited Iraq in April and hosted Egypt's president the end of June. Other contacts involved Syria and Yemen.

Relations with Yugoslavia remained correct, although the latter complained about discrimination against the Macedonian minority in Bulgaria.

The *State Gazette* on July 9 published ratification of the consular convention with the United States. A former Bulgarian economist and U.N. employee, sentenced in Sofia to be shot for espionage, was released and arrived in Tel Aviv on August 22. The following month Bulgaria celebrated the thirtieth anniversary of Communist power, attended by Soviet president Nikolai Podgorny. Visits during the year from officials of Kaiser Steel, Exxon, and Food Machinery Corporation showed that Bulgaria wants American technology.

Czechoslovakia did not publicize the death in mid-January of Josef Smrkovsky, a prominent figure during the 1968 Prague "spring." However, former party leader Alexander Dubcek, in a letter to the widow, denounced persecution of the deceased and repressive rule throughout the country. Another courageous man, President Ludvík Svoboda, became too ill in late March to exercise his duties.

Economic problems due to shortages of manpower and oil forced the government to introduce steep price increases. Party leader Gustáv Husák spoke on April 20 to allay rumors about currency devaluation. The following month a Central Committee plenum dealt with scentific research and development. During the summer, all schools and social institutes underwent a purge of "unreliable" teachers.

The West German parliament by a vote of 262 to 167 ratified the state treaty with Czechoslovakia on July 10. Five days before that, a preliminary agreement had been reached with the United States for return of gold impounded since the end of World War II and compensation for nationalized American property by the regime in Prague.

That same month a new law on national security went into effect. It allowed for investigation, detention, house search, and listening devices, with subsequent approval by the courts. In August, a group of young people in Bratislava were given prison sentences of up to fifty-two months for "ideological subversion."

East Germany held district conferences during early February to elect officials in its ruling Communist party. Toward the end of the month, leader Erich Honecker visited Cuba where he signed a friendship declaration with Castro. The arrest on April 24 of West German chancellor Brandt's political assistant and revelation that he had been an East German secret police officer indicated the high level to which espionage had penetrated.

Local elections held throughout the German Democratic Republic (GDR) on May 19 resulted in 99.9 percent of the voters allegedly supporting the national front single slate. Negotiations for exchange of diplomats with Washington were suspended at the end of July because of incidents on access routes into West Berlin. In early September an agreement was signed, and the United States became the 105th government to recognize the GDR. The first ambassador will be John Sherman Cooper, a former U.S. senator from Kentucky.

Leonid Brezhnev visited East Berlin on October 7 to honor the twenty-fifth anniversary of the GDR, the same day

THE CASTLE at Jindrichuv Hradec in southern Bohemia is one of more than 2,500 castles in Czechoslovakia. In 1974 restoration work on historic buildings was visibly speeded up throughout the country.

that constitutional amendments went into effect. They delete such terms as "German unity" and "German nation," eliminating the goal of eventual reunification. Powers of the state council are reduced, and the duration of parliament is now five years which coincides with the economic plan.

Hungary appeared to be in the midst of policy changes when two Central Committee secretaries, responsible for economic reform and ideology, were relieved on March 20. These moves probably will take the country back toward protection against the market and cultural orthodoxy. The previous month Pope Paul VI had dismissed exiled Cardinal Mindszenty as primate and appointed an apostolic administrator to head the archdiocese, indicating an accommodation with the Budapest regime.

During the summer it was disclosed that Siemens in West Germany and Volvo in Sweden had agreed to establish joint enterprises in Hungary which will retain 51 percent ownership of each. Also of interest is a $100 million loan from a consortium of U.S. and Canadian banks, announced on June 29. The previous month, a long-term economic and technological agreement had been signed with Italy.

Party leader Janos Kadar traveled to the Crimea for a meeting with Brezhnev. The communiqué on August 4 did not reveal the reason for the trip, although Radio Moscow announced two days later that Hungary would receive 5.7 million tons of crude oil during 1974 and 1 billion cubic meters of natural gas in 1975 from the Soviet Union. The end of September witnessed Kadar again in the U.S.S.R., heading a party government delegation.

Poland began the year with a worsening of relations vis-a-vis West Germany. Emigration of ethnic Germans subsequently declined, and the Warsaw regime again raised a demand for compensation to wartime concentration camp inmates. These developments may have been due to Soviet and East German pressure. A reshuffle of the party secretariat brought back two hard-liners, previously identified with repressive ideological policies. This coincided, however, with an official visit in February by an emissary from the Vatican, emphasizing relatively good church-state contacts.

Inflation, fuel and energy problems, a negative trade balance, and overinvestment continued to plague economic planners. A report from Warsaw, appearing in *Pravda* on July 9, quoted the number two man in Poland as advocating economic integration with the U.S.S.R. That same month, Soviet leader Brezhnev attended the thirtieth anniversary of Polish Communist rule. He was awarded the highest decoration of *virtuti militari*. Aerial maneuvers and a parade were part of the festivities, accompanied by an amnesty which resulted in release of more than 2,000 criminals.

A new law, adopted in the fall, which eased taxes on private entrepreneurs follows previous legislation covering artisans. Placing these two groups on a par with state-controlled enterprises should result in more efficient service. Party leader Edward Gierek visited Washington, D.C., and was honored on October 8 with a White House dinner given by President Gerald Ford. The U.S. Department of Agriculture announced a $28 million commercial credit package, for which Poland may purchase cotton, tobacco, rice, and tallow. About 60 percent of Polish trade remains within CMEA.

Rumania also experienced institutional and personnel changes toward the end of March. The old Permanent Presidium became the Permanent Bureau, with mostly ex officio members. It will be responsible to the party's executive committee. On the government side, the premier retired for health reasons, and other important younger functionaries were replaced. All of this occurred well in advance of the eleventh Communist party congress held the end of November. It approved the economic plan for 1976-1980 as well as directives for the long-range plan through 1990.

Party leader Nicolae Ceausescu traveled throughout parts of the Middle East early in the year and negotiated an agreement with Libya for 12 million tons of petroleum over the next four years. Subsequently, he visited Argentina, Liberia, and Guinea in an attempt further to identify his state with the lesser developed countries. Argentina accepted a $100 million loan and signed a treaty of friendship with Rumania. President Anwar Sadat of Egypt came to Bucharest in June and also received credits of $100 million. Syrian president Hafez al-Assad arrived in early September.

By contrast, Rumania obtained two loans totaling $130 million from the World Bank to build fertilizer and steel plants. A third loan of 3 million pounds sterling came in July from the National Westminster Bank to finance purchases of British equipment. The U.S. Senate approved most-favored-nation status for Rumania in early August. On the other hand, Bucharest's trade was heavily dependent upon the bloc, some 43 percent inside CMEA and half of that with the U.S.S.R. Aleksei Kosygin attended the thirtieth anniversary of Communist rule in Bucharest at which time Ceausescu called the Soviet Union his country's top ally. Exactly one month later, on September 23, Rumania agreed to pay 2½ percent on account for Americans holding 1929 government bonds that went into default some forty years ago.

Yugoslavia opened the year by announcing that trade with the Soviet Union would reach $1 billion in 1974, for an increase of one-fifth. The daily *Vesnik* on January 14 attacked Aleksandr Solzhenitsyn for allegedly spreading anti-Socialist propaganda. Milovan Djilas, former deputy to Tito, and the writer Mihajlo Mihajlov (arrested in early October) were denied passports for a visit to the United States.

Tito himself flew to India where he received the Nehru award for international understanding and then stopped in Bangladesh. Early in February, he traveled to Syria. Tito came back from West Germany the end of June with $300 million in credits. The World Bank gave Yugoslavia a $176 million loan, and the U.S. Export-Import Bank authorized $176 million low-cost financing for a nuclear plant during July.

In domestic affairs, a new constitution was adopted on February 21. It is similar to a detailed labor relations agreement, based on the principle of self-management. Tito, eighty-two, will remain president for life and will be followed by a presidency rotating among nine members of the Presidential Council. The League of Yugoslav Communists numbering about 1 million members held its tenth congress May 27-30 and reelected Tito chairman. The end of September, thirty-two persons received up to fourteen years in prison for belonging to a clandestine "Cominformist" organization having contacts with emigrés in Kiev. The ninth congress of the Socialist Youth Federation met at Belgrade during November 20-22, followed by the seventh trade union congress December 17-20.

50 Years Ago: The Vienna Boys' Choir, Austria's most famous cultural ambassador, was refounded by Monsignore Josef Schnitt.

Ecology/Environment

FRESH, CLEAN AIR is essential to healthful life. In October the National Academy of Sciences released a four-volume report on U.S. clean-air standards which found that the health benefits of federally mandated auto-emission controls justified their cost to the auto industry and the public. The report concluded the academy's year-long investigation of EPA standards set under the Clean Air Act of 1970.

The Sagging Environment. The overall level of environmental quality in the United States sagged slightly in 1974, according to the National Wildlife Federation. In its fifth annual assessment of the country's livability, the nation's largest conservation organization found improvement only in air pollution among the seven elements on which the study is based — air and water pollution, wildlife, minerals, timber, soil, and "living space."

Most cities remained overcrowded as three-fourths of the U.S. population continued to live on 2 percent of the land, although only 13 percent of the nation's citizens would live in cities if they had a choice. The Department of the Interior's list of endangered wildlife species rose from 101 to 109 as habitat destruction continued.

The Great Lakes, the world's largest fresh water reservoir, have been used as a sewer by the United States and Canada for two hundred years, but the resultant severe pollution was rated as beginning to diminish in 1974. Lake Erie, once thought by environmental scientists to be dead, is now the home of brown trout and salmon. According to the Environmental Protection Agency (EPA), the total amount of phosphorus flowing into Lake Erie has dropped from 29,300 tons in 1971 to 18,100 tons. For Lake Ontario the reduction was from 13,900 tons to 11,425 tons.

Flushing is the basic strategy being pursued by the United States and Canada through the International Joint Commission on the Great Lakes in attempting to clean up the pollution. Water flows from the upper lakes — Superior, Michigan, and Huron — generally viewed as being relatively clean — into the lower lakes — Erie and Ontario. The theory is that if industries and municipalities are stopped from dumping pollutants into the lower lakes, the latter will eventually be flushed out and made tolerable again by the clean water flowing through them from the upper lakes to the St. Lawrence River.

In the dual attack on pollution in the lakes, Canada, which has a 10 percent share of the program, has modified some eighteen sewage treatment centers, and built sixteen new ones. The United States, meanwhile, has not acted as fast, slowed down by the Nixon administration's impoundment of $9 million of the $18 million Congress authorized for fiscal years 1973 through 1975. One of Richard Nixon's last presidential actions was to veto the $175 million allocated to the EPA for the Great Lakes clean-up.

CONCENTRATIONS OF BACTERIA, a consequence of improper sewage treatment, have occasionally forced the closing of this Indiana state park beach on the southern end of Lake Michigan.

Environment Bills to improve the quality of life were passed by virtually all the states during 1974. Although Congress rejected as unwarranted interference with local prerogatives a program to give states grants for planning land use, land-use problems led the list of environmental legislation across the country. In general, bills to protect environmentally choice land areas fared well, while proposals for comprehensive state regulation of land use encountered stiff opposition. The most popular type of land-use legislation provided for state acquisition of park lands.

Several states acted in ways that environmentalists considered retrogressive. Foremost among these was New Mexico's repeal of its Environmental Quality Act which had required advance environmental impact assessments on major projects.

Economy

by
ROBERT I. MEHR

Professor of Finance
University of Illinois at Urbana-Champaign
Editor, *The Journal of Risk and Insurance*

The Year 1974 proved to be a continuation of the previous year. Most of the records set in 1973 were surpassed in 1974. The interest rates rose to levels untouched in the recorded past, inflation continued its rapid increase, and unemployment rose. The basic areas in which there were significant declines are the stock market and the Gross National Product.

Interest Rates. The prime interest rate (the rate charged by banks to their most credit-worthy customers) once again reached a record high. At the start of the year the prime rate was 10 percent. Less than two years earlier (1972) that rate was as low as 4.5 percent. As 1974 progressed so did the prime rate, reaching a new record high of 12 percent. This 12 percent rate was in effect from July 5 until September 26 when some bellwether banks reduced it to 11.75 percent. The downward trend continued into November with the prime rate falling to 10.25 percent.

High interest rates continued to plague the housing industry. Savings and Loan associations were unable to attract capital to lend to home builders or buyers because of the low ceiling placed by the government on the rate of interest that they could pay depositors. Yields on Treasury Bills soared to above 9.25 percent whereas passbook accounts were paying only 5.25 percent and four-year certificates of deposit paid 7.5 percent. Housing starts dropped to an annual rate of 1.1 million, 40 percent below that of a year ago, and the lowest level since May, 1970. The effective mortgage rate on newly purchased homes set a new record of 9.2 percent in September.

Recession. In the nearly thirty years following World War II (not counting the present one) five recessions were experienced: November, 1948 - October, 1949; July, 1953 - August, 1954; July, 1957 - April, 1958; May, 1960 - February, 1961; and November, 1969 - November, 1970. The declines in the Gross National Product (GNP) for those periods were 1.6 percent in 1948-49, 3.4 percent in 1953-54, 3.9 percent in 1957-58, 1.4 percent in 1960-61, and 1.4 percent in 1969-70. The peaks in unemployment rates were 7.9 percent in 1949, 6.0 percent in 1954, 7.4 percent in 1958, 6.9 percent in 1961, and 5.8 percent in 1970. The rule-of-thumb definition of a recession has been two consecutive quarters with a decline in the "real" GNP, that is the value of the economy's total

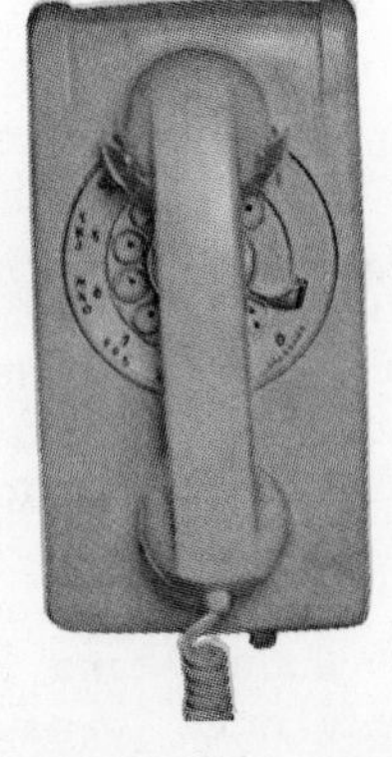

MA BELL, the mammoth American Telephone and Telegraph Company, was being investigated by the federal government in an anti-trust suit in 1974. Alexander Graham Bell started this communications industry with his liquid telephone in 1876, top left. Later innovations included, left to right, the decorative, compact 1892 desk set, the Magneto Wall set of 1907 with a built-in generator for signaling the operator, the 1919 dial telephone, the 1930 desk set, the 1956 wall telephone, and the 1964 pushbutton model.

output of goods and services after adjusting for inflation. In 1974 there were three such quarters: a 7 percent decline in the first quarter followed by a 1.6 percent decline in the second quarter and a 2.9 percent drop in the July-September period. Even with this continuous decline in the nation's output a few U.S. government economists persisted most of the year (until mid-November) in maintaining that the downturn was merely a "sideways waffle." However, economists in the private sector and some in the public sector were quick in calling this economic slump the sixth recession since World War II. By October the recession had already become more severe than three of the previous ones, and the end was not in sight.

The annual rate of inflation during the first three quarters of 1974 was 11.5 percent. In the past the administration had relied on a tight money policy of the Federal Reserve Board to control the rate of inflation. In the present circumstances, however, the policy succeeded only in increasing interest rates, drawing vast amounts of capital away from the mortgage market, placing a severe strain on credit, and slowing production. But it failed to accomplish its avowed purpose of dampening the rate of inflation.

Adding to the problem was the increase in unemployment. In October more than 6 percent of the labor force was unemployed, and the rate was still climbing. Especially for those with unemployment insurance as their only source of income, their lack of work coupled with the double-digit inflation made it difficult, if not impossible, to maintain even a meager standard of living. The jobless rate in some industries, such as construction, was more than 12 percent. The rate for white-collar workers was only 3.3 percent compared to 7.3 percent for the blue-collar workers. The rate for blacks was 9.8 percent compared to 9.2 percent one year earlier.

The increase in inflation and unemployment naturally caused economists great concern because it did not fit neatly into their "Phillips curve." Professor Phillips of the London School of Economics has shown, with his famous curve, trade-offs between the intensity of growth rates, price increases, and unemployment. Today with "stagflation," or inflationary recession, an increase in both unemployment and inflation is being experienced. It appears that no one knows how to cure inflation without causing a significant and unacceptable increase in the rate of unemployment.

Another fundamental problem of the economy was in worker productivity, or output per hour of work. It fell in the first and third quarters with only a slight increase experienced in the second quarter. For the twelve months ending September, 1974, the productivity rate had fallen 2.5 percent over the previous twelve-month period. Falling productivity together with rising pay scales caused the employers' unit labor costs to rise at an annual rate in the third quarter of 13.9 percent. The workers' paycheck after adjustments for inflation nonetheless was worth 2.3 percent less in the third quarter of 1974 than in the same quarter of 1973.

Nearly every American was affected by the problems of inflation. Those who wished to purchase a home found that they could no longer afford the one they desired because of the rapid increase in construction costs. The national median price of a new single-family house was $35,000, a 50 percent increase since 1970. The median price for a previously owned home was $32,860, an increase of 40 percent for the same period. The single-family home is becoming a luxury. In many instances, those who could afford a home and were willing to pay in excess of 10 percent interest and a down payment equal to one-third of the purchase price found themselves unable to obtain a mortgage loan because of the aforementioned shortage of funds in the lending institutions.

Unfortunately those who suffer most in time of inflation are the poor. The price of basic foods had increased at a more rapid rate than the consumer price index which had increased at an annual rate of 11.2 percent through August. In the past year the price of rice has increased by 90 percent, sugar by 132 percent, bread by 27 percent, and milk by 20 percent. The president declared that inflation was America's number one problem and openly declared war against it but seemingly without sufficient weapons to fight a winning battle.

In hopes of finding a solution to the economic ills of the nation the president and his top economic aides met with some 800 leaders from labor, business, agriculture, and finance. When the summit concluded it was felt by many that nothing more had been accomplished at the meeting than to point out, to the surprise of no one, that the economists could not agree on a solution to the problem.

The Stock Market. The Dow Jones Industrial Average (DJIA) which stood at 850.86 on December 31, 1973, was down considerably from the record high of 1051.70 set earlier that year. In 1974 it continued the downward trend to reach a low of 584.56 on October 4. This was a drop of 467.14 points or 44.4 percent from the high and a 266.30-point or 31.3 percent decline for 1974. All industries appeared to be affected. (The Dow Jones twenty-transportation-companies average was 196.19 at the first of the year and bottomed out at 125.93 on October 1, 1974, for a drop of 70.26 points or 35.8 percent. The DJ average of fifteen utilities declined from 89.37 at the start of the year to 57.93 on September 13, 1974, a decrease of 31.44 points or 35.1 percent.)

The close of 584.56 was the lowest for the DJIA in twelve years since October 29, 1962, when it closed at 579.35. In October, 1974, the stocks which make up the DJIA sold for 85 percent of their combined book value, and these securities at current dividend payments were yielding approximately 16 percent. This was the highest yield in a quarter of a century. While the DJIA fell 44 percent,

THE EXECUTIVE earned more money than ever in 1974, with average executive salaries up by 11.5 percent over 1972. The following five were the top-paid U.S. executives: Philip B. Hofmann of Johnson and Johnson, $978,000; Richard C. Gerstenberg of General Motors, $938,000; Henry Ford II and Lee A. Iacocca of Ford, both $878,746; and Edward N. Cole of General Motors, $846,500.

this group included only thirty blue chip stocks. Many securities fell 70 percent, or in some cases as much as 90 percent, from their previous highs. This latter list includes a number of securities that were popular and considered to be stable and conservative investments.

The common stocks of a much smaller list of companies moved against the downward trend and showed substantial gains. These gains were mainly attributable to shortages of steel, aluminum, paper, and chemicals or to the soaring prices of gold, copper, and sugar.

The decline in the market affected not only those who held shares directly but also many persons who were indirect and possibly even unknowing investors. Those individuals and institutions that rely heavily on grants from institutions fell into this latter category. The level of the market can have an adverse effect on the size and the number of grants awarded in the coming year. Most foundations make payments only from dividend and interest income. As long as the income continues the grants will continue, and up to this time most of the firms they have invested in have not been forced to reduce or discontinue their dividends. Some exceptions, however, such as Consolidated Edison and General Motors had lower total payouts in 1974 than in 1973. Some of the large foundations have made payments in excess of their income using capital gains to absorb the difference. With a decrease in the market value of the portfolio this practice cannot continue indefinitely without a steady erosion of the portfolio occurring.

Another group falling in this latter category are millions of people affected by the large numbers of private pension plans. Private pension plans were more than 60 percent invested in common stocks, the decline of which severely reduced their funded ratio. Nonlife insurance companies also were heavily invested in common stock, and the market decline severely reduced their surpluses and consequently their ability to write

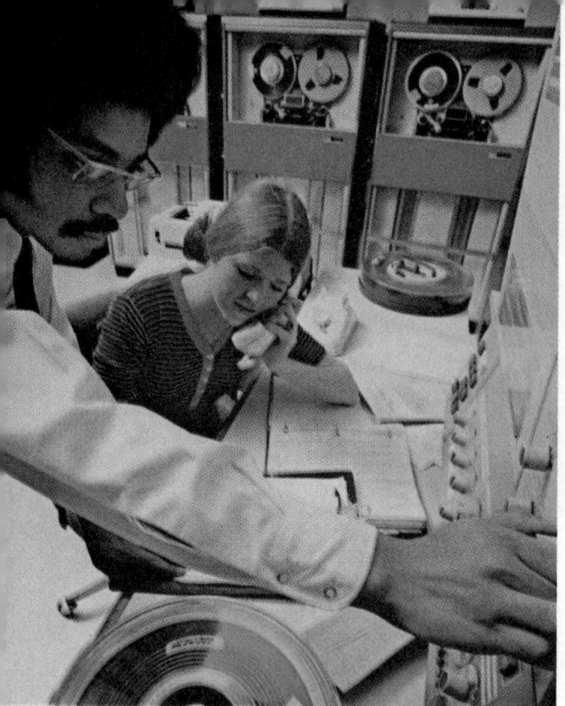

EQUAL EMPLOYMENT OPPORTUNITY for minorities and women is government regulated by a tangled thicket of rules on hiring and advancement. Costly settlements in federal discrimination suits during 1974 spurred companies' efforts to end bias. Personnel people with a knowledge of equal employment law commanded annual salaries ranging up to $60,000.

insurance in the amounts demanded by the public.

A larger number of unsuspecting individuals affected by the market decline is the group of persons retired on pensions. With the steady increase in the cost of living in the past two decades the retired person living on a fixed pension income found himself unable to continue to maintain the standard of living he had expected for his retirement years. For this reason many pension managers adopted the concept of the variable annuity pension. Under this plan the retirees would receive annuity payments that would fluctuate with the market value of the securities supporting their pensions. It was thought that common stocks would fluctuate generally in the same direction as the cost of living and thus the retirees' purchasing power would not diminish. The opposite occurred: double-digit inflation and a severe decline in the market value of the securities. So, as the cost of living increased, the size of the pension check was reduced.

It is too early to conclude that the concept is unworkable. However, in the short run it obviously has not worked as anticipated, to the dissatisfaction of many with high expectations. In the longer run the plan may be satisfactory but that empty hope meant little to those who saw not only a rise in prices but also a decrease in dollar incomes.

Not only were the variable-annuity type pensions under fire but many other plans were also in possible trouble. Any pension manager who had invested the contributions in corporate stocks or bonds was faced with the fact that the value of the fund purchased from contributions was less than the amount of the contributions. This problem of a decrease in the value of the fund was magnified by the increase in inflation and loss of purchasing power.

Banking Crises. The year 1974 saw one of the worst banking crises in U.S. history. The Franklin National Bank, the twentieth largest of the nation's approximately 14,000 banks, became insolvent. The assets and liabilities of the bank were sold to the European-American Bank and Trust Company, and it continued to operate as a going concern. This move was taken in order to maintain continued confidence in the banking system, a problem not being overlooked by the international monetary community.

Balance of Payments. For the first three quarters, the United States registered a $2.35 billion trade deficit, an increase from a $15.6 million deficit for the first nine months of 1973. An improvement of $900 million was experi-

BLANKETS are silk-screen printed in a northern factory. Wage and price controls were lifted from textiles and fifteen other sectors of the economy on April 15.

enced from August to September, partly because of the sluggishness of the domestic economy which caused a softening of demand for foreign goods. The major factor in the improvement was the large decline in oil imports as a result of the huge buildup in oil inventories in earlier months.

Energy. As the year drew to a close, the government was advising the consumer to conserve energy, reduce speed on the highways, and set the thermostat lower. Service stations were requested to close early. At the same time the oil companies were pressuring their dealers to sell more gasoline and stay open longer hours and on Sunday. In September the average price of regular gasoline was 55 cents a gallon compared with 40.2 cents a gallon one year earlier. The price peaked at 55.8 cents in July. The price range varied widely throughout the country, and in October the price was as low as 39.9 cents in one area and as high as 59.9 cents a gallon in another. A surplus of fuel existed at that time but there was uncertainty concerning the future supply.

Accounting methods. Many corporations changed their accounting methods from first in, first out (FIFO) or average cost, to last in, first out (LIFO). In times of inflation FIFO and average cost produce higher profits and also higher taxes. It was estimated that at least 100 of the largest 500 companies were considering making a change. One large corporation projected a decrease of pretax earnings of about $300 million and a tax savings of about $150 million as a result of the change in its accounting method. The government estimates that the change to LIFO could cost $5 billion to $9 billion in tax revenues. In addition to the loss in tax revenue the change in inventory accounting will make it more difficult to compare earnings results from one period to another and also could distort such vital indexes as the GNP.

Education

by

W. RICHARD STEPHENS

Vice-President for Academic Affairs
Greenville College
Greenville, Ill.
Author of *Social Reform and The Origins of Vocational Guidance* (1970) and *Education in American Life* (with William Van Til, 1972)

A Troubled Opening. America's schools opened this year with an atmosphere of apprehensive peace, buffeted by a social climate which was poisoned daily by reports of Watergate revelations and the crises of declining energy resources and spiraling inflation. Pencils which cost elementary school children 90

THE ONE-ROOM SCHOOL, here depicted by a Winslow Homer painting, is a cherished American tradition. There are still 1,815 one-room schools in the United States. Nebraska has the most, 674, and South Dakota ranks second with 315. Calling it "innovation," institutions of progressive education are returning to the one-room-school way of teaching with mixed and open classrooms.

cents a gross four years ago were on the market for $2.25. School lunches increased 50 cents over last year's and contained less meat and more macaroni and cheese. Within the schools classroom crime made teachers and students nervous. For examples, in Los Angeles 66,000 broken windows and other vandalism cost the school system $2.5 million; New York City hired 935 guards to patrol its high schools and 818 for its elementary and junior high schools. In St. Louis last year an eighteen-year-old student was shot and killed when he refused to give up his new black leather jacket. But perhaps most serious of all was the moral confusion school children experienced in the climate of crisis which characterized 1974. One study of fifth through eighth grades in a metropolitan center found that 43 percent of the students thought it proper for the president of the United States to do whatever he believed was good for the country whether ethical or unethical. Even so, others believed that Watergate, while bad for the country, could help produce more responsible voters. Said one representative gradeschooler in this study: "When I begin to vote, I'll look at the candidate's record and how he has kept his past promises. Then I will decide for myself how he will carry out new promises."

Even though the schools experienced to an unusual degree the stress and turbulence of 1974, surveys of parents and professional educators revealed an increasing level of confidence in schools. It is true that many were concerned about the problems of discipline, racial integration/segregation, financial support, and drugs. But it was also the case that many parents and educators gave schools excellent marks for their teachers, facilities, curricula, and teaching methods. Parents in one survey said, by a margin of three to one, that schools were better this year than when they were children, and that their children were being better educated by the schools than they had been.

Enrollments and Teachers. Based on rapidly declining birth rates, educational statisticians forecast continuing decreases in school enrollments at all levels. The actual number of five-year-olds dropped 15 percent between 1960 and 1970. The actual number of births dropped 12 percent between 1970 and 1972. The nation's birth rate reached its lowest point in history, a rate below zero-population growth, and it had not yet stabilized.

Using Illinois, one of the heavily populated and economically thriving states, to represent the meaning of these declining population figures for schools, forecasters projected a 20 percent drop in school enrollment by 1983 based on 1970 figures. The public school enrollment in Illinois in 1973 was 2,311, 797, a decrease of 61,862 students from the record high enrollment two years earlier, 1971.

Parochial schools also were affected by declining enrollments. The number of full-time students in Roman Catholic schools decreased by 174,300. About 235 elementary and high schools were closed or merged with others last year, leaving American Catholics a total of 10,350 schools. Catholic college and university enrollments were 407,081, down 11,000 from 1973.

By the early 1980s, due to the decline in the nation's population of eighteen- to twenty-four-year-olds, all institutions of higher education are due for a sharp enrollment drop. The U.S. Office of Education projected in 1973 that the collegiate enrollment figure will continue its slow rise through the remainder of the 1970s to a total of 10 to 15 percent over 1972-73; but, that collegiate-level enrollments will drop precipitously, conceivably by as much as 25 to 30 percent, during the 1980s.

While enrollments were down this

EDUCATION

year, not all school programs suffered student reductions equally. Some academic programs even grew. For example, vocational and career education programs experienced marked student increases. Community college enrollments, with their emphasis on adult and continuing education, increased between 8 and 10 percent. The Community College of Vermont (CCV), founded in 1970, illustrates the robust growth many other such colleges have experienced. More than 1,300 adult students, of all ages, enrolled there this year, attracted by courses tailored to their personal needs and designed to impress their would-be employers. CCV sought out "nontraditional" students—older women, young housewives, and family men who needed better job skills. The college had no buildings, no paid full-time faculty, no set course offerings, no credits, hours, or requirements. In line with Vermonters' expressed needs, CCV offered courses on demand which were taught by volunteers with specific skills.

Reserve Officer Training Corps (ROTC) programs did not fare so well in student enrollments. The combined total for the army, air force, and navy dropped from 212,400 in 1968 to 75,000 this year. The army took the biggest percentage loss, going from 174,173 at its peak in 1966 to about 38,000 in the fall of 1973.

An important consequence of declining school enrollments this year was a drop in the number of college graduates who were prepared to teach. Between 1968 and 1972, approximately 35 percent of all college graduates were prepared to teach. That figure dropped this year to 29 percent. With the tightening of academic standards in professional education courses and more selectivity of teacher education students by departments of education, the percentage of teacher graduates is forecast to drop to 19 percent in 1976.

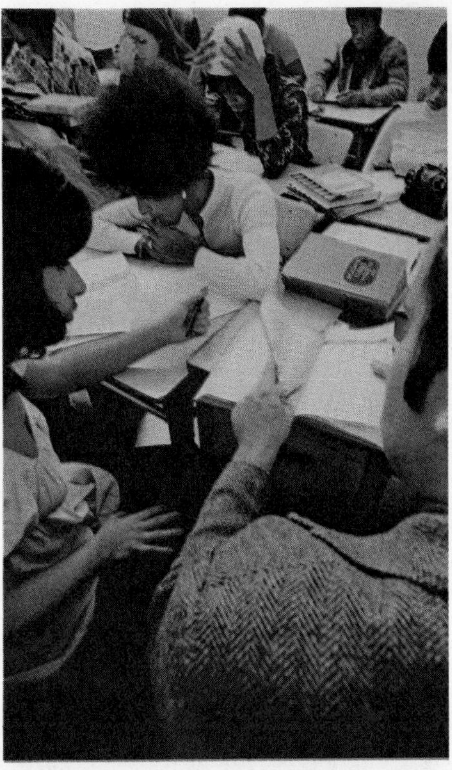

OF EVERY ONE HUNDRED STUDENTS attending school across the nation, twenty-three drop out, seventy-seven graduate from high school, forty-three enter college, twenty-one receive a bachelor's degree, six earn a master's degree, and one earns a doctorate, according to James A. Harris, president of the National Education Association.

As school enrollments declined, governing boards of education made massive cuts in teaching positions. In response to this tightening of the job market, teachers (including college professors) resorted to strikes as a means of gaining job security, improved pay, and better teaching conditions. Historically, teachers had been reluctant to strike or engage in work stoppages. But between 1941 and 1961 teachers' groups struck 105 times, and during 1968-69 alone teachers' organizations struck 131 times. As this trend continued almost every major metropolitan center experienced an actual strike or strike threat. Usually strikes resulted from the refusal of school boards to engage in collective bargaining with teachers' organizations. Boards argued that in the absence of state laws permitting them to bargain collectively, their hands were tied. Quickly, state legislatures began to pass laws legalizing collective bargaining between school boards and teachers' organizations. By 1974 several states had passed such laws, and other states were considering them. These laws applied to faculties in public colleges as well as to teachers in elementary and secondary schools. For example, nineteen states had put laws on the books permitting collective bargaining by college faculties. At the close of this year, eleven more states were about to be added to that number.

Though teachers were able to win victories with state legislators to bargain collectively, their efforts to close ranks in a single professional teachers' organization faltered and at times throughout the year came to a halt. For several years the National Education Association (NEA) and the American Federation of Teachers (AFT) had pursued a merger of the two groups. Some states and local affiliates of these two groups actually had achieved merger. But merger negotiations at the national level broke down in 1974 when Helen Wise, president of the NEA, announced in February that no progress was being made. The AFT deplored the NEA's break-off of merger talks, saying: "Most of the nation's more than 3 million teachers want unity. They will be bitterly disappointed by the irresponsible action of the NEA." It is unlikely that these two organizations will come together soon into a new organization, given the bad blood which has characterized their relationships since the founding of the AFT in 1916. But, undoubtedly, they will be forced to continue merger discussions now that local school boards increasingly must bargain collectively with a single teachers' organization.

Cost of Education. With college enrollments declining, inflation spiraling, and the relative scarcity of energy resources increasing costs, parents could look forward only to heavier economic burdens. The College Entrance Examination Board projected a 9.4 percent increase for a college education for the fall of 1974, 35.8 percent more than it was four years ago. Columbia University projected a fuel bill this coming year of $1,926,000; the University of Maine, $925,000 compared to $475,000 last year; and Mount Holyoke, $173,000 compared with $100,000 last year. When cost increases like these were passed on to the students, the dollar amount increased to an average high price of $4,039 at private colleges and $2,400 at public colleges. This private/public difference, however, reflects only the charges which were passed on to students; it does not reflect the increased costs to private and public colleges, which are nearly equal.

Some results of skyrocketing costs were the closing of forty-five private colleges and the opening of more than fifty state or community colleges last year. The ratio of part-time to full-time students increased as students "stopped-out" or dropped out to take part-time jobs. Massive faculty layoffs occurred. For examples, Southern Illinois University at Carbondale released 104 faculty, the University of Wisconsin dismissed 88 faculty, and little Bloomfield College in New Jersey reduced its full-time faculty of 67 by 25 percent. Many colleges reduced their course offerings: Princeton dropped its graduate department of classic languages and many smaller colleges cut out courses in science, English, philosophy, and foreign languages.

It was obvious that increased costs

A LONE STUDENT descends the steps of Reed Library at the College of Fredonia, near Buffalo, N.Y. An enrollment drop caused by the lower numbers of school-age youth as postwar baby-boom youngsters grew up, the disappearance of those studying to escape the draft, and a diminishing belief in the U.S. ethic that college is a prerequisite for success, forced the closing of more than fifty small colleges and a shift to hard sell in recruiting students in 1974.

were making access to higher education more difficult, especially for low and middle-income students. That unequal access was deleterious to the democratic ethic and to individual and national well-being was obvious. Hence, a National Commission on the Financing of Postsecondary Education was formed and made its report to the president and Congress. The commission affirmed the principle of universal postsecondary education for all American citizens according to their needs and abilities. The commission further recommended that the economic burden for postsecondary education should continue to be borne by federal, state, and local governments, by students, parents, and other concerned individuals and organizations. No specific financial proposal was put forth. Nor does it seem likely that the historic principle of free and universal education, tax supported, will be extended upward in the near future to include all of postsecondary education.

Educational Achievements and Problems. The American school system maintained its position of leadership among the nations. Medical schools produced more physicians than ever before, and teaching hospitals continued to receive an increasing number of foreign-trained physicians as interns. The U.S. Bureau of the Census reported a continuing rise in the economic benefits of a college education. A person with a college degree, said the report, could expect to earn $758,000 before he dies. Though many job-seeking graduates may not agree, the bureau reported that the yearly income of men with college degrees in 1972 was $16,200 compared to $10,430 for high school graduates.

However, all was not well. The age-old problem of illiteracy was still around in 1974. Two years ago a national right-to-read program was initiated by former President Richard Nixon. The brilliant black educator, Dr. Ruth Holloway, was made its director. Her report on illiteracy was a discouraging one.

Five percent (1 million) of all Americans aged twelve to seventeen were discovered to be illiterate—unable to read at the fourth grade level. Boys, black and white, demonstrated a higher percentage of illiteracy than girls (6.7 percent for boys as compared to 2.8 percent for girls). Generally, Dr. Holloway found higher illiteracy rates among black youths than among white, a continuing consequence of racism in the history of American education. If parents had little or no formal education, 22 percent of whites and 53 percent of blacks could not pass the fourth grade test. But when one parent had finished elementary school, the illiteracy rate fell to 6 percent for white youths and 18 percent for blacks, reflecting the effectiveness of the public schools.

National attention was focused in 1974 on a disturbing ten-year decline in the average Scholastic Aptitude Test (SAT) scores of high school seniors. The SAT purports to measure a person's verbal and mathematical abilities. In 1962 the average verbal score was 478, while in 1972 it was 443. Some observers tried to blame the schools for this decline, but Dr. Sidney P. Marland, Jr., president of of the College Board which administers the SAT, disagreed. He argued that there were many factors involved in the declining trend such as a changing test population and the fact that many high ability students simply did not take the SAT because they did not intend to enroll in college. Educational Testing Service researchers reported that some of their test findings suggest that young Americans have been getting brighter over the years.

Law and Education. The rising trend of court involvement in education continued unabated in 1974. For examples, the Supreme Court struck down school regulations that forced teachers off the job in the early months of pregnancy. It ruled that the San Francisco schools illegally discriminated against non-English-speaking Chinese students by failing to help them surmount the language handicap. The Supreme Court let stand a lower court decision which declared unconstitutional a New Jersey plan to provide reimbursement up to $20 a year to parents of nonpublic school pupils for purchases of textbooks. Bob Jones University, an archconservative institution in Greenville, S.C., was judged by the Supreme Court no longer to qualify for tax-exempt status. Bob Jones, an allegedly Christian college, was found by the court to be guilty of racial discrimination in its policy not to admit black students because, the college claimed, that is what the Bible teaches. A federal grand jury in Cleveland, Ohio, reopened the case of the Kent State University killings and indicted seven former and one present Ohio National Guardsmen. They were members of the units that fired their weapons into a crowd of about 500 students who assembled on May 4, 1970, to protest — some by throwing rocks — the U.S. invasion into Cambodia. A state grand jury had absolved the guardsmen in 1970, but the stain of that tragedy would not go away. Hence, the reopening of the case by a federal grand jury.

Prayer and Bible reading were in the news again when the Massachusetts legislature passed a law permitting school officials to establish a short period of time during each school day for students to use for "meditation" or "prayer." The Supreme Court ruled several years ago that school-sponsored prayers and Bible reading were unconstitutional. However, the court explicitly encouraged the academic study of the Bible as a literary and historical document. A survey of fifty states revealed that since the court's decision ten years ago, very little had been done to offer formal study in religion at the high school level. However, another survey of 580 Michigan high schools found that 300 of them were now offering courses in world religions, comparative religion, the Bible as literature, and religious history. Michigan, Wisconsin, and California had made provisions to certify public school teachers in approved religious studies as an area of teaching specialization. It appeared that the development of religious studies in public schools occurred when enough public demand was generated to persuade school officials.

Education and Minorities. Sexism in the conduct of schools became a matter of national concern, especially when the U.S. Office of Education held nationwide conferences on the implementation of Title IX of the law which prohibits discrimination against women. Women's studies caught on this year with 300 colleges offering more than 2,000 courses. Approximately eighty-five colleges had developed full women's studies programs. Also, more women participated in interscholastic sports programs, normally reserved for men, than ever before.

Two decades ago this year the Supreme Court declared "separate but equal" schools unconstitutional. In 1955 the court said that its desegregation order must be implemented "with all deliberate speed." However, in many cities the schools actually were more racially segregated in 1974 than they had been twenty years before. Two out of three black children outside the South attended schools which had become increasingly segregated. To illustrate, nearly half of Chicago's 537 elementary schools were more than 90 percent black, and 144 primary schools had 100 percent black enrollments. In New York City 80 percent of the public school students attended mostly black schools.

Black studies programs which sprang up like wildfire during the 1960s found their way into more than 1,200 colleges by 1972, and majors were offered in 182 colleges. But during 1974 black studies began to fold at a rapid rate. Some of the reasons were: declining student interest, insufficient funding, faculty skepticism, and growing student concern for marketable skills. Whatever the reasons, this decline was part of a growing apathy toward black Americans.

In a significant case this year, the Supreme Court ruled against the special admission program of the University of Washington Law School for Negroes, Chicanos, Indians, and Filipinos. Marco De Funis, Jr., a white applicant to the law school, was denied admission even though thirty-six minority students were admitted who had lower scores. De Funis sued the University of Washington Law School and won. This case involved not a quota but an effort by the school to assemble a diverse student body and to rectify past discriminatory inequities. The final outcome of this case was not clear, but it stood as a possible deterrent to the progress of minorities in civil rights.

EDUCATION IN GREAT BRITAIN

by

MARK HANKEY

Secretary of the Incorporated Association of Preparatory Schools and of the Common Entrance Examination Committee. Formerly Headmaster of Clifton College Preparatory School, Bristol, England.

The Importance of Education. It is becoming increasingly clear that education matters more and more to more and more people. The *London Times* now produces not only a weekly educational supplement but also one specifically devoted to further education. Toward the other end of the spectrum is the thought being given to nursery schools. It may be significant that Mrs. Margaret Thatcher remained secretary of state for education and science for four years. It is a long time since there has been such a degree of continuity in the leadership of this department. Moreover the Schools Council, a body in which teachers predominate and which was created in 1964 to consider the relationship between curriculum and examinations, seems now to be widening its range, for it is commissioning research into such matters as moral education.

Teacher Training. Of great importance is the training of teachers, a matter into which there has been an official inquiry by a distinguished panel of educational pundits under the chairmanship of Lord James of Rusholme, vice-chancellor of the University of York and formerly high master of Manchester Grammar School. The "James Report" certainly generated some heat, and one of its results has been a move toward more in-service training. At present a teacher, having completed his or her course at a college of education, must, in order to become fully qualified, work a year's probation in a state-maintained school. It may now be that the probationary year will be replaced by the inductory year, a specific part of the course of training, served in a school under the instruction of a member of its staff.

This plan, admirable in many ways, will create certain staffing problems, for it is clear that a teacher cannot combine a full-time teaching program with part-time supervision of a trainee. Moreover the best trainers are likely to be the best teachers, whose impact on the pupils will be lessened owing to the reduction of the time they spend in the classroom. It may indeed be difficult to find part-time teachers of equal caliber. It does however seem that the implementation of this part of the James inquiry will make for a more effective teaching force. Lucky is the novice who can make the mistakes of inexperience under close and benevolent supervision.

Standards of Literacy. Another important inquiry is that into reading and the use of English, conducted by a powerful team led by Sir Alan Bullock, vice-chancellor of Oxford University from 1969 to 1973 and master of St. Catherine's College, Oxford. This arises from a widespread concern about standards of literacy, for which blame is sometimes laid on modern methods of teaching. This concern is expressed in the publication of three "Black Papers" (the title contrasts with the government's traditional "White Papers"). It does not derive from a reactionary pressure group; it is a concern felt by some distinguished teachers in the maintained system. When Sir Alan Bullock's working party has had time to sift written and verbal evidence and to make its own investigations, its report may prove of great significance in British education.

Education and Politics. It is, sad to say, impossible to keep education and politics apart. The previous British secretary of state was criticized for refusing to impose comprehensive schools on local authorities who might not want them. Her argument was simple: where there are local grammar schools which are doing a good job, why cause disruption by insisting that they become comprehensive? In any case, there is a growing disenchantment among parents which may in part explain the increasing demand for places in independent schools, both elementary and secondary.

On the other hand there is a very strong doctrinaire lobby, especially in the Labour party, for the imposition of a wholly state-maintained system of comprehensive schools. Indeed the Labour party has declared its intention to abolish the direct grant, by means of which certain independent grammar schools, some of them among the most distinguished in the country, are enabled to admit pupils from elementary schools run by local education authorities. The result would be that these schools would become either wholly independent or comprehensive. Further down the list of intentions is the abolition of all independent schools. This might not be an altogether easy process, would be expensive, would arouse considerable opposition, and might involve the loss of a large number of "fringe" votes. For example, some independent schools are run by religious orders or are specifically religious foundations. Others are sponsored by powerful city guilds. Even the most rabid opponents of independent schools are doubtful whether their destruction could be achieved unless Labour were returned for two successive five-year terms of office. But the threat to their existence has been stated and cannot be ignored by the schools.

ISIS. Even before this policy had been enunciated much thought had been given to a project which was fulfilled in October, 1972, when the Independent Schools Information Service (ISIS) came into being. For the first time all the hitherto separate associations of independent schools were united in contributing to the cost of an organization whose purpose is to make their merits more widely known. This national ISIS, the culmination of a series of similar organizations serving limited areas, now covers England, Wales, Scotland, and Northern Ireland. It is not a pressure group, it has no intention of dabbling in politics, it is not propagandist. Its aim is simply to make the facts about independent schools more widely known. It publishes regular news letters and pamphlets on such subjects as relations with the media and means of covering the payment of fees. Its director is D. D. Lindsay, formerly headmaster of Malvern College, a famous "public school." It has a mobile display unit and an office in London, where the ever-increasing flow of inquiries is dealt with. It employs a well-known consultant in public relations.

STUDENTS gather before the mellow redbrick buildings of Eton on a Sunday morning. "Old Etonians" from this prestigious British boarding school made up over 10 percent of the House of Commons and 25 percent of the cabinet under Prime Minister Edward Heath. The 7 percent of British schoolchildren who are privately educated in the country's 2,700 independent schools retain an iron grip on Britain's top professions.

Energy Crisis

by
PAUL H. OEHSER

Editor, Research Reports
National Geographic Society
Member, Governing Council,
The Wilderness Society

STRIP MINING created this ugly "high wall" in Appalachia. The mining and power industries endorse more strip mining as the quickest, easiest, and cheapest way to mine coal. A 1974 report from the Ford Foundation's Energy Policy Project called reclamation of stripped lands "difficult if not impossible" in much of mountainous Appalachia, "feasible" in the flatter terrain of the Midwest, and "an unresolved problem" in the West where it is not possible in arid regions with less than ten inches of annual rainfall.

Who's to Blame? Long predicted by some geologists and economists — who warned of diminishing fossil fuels and other natural resources, particularly in the wake of the increasing world population — the energy crisis hit everyone in one way or another in 1974, for civilization is today geared to the production of enough gasoline and oil to heat our homes, run our automobiles, tractors, and industrial machinery, manufacture electricity, and provide all the other necessities of modern life. The average citizen was quite confused as to how and why it all came about—whether it was a "put-up" job of the oil companies to raise prices, a result of the Arab oil embargo, or a failure of technology to develop new sources of power. Some, in fact, blamed it on the "environmentalists," charging them with unreasonably blocking location and construction of nuclear power plants, insisting on air-pollution controls that hampered industry, and opposing the Alaska pipeline, strip mining, and other projects that tended to desecrate the landscape and endanger human health and the earth's habitability.

Environmental Backlash. This situation only points up the fact of the great complexity of the total environment-energy-economy picture, but as Russell Train, administrator of the federal government's Environmental Protection Agency (EPA), stated: "To blame the 'crisis' solely on an increased concern over environmental quality would be a grave failure to face the problem honestly and squarely." It is true that the energy crunch seemed to slow down the momentum of the great progress the country had been experiencing during the past five years or so and gave "anti-environmentalists" a chance to say "We told you so." It is true also that the crisis came along at a time when, as one commentator expressed it, "the environmental movement was beginning to lose the rosy flush of fashion it had a couple of years back."

It is no wonder that the public has been confused, worried with two problems — on the one hand people were urged to do everything possible to conserve energy and on the other to protect the environment, fight pollution, oppose nuclear-energy installations and strip mining, and recycle their paper and bottles. The two aims were not always in harmony. Obviously, for most a middle ground had to be assumed.

The overall effect of the environmental "backlash" (as some have termed it) has been two-fold: A slowing down of environmental legislation and a relaxing of environmental regulations already in force. For example, two long-debated bills in the U.S. Congress in 1973-74, one regulating strip mining, the other establishing a national land-use policy, were still unenacted when President Gerald Ford took office in August, 1974.

The federal Clean Air Act, despite its stringent demands, allows the EPA to grant waivers to meet special circumstances. In August, 1974, for example, the agency proposed to allow the states to give industrial and economic growth priority over protection of pure air. It would permit construction of 1,000-megawatt coal-burning power plants, petroleum refineries, shale oil processors, and other air-polluting installations in certain areas, particularly in the West. The proposal is likely to be challenged in the courts, but it is an indication of the temptations confronting administrators to ease restraints in the face of demands for increased power production and of pressures for industrial and economic growth deemed to be more important than clean air policies. The environmentalists are accused of being unrealistic in the face of national emergencies; their opponents are accused of being shortsighted in the face of dwindling resources and the constant erosion of the environment and of being too much concerned with profits.

Thus the plot thickens and compromises will be necessary. "Both sets of problems," states Train, "are real and serious. They will not be solved by wishful thinking or simply by ignoring them. Those who call for 'more energy and damn the environment' ill serve their country, their companies, or their constituents. Those who try to stop every energy project ill serve that which they most wish to serve—the environment." Or, as Luther J. Carter expressed it in an article in *Science:* "More encouraging, if less obvious, is the possibility that persistent energy shortages will make for desirable changes in the nation's social and economic development, including some wholesale changes in life styles. The essential point is that crisis is perhaps necessary to teach the body politic that the conservation of energy and the attainment of environmental quality are complementary goals, both demanding that resources be used with care and restraint."

New Energy Sources. All agree that new energy sources must be found. In simple terms, what seems to be required is to reduce the use of energy and at the same time encourage the production of more energy in every practical way. Americans found that they can adjust to using less gasoline, gas, heating oil, and electricity if they have to, even though they characteristically do a lot of griping about it and blame the government for the inconveniences. Most citizens concluded that until, if ever, the energy gap is closed, they would have to accommodate themselves to a decelerated way of life—and could be just as happy. But the research, technology, and construction problems that are entailed in developing new energy sources and making better use of old ones, will take time; they will not be solved overnight. And the choices, as far as can be seen in the future, are somewhat limited. But these choices are being actively explored, and some of them will surely pay off.

Nuclear Energy. One of the most promising choices, even though fraught with controversy, dangers to health, and environmental hazards, is nuclear energy, which is coming whether we like it or not. It is likely that we shall be committed to it as long as our plutonium holds out and the dangers from radio-

A TRANSMISSION TOWER on a power line: the president's Energy Resources Council (ERC) called for U.S. business and industry to achieve a 20 percent energy savings by 1980. Andrew E. Gibson replaced John C. Sawhill as federal energy administrator in November.

active wastes are minimized. A Ford Foundation report, "Exploring Energy Choices," predicted that nuclear power will become larger and larger in the national economy "because units already committed and under construction equal 20 to 30 percent of the normal growth in total energy consumption for the next few years . . . Nuclear power capacity is expected to jump from 24,000 megawatts to about 60,000 megawatts by the end of 1976 . . . If we pursue conservation aggressively, nuclear capacity might even meet half our growth needs in the 1970s."

Still, there are reservations. Labor, materials, and technical problems may impede development, and there is a great difference of opinion that needs resolving concerning the dangers to human and other life from possible accidental radiation emission from waste from nuclear plant installations. Environmental problems resulting from nuclear reactor operations would perhaps be less than those from combustion of fossil fuels, and nuclear power would lessen the dependence on fossil fuels; but there are many factors which indicate that nuclear energy may not be the total long-term answer, in spite of its present rapid growth. The Atomic Energy Commission estimates that there will be more than a thousand nuclear power plants in operation in the United States by the year 2000, costing $500 billion and providing half the U.S. electrical generating capacity. At the beginning of 1974 there were 36 in the United States and 146 under construction or on order. There is a similar growth in Europe, U.S.S.R., Japan, and Latin America.

Geothermal Energy. Development of geothermal energy has also received much attention. Research of this energy source promises possibilities in some areas. The environmental effects would appear to be minimal if installations are kept out of wilderness and other areas critical to land use. In the United States and some other countries there is a growing effort to tap deposits of hot water deep within the earth for the generation of electricity and for home heating. Conversion of geothermal heat to a usable form involves technological problems for scientists and engineers, but eventually it may prove to be one of the several developments that will contribute to the closing of the energy gap. Iceland now leads the world in per-capita use of geothermal heat and furnishes an outstanding example of what might be done in other areas. In Iceland's capitol, Reykjavik, which is situated advantageously directly over deep reservoirs of water as hot as 275° F., 99 percent of the city's 85,000 residents heat their houses by this hot water. Certainly this harnessing of one of nature's abundant resources is ingenious and of great potential as a pollution-free power source.

Solar Energy is another choice and is especially inviting because (so far as we know) it is inexhaustible. There is enough to supply all the conceivable needs of the world. It is not new; for decades it has been utilized in regions of more or less constant sunshine for various purposes, and scientists have long been working on the problem of devising means for its wider application. Dr. Charles G. Abbot, of the Smithsonian Institution, spent many years on the problem. In the 1930s he invented a "solar cooker" and built a "solar engine" that generated enough power to run a small electric motor. He was not alone in seeing the potential, but so far technology has not come up with a means of converting solar energy into electrical power that can compete in cost with other methods. The federal government is sponsoring increased research in this field, in an effort to catch up the lagging technology and close another gap in the energy complex. Costs are at present a deterrent. Sunshine will always be undependable over much of the earth, but many believe that technology will produce a low-cost process for collecting this free pollution-free power from the sun and storing it and making it serve mankind in ways we now little dream of. In fact, its use may not be as far off as some think. An article by Egan O'Connor in *High Country News* in January, 1974, listed more than a dozen examples of solar-energy equipment and components working today, including solar-heated homes, solar-powered refrigerators, solar-electrified homes (with wind generators), stoves and cars running on solar-made methane (or hydrogen), solar cells converting sunlight to electricity, fuel cells producing electricity without thermal pollution, and electrolyzers converting solar energy to clean hydrogen fuel. Solar energy, we may add, is used in our space programs. The present Skylab operation has massive solar panels to catch sunshine and convert it directly to electricity to operate the station, but the solar cells covering an area of about 1,000 square feet can provide only seven and a half kilowatts of power.

THE DIPPER of a surface coal mining shovel dwarfs a mechanic, left, as it lifts 140 cubic yards — about 210 tons — of earth and rock. Coal, the energy resource the United States has in great abundance, accounts for only 18.2 percent of the energy used in the country.

The Alaska Pipeline. The energy crunch has of course spurred all the world into frantic action not only to develop new sources of energy but also to accelerate the exploitation of the old ones. A shining example was the mad rush to build the oil pipeline from the North Slope of Alaska to Valdez in order to get the newly discovered oil out—this against all odds, environmental and economic, and with the knowledge that the Alaska oil would be only a "drop in the bucket" in solving the energy crisis in the United States. Delayed by litigation instigated by a group of citizens' conservation organizations, the permit for the pipeline was finally approved by Congress, with the environmental impact on Alaska and its people, as well as the efficiency of the total operation itself, still in doubt.

Strip Mining. Equally controversial is strip mining, likewise accelerated by increased demands for power generated from coal. In vast areas of the American continent this practice has been going on for scores of years, and there is little argument as to its devastating effects on the land. Some states have been somewhat successful in requiring mining companies to restore the landscape destroyed by strip mining operations; and conservationists have been diligent in attempting to get legislation through Congress for an orderly phasing out of strip mining, but its opponents have so far delayed its enactment.

The environmental argument was well stated editorially in the *New York Times:* "No more than 10 percent of this country's recoverable coal reserves can be reached by surface mining. That should be a salient consideration in the debate on strip (surface) mining. There is neither sense nor sincerity in making the energy shortage a pretext for rejecting environmental curbs on surface mining when all the strippable coal in the country would in any case be exhausted in a few years of unrestricted operations. Such a course would leave great areas of the West in dismal ruins and the energy need as great as ever. In the energy shortage which confronts it, the country must draw on its vast coal supply. But it needs its land too. It cannot afford to have it raped and abandoned at the rate of 1,000 acres a week for coal alone."

The Great Lesson that has been forcefully impressed on people by the energy crisis is that the earth's resources of fossil fuels on which we have long depended for energy are finite—when they are gone they are gone for good. People sometimes become overly optimistic when they hear of new oil and gas discoveries or read of the vast reserves hidden under the seabed recoverable by offshore drilling, or of the 600-billion-barrel shale-oil reserves in our Western public lands, or of the coal still unmined around the world. But some day these too will be gone. Their recovery will be costly and in some cases will ravage the earth; for example, even with modern equipment shale oil is expensive; more than a ton of the richest rock yields only one barrel of oil, and to get significant quantities of oil entire mountains may be gouged open. The energy crisis has been enough to scare us—not that we expect disaster to strike in this generation, or perhaps the next, or the next. The real job ahead is to stretch this time period out as far as humanly possible.

Man must exploit the earth's resources in order to live. The earth was put here for his use, but unless he applies his wisdom not only to use its resources wisely and providently but also at the same time to preserve some of its pristine beauty and wonder and its physical habitability, our present civilization will progressively retrograde and, some predict, vanish. Survival can no longer be taken for granted. The road ahead will be hard, and the contest between "quality of the environment" and wanton and shortsighted exploitation will not disappear soon. But somehow they must be reconciled until every man will be proud to be called an environmentalist. If we are to save the earth and preserve its resources for man, we must no longer be divided into two camps.

Exorcism

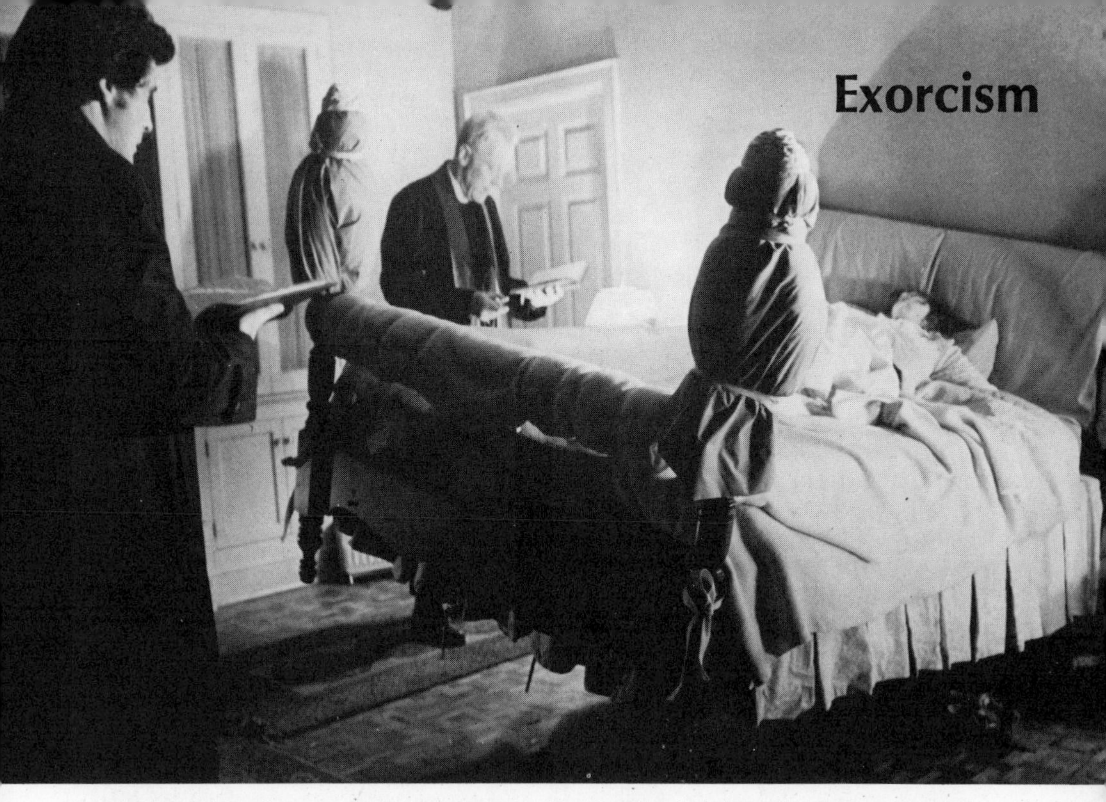

FATHER KARRAS (Jason Miller) and Father Merrin (Max von Sydow) attempt to help Regan (Linda Blair) in *The Exorcist*. The film's author, William Peter Blatty, won the Academy Award for the best screenplay based on a work in another medium.

by

MARTIN EBON

Administrative Secretary, Parapsychology Foundation (1953-1965); Author, *The Devil's Bride: Exorcism, Past and Present;* Editor, *Exorcism: Fact, Not Fiction*

The Power of the Picture Show. Despite the influence of television on the political and cultural life of the United States, the motion picture retains its power to lead changes in a great variety of fields. This can be noted in patterns of speech and musical tastes and in areas as diverse as fashions and religion. During 1974, the motion picture *The Exorcist* dramatized this point: it became a national phenomenon that had an impact far beyond the nation's movie theaters.

Earlier, *The Godfather* had suddenly focused wide attention on the "human side" of organized crime. Earlier still, the film *Rosemary's Baby* had aroused an interest in witchcraft that lasted for several years. In the case of this film, as well as in that of *The Exorcist,* the novels that had preceded the filmed versions had much less impact. Certainly, when William Blatty's novel first appeared in a hardcover edition in 1971, and then as a paperback in 1972, it attracted wide attention. But it was as a motion picture, produced by William Friedkin, that *The Exorcist* set off waves of public attention, criticism, approval, revulsion, and attraction, as well as a certain number of apparently delusional experiences. For several months, clergymen and psychotherapists reported that people had come to them in relatively large numbers, claiming to be "possessed by a demon," more or less as the young girl, named Regan, had been in the movie.

The Exorcist. The plot of both the novel and the film suggested that the twenty-year-old girl showed physiological and psychological phenomena that were outside medical and psychiatric knowledge. Eventually, the devoted and exhausting work of two Roman Catholic priests helps to "exorcize" the demon that had taken over the body of the young girl. The elder priest, an experienced exorcist, dies during the proceedings, apparently of a heart attack; the younger, somewhat emotionally troubled priest who is given the name of Demian Karras, is hurled or hurls himself out of the window of the child's room—seemingly sacrificing himself, lovingly, for the little girl's freedom from possession. He is found dead on the ground. Regan's demon is "exorcized," and the child does not remember the experience, as if it had been blocked by amnesia.

The Clinical Base of the Blatty Novel. The producers of the motion picture, and notably the novelist William Blatty, have alleged that actual possession cases are rare but that Blatty's novel was based on an actual and well-documented case that occurred in Washington, D. C., in 1949. It can be argued, quite strongly, that the Washington case was more psychological than demonic, and that three factors should be considered in judging the novel in relation to the clinical evidence:

1. that the so-called Washington case, which involved a fourteen-year-old boy who became known, presumably pseudonymously, as Douglas Deen, was never given the detailed ecclesiastical diagnosis required by the Roman Catholic church's *Rituale Romanum,* and that the decision to undertake an exorcism was made much too hastily;

2. that the records kept on the actual exorcism proceedings, which took place in St. Louis, Mo., rather than in Washington, were less a purely factual transcription of events than a diary that reflected the emotional involvement, memory distortions, and often near-hysterical conditions of the exorcists and their assistants;

3. that the novel and motion picture *The Exorcist* went still further in dramatizing and oversimplifying the records of the St. Louis proceedings, adding visual phenomena through technical devices, as well as a terminology and actions likely to arouse prurient interest.

The Film Translation. The skillful technology of motion picture production translated the novel into an intensive, horrifying experience. Both its use of physiological phenomena, aided by subtle film-making technology, and its exploitation of sexual, pseudosexual, and blasphemous acts and language added to the shock value of the film. National news weeklies, the daily press, and periodicals directed at varying audiences, described aspects of the film and its phenomenal impact. Mass audiences listened to the views of priests and laymen on television talk shows, and the whole age-old question of possible possession and exorcism was aired freely and extensively.

The Fascination of the Forces of the Unknown. Public fascination with forces of the unknown, preferably evil, can be gauged by the persistent popularity of horror films. The impact of fiction on life has been particularly great in the area of so-called psychic phenomena. Originally, stories of the supernatural and ghostly emerged from allegedly true accounts of hauntings and witchery. Fact and fiction have been trespassing on each other's territory for centuries, and their intercourse has brought forth offspring that are quite often a mixture of both. Daniel Defoe, who is best known for his *Robinson Crusoe* (an elaboration of a brief account of a shipwrecked sailor), published *A True Relation of the Apparition of One Mrs. Veal* in 1706, and literary historians are still wondering whether it is a factual account of an apparition viewed in Canterbury on September 8, 1705, or yet another fictional Defoe elaboration, based on evidence that was dubious to begin with.

The Impact of *The Exorcist*. To the degree that the movie *The Exorcist* pushed the Defoe tradition to the outer limits of modern technology, the impact of its peculiar combination of doubtful fact and outright fiction was many times that of its predecessors. This prompted one psychiatrist, Dr. Ralph R. Greenson, of Los Angeles, to call the film a "flagrant combination of perverse sex, brutal violence, and abused religion." Writing in the *Saturday Review World* (June 15, 1974) he added: "Like most psychiatrists, I have seen patients with one or another of the hair-raising symptoms that plague Regan, but I have never encountered, or even heard of, any single patient bristling with all the bizarre, morbid symptoms the girl in the movie exhibits. It is my conviction that *The Exorcist* was contrived to appeal to a wide audience, to attract and scare the wits out of troubled and disoriented people — by appealing to their voyeuristic impulses, their sadism, and their masochism. It also tried to titillate these unfortunates by making their panic-fears sexually exciting."

Possession Phenomena. While television shows — which tend to emphasize controversy over information for enlightenment's sake—are not ideal educational media, the talk shows on exorcism in 1974 nevertheless made one point quite clearly: there is little agreement, even among Roman Catholic priests, concerning the extent and nature of possession phenomena. That is not surprising, as Christian, pre-Christian, and non-Christian concern with possession has historically seen it in many forms. If we keep in mind that modern concepts of mental illness—including those of psychosomatic medicine—are relatively young, the view or explanation that any otherwise inexplicable illness or form of behavior must be due to an outside force has a good deal of superficial logic.

Within the history of so-called possession, there is a good deal of overlapping between possession of human beings by *the* Devil, by *a* devil, by a demon, or by an evil spirit. Traditionally, exorcists have confronted the apparently possessing entity with ritual and exhortation, with prayer and with threats. Usually, demon possession—to use this category as a common denominator for simplicity's sake—showed itself by aberrant behavior that went against the social mores of a given society as well as contrary to the established personality characteristics of the possessed person.

In all their suffering, which is undoubtedly real, both exorcist and possessed are centers of dramatic attention. Their relationship to each other is subtle and ambivalent. Theirs may be compared to the relationship between hypnotist and the hypnotist's subject, between interrogator and suspect. The "victim's" tendency to act as is expected of him or her is notable in many cases. Underlying psychological factors, often of a sexual nature, can frequently be noted. In many cases the possessed person has been a woman, the exorcist always a man.

The History of Exorcism. While in western society the Roman Catholic church, the Anglican and Episcopal denominations, and the Eastern Orthodox church have remained relatively consistent in their views of possession through the centuries, there have been fewer and fewer publicly reported cases of either possession or exorcism—that is, until the film *The Exorcist* made these concepts, in a manner of speaking, fashionable once again. Possession, like other emotional conditions, has tended to come in spurts, in the form of minor epidemics. The phenomena of the condition have tended to be imitative, or responsive to suggestion.

In such ancient civilizations as China and Assyria-Babylonia, possession by demons or spirits was taken for granted, and various means of ousting such entities, by threatening or appeasing them, were used. During the Middle Ages exorcism was so widely practiced that in Europe the Christian church saw itself forced to establish firm rules. These were incorporated into the *Rituale Romanum* (1614) at the behest of Pope Paul V. Few revisions have been made in this text. The most recent modernization took place in 1952 when mental illness was specifically mentioned among the illnesses that did not indicate valid possession.

Modern Views of Possession. Just how different modern views of possession can be was illustrated in 1974 by two Catholic priests, both associated with Georgetown University in Washington, D.C. One of them, Father John J. Nicola, who collaborated in giving the motion picture its theological and practical authenticity, said that the church's explanation for phenomena of possession remains "as plausible today as the doubtful answers of science." He added: "The mystique is still there. If exorcism is to satisfy a certain need, what is its effect on the general public? There is a good deal of danger. That is why the Catholic church has been so reserved. In the Middle Ages, use of exorcism in cases of common diseases and mental problems resulted in a case of mass hysteria."

Father Juan B. Cortes, also of Georgetown University, wrote in *Science Digest* (April, 1974): "The Catholic church still permits a priest to perform the ritual to send the devil back to hell. Each session takes three to four hours, and often the terrifying treatment must be continued for years before the possession can be ended. From a psychologist's point of view, the whole process is perilous." He argued that "reported demons are often the outward signs of organic brain damage, neurosis or psychosis—problems that can be treated today without cant."

In Great Britain, the Anglican Bishop of Exeter commissioned a study, published under the title *Exorcism* (1973) that described precautions, ritual, participation, and procedures in exorcism in manner and detail which suggested that cases of possession were being encountered frequently throughout the United Kingdom. It specified the ecumenical approach and concern felt by Anglican authorities, urging that each diocesan bishop should "appoint a priest as diocesan exorcist, and that in each province centers of training should be established, if possible in collaboration with our Roman Catholic brethren." It is well to keep in mind, at this point, that a number of Protestant denominations in Europe and the United States also hold the view that demonic possession is a contemporary reality which must be dealt with by means of exorcism rites.

The Anglican instructions emphasized that caution should be observed in diagnosing, as it were, the condition of possession; that priests undertaking exorcism should preferably do so in teams of at least two; that merely curious participants or onlookers should be excluded; and that good judgment and confidentiality should be preserved. While these rites—as well as those of the Roman Catholic and Eastern Orthodox churches —are elaborate and may, as Father Cortes points out, take up a good deal of time, the Anglican instructions noted that in case of emergencies the exorcist must "make a quick, deep act of Recollection, calling upon the help and power of the Holy Spirit," and then speak a brief command such as this: "In the name of Jesus Christ our Lord, I command you, evil spirit, to harm no one, but depart to the place appointed you."

As the wording of this Anglican exorcism indicates, the term "evil spirit" is used in this context, suggesting that some entity that is neither strictly diabolical nor demonic may be "possessing" the afflicted person. One Anglican priest, Canon J. D. Pearce-Higgins, former canon residentiary and vice-provost of Southwark Cathedral in London, acts on the assumption that possessing entities are indeed spirits of deceased persons: not actually "evil," but merely misguided and, in a sense, "misplaced" in their efforts to act through the bodies of living persons. His efforts are designed to alert such spirits to their condition and, through prayer and ritual, to free the possessed individual. This approach is related to that used by a U.S. psychiatrist, Dr. Carl A. Wickland, who treated seemingly possessed patients first in Chicago and then in Los Angeles in the 1920s and 1930s by means of such "re-education." He attempted to induce spirits to enter the body of his wife, a spiritualist medium, to enable him to speak to them and use such dialogue literally to "talk them out of" the bodies of the patient.

The Medical Borderline. The borderline between what in ecclesiastical terms is regarded as "possession" and what in modern medical terms is either a psychophysiological, mental, or psychosomatic condition, is obviously so elusive as to be almost nonexistent. My own impression, after a good deal of research on this subject, suggests that one or another approach or method may be effective within specific religio-cultural environments. The upbringing, emotional maturity, intellectual development, and mental response of each afflicted individual may well provide the clue to whatever method may be best for combating the phenomena of apparent possession.

The exorcist may well be regarded as the forerunner of the psychotherapist of the twentieth century. One aspect of *The Exorcist* that has been quite rightly criticized is the rather crude line drawn between the psychiatric and the religious approach. In actual fact, psychotherapists who have a deep understanding of religious viewpoints and clergymen with psychological training are, in my view, among the most successful in solving emotional problems.

The Harris Survey, a public opinion poll, reported after *The Exorcist* was shown in 1974 that 36 percent of persons interviewed thought that "people are sometimes possessed—taken over in mind and body by a demon or the devil." The survey found that a total of 5 percent of Americans eighteen years or over, or one in twenty, claimed that either they or "someone close to them" had actually been "possessed by the devil." Overall, of those questioned, only 16 percent felt that "modern medicine and psychiatry have successfully diagnosed" the cause of such aberrations, while another 30 percent felt that it had been "somewhat explained." A majority, 54 percent, either felt that all explanations thus far had been inadequate or simply did not know how to explain the reported episodes.

The very arrangement of questions in a poll such as this assumes that all or most aspects of human behavior can in fact be "explained" in the manner of phenomena in the natural sciences. But explanations of such depth cannot be made within the contemporary framework of science. Physical events, such as landing men on the moon, have aroused expectations that have simply risen too high. As man seeks to fight illness or combat evil, he suddenly discovers that the present offers no total answers, and so there is a tendency to look to the past for enlightenment.

Expo '74

AN EXPO '74 HOSTESS hands Mrs. Richard Nixon lilacs as the president opens the Spokane, Wash., world's fair on May 4. Dedicated to "preservation of the environment," Expo '74 attracted 5.2 million visitors in its 184-day run.

WORKMEN secure clamps on the cables designed to support the vinyl canopy of the $11.5 million U.S. pavilion. The exhibit was criticized for showing ecology solutions of only government and industry. No environmental organizations were represented in Expo '74.

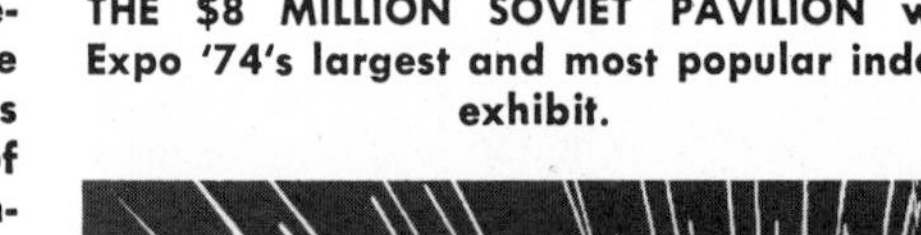

THE $8 MILLION SOVIET PAVILION was Expo '74's largest and most popular indoor exhibit.

Farming

A GALLON OF MAPLE SYRUP cost $12 in 1974. New York state was the leading producer of maple syrup with 326,000 gallons. Vermont was second with 323,000 gallons.

by
LANE PALMER

Editor and Vice-President
Farm Journal

High Hopes. After more than twenty years of worrying about farm surpluses and subsidies, the United States had reason during 1974 to wish that its "farm problems" were again so simple.

The year started off with high hopes and bright prospects. The government had taken all remaining acreage controls off grains, soybeans, and cotton. Farm leaders talked confidently of producing a 6.5 billion-bushel corn crop. The 1973-74 winter wheat crop was off to a great start and indeed turned out to be the biggest on record. Meat prices were beginning to come down from the heights reached after price controls had been taken off in 1973. Dairymen were rejoicing over a combination of high prices and good milk yields. And cotton growers looked forward confidently to their second straight year of 60 to 70 cent cotton.

A Changed Picture. But by November, the whole picture had come unstuck. Instead of celebrating their first 6 billion-bushel crop, corn growers had to settle for less than 5 billion. Some livestock farmers were killing young calves in front of television cameras to dramatize the losses they were suffering from high feed-grain prices. Consumers were organizing a boycott against sugar, which had gone up in price 300 percent in one year. Hardest hit of all were the poor and the elderly: Prices of the traditional poverty foods—dried beans, peas, and rice—had climbed as much as 400 percent.

World Food Crisis. In the United States, it was deprivation and discomfort;

FARMING

in parts of Asia and Africa, it was mass starvation and death. Floods had wiped out the summer crops in Bangladesh and parts of India; four years of drought had parched the whole sub-Sahara region of Africa. The World Food Conference in Rome, which had been scheduled for more than a year, became a natural focal point. The developing countries, which had always been able to fall back on the United States for food aid, now attacked bitterly because the United States and other wealthy countries were not promising enough food. The world food crisis, which had been predicted for almost a decade, had finally arrived.

Three Strikes Against Crop Farmers. With no limit on the acres they could plant, farmers could hardly restrain themselves as warm weather arrived in April. They knew they would not be able to buy all the fertilizer they needed —the industry just could not expand fast enough to handle all the additional acres. Many farmers were still waiting six to eight months for new tractors and field machinery they had ordered. Fuel and pesticides were still in tight supply. But these all turned out to be the least of their problems.

SUGAR BEETS are harvested by machine. A tight supply-and-demand situation and speculative buying by Middle East interests who decided sugar was an excellent inflation hedge drove sugar prices through the roof. Congress killed the Sugar Act on June 5, ending import quotas that had guaranteed U.S. farmers a large share of the American market for the last forty years.

Some corn belt farmers moved into their fields on schedule and had part of their corn crop planted by early May. But then the rains came. Tractors, with corn planters attached, stood in Illinois fields for three weeks or more, waiting for the rains to stop. Iowa hillsides, normally left in pasture but now plowed to produce more corn, were creased with gulleys washed out by the rains. Some of the corn that had been planted rotted in the ground from cold and wetness.

Not until June did many of the planters roll again. The farmers in the tractor seats were already counting their losses by the old rule of thumb: "a bushel of yield per day, after the first of May." Now they were planting corn when they should have been planting their other important crop — soybeans. Many soybeans went into the ground in July—and were set up for the twin disasters that followed.

The rains stopped almost as abruptly as they had started. At first, farmers were happy with the chance to play "catch up." A rainless June was all right—still plenty of moisture in the soil. But then the hot, dry days continued into July. The rapidly growing corn quickly sapped the subsoil moisture. Corn leaves rolled into tight spirals. Pollen from the tassels withered before it could fertilize the emerging silks below. By early August, when the first showers began to skip through the central corn belt, farmers knew that their former hopes of a record crop had been shattered.

What is more, they knew they were vulnerable to a third blow: an early frost. And sure enough, it hit. During the first week of September, the first traces of early-morning white appeared on the still-tender leaves in Minnesota, the Dakotas, and northern Iowa. A week or so later, it had crept southward into northern Illinois and Indiana. By the first of October, the freeze was general. Late-planted soybeans, some of them still only eighteen inches high, turned black under the mid-morning sun. Seeds in many of the pods were only half their normal size. The corn belt's long series of favorable growing seasons had come to an end.

The Story Behind the Calf Kills. What was a disappointment for feed-grain growers became a disaster for livestock feeders. Corn growers could expect to make up in price part of the losses they were suffering in yields. But cattle feeders particularly had no way to make up their losses. This is why: Beef production in the United States is a complicated chain of steps lasting two or three years and involving three or four different types of livestock specialists. The first specialist is the *purebred breeder* who furnishes seed stock (bulls and cows) to the *commercial breeder*. Commercial breeders usually run their cow herds on the open range or in large pastures and often sell the resulting calf crop to *backgrounders* or *grow-out specialists*. These stockmen "carry" a 500-pound calf for a few months on corn stalks, hay, or other roughage and then sell them to *commercial feedlot owners*. It is during this final step that the finishers feed a ration high in grain and soybean meal to put marbling in the meat—deposits of fat which give fine steaks and roasts their juicy, succulent flavor.

If something happens to any one of these specialists, it takes several months — maybe a year or more — before the effect is felt by other specialists in the chain. The sudden climb in corn prices in early summer whiplashed the commercial feedlots. Because of high meat prices in late 1973, feedlots in 1974 were packed full of calves that had cost the

THE U.S. SHEEP POPULATION has declined from a high of 56 million in 1942 to 16.5 million, the lowest level since the Civil War, according to the American Sheep Producers Council.

operators 60 cents, as high as 75 cents a pound. Now consumers suddenly were not eating as much beef as they had before prices had soared. So slaughter prices fell to 50 cents, 45 cents, and in some areas, as low as 35 cents. That meant the feedlot owner might recover only half as much per pound as he had paid for the original weight of the calf. And the pounds he was putting on in the feedlot were with \$3 corn—not the \$2 corn he had counted on. Many cattle feeders lost \$100 to \$200 per head on animals sold during the summer months. By fall, the effect had backed up to the commercial cowmen, and they were being offered 40 cents or less per pound for their feeder calves.

Broiler and egg producers, hogmen, and dairymen were under similar pressures. Poultry producers could cut their losses because the life cycle of a broiler is only eight to ten weeks. They simply placed fewer hatching eggs in the incubator. But dairymen, like the cattle feeders, were stuck. Whereas milk prices had reached nearly $10 a hundred pounds during the winter, they plummeted to $7 or less when the spring milk "flush" hit in June. What's more, dairymen could not get Congress or the president to raise support prices on dried milk and butter, which would have boosted their fluid milk prices. All dairymen had gotten a "black eye" from the involvement in the Watergate mess of one big dairy co-op.

Frustrated on this front, some dairymen dramatized their troubles by killing baby calves in front of television cameras. In years gone by, dairymen frequently got rid of unwanted bull calves by "knocking them in the head." Some dairy breeds do not gain well enough to compete as beef animals. Now, with beef prices in the doldrums, these were again the least-wanted calves, and the owners really could not afford to feed them. The televised "calf shoots" offended the public at a time when millions were starving in other countries.

Pressures to Feed the World. Because U. S. exports of grains are so important in paying the bills for oil and other imports, Secretary of Agriculture Earl Butz had made special trips to both Europe and Asia after the big 1973 crop was harvested. His purpose was to assure governments there that we had enough wheat, feed grains, and soybeans to fill all their orders. "The embargo we placed on soybean exports (in mid-1973) was something we had to do to learn that we should never do it again," he said everywhere he went.

His promise lasted less than a year. In October, Russia again placed a sizable order for corn and soybeans. Butz had approved it before he knew its true size, but the White House interceded and canceled the order. Once more, crop farmers fumed over controls on exports.

But the need to parcel out our supplies was readily apparent at the World Food Conference less than a month later. Pressures for the United States to greatly increase its food aid began building up well before the meeting began. An enormous contingent of senators, congressmen, churchmen, environmentalists, farmers, and agribusiness leaders journeyed to Rome and became lobbyists for their varying viewpoints.

Secretary Butz and Secretary of State Henry Kissinger deliberately delayed making any commitments in an effort to get the oil-producing nations, Western Europe, Russia, China, and other countries to carry part of the load. Also they made it clear that they had the power only to propose aid levels to Congress. In fact, the U.S. Department of Agriculture's own appropriations bill for 1974-75, including almost $1 billion in food aid, still had not passed Congress.

The newly elected Congress already faced an expected deficit of $10 to $20 billion for 1975-76. And President Gerald Ford had asked Congress to balance the budget to fight inflation.

So whatever level of food aid Congress finally settled on, there was bound to be disappointment—in the United States, as well as abroad. Respected scientists, such as Dr. John Hannah, former administrator of the Agency for International Development, and Dr. Philip Handler, president of the National Academy of Sciences, warned that the food needs of the world were already outrunning the capabilities of even the American farmer. Whatever they did, the people faced the prospect of seeing on their television screens, with increasing frequency, the gaunt faces and bloated bellies of the starving.

Fashion

THE BLUE JEAN REVOLUTION

Blue jeans have become for the American wardrobe what the hamburger is to the national menu. They have shattered barriers of age, economic status, and fashion. The sea of denim has even inundated Europe, where used, U.S.-made jeans bring as much as $150 a pair.

Denim, which originated in Nimes, France (**serge de Nimes** was the original name), was one of the most popular cloths in the world in 1974. More than 450 million square yards of denim were manufactured in the United States during the year. More than 30 million dozen blue jeans, denim overalls, and jackets were produced. Levi Strauss, the pioneer blue-jean manufacturer, made $900 million in sales in fiscal 1974 and was expected to break through the $1 billion-a-year sales level in fiscal 1975.

The denims on this page, part of fashion's "peacock revolution," are prizewinners in Levi's Denim Art Contest.

ELEVEN POUNDS of silver, brass, and jewel-toned studs, a police whistle, a removable ashtray, and a desk bell decorate the first-prize winner by Bill Shire of Los Angeles, Calif.

***WORKER BLUES* is the title of this appliqued jacket. It won Kay Aronson of Lafayette, Calif., a second place award.**

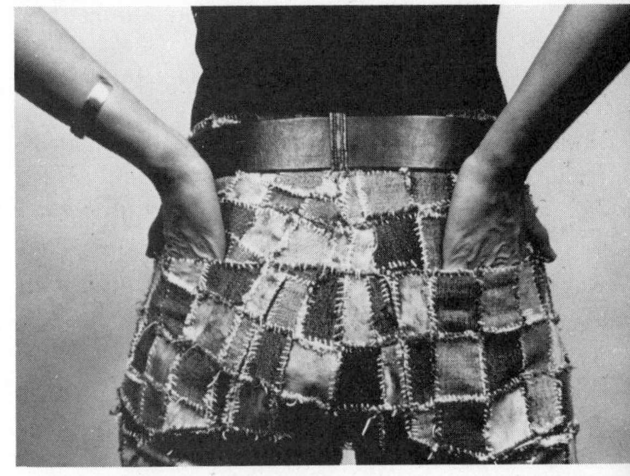

THE ULTIMATE in patched jeans won a second place for Steve Ostrow of Portland, Ore.

Films

ROBERT SHAW, ROBERT REDFORD, AND PAUL NEWMAN meet a new challenge in *THE STING*. The film won seven Academy awards: best picture, best director, best original screenplay, best scoring adaptation, best film editing, best art direction, and best costume design.

Business is Better. Since the smashing success of *Love Story* in 1971 and *The Godfather* in 1972, public interest in motion pictures has revived. Box office receipts were higher in 1974 than in the previous year and several polls showed that movies gained in popularity over other forms of entertainment outside the home. Even with higher prices, they cost less than theater tickets or "eating out." Another factor is the trend to "spectaculars." By this term is meant a film that deals with the wildest adventure or the most colossal catastrophe, that presents not one but a whole galaxy of stars, that costs millions, and that is promoted by saturation advertising. Among these are *The Towering Inferno,* focusing on a skyscraper conflagration, produced by Twentieth Century Fox at a cost of \$12.5 million; *Earthquake,* which concerns the destruction of Los Angeles; *Airport 1975*, depicting the mid-air crash of planes; and *The Day the World Ended.* High-budget films of this sort tend to crowd out the more serious, low-cost offerings, including those from Europe, that have a simple, human appeal. The trend to depict bizarre, if not perverse, situations and off-beat characters persists.

Film Festivals. Film festivals are usually organized around a certain star, a certain director, or a type of subject matter — such as horror or science fiction. Once confined to the large cities, they have spread across the country, and now number in the hundreds — requir-

FILMS

ing only an entrepreneur with capital to select films, advertise, and provide for nightly showings for a week or more.

Topping the list of film festivals in point of fame is the one held each May in Cannes, on the French Riviera, under the auspices of the ministry of culture. Here hundreds of carefully selected films from all over the world are shown to a cosmopolitan audience of critics and others connected with the industry who are competent to establish criteria and make judgments. In 1974 the United States carried off honors, with the Golden Palm awarded to Frank Coppola's *The Conversation;* and the awards for best scenario given to *The Sugarland Express,* and for best actor to Jack Nicholson in *The Last Detail.*

Unlike the Cannes Festival, the New York Festival, held in the fall, is non-competitive. It is also less commercial. Founded in 1963, it shows at Lincoln Center a selection of superior films in various categories.

Film Rentals. The renting of films has become big business, bringing prosperity to several companies. The films are mainly of the sixteen-millimeter type, and the renters are schools and various organizations, as well as private individuals. The cost may vary from a few dollars to several hundred, depending on the length and popularity of the film. The full-length features are not rented until a year after their release. The short, creative films once shown in little "art" theaters are now enjoyed by groups in classrooms, clubs, and libraries.

TATUM O'NEAL shows her grandfather, Charles O'Neal, the Oscar she won for best supporting actress for her role in *Paper Moon* at the Motion Picture Academy awards celebration on April 2.

SHELTON DIGGS, on ground, catches a game-winning two-point conversion pass to give Southern California an 18-17 win over Ohio State in the Rose Bowl. Southern California's John McKay, jumping with joy at left, had caught a touchdown pass a moment before to narrow the gap to one point.

Football

by

ART DUNN

Editor, Sunday Sports Section
Chicago Tribune

The College Season was in many respects a carbon copy of the previous years as Penn State, Alabama, Ohio State, Oklahoma, and Southern California again emerged as regional powerhouses.

Penn State won nine of eleven games to capture the Lambert Trophy, symbolic of the best team in the East, for the fourth straight year. Ohio State, the preseason choice to win the national title, again needed a vote by the Big Ten athletic directors to send the Buckeyes to the Rose Bowl after tying Michigan for the conference crown. And for the third year in a row, Ohio State would face Pacific Eight Conference champion Southern Cal in Pasadena, Calif.

Alabama marched through the Southeastern Conference toward a perfect season (one of only two major teams to do so) and an Orange Bowl date with independent power Notre Dame, a rematch of last year's Sugar Bowl. Oklahoma also won eleven without a loss, but was ineligible for a bowl appearance because of a two-year probation for recruiting violations imposed last season by the National Collegiate Athletic Association (NCAA). Just as a year ago, the Sooners were thought by many to have the nation's strongest team.

There were two major changes in the power structure. The Baylor Bears, long a doormat in the Southwest Conference (SWC), turned a 2-9 record from 1973 into an 8-3 season and terminated Texas's seven-year reign as SWC winner. The abrupt reversal earned Grant Teaff coach-of-the-year honors and Baylor a Cotton Bowl appearance for the first time.

Though there was confusion at the top of the ratings due to Oklahoma's probation, one thing was certain — Notre Dame would not repeat. The Irish finished 9-2 as Purdue beat them early by scoring twenty-four points in the first quarter, and Southern Cal humiliated them the last week of the season.

Notre Dame was leading long-time rival USC 24-6 at halftime, but speedster Anthony Davis ran the second half kickoff back 103 yards, and the Trojans rolled a 55-24 victory with Davis scoring four times in all.

The pivotal week in the college campaign was November 23. Ohio State hosted Michigan to decide the Big Ten title as the two unfriendly neighbors had done so often. The number one-rated Buckeyes spotted Michigan a 10-0 lead in the first ten minutes, then chipped away with four field goals by Czechoslovakian-born kicker Tom Klaban to win 12-10. The last one covered forty-five yards in the third quarter. With sixteen seconds left, Michigan's Mike Lantry teed up a thirty-three-yard field goal

FOOTBALL

attempt which sailed just wide.

The next day, Big Ten directors settled the title tie in the Buckeyes' favor. Thus Michigan, which compiled a three-year record of 30-2-1 stayed home for the holidays again because neither the Big Ten nor Pac-Eight allows runnerup teams to make bowl appearances.

While Ohio State was kicking its way past Michigan, Southern Cal earned its seventh Pacific-Eight conference championship in nine years by drubbing crosstown rival University of California at Los Angeles 34-9. The Trojans scored the first three times they had the ball, and Davis shredded UCLA defense for 195 yards.

Meanwhile, Oklahoma was withstanding its stiffest test of the season in Lincoln, Neb. The Sooners fell behind 14-7 in the third quarter, then roared back to whip Nebraska 28-14, amassing 482 yards rushing in the process. It was the twenty-eighth straight game without a loss for the Sooners and their nineteenth victory in a row.

The Rose Bowl. Southern Cal (10-1-1) gained the national title in the coaches' poll (where Oklahoma was ineligible) by nipping Ohio State in the Rose Bowl 18-17. The Buckeyes were up 7-3 after three lackluster quarters, then their pass defense came apart as Rhodes scholar quarterback Pat Haden pitched two fourth-quarter touchdown passes and a two-point conversion for the victory. Trailing 17-10 with 2:03 left, the Trojans scored when Haden passed thirty-eight yards to J. K. McKay, son of the Southern Cal coach. Then Haden hit Shelton Diggs, who made a lunging catch in the end zone, for the two extra points.

The expected duel between Davis and Ohio State's Archie Griffin never materialized. Davis was injured late in the first half and never returned. Griffin, who became the fifth junior to win the Heisman Trophy, fumbled twice deep in USC territory and was held to 76 yards rushing to break his string of twenty-two games with over 100 yards gained rushing.

ALL-AMERICAN TEAM

OFFENSE

Wide receiver	Pete Demmerle, Notre Dame
Tight end	Bennie Cunningham, Clemson
Tackle	Kurt Schumacher, Ohio State
Tackle	Marvin Crenshaw, Nebraska
Guard	John Roush, Oklahoma
Guard	Gerry DiNardo, Notre Dame
Center	Steve Myers, Ohio State
Quarterback	Steve Bartowski, California
Running back	Archie Griffin, Ohio State
Running back	Joe Washington, Oklahoma
Running back	Anthony Davis, Southern California

DEFENSE

End	Van Decree, Ohio State
End	Pat Donovan, Stanford
Tackle	Randy White, Maryland
Tackle	Mike Hartenstine, Penn State
Middle guard	Rubin Carter, Miami of Florida
Linebacker	Rod Shoate, Oklahoma
Linebacker	Richard Wood, Southern California
Linebacker	Woodrow Lowe, Alabama
Defensive back	Neal Colzie, Ohio State
Defensive back	Dave Brown, Michigan
Defensive back	Randy Hughes, Oklahoma

The Orange Bowl. Notre Dame, an eleven-point underdog, ruined Alabama's bid for a perfect season for the second straight year and left Tide Coach Bear Bryant without a bowl victory in his last eight tries. The 13-11 victory ended the Notre Dame coaching career of Ara Parseghian, who had announced his retirement after eleven years because of the escalating pressures of college coaching.

The Irish dominated both lines of scrimmage and relied mainly on the running of Wayne Bullock, Al Samuels, and Mark McLane. Alabama scored its long touchdown with 3:13 to play, then the Tide's last gasp was blunted when defensive back Reggie Barnett intercepted a Richard Todd pass.

Sugar Bowl was a sweet treat for Nebraska as the Cornhuskers won their sixth straight postseason game, 13-10, from Florida. Nebraska, bowling in Oklahoma's stead, finally got untracked in the final fifteen minutes to overtake still another Southeastern Conference representative.

The Cotton Bowl was the scene of more fourth-quarter heroics. Penn State, held to a 17-14 advantage after three quarters, blew gritty Baylor out with twenty-four points in the final fifteen minutes. The Nittany Lions, angered when a long touchdown pass was nullified by a penalty, were keyed by freshman flanker Jimmy Celafo and quarterback Tom Shuman.

The Gator Bowl. Texas, away from the Cotton Bowl for the first time in eight years, received a rude comeuppance from number six-rated Auburn in the form of a 27-3 pasting. The Alabama Tigers were one of five Southeastern Conference teams in postseason bowls.

Pro Football. Before the first shoulder hit a training-camp tackling sled, it appeared certain the fifty-fourth National Football League (NFL) campaign would be a difficult, dissonant season.

In July the NFL Players' Association, which represents the league's veterans, struck the owners when their four-year collective bargaining agreement ended without resolution. The players' group issued a list of sixty-three demands, and the camps started with rookies and free agents. The veterans busied themselves by picketing the camp sites while their lawyers haggled with management.

The annual College All-Star game was canceled and exhibitions were staged without stars in front of small audiences.

As the regular season approached, federal mediator W. J. Usery, Jr., suggested a two-week cooling-off period

FRANCO HARRIS (32) of the Pittsburgh Steelers is stopped for a loss in this first quarter carry against the Minnesota Vikings in Super Bowl IX. Throwing a block is the Steelers' John Kolb (55).

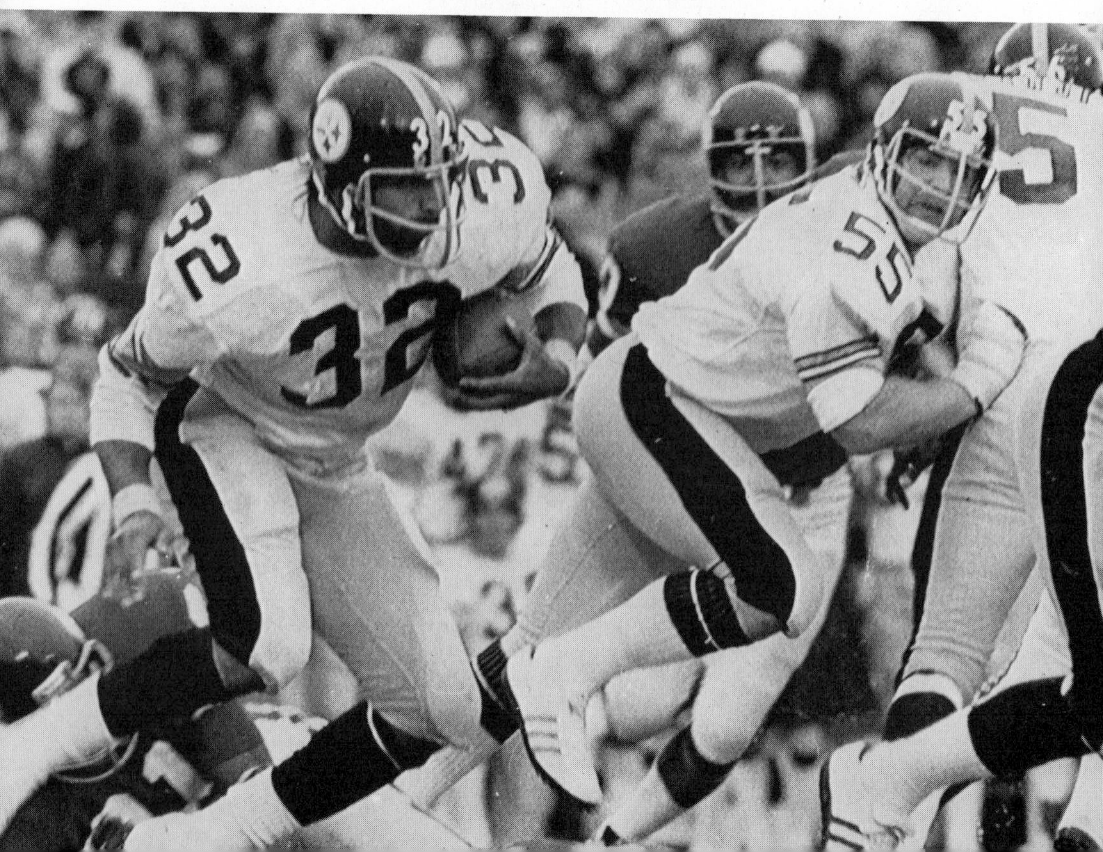

FOOTBALL

which the players accepted. After a fortnight, the veterans decided to remain in camp, thus ending the unsettled strike.

Chief among the players' complaints was the "Rozelle rule," whereby Commissioner Pete Rozelle compensates a team when a man plays out the option year of his contract, signs with another club, and the two teams cannot agree on an exchange. At year's end, the players won an apparent victory on this front. A federal district court judge in San Francisco handed down a decision on an antitrust suit brought by former New England quarterback Joe Kapp that declared the Rozelle rule illegal.

Another thorn — much smaller as it turned out — in the side of the NFL was the World Football League (WFL), a rival pro circuit which started in late summer with twelve teams and attendant dreams of glory. The dreams all but drowned in a sea of red ink when the rival league lost an estimated $20 million, and prospects for a second season appeared dim at best.

Birmingham beat Florida 22-21 in the WFL World Bowl, but Florida won the battle of back checks. The winners had not been paid in three and a half months, the losers in five weeks.

When the NFL season began it seemed the rancorous summer had left its scar on the traditional pro powers. Miami, winners of the last two Super Bowls, discovered that Toronto (which later moved to Memphis) of the WFL had signed fullback Larry Csonka, running back Jim Kiick, and flanker Paul Warfield for a combined $3 million to perform in 1975. Then the champion Dolphins lost their first game to upstart New England.

That same Sunday, Buffalo squeezed past Oakland, another defending division champion. St. Louis, which hadn't won a title since 1948 when the Cardinals were in Chicago, jumped off to seven straight victories. New England won five in a row off the mark, counting Miami, Los Angeles, and Minnesota—a trio of past and future playoff teams—among its victims.

But as the season wore on, the old headliners reasserted themselves. Miami, Oakland, Los Angeles, and Pittsburgh repeated as division titlists, and Washington made the playoffs again. The Cardinals had to defeat the Giants on the final Sunday to edge the Redskins for the NFC East crown. Miami stopped last year's record runner O. J. Simpson and the Bills in both meetings to win again.

Most, but not all came back. Dallas lost three of its first four and relinquished its title to St. Louis. The biggest turnabout was Houston, which had compiled successive 1-13 records. Coach Sid Gillman and quarterback Dan Pastorini guided the Oilers to a 7-7 mark, including a victory over Pittsburgh and two over Cincinnati. The inability to beat Houston kept the Bengals out of postseason play.

A final sour note was sounded on the last Sunday in Atlanta when some 10,000 turned out to watch the Falcons beat the once-mighty Packers in a driving rain. The game was a sellout, but 48,830 stayed home, a "no-show" record in the second season without the home television blackout in effect.

The Playoffs. In the minds of many, the Super Bowl was played on the opening day of the playoffs when Oakland, often a bridesmaid, stopped Miami from advancing to its third straight title game.

It was superior football after a season filled with boredom and lower television ratings. The lead changed six times as the Raiders won 28-26 by scoring in the final twenty-six seconds. Quarterback Ken Stabler completed six passes in a row in the last drive, three to his wide receiver Fred Biletnikoff, who had earlier

MINNESOTA'S ALAN PAGE sacks Pittsburgh quarterback Terry Bradshaw (12) during first quarter action in Super Bowl IX.

caught one for a touchdown.

Stabler's last, though, was a soft, wobbly, floater thrown as he was being tackled from behind. Clarence Davis outwrestled two defenders for the ball in the end zone. Rookie Nat Moore had run the opening kickoff back eighty-nine yards for a touchdown and the Dolphins had led 16-14 after three quarters.

Pittsburgh routed Buffalo 32-14, scoring twenty-six points in the second quarter. Quarterback Terry Bradshaw paced the Steeler blitz, complemented by running backs Rocky Bleier and Franco Harris. Bleier, a wounded Vietnam veteran, caught a touchdown pass and Harris plunged for three scores. The immovable Pitt defense held Simpson to forty-nine yards in fifteen carries.

Minnesota and Los Angeles survived the first round of the National Conference playoffs. The Vikings ended St. Louis's visions of Super Bowl grandeur by converting two turnovers into ten points within sixty seconds. Again the second quarter was pivotal as Fran Tarkenton threw two scoring passes to flanker John Gilliam in a 30-14 victory.

Los Angeles eliminated Washington 19-10 on the strength of defensive tackle Merlin Olsen, who made three key plays —forcing a fumble, intercepting, and sacking quarterback Sonny Jurgensen. Ram linebacker Isiah Robertson picked off Jurgensen's pass and ran it back fifty-nine yards for a touchdown.

The conference title games produced a newcomer a and three-times repeater for Super Bowl IX. Minnesota, the Dolphins' victim in SB VIII, bored past Los Angeles 14-10 in a game with eight fumbles and three pass interceptions.

The winners fumbled five times, but recovered three; the Rams lost three of three and contributed two interceptions. Tarkenton hit Jim Lash for twenty-nine yards and the first score. Dave Osborn dived over from one inch in the fourth quarter, and that was all the sturdy Viking defense needed.

The Steelers sealed their first conference title in forty-two years by shutting off Oakland's ground game and scoring three times in the fourth quarter for a

NATIONAL FOOTBALL LEAGUE STANDINGS

Final

NATIONAL CONFERENCE

East Division

	W	L	T	Pct.
St. Louis	10	4	0	.714
Washington	10	4	0	.714
Dallas	8	6	0	.571
Philadelphia	7	7	0	.500
N.Y. Giants	2	12	0	.143

Central Division

	W	L	T	Pct.
Minnesota	10	4	0	.714
Detroit	7	7	0	.500
Green Bay	6	8	0	.429
Chicago	4	10	0	.286

West Division

	W	L	T	Pct.
Los Angeles	10	4	0	.714
San Francisco	6	8	0	.429
New Orleans	5	9	0	.357
Atlanta	3	11	0	.214

AMERICAN CONFERENCE

East Division

	W	L	T	Pct.
Miami	11	3	0	.786
Buffalo	9	5	0	.643
New England	7	7	0	.500
N.Y. Jets	7	7	0	.500
Baltimore	2	12	0	.143

Central Division

	W	L	T	Pct.
Pittsburgh	10	3	1	.750
Cincinnati	7	7	0	.500
Houston	7	7	0	.500
Cleveland	4	10	0	.286

West Division

	W	L	T	Pct.
Oakland	12	2	0	.857
Denver	7	6	1	.536
Kansas City	5	9	0	.357
San Diego	5	9	0	.357

24-13 victory. The entire Raider team gained just twenty-nine yards in twenty-one attempts. Pitt's last two touchdowns were set up when J. T. Thomas and Jack Ham picked off Stabler passes.

Oakland's loss was its fifth straight in the American Conference title game, dating back to 1968. Their four previous conquerors all went on to win the Super Bowl.

SUPER BOWL IX — The Steelers ended forty-two years of frustration by dumping Minnesota 16-6 in the New Orleans spectacle, the third Super Bowl setback in three tries for the Vikings. Again it was Pittsburgh's impregnable "Steel Curtain" defense which salvaged the N.F.L. title trophy for popular owner Art Rooney.

Pitt's front four of Joe Greene, L. C. Greenwood, Ernie Holmes, and Dwight White held the Vikings to 17 net yards in twenty-one carries, forced three fumbles, three interceptions, and deflected four passes. The Vikings' only score came on a blocked punt early in the fourth quarter.

The Steelers didn't exactly overwhelm Minnesota on offense, though Harris set a Super Bowl record with 158 yards rushing. The lone score in the first half was a two-point Steeler safety when Tarkenton fell on his own fumble in the end zone. They made it 9-0 when Marv Kellum recovered Bill Brown's fumble of the second half kickoff and four plays later Harris skirted nine yards around left end.

The final drive of the season, seven minutes after Minnesota scored, was capped by Bradshaw's four-yard pass to Tight End Larry Brown. The key play, in the drive and perhaps the game, was a thirty-yard completion to Brown at the Vikes' 28. Brown fumbled, but Minnesota's recovery was nullified when officials ruled the fumble occurred after the whistle. Thus Pittsburgh marched on to the end zone and the long-awaited victory.

Gerald Ford

BORN on July 14, 1913, the same year as Richard Nixon, Leslie King, Jr., was two years old when this picture was taken. His parents had just been divorced.

THE FUTURE PRESIDENT plays with his dog at age three. His stepfather had adopted him and given him his name.

IN THIS HOUSE in Grand Rapids, Mich., the boy who was to become the thirty-eighth president of the United States spent much of his childhood. His mother had remarried and the boy's new stepfather was Gerald Rudolph Ford, the owner of a Grand Rapids paint store.

AS A CENTER for the University of Michigan, Ford helped the Wolverines win the national championship in 1932 and 1933 and was named most valuable player in his senior year.

CONGRESSMAN-ELECT FORD shows his bride the Capitol. He met the former Elizabeth Bloomer while she was helping with his campaign, and they were married on October 15, 1948.

THE REPUBLICAN CONGRESSMAN from Michigan, freshman year, 1949. Before coming to Washington, Ford had earned his law degree from Yale University (1941), served in the Navy during World War II, and practiced law in Michigan for several years. For the next twenty-five years his constituents returned him to Congress with majorities of 60 percent.

ELECTED HOUSE MINORITY LEADER in 1965, Ford receives a pen used by President Lyndon Johnson to sign the bill setting up the Herbert Hoover National Historic Site at West Branch, Iowa.

WITH PRESIDENT RICHARD NIXON watching, Gerald Ford takes the oath of office as fortieth vice-president of the United States on December 6, 1973. He was the first non-elected vice-president to take office under the twenty-fifth amendment.

NINE MONTHS LATER, Betty and Gerald Ford wave farewell as a helicopter takes President Nixon from the White House after his resignation on August 9. Later that day Ford was sworn in as the thirty-eighth U.S. president.

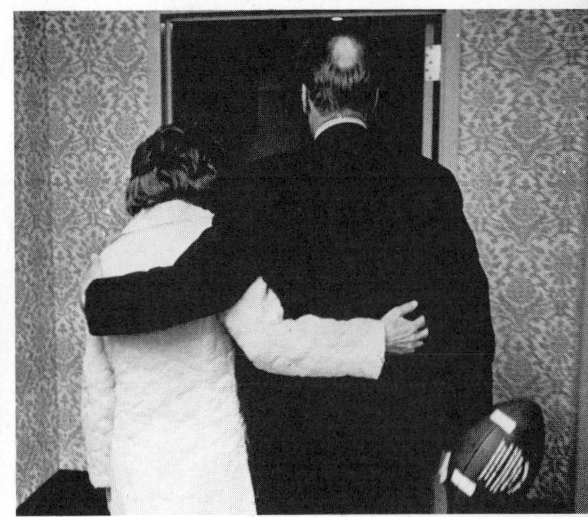

"A FULL, FREE, AND ABSOLUTE PARDON" for Richard Nixon was signed by President Ford on September 8. His clemency caused a sudden and severe dip in his popularity with the American people.

IN SEPTEMBER Betty Ford was operated on for breast cancer. The president, holding the game ball from the Washington Redskins game with Denver, visited her in Bethesda Naval Hospital's presidential suite.

THE FIRST FAMILY: Jack, twenty-two; Steve, eighteen; Mrs. Betty Ford; the president; Susan, seventeen; daughter-in-law Gayle; and her husband Michael, twenty-four.

FORD

IN MEETING THE PRESS, Ford is friendly and at ease. Observers expected his administration to be more open than Nixon's and more attuned to Congress and the American people.

WITH HIS GOLDEN RETRIEVER *Liberty* at his side, Ford studies budget statistics at his desk in the oval office of the White House. Grappling with the shaky U.S. economy was to be one of the president's major problems in the year ahead.

Ford Administration

DRAFT EVADER Doug Bittle returned from Canada in September to take advantage of President Ford's amnesty plan. Of the 12,500 deserters and evaders (now officially called absentees) eligible, only 1,989 had applied for clemency by December 7. The deadline for application was January 31, 1975.

by
GODFREY SPERLING, JR.

Washington Bureau Chief,
Christian Science Monitor

The Ford Style. The new president had been in office only a few days, and he was meeting with the press for the first time. Soon the question that the American people were waiting to have answered was asked:

"Mr. President," a reporter queried, "What do you plan to do as president to see to it that we have no further Watergates?" There was no pause before the reply. Gerald Ford, quite clearly, had been waiting eagerly to express his views on this vital subject.

"Well," he said, "I indicated that one, we would have an open administration. I will be as candid and as forthright as I possibly can. I will expect any individuals in my administration to be exactly the same. There will be no tightly controlled operation of the White House staff. I have a policy of seeking advice from a number of top members of my staff. There will be no one person, nor any limited number of individuals, who make decisions. I will make the decisions and take the blame for them or whatever benefit might be the case." A slight pause here and then he added:

"I said in one of my speeches after the swearing in, there would be no illegal wiretaps, there would be none of the other things that to a degree helped to precipitate the Watergate crisis."

Here the reporter followed up with this question: "Do you plan to set up a code of ethics for the executive branch?"

Setting his jaw firmly and speaking with resolve, the president answered:

"The code of ethics that will be followed will be the example I set."

So it was that the new president, right from the outset, set the theme of his administration. He was telling Americans that his approach would be just the opposite of his predecessor's. Unlike Richard Nixon, he was saying, he would be open and aboveboard. Further, he, as president, was accepting the responsibility of setting a high, ethical example that would set the moral tone of the new government in Washington.

So it was, too, that an earnest, sincere Gerald Ford rallied Americans of both parties and all varieties to his side. Polls showed that three-fourths of the public approved of the way he was handling the presidency. And only about 4 percent disapproved. Ford was riding high. Observers in Washington were calling the new, hopeful attitude sweeping the nation an era of good feeling.

The new president was off to a remarkably good start.

And then, as is inevitable with presidents as they begin to make decisions, this widespread support subsided.

However, this president did not nibble away at his popularity.

The Pardon of Nixon. Instead, within a few days of his first press conference, he announced over television that he was pardoning Richard Nixon for any Watergate-related crimes he may have committed.

It was a stunning announcement, particularly since, at the press conference, the president had indicated that he intended to let the legal processes run their course before considering the option of a pardon.

Ford gave this explanation for the sudden shift in direction: that, in mercy, he decided he would not put Nixon through the anguish of waiting for a pardon which he—the president—had decided would be eventually forthcoming.

Sources close to the president at the time said there was an additional reason, a reason he later emphasized in a dramatic appearance before the House: Ford thought that by pardoning Nixon he could get Watergate behind him so that he could give full attention to urgent problems facing the nation, particularly soaring prices and the stagnant economy.

But the president clearly misjudged the national mood. Instead of ending the public obsession with Watergate, he put the issue right back on the front burner of public attention.

Polls indicated that the only Americans who welcomed the pardon were those who made up that one-fifth of the nation which still supported Nixon at the time he resigned.

Among the others the dissent was, largely, an angry one.

Many people felt that Richard Nixon should not have been entitled to any special privileges. This complaint was usually worded: "Just because he was president he should not be above the law."

Many people, too, saw in the pardon an extension of the Watergate cover-up. This complaint was often phrased in this way: "Without Nixon being tried, we will never find out the facts now."

Other dissenters were concerned over what the Nixon pardon would do to the trials of other Watergate defendants—that, perhaps, they would be fatally flawed to the point that convictions would not stand up on appeal.

There were charges, too, in some quarters that the pardon was the result of a secret "deal" between Nixon, when he was still president, and his then vice-president, Gerald Ford.

New polls showed Ford taking the biggest drop in popularity ever recorded in such a short length of time. He was now down to barely over 50 percent and, apparently, still descending in public favor.

At a new press conference the president admitted he had miscalculated the amount of public disfavor his pardon would evoke. But he still stuck to his guns on what he saw as the rightness of his decision. It was the merciful thing to do, he said again.

The president denied that he had tied his decision to reports of Nixon's failing health—although he said he was aware of such reports.

The president said he had acted alone. Not only did he so act—but it soon became apparent that all of the Ford inner-circle of advisors, both in and outside the White House, were opposed to the decision. They had not been consulted. And they were all upset when they heard what the president had done.

Within a few days the president, again on his own, was dropping a hint that he might issue a blanket pardon to all Watergate-related defendants.

A Ford statement issued through his new press secretary, Ron Nessen—his first press secretary, Jerald terHorst, had resigned in protest of the pardon decision—that such a pardon was under study, was widely interpreted as a prelude to a blanket act of clemency.

And, again, the negative stir across the country was immense. This time the president appeared to pull back, asserting that no blanket pardon was ever contemplated—that he merely was saying that in accordance with what was only routine, he would naturally study any Watergate-related request for a pardon that might come to his attention.

Here, too, Ford advisors said that had they been consulted they would have sought to prevail on the president not to get into the subject at all—and thus avoid the tempest that was certain to follow.

The Amnesty. Even before the pardon the president had dipped into controversy by indicating he favored a qualified amnesty for Vietnam draft dodgers and deserters.

This, of course, hurt Ford among the old, hard core of Nixon supporters.

The Economic Proposals. It was against this background of fading public approval that Ford moved into his greatest challenge, that of dealing with the economy.

First, he set up a number of presummit meetings, bringing forth an input of recommendations from a wide variety of economic experts and interested parties from across the nation.

Then, in late September the president himself presided over a summit meeting of economy-related experts and American leaders.

From the suggestions coming out of all these meetings the president and his top economic assistants then came up with a number of proposals, most controversial of which was a request that Congress pass a 5 percent surcharge on family incomes of $15,000 and above.

The president also asked for an increase in public service jobs for the poor, a remedy for unemployment; and for legislation that would encourage business investment and home building. And he clearly put himself behind a policy of relaxed, not stiff, interest rates.

Was this the right medicine to deal with runaway inflation? Was it too much? Was it not enough? How much of this would Congress enact?

These were all questions yet unanswered as Congress took a preelection break. It was to return for a rump session in November and December. But few observers in Washington thought there was time in such a session for much economy-related legislation to be passed and put into effect.

France

FRENCH PRESIDENT VALERY GISCARD D'ESTAING, left and West German Chancellor Helmut Schmidt face the press after a series of talks on French-German relations and the European Common Market in June.

by
BRIAN WEINSTEIN

Associate Professor
Howard University
Author of *Eboue* (1971) and Coauthor of *Introduction to African Politics: A Continental Approach* (1974)

From Pompidou to Giscard. Speculation about President Georges Pompidou's health continued from 1973 into 1974 as his physical appearance deteriorated. Trips within France and without and vigorous speechmaking belied predictions of his resignation or death. At Poitiers in January he announced new economic measures, notably his decision to float French currency which meant the end of fixed parities between the franc and other monies of the world. The president then asked for the resignation of his prime minister, Pierre Messmer, amid growing complaints about the weakness of the government. Against all predictions he reappointed Messmer instead of the powerful minister of finance, Valéry Giscard d'Estaing, who waited coolly on the sidelines.

Suddenly, at the very end of March the president's secretary began to cancel appointments for him, and it was reported he had been moved by ambulance to his private home. On April 2 he died. Georges Pompidou was then quietly and simply buried near his country home.

Although the disappearance of the second president of the Fifth Republic opened no floodgates of emotion as had General Charles de Gaulle's death three years before, it did unleash the politicians of all parties and groups in the scramble to replace him. As Alain Poher, president of the senate, once again fairly and serenely presided over the presidency of the republic, as the constitution stipulates, Gaullist rule of France came briskly to an end.

The Gaullist UDR (Union for the Defense of the Republic) party, in control of the National Assembly, tried to put forward one strong candidate, but calls for continuing unity went unheeded as ambition ruled other feelings. Jacques Chaban-Delmas announced his candidacy shortly after the president's death, then Pierre Messmer, and Edgar Fauré. Finally all withdrew except Chaban-Delmas, mayor of Bordeaux, World War II companion of General de Gaulle, and former prime minister. The leader of the Independent Republican party, Valéry Giscard d'Estaing offered his name, and François Mitterand was the clear choice of the unified Left. There were nine other candidates ranging from environmentalist Professor René Dumont to Jean Royer, ultraconservative. Until he was disqualified, one candidate claimed to represent the cultural minorities of the country.

Giscard proved himself to be more dynamic and less conservative than was previously believed. He emphasized his relative youth—forty-nine years of age, compared with François Mitterand's fifty-seven and Chaban-Delmas's fifty-nine. He promised new rights for women, more aid to the old and the handicapped, better conditions for workers, and improved urban planning. His opponents attacked him, saying that he had had many years in the government to undertake all the reforms he claimed he would undertake as president. He had been President de Gaulle's and President Pompidou's minister of finance and had not shown any particular reforming zeal. Nonetheless, he and François Mitterand won the most votes: Mitterand received 43 percent of the 25,775,000 votes cast, Giscard 32.6 percent, and Chaban-Delmas only 15 percent for the first round of the elections on May 5.

Because no candidate obtained a majority of the votes cast, a second round between the two highest vote-getters was scheduled for two weeks later. Giscard and Mitterand debated the issues on television while Giscard worked to mobilize UDR votes for himself. Whispered treats of a Communist takeover of France should Mitterand be elected became shouts as public opinion experts showed that the election would be extremely close. In the second ballot on May 19 a record 25 million Frenchmen voted, with only about 15 percent abstaining.

Giscard barely won. His margin of victory was only 200,000. Mitterand thus won 49.3 percent of the popular vote. Considerable credit for the victory, razor-thin as it was, was given to Michel Poniatowski, or "Ponia," an old friend of Giscard from his days as a student in the Ecole Nationale d'Administration. Depressed Gaullists were unsure about the future while a disappointed Left promised further challenges.

Pompidoulians to Giscardians: A Sixth Republic? President Valéry Giscard d'Estaing began his seven-year term of office with gestures of informality and innovation which brought no basic changes. He asked his compatriots to suspend judgment of him and his cabinet for 500 days during which time he would set France on a new course.

In deference to the Gaullists he named one of their number, Jacques Chirac, to be his prime minister, but at the same time he made clear his intention to treat him as a subordinate. He then named a woman, Simone Veil, to be minister of health in a cabinet numbering fifteen ministers and twenty-one secretaries of state. He appointed another woman,

Françoise Giroud, who had supported Mitterand for president, to be secretary of state for woman's affairs, a new position. He also created a ministry for growing problems of pollution, noise, and congestion and called it the ministry for *qualité de vie* or quality of life.

In order to reassure African countries of France's continuing interest in aid programs, Giscard raised the Secretariat for Cooperation to a full-fledged ministry. African states had been concerned about their future relationship with France, because the president abolished the Secretariat for African Affairs headed by the powerful Gaullist, Jacques Foccart, but the new ministry would take up the slack. On the other hand, Giscard's orientation did seem to most to be toward Europe, the Mediterranean, and America, as well as toward the solution of many internal problems in France.

To help solve domestic problems, the president appointed his close friend Michel Poniatowski to be minister of the interior, probably the most important post in the cabinet. This ministry is a key to France's centralized system of government because of its control over the police and the prefects who head the administrative districts. To show that he had a more liberal outlook than his predecessors, Ponia announced an end to most of the telephone taps. People who used to boast that they were important enough to have their telephones tapped thus lost one sign of their prestige.

To symbolize the importance of France's relationships with Germany, Giscard appointed France's ambassador to Bonn as minister of foreign affairs. Germans and Frenchmen who support the idea of a united Europe were pleased with the appointment of Jean Sauvagnargues to this post because of his close ties with the Germans and because of his well-known work for a more European economic community. Jean-Jacques Servan-Schreiber, who has similar ideas, was also appointed to the cabinet for what must have been one of the shortest terms of office in French ministerial history. This dynamic journalist, writer, and head of the middle-of-the-road Radical party has long opposed France's nuclear tests so that when the government announced the resumption of the Pacific tests, he promptly criticized the action in a press conference. Giscard unceremoniously fired him just thirteen days after he was named to the cabinet.

Some of the innovations then undertaken by Giscard and his cabinet seemed purely cosmetic albeit useful. After his election, for example, the president spoke in English to symbolize his lack of the chauvinism for which the Gaullists had been famous. He walked to his inauguration in a plain business suit thus shunning the expected pomp and circumstance. He spent a day in a submerged nuclear submarine to show how safe it was and how important for France. And, he inaugurated cabinet meetings outside of Paris, the first in Lyon, to show that he intended to decentralize the government.

In another gesture of decentralization, the new government approved the breaking up of the famous ORTF (French Radio and Television Office), which monopolized broadcasting. The ORTF was well known for its attempts to stifle the views of those opposed to government policy, and some thought that the media of communication might eventually reflect more diverse opinion than in the past. Giscard also ordered an end to construction of the highways through Paris which his predecessor had vigorously promoted to the consternation of architects, Parisians, and all people around the world who view the French capital as one of the most beautiful cities on the planet. He also promised a more attractive development for Les Halles,

A FRENCH BUTCHER cuts up a side of beef in a Paris shop. At 3,600 *boucheries chevalines* (horsemeat butcher shops) Frenchmen buy horsemeat because they feel it is good for their health. (French doctors began prescribing horsemeat as a "fortifier" in the mid-nineteenth century.) Per capita consumption of horsemeat in France in 1974 was about 4½ pounds a year, compared to about 15½ pounds of beef.

the market area of Paris.

Significantly, the new government led the National Assembly to lower the official age of adulthood from twenty-one to eighteen and to liberalize restrictions on abortion. A 1920 law prohibited all abortions in the country, but Giscard ordered an end to prosecutions of women for having them. Further, he proposed that women could legally have an abortion up to the tenth week of pregnancy even though there might be no threat to their lives or health in letting the pregnancy continue. After the tenth week abortions could be performed only in case of a threat to the woman's life. Because some Roman Catholic groups are very powerful in this nominally Catholic country and because one of the pillars of Gaullism has been the need for a larger French population, the proposal ran into trouble. It passed the legislature after the government agreed to remove provisions that would have permitted reimbursement of medical expenses under social security.

Giscard's ministers continued a study of educational reform begun in the previous government. At issue were the secondary schools and the *bac* or diploma examination given. Amid reports that conditions for these lycee students are the worst in Europe, the minister of education proposed two basic streams of education—university-oriented and non-university-oriented. The former group would receive a highly academic education, while the latter would be encouraged to choose a trade. Protests came immediately from those who saw this reform as a technique to maintain a certain elite in power and to deny poorer people even the hope that their children might get a university degree. More than 30,000 high school students had marched through Paris to protest the project when it was first proposed by Pompidou's minister of education, but René Haby, the new minister, said he would propose similar changes.

Despite these and other plans for change, and despite a seemingly increased informality in the government, the most important problems went unresolved. Near the end of a most difficult year 89 percent of the French people polled believed the most important problem would not be solved in the near future. This issue was, of course, the economic crisis caused by a rate of inflation in France of nearly 15 percent per year which was in large part caused by the oil crisis.

Oil. Fueling the fires of inflation was the petroleum price increase. About 70 percent of France's energy is imported in the form of petroleum from Arab countries. Since the end of the war in Algeria in 1964 relations between France and the Arabs had steadily improved. France purchased oil and gas from Algeria and from other oil-producing countries such as Saudi Arabia.

After the six-day war in the Middle East in 1967, France turned more openly and enthusiastically toward the Arabs, hoping to become a major influence in an area where America was viewed with intense hostility. France rushed to sell arms to the Arabs and refused to supply arms to the Israelis. France claimed neutrality, but sold jets to Libya, who had no pilots to fly them. Most analysts knew these airplanes would go to Egypt. French businessmen and technicians flew into Saudi Arabia and elsewhere. In the United Nations France sided most often with the Arabs on key matters. In his September 23 speech before the U. N. General Assembly, French Foreign Minister Jean Sauvagnargues said that although all countries should live in peace with "secure and recognized boundaries," his own government "believes it is high time for the international community to recognize the legitimate aspirations of the Palestinian people . . ."

Outside the United Nations France engaged in intense bilateral negotiations with the Arabs. Michel Jobert, Pompidou's last foreign minister, had traveled to Saudi Arabia, and his successor traveled to Beirut to meet with Yasir Arafat, head of the Palestine Liberation Organization (PLO), thus giving more prestige to the latter. At the U. N. debate concerning Palestine France abstained rather than vote pro or con on the resolution allowing the PLO observer status.

In Paris President Giscard d'Estaing welcomed the Shah of Iran. In discussions about economic matters they agreed that over the next three years Iran will deposit a total of $1 billion in the Bank of France. Furthermore, France agreed to build nuclear power plants in Iran and a subway in Teheran, the capital, and to sell goods and technical skills to the country. The total price will be $4 billion, thus bringing Iran and France much closer together than they have ever been. France also hoped for closer relations between the Arab League and the Common Market countries after meetings between the two groups at the end of 1974 and the beginning of 1975.

While trying to ensure a continuing flow of petroleum into France, other measures were being taken to conserve energy and even to cut down on imports. For example, the government announced it would try to decrease oil imports by 10 percent. It also rushed to finish construction of the new oil port of Antifer near Le Havre. Antifer will serve the supertankers and will be a refining center. Pipelines extending into Belgium and Germany will supply some oil to these countries.

Meanwhile France attended conferences sponsored by the United States, but tried to challenge American leadership and American projects for joint efforts concerning oil. Giscard criticized American attempts to set up an association of oil-consuming countries and insisted that one organization should bring consumers and producers together.

But, oil prices went up for France as for other countries. The search for oil in France and offshore brought no great discoveries yet. Other prices rose accordingly, and the country was in no mood to hear anyone criticize the quality of its exports, notably its arms and airplanes.

No wonder that most French people reacted violently to General Paul Stehlin's suggestion that North Atlantic Treaty Organization (NATO) countries ought to purchase a new American fighter airplane rather than a French airplane. Stehlin, a vice-president of the National Assembly and distinguished member of the UDR party, had submitted a memorandum to the president of France analyzing the relative merits of the American and French fighters. His conclusion that the American airplane is superior brought forth a storm, and as a result he had to resign his post in the National Assembly. Leading Gaullists refused to shake hands with him, the ultimate insult in France. An attempt was allegedly made on the life of his son.

Strikes. Naturally, the 15 percent increase in prices brought about largely by the inflation of oil prices impelled labor unions, notably the communist-led General Confederation of Labor (CGT), to demand higher wages. The possible disruptive results of unreasonable demands fit into the Communists' desire to reshape French society. Refusals on the part of owners and government brought strikes at the Saviem truck manufacturing corporation. Students joined the strikers and tried to form links which might lead to a general strike similar to that of May, 1968. Workers here and elsewhere demanded more money and a guaranteed annual wage, and the government made the extraordinary promise that it would guarantee the salary for one whole year of those who become unemployed.

Workers of the Credit Lyonnais, one of the largest banking systems in France, struck for a different reason. Management-introduced computers threatened many jobs, and workers protested. The luxury liner *France* was taken out of service but not before its crew and employees protested by seizing the vessel, an act similar to the takeover of the Lip watch company last year. (The Lip affair had been more or less settled by the company's incorporation into a larger conglomerate.)

In urban areas apartment tenants refused to pay their monthly rents because of a 30 percent increase due to fuel costs. In rural areas farmers demonstrated because of a constant decline in their income as the famous French middle men swept up the profits realized from higher prices. Postal employees then went on strike, leaving a country which is accustomed to what is probably the world's most efficient postal service without the daily mail. The large Neogravure printing firm then closed, so that many magazines were not being printed. To top it all off, the trash collectors struck, and thus all the labor troubles took on a new odor.

Events in Great Britain affected the French economy. The government across the channel changed and threatened to leave the Common Market as well as to give up its support of the Concorde airplane, a joint Franco-British project. If the Concorde were dropped, French unemployment would rise above the estimated 600,000 already out of work. In the end, it seemed the British might not leave the Common Market and that sixteen airplanes would be produced. Perhaps only the oil producers would be able to purchase the mammoth airplanes.

Other Social Disorders were less directly related to the economy, but they contributed to the general pessimism hanging over France like storm clouds. Prison uprisings led people to investigate conditions within these institutions. And, on the island of Corsica, bombings and other disorders occurred as people objected to Paris policies and high prices. The government reacted by suppressing ethnic movements in Corsica, in Brittany, and in the Basque country along the Spanish frontier.

During his press conference on October 24 President Giscard d'Estaing summed up the feelings of his government and the people of France. He admitted the crises his country and the world face will not soon pass away; they are the result of population growth, shortages, lack of food, and financial deficits in industrial countries. He suggested France might be willing to give up some sovereignty to a confederal Europe and that it would press forward to promote agreement on oil between producers and consumers. But he admitted he saw no easy solution and added that according to his calculations the world is heading toward catastrophe.

The Brighter Side. All was not gloom. In spite of the economic situation, exports of French clothing increased, and the governing Independent Republicans were cheered by reported tensions between Communists and Socialists in the supposedly united Left.

Although the country lost one brilliant composer with the death of Darius Milhaud, another figure in music, Pierre Boulez, agreed to come home from America to head an electronic research center. A giant of French theater, Jean-Louis Barrault, opened a new theater in the Gare d'Orsay railway station. A new film by Jean Yanne, *Les Chinois à Paris* which tells the story of a supposed Chinese invasion of France in a humorous way, was not considered at all humorous by the very serious representatives of the Chinese Peoples' Republic, who threatened to refuse visas.

Another film, *Lacombe, Lucien,* was the latest in a series about the effects of German occupation in World War II. The treatment of Lacombe who, more out of boredom than anything else, joins a group of Frenchmen working for the German police, reflected the self-questioning and subtle criticism which began most spectacularly with *Le Chagrin et la Pitie.* These echoes of World War II became real when Beate Klarsfeld tried to kidnap a former Nazi who had been condemned in France for the alleged murder of countless French citizens. A large delegation from France attended the trial of Klarsfeld, and many Frenchmen protested her condemnation by a German court.

The irreverent had a last laugh when a distinguished cardinal of the Roman Catholic church, Jean Danielou, unfortunately died from a heart attack in a beautiful dancer's apartment. Amid suspicions that important figures in the church were not exactly following rules of celibacy, red-faced clerics denied there had been anything improper about his visit.

All Frenchmen — reverent and irreverent — might have stopped to think about problems of leadership when a new Paris airport was officially opened. The capital's third large airport, built at a cost of more than $325 million, was named after General Charles de Gaulle. The name still evoked strong images and strong passions pro and con, but no one could deny that the age of the political giants seemed to be over, although France, like other countries of the West, needed strong inspiration and direction to help preserve its values and integrity in a world turned upside down.

GARAGE SALES

THE FAMILY GARAGE has turned into everyone's favorite discount supermarket.

The Garage Sale is a modern American development. The term is used for any sale where a large number of items are offered at small prices. Depending on location it might be called a lawn sale, or basement, backyard, porch, barn, carport, or patio sale.

Everyone wins—the buyer and the seller. The buyer may be enabled to furnish or decorate her home at little cost, clothe her family in fine style, pick up presents, match a missing plate from a set of china, and sometimes find a real treasure. The seller can clean out the attic, basement, garage, dresser drawers, and closets, and make money at the same time.

There are several reasons why buying and selling second-hand goods is so popular. There no longer is a stigma attached to purchasing used goods as there was in the past. People by choice or necessity may prefer to pay less for something new or slightly used at a sale than to buy it at current high prices in a store. Older items were often made better than their modern counterparts, and will last longer. Then, too, the warm, human expression of love found in a handmade item is becoming more valued in our more materialistic, plastic world. Affluence has enabled many persons to have second homes in the woods, by the lake, or in the mountains. Garage sales provide an excellent source for that second set of everything. Environmental control has convinced many that it is better to recycle through a garage sale than through a junkyard. One man's junk is another man's treasure. Anything can be sold. Anything will be bought.

Going to a Garage Sale. Imagination and vision play a big part in the successful quest for needs or knicknacks. The buyer should try to picture some items in roles other than the ones they were made for. Many things can be converted into plant holders, coffee tables, lamps, and wall hangings, for example. She should learn to bargain ("What is the least you'll take for this?" "I like this but it's too expensive. Will you take . . .?" and "I'll give you . . . for this whole batch of items."). Best buys are often seasonal, such as ice skates in the summer, or out of favor, such as silver goods that no one wants to polish anymore.

The shopper should read garage sale ads carefully so that she doesn't waste her time on any that are too far away or do not seem to offer things she has in mind. She also should plan to get to a sale early for the best choices. Sales are mostly cash-and-carry transactions. Personal checks are not accepted by many sellers because too many of them bounce. Boxes or paper bags in the car will help the buyer carry home everything without losing it en route. A tape measure helps immeasurably when deciding on an item of clothing or a piece of furniture.

Giving a Garage Sale is fun and satisfying if it is well organized. The following list may help:

1. Gather together the sale items.
2. Clean and repair merchandise.
3. Price the goods.
4. Place ads in newspapers and on bulletin boards in your area.

"WHAT does it mean, Doctor? I keep having this recurring dream that I'm always putting everything I have into a garage sale!"

5. Make and put up signs in the neighborhood.
6. Clean the garage (or other sale area).
7. Set up display tables and arrange articles and lighting.
8. Get plenty of change.
9. Have bags, boxes, packing material, paper, pencils, and tape measures available.
10. Open the garage door and sell!

If you are moving, or the house is full of things no one likes any longer; if objects have been outgrown or replaced, or you want some extra cash (perhaps to go to a garage sale), hold a sale. There is no positive way to predict what someone may want to buy, so accumulate all things you want to get rid of. Dishes, glasses, bowls, vases, pitchers, and mugs sell well singly or in sets. Small appliances are popular, and so are *Popular Mechanics, National Geographic,* and other magazines that do not outdate themselves rapidly. Books attract buyers, and so do used radios and TVs (men and boys like to tinker with them or use their parts to repair other sets they may have).

Antiques are fine if marked below shop prices. In fact, anything that is old is "in"—tin cracker boxes, antimacassars, shawls, bottles of various sizes, shapes, and shades, lead soldiers, mustache cups, and so on. People never seem to have enough tools or pieces of kitchen equipment (you can sell the gadgets that are so appealing in ads but which you never used, to someone who has always wanted them but would never pay full price).

Clothing moves rapidly, especially children's clothes. Young people like a variety of items, and if they are well worn, so much the better. If you are artistic, offer your own efforts. Desks, straight chairs, and chests sell themselves. And don't forget all the five to twenty-five cent goods for the neighborhood children—or adults—such as costume jewelry, toys, key rings, marbles, games, scarfs, door knobs, pet supplies, garden tools, and the like.

Everything should be as clean and in as good repair as you, a washing machine, needle and thread, glue, tape, soap and water, hammer, saw, nails, and screwdriver can make them. The more effort you put into preparing the items you want to sell, the bigger your profits.

Everything should be clearly marked, perhaps with little commercial white stickers or torn masking tape on hard materials, and stapled pieces of paper on clothing. Sizes on clothing, measurements on furniture, or any other pertinent information helps. Price articles as if you were seeing them at someone else's garage sale. What would they be worth there, divorced from your sentimental attachments? Some merchandise will be underpriced and some overpriced, but you will probably come out even. You will be rid of the cheap goods and the higher priced items leave room for negotiation. One garage sale expert advises pricing anything in good condition at one-fourth its original cost.

Place an ad in the local newspaper or weekly shopping news to run the day before the sale and each day it is on. Give the days, hours, location, and special features—if any—of your particular garage sale. Most sales run one to three days, with Saturday the best day, Sunday next, and Friday a good lead-in. A one-day sale is fine if you do not have too many items or too much time, but it can be very unproductive if the weather that one day is poor. Bulletin boards are available for thumbtacked advertisements in many grocery and drug stores, at churches, in youth centers, and many other spots. Make large posters that are easy to read from passing cars, and tack them to strategic trees or telephone posts.

The garage or other sale area must be as clean and open as possible. People prefer wandering in and out of readily accessible places to squeezing past the proprietor in a small spot. Displays should be as attractive and spread out as possible, and lighting should be bright. Don't leave anything around that you don't want to sell.

Be ready to open at the appointed hour, with plenty of cash on hand, and for safekeeping take money into the house from time to time during the sale. Customers will come in largest numbers early in the day and in spurts the rest of the time. If anything should happen to be left over, you can give a sigh of relief and be glad that it will be yours for a while longer—or you can give it to the Salvation Army. Or save it for your next garage sale.

Gardening

by
R. MILTON CARLETON

Research Director
Growth Systems, Inc.

High Prices and Shortages During 1974. American housewives were shocked to find prices for fresh produce at the highest level in history and still rising. Equally disturbing were actual shortages of such staples as potatoes, onions, lettuce, and cabbage — vegetables which housewives had always taken for granted would be freely available.

Adding to their uneasiness were newspaper reports of semistarvation and rumors of famine ahead for much of the world. Americans were told bluntly that they could no longer expect to enjoy lavish table but that production of this food-rich nation must be shared with hungry hordes of other lands, where populations kept swelling in numbers with each passing day.

One economist went so far as to urge abandoning cities for safety and survival in a crisis that might come even before preparations could be made to meet it. "Buy a farm at a safe distance from big cities, raise all your own food as far as you can, stock up on necessities that cannot be produced at home and sit out the chaos that is to come" were some of his recommendations.

Garden Boom. Spurred by cold facts and disturbing rumors, Americans tried to find answers. As one of the few actions possible for most families, they turned to growing their own vegetables. Estimates of the number of home vegetable gardens planted in the spring of 1974 range between 35 million and 40 million, exceeding those cultivated during World War II.

The sudden demand found seedsmen and suppliers of garden materials unprepared. To increase the supply of seeds requires two years, one to build up foundation stocks, a second to grow seeds for sale. By early spring of 1974, most seed bins were so low that remaining stocks were set aside for increased production to sell in 1975.

Similar shortages in tools and other equipment caught both manufacturers and dealers without enough to go around. Particularly critical was the fertilizer supply, which depended upon scarce chemicals, particularly crude oil, as raw materials.

In spite of these limitations, millions who had never before thrust a spade into the earth rushed into gardening on whatever bit of soil was available to them. As might have been expected, there were many failures, but the miracle was that percentagewise, these were amazingly low. An extensive survey shows that only one garden in twenty was considered a complete failure. Of the rest, three out of seventeen showed no actual savings in the value of produce consumed as against vegetables purchased on the open market. Of the latter, at least half the gardeners felt their efforts had not been wasted, since they not only ate fresher, tastier produce, but were sure of an adequate supply. Too, they were happy to share surpluses with friends and neighbors.

Successful Gardeners. Of those who felt their gardens were a success financially, crops produced had values ranging from slightly above cost up to five times the total of all purchased supplies. Those who showed the highest return were usually old-time gardeners who used every means of increasing and using what they had grown. They *planned* production to equal demand as contrasted with beginners who sowed once in spring and hoped this one sowing would feed them all summer.

CAULIFLOWER SNOW CROWN, an All-American winner for 1975 introduction, produces well-rounded, pure white heads a week earlier than other snowball types. In the stores, cauliflower is one of the costliest vegetables to buy, so growing your own makes good sense.

Highly successful gardeners not only seeded main crops of the most used vegetables, but resorted to catch crops, intercropping, and succession crops to use every inch of space productively.

A Catch Crop is an early vegetable seeded as soon as the soil can be worked in spring, one which can be harvested before a later one will need the space. For example, radishes can be sown early and harvested before the soil is warm enough to sow snap beans. Leaf lettuce can be harvested before cauliflower and fall cabbage are ready to transplant.

Intercrops occupy the same garden area for at least part of the same season. For example, tomatoes can be interplanted with leaf lettuce or turnips which will be out of the way before the tomato vines can spread. An interesting intercrop is radish seed sown in the same row as carrot seed. The latter germinates so slowly that the radishes will have been eaten before the carrots need the space.

Succession Crops. In addition to making full use of garden space, experienced growers do not overplant. Most beginners might sow a whole packet of Swiss chard seed, for example, and cultivate a twenty-five- to fifty-foot row, of which perhaps only ten feet will ever be used. A five-foot row of parsley is plenty for most families, but many a first-year garden will struggle with an unused twenty-five foot stretch of it. Instead of a fifty-foot row of snap beans, old-timers usually sow succession rows fifteen feet long every ten days.

Sowing Errors. When reasons for failures among first-time gardeners were analyzed, errors in sowing of seed were common. Planting too deep or too thick, as well as too early or too late, were common mistakes. Experienced gardeners once followed a rule of thumb, "Sow thick, thin quick." This was sound practice designed to avoid gaps in a row due to low seed germination. Today, practically all seeds are subject to government laws which penalize seeds of low vitality, so thinner sowing avoids the need to do severe thinning.

Pulling surplus seedlings disturbs the roots of those left standing so they are set back in growth or sometimes killed. To fill in an occasional gap, a few extra seeds at the end of the row will produce enough transplants for a solid row.

Another cause of reduced production among novice gardeners was too much dependence on purchased transplants instead of reliance on direct sowing of seeds. Although most commercial growers of bedding plants and vegetable transplants try to turn out reasonably good plants, in areas that remained cold and wet these often did not sell early and were overgrown, weak, and poorly fitted to grow by the time the weather changed.

WATERMELON YELLOW BABY, a bronze medal winner in the 1975 All-America selections, is sweet-flavored, long-lasting, and early-ripening, with fewer seeds than other "ice-box" watermelons. Color is an attractive, mouthwatering pineapple-yellow.

Although there are advantages to the use of transplants, this practice is not all gain. Like an operation on a human body, transplanting may place the seedling in a better condition to survive, but the plant needs time to recover afterwards. There is always a setback, often one severe enough to offset any gain in growth over direct-sown seedlings which have been spaced out properly.

Too-deep planting of seeds was a frequent cause of failure in new gardens. Experienced gardeners were found to be using the accepted standard of covering the seed with only enough soil to equal two to three times the smallest dimension of the seed. For example, while a squash seed might be over an inch long, it is so thin that it needs only about a quarter of an inch of soil over it. If the soil in which it is planted is stiff, heavy clay, even this covering may be too deep. The use of well-sifted compost or a mixture of half sand and half peat moss was frequently recommended by old-timers.

Even when seeds were planted at the proper depth, there were failures caused by a sinking of the seed into a soft, loose soil. Common practice calls for pressing down the soil in the furrow before sowing, using a rake handle or other tool to firm the row to prevent seeds from sinking.

Proper timing of seed sowing was particularly difficult to schedule in the spring of 1974, because of the unseasonably cold weather during May and June in many parts of the United States. Recommendations made in newspaper and magazine articles and in garden books call for waiting until May and June to plant seeds of tender crops such as snap beans, peppers, eggplant, cucumber, squash, melon, and okra. Inexperienced gardeners followed these recommendations to the letter, only to have their seeds rot in the ground.

Most experienced growers were aware of the possible effects of cold soil on such tender crops and either waited to sow them until the weather warmed up, or passed up first plantings entirely. The weather even affected cool weather crops. For example, in New England the traditional planting date for peas is St. Patrick's Day, March 17. There was snow on the ground in many locations on that date, but peas were sown in many gardens, only to rot. Even sowings in May failed in Maine, where peas are often several inches high at that time in normal years. The only successful plantings reported from May seeding were those that had been treated with a fungicide to prevent rotting.

Neophyte gardeners did not realize that soil can be too warm for success with some vegetables. Lettuce, for example, may not germinate at soil temperatures above 75 degrees, which means that midsummer sowing to grow a fall

"CAN'T YOU SEE IT? Our own low-cost garden tomatoes, lettuce, cukes, corn, parsley, a few chickens, maybe a turkey . . . ."

crop requires special treatment. Sometimes the seed is mixed with damp sand and stored in a refrigerator—but not in the freezing compartment—for a week to ten days before sowing.

Timing had its good and bad effects on other crops too. Chinese cabbage, sometimes called celery cabbage, sown before July 1 disappointed many a new gardener looking forward to fall salads. Planted before this date, it refuses to head up and sends up a seed stalk instead.

Choosing the Right Seed. A common error which reduced the yield from new gardens was the use of varieties bred originally for commercial growing. Unfortunately, many seed display cases in supermarkets, garden centers, and other outlets are stocked with these varieties, largely because the names are familiar to customers. Although they produce leaves, fruits, or roots which may be satisfactory in flavor, they have the drawback of having been bred to mature so the entire crop can be harvested at the same time. This is done so the truck gardener can sell his produce, plow up the old plants and sow a succession crop. As a result, a beginning gardener who plants these varieties finds himself with a harvest of far more beans, peas, or corn than he can possibly use, with nothing for the table either before or after this peak production.

Experienced gardeners read catalog descriptions carefully for phrases such as "concentrated set," "a cropper," or "good market variety" so they can avoid ordering commercial types. Instead, they look for those seeds described as "home market variety," "good for local markets," or "long harvest period."

Location. Another factor in partial or complete failure is the location of a new garden. In cities and suburbs about the only place available is on the owner's property, whose site determines such factors as soil, sunlight, drainage, water supply, and weeds. Few homes are chosen on the basis of whether or not these factors are favorable for gardening.

Sun. All of these factors are important, even critical, but the one which is usually impossible to correct is a lack of sunshine. Occasional improvement can be effected in cutting away the lower limbs of trees or removing trees entirely, but in about 95 percent of the situations, the gardener must accept what he has. Lack of sunshine all but prohibits growing vegetables of which the fruit is eaten, such as beans, peas, tomatoes, sweet corn, and melons. Experts do not recommend growing these unless the plot receives at least seven hours of full sunshine on July 4th, which means that with shortening days in fall, it may enjoy about six hours.

Leafy vegetables such as spinach, chard, parsley, lettuce, endive, and cabbage can do reasonably well with as little as five hours, while root crops such as beets and carrots need about six hours.

Soil. Survey reports of last spring's results showed poor soil as the second most important cause of failure, but since most problem soils can be modified by the addition of organic matter, experts feel it is less serious than the problem of shade.

Compost. Renewed interest in organic matter has stimulated the making of compost to a degree that worries some authorities. They do not question the extreme importance of this means of increasing humus and other forms of organic matter in soils, but feel that too much reliance on compost as a source of fertility could reduce yields of early crops. Even many dedicated organic gardeners bend a little and use some chemical form of nitrate nitrogen to spur growth of crops such as peas, spinach, and lettuce before soil reactions can release nutrients from compost.

The use of home-saved organic matter becomes more important, however, with the critical shortages of fertilizers made from petroleum.

Weeds. Possibly the most irritating problem encountered by beginning gardeners was that of weeds. Most serious was that of quack grass, also called witch grass in some areas. Even chemical weed killers (which would also damage desirable plants) were only partially successful. Older gardeners use dalapon, sold under various trade names, but this takes the treated plot out of use for several weeks. Covering infested ground with tar paper or black plastic requires two years plus cultivation. Experts recommended avoiding infested soil if possible.

Sources of Gardening Information. One factor stressed by reports of 1974 gardens was the lack of accurate information for the completely inexperienced gardener. Perhaps the best source, although often tending to be too conservative, are recommendations of the horticultural departments of state universities. These can be secured either directly from the university (address department of horticulture) or from the county farm advisor, usually located at a county seat.

From the signs already flying, 1975 threatens even greater food shortages than already exist, a situation which will result in millions of new vegetable gardens. Hopefully, the successes and failures of 1973-74 will be a guide to better results.

JOHNNY MILLER hits from the rough on the seventeenth fairway enroute to his victory in the Kaiser International Open at Napa, Calif., on September 29.

Golf

by

ART DUNN

Editor, Sunday Sports Section
Chicago Tribune

Johnny Miller dominated the men's professional golf tour as no player has since World War II. He teed off on his remarkable year by winning the first three events, something no one else had accomplished.

In all, the blond San Franciscan won eight times on the U.S. tour and once in Japan. Only Byron Nelson and Sam Snead ever won more tournaments in a year. Miller also banked $353,021 in official Professional Golfers' Association (PGA) money, shattering Jack Nicklaus's money record by more than $30,000.

But Miller, named player of the year by the PGA, did not count a major tournament in his string of victories.

Gary Player, stylish and popular South African, captured half of the modern Grand Slam for his seventh and eighth major titles. Before the year was out, Player won his 100th golf title by winning the Australian Open.

His victory in the Masters was his second at Augusta, Ga., over a thirteen-year span. Player all but clinched the Masters' green jacket on the third day by shooting a brilliant 66 after two 71s. His 6-under-par round included five straight birdies on the treacherous back nine. A final round of 70 brought Player home two shots ahead of Dave Stockton and Tom Weiskopf.

Player continued his excellence in major events with a four-shot triumph in the British Open at Royal Lytham's in Lytham St. Annes. He was the only contestant under par in the wind-swept British. Peter Oosterhuis again was second, a stroke ahead of Nicklaus.

Lee Elder, a quiet and competent black man from Washington, D.C., birdied the last four holes to tie Oosterhuis, then birdied the fourth extra hole to win the Monsanto Open in Florida. His first PGA tour victory in six years qualified Elder for the 1975 Masters, where he will be the first of his race to compete.

The U. S. Open returned to Winged Foot, north of New York City, where slick greens and narrow fairways had the country's best golfers talking to themselves. No one came close to matching par as Hale Irwin, a former all-Big Eight football safety at Colorado, won with a 287 total, 7 over par and one in front of Forrest Feezler.

The victory was the first major title for the bespectacled Irwin, who has lacked golf glamor, though he finished

LEE TREVINO poses with the World Series of Golf trophy on September 9.

seventh in money winnings the past two years.

Lee Trevino, the merry Mexican-American who is often moody, grabbed his fifth major championship in six meteoric years on tour. He won his first PGA title by one shot over Nicklaus at Tanglewood, N.C., with ageless wonder Sam Snead, sixty-two, tied for third.

Women's Tour. JoAnne Carner, a five-times U.S. Amateur winner, and veteran pro Sandra Haynie shared the Ladies Professional Golf Association (LPGA) limelight. Carner won the money and Miss Haynie the major titles.

The gals played for a record $1.8 million on their worldwide swing, and Carner garnered the lion's share, winning six times for $87,094, also a record. Texan Haynie matched Carner's victory total, including the LPGA and Women's Open. Joanne Prentice won the richest event, the Colgate Dinah Shore, to pocket $32,000. Janie Blalock, embroiled in legal problems last year, won four times and just $652 less than Mrs. Carner.

Amateurs. Two college students earned top marks in the men's ranks. Jerry Pate of Alabama won the U.S. Amateur and paced the United States to victory in the World Team competition. Freshman Curtis Strange of Wake Forest became the school's only National Collegiate Athletic Association (NCAA) medalist as the Deacons won their first team title.

The third time was the charm for Cynthia Hill, twenty-six, who won the Women's Amateur after twice failing in the finals.

CHAMPIONSHIP FORM **helped win the Military Photographer of the Year award for Paul J. Harrington.**

Government Changes

The year 1974 was marked by turmoil and unrest in many of the countries of the world. Here are some major changes in leadership.

ARGENTINA	Juan de Perón, president, died on July 1; he was succeeded by his wife, Isabel Martínez de Perón, who had been vice-president.
AUSTRIA	Franz Jonas, president, died on April 23; following general elections, Rudolf Kirchschlager, foreign minister, was sworn in on July 7.
BANGLADESH	Abu Sayeed Chowdhury, president, resigned December 24, 1973; Muhammadullah, speaker of Parliament and foreign minister, was elected January 24 and sworn in on January 27.
BELGIUM	Caretaker government under Edmond Leburton resigned on January 26; general elections of March 10 brought Leo Tindemans, Social Christian party, to power as premier on April 25.
BURMA	U Ne Win, prime minister, announced on March 2 the dissolution of the ruling Revolutionary Council and the turning over of its powers to the newly formed Peoples Assembly, in accord with the new Constitution adopted on January 4, establishing Burma as a Socialist Republic under one-party rule.
CHILE	Military junta which overthrew Salvador Allende Gossens in 1973 brought country toward bankruptcy and anarchy; General Augusto Pinochet Ugarte, army commander and junta member, assumed executive power as president on June 26.
COLOMBIA	Alvaro Gomez Hurtado, whose Conservative party had held power for sixteen years, was defeated in general elections on April 21 by Alfonso López Michelsen, Liberal, who was sworn in on August 7.
COSTA RICA	José Figueres Ferrer, president, barred by Constitution from running for reelection; he was replaced by Daniel Oduber Quirós, foreign minister and leader of National Liberation party, in election of February 3.
CYPRUS	Archbishop Makarios, president, fled to London in June to avoid possible assassination in military coup led by Greek-officered National Guard. Rebel-proclaimed President Nikos Giorgiades Sampson resigned July 23; he was replaced by Glafkos Clerides, moderate, speaker of Cyprus House of Representatives. Makarios returned December 8 to be reinstated.

ETHIOPIA	Haile Selassie I, emperor, in a year of continual violence was deposed September 12 and held in protective custody; Endalkachew Makonnen, named premier in February, yielded to Armed Forces Committee in July, and Aman Michael Andom became head of military junta. Andom relinquished this post but remained chairman of Council of Ministers; he was assassinated in November and succeeded by Brigadier General Tafari Banti.
FRANCE	Georges Jean Pompidou, president, died on April 2; Valéry Giscard d'Estaing, finance minister, was sworn in as president on May 19, following general elections and a runoff election.
GREECE	George Papadopoulos, head of the military junta which seized power in 1967, relinquished office under pressure in June; Constantine Caramanlis, former premier, representing New Democracy party (conservative-moderate), returned from exile in July and was sworn in as head of caretaker government on July 2. He resigned October 2; his position was confirmed in election of November 17. Papadopoulos and aides were banished to island of Keos to await trial. In general elections of December 8 the exiled monarch, King Constantine, and the institution of monarchy were rejected by a vote of more than two to one.
GUATEMALA	Carlos Arana Osorio, president, was defeated in election of March 3; after period of dissension over results, General Kjell Laugerud García, head of Nationalist Coalition, was sworn in on July 1.
ICELAND	Olafur Johannesson, premier, resigned on July 2 after his Left-wing coalition lost its majority in Parliament; on July 5 Kristjan Eldjarn asked Geir Hallgrimsson, Conservative Independent party leader, to head a new coalition government.
ISRAEL	Golda Meir, prime minister, resigned on April 1, following Cabinet dissension; Yitzhak Rabin, Labor party leader, chief of staff in 1967 war, a former ambassador to United States, assumed power.
ITALY	Mariano Rumor, premier, submitted his and his cabinet's resignation to Giovanni Leone, president, on June 10; was persuaded to stay. Rumor resigned again in November, and Aldo Moro formed a coalition government on November 23.
JAPAN	Kakuei Tanaka, premier, Liberal Democratic party, accused of illegal acquisition of great wealth, resigned early in December; he was succeeded by Takeo Miki, a compromise choice of the ruling party, after a special session of Parliament on December 7.

LAOS	Prince Souvanna Phouma, premier, became inactive because of poor health: On July 12 King Savang Vatthana signed a decree establishing Souvanna as head of a new government, sharing power with his half-brother Prince Souphanouvong, Pathet Lao leader, as president of National Council and Phoumi Vongvichit as foreign minister, resulting in a government of left, right, and neutralist elements.
LEBANON	Takiedden Solh, premier, and cabinet resigned on September 25; Suleiman Franjieh, president, designated Rashid Solh, independent member of Parliament, as premier.
NICARAGUA	Edmundo Paguaga Irias, president, Conservative party, was defeated in general elections of September 14 by General Anastasio Somoza Debayle, former president and nation's strong man, the Constitution having been rewritten to permit him to run.
PORTUGAL	General Antonio de Spinola, head of seven-man military junta was proclaimed president on May 15. He resigned September 29; he was replaced by Francisco da Costa Gomes, chief of joint military staff, in peaceful change. Colonel Vasco dos Santos Gonçalves was appointed premier on July 14.
SPAIN	General Francisco Franco Bahamonde, dictator, in poor health, on July 19 delegated power as head of state to Prince Juan Carlos de Borbon, named as his successor; Franco reassumed power on August 31.
TURKEY	Naim Talu, acting premier, resigned on January 10; Fahri Koruturk, president, on January 15 asked Bulent Ecevit to form coalition government; Ecevit acceded but resigned on September 18, due to split in coalition. He tried again in November, but failed; Koruturk then asked Sadi Irmak, independent senator, to assume office as premier.
UNITED STATES	Richard M. Nixon, president, Republican, resigned under pressure on August 9; he was succeeded by Gerald R. Ford, whom Nixon had earlier appointed vice-president, following resignation of Spiro T. Agnew.
WEST GERMANY	Willy Brandt, chancellor, Social Democratic party, resigned on May 6 under attack; Gustav Heinemann, president, asked Walter Scheel, foreign minister, to head caretaker government until Bundestag elected new chancellor. Helmut Schmidt, finance minister, was elected on May 7 and sworn in on May 16; supported by Social Democratic party and Free Democratic party.

Great Britain

THE HARBOR at Aberdeen, the Scottish city now called the "oil capital of Europe," is being expanded to cope with booming traffic connected with the exploitation of North Sea oil.

by
THOMAS P. PEARDON, Ph.D.

Professor Emeritus of
Political Science
Barnard College, Columbia University

The Fall of Mr. Heath. Prime Minister Edward Heath resigned on March 4. He had come to power in 1970, proposing to solve British problems by a policy of free market competition, a minimum of government interference in the economy. But circumstances proved stronger than doctrine and the Heath administration shifted to "pragmatic intervention." Loans were advanced to ailing companies, the money supply was expanded, taxes were reduced (especially in the upper brackets — this was supposed to stimulate initiative), the pound was allowed to float in value so as to encourage exports. To control inflation a program of wage and price controls was adopted, while an attempt was made to curb industrial disorder by the rules and procedures laid down in the industrial relations act. Finally, Great Britain was led into the European Economic Community (EEC, the Common Market) in the search for new markets and the bracing shock of competition. For a time this policy of "going for growth" attained a considerable measure of success. Then disaster struck in the winter of 1973-1974.

The price of world commodities such as food and raw materials that must be imported to feed men and machines continued to rise at explosive rates. In particular, the price of crude oil quadrupled. The balance of trade was disrupted—the 1974 deficit was estimated to be about $10 billion, while the rate of inflation soon rose to 17 percent and threatened to reach 20 percent by the end of 1974.

Moreover, the economy was disrupted by labor disputes in the winter of 1973-1974. The unions had never responded well to the restraints of wage and price controls or the prohibitions of the Industrial Relations Act. But now more and more categories of workers, their standard of living threatened by inflation, sought pay increases that

GREAT BRITAIN

would exceed the norm of the 7 percent prescribed by law. Some of them resorted to direct action. Travel was interrupted when the engineers decided to "work by rule." The output of coal fell some 40 percent when the miners first declined to work overtime after November 11, 1973, and then went on strike on February 10, 1974. Since 70 percent of British power is produced by coal, a miners' strike is a catastrophe of the first magnitude. To try to avert it the government had exceeded even its own norms by offering a pay increase of 16 percent. The miners declined the offer. The shortage of coal combined with the Arab oil embargo to produce an energy crisis.

Here then was a bewildering complex of troubles: a rising rate of inflation, the worst trade balance on record, labor unrest, a shortage of energy. Beginning in the middle of November, 1973, emergency measures were taken. (1) To curb demand, public expenditures were cut, the supply of money was tightened, interest rates were raised, and installment buying was made more difficult. (2) Various conservation measures — including the reduction of street lighting and the prohibition of display advertising and lighted shop windows — were tried. Evening television programs had to be ended at 10:30! (3) Finally, on January 1, 1974, a three-day work week was imposed on industry.

It was certainly a dark time for the British (in more ways than one), yet not as dark as it might have been or as the outside world sometimes believed. The British seem to know how to accept inconvenience. The three-day work week (which lasted until March 11), while costly, did not have the catastrophic impact that had been feared. Production remained at about 75 percent of normal because workers and management cooperated in meeting the crisis. Many companies proved to have stand-by generators that were pressed into service. Some used old steam engines, and manual power was used where mechanical power was lacking. The old-fashioned screw driver became popular again. And the mild winter helped stretch what coal and oil were available. It was an example of how men can rise to meet emergencies.

In the meantime Prime Minister Heath kept trying to reach a settlement with the miners. When all his efforts failed, he resorted to a policy of confrontation. Parliament was dissolved and a general election called for February 28 on the issue Who Rules Britain?

The February Election. Confrontation, too, was the keynote of the Conservative electoral program and campaign. Tough action was to be taken against the unions, social security benefits were to be denied to strikers' families, strict control on wages (and prices) was to be continued. Much was made of the charge that the Labor party had fallen into the hands of extremists. Observers agreed that there was an unaccustomed shrillness in the tone of Heath's speeches.

Harold Wilson and the Labor party, on the other hand, tried to project an image of dignity and moderation. They proposed to settle the miners' strike by negotiation and then to regulate future wage increases by agreement rather than by legal command. They talked of consultation and conciliation, a social contract between government and unions, instead of confrontation. They promised to give immediate help to the poor by higher pensions and food subsidies. For the long run they proposed an expansion of public ownership. In defense they offered a reduction of expenditures, and in foreign affairs a renegotiation of the terms of British membership in the EEC. The people would be asked to decide by a referendum or in a general election whether the membership in the Common

Market should be continued.

Seeking to profit by the widespread disillusionment with both major parties, the Liberals nominated 517 candidates for the 635 seats in the House of Commons. They hoped to shatter the two-party system by capturing the balance of power in the new Parliament.

The campaign went badly for the Tories. Rising prices were blamed on them. There was also the sensation caused by Enoch Powell's refusal to seek reelection. He urged the voters to support the Labor party because of its stand on the EEC. Finally, shortly before polling day, the National Pay Board announced that it had miscalculated the miners' pay. They were actually earning 8 percent less than the average pay of workers in manufacturing, not 3 percent more, as the government had claimed.

No party gained a majority of the 635 seats in the new House of Commons. Labor led with 301; followed by the Conservatives with 296; Liberals, 14; Scottish Nationalists, 7; Welsh Nationalists (Plaid Cymru), 2; United Ulster Unionists, 11; others, 4. In terms of votes cast, however, the Conservatives with 11.9 million (38.1 percent) outpolled Labor—11.6 million (37.3 percent) by a small margin. The Liberals derived great encouragement from winning approximately 6 million votes (19.3 percent) but were disappointed by the small number of seats these votes secured for them. More striking than these Liberal results was the fact that the Scottish Nationalists had gained five new seats, and the Welsh Nationalists two, and that eleven of the twelve Ulster seats were now held by Protestant extremists.

Following the election, Heath made an unsuccessful attempt to have the Liberals join in a coalition (he would still have been short of a majority). When this failed, he resigned office and was succeeded by Harold Wilson, leader of the opposition Labor party.

Minority Government: March to October. Labor took office on March 5. Prime Minister Wilson quickly settled the miners' strike (the price being a 35 percent wage increase), ended the three-day work week, abolished control of wages while keeping controls on prices, and moved to repeal the Industrial Relations Act. To help the poor, rents were frozen until the end of the year, pensions were increased sharply, food subsidies were adopted, and more than a million persons of low income were exempted from income tax. Business and the well-to-do on the other hand were subjected to higher taxes. The nationalized industries, which had not been favored by the Conservatives, were now allowed to raise their prices. They were also helped by loans.

Most of the fiscal measures mentioned above were taken in the March budget. Their general effect (except for those with the lowest income) was to curb demand. In particular, business profits were squeezed between the necessity of paying both higher taxes and higher wages. The economy was slowing down, unemployment was growing, prices were rising.

To counter some of these bad effects, the chancellor of the exchequer, Denis Healey, issued a new budget in July. The value added tax, by which a levy is made on the value added to any commodity at every stage in its production, was reduced from 10 percent to 8 percent. Additional food subsidies were adopted in the amount of $120 million. Those higher up the scale were helped by raising from 5 percent to 12.5 percent the limit allowed for dividend increases. Some relief was also extended to property owners who were faced by very high increases in local taxes.

The Balance of Payments deficit was attacked by the usual drive for increased exports, but more directly by the arrangement with commercial banks of a \$2.5 billion loan and by securing a credit of \$1.2 billion from the Iranian government. These loans are to be paid in the 1980s. Thus Great Britain is already mortgaging the hoped-for profits from North Sea oil.

The Social Contract. Much was heard during these months about an informal and unwritten understanding supposed to exist between the unions and the Labor government. The unions were to seek only one wage settlement a year, with wage demands limited to the rise in the cost of living. On its side the government was to strive for a more just society by a wiser distribution of wealth and income. The Social Contract was a good slogan and may even have had some influence on the course of events, but wages continued to rise sharply and strikes to occur—sixty of them in June alone.

The extension of public ownership was also said to be a part of the social contract. Announcements were made about industries that would be nationalized (especially shipbuilding), but not much could be done by a minority government except in the case of one or two industries so hard-hit that they had to be taken over.

Renegotiation of the terms of British membership in the European Economic Community was slowed by the expectation of an early election. It will not be completed until some time in 1975.

The Cash Squeeze. The plight of the businessman grew worse in the course of the year. He was forced to pay more for labor, fuel, and raw materials, and more to the government in the form of higher taxes. Yet he was forbidden to raise his prices as much as he deemed necessary; nor could he borrow freely because of high interest rates and a declining supply of money. Business confidence sank and along with it output and the willingness to make capital investments.

Democracy Under Strain. Lack of confidence seemed to spread beyond the economy. The successful strike of the miners and later of Protestant workers in Northern Ireland seemed to prove that direct action was stronger than parliamentary government. Moderate men in all parties, including Labor, were worried about the undue influence that appeared to be exercised by extremist minorities. Left-wing students at the University of Essex refused to hear views with which they disagreed. Two retired officers started to organize groups on quasi-military lines to operate essential services in the event of breakdown through industrial strife. One of their bright ideas was to use helicopters to leap over picket lines. Of course they were laughed at but perhaps less than would have been true a few years earlier.

There were complaints about adolescent rowdiness at football games. Crime in London in the first quarter of 1974 rose 19 percent over that of the first quarter of 1973. Irish Republican Army (IRA) bombings continued to occur in various parts of London, including Parliament and the Tower. There were instances of corruption in public life, and a royal commission was appointed to investigate the extent to which it occurs.

Too much must not be made of these scattered examples. There is still a great deal less crime, violence, and corruption in Great Britain than in most other countries. The speakers still spout freely at Hyde Park Corner. But both the law and Parliament have declined in public respect, and this gives cause for worry.

The October Election. October 10 was the date chosen to try to solve the deadlock of February. Labor (626), Conservatives (622), and Liberals (616) each entered more than 600 candidates

GREAT BRITAIN

for the 635 seats in the House of Commons. The Scottish Nationalists contested all 71 seats in Scotland, the Welsh Nationalists all 36 in Wales. But it was a very quiet campaign. The Conservatives this time talked about national unity rather than confrontation. If elected, they said, they would consult all parties and all great interests in the process of shaping policy. Toward the end Heath even talked about a possible coalition.

The Labor party rejected all proposals for coalition, although there seemed to be a good deal of popular sentiment in its favor. The Labor platform stressed the social contract as the only possible way to maintain industrial peace while fighting inflation. It reaffirmed the promises previously made — extended social benefits, more nationalization, a popular vote on the Common Market, public control and even ownership of North Sea oil.

The Liberals still asserted that they were seeking to destroy the existing two-party system, thus bringing about a realignment of politics. Their most important specific commitment was to a pay freeze and statutory price and income controls.

All three parties committed themselves to some sort of legislative assembly for Scotland and Wales.

The Results gave Labor 319 seats for an overall majority of three; Conservatives, 276; Liberals, 13; Scottish Nationalists, 11; Ulster Unionists, 10; Welsh Nationalists, 3; others, 3. None of the major parties could derive much satisfaction from this result. Labor won a small majority, but its share of the popular vote was barely 40 percent. The Conservatives with only 36 percent made their worst showing in this century. The Liberals, too, suffered disappointment; although they had entered more candidates than in February, their percentage of the popular vote shrank from 19.3 to 18.3 and their seats from 14 to 13, a blow to Liberal hopes of a sustained revival.

It was the regional parties that did best. In Scotland the Nationalists added four seats to their previous total and passed the Tories in popular votes to become the second party in the country. In Wales the Nationalists added one seat to their previous total. Celtic nationalism appears to be growing stronger, especially in Scotland which has visions of wealth and prosperity from North Sea oil (much of which lies off the Scottish coast). As for the Protestants (Ulster Unionists) of Northern Ireland, although they had one less seat than in February, their share of the popular vote went up.

It was predicted after the election that Heath, having lost three of the last four elections, would not remain long as leader of the Conservative party.

Above all, the campaign and its outcome reflected the boredom and disillusionment of the electorate. The Conservatives were rejected emphatically, Labor was endorsed grudgingly.

Prospects. Observers thought that Labor's narrow margin of victory would mean that cautious policies must be adopted by the new government. This was not true, however, of the program laid before Parliament in the queen's speech on October 29th. Its emphasis on the expansion of public ownership pleases the Left more than the Right. It was noted that nothing was said about coming to the aid of industries that need help to avoid bankruptcy. Some thought, however, that this action would be necessary before long.

Everyone agreed that another grim winter—and probably more than one—lay ahead. But hope was buoyed up by the prospect that in the 1980s there would be oil in abundance and that this, along with coal and nuclear fuel, would trigger a breakthrough to prosperity.

GREECE

by
MICHAEL COPE
Internationally Syndicated Columnist

An Eventful Year. For the 8 million Greeks 1974 was a significant and eventful year in the country's long and turbulent history: democracy was restored following collapse of the authoritarian military junta which seized power in 1967. The year also saw the first free elections in Greece in eleven years, followed by a national plebiscite which overwhelmingly rejected a return to monarchic government.

The Downfall of the Junta. It was the humiliation of the Turkish invasion of the predominantly Greek-speaking island of Cyprus which triggered the downfall of the dictatorial junta, although resentment at the brutal enforcement of the regime's will by the army had been building up for the previous three years.

But even earlier events and factors, dating back to the end of World War II, led up to the 1974 changes. It was the widespread Communist insurrection following the war and the subsequent outlawing of Communism which spawned the political bitterness and jealousies which led the twenty-two-year-old King Constantine to dismiss the elected government in 1965. Dominated by the dowager Queen Frederika, he persuaded nonelected governments to rule under his direction for the next two years. But such was the interference and manipulation from the throne that in 1967 a group of Greek army officers seized control, suspended the constitution, and ruled as a junta by decree. Later, having driven Constantine into exile, they abolished the monarchy following an outrageously rigged plebiscite.

GREEK VILLAGE WOMAN'S PORTRAIT won Albert Leonard, Jr., of Wellesley, Mass., the first prize in the Modern Greece Photo Contest sponsored by the Greek National Tourist Office.

During these troubled years an increasingly restless Left-wing element emerged in Greece, particularly among the nation's disaffected students. There were repeated demonstrations throughout the country. In Athens, the junta sowed the seeds of its own eventual downfall in November, 1973, when it ordered tanks and troops to smash through student barricades at the Athens Polytechnic. The sixty young Greeks who died in that confrontation became instant martyrs and the focal point for growing opposition.

The instrument of the junta's final downfall was Cyprus where the 482,000 Greek-Cypriots — their traditions and ethnic origins still firmly bound to the Greek motherland by language, custom,

A GREEK FISHERMAN prepares for a day's work in the harbor at Iraklion, Crete. The picture won a second prize in the Modern Greece Photo Contest.

and religion — were defeated by the invading Turkish army. The Turks had gone to the aid of the 118,000 Turkish-speaking Cypriots after the fanatical Right-wing EOKA movement, led by Greek army officers, deposed the elected Greek-Cypriot president, Archbishop Makarios, in July. The Turks partitioned one-third of the island, displacing thousands of prosperous Greeks.

Open rebellion threatened across mainland Greece over this international humiliation, while at the same time relations with neighboring Turkey deteriorated to the point where war between the two countries seemed inevitable. The military junta in Athens prudently decided the time had come to step down.

Caramanlis. It is a paradox of history now that the person invited by the outgoing junta to salvage the country was sixty-seven-year-old Constantine Caramanlis, a veteran politician. Caramanlis's conservative Right-wing National Radical Union, which he founded, had formed the Greek government from 1955 to 1963, when he resigned following unsubstantiated opposition charges of vote-rigging in the 1961 election. He had gone into self-imposed exile in Paris.

Caramanlis was the most favored politician with the electorate when he called the general election. As caretaker prime minister during the weeks following the junta's demise he opened the nation's jails and released thousands of political prisoners; he drew Greece back from the brink of war with Turkey, and he brought the one ingredient so many Greeks had sorely missed in the past decade — hope.

The Election. The political spectrum of Greece was at that time jumbled and unclear after the political juggling by the deposed king and the military junta. Caramanlis campaigned under the banner of his hastily reformed right-of-center party which he shrewdly renamed the New Democracy party and which swept 220 of the 300 parliamentary seats at stake. His nearest rival was the Center Union/New Forces party, led by George Mavros who had served as foreign minister in Caramanlis's interim caretaker government. Center Union/New Forces party won 60 seats. The surprise of the election was the poor showing of the Pan-Hellenic Socialist Movement which took only 12 seats. The remaining 8 parliamentary seats were won by the United

Leftists, primarily Communist candidates who emerged with less than 10 percent of the overall popular vote, a significant decline of influence from the immediate postwar years when the Communists nearly won office. The deep divisions between the Communists, despite the irony of their United Leftist banner, an uneasy ideological truce for the election only, were reflected by the unexpectedly poor support.

The result of this important election reflected the previously unknown political mood of the people. There was still cautious conservatism (long the traditional standpoint of the Greek voter), but also suspicion, even distrust of the left. Caramanlis was undoubtedly in a strong position. He had returned to the political stage in Greece not only as an established and respected politician, but also one of the few untainted by the previous junta or discredited by his earlier uneasy partnership with the monarchy. The solid parliamentary majority he won in November represented a vote for moderate, stable, reformist government, conservative enough to avoid provoking another military intervention, but reformist enough to allow for genuine democracy to develop again.

The Constitution. The first question to be settled was the constitution. Was Greece to revert to its traditional monarchism or to adopt a new republican constitution? The campaign was a heated

SYMBOL OF GREECE, the Acropolis at Athens is in danger of collapsing, according to Athens University geology professor John Trikkalinos. A series of dangerous rifts and hollow caves underneath the foundation are threatening the famed structure. Certain spots were closed off in 1974 and scaffolding to reinforce splitting columns was set up. In December the Greek government announced a grant of $1.6 million for the restoration of the Acropolis, including the Parthenon.

GREECE

one. The antimonarchists, led by the left-of-center political parties, staged powerful campaigns throughout the country with massive crowds chanting antiroyalist slogans. Prime Minister Caramanlis earned much respect at home and abroad during this time by remaining scrupulously neutral and insisting his cabinet do the same. The result was that on December 8 two out of three Greeks voted for republicanism. The monarchy, which most Greeks blamed for the political interference and manipulation which led to the seizure of power by the military junta was clearly and irrevocably discredited. In England, exiled King Constantine lost graciously with the statement: ". . . true normalcy, progress, and prosperity for our country demand that national unity must come first. I pray with all my heart that future developments may justify the outcome (of the plebiscite)." So he joined the growing and melancholy club of exiled and deposed royalty and pretentious claimants to nonexistent crowns and thrones.

Foreign Policy. Prime Minister Caramanlis's next problem was to mend Greece's broken fences with the rest of Europe, and at the same time maintain a cautious but firm stance on the unresolved Cyprus question. Already he had decided, even before the election, to withdraw Greek military forces from the North Atlantic Treaty Organization, because NATO had, as he put it, "failed to avert and tolerated the Turkish invasion of Cyprus." He went on: "But this does not mean that Greece proposes to break off political, cultural, or other relations with the West."

This move, together with massive defense cuts announced about the same time by Great Britain — which maintains large air and land bases in Cyprus, both of which will be reduced under the London cuts — threatened to weaken seriously NATO's southern flank. Prime Minister Caramanlis also indicated his new government would "request revision of the agreements concerning American (mostly naval) bases in Greece."

Against this background, Caramanlis appeared to emerge as a new Gaullist-type moderate strong man in southern Europe, dedicated to democracy, but conscious of the groundswell of nationalism among his people. In speeches and press conferences he emphasized that he saw the new Greece integrated in the European community and playing a role in Europe's eventual political, economic, and industrial unification. He was using Europe — particularly the weakened NATO alliance which sorely needs Greece's 120,000-man army and ten squadrons of attack aircraft — as well as the Greek bases so essential to the U.S. Sixth Fleet policing the troubled eastern Mediterranean, as a bargaining ploy to settle the Cyprus question. To consolidate his electoral victory, it was essential he get the Turkish army out of Cyprus. "Greece prefers consultation to confrontation," he said, but added pointedly, "but knows how to defend her national interests. The Greek government always hopes Turkey will revise her provocative behavior and cease being a threat to peace in this sensitive region of the world."

The Future. Greeks had much to be thankful for and even more to hope for in the future under their first democratically elected government in eleven years. Nor would there seem to be reason why their expectations should not be realized; Prime Minister Caramanlis is respected both at home and abroad and enjoys the biggest parliamentary majority ever accorded to a modern political party in Greece. He also has the political skill, experience, and firmness to reestablish Greece's temporarily relinquished position among the world's democracies.

Hockey

TEAM CANADA GOALIE Gerry Cheevers, right, blocks a shot by Soviet player Valeri Kharlomov, center, after Canadian Pat Stapleton failed to stop the Russian during the Canadian-Soviet ice hockey series opening game in Moscow.

by
ART DUNN

Editor, Sunday Sports Section
Chicago Tribune

Gordie Howe. The old and the comparatively new were the best skaters in the country's two professional hockey leagues. The two-year-old World Hockey Association (WHA) scored a promotional coup when graying Gordie Howe ended a two-year retirement to join the Houston Aeros.

Howe, forty-five, came back to play with his sons Marty and Mark and quickly proved he had not left his skills in the National Hockey League (NHL) where he was its greatest scorer in a twenty-five-year career. Poppa Gordie was the league's most valuable player and third leading pointmaker as Houston romped to the World Trophy.

Stanley Cup. The Philadelphia Flyers, NHL babies at six, bulled their way to the Stanley Cup — the first expansion team to do so. They did it by following team leader Bobby Clarke's credo: "We take the shortest route to the puck and arrive in ill humor."

The Flyers won the West and the cup from the favored Boston Bruins by combining short tempers, skating skills, and the goaltending of Bernie Parent who won a record forty-six games and topped the league with a goals against average of 1.89.

Philly needed just four games to eliminate Atlanta in the first round, then squeezed past the New York Rangers in seven, in a series which set a record for penalties. Boston, meanwhile, steamrolled Toronto and Chicago behind Phil Esposito, who won his fifth scoring title, and incomparable defenseman Bobby Orr.

The pugnacious Flyers led three games to two as the series went back to Philadelphia on the third Sunday in May. The game's only goal was scored in the first period during a Flyer power play. Rick MacLeish steered Andre Dupont's shot over goalie Gilles Gilbert's arm and Parent recorded his second playoff shutout.

W.H.A. Houston had an easier time in the WHA, blitzing Winnipeg in four and Minnesota in six, before taking on Chicago in the finals. The Cougars, who just barely made the playoffs, needed fourteen games to edge New England (East Di-

HOCKEY

vision winners and defending champions) and Toronto.

But the gritty Cougars were no match for the Howe family and mates. The Aeros clicked on ten power play goals in the four-game final to rout Chicago and bring a pro sports title to Houston for the first time in twelve years.

Team Canada II: The WHA, taking a page from the NHL's book on international hockey diplomacy, rounded up an all-star team in September for a series with the Soviet Nationals. It was similar to the older league's ice-breaking confrontation two years ago in all respects save the result.

Canada, though rated a decided underdog, held its own in the North American portion, winning once and tying twice in four games. But in Moscow, the Russians unnerved the visitors on the ice and off, and Team Canada lost three and tied one. Winnipeg's Bobby Hull led all scorers with seven goals.

1973-74 NATIONAL HOCKEY LEAGUE STATISTICS

FINAL STANDINGS

East Division

	W.	L.	T.	PTS.
Boston	52	17	9	113
Montreal	45	24	9	99
N.Y. Rangers	40	24	14	94
Toronto	35	27	16	86
Buffalo	32	34	12	76
Detroit	29	39	10	68
Vancouver	24	43	11	59
N.Y. Islanders	19	41	18	56

West Division

	W.	L.	T.	PTS.
Philadelphia	50	16	12	112
Chicago	41	14	23	105
Los Angeles	33	33	12	78
Atlanta	30	34	14	74
Pittsburgh	28	41	9	65
St. Louis	26	40	12	64
Minnesota	23	38	17	63
California	13	55	10	36

TOP SCORERS

	G	A	PTS
P. Esposito, Boston	68	77	145
B. Orr, Boston	32	90	122
K. Hodge, Boston	50	55	105
W. Cashman, Boston	30	59	89
B. Clarke, Philadelphia	35	52	87
R. Martin, Buffalo	52	34	86
S. Apps, Pittsburgh	24	61	85
D. Sittler, Toronto	38	46	84
L. MacDonald, Pittsburgh	43	39	82
B. Park, N.Y. Rangers	25	57	82

G-goals. A-assists. PTS-points.

WORLD HOCKEY ASSOCIATION

FINAL STANDINGS

East Division

	W.	L.	T.	PTS.
New England	43	31	4	90
Toronto	41	33	4	86
Cleveland	37	32	9	83
Chicago	38	35	5	81
Quebec	38	36	4	80
New Jersey	32	42	4	68

West Division

	W.	L.	T.	PTS.
Houston	48	25	5	101
Minnesota	44	32	2	90
Edmonton	38	37	3	79
Winnipeg	34	39	5	73
Vancouver	27	50	1	55
Los Angeles	25	53	0	50

TOP SCORERS

	G	A	PTS
M. Walton, Minnesota	57	60	117
A. Lacroix, New Jersey	31	80	111
G. Howe, Houston	31	69	100
B. Hull, Winnipeg	53	42	95
W. Connelly, Minnesota	42	53	95
W. Carleton, Toronto	37	55	92
D. Lawson, Vancouver	50	38	88
B. Campbell, Vancouver	27	61	88
S. Bernier, Quebec	37	49	86
L. Lund, Houston	33	53	86

G-goals. A-assists. PTS-points.

CANNONADE, with Jockey Angel Cordero aboard, crosses the finish line to win the 100th running of the Kentucky Derby.

Horseracing

by

ART DUNN

Editor, Sunday Sports Section
Chicago Tribune

The Triple Crown. In the wake of Secretariat's record-breaking year in 1973, the three-year-olds of 1974 were a rather plebeian collection.

The Kentucky Derby staged its centennial Run for the Roses in Louisville before 163,628 spectators, including England's Princess Margaret. An unwieldy field of twenty-three went to the post, the largest in the history of the race. Among the contestants was Sir Tristram from France, the first European colt ever to compete in the American classic.

Cannonade, the well-bred son of Bold Bidder—Queen Sucree, by Ribot, muscled to a 2¼-length victory despite being roughed up at the start. Jockey Angel Cordero kept Cannonade on the rail for the first half mile, then swung outside to avoid traffic.

The time for the mile and a quarter was 2:04, far off Secretariat's 1:59 last year. But Trainer Woody Stephens's horse did earn an American record of $274,000 for owner John Olin out of the richest Derby purse ever—$326,500.

Hudson County was second and Agitate took show money. Little Current, who later won the other jewels of the Triple Crown, finished fifth.

The Preakness at Pimlico outside Baltimore produced the third fastest time in the ninety-eight previous runnings of the mile and three-sixteenths race, as Little Current won in 1:54 3/5.

Rider Miguel Rivera guided Little Current along the rail and the son of European champion Sea Bird roared through a narrow opening to win by seven lengths over long shot Neapolitan Way. Cannonade, who was first at the stretch, finished third.

Little Current and Rivera repeated their Preakness triumph in the 106th Belmont Stakes, again winning by seven lengths. This time Rivera took the outside route to win in 2:29 1/5, a full 5½ seconds off Secretariat's time last year.

Jolly Johu was second by a nose. Cannonade was again third.

Cannonade never again attained the flawless form he exhibited at Churchill Downs and was retired to stud by midsummer due to injury. Later in the summer, injury forced Little Current to be retired.

Other Big Stakes. French import Dahlia, the first horse ever to win stakes in five countries (Canada, the United States, England, France, and Ireland) was installed as a heavy favorite in the prestigious Washington, D.C., International. But the filly was upset by Admetus, at 31-1 the longest shot ever to win that race.

Forego, a massive four-year-old, was named Horse of the Year for winning eight times in thirteen starts, all under high weights.

Hollywood (Calif.) Park arranged a match race between Chris Evert, winner of New York's Triple Crown for fillies, and Miss Musket, rage of the West Coast three-year-old filly set. The $350,000 prize made it the richest match race in history.

It was a race in name only. Chris Evert romped to an awesome fifty-length victory in the mile and a quarter event.

Harness Racing. Christopher T., driven by Billy Haughton, won the Hambletonian for three-year-old trotters in straight heats. Haughton also teamed up with Armbro Omaha to annex the Little Brown Jug, the top event for three-year-old pacers. Delmonica Hanover (Del Miller) took the $200,000 Roosevelt International.

Jockey Record. Rookie rider Chris McCarron set a world mark for winners in a year when he registered his 516th victory December 17 to break Canadian Sandy Hawley's year-old standard of 515.

Off-Track. Secretariat and his Meadow Stable mate Riva Ridge were both pronounced fertile at stud after their potency had been suspected earlier in the year, and on November 15 Secretariat became a father. His first foal was born to a thirteen-year-old Appaloosa test mare on a farm in Minnesota.

Incas

MYSTERIOUS FLAT-TOPPED MOUND in an Ecuadorian highland valley near Cuenca has been marked through aerial photography as the site of an Inca settlement. The use of aerial photography in archaeology, including images transmitted by orbiting satellites, is greatly increasing the scope and accuracy of exploration. Photographs from above reveal potential excavation sites that are impossible to see on the ground.

The Incas never created an alphabet. They never discovered the marvelous uses of the wheel. Yet they constructed well-planned urban centers and sophisticated systems of irrigation for their terraced fields, and were the first to cultivate the potato, now a staple food throughout the world. The Inca empire stretched from northern Ecuador to central Chile. It was ruled from fortress cities, so well constructed that even today a fingernail will not fit between the stone building blocks held together without mortar.

Mysteries of Inca life remain unsolved because there were no written histories. Knowledge of their culture comes largely from Spanish chronicles. Among the puzzling features in these accounts is the "spring run" on the vernal equinox, when 400 runners assembled in the Inca capital, now Cuzco, Peru. In preparation for the ceremony the city was cleansed of dogs and foreigners. At a signal the

MACHU PICCHU, the "Lost City of the Incas," was discovered by U.S. explorer Hiram Bingham in 1911. Perched 6,750 feet above sea level in the Peruvian Andes, it attracted 80,000 tourists in 1974.

runners set out along four roads radiating from the Temple of the Sun in the city's center, shouting to banish evil from the town. Outside the city the "shout" was relayed to other runners who carried it far out into the empire.

In March Gary Vescelius, director of Cornell University excavations in the Peruvian highlands, made public a study that seemed to prove that the 328 Inca shrines around Cuzco and the paths of the "spring run" comprise the Inca calendar system. It is known that the Inca year was divided into twelve months of three ten-day weeks each. Vescelius believes each shrine represents one day. With a sabbath for each of the thirty-six weeks plus one special festive day, the total would be 365, a full year.

The famous Sun Gate of the Incas at Tiahuanaco, Bolivia, dating to A.D. 500, shows a trumpeter in the months of the summer and winter solstices. When the sun seemed to stand still in its seasonal progress to the north or south, the Incas are believed to have sent a trumpeter to the heights to summon its return. The Vescelius theory would date the Inca calendar system's origin at least 1,000 years before the height of the Inca empire and dispel assumptions that the Incas were not greatly concerned with time reckoning.

India

THE INDIAN CAMEL CORPS patrols the 600-mile desert frontier with Pakistan. As a legacy of British rule, Indian soldiers snap to attention with the classic British hop and their officers slap their jodhpur-clad legs with Sandhurst-style riding crops.

by
ASHAKANT NIMBARK, Ph.D.

Professor of Sociology
Coordinator, Sociology and Anthropology
Dowling College
Oakdale, Long Island, N. Y.

Quiet Outside, Nervous Inside. Quiet and calm externally, but exploding and upset internally—that is the most concise way of summarizing India in 1974. While India maintained cordial relationships with other Third World countries, kept up its goodwill pact with the Soviet Union, repaired its ties with the United States, and reestablished trade relations with its traditionally hostile neighbor, Pakistan, it went through a year of internal calamity and strife—natural, economical, and political. India's dramatic entry into the sphere of nuclear power which was greeted with pride and self-confidence at home, was viewed with mixed feelings by the outside world. Ironically, instead of covering up the strains and scars on India's face, the nuclear blast simply illuminated them.

Nationwide Student Revolt. While the West in general — and the United States in particular — was witnessing apathy among nonpolitical youth and a return of quiet on college campuses, political activism among youth was at the highest peak in India's twenty-seven years of independence.

In the western state of Gujarat, famous for its textile industries, student revolt exploded from a small incident involving dormitory students at a college in Ahmadabad who were protesting

INDIA

higher food costs and led to large-scale public protest against corruption among high-level state ministers and their economic and political wrongdoings. After a two-month-long popular uprising in which students as well as faculty and workers as well as farmers participated, and which cost nearly eighty lives and more than $50 million in property, the chief minister was ousted. The state assembly was forced to dissolve and presidential rule was enforced for six months. The students' struggle was essentially against political corruption, unemployment among educated people, inflation, and educational obsolescence. They innovated highly effective techniques for mass unity involving dramatic slogans and symbols such as a Death Knell (at a given moment, millions of people would bang metal plates dramatizing popular demand). Following a series of statewide debates for reforming the government, presidential rule was imposed for another six months, until February, 1975.

In Bihar a youth-led movement virtually paralyzed the state government. Bihar is a large northeastern state with 60 million people, 80 percent of whom are illiterate. Despite the state's natural resources, such as steel and coal, Biharis are economically poor, due largely to corruption and ineffectiveness within the state bureaucracy.

Inspired by the Gujarat students, Bihari youth, under the leadership of Jayaprakash Narayan, attacked the problems of inflation, unemployment, high-level corruption, and social ills. Their leader was a seventy-two-year-old man, popularly known as JP, who has been advocating the cause of a partyless people's democracy, free from elitism and centralized power. In the tradition of India's "father of nation," the late Ma-

HUNGER is the only leftover among Indian families of marginal means, who had to spend from 80 to 90 percent of their income on food in 1974.

FAKHRUDDIN ALI AHMED was elected president of India on August 17.

hatma Gandhi, JP's leadership is charismatic and moral, not political and legal; and his focus is on the rural-agricultural masses even though his movement is supported by intellectuals and students. Toward the end of the year, Bihar encountered a series of confrontations between JP's youthful followers who demand a dissolution of the state assembly and the central government which is resisting such a move, lest other states follow suit. India's prime minister, Mrs. Indira Gandhi, and other leaders are openly challenged by JP's movement which has attracted, locally and nationally, many sympathizers as well as critics. As yet, the exact direction of this conflict remains unpredictable.

India's Nuclear Test. On May 18 India, by conducting an underground nuclear test in a western region, became the sixth member of the exclusive nuclear club which includes the United States, the U.S.S.R., Great Britain, France, and China. Prime Minister Gan-

FERTILIZER is loaded on a bullock-powered cart in India. The Indian government attributed lagging of food output to a scarcity of imported fertilizer. Indian fertilizer plants, of which there are too few, ran at less than 60 percent of capacity in 1974 due to power shortages.

INDIAN ELEPHANTS, loaded with passengers, cross a river. On many roads in southern India government signs state: "A Stray Tusker May Mean Your Life!" Elephants do have the right of way.

dhi, as well as India's sophisticated nuclear scientists, promptly announced that they have no intentions of making a bomb, and were opposed to military uses of nuclear power. The test came as a tremendous boost to the declining morale of a country beset for some time with unprecedented economic difficulties. However, it drew considerable criticism from the West, especially Canada and the United States, who pointed out that a poor nation should not divert its scarce resources to such a costly and potentially dangerous activity. Indians defended their position by stating that they were the first to have conducted such a test underground and at a low cost. They emphasized the peaceful uses of atomic explosions which include digging canals, producing electrical power, extracting natural gas from below rocky mountains, and mining. They further pointed out that such a test would encourage their scientists at home to achieve further breakthroughs in technological advances, and would appeal to India's expatriated nuclear scientists.

Food Crisis and Famine. While population control programs lagged and inflation hit a peak of 30 percent, several states reached the starvation point in 1974. Food shortages were especially acute in Bihar, West Bengal, Orissa, Madhya Pradesh, Rajasthan, and Gu-

A BAG OF WHEAT FLOUR, used in making chappatties, the unleavened pancakes that are the staff of life for Indians, is weighed in India. In the 1973-1974 agricultural year ending in June, Indian food production fell to 103 million tons, down from 108 million tons in 1970-1971, while the Indian population increased by 36 million.

jarat due largely to spring and summer drought leading to grain hoarding and black-marketing.

Mrs. Gandhi, under heavy attack for unsuccessful economic policies and the slow progress in family planning, was forced to overhaul the central cabinet. Jaglivan Ram, a tough figure, was named agriculture minister, and Chidambara Subramaniam became finance minister. Alarmed by an annual increase of 13 million people, the government also stepped up its birth control plans, especially in the countryside.

Central Government: Setbacks and Victories. India's ruling Congress party was heavily criticized by other politicians as well as the economically suffering masses. Perhaps, for the first time in the country's twenty-seven years, another strong party may emerge in opposition to the Congress party. The new Bharatiya Lok Dal (Indian People's party) was formally launched in August. It was a coalition of socialists as well as free enterprisers, and may yet prove to be a serious challenge to the present Congress leadership, which is showing signs of internal disunity. At least three other events during the year caused this disunity. JP, who enjoys mass support and who openly attacks the Congress party, has some admirers within the party. The government authority of MISA (Maintenance of Internal Security Act) has been frequently misused in curbing legal rights of political opponents and is also criticized for its less controversial use in curbing the major smugglers. The dismissal of the editor of the prestigious newspaper *Hindustan Times,* an outspoken critic of the government, was viewed as a blow to the country's traditionally free media.

In 1974, Mrs. Gandhi's leadership scored at least three crucial victories at home. A nationwide train strike, beginning May 8, which involved 2 million workers and crippled the country's travel and trade, collapsed after twenty days. Due to Mrs. Gandhi's decisiveness, the striking railroad workers' demands were only partially met. The train strike and other similar antigovernment labor demonstrations were skillfully controlled. In August, when an election for India's president took place, Fakhruddin Ali Ahmed, a Congress candidate and a Moslem, won a dramatic victory scoring 80 percent of the votes against the opposition candidates. This victory also enhanced India's claim to be a secular state. In September, India managed to incorporate Sikkim, a tiny but strategic northern mountain state, as an associate state of Indian union due to internal feuds and protest there against the traditional ruler, the Chogyal. This involved a successful amendment of the Indian Constitution and created a favorable condition on India's frontier.

External Relations: Cordial and Improving. Toward the end of the year India, after a ten-year embargo, renewed trade ties with traditionally hostile Pakistan, maximizing the possibility of peaceful coexistence and cooperative development in the subcontinent.

India's relations with the United States, which had been strained during the Nixon administration, were significantly improved due to a visit by Secretary of State Henry Kissinger in October. New, friendly exchange pacts were made and promises for much-needed U. S. aid were offered during this visit. Commenting on India's independent posture, Kissinger had this to say: "Our attitude toward the nonaligned will be based on the principles of equality, mutual respect, and shared endeavors and on the premise that all countries have a stake in a peaceful world. Condominium, hegemony, spheres of influence are historically obsolete and morally and politically untenable."

NAVAJO tend sheep in Monument Valley, Ariz. In November a record 75 percent of the registered voters on the 250,000-square-mile Navajo reservation in Arizona, New Mexico, and Utah went to the polls to reelect Peter MacDonald to a second four-year term as chairman of the Navajo Tribal Council. MacDonald is the tribe's first leader with a college degree.

> "No white person or persons shall be permitted to settle upon or occupy any portion of the territory or without the consent of the Indians to pass through the same."
>
> —Fort Laramie Treaty of 1868

The Wounded Knee Trial was a major test of the Fort Laramie Treaty of 1868 between American Indians and the federal government. Held in St. Paul, Minn., it brought national focus on the American Indian Movement (AIM) and the plight of reservation Indians.

The Defendants were militant AIM

INDIAN JEWELRY: An Indian silversmith might spend a month on an ornate silver and turquoise belt or necklace and sell it for $600.

INDIAN OR IMITATION?

As the value of authentic Indian arts and crafts has soared, imitations have flooded the market. Mass-produced by factories in Hong Kong and Japan and even hand-made by U.S. artists, copies of traditional Indian designs are fooling collectors and cutting into the income of Indian artisans.

Indian protests have prompted legal action across the nation. In the spring Oklahoma became the tenth state to pass strict laws against misrepresentation of non-Indian articles. Six shops in the Pacific Northwest were sued by the Federal Trade Commission for falsely labeling some of their merchandise as being made by Alaskan Indians, and three Arizona Indian trading posts were taken to court by the state's consumer-protection division for selling imitation Indian rugs.

NAVAJO WEAVER takes about 350 hours to finish a three-by-five-foot rug which sells for between $350 and $700. Mexican imitations can sometimes be detected by the ridges woven along the top and bottom edges.

leaders Russell Means, an Oglala Sioux, and Dennis Banks, a Chippewa. They were charged with leading 200 AIM members and sympathizers in the seizure of Wounded Knee, S. Dak., on the night of February 27, 1973, and holding the area until surrendering on May 8, 1973, to a force of approximately 250 Federal Bureau of Investigation (FBI) agents and U.S. marshals. Beginning in January, 1974, the trial lasted over eight months, developing further strain between Indians and the Bureau of Indian Affairs.

The Prosecution insisted that the sole question for the jury was whether the Indians had violated laws when they raided stores, seized homes, held hostages, and fired at the FBI agents and marshals during the seventy-one-day occupation.

The Complex Indian Defense involved provisions of the Fort Laramie Treaty. The defense argued: 1) that the Pine Ridge Sioux reservation where Wounded Knee is located is governed illegally through a system imposed on the reservation by the Indian Reorganization Act of 1934 and not in accordance with the terms of the 1868 treaty;

2) that the marshals and FBI agents were on the reservation unlawfully because the Indians had not requested them to help put down the demonstrations that began at Pine Ridge a month before Wounded Knee was seized;

SITE OF CUSTER'S LAST STAND clearly conveys the story of Montana's epic Indian battle on the Little Bighorn River where the Sioux led by Sitting Bull and Crazy Horse wiped out George Custer's troop.

2) that if laws were broken by the demonstrating Indians, it was a matter to be judged by the Sioux Indians, not the federal government.

The Dismissal. On September 16, U.S. District Judge Fred J. Nichol dismissed charges against the AIM leaders, citing "government misconduct." In a seventy-five-minute lecture he criticized the Justice Department for "refusing to let eleven jurors try the case after the twelfth became ill"; accused the chief prosecutor, Assistant U.S. Attorney R. D. Hurd, of seeking conviction rather than justice; and berated the FBI for "stooping to a new low," a reference to times during the trial when FBI agents were shown to have testified untruthfully and to have withheld evidence from the court.

The judge's decision led U.S. Attorney General William Saxbe to order an investigation of the Wounded Knee trial and other trials where defendants pleaded they were being tried for political reasons.

Italy

by
NORMAN KOGAN

Director, Center for Italian Studies
University of Connecticut

Economic Distress. The economic plight in which Italy had been floundering since the beginning of the decade continued to worsen during 1974. The country is particularly deficient in and is required to import on a large scale major raw materials and some critical foodstuffs such as meat, grain, and dairy products. The prices of raw materials and foodstuffs on international markets had been rising for several years, putting increasing pressure on Italy's foreign exchange reserves and stimulating a growing rate of inflation. In the fall of 1973 the quick quadrupling of the price of crude petroleum by the Organization of Petroleum Exporting Countries (OPEC) created a major economic crisis in the country. Italy imports 94 percent of its petroleum, mainly from Middle Eastern and North African countries. By the beginning of 1974 the strain on the Italian balance of payments was enormous, and more than two-thirds of Italy's foreign exchange payments were made to cover the cost of petroleum imports, leaving what was left to pay for the imports of other raw materials such as coal and iron, foodstuffs, and manufactured items. The Italian lira continued its downward course.

THE TOWER OF PISA in Tuscany has been leaning since construction began on shifting ground in 1173, and Italian authorities say any more lean could endanger nearby buildings and perhaps the tower itself. An international competition for the best way to stop the tilt was sponsored by the Italian Public Works Ministry in 1974, but no one won. A commission of experts turned down all the projects entered by architects and engineers from three continents.

ITALIAN SAFETY LEGISLATION banned those under twenty-one and over sixty-five from driving powerful luxury cars in 1974. Italy had more than 12,000 deaths on the road and some 250,000 injuries from automobile accidents during the year.

The impact of the oil crisis was not limited to Italy's foreign trade problems. It spread throughout the domestic economy. Agricultural fertilizers are made from petroleum by-products as are numerous plastics, and the Italian public had

ITALY

become an avid consumer of plastics in the two previous decades. In a futile effort to control inflation the Italian government had put a freeze on food prices in the middle of 1973. By 1974 Italian agriculture was approaching a state of collapse. Farmers complained that they were going broke because permitted prices no longer covered increasing costs of production. Farm laborers were striking because their wages were worth less. This was true, of course, for all income earners, and on February 28 the three major trade union confederations called a general strike to protest against the increasing cost of living. There was little or no violence, the walk-out was staggered from two to twenty-four hours in different fields, and it was clear that moderate rather than extremist forces were in control. It was not intended to overthrow the government or paralyze the economy.

Protests in the form of strikes and shutdowns, in agriculture, industry, public services, and commerce would continue throughout the year, but on a substantially lower scale than during the previous year. By the end of 1974 the analysts were forecasting a 4 to 5 percent growth in real productivity for all of 1974, the only positive sign in a generally dismal picture. This real growth is even more impressive when considered in relation to the drastic decline in automobile production which took place. Automobile manufacturing is one of Italy's most important industries. It should also be measured against the decline in real production which occurred in the United States in the same year. Price controls on foodstuffs naturally produced continuing shortages since more and more staples, such as pasta, disappeared into the black market.

The Fiat Motor Company, Italy's largest private company, was particularly hard hit. Domestic sales of its autos were down 35 to 40 percent over the year, and foreign sales were also reduced, although to a lesser degree. In 1973, it lost money for the first time in the postwar period and in 1974 its losses mounted. At the same time its workers were pressing for substantial wage increases to match the rising cost of living. Forced by the government to grant these demands, the company was caught in a trap. Rumors circulated to the effect that Fiat would throw in the towel and sell out to the government holding corporation, the Institute for Industrial Reconstruction. At the end of April, however, Giovanni Agnelli, the company's president, announced that he would not sell. Instead he asked the government for subsidies on the ground it was responsible for forcing the increasing labor costs on the company. The government agreed. Fiat workers were put on a three-day week while the government paid them almost the equivalent of two days' wages in unemployment compensation. The total received by the workers was 85 to 90 percent of a full week's pay. At a time when inflation was running at an annual rate of 20 percent, this still meant a considerable loss in real income.

By the late spring and early summer the economic crisis led to public forecasts of disaster. At the end of May, Guido Carli, governor of the Bank of Italy, made his annual report on the state of the economy, warning of catastrophe and demanding drastic measures

> "The Italy of the families is definitely the real Italy, the quintessential Italy distilled from the experiences of centuries, while the Italy of the laws and institutions is partly make believe, the country Italians would like to believe will be but know is not."
>
> Luigi Barzini, **The Italians**

MY NAME is Marco. I am ten and live in Venice. As I come out of school carrying my books in a bag over my shoulder, I look pleased because I recited a canto of Dante's *Divine Comedy* perfectly from memory. It is important to do well in class, because in my country if you fail a grade twice you cannot be readmitted to school.

MOMMA likes to watch passersby from our living room window. In a recent study in which young Italians were asked to rate the persons they looked upon with confidence, mother came first and politicians were last with one-half of 1 percent.

MARCO
A Boy of Italy

WHEN THIS STREET PUPPETEER performs, we often stop to watch and throw him a few lire.

ELENA, my married sister, always meets me at the school door with my baby niece, Marissa. My mother is afraid of traffic and of kidnappers. Sometimes we stop for *gelati* ("ice cream") on the way home.

ON HOLIDAYS we sometimes drive to Lake Como for a picnic. We have seventeen Italian holidays (more than anywhere in Europe). On bridge holidays when an extra day is thrown in to bridge a holiday to a weekend, we used to go on long trips, but this summer my father said we could not drive very far because gasoline costs $1.85 a gallon, almost double the 1973 price.

ON WEEKENDS my friend Guilio and I play in the courtyard behind our apartment building.

MY FATHER reads his newspaper as he rides a Venetian "taxi" to his job. To meet our 25 percent Italian inflation this year he had to take on after-hours work.

of austerity to reduce inflationary pressures and conserve scarce foreign exchange. This immediately provoked a major debate with the Left-wing parties charging that the government wanted to fight inflation by putting the major sacrifices on the working classes and the poor. They demanded that the well-to-do be required, instead, to make the sacrifices. Nevertheless, on June 27, Prime Minister Mariano Rumor announced that the government was introducing additional measures of austerity including $5 billion of increased taxes. Since the Italian tax system is essentially regressive, most of the additional taxes would be paid by the lower income groups. The government hoped that in this way two of the major causes of inflation, heavy government deficits and money in circulation, would be somewhat reduced. Although the governing Center-Left coalition was divided on these measures, they were passed—adding, however, to strains in the government's supporting alliance of parties. At the same time, government spending was held back, leading to the closing of museums, galleries, and other enterprises dependent on state subsidies.

Strikes were called by the trade unions to protest the higher taxes, but again they were more for the record than a serious effort to reverse policy. In the meantime, various businesses reported heavy losses, and a process of economic consolidation continued. The controlling interest in the largest newspaper in Italy, the *Corriere della Sera* of Milan, was sold in July to the Rizzoli publishing company, already a major holder of magazine, book, and cinema firms. This reduced further the number of independent voices in Italian journalism. All newspapers in Italy were losing circulation as a result of price rises and all were running large deficits, covered by subsidies from interest groups, political parties, or indirect government subventions. The crash of the international banking empire of the Italian financier Michele Sindona, (whose American bank, the Franklin National of New York, was forced to close), put additional burdens on the Italian state, for the Bank of Italy and several other government-owned banks were forced to come to the rescue, at a substantial price, in order to maintain the international credit and good name of the country.

In the fall and winter of 1974, the

VENICE had sunk a full foot deeper into the Adriatic between the turn of the century and the end of 1974. Although the Italian Parliament passed a special law in April, 1973, in which "the safeguarding of Venice" was "declared to be a problem of paramount national concern," none of the funds appropriated had been spent in 1974. The approximately $2 million spent by private groups on the restoration of the city has been subjected to the nation's value-added tax, causing one organization to complain, "We are saving your monuments and you are charging us for the privilege."

economic situation showed no signs of improvement. While production held up, the rate of inflation continued to increase, and it was estimated that by November and December of the year inflation was running at an annual rate of about 25 percent.

Political Instability. The economic problems naturally led to substantial political turmoil. The Center-Left coalition was divided on how to fight the inflationary squeeze. Some demanded severe austerity and others rejected austerity on the basis of its consequence for unemployment and for lower income groups. In addition, oil scandals broke out in February with evidence that the oil companies, domestic and foreign, had been making large gifts to the parties in return for favorable treatment. One of the results of the scandals was the passage of new legislation on April 17 providing for public subsidies for the political parties. The money from the state treasury would be distributed in proportion to the size of the parties, and restricted to those having representation in parliament. The bill also forbids state-controlled agencies and firms from contributing to political groups.

At the end of February the Treasury minister, Ugo La Malfa, resigned. He is the leader of the Republican party, one of the four in the Center-Left coalition. La Malfa is one of the strongest voices calling for a policy of austerity. His departure led to the resignation of the entire cabinet. On March 6, President Giovanni Leone formally asked Prime Minister Mariano Rumor to form a new government. In a week he had recreated practically the same coalition, and on March 14 the thirty-sixth Italian government since World War II was formed. The Christian Democrats, Social Democrats, and Socialists remained in the cabinet. The Republicans stayed out but agreed to support the government in parliament. Most of the previous cabinet ministers returned to their very same posts.

For the next two months the major issue on the political agenda was the national referendum on the divorce law. For the first time in Italian history divorce had been legalized in 1970. Catholic forces in the country had been trying ever since to overthrow the law by a popular referendum. For more than three years the issue had been stalled by politicians who realized the divisive effects of such a referendum on the country. All the delaying maneuvers had finally been exhausted and the date had been set for May. The Catholic church threw all its weight into the campaign. Priests who spoke up in favor of divorce were suspended. Amintore Fanfani, secretary-general of the Christian Democratic party, mobilized his party organization on the side of the church. The neo-Fascist *Movimento Sociale Italiano* (MSI) Party also opposed divorce. All the other parties in parliament supported the divorce law. Up to the very end it appeared that opinion in the country was almost evenly divided. The referendum was held on May 12 and 13. To the surprise of everyone the results were a sweeping victory for the pro-divorce forces who won by a margin of 60 percent to 40 percent. Their strength was spread all over the country, in the North and South, in urban areas and rural ones.

Political consequences from the result soon became apparent. In June, regional elections were held in Sardinia, and the vote of the Catholic party declined while the Left parties increased. At the end of the month dissident Left-wing Catholics met in Rome and threatened to form a new Catholic-political party. This threat has been raised a number of times during the postwar period, but the Christian Democratic party and the Vatican — committed to the principle of the political unity of Catholics — have always successfully fought it off.

On June 11, Premier Rumor submitted the resignation of his cabinet once more, because of the divisions over the issue of economic austerity. President Leone refused to accept the resignation, however, and after a few days of consultation the government was persuaded to remain in office. It did not, therefore, count as a new government. The tax plan referred to earlier was the result of the compro-

ROMANS meet on the Ponte Sant' Angelo, a bridge decorated with Giovanni Bernini statues of angels. Rome's 3.5 million citizens enjoy less green space for recreation than do residents of any other European city — two square yards of scorched grass per person.

mise reached between the parties.

Throughout the year incidents of sporadic violence had occurred throughout the country. Extremist neo-Marxist and neo-Fascist groups engaged in a variety of attacks, bombings, and riots, against each other and the rest of society. The worst incident occurred on August 4, when a bomb exploded on a train just emerging from a tunnel on the main line between Florence and Bologna. Twelve people were killed and forty-eight injured. It was the worst terrorist attack since the bombing of a bank in Milan in 1969. Arrests were made a few days later of members of a neo-Fascist group called the Black Hand.. The MSI denied any involvement and insisted it was a legal, non-Fascist party, although there were continuing charges it was linked to the extremist groups.

The threat to the polity did not come only from young extremists. Throughout the year there were arrests of army officers suspected of plotting against the republic. In January a certain Lt. Col. Amos Spiazzi was arrested when an arsenal of weapons was discovered in his private quarters. Other officers, some retired and some on duty, were under suspicion. On October 31, General Vito Miceli, former head of the Secret Service, was arrested on charges of using his position to foment disorder and of plotting an insurrection. He was also charged with having known of various other plots and doing nothing to inform his political superiors or stop the plotters.

One of the major issues causing cabinet instability was the disagreement over the role of the Communist party, second largest in the country. The Socialists insisted that no solution to the country's problems was possible without the Communists who dominated the major trade union confederation, the General Union of Italian Workers (CGIL), and the largest number of workers in the country. The Communist leadership proclaimed in January that it was ready to collaborate in a solution to the crisis, but insisted that the government would have to treat it as a serious and valid participant in the critical decisions. The leaders did not demand immediate entry into the cabinet. At the time of the June crisis the Communists once more announced that they wanted a say in decision-making at the highest level. The Christian Democrats, however, rejected their overtures, turning down—as the Church as always turned down—the demand for an "historic compromise" between Catholicism and Marxism. At the beginning of September, the Communists returned to the attack, offering their availability for government responsibility. They said it was time to forget prejudicial anti-Communism and assured the public that they would respect Italy's current foreign policy commitments to the North Atlantic Treaty Organization (NATO) and the European Economic Community (EEC). They reiterated their indifference to the issue of holding posts in the cabinet.

On September 5, Giovanni Agnelli, president of the Italian Confederation of

AN ITALIAN LABORER starts out for work. In October northern Italian workers tried "civil disobedience" to fight inflation. Backed by their unions, in Turin they refused to pay a 15 percent price hike on bus tickets and paid only half of their electric bills which had been increased by 70 percent. In Milan some 20,000 families in public housing refused to pay higher rents.

Industries as well as of Fiat, publicly argued against Communist participation in the government. He did not accept Communist assurances concerning Italy's international commitments and warned against the danger to "free and efficient" private enterprise. The conflict over the issue within the governing coalition continued and was aggravated by claims and counterclaims of disloyalty. Finally, on October 3, the cabinet collapsed and Prime Minister Rumor turned in its resignation to President Leone.

The crisis this time was a long one. Leone, after a week of consultation with political leaders, called on Amintore Fanfani to try to unite the parties. Fanfani reluctantly agreed, but after more than a week of negotiations gave up. On October 29, Leone asked Aldo Moro, a former Christian Democratic prime minister, to try. It took Moro more than three weeks but finally he succeeded in forming a new government on November 23. By December 7, the cabinet had received votes of confidence from the Senate and Chamber of Deputies. The crisis had lasted more than two months.

Moro's government was a two-party coalition of Christian Democrats and Republicans, therefore a minority government. The Socialists and Social Democrats promised to support it in parliament and did give it their backing when the confidence votes were taken. Since the Republicans are identified with the policy of severe austerity, the declared program of the new government emphasized retrenchment and sacrifice. It was natural for the two Socialist parties to let the onus of such policy fall on others. Moro also reiterated his country's fidelity to existing international commitments and rejected any prospective alliance with the Communists. He called for a reduction of imports and an increase in exports to reduce the deficit in the balance of payments and reestablish Italy's "political and financial credit."

Foreign Policies. With one exception Italy's foreign policy actions were linked to its economic problems. It needed foreign loans desperately to obtain funds to import oil and other necessary raw materials. The International Monetary Fund offered a $1.2 billion standby credit in February on condition that Italy undertake the necessary domestic belt-tightening. At the same time the

United States extended and increased a loan it had given in 1973. La Malfa, then the Treasury minister accepted, but the Socialists reacted violently, calling it interference in Italy's internal affairs and accusing the bankers of imposing unemployment and reduced living standards on the working class. It was the controversy over the loan that caused the Republican withdrawal from the cabinet the first week of March.

At the same time Italy was making separate deals with Arab oil exporting nations. On February 25, a pact was announced with Libya which involved an exchange of North African oil for Italian investment and technological aid in the steel, shipbuilding, and petrochemical sectors. A week later Italy abandoned its effort to stay equidistant in the Arab-Israeli dispute and called upon Israel to give up all the territories occupied in the 1967 six-day war.

The deteriorating economic situation also forced a revival of economic nationalism. In late 1973, an Italian oil processor and wholesaler, Monti Petroleum, had bought out the complete British Petroleum investment in Italy. At the beginning of 1974, the Italian government petrochemical holding corporation National Hydrocarbons Agency (ENI), bought out most of the Royal Dutch Shell petroleum operations in Italy, including its refineries and distribution network. These were not forced sales imposed by a political policy of nationalization; the foreign concerns were happy to sell. Nonetheless it meant a reduction in the interdependence of the members of the Common Market.

Italy's relations with the Common Market were strained further when on April 30 it unilaterally announced protectionist measures discouraging the importation of finished goods. It used a special emergency clause in the EEC treaty to justify its move, which also was a violation of its commitments under the General Agreement on Tariffs and Trade (GATT). The government justified these curbs as temporary. Both the EEC and GATT accepted these actions under the emergency clauses, but it was obvious they had been presented with a *fait accompli*. Italy had violated the free trade principles of both organizations and given an indication of growing protectionism in response to an international crisis. Italy later eased the import restrictions on foodstuffs from other Common Market countries.

During the summer, Italy continued to seek foreign loans and at the end of August announced a $2 billion loan from the West German government. The announcement temporarily stabilized the precarious government coalition. American worries about possible Communist participation in the government led to a presumed warning by Secretary of State Henry Kissinger in September. In November, Italy received an extension of repayment of a loan received from the Common Market during an earlier period. In such manner it staggered along to the end of the year.

The one foreign policy issue not tied up with oil, loans, and international finance was the question of NATO bases. As a result of the Cyprus coup and the Turkish invasion of the island, the new Greek government which replaced the military regime announced it was removing Greek military contingents from NATO and would request the removal of NATO military bases from Greece. It was immediately speculated in Italy that the government would be asked to grant additional bases to the American fleet as a substitute. The Left wing objected loudly, arguing this would increase American "colonialism" and interference in Italian politics. At the end of the year the issue was dormant since the Greek government had not carried out its threat.

THE JAPANESE WORKER, educated in the Confucian idea that a company is an extension of the family, not an impersonal corporation, feels a sense of loyalty to his factory; and it is Japanese practice to guarantee lifetime jobs to those hired. The 1974 economic slump caused Japanese companies to cut back production, but instead of firing workers most businesses put all employees on *ichiji kikyo* ("temporary home rest") for short periods. The productivity, or output per man-day, of Japanese labor rose a record 20.1 percent during the year.

Japan

by
THEODORE McNELLY, Ph.D.
Professor, Department of Government and Politics
University of Maryland

The Energy Crisis. In 1974, as in 1973, economic difficulties were the dominant concerns of the Japanese people. The slow-down of oil shipments from the Middle East at the end of 1973 was a more severe shock to Japan than it was to some of the other major industrialized countries. In Japan, petroleum was used not only to power trucks and automobiles but also to produce most of the electricity. Japan's industries and nearly all of her trains and subways depended upon this electrical power. The Japanese, like Americans, being fond of air conditioning and brightly lighted streets and shops, had become prodigal users of electricity. Japan produced very little coal and virtually no oil in her own territory and was almost entirely dependent on imports of these fuels. It was not possible, given her short rivers and limited territory, to enlarge substantially her capacity to produce electricity by harnessing water power. Atomic power plants were still rare and could not be increased rapidly.

The Kyushu Power Company planned the construction in southern Japan of a geothermal power plant, which would convert subterranean heat into electricity. Japanese scientists were hard at work developing systems for the extraction and use of hydrogen (abundantly available in water) as an economical and non-polluting source of energy. However, it would take several decades before new types of power plants could be designed and put into large-scale operation. In the meantime, Japan would continue to depend on oil imports for most of her energy.

Under pressure from the oil-producing nations, the Japanese government, at the end of 1973, announced a pro-Arab stance in the Arab-Israeli dispute. (A Jewish-organized boycott of Japanese goods in America was threatened but did not materialize.) The Arabs assured Japan of a continuous supply of oil, and the oil shortage was overcome by the spring of 1974. However, the new higher price of oil remained a grave, unresolved problem. As the cost of energy rose, the competitive position of Japanese products in the world market was seriously threatened. Japan's dependence on other countries for fuel and raw materials was the Achilles' heel of her booming economy. The Japanese government embarked on "resources diplomacy" to strengthen economic relations with nations rich in natural resources, including the Soviet Union, Canada, and Australia.

Nuclear Power. The difficulties experienced by Japan's only nuclear-powered cargo ship raised serious doubts about the future of nuclear energy in Japan. For months, local fishermen had managed to delay the launching of the ship until they had been generously compensated for losses they feared would result from contamination of their fishing grounds. In September, shortly after slipping out of the harbor during a storm (the departure had been blocked by the boats of protesters), the ship's nuclear reactor sprang a dangerous leak. For weeks the local inhabitants would not permit the ship to return to its home base at Mutsu for servicing and repairs, and the seamen's union ordered the crewmen to leave the ship. Advocates of nuclear power feared that the adverse public reaction would seriously delay the future development of nuclear energy as an alternative to oil.

The Ocean's Potential. The Japanese

JAPAN

government and some leading industrial firms invested heavily in the construction of the International Ocean Exposition to be held in Okinawa in 1975. Okinawa, Japan's southernmost prefecture, consisting of a chain of islands between the main Japanese islands and Taiwan, had been returned to Japanese rule by the United States in 1972 and was in severe need of economic development. The focus of Expo '75 would be the relationship of mankind to the oceans. In addition to unique exhibits depicting marine life and the ocean ecology, the exposition would feature the Aquapolis, the world's first floating city. The Aquapolis, measuring 100 meters (328 feet) in width and length, would have its own power generation plant, water supply, and garbage and sewage disposal equipment, making it independent of land facilities. It represented one possible answer to the problem of urban congestion for overcrowded countries like Japan. The Japanese were great consumers of fish, including shellfish, and of seaweed, and since World War II had developed a fish farming (in addition to a fish catching) industry. With the application of ingenuity and hard work, the food, fuel, and mineral resources in and under the ocean apparently represented a great potential for development.

The Economy. The economy planning agency announced in February that the gross national income had reached a new high in 1973: $415.7 billion or $3,839 per capita. However, the belief grew among bureaucrats, businessmen, and economists that the Japanese economy could no longer grow at the rate of 10 percent or more per year as it had been doing for two decades. An annual growth rate of 6 to 8 percent seemed more likely because of shortages of fuel, raw materials, and industrial sites and because of the costs of pollution control.

The Conservatives. Ever since 1948, the conservatives had ruled Japan. Until 1955 these were either Liberals or Democrats, and after 1955, they were members of the Liberal-Democratic party, which had resulted from a conservative merger. The Liberal-Democrats held a majority of seats in both the upper and lower houses of the Diet (parliament), and the prime minister and his cabinet ministers were Liberal-Democrats.

Conservative leaders had placed priority on the restoration of the economy, which had been destroyed in World War II, and the promotion of high productivity. Under the conservatives, Japan had attained by 1968 the world's third largest gross national product and her standard of living approached that of western Europe. By 1970, however, it was clear that part of the price of Japan's economic miracle had been the pollution or destruction of much of the environment. The fish and shellfish in the waters in some of the principal fishing grounds around Japan were poisoned, the air in the great cities was dangerously contaminated, much of the scenic beauty was ruined. By 1973 there were shortages of lumber, cement, paper, housing, and other necessities, and inflation seemed to be getting out of control.

Prime Minister Kakuei Tanaka hoped to carry out his famous plan for the reconstruction of the Japanese archipelago, which would relocate industries from overly congested areas to economically depressed areas and greatly improve the transportation system. These proposals, unfortunately, seemed only to aggravate land speculation and inflation and threatened to expand pollution rather than contain it. Political and business leaders seemed to have great difficulty in shifting their priorities from high productivity to preserving the environment and stopping inflation. The Socialist and Communist parties blamed the Liberal-Democrats and monopoly capitalists for all of Japan's problems. Since 1967 the conservatives had been unable to capture a majority of the popular votes in Diet elections (although they managed to hang onto a majority of the seats in both houses of the Diet). Many of the large cities of Japan (including Tokyo) had elected "progressive" (Socialist- or Communist-sponsored) mayors, who were trying to come to grips with urban problems. Within the conservative party there had recently emerged a right-wing hawkish faction, the Seirankai, which opposed the prime minister's policy of rapprochement with Communist China. The Seirankai provoked a bitter feud with the moderates of the party and threatened to withdraw its support from the Tanaka cabinet.

The Challenge of the Election. The 1974 upper house (House of Councillors) election was a severe challenge for the governing Liberal-Democrats. Councillors serve for staggered six-year terms, with half the seats up for election every three years. Of the total of 252 members, 152 represent the forty-seven prefectures, and 100 represent the nation at large. In this system, each voter casts one vote for a candidate to represent his prefecture and one vote for a candidate on the nation-at-large list. This system makes it possible for minor parties and prominent nonpoliticians to win seats in the House of Councillors. In the upper house election of July 7, 130 seats (including four vacancies) had to be filled.

Popular interest in the election was intense, as there was a real possibility that the Liberal-Democrats might, for the first time, lose their majority in the upper house. In spite of torrential rains, a record 73 percent of the voters went to the polls. As a result of the 1974 elections the Liberal Democrats ended up with 126 seats (including members elected in 1971), a number which was converted into a bare majority when the support of two conservative independents is taken into account. The only dramatic winners in the election were the Communists, who won 9 seats, for a total of 20 seats, nearly twice their previous representation. Although the Socialists (the number two party) increased by 3 the number of their seats, they could gather no comfort from the fact that their percentage of the popular vote had dropped from 21.27 in 1971 to 15.18 in 1974.

The results of the election were as follows:

Parties	% of votes won in 1971	% of votes won in 1974	Preelection Strength	Seats won in 1974	Grand total of seats held after 1974
Liberal Democrats	44.48	44.34	134	62	126
Japan Socialists	21.27	15.18	59	28	62
Komeito	14.09	12.09	23	14	24
Japan Communists	8.06	9.37	11	13	20
Democratic Socialists	6.11	5.92	11	5	10
Minor	0.12	0.14	0	1	1
Independents	5.87	12.96	6	7	9
Vacancies	—	—	8	—	—
Totals	100.00	100.00	252	130	252

Obviously it was possible that if there was the slightest defection from the conservative party in the upper house, its proposals there could be defeated. The Liberal-Democrats would need the cooperation of the middle-of-the-road parties (Democratic Socialists and Komeito).

The Liberal-Democrats' poor showing in the election gravely weakened Prime Minister Tanaka's leadership in the par-

DINING OUT can cost $100 per person in Tokyo, which claims some of the most expensive restaurants in the world. Beef *sukiyaki* is cooking in the pan at left with scallions, watercress, bamboo shoots, and mushrooms. At right is a plate of *sashimi* (raw tuna, squid, and striped bass).

MUSKMELONS, gift-packaged with *noshi* (paper decorations), are priced at $12 each. In June peaches sold for 45 cents apiece and grapes for $6 a pound.

FOOD IN JAPAN

As inflation turned Japanese affluence to economic gloom in 1974, many Japanese began reverting to traditional frugal habits developed over centuries of living on their crowded, largely resourceless islands.

The oil crisis was little felt in heating cutbacks or gasoline shortages. Japanese women have always done their food buying in little neighborhood shops, not massed shopping centers, and have traveled to the market on foot. The oil crisis did cause panic buying and hoarding of daily necessities, it hampered the farming of vegetables as the vinyl used in greenhouses became scarce and soared in price, and it resulted in a cutback of fishing by boats.

Food prices jumped sharply. Sales slumped at the many cake shops. Women began buying fish heads instead of more expensive sea food, and what had been a growing trend to beef-eating was reversed.

Many younger Japanese women, raised in the era of prosperity, continued spending a large percentage of their salaries on clothes from the presitge shops, while reducing their meals to bowls of rice and vegetables eaten in company cafeterias. Appearances have always been important in Japanese society, a tradition illustrated by the old Japanese proverb: "The samurai uses a toothpick, even if he didn't eat dinner."

A JAPANESE HOUSEWIFE buys a few strips of thinly sliced beef at $15 a pound. By the end of the year sirloin was selling for $40 a pound in Tokyo.

ASA (MORNING)

by

Mrs. Shizue Iwatsuki

In the light of the morning sun
On the Columbia River
Sails a wheat-laden Japanese ship
Led by a tugboat

In 1974 30,000 poems of thirty-one syllables were entered in the yearly Japanese competition. The poem by Mrs. Iwatsuki, a seventy-seven-year-old naturalized U.S. citizen of Hood River, Ore., was one of ten selected to be read at Emperor Hirohito's annual poetry-reading party on January 10.

ty. A published exposé of the alleged ways in which he had used his political power to enhance his vast personal business enterprises proved politically fatal. In November, immediately after President Gerald Ford's visit to Japan, Tanaka announced his resignation.

Foreign Relations. The Japanese were greatly shaken by India's testing of an atomic weapon in 1974. It was a keen disappointment that a fellow Asian country, which had so vigorously proclaimed its devotion to peace and its concern for the poor, would use its limited resources to develop an atomic weapon. In protest, the Japanese government reduced its economic aid to India. Among the three leading Asian states, China, India, and Japan, only Japan did not have the bomb. Japan had signed, but not yet ratified, the nuclear nonproliferation treaty. Her policy continued to be not to manufacture, possess, or permit the introduction (by American forces) of nuclear weapons. The Japanese, with their well-known "allergy" to nuclear weapons, were hopeful that the international situation would not become unstable and that they would never feel constrained to acquire nuclear weapons. Japan's relations with Communist China continued to show slow improvement. In September, exactly two years after the establishment of diplomatic relations between the two countries, regular direct air service between Tokyo and Peking was established.

Shortly after President Richard Nixon's resignation in August, it was announced that President Ford would visit Japan in November. Leftists and pacifists in Japan hoped that with their demonstrations they would be able to prevent the presidential visit as they had done in 1960, when they had forced the Japanese government to "postpone" (actually cancel) President Dwight Eisenhower's scheduled visit to Japan. Several weeks before Ford's arrival, it became known that American naval ships had for some years been carrying nuclear arms, in transit, into Japanese harbors. This very sensitive issue threatened to heighten further anti-American feeling on the eve of the presidential visit. However, massed police forces and the use of a helicopter instead of an automobile to take the president from the Tokyo airport to his guest quarters prevented demonstrators from disrupting Ford's welcome. The visit apparently accomplished its main function of reaffirming the close ties between America and Japan, and it was announced that the Japanese emperor would visit the United States in 1975. From Tokyo, the president and Secretary of State Henry Kissinger flew back and forth across the Japan Sea to visit first South Korea and then the Soviet Union. In Seoul, the president reiterated America's determination to maintain a military presence in South Korea against the threat of Communist North Korea. In Vladivostok, the president met the Soviet Communist party chief Leonid Brezhnev,

AT THE TOKYO STOCK EXCHANGE prices registered their heaviest plunge of the year in August, as volume rose to 200 million shares. The setback was triggered by unconfirmed reports that the Bank of Japan might raise the discount rate to tighten credit.

and the two leaders announced substantial progress in the Soviet-American strategic arms limitations talks (SALT). Kissinger made a side trip to Peking, where he arranged a presidential visit to China for 1975. Before returning to Washington, Kissinger reported on his China trip to Japanese officials in Tokyo, reassuring them that the American policy of detente with the Soviet Union and China would not be at the expense of Japanese-American friendship.

The Korean Problem. Japan's relations with her nearest neighbor, South

Korea, gravely worsened in 1973 and 1974. The events of these years, of course, must be seen in the context of the persistent fears of the Koreans that Japan might once again achieve a position of dominance over them. (From 1910 to 1945 Korea had been part of the Japanese empire.) From the end of World War II, when Korea obtained her independence from Japan, until 1965, when Japan and South Korea signed a treaty normalizing their relationship, there had been no regular diplomatic relations between Japan and either of the two Koreas. Following the 1965 treaty, Japanese trade with and investment in South Korea grew rapidly. Many Koreans feared that the conspicuous Japanese economic involvement in Korea might compromise her independence. At the same time, Japan's recognition of Communist China in 1972 and tentatives towards improving her relations with North Korea deeply disturbed the South Korean government. Reports that the Japanese practiced widespread discrimination against the some half million Koreans living in Japan, kept alive the feeling of distrust between the two countries.

In 1973, Japan-South Korea relations were soured by the Kim Dae Jung affair, in which a leading Korean politician was mysteriously kidnapped from his hotel in Tokyo. Japanese police officials, citing circumstantial evidence, charged that officials in the Korean embassy in Tokyo were involved in this, and if this were the case, South Korea had violated Japanese sovereignty. In 1974 the increasingly despotic character of the Park Chung Hee regime in South Korea again raised the question of the propriety of the Japanese government's economic and diplomatic support of South Korea. On August 15, 1974, a Japan-born Korean with a forged Japanese passport and a stolen Japanese police revolver attempted to assassinate President Park, but failed, killing Mrs. Park instead. There were charges in Korea that the Japanese were in some way responsible for this incident.

There were repeated protest demonstrations, some very violent, at the Japanese Embassy in Seoul. The South Korean government demanded that the Japanese apologize for their alleged involvement in the assassination and suppress the pro-Communist league of Koreans residing in Japan, which was accused of planning the assassination attempt. The United States, which maintained military bases in both South Korea and Japan, feared the consequences of a split between her two allies in Asia and reportedly urged a compromise settlement. Japan (after the United States) was South Korea's second biggest customer and foreign investor.

It would appear from the Kim Dae Jung affair and the Park assassination attempt that the Japanese government was caught on the horns of a dilemma. Friendly relations with the Park regime were criticized as supportive of dictatorship, but any appearance of sympathy with or involvement in an effort to overturn the Park government would be interpreted as an imperialistic plot.

No Easy Solution. In some ways it would seem that Japan's economic and diplomatic problems were the price of her postwar successes. Her rise to the position of the world's third largest economy had made her (like Western European countries) excessively dependent on Middle Eastern fuel. Her economic expansion into Korea and Southeast Asia had aroused fears in those countries that Japan was a threat to their independence. The dependence of the Japanese economy on foreign trade (including oil imports and the exports necessary to pay for the imports), meant that there was no easy solution for Japan's problems in relating to the rest of the world.

Judaism

by
JAY B. STERN, D. R. E.

President, Midrasha College of Jewish Studies
Southfield, Michigan

Soviet Jewry. The efforts of large numbers of Russian Jews to leave the Soviet Union continued to receive worldwide attention in 1974. American Jews tried to tie the question of Jewish emigration from Russia to the issue of American trade with the Soviet Union. Senator Henry Jackson was the sponsor in the U.S. Senate of an amendment to a bill which would withhold certain American trade rights from nations restricting free emigration of their citizens. The bill was obviously aimed at Russia. The Soviets claimed that the matter of emigration was purely an internal affair of their own, while proponents of the Jackson amendment contended that in the face of overt inhuman acts, such as the virtual imprisonment of innocent people, there can be no such thing as a purely internal matter.

The Soviets engaged in the tactic of increasing and then slowing Jewish emigration. President Richard Nixon visited Russia in June, discussing with the U.S.S.R.'s Leonid Brezhnev U.S.-Soviet detente, nuclear arms limitation, the Middle East, "most favored nation" trade status, and, presumably, the emigration issue. His visit was preceded by the arrest by the Russians of dozens of Jewish activists in the Soviet Union, and, surprisingly, the release of the famous dancer Valery Panov and his wife. The couple was finally permitted to move to Israel after a two-year wait which included the exclusion of the Panovs from all Russian artistic activity. Panov is Jewish. His wife is not.

LEONARD BASKIN'S PAINTING of the four mothers of Israel — Sarah, Rebecca, Leah, and Rachel — is one of the modern illustrations in *A Passover Haggadah*, Reform Judaism's first new rabbinically approved prayer book in fifty years.

The Yom Kippur War. War broke out in the Middle East in October, with a combined Egyptian-Syrian attack on Israel on Yom Kippur, the holiest day of the Jewish year. While the intention was apparently to catch Israel off guard, the choice of Yom Kippur made the mobilization of Israel's civilian army somewhat easier, since virtually the entire population was in synagogues or at home that day.

The war changed certain presumptions about Israeli military strength and preparedness and opened the way for Secretary of State Henry Kissinger's diplomatic missions to the Middle East. Kissinger's efforts resulted in some Israeli pullbacks, the placement of U.N. troops between Israel and Egypt and Syria, the reestablishment of diplomatic relations between the United States and several Arab states, and some tentative discus-

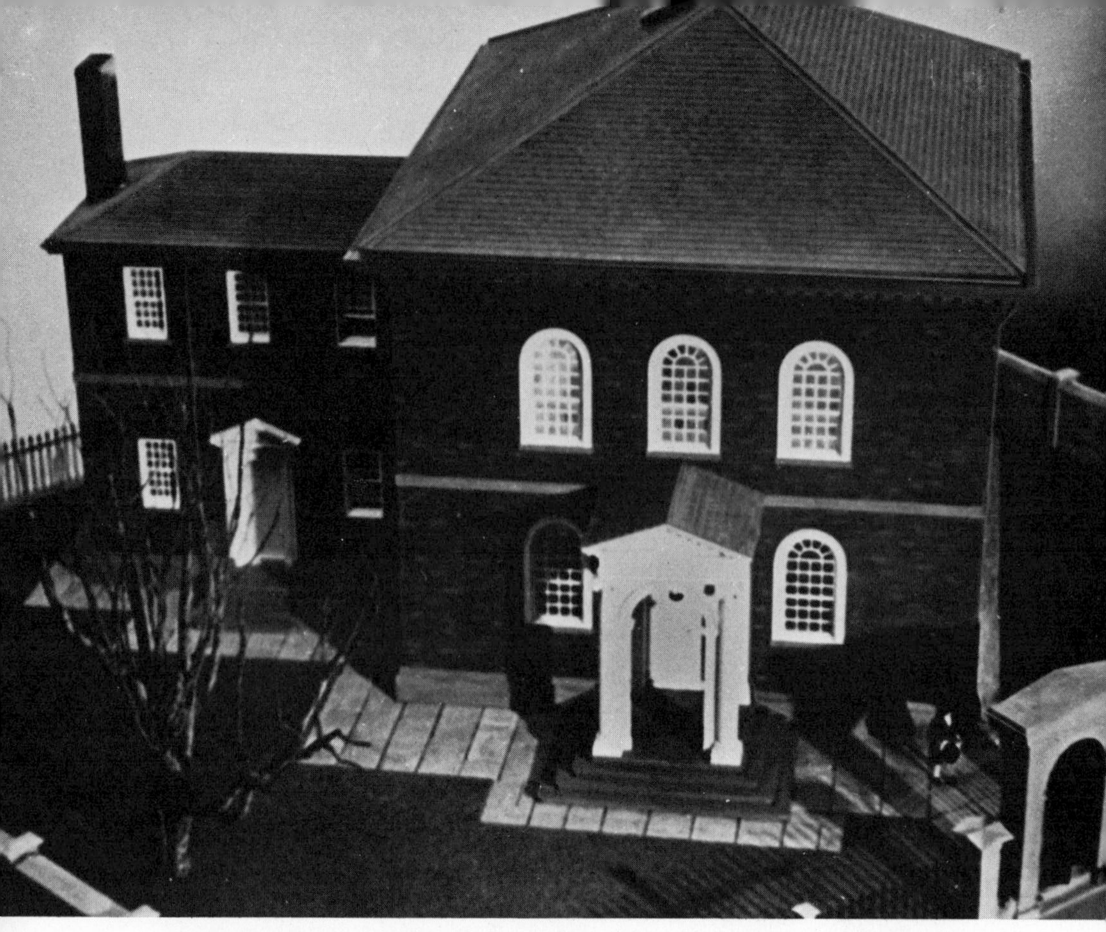

MODEL OF TOURO SYNAGOGUE, an eighteenth-century temple in Newport, R.I., is on permanent display with nine other meticulously crafted scale models in the exhibit "Synagogues Through the Ages" at New York City's Yeshiva University Museum.

sions between Israel and the Arabs. Secretary Kissinger, interestingly enough, is Jewish. He came to the United States as a young boy, having escaped from Nazi Germany.

Arab terrorist attacks against Jewish settlements in Israel were frequent in 1974, with the apparent aim of breaking up the Kissinger peace initiatives. A teenage hiking group was brutally murdered in the northern village of Maalot, and families were killed in Kiryat, Shemoneh, and Nahariya. These attacks on civilians were reminiscent of the murder of the Israeli Olympic team in Munich in 1972. Jewish communities throughout the world protested the U.N. condemnation of Israeli retaliatory raids against terrorist bases while ignoring the massacre of Jewish civilians, the cause of these retaliatory raids.

The DeFunis Case. The question of compensatory treatment of minority groups, particularly blacks, split the Jewish community during 1974. The Reform Union of American Hebrew Congregations and the National Council of Jewish Women found themselves arrayed against the American Jewish Committee, the Anti-Defamation League of B'nai B'rith, the American Jewish Congress, and the Jewish Rights Council in the U.S. Supreme Court case of Marco DeFunis.

DeFunis, a Phi Beta Kappa magna cum laude college graduate, was denied admission to the Washington University law school. He took his case to court claiming that he had been passed over in favor of far less qualified candidates who were admitted under a compensatory program designed to give blacks a chance to make up for past discrimination.

DeFunis was eventually admitted to law school and graduated, but the question of the stance of the Jewish community on the issues raised by the case is by no means settled. The Union of American Hebrew Congregations-National Council group claims that minorities — in this case blacks — deserve special favored treatment. Other Jewish groups contend that compensatory treatment of one group inevitably means discrimination against another group, as the DeFunis case illustrated.

Jewish Population. The Zero Population Growth movement seems to have had a strong effect upon the population of American Jews, whose family size tends to be smaller than average. Had American Jews reproduced at the same rate as the rest of the population after 1940, there would now be a Jewish population in the United States of 7½ million, instead of less than 6 million. For a minority people, the loss of that potential 25 percent increase is extremely important, particularly when one considers the serious inroads intermarriage has made upon the Jewish population. In terms of world Jewish population, Jews constitute the only group which has lost numbers since World War II. Other ethnic groups which lost large numbers in the war have since replaced this lost population by internal growth. For this reason population growth and intermarriage remain serious Jewish concerns.

Watergate. The Watergate affair began to have its Jewish overtones in 1974. The Jewish community was relieved to learn that none of the conspirators or defendants was Jewish. When the White

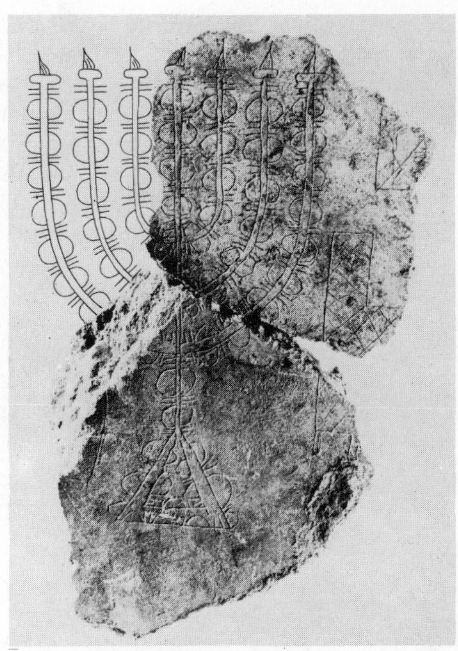

THIS DEPICTION OF A MENORAH, or seven-branched candelabrum, was made when a vessel of this kind was standing in the Second Temple and is probably the most authentic representation of a temple menorah yet found. Discovered in Jerusalem's Jewish Quarter, it is believed to have once decorated a wall of a Herodian palace in the area.

House released transcripts of some of the tape recordings in its possession, however, rumors immediately began to circulate that some of the deletions and inaudible sections actually contained antisemitic references. *The New York Times* carried a version in which the president and his aides were reported to have complained about Jews on the special prosecutor's staff. True or not, the matter turned into a tempest in a teapot when one of the three so-called Jews turned out to be an Episcopalian.

Jews were generally divided on the impeachment issue. One group, The Committee on Fairness to the President, was formed and headed by a rabbi.

Arrayed against this group were several Jewish organizations calling for impeachment or resignation.

Women's Rights. Judaism did not escape the efforts of the women's rights movement in 1974. Reform Jews had already ordained their first female rabbi and had a number of candidates in prospect.

The more traditional Conservative Jews refused to admit female rabbinic students to their Jewish Theological Seminary, though the seminary does train women teachers and professors of rabbinic studies. However, the Conservative movement did go on record permitting certain synagogue functions to women. Among these was the right of women to be called to the scriptural reading at synagogue services, a function previously reserved for men.

Opponents of the move ranged from those few who thought the change to be in violation of Jewish law to a larger minority who decried the erosion of male religious responsibilities at a time when family sexual roles were becoming less clearly defined.

Orthodox Judaism, the most traditional of all the movements, has not seen the role of women as being problematic in Jewish life.

Jewish Defense League. Rabbi Meir Kahane, founder of the Jewish Defense League, resigned his position as chairman of that organization in April. Kahane's militant group claimed responsibility for bringing the plight of Soviet Jewry to the attention of the organized Jewish community and the world. But Kahane's militant tactics had gotten him into difficulties with police authorities throughout the world, including Israel where he had recently settled. Kahane claimed that Jewish leadership was bankrupt and cowardly, and that too little money was available to carry out the Jewish Defense League program.

Rabbinical Questions. In May the Rabbinical Assembly of America, professional organization of the Conservative rabbinate, expelled two of its members for agreeing to serve in the pulpit of a Toronto congregation before a case involving the incumbent rabbi had been properly adjudicated. At issue was the responsibility of these men to maintain professional discipline in the face of requests by a congregation for their services. Jewish congregations are usually totally independent of any ecclesiastical control in terms of ideology and staffing. In this they are unlike Roman Catholic and some Protestant groups. In an attempt to maintain discipline among its men, if not among congregations, the assembly expelled the two rabbis from membership.

In a similar vein, the Union of Orthodox Jewish Congregations decided to suspend its membership in the Synagogue Council of America, the umbrella organization of the Jewish religious community, over the issue of Reform and Conservative Jewish attitudes toward conversions in Israel by non-Orthodox rabbis. At present, religious matters in Israel are totally under the control of the Orthodox rabbinate. Conservative and Reform rabbis objected to what they felt was discrimination. This prompted the pullout by the Orthodox. The problem has worldwide dimensions because conversions, marriages, and divorces are arranged by non-Orthodox rabbis outside of Israel. This has led to problems when such converts, couples, or divorced people moved to Israel. There has been some questioning of their legal status. The problem is further complicated in the case of Russian Jews moving to Israel. Lacking the services of rabbis, Orthodox or otherwise, in Russia, the marital status of Russian Jews is often in doubt, giving rise to serious problems upon their arrival in Israel.

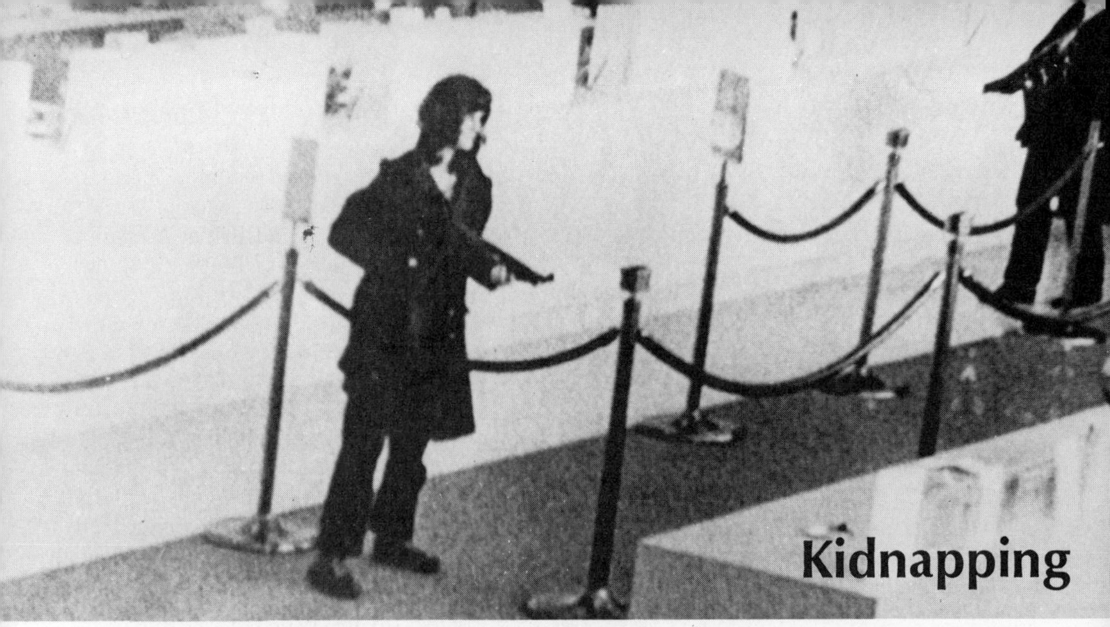

ROBBERY PHOTOGRAPH shows Patricia Hearst holding a weapon in a San Francisco bank holdup on April 15.

Patty Hearst: Masses of Words, Few Clues. On February 4 Patty Hearst, daughter of Randolph Hearst, the San Francisco newspaper publisher, was dragged from her apartment in Berkeley, Calif., by a little-known group of armed revolutionaries calling itself the Symbionese Liberation Army (SLA). By year's end ten months later, masses of words had been written about the Hearst kidnapping, but Patty Hearst was still missing. The twenty-year-old victim had gone from captive to comrade while the Federal Bureau of Investigation (FBI) checked one false report after another of her whereabouts.

The police found the 1964 green-and-white Chevrolet that was used in the kidnapping and a one-story bungalow in the San Francisco suburbs where they say she was held immediately after being abducted, but could not trace Patty from the messages the kidnappers sent. The Hearsts quickly gave in to the SLA demand for a food giveaway program. Through the threat of death for Patricia Hearst tens of thousands of Oakland, Calif., residents received free food, a fact that tended to neutralize the normal public response to the lurid kidnapping.

Meanwhile, Patty Hearst's conversion from rich man's daughter to armed revolutionary was made public through tapes of her voice and a photograph sent to a California radio station. The Hearsts identified the recordings and picture as being authentic. In April Miss Hearst surfaced with other members of the SLA to hold up a San Francisco bank. Here she was identified through a photograph taken by the bank's security mechanism.

On May 17 the police followed a telephone tip that members of the terrorist group were holed up in a small bungalow in a Los Angeles ghetto and went into a shoot-up that achieved nothing but the death of all six SLA members inside the house and the destruction of possible leads in the search for Miss Hearst and Emily and William Harris, the surviving flag-bearers of the SLA. Patricia Hearst's last public word came in late May in a tape recording in which she attested anew to her commitment to the SLA and her love for William Wolfe who had been killed in the May 17 gun battle. On June 6 Miss Hearst was indicted by a federal grand jury for the

San Francisco bank robbery and for the use of a weapon during a felony.

In May 375 federal agents were on Patty Hearst's trail. By year's end only 20 FBI men were still working on the Hearst case, and Randolph Hearst had withdrawn the $50,000 reward he had offered for his daughter's safe return.

Other Kidnappings. Kidnapping had been a fairly infrequent crime in the United States since the Lindbergh case in 1932. Since highly publicized crimes often generate similar crimes, there was a wave of abductions after Patty Hearst's made headlines. Among the most important of these was the February 20 kidnapping of the editor of the *Atlanta Constitution,* Reg Murphy, whose abductor extorted $700,000 from the newspaper. March saw the kidnapping of Mrs. Gunnar Kronholm of St. Paul, Minn. — who was freed after her husband paid a $200,000 ransom — and a kidnapping attempt on Princess Anne of Great Britain near Buckingham Palace, London.

TANIA was the name Patty Hearst said she had chosen as a member of SLA when this picture was sent to a California radio station along with a tape recording on April 3.

Legislation. Since the Supreme Court struck down the death penalty, the maximum penalty for kidnapping has been life imprisonment. Convicted kidnappers are often eligible for parole after a few years. The kidnappers of Melvyn Kahn, president of a Chicago drug company who was held for forty-eight hours before he made his escape and led the police to his abductors' hideout, were sentenced to terms of twelve and fifteen years in prison, which made them eligible for parole in ninety days.

The increase in kidnappings gave added impetus to the trend toward reinstatement of the death penalty by states, and legislation was introduced into Congress that would restore the death penalty in kidnapping cases in which the victim is killed.

Precautions. To help citizens guard against the chances of being kidnapped, the FBI issued a list of precautions that included the following: vary daily travel routines, keep doors of house and cars locked at night and during the day, provide no personal or family information to strangers, check that children's rooms are not readily accessible from the outside.

In March American Underwriters Corporation of Detroit began advertising a kidnapping and ransom policy for those individuals open to this "financial devastation." Although the policy was written by American Underwriters, it was carried by brokers of Lloyd's of London which has been insuring kidnap risks since 1933. Lloyd's declines to divulge the names of any persons they have insured as ransom risks, believing that such clients would become the first targets of kidnappers.

EVEL KNIEVEL TOYS are big sellers among children. Bitten by the Evel bug, the youngsters often attempt to imitate their hero in bicycle jumps from homemade ramps and land in the hospital.

EVEL KNIEVEL, the thirty-four-year-old darling of the motorcycle set, holds a model of his Sky-Cycle X-2 as he tells a press conference his plans for jumping across the Snake River Canyon in Idaho on September 8. When an NBC television cameraman asked the stuntman to smile, Knievel shoved his camera in his face, breaking the lens, and said, "Today and Saturday and Sunday, nobody tells me what to do except God."

Knievel

IN A CHRISTENING CEREMONY on September 7, Knievel breaks a bottle of champagne over the Sky-Cycle X-2. The vehicle's design was simple: seventy-seven gallons of water heated to 740 degrees was pumped into the rocket under pressure shortly before launching and at the go signal was released as steam through a rear nozzle, propelling the X-2 at a speed of about 350 miles an hour within five seconds.

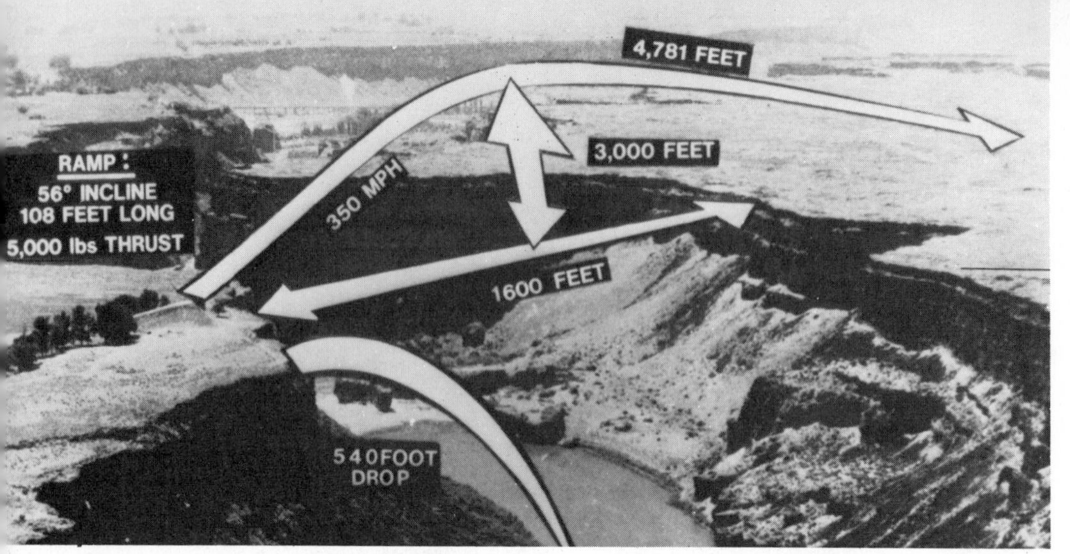

PHOTO-DIAGRAM shows the path of the planned feat.

KNIEVEL, who could make a gross income of $10 million from the closed-circuit television broadcast of the Snake River fiasco plus the spin-offs and endorsements it engendered, plans to tour Japan in 1975, and there are rumors he would skyjump Mount Fuji for $10 million. Governor Cecil Andrus of Idaho suggested Knievel would not be welcomed back to Idaho to repeat his canyon jump because of the vandalism of the crowd attracted on September 8.

AFTER LAUNCHING, the rocket streaked about 1,000 feet above the Snake River before floating into the canyon to make a nose-down crash landing on a rocky bank at the river's edge. A tail parachute had deployed prematurely on the take-off to spoil the flight. Several minutes later Knievel was pulled uninjured from the craft by a rescue team.

***KUMJE BRIDGE*, a scene in South Korea, won Billy L. Mason of the U.S. Navy a second place in the pictorial class in the Military Pictures of the Year Competition.**

South Korea and Democracy. Sooner or later South Korea must crystallize politically, either as a totalitarian police-controlled state under the continuing autocratic rule of President Park Chung Hee, or as the sort of real democracy which 324,000 American and other U.N. troops were killed and wounded defending during the Korean War, 1950-1953. The two decades since the uneasy peace was signed have seen remarkable economic growth in South Korea, but political stability has thus far eluded the nation.

Emergency Decrees. In January President Park countered growing opposition to his stern regime by proclaiming two presidential "emergency decrees" under which anyone criticizing the constitution of the republic or advocating its revision was liable to arrest without warrant, trial by court-martial, and imprisonment for up to fifteen years. He relied on his powerful army of secret police—the 20,000 agents of the Korean Central Intelligence Agency (KCIA) and its 50,000 informers—to enforce the new laws.

The proclamation followed waves of unrest among and demonstrations by the huge student population (in Seoul, the capital, alone there are thirty-seven universities), criticism from intellectuals and religious leaders, and challenges from his political opponents.

Kim Dae Jung. Before the secret police began rounding up dissidents, the seriousness and bitterness of the political and ideological divisions in Korea had been manifested by two earlier important events: The first was the kidnapping in Japan and abduction to Korea by the KCIA of Kim Dae Jung, a politician who polled 46 percent of the popular vote in the last presidential election in Korea three years before. Kim was charged with spreading defamatory rumors during the 1971 election. The precise "rumor" was: If there is not a change of president now, there will be no more popular elections to choose the head of state. Speaking to a British correspondent as he awaited trial in June, Kim said with almost philosophic fatalism: "My death would not be valueless if it aroused my people." To President Park, Kim—exiled but vociferous in Japan—had represented the rallying point for the growing opposition to his regime, and an obvious successor.

Assassination Attempt. The other event was an unsuccessful assassination attempt on President Park's life in August. His wife and a teenage girl bystander died in the hail of bullets fired by Mun Se Kwang, a twenty-three-year-old Korean-born Communist who had lived in Japan. Mun was sentenced to death by hanging in the Seoul District Criminal Court in October. The incident triggered violent anti-Japanese demonstrations which culminated in the macabre spectacle of fifteen Koreans amputating their little fingers which they wrapped in Korean flags, and tried to deposit at the Japanese Embassy as a grizzly protest. They were prevented only by riot police firing tear gas shells.

Economic Picture. The tragedy of South Korea is that its political divisions have seriously affected its previously dynamic industrial and economic growth. As anti-Japanese demonstrations continued and mass round-ups and trials of dissidents and political opponents increased, the Gross National Product growth dropped from 12 percent in the first half of 1974 to an estimated 2 percent in the second half, and economists predicted it would not exceed 5 percent for the whole of 1975. Falling confidence in South Korea was reflected also in the slump in foreign investment on which President Park's administration relies heavily. The first half of 1974 saw only $89 million invested, compared with $165.4 million in the same period of 1973. President Park's abduction of his political rival Kim Dae Jung from Japan, his tolerance of the violent anti-Japanese demonstrations, and the twenty-year jail sentences he allowed his military courts to impose on two Japanese nationals accused of subversion were perplexing in view of South Korea's heavy dependence on Japan—the source of 94 percent of all foreign investment during 1973.

Concern about events in Korea spread across the Pacific to the United States where two Congressional subcommittees were urged to reduce drastically aid to South Korea which has received nearly $12 billion in the past twenty-five years. Seoul dispatched investment missions to Europe and South America in search of new fund sources, but both regions, beset by inflation, had little to offer.

Communist Fears. President Park justified his heavy-handed autocracy with the almost obsessional belief that Communist North Korea was readying to invade the South again and that much of the unrest among his 33 million people is directed by Japan-based Communist organizations. His defense ministry cited the North's recent acquisition of Soviet-designed MIG-21 supersonic interceptors, as well as another fifty MIG-19 fighter-bombers; wide-scale reorganization, reequipping, and redeployment of the army; establishment of new bases near the Demilitarized Zone (the 38th Parallel which physically divides the ideologically different Communist North and Republican South); and six new submarines supplied by Russia to the North Korean navy. But U. S. command sources in Korea described the North's military modernization and exercises as "entirely normal"; compared with the North's 370,000-man armed forces, President Park maintains 600,000 soldiers.

U. S. Relations. But it was the likelihood of the U. S. withdrawal of its remaining 38,000 troops in South Korea that particularly worried President Park at year's end, despite a reassuring state visit by President Gerald Ford in November.

N THE CHINESE CONNECTION, Bruce Lee inishes off the last of an entire Japanese boxing club.

The Newest Fad. Since television's kung-fu series with David Carradine and the kung-fu films starring Bruce Lee, there has been an enormous increase in U.S. interest in this ancient martial art. There are approximately 100 kung-fu schools across America, but because many karate instructors, hoping to cash in on changing tastes, have switched from this Japanese-originated method of

KUNG-FU

defense to kung-fu without proper training, it is advisable to write to the newly founded Eastern U.S. Kung-Fu Federation, 740 Sixth St., N.W., Washington, D.C. 20001, for information on kung-fu schools and teachers.

History. The patriarch of the martial arts, *kung-fu wu-su* (discipline and martial arts training) is older than judo, jujitsu, and karate. According to official Chinese records, Huang Ti used kung-fu in 2674 B.C. Originally, the kung-fu expert knew how to cure as well as to inflict pain: he was a Chinese counterpart of the European Christian knight. While kung-fu is usually taught as merely a fighting technique, it is also a method of healing, a code of conduct, and a philosophy of life emphasizing humility, virtue, purity, oneness with the universe, and the sacredness of life. As a system of self-defense, kung-fu was considered so dangerous that its first practitioners, Chinese Buddhist and Taoist monks, forbade its teaching to the common people.

Characteristics. There are about twenty major styles of kung-fu, each with its own characteristics. As in karate, muscular strength and speed are important. Punching, kicking, and blocking techniques are used, but instead of karate's single punches and kicks, continuous fluent movement is stressed. Muscle tone is attained with the goal of relaxation, since one can move faster when relaxed.

All kung-fu styles have in common the development of inner as well as external strength. Controlled breathing and meditation are used in a search for a higher sense of awareness in the union of mind and body.

In Tai Chi style, slow motion is used to achieve the goals of kung-fu. Chinese leader Mao Tse-tung is said to practice Tai Chi for forty-five minutes before he has his breakfast each morning. Shaolin, a form of boxing, was perfected by the Shaolin Buddhist monks.

The Lost Track style emphasizes using the blind spots of the adversary; in the Southern Praying Mantis style the practitioner sticks his elbows in to protect his midsection. In the Drunken style the fighter acts as if intoxicated.

Americans, drawn to this oriental martial art, in a time when Western values are being questioned, find kung-fu builds confidence in one's ability to survive and helps to banish fear. Shaolin and Tai Chi are the most popular styles in the United States.

BRUCE LEE, who achieved international fame as a star in kung-fu films, was found dead in his home in Hong Kong on July 20, 1973. He was thirty-two years old.

BRIDGE WORKERS **by Fred Comegys of the *Wilmington News-Journal* won the $2,000 first prize in the Third National Construction Photography Contest. It depicts two workers taking a break from clearing debris from the Penn Central Railroad bridge over the Chesapeake and Delaware Canal.**

Labor

by
HOWARD J. ANDERSON

Senior Editor for *Labor Services*, The Bureau of National Affairs, Inc. Editor of *Major Principles, Established by the NLRB and the Courts; the Primer of Labor Relations; The Labor Board and the Collective Bargaining Process* (1971); *The Role of the Neutral in Public Employee Disputes* (1972); and *The Equal Employment Opportunity Act of 1972* (1973).

Militancy, Restiveness, and Discontent characterized the mood of labor during 1974. It led to heavy wage-fringe demands in collective bargaining negotiations, a high rate of union-membership rejections of tentative settlements negotiated by bargaining committees, and the highest rate of strike activity since 1970.

The 1974 experience was in sharp contrast to that in 1973. In 1973, union demands were moderate, the rate of rejection of settlements was down, and strike activity was at a low ebb.

Many factors played critical roles in labor relations in 1974—the confused economic picture, the increase in strikes, the Experimental Negotiating Agreement in steel, the emergence of the Equal Employment Opportunity Commission as the dominant federal agency in the regulation of employment relations, and

LABOR

the adoption of legislation affecting private pension plans and private nonprofit hospitals.

The Cost of Living and the Unemployment Rate were the key economic factors affecting labor relations in 1974.

By October, the consumer price index was climbing at an annual rate of 12.2 percent. The result was an erosion of the workers' real wages and the wage gains achieved in prior negotiations. The average U. S. worker's buying power in September, 1974, according to the Bureau of Labor Statistics, was down 5.2 percent from September, 1973, and 7.4 percent from the same month in 1972. Although slightly more than 50 percent of union members were covered by cost-of-living escalator clauses, these clauses were falling short of keeping wages abreast of price increases. This could affect 1975 negotiations, with some unions seeking to reopen their contracts to negotiate higher wages.

In the past, rising prices had been considered incompatible with rising unemployment. But while prices were skyrocketing in 1974, the unemployment rate rose to 6 percent by October. Moreover, there were predictions by economists that the unemployment rate would rise to 7 percent or higher by mid-1975. Even a 5 percent rate had been considered unacceptable in prior years.

The Pivotal Auto Industry was hardest hit by the unemployment rise. In October, the United Auto Workers reported that 150,000 of its members had been laid off. The number was expected to climb to 250,000 or more in December as a result of the decision of Chrysler Corporation to close down five of its six assembly plants in the United States and the additional layoffs contemplated by General Motors. Moreover, the layoffs and production cutbacks in auto manufacturing had a crippling effect on suppliers, causing additional layoffs.

All of this led Auto Workers' Vice-President Irving Bluestone to remark: "The auto industry is not in a recession —it's in a depression."

The Collective Bargaining Schedule was heavier in 1974 than in 1973. Major contracts covering at least 5½ million workers were due to expire or were subject to reopening on wages during the year. A major contract is defined by the Bureau of Labor Statistics as one covering 1,000 or more employees.

Included on the list were contracts in such key industries as can, aluminum, steel, copper, clothing, communications, airlines, bituminous coal, and railroads.

Agreements were reached by peaceful negotiations in such industries as steel, aluminum, can, copper, longshoring, and communications. A strike of 500,000 employees of the Bell System was averted only when an agreement was reached two hours before the deadline.

The settlements in these and other industries, however, were higher than those reached in 1973. The average first-year wage increase under major settlements during the first nine months of 1974 was 9.6 percent. Most of the contracts were for three-year terms. In all of 1973, the average first-year wage increase under major contracts was 5.8 percent. These figures were released by the Bureau of Labor Statistics.

The Economic Stabilization Act, which neither the administration nor Congress wanted to extend, died on April 30, 1974. It had had little effect on wage settlements negotiated during the first quarter of 1974.

Steel Negotiations were conducted the first time in 1974 under the Experimental Negotiating Agreement. Under the agreement, an April 15 deadline for negotiations was established. The deadline later was moved back to April 11. Any issues not resolved by the deadline were to be submitted to binding arbitration. The union, however, retained the right to strike on local issues.

The objective of the agreement was to avoid the crisis bargaining that had led to heavy stockpiling by steel users each time the major steel companies and the steelworkers entered into negotiations. The stockpiling caused layoffs of workers after an agreement was reached and loss of business to other industries by the companies. A settlement was reached on April 12 which provided for a 28-cent wage increase effective May 1, 1974, and increases of 16 cents an hour on August 1, 1975, and August 1, 1976. The cost-of-living escalator formula was revised to provide a one-cent-per-hour wage increase for each 0.3 point increase in the consumer price index.

The contract also provided what union spokesmen described as "a number of breakthroughs." There is an inflation adjustment for retirees, the retirement age was reduced from 65 to 62, and full pensions for life were provided for those retiring at 62. Both the companies and the union were sufficiently satisfied with the way the Experimental Negotiating Agreement worked that they plan to use it in the 1977 negotiations.

Bituminous Coal Negotiations, in contrast to those in steel, were stormy. Adhering to their policy of "no contract, no work," the Mine Workers struck in mid-November. The strike continued until the first week in December. The number of miners on strike was about 122,000.

On November 13, the negotiators reached agreement on a tentative settlement providing a 50 percent increase in wages and fringes over a three-year term. But the union's bargaining council rejected the settlement.

So the negotiators went back to the bargaining table. On November 24, agreement was reached on a new settlement providing wage-fringe increases of 54 percent over a three-year term. The union also obtained its first cost-of-living escalator.

The union's bargaining council first rejected and then reconsidered and approved the settlement. It then was ratified by the union's membership.

The 54 percent settlement was the largest ever reached for an entire industry. As a result of the strike, about 22,000 employees in related industries, such as coal hauling, were laid off. Government economists estimated that if the strike had continued until mid-December the number of layoffs in other industries would have reached 400,000.

Strikes in 1974 reached the highest level since 1970. During the first nine months, the idleness ratio reached 0.26 percent of estimated working time. In 1973, the ratio for the entire year was 0.14 percent.

The Federal Mediation and Conciliation Service (FMCS) put most of the blame for the rash of strikes on inflation. It pointed out that many of the strikes involved individual companies and generally were of short duration.

But there were some major strikes. There was a brief strike by 110,000 clothing workers represented by the Amalgamated Clothing Workers. It was the first nationwide strike in the clothing industry in fifty-three years.

There was a two-week strike by 12,000 drivers and other employees of the Greyhound Bus Lines; there was a two-month strike by the Machinists Union against National Airlines; and there was the coal strike.

Rejection of Tentative Settlements negotiated by union bargainers by rank-and-file union members was one reason for the increase in strikes.

During the first eleven months of the 1974 fiscal year, ending June 30, according to the FMCS there were 897 rejections of tentative settlements that were

LABOR

worked out in joint meetings between the parties and FMCS. This number represents 12.3 percent of FMCS's active cases.

Both the number and the percentage of rejections were higher than in the entire 1973 fiscal year. There were 697 rejections of tentative settlements in 1973. This represented 9.6 percent of the FMCS's joint meeting cases.

The Equal Employment Opportunity Commission (EEOC) has replaced the National Labor Relations Board (NLRB) as the dominant federal agency in the regulation of employment and labor relations.

The annual case intake of the EEOC is more than double that of the NLRB. Estimates place the case intake at close to 100,000 a year, and the EEOC has a backlog of about 80,000 cases.

But the EEOC represents only the tip of the iceberg. Numerous federal, state, and local agencies are involved in policing employment discrimination based on race, color, religion, sex, national origin, and age. In the federal hierarchy are the Office of Contract Compliance, the procurement agencies, the Justice Department, the Labor Department's Employment Standards Administration, the Civil Service Commission, the U.S. Civil Rights Commission, and the Department of Health, Education, and Welfare.

Then there are the state and local fair employment practices agencies. There are forty state agencies, and seventy local commissions.

Some significant decisions involving equal employment opportunity have been handed down by the Supreme Court in the past year. In *Alexander* v. *Gardner-Denver Co.*, the court held that an employee who presses a claim of alleged racial discrimination through the grievance-arbitration procedure under a collective bargaining contract and loses, may still file an action involving the same claim in court under Title VII of the Civil Rights Act. The court must afford the employee a trial *de novo* on his claim.

There also have been cases involving pregnancy and sex discrimination. In *LaFleur* v. *Cleveland School Board* and *Cohen* v. *Chesterfield County School Board*, the court held that it was a violation of the due process clause of the Constitution for a school board to require a teacher to take maternity leave after a specified period of pregnancy.

In *Geduldig* v. *Aiello*, the court held the Equal Protection of the Laws clause of the Constitution was not violated by a state disability insurance program that excluded disability resulting from normal pregnancy.

One of the most sacred principles of the unions — seniority — has been involved in some Title VII cases. In *Watkins* v. *Steelworkers* a federal district court in Louisiana held that seniority could not be determinative on the order of layoffs where it tended to perpetuate past discrimination. But in *Waters* v. *Wisconsin Steel*, the U.S. Court of Appeals for the Seventh Circuit upheld the use of seniority in determining the order of layoffs, stating that the principle of "last in, first out" still applies. The issue is expected to go to the Supreme Court.

Pension Reform Legislation finally was passed by Congress in 1974. The law establishes stricter fiduciary standards for pension plan administrators, requires compliance with vesting and funding standards, and sets up a system of insurance to protect beneficiaries in the event of the termination of a plan.

Congress also passed an amendment to the Taft-Hartley Act extending the act's coverage to private nonprofit hospitals. The NLRB already had asserted jurisdiction over proprietary hospitals.

Latin America

by
GEORGE BLANKSTEN, Ph.D.

Professor of Political Science
Northwestern University
Author of *Argentina and Chile* (1969)

TWO WOMEN CASTROITES walk purposefully in Havana. In Cuba, loafing is a punishable crime and brings sentences of up to two years in a labor camp.

General. The year was marked by a pronounced increase in terrorism, repression, dictatorship, violence, and natural catastrophe in Latin America. The countries mainly affected by these developments were Chile, Argentina, and Honduras.

The Inter-American Press Association (IAPA), which held its annual convention at Miami, Fla., early in April, adopted a resolution declaring that in 1974 problems of censorship of the press were more serious and widespread in the Americas than in any other year in the history of IAPA. Especially censured for repressive restrictions against the press were the governments of Brazil, Chile, Uruguay, Cuba, Haiti, and Panama. The Second Bertrand Russell Tribunal, meeting at Rome, Italy, in April, added its formal condemnation of the governments of Brazil, Chile, Bolivia, and Uruguay for their "crimes against humanity." When the General Assembly of the Organization of American States (OAS) met at Atlanta, Ga., late in April, U. S. Secretary of State Henry Kissinger called upon the member governments to strive toward renewed attempts to reach "new horizons" of inter-American cooperation in a variety of fields of activity.

Chile. In the wake of the bloody military coup of September 11, 1973, Chile continued to hold the limelight as a major theater of violence and repressive dictatorship in 1974. The ruling military junta decreed full press censorship early in January, and later that month the forced "recess" of all of the country's civilian political parties was ordered. Under that decree of January 21, the parties were required to terminate all of their activities, although they were allowed to keep their property. Political refugees left Chile by the thousands. It was estimated that 2,225 had left the country by January 1, and, as of that date, over 1,000 Chilean refugees had arrived in France alone. Chilean Senator Carlos Altamirano, exiled in Cuba, charged that since the 1973 coup in Chile the military regime there had "assassinated" over 15,000 Chileans; that over 30,000 had been arrested; more than 200,000 had been fired from their jobs; and over 25,000 had been expelled from the country's various universities. Amnesty International charged on January 20 that political prisoners were being tortured on a widespread scale in

LATIN AMERICA

Chile, often with the help of foreign police "experts" in torture made available by the military government of Brazil. Although the Chilean regime claimed that it had killed only 2,500 Chileans, most unofficial estimates ran closer to the figure of 15,000.

Economic conditions also became increasingly severe in Chile. In the first five months of 1974 the cost of living in that country rose by 103.3 percent. Living conditions deteriorated in low-cost housing communities, and disease and crime increased at accelerated rates in Santiago and other principal cities of Chile.

Foreign and international censure of the Chilean dictatorship grew in 1974. On January 3 and 7, the Argentine government lodged formal protests against Chile for the shooting in the Argentine Embassy at Santiago of Sergio Leiva Molina, a political refugee who had sought diplomatic asylum in the Argentine mission. The U.N. Commission on Human Rights on February 28 condemned repression in Chile and called upon the junta to cease "all violations of human rights." The government of the United Kingdom moved on March 27 to terminate its military sales and other aid to Chile, asserting that the British government wished to see "democracy and human rights fully respected" by the Chilean regime. And on April 24 the Roman Catholic church assailed the junta in Santiago for its economic policies, political repression, and violations of human rights.

But the government of the United States became distinguished for its support rather than censure of the Chilean dictatorship. On February 3, U.S. Senator Edward M. Kennedy (D., Mass.) unsuccessfully called upon then President Richard M. Nixon to curtail U.S. foreign aid to the junta. When Hortensia Bussi de Allende, the widow of the late Chilean president, Salvador Allende, who had been killed in the 1973 coup, arrived in the United States in February, the Washington administration permitted her to go to New York to appear at the United Nations, but prohibited her from going to Washington to take part in a press conference about Chile organized by Senator Kennedy.

By far the most far-reaching indications of U.S. involvement in the Chilean affair came with the revelation on September 8 that the U. S. Central Intelligence Agency (CIA) had been authorized by a panel headed by Secretary of State Kissinger to spend over $8 million in Chile between 1970 and 1973 to "destabilize" the Allende government before the 1973 military coup. In his first press conference after becoming U.S. president, Gerald R. Ford admitted on September 16 that the CIA had been involved in anti-Allende activities, but claimed that the purpose of this activity had been to discredit the Allende administration at the polls in Chile rather than to promote its overthrow in a military coup. Interest in the CIA matter grew in the United States, where there was some discussion, as the year drew to a close, of a Congressional investigation of the full extent of the role of the CIA in the overthrow of the Allende government.

Meanwhile, the Chilean ruling military junta moved to discharge its obligations to its foreign friends and benefactors. On January 30, the International Monetary Fund loaned the junta $95 million to overcome Chile's foreign exchange deficit, and the junta announced on February 23 its intention to pay foreign debts of about $4 billion. Chile's twelve creditor nations, the United States prominent among them, agreed on March 25 to refinance 80 percent of the foreign debt of Chile.

The junta declared in January that it would return all commercial banks na-

HURRICANE FIFI destroyed this little girl's home in Choloma as it ravaged Honduras in September.

tionalized during the Allende administration to their previous owners. Two Chilean affiliates of the Dow Chemical Company, which had been "requisitioned" by Allende in October of 1972, were returned to Dow by the junta on January 4; the combined value of the two affiliates was estimated at approximately $32 million. On March 12 a new agreement was announced under which the junta would pay $42 million to the Cerro Corporation for its Chilean copper interests, which had been nationalized by the Allende government in 1971. Finally, a settlement with the Anaconda Copper Corporation was announced on July 24. This provided that the junta would pay $65 million immediately and sign an additional $188 million in promissory notes in compensation for the Anaconda interests nationalized in Chile in 1971.

Argentina. Terror and violence, together with a dramatic change in government, also visited Argentina in 1974. Politically motivated murders and kidnappings, many of them the work of the left-leaning Peoples Revolutionary Army (ERP), increased in number and importance during the year. Alejandro Giovenco, a *Peronista* leader, was wounded by assailants on January 2. Less than a week later, Douglas Roberts, an executive of Pepsi-Cola South America, and José Ludvik, a Buenos Aires businessman, were abducted in separate incidents. Late in January, with such violent incidents increasing in number and scope, the Chamber of Deputies approved an antiterrorism bill doubling the prison sentences for convicted kidnappers and conspirators.

Violence and terrorism were especially serious during the year in the city of Córdoba, capital of the province of the same name. This took place against the background of a bitter division within the ranks of the *Peronista* party in Córdoba. The extreme left wing of the *Peronista* party, opposed to President Juan Domingo Perón, had gained control of a number of offices of provincial and municipal government in Córdoba. These leftists were attacked by more moderate *Peronistas*, supported by the Perón government at Buenos Aires. With the blessing of the national government, the Córdoba city police, led by moderate *Peronistas*, rose in rebellion against leftist municipal officials on February 27. In sympathy with this uprising, President Perón intervened in Córdoba on March 12, replacing its elected governor with Diulio Brunelli, a moderate *Peronista*. Violence and terrorism nevertheless continued in Córdoba. Roberto Francisco Klecher, a Fiat executive, was killed there by guerrillas on April 4. In a dramatic episode the following week, Alfred A. Laun III, director of the U.S. Information Service office at Córdoba,

LATIN AMERICA

was wounded on April 12 when he resisted capture by guerrillas. He was released three days later.

Similar terrorism continued in other parts of the country. Victor Samuelson, a petroleum refinery manager, was abducted in March. Esso Argentina paid $14.2 million to the ERP for his release. In mid-April, Antonio Magaldi, a labor leader, and Fernando Quinteros, a *Peronista* organizer, were killed by guerrillas, again in separate incidents.

But for Argentineans the greatest blow of all came on July 1, when President Juan Domingo Perón died of a heart attack at the age of 78. The aged leader, who had ruled Argentina from 1943 to 1955, and again from 1973 until his death, had become a virtual legendary figure among his countrymen, and his passing constituted a turning point of major significance. He was succeeded in the presidency by his third wife, Isabel Martínez de Perón, who had been vice-president in her ailing husband's administration. The new President Perón thus became the first woman chief of state in all of the histories of all of the countries of the Western Hemisphere. The road ahead promised to be rough for her, with violence, terrorism, and widespread political unrest continuing to mar Argentine national life as the year drew to a close.

IN BOOMING BRAZIL, slum mothers still hire children out to panhandle. The benefits of the seven-year-old business prosperity have not trickled down to most of the 100 million Brazilians. While the country's Gross National Product rose 56 percent during this period, the real value of the minimum wage dropped 55 percent.

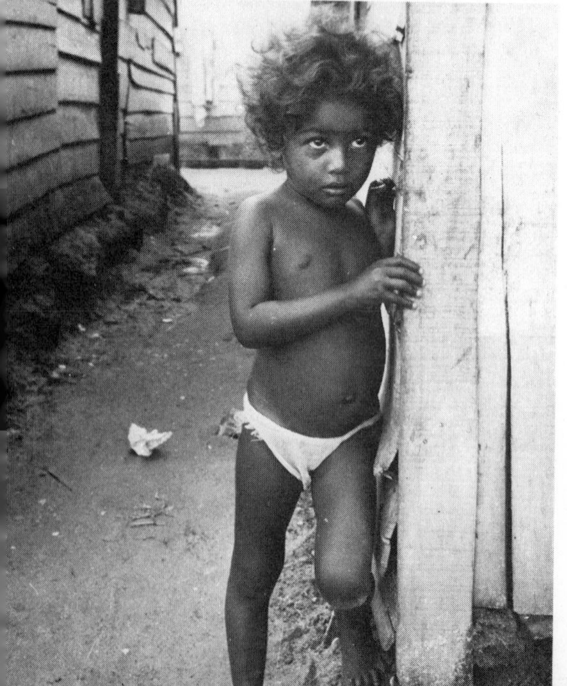

Honduras. In September, Hurricane Fifi visited Central America and the Caribbean, leaving its most devastating damage and destruction in Honduras. It was estimated that more than 8,000 died in the disaster, making it one of the largest natural catastrophes in the history of twentieth century Latin America. An inter-American relief effort was mounted to aid the hurricane victims, among whom disease and hunger reached catastrophic levels.

Cuba. If 1974 was a good year for any Latin-American country, that country was Cuba. During the year economic conditions improved for the island, and it appeared that Cuba was emerging from the diplomatic, political, and economic isolation in which the country had lived for over a decade.

On January 7, Fernando López Murino, Cuba's ambassador to Mexico, declared that the Castro regime would be interested in holding general talks with the United States, if Washington would end its economic blockade of Cuba. The following day, a U.S. State Department spokesman expressed "cautious interest" in the Cuban overture. Leonid Brezhnev, Secretary-General of the Communist party of the Soviet Union, visited Havana from January 28 until February 3, discussing a wide variety of problems with Cuban Premier Fidel Castro. A joint Cuban-Soviet communiqué published on

February 4 endorsed the Soviet Union's detente with the United States, reaffirmed Cuban-Soviet solidarity, and assailed policies of the Chinese Communist government. A number of Latin-American governments during the year launched moves toward Cuba's reincorporation into the OAS, from which the Castro regime had been expelled in 1962.

On the economic front, 1974 was a hopeful year for the island. Figures released in May showed that in 1973 Cuba's foreign trade had reached a record $2.6 billion, double the volume of 1968. As the inter-American blockade of Cuba progressively weakened, the Argentine subsidiaries of the Chrysler and Ford companies on April 23 signed contracts to sell automobiles and trucks to Cuba under a $1.2 billion credit granted to Havana by Argentina.

An interesting turn in U.S.-Cuban relations appeared to be in the making late in September, when two U.S. senators, Claiborne Pell (D., R.I.) and Jacob K. Javits (R., N.Y.) arrived in Havana. They held extensive discussions with Premier Castro, Foreign Minister Raúl Roa, and other Cuban officials. By the end of the year predictions were growing that Cuba might soon be readmitted to the OAS, and that the island's diplomatic relations with the United States, suspended since 1961, might be resumed in the near future.

Mexico. Under the auspices of the OAS, the foreign ministers of the various American republics met at Mexico City from February 21 to 24. In a major address at that meeting, Secretary of State Kissinger, while avoiding mention of the Cuban question, called for a "new community" among the American republics, emphasizing economic and technological cooperation.

Mexico had its share of terrorism and kidnappings during the year. John Patterson, U.S. vice-consul in Hermosillo, was abducted on March 22; his body was at length found on July 8. Mexican Senator Rubén Figueroa was kidnapped on June 27. But Mexico's most celebrated kidnap victim was José Guadalupe Zuño, eighty-three-year-old father-in-law of President Luis Echeverría. Zuño was released unharmed after the Mexican government adamantly refused to pay ransom.

In his first journey outside the United States after becoming president, Gerald Ford met at Nogales, Mexico, with President Echeverría on October 21. Their talks ranged over a variety of subjects, including oil. Echeverría declared that while Mexican petroleum would be available, it would be sold to the United States at "world prices." The Mexican president also expressed interest in his government's joining the Arab-dominated association of oil-producing countries.

Governmental Changes. Presidential elections were held in 1974 in Costa Rica, Guatemala, Venezuela, Brazil, Colombia, and the Dominican Republic. Daniel Oduber Quirós was elected president of Costa Rica on February 3; he was inaugurated on May 8. General Kjell Laugerud García was chosen president of Guatemala on March 3 after an unusually violent political campaign. In Venezuela, Acción Democrática candidate Carlos Andrés Pérez was chosen president. The U.S. delegation at his inauguration on March 12 was led by Mrs. Patricia Nixon, then first lady, and General Vernon Walters, deputy director of the CIA. On March 15, the Brazilian Army designated General Ernesto Geisel as the new head of the military dictatorship in Brazil. The Liberal party's candidate, Alfonso López Michelsen, was elected president of Colombia on April 21; and on May 16 incumbent president Joaquín Balaguer was reelected in the Dominican Republic.

THE READING PUBLIC found its local library forced to cut back on the very items it existed to provide — books and periodicals.

by
JESSE H. SHERA, Ph.D.

Emeritus Dean, School of Library Service
Case Western Reserve University
Member, Tangley Oaks Board of Educators
Author of *The Compleat Librarian* (1971) and *Foundations of Education for Librarianship* (1972)
Recipient, The Scarecrow Press award for the best book on librarianship published during the past three years.

The Economic Malaise that has infected all parts of our national life has not left libraries untouched. Confronted by this paradoxical time of inflation-deflation, of rising costs and declining revenues, the librarians are finding it increasingly difficult to maintain even their minimum services. The severity of this crisis is illustrated by the Cuyahoga County, Ohio, Public Library, the director of which reported in the spring that his library would be unable to purchase any new books until November. Many other libraries have reduced book purchases by as much as 60 percent, due to sharply rising costs and reduced income. Funds from the federal government for library expansion and support have been virtually eliminated, and there is growing voter resistance to increasing taxation to relieve the library of its financial plight. Many libraries have been compelled to cut back on much-needed additional staff in order to meet the demand for cost-of-living salary increments for those already in their employ. In many instances vacancies created by resignation and retirement have been permitted to go unfilled. School, public, and academic libraries have shared in this general misfortune, although the situation is probably worst among the private schools, colleges, and universities.

A hardcover book, which in 1968 cost $8.77, rose in 1972 to $12.99, the latest year for which figures are available. Periodical subscriptions have increased proportionately. For example, *Chemical Abstracts*, an index to the literature of research in chemistry and chemical engineering essential to every college and university library, increased its annual subscription from $700 in 1965 to $2,400 for the current year. General periodical subscriptions increased from an average of $8.77 in 1968 to $13.23 by 1972. The

LIBRARIES

problem has been intensified by a rise in second-class postage rates, the class for most newspapers and magazines, which have more than doubled since 1968, an average increase from two to five cents. At the same time, federal revenue sharing has been of little aid to libraries since they are generally low on local priority lists. All of these factors have severely limited the buying power of libraries. The graduate library of the University of Michigan, for example, has seen its buying power cut by nearly 50 percent.

Budget Trimming. Libraries have sought relief in several ways. Sacrifice of the budget for the acquisition of library materials to maintain salary levels is, perhaps, the easiest and least painful of expedients, but it can do irreparable damage to the library's services for years to come. Failure to keep pace with the current output of print can destroy public confidence in the library and impede its ability to elicit future support.

Many libraries have ceased to purchase multiple copies of periodicals and in large numbers are substituting paperbacks for hardcover editions. Yet for titles in heavy or continuing demand, paperbacks may be a dubious economy. In the past, libraries tried to acquire materials in reenforced bindings, an additional cost that seemed justified by extended viability.

Interlibrary Lending has long been a practice among libraries, but in the past decade resources of the system have been made available to all members of the group. The obvious advantages of sharing points to the likelihood the system will continue in the future regardless of economic necessity. The success of the Ohio College Library Center, in Columbus, Ohio, which unites a cluster of college libraries in a computerized network, is indicative of what the future holds. The center not only promotes the sharing of resources but also through centralized cataloging has reduced the processing costs of the individual member libraries.

Organizations such as the Friends of the Library, the objectives of which are to promote public concern for the institution and to encourage gifts for its support, may be expected to increase their activities in the near future. Also, the American Library Association's Washington office will intensify its efforts for library legislation, and the state libraries of the several states will redouble their efforts for legislation to benefit libraries. An increase in the employment of consultants to local library boards to inquire into the efficiency and effectiveness of library programs and procedures may also be anticipated, though it may not be regarded as extreme to say that library dollars are more efficiently used than those for most public services. That the public gets better library service than its pays for has long been a bromide among librarians, and there is considerable evidence to support the belief. Librarians are generally a dedicated group of people who put service above all other considerations.

The Benefits of Good Libraries. That good libraries are essential to democracy was an effective argument used by the proponents of free public libraries as early as the opening decades of the nineteenth century, and it is still true today. The growing complexity of our society has made access to recorded knowledge more important than it has ever been in our national life. We cannot allow libraries to suffer starvation, for a free public library system is a necessary adjunct to a free press and the right of assembly. The benefits that libraries confer may be more subtle and less apparent than those of highways or shopping centers, but they are far more important to our national welfare.

Literature

EXILED SOVIET AUTHOR Aleksandr Solzhenitsyn receives his 1970 Nobel Prize for literature from King Carl Gustav of Sweden in Stockholm on December 10. Although his $90,000 award money was deposited in a Swiss bank account four years ago, his medallion and diploma have been held by the Swedish Academy, because Russian authorities had refused Solzhenitsyn a visa to leave the country. He was banished from his homeland in February.

by
CHARLES MONAGHAN
Assistant Editor
The National Star

Sales. As dark economic clouds hung over the United States at the end of 1974, the wails in the publishing industry were more muted than in other sectors of the economy. In fact, sales statistics showed that sales through the end of November, 1974, were ahead of 1973.

And this in a year when publishers had good cause to worry—they had of necessity given a big hike to book prices to meet skyrocketing costs, especially of paper.

Prices. William Manchester's 1,302-page *The Glory and the Dream: A Narrative History of America—1932-72* was climbing the best-seller lists as 1975 began, despite the fact that it cost $20. But as one observer pointed out, there are several nights of entertainment in the mammoth Manchester volume, and its cost was a lot less than the price of several nights at restaurants, concerts, or even the movies.

So perhaps publishing was benefiting from the recession that seemed so harsh elsewhere.

Publishing Conglomerates. There was one major exception. The big Macmillan Publishing Company laid off 179 editorial staffers in one fell swoop in October, attributing the move to "belt-tightening." No other publishers saw fit to tighten belts in quite so radical a way, though stories of editorial posts left deliberately unfilled abounded in the industry.

The irony of the Macmillan firings was that they occurred in one of those publishing conglomerates that several years ago were hailed as the salvation of the fuddy-duddy publishing game. The conglomerates were expected to bring big business efficiency to bear where previously there had been only gentlemanly handshakes.

Macmillan, Inc., is heavily into the business of band instruments, owns the Berlitz language schools and the Gump's and Brentano's bookstore chains. It was clear that publishers who were part of big corporate setups were even more vulnerable to the general economic downturn than smaller firms that kept to their known market.

Art Books. One example of a smaller publishing house that seemed to be weathering the economic storm well was the New York firm of George Braziller.

Braziller has traditionally had a tiny though tasteful list of novels, poetry, and general-interest books, but it has become known in the past few years as an innovator in a booming aspect of publishing—the art book.

Braziller's prosperity in this area is due to a series of book reproductions of illuminated manuscripts that have drawn critical huzzahs.

It began in 1967 when Braziller published *Catherine of Cleves*, an illuminated manuscript from New York's Morgan Library. It cost $17.50 and sold 25,000 copies. It has been out of print for two years but Braziller intends to reissue it soon—at a higher price.

The two best-known illuminated manuscripts published so far in what Braziller projects as a nine-volume series over fifteen years are the *Tres Riches Heures* of Jean, Duc de Berry (published in 1972) and this year's entry in the Christmas race, the *Belles Heures* of the Duc de Berry.

The *Tres Riches Heures* came from the Chantilly Museum in France and the *Belles Heures* from the collection of the Cloisters in Manhattan. They were both printed—and magnificently—at the esteemed Paris firm of Draeger and are selling for $45. The *Tres Riches Heures*, universally hailed by the critics, has already sold 18,000 copies.

Reproductions of illuminated manuscripts are caught in their own particular price squeeze. More than most art books, they use a great deal of gold. The ink that is used actually contains powdered gold, whose price has recently jumped to four times its previous cost.

Braziller's main competition in the illuminated manuscript market this year came from Random House, which issued a well-received reproduction of the most famous example of all illuminated art, *The Book of Kells*, from the library of Trinity College, Dublin. The text is by the great authority on Celtic art, Françoise Henry. *The Book of Kells* sold for $55 until January 1 and $65 thereafter.

(The practice of jumping the price of art books after the holidays so as to entice Christmas buyers at the lower tariff is now widespread in the industry.)

Braziller knows he is onto a good thing with his art book series because of the vogue for illuminated manuscripts and medieval art. But he sees problems on the horizon for art books in general.

"A few years ago," he says, "there were only five or six publishers in the art book field, producing thirty or forty books a year. This year, nearly every publisher has a big illustrated book. There are probably 300 such books competing for the Christmas dollar."

Christmas Books. Braziller's comments underline a trend of the past half-decade—the popularity of books as Christmas presents. Some 70 percent of the total book sales take place between October and Christmas.

This has caused publishers to invent more and more ideas for the Christmas market alone. Which explains the fre-

LITERATURE

THE RETURN OF SHERLOCK HOLMES

Although a perennial favorite, Sherlock Holmes, that master detective from the pen of A. Conan Doyle, experienced his greatest popularity in four decades during 1974. Christopher Morley called the fifty-six Holmes stories and four Holmes novels by Doyle "pure anesthesia," but modern analysts ascribe the revival to nostalgia for a less chaotic age and the yearning for an admirable and powerful character to fill the hero void of modern literature.

Holmesian books, parodies, films, pastiches, ads, plays, musicals, and even ballets made headlines during the year. The London production of the 1899 Doyle-William Gillette play which became a Broadway success in the fall was joined by the Off-Broadway **Holmes and Moriarty** by Allen Sternfield.

SHERLOCK HOLMES PORTRAIT by Frederic Dorr Steele, a major U.S. illustrator of the Holmes stories, is used as a club symbol by the Baker Street Irregulars.

HOLMES'S DEERSTALKER HAT and checked jacket hang on the hall tree at 2212B Baker Street. Fashion designers were busy in 1974 exploiting Holmes's style in clothes.

In **The Seven Percent Solution** (Dutton) Nicholas Meyer links the detective and Sigmund Freud in solving a case. Ian McQueen points to errors in the Holmes canon in **Sherlock Holmes Detected** (Drake). It took Ronald De Waal six years to compile the 608-page **World Bibliography of Sherlock Holmes and Dr. Watson** (New York Graphic Society, $60). In **The Memoirs of Schlock Homes, A Bagel Street Dozen** (Bobbs-Merrill) Robert L. Fish mines Holmes for laughs with such apocrypha as a Scottish story called "The Adventure of the Steamed Clans." Serious studies published by Drake included: Michael Harrison's **The**

LITERATURE

London of Sherlock Holmes and **In the Footsteps of Sherlock Holmes,** and **The Public Life of Sherlock Holmes** by Michael Painter. Albert Mendez's **The Sherlock Holmes Quiz Book** was scheduled for 1975 as was a sequel to John Gardner's account of the villainous master mathematician, **The Return of Moriarty** (G. P. Putnam).

In London the Sherlock Holmes Society, which meets six times a year and boasts 720 members scattered throughout the world from Czechoslovakia to Japan, publishes **The Sherlock Holmes Journal** semiannually with lead articles on such subjects as "Holmes's University Career."

In the United States the Baker Street Irregulars, a Holmes fan club founded in 1933 by Christopher Morley and Vincent Starrett has 150 members and acts as a parent organization for about sixty "scion societies" spread across the nation, among them The Hounds of the Baskerville in Chicago, Ill. Its quarterly, **The Baker Street Journal** (circulation 1,500), will be published by Fordham University Press beginning in March, 1975. In February, 1975, the world's second Sherlock Holmes symposium was scheduled at Colorado State University.

Sherlock Holmes gives every indication of staying alive forever.

SHERLOCK HOLMES (John Wood) listens to Dr. Watson (Tim Pigott-Smith) in a scene from the Royal Shakespeare Company production of the Gillette-Doyle play that opened in London on January 1 and in New York City on November 12. Wood reread every Holmes story and wrote down "every single physical description of Holmes" to prepare himself for the part. William Gillette was the first Holmes, but the actor who made the deepest modern impression on the character was Basil Rathbone.

quency at Christmastime of books devoted to the subject of . . . Christmastime.

The one book of this ilk that is expected to be the biggest seller this year is *The Glory and Pageantry of Christmas,* by the editors of Time-Life Books. It is like a giant *Life* magazine article, containing a historical survey of paintings with Christmas subjects, a historical commentary, and a grab bag of poems, songs, and stories about the holiday.

Fiction. As tastefully produced as it may be, this type of book is becoming the bullyboy of the publishing world, elbowing out more traditional fare. Its main victim is the novel, which at one time was the Christmas gift staple (and still is in England and France).

In fact, the subject most widely discussed in serious publishing circles as 1975 blew in was the future of the hardback novel. Even the shortest novel now retails for $6.95. And when libraries—which publishers rely upon to take a deficit-eliminating minimum of books—find themselves in a budget squeeze, it seems that fiction is the category that suffers first.

All voices in the industry say that a greater amount of fiction will begin to originate in paperback, published both by the mass market paperback houses or in paper cover by the normal trade houses.

As it is now, an estimated 90 percent of fiction titles in certain genres—science fiction, thrillers, gothics, westerns, and love stories—are now issued in paperback and never appear in hardback. The same future beckons for general fiction.

Of course, there will always be a place in hardback publishing for a certain number of fiction titles. The two big fictional sellers of 1974 serve as cases in point.

One was *Watership Down* by Richard Adams, which had been a hit in England. This is an epic of sorts about the journey of a group of rabbits from one habitation to another on the English downs. The subject matter was fresh and the books of Tolkien had created an appetite among a whole generation of readers for fantasies of this sort.

Undoubtedly, successful English authors such as a Graham Greene, a Kingsley Amis, or a John LeCarre will have a hardback market in America for years to come.

The second big fiction seller was *Centennial* by James Michener, which was well up on the lists at year's end. Established commercial authors like Michener and Arthur Hailey will always have a good run in hardback, even if more and more of their sales come through the book clubs.

Nonfiction. On the nonfiction side, the bestseller early in the year was *Plain Speaking,* Merle Miller's round-up of the wit and wisdom of Harry S. Truman.

But after the sales figures were in, the top seller of the year was likely to be *All the President's Men,* the Watergate book by Robert Woodward and Carl Bernstein of the *Washington Post.*

Robert Redford's movie of the adventures of the two *Post* reporters as they picked apart the Nixon administration will follow soon. *All the President's Men* also got the top price for a paperback sale—$1 million from Bantam Books.

The trend of huge paperback bids, exceeding movie rights by far, is likely to continue for years to come.

Albert Murray. The most distinguished book from a new writer of fiction in 1974 came from a man already established as an essayist and literary theorist.

He is Albert Murray, a retired Air Force major, university professor, and resident of Harlem. With the publication of his first novel, *Trainwhistle Guitar,* Murray joined his friend Ralph Ellison in the top rank of American writers, black or white.

Medicine

by
JOAN HOLLOBON

Medical Reporter, *The Globe and Mail* (Toronto, Ont.)

Quality Control of medical care was one of the most notable, and controversial, developments in medicine in North America in 1974. In the United States, professional standards review organizations were set up, while in Canada the medical profession's provincial licensing bodies addressed themselves to the same problem in various ways with varying effectiveness.

Both are peer review systems—doctors scrutinizing doctors — but the impetus came from lay people, reflecting rising "consumerism" in health care as in other aspects of contemporary society. It also reflects increasing public participation, through taxes, in the provision of health services, with consequent concern about ensuring the quality of what is provided.

Canada has had a countrywide medicare scheme covering treatment in hospital and in doctors' offices, for some years. The United States, on the verge of national health insurance,, already pays for a substantial amount of health care through Medicare and Medicaid programs for the old and poor and through other government agencies, such as the Veterans' Administration.

Peer review of medical care is supported by those inside and outside the medical profession, who consider the profession has policed itself poorly. It is attacked by those who see it as the beginning of ever-increasing surveillance and the end of the individual doctor's freedom of practice. Others attack it as a means of controlling costs more than quality.

HMOs. The year also saw establishment of Health Maintenance Organizations (HMOs) for which legislation was signed on December 29, 1973. HMOs signal new directions for delivering health care, as well as stressing prevention. Rapidly rising health costs are another impetus toward more emphasis on prevention in efforts to stem the rising tide of degenerative diseases—heart disease, strokes, cancer—costly to treat, costly in the social consequences of disability. The energy crisis of 1973, with its continuing threats of fuel shortage at home and imminent famine abroad, also influenced public attitudes toward a more abstemious lifestyle, with greater emphasis on physical fitness through

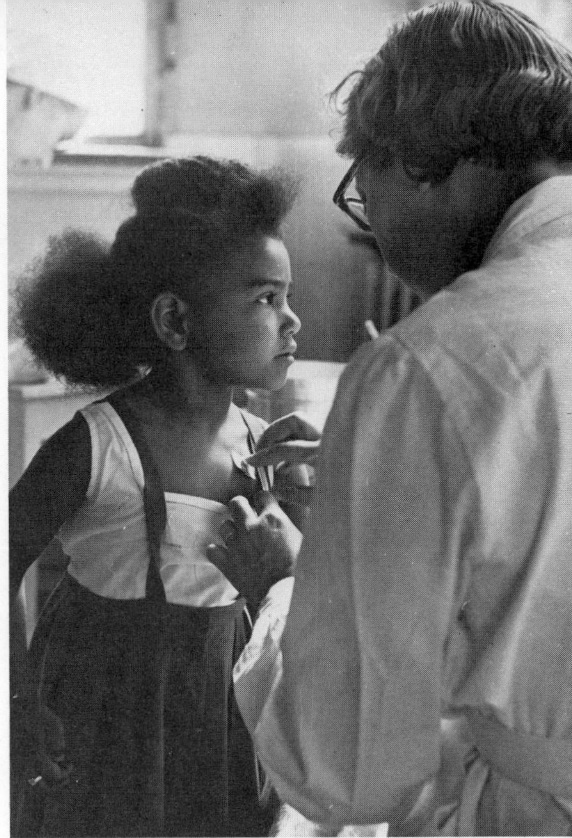

A WOMAN DOCTOR checks a tuberculosis test. American women are entering the medical profession in dramatically increasing numbers. In the past three years the number of women enrolled in U.S. medical schools has more than doubled, from 3,894 or 9.6 percent of the total enrollment to 7,824 or 15.4 percent.

moderation in eating, drinking, and smoking and through more exercise.

Disease and Environment. Consumer concern also provided much of the drive that kept the spotlight on environmental factors in disease, ranging from air pollution and dangerous industrial chemicals to food additives.

It is estimated that some 100,000 people die in the United States every year from occupational diseases, while nearly 400,000 are disabled. This toll is largely hidden, because the deaths and disabilities may occur years after the individuals quit the jobs that caused them, so the association is missed. Tragically, when the association is finally made and protective steps taken, many victims are already doomed, because chemicals often take many years to exert their effects which then are irreversible.

A horrifying example of this was revealed last year when vinyl chloride was found to cause a rare liver cancer. Vinyl chloride is used to make a plastic—polyvinyl chloride—used in food wrappers, toys, and other common products. Vinyl chloride was widely used as a propellant in such household aerosol sprays as hair sprays and pesticides, until banned last year.

Angiosarcoma of the liver is so rare (twenty or so deaths a year in the whole country) that vinyl chloride was rapidly implicated when six plastics workers were found to have died of it. Thalidomide was incriminated relatively quickly because it caused a rare deformity. However, if thalidomide has caused a common defect or vinyl chloride a common cancer (such as lung cancer) both might have gone undetected for years.

How many similar hazards lurk among the 50,000 or so chemicals now used in industry or the 3,000 new ones introduced every year? And what about possible effects on the unborn?

A U.S. National Cancer Institute official suggested that prenatal chemical exposure may influence an individual's lifetime risk of developing cancer. There is concern about chemicals, such as phenyl mercury commonly used in fabrics, paint, and even contraceptive foams, because many chemicals are known to be able to cross the placenta. Researchers at Laval University, Quebec City, found that children who died of cancer before they were five years old were twice as likely to have fathers whose jobs were associated with hydrocarbons, such as auto mechanics or mining. They have not yet determined whether the disease results from hydrocarbons in the infants' environment or through direct effects on spermatogenesis.

The U.S. Center for Disease Control at Atlanta, Ga., has now set up a national computer monitoring system that will check for some 250 known birth defects among one-third of the 3.2 million babies born every year.

If the computer shows an increase in defects, the medical sleuths will try to trace any possible environmental influence. Birth data from 1970 through 1973 were available when the program began at the end of the year, and additional data will be added by the 1,500 participating hospitals on an ongoing basis.

Food Additives are another area causing anxiety. There are some 3,000 to 10,000 in use now. As improving technology permits detection of ever smaller amounts of substances found to cause cancer in animals, more and more of these materials—considered safe now—are likely to be withdrawn.

Diethylstilbestrol (DES) created some slight across-the-border friction last year, when Canada banned imports of U. S. beef from cattle treated with DES. Now, some experts say the minute amounts of any residue would be harmless. DES was also implicated in causing cancer in some young girls whose mothers had been treated with the hormone during their pregnancies eighteen or twenty years earlier.

Nutrition, long the Cinderella of medicine, came in for more professional interest.

Medical Letter said clinical trials showed that large doses of vitamin C do not prevent colds, reduce their severity, or shorten their duration, but in other studies vitamin C came off better. New York University School of Medicine researchers suggested that large doses may prevent toxic build-up of drugs in the body; British investigators at Manchester said such doses helped bed sores heal faster; at Vanderbilt University Dr. G. V. Mann said high doses taken with their insulin might protect diabetics from the vascular complications of their disease; and at the British National College of Food Technology vitamin C got a plug as a booster of mental alertness. Scientists suggested it exerts this effect by raising levels of cyclic AMP, known to be reduced in the brains of depressed people.

Dietary chromium received attention from Dr. Richard J. Doisy, a biochemist at New York Upstate Medical Center, Syracuse. He said the bland North American diet may be seriously depriving elderly people of this vital trace element, thus contributing to the high rate of chemical diabetes seen among the old. Chromium in a form usable by the body is found in brewer's yeast, liver, kidneys, mushrooms, black pepper, and spices.

But it was an English surgeon who caused the biggest dietary changes, especially in prescribed diets. Dr. Denis Burkitt (for whom a jaw cancer among African children is named, Burkitt's lymphoma) observed when he lived in Africa that many of the diseases plaguing Westerners today are rarely seen among Africans, especially diseases of the intestinal tract, such as colon cancer, on the rise here. He noted that Africans eat a diet high in fiber, which speeds material through the intestinal tract. Others have confirmed his observations and extended the association to other diseases causing concern in the West, such as heart disease, gall bladder disease, inflammation of the intestines, and even obesity. So, "roughage" is in, and the bland diets formerly prescribed so freely are on the way out.

Dr. Charles E. Butterworth, Jr., of the University of Alabama, Birmingham, chairman of the Council on Foods and Nutrition of the American Medical Association, took a scandalized look at the standards of nutrition in the place where it is most vital and where the individual has least control over what he eats—hospitals.

The professor of medicine and pediatrics and director of the nutrition program at Alabama said that "iatrogenic (meaning physician-induced) malnutrition has become a significant factor in determining the outcome of illness for many patients." In an article in *Nutrition Today* Dr. Butterworth said he suspects that "one of the largest pockets of unrecognized malnutrition in America, and Canada, too, exists not in rural slums or urban ghettoes but in the private rooms and wards of big city hospitals." He cites a number of cases in which serious malnutrition — even one death, literally, from starvation — occurred because doctors and nurses absorbed in the most meticulous attention to drugs and technology failed to consider nutrition or recognize evidence of severe vitamin and other deficiencies.

Diabetics could take heart from advances made in 1974 that offer real hope for them. The advances were in three directions — toward transplantation of insulin-producing Beta cells from the pancreas, that seem not to be rejected; toward an artificial computer-controlled

MEDICINE

pancreas; and through improved hormone control which may protect against the vascular complications.

Researchers at the University of Minnesota Hospitals, Minneapolis, predicted they would begin transplantation of isolated islets of Langerhans in patients next year.

At Toronto, Dr. Bernard Leibel and engineer A. M. Albisser produced equipment that successfully controlled blood glucose levels, but is too large yet for wide application. It is now being miniaturized. Dr. Roger Guillemin of the Salk Institute, San Diego, Calif., identified a hormone from the hypothalamus in the brain, which he called somastatin, that may provide better control of juvenile diabetes. It is still under clinical investigation.

In Reproductive Research the most startling event of 1974 was the announcement by a British doctor that three children had been born from human eggs fertilized in a test tube and then implanted back into the women from whom they had been taken. A number of researchers have been trying to achieve this, but this was the first report of success. The method offers a way in which women who cannot conceive normally because of blockage of the Fallopian tubes can become pregnant.

However, Dr. Douglas C. A. Bevis of the University of Leeds was criticized for the manner of his announcement—a press release handed out prior to a talk he gave to the British Medical Association in which he made no mention of the three successful pregnancies. Dr. Bevis has not presented any scientific paper on the research. He said the children are well and reported their ages between twelve and eighteen months.

Cancer Research in 1974 continued to stress immunology—the study of the body's defense system—and the possible role of viruses. The strongest evidence yet for a human leukemia virus was provided by two Toronto researchers, Dr. T. W. Mak and Dr. A. F. Howatson of the Ontario Cancer Institute. The particles isolated, photographed, and grown in culture passed chemical and physical tests, were the correct size, and had the appropriate appearance. The team still awaits final proof that they can turn normal cells into malignant cells.

Lung cancer remained the number one cancer killer among men and has moved up to number three among women, presumably as women smoke more, but the leading cause of female cancer deaths remains breast cancer.

Last year the wife of U. S. President Gerald Ford turned a spotlight on breast cancer when she underwent a radical mastectomy at Bethesda Naval Hospital. Because of Mrs. Ford's open and courageous attitude, women across the world who otherwise would not have done so were encouraged to go for a medical check-up. Indirectly, Mrs. Ford may have helped save many lives, because the National Cancer Institute's breast cancer task force reported that screening by thermography, mammography, and physical examination may, through earlier detection, save 22 more lives among every 100 women with the disease. Thermography measures heat emitted by body tissue: malignant tumors give off more heat than normal tissue. The estimate came from computer analysis of the first 42,000 women screened of the 270,000 slated for such screening at twenty-seven demonstration clinics across the United States. The analysis showed that in 77 percent of women who had mastectomies as a result of screening the cancer had not spread into the lymph nodes, compared with the average of 40 to 50 percent. When the cancer remains confined to the breast, the individual has an 85 percent probability of a five-year survival.

GOLDA MEIR resigned as Israeli premier and was succeeded by Yitzhak Rabin in June. This portrait of Mrs. Meir won Jorma Pouta of *Lehtikuva* Oy, Finland, third prize in the personalities class of the World Press Photo Holland contest.

by
AARON R. EINFRANK

(Mr. Einfrank is a journalist who has lived in Israel and has visited the Arab world. In 1973 he covered the Yom Kippur conflict from the Israeli side as a war correspondent. At the United Nations and in Washington he has written extensively on the diplomatic aspect of the Arab-Israeli conflict. He is a two-time winner of the Award for Distinguished United Nations Reporting.)

The Possibility of Peace. During the first half of 1974, there seemed to exist a real possibility of achieving a lasting peace settlement in the Arab-Israeli conflict which has tormented the Middle East for so long.

But as the year came to a close, the clouds of war were again on the horizon, and the bright promise of peace seemed to become as illusory as a desert mirage.

Between January and June, U. S. Secretary of State Henry Kissinger performed the role of diplomatic magician with an extraordinary display of shuttle diplomacy and artful wheeling and dealing. Thanks largely to Kissinger, troop disengagement agreements were worked out between Israeli and Syrian forces on the Golan Heights and between Israeli and Egyptian forces in the Sinai. Israel even gave up some of the territory seized in the 1967 June war as well as land occupied during the 1973 Yom Kippur conflict. Kissinger also got the Arabs to lift their oil boycott against the United States. Before resigning, President Richard Nixon was able to make a triumphant tour of the Middle East, including visits to Israel, Syria, and Egypt.

A most heartening development was that the prime Arab combatants—Egypt,

Syria, and Jordan—seemed ready to accept Israel as a permanent factor in the Middle East equation.

Why Things Went Sour in the latter half of 1974 is a complex and even disputable question. For one thing, Watergate played a role. The political "execution" of Richard Nixon removed a U.S. chief of state who was willing to pressure Israel into making concessions for a peace settlement. A politically weak President Gerald Ford, who was not elected by the American people, had to face a U. S. Congress where Zionist influence is predominant. To make matters worse, America was so wrapped up with Watergate and the change of presidents that the Middle East seemed at times to be forgotten in Washington.

Another element in the darkening picture was the Israeli reluctance to give up more occupied Arab territory. Even though the 1973 war showed that Israel's 1967 conquests were not easily defended, Israelis still tended to equate security with conquered territory.

PLO. A factor which upset Kissinger and others was the amazing rise to prominence of the Palestine Liberation Organization (PLO) led by Yasir Arafat. For years the Arab states had ignored Arafat and the plight of the Palestinians, giving only token aid to the PLO. But in 1974 the PLO came into its own. Thanks to a series of terrorist raids against Israel plus Tel Aviv's reluctance to make a deal with the Arab states, Arafat could strut on the Arab and world stages as never before.

Arafat was able to persuade the Arab leaders at the Rabat summit meeting of Arab states in October to accept the PLO as the only representative of the Palestinian people. The next month he went on to a greater triumph at the United Nations where the General Assembly treated him as a head of state. The PLO was accorded observer status in the world organization, tantamount almost to recognition of statehood.

How Arafat and Israel combined—no doubt unintentionally—to make things difficult for Kissinger's peace campaign was demonstrated by the case of King Hussein of Jordan who has generally taken an anti-PLO line. Before the 1967 war, Hussein was not willing to give the West Bank of the Jordan river to the PLO. Israel's seizure of the West Bank in 1967 put the West Bank up for grabs. Had Tel Aviv returned the West Bank to Hussein, the Jordanian king could have been expected to continue his anti-PLO policy. But Israel stalled. At Rabat Hussein had to accept the summit decision that the West Bank would be the nucleus of a PLO-dominated Palestinian state. At the time of the summit, Israel announced it was willing to deal with Hussein on the West Bank issue. But it was too late. Hussein was no longer in the West Bank picture, and this means a stalemate as long as Israel refuses to negotiate with the PLO. The PLO factor created a further obstacle to the resumption of the stalled Geneva Conference on the Middle East.

Israel. Concerning domestic events in Mideast states, the most startling phenomena were evident in Israel which lost its reputation in 1974 for being a stable, solid island of prosperity in the midst of the Middle East whirlwind. The aftermath of the Yom Kippur war was marked by political and economic turmoil that the Jewish state had not known since its early days.

The war smashed the myth of Zionist invincibility, and resulted in a national trauma. The confusion was complicated by the resignation of Prime Minister Golda Meir and a complete shake-up in the Israeli military establishment. The Israeli chief of staff General David Elazar had to resign after a government commission found inadequacies in the performance of the Israeli defense forces. Moshe Dayan lost his job as defense minister when the new prime minister, Yitzhak Rabin, formed his cabinet.

The economic impact of the war on Israel was perhaps greater than the political effect. Prior to the 1973 war, Israeli lived very well on foreign handouts. United Jewish Appeal money and U.S. aid could be used to subsidize a standard of living which was far too high for a tiny, rocky, and arid country which has few natural resources and only a small internal market. Israelis had come to expect automobiles, modern apartment houses, air conditioning, and other *dolce vita* conveniences. Food prices were low because of state subsidies. It was a dream world paid for by foreign money which had not been earned by economic productivity.

The war meant that foreign assistance to Israel could no longer be used for consumerism. Instead, the money now had to go for defense purposes to maintain large standing armed forces ready to repel a Yom Kippur-type attack. The cost of living soared. Food subsidies and other supports had to be discontinued. The Israeli pound was devalued by nearly 43 percent. There were strikes and protest demonstrations. Jewish police battled Jewish demonstrators in the streets of Tel Aviv following the announcement of government austerity measures.

Some observers noted a "Masada" complex developing in Israel similar to the attitude of the fanatical Jewish rebels who fought to the last man against Roman troops in the fortress of Masada two thousand years ago. Others called this attitude a "Samson" complex or a willingness to tear the world down if Israel does not get its way. The danger of such "complexes" is that Israel possesses missiles and a nuclear capability. In addition, another Mideast war could mean a world conflagration with the super powers being dragged in.

Paradoxically, Prime Minister Rabin is a moderate. As former Israeli ambassador to Washington and a distinguished soldier (former chief of staff), he is aware of the dangers of war and well-versed in the realities of the outside world. His relationship with Kissinger has been particularly good, and Rabin on several occasions has shown himself far more flexible than previous Israeli leaders. However, Rabin is weak domestically. A combination of the right-wing Likud opposition and the hard-liners in Rabin's own Labor coalition could oust Rabin at any time. Adding to the prime minister's difficulties is the fact that a member of the ruling coalition is the National Religious party which opposes giving land back to the Arabs. (The West Bank used to be part of biblical Israel). One of Rabin's most difficult decisions in 1974 was to order Israeli troops to remove religious fanatics and nationalists who tried to set up illegal settlements on the West Bank.

Israel was plagued by terrorist raids and by unrest in the occupied territories. There were signs of unrest even among Christian and Moslem Arab citizens in the Jewish state. Israeli authorities had to resort to mass arrests of Arabs. In one protest demonstration an Arab girl was killed on the West Bank. A sensational incident was the twelve-year prison sentence that Greek Catholic Archbishop Hilarion Capucci received from an Israeli court in Jerusalem which convicted him of smuggling arms to Palestinian resistance fighters. (The Vatican protested the Capucci sentence.)

The worst Palestinian terrorist attack occurred in May in Ma'alot when twenty-one children and three guerrillas were killed after the guerrillas had taken a whole school hostage. Israeli authorities ordered troops to storm the school

A PUPIL studies an Arabic reader in a school near Jericho, Jordan. The study of Arabic in the United States rose 50 percent in 1974.

rather than submit to guerrilla demands that certain Arab prisoners be released from Israeli prisons.

A particularly ghastly incident took place at Beit Shean when three Palestinian guerrillas killed four Israelis. Israeli troops killed the guerrillas. However, an Israeli mob ran amok and burned the bodies of the guerrillas in a public display of race hate. By mistake the mob in its fury defiled and burned the body of one of the Israeli victims of the terrorist attack.

Israel resorted to terror of its own by attacking neighboring Lebanon. Refugee camps suspected of harboring guerrillas were bombed and shelled. There were also mini-invasions of Lebanese soil by Israeli troops similar to the "incursion" by U.S. troops into Cambodia in 1970 during the Vietnam War. But Israeli counterterror did not stop the guerrillas. On December 11 a terrorist threw grenades in a crowded Tel Aviv theater, resulting in three deaths and injuries to nearly sixty. Israel then retaliated with an air attack on a refugee camp near the Lebanese capital of Beirut. Israeli long-range artillery resumed bombardment of border areas in Lebanon.

The holy city of Jerusalem became a focal point because of its importance to Christians and Moslems as well as to Jews. Israeli housing projects in Jerusalem are designed to make the city more Jewish and less Arab. The housing projects are run on an apartheidlike basis—Arabs do not live in them, only Jews, many of them recent immigrants from the Soviet Union. Questions were raised in UNESCO about Israeli archaeological excavations in Jerusalem. Israel found itself excluded from certain UNESCO activities because of the Jerusalem question, thus increasing the isolation of the Jewish state in the world arena.

Peace in the Mideast depends to a great extent on Israel's returning Arab lands taken in 1967 in accordance with U.N. resolutions.

However, the problem of giving up occupied territory was complicated by other factors than just the question of military security. Israeli settlements have been established on the Golan Heights and on the West Bank. It is difficult to tell settlers to pull up stakes after they have risked their lives defending these settlements. The oil fields in the Sinai are vital to the Israeli economy, and if Israel gives them back to Egypt, the United States must be ready to come up with even more assistance in order to help pay Israel's oil bill. The immigration of Soviet Jews to Israel was also a factor. Since the end of 1970, more than a hundred thousand Soviet Jews have been allowed by Soviet authorities to emigrate to Israel. Land is needed for these new immigrants.

The influx of Soviet Jews to Israel was not an unmixed blessing for Israeli officials. Many Soviet Jews "defected" before reaching Israel, choosing instead to live in Europe and North America. Many

Soviet Jews left Israel when they found they could not adjust in the country. Economic conditions did not make things easy for the new settlers in spite of Israeli government aid to immigrants (aid which causes jealousy among native-born Israelis). Soviet Jews with non-Jewish wives have a particularly difficult time if their wives do not convert to Judaism.

Total Soviet Jewish immigration to Israel was expected to top 18,000 in 1974, down by more than one-third from 1973. (The decline was due to Soviet government restrictions as well as to "defections.") In November, 1974, 1,700 Soviet Jews emigrated from the U.S.S.R., ostensibly to go to Israel. But only 1,100 showed up in Israel, the rest choosing to live elsewhere (even choosing Germany where Jews were massacred only a few decades ago). And it was not only Soviet Jews who were reluctant to live in Israel. In the first six months of 1974, only 1,177 American Jews moved to Israel, down from the 1,908 figure of the same period in 1973.

Arab Oil Power. The tremendous importance of oil gave the Arab world a bargaining position which it had not possessed before. This explains why some Western nations who previously were unconcerned about the rights and wrongs of the Mideast tragedy have suddenly become aware of the virtues of the Arab position vis-a-vis the Arab-Israeli conflict.

Arab oil power brought problems as well as benefits to the Arab world. There was speculation about possible U.S. intervention to get control of Arab oil resources. U.S. officials denied such intervention was being planned, but the speculation continued. The four-fold increase in oil prices meant that the oil-producing states of the Mideast were amassing huge sums of "petrodollars" which if not properly utilized could cause havoc in the Western world. Concern was also voiced in the West about oil money buying up property and financial interests in the United States and Europe. Kuwait purchased shares in the West German auto-maker Mercedes, and Iran acquired an interest in the mighty West German steel-maker Krupp. An Arab attempt to purchase a financial interest in Lockheed Aircraft was turned down. In spite of worries about Arab takeovers in the West, investment by oil producers could lay the basis for constructive cooperation between the West and the Arab world. A world depression or a world war would benefit neither the Arabs nor the West.

Iran. Oil was a principle factor in the sudden rise of Iran to the status of being almost a world power. With American aid, the Shah was able to build up his military forces to counter growing Soviet influence in the Persian Gulf and Indian Ocean area. Iran, like Israel, has a nuclear-weapons capability.

In Egypt President Anwar Sadat accomplished domestic reforms, including some which called into question many of the policies of the late president Gamal Nasser. Political prisoners were released and exiles allowed to return home. Requisitioned property was in some instances returned to former owners. The country became less of a Soviet police state. There was also some liberalization of the Soviet-style state planning system which Nasser imposed on the economy. (All this made Moscow very uneasy.) Plans went ahead for opening the Suez canal, much of which was cleared of wreckage and explosives. The United States and Great Britain helped with the clearing of the canal, while the Soviets cleared mines from the Gulf of Suez. The Cairo government announced a grandiose plan for reconstruction of destroyed communities along the canal which had been the front-line of the Egyptian-Israeli conflict since 1967.

Sadat looked to the United States as a means of countering the Soviet influence which Nasser so depended upon. He eagerly accepted a U.S. offer of a nuclear power reactor which Nixon made during his visit. The deal, however, was stalled following Nixon's resignation, due to Congressional opposition. (Egypt accepted the U.S. demand that there be safeguards to ensure that the reactor not be used for military purposes. Israel received the same offer from Nixon, but Israeli officials did not like the idea of safeguards because it would mean U.S. inspection of Israeli nuclear facilities which are capable of turning out nuclear weapons.) The Soviet Union immediately offered Egypt a reactor, thus undercutting both Sadat's efforts to become independent of Moscow and U.S. influence in Egypt. The announcement of a visit to Egypt in January, 1975, by Soviet Party Leader Leonid Brezhnev was another indication that the U.S.S.R. was not content to allow Kissinger to call the shots in the Mideast.

In Syria President Hafez Assad concentrated on building up the country's defense might, thanks to massive Soviet arms shipments. There was also reconstruction of installations damaged in the 1973 war, particularly the refinery and port at Homs. There was a war scare on the Golan Heights front toward the end of the year as Israel mobilized and Syrian troop build-ups were reported. However, Kissinger was able to step in and cool tempers. The mandate of the U.N. forces on both the Golan Heights front and the Sinai front were extended, giving the world a few more months of peace in the Mideast. Showing that Arabs can be just as inflexible as Israelis, the Syrians refused to allow the tiny Jewish community in Damascus to emigrate to Israel, thus in effect holding this community hostage.

Saudi Arabia and Kuwait applauded Kissinger's peace efforts. But even Saudi King Faisal, a longtime friend of the United States and a foe of communism, expressed impatience over Kissinger's inability to achieve a final settlement.

Divisions and Difficulties. Although the Rabat summit showed the Arab world was united as seldom before, there were still divisions. Libyan leader Muammar Qaddafi played the role of Young Turk in opposing any Arab-Israeli settlement. Qaddafi did not even show up at Rabat. President Sadat accused Qaddafi of trying to overthrow the Egyptian government. The Kurdish revolt continued in Iraq, and this contributed to border clashes between Iranian and Iraqi forces. Turkey was too busy with Cyprus to play an active role in Middle East politics.

The Palestine Liberation Organization faced challenges from the more militant branches of the Palestinian movement. As Arafat sought to make the PLO more respectable, Palestinian extremists often found themselves at odds with the PLO. The condemnation by the PLO of the hijacking of a British airliner at Tunis was an indication of Arafat's effort to win international respectability, but it also intensified the extremist opposition against Arafat, particularly from the Popular Front for the Liberation of Palestine which is led by George Habash.

Arafat's reluctance to follow Egypt and Syria in according de facto recognition to the existence of Israel is no doubt due in part to this extremist opposition within the Palestinian ranks. In his U.N. speech Arafat talked in terms of a secular state in which Jews, Christians, and Moslems could live in peace. Of course this is not acceptable to Israel because such a secular state means the destruction of Israel as a strictly Jewish state.

In 1974 it was evident that any real

Mideast peace settlement must provide some sort of "national home" for the Palestinian people in the Gaza Strip and on the West Bank of the Jordan River. The world can no longer ignore the plight of the Palestinians who have been without a homeland, living for the most part in refugee camps, for a quarter of a century. Yet the PLO refuses to recognize Israel. And more important, Israel tries to ignore the Palestinian question by refusing to deal with the PLO (which explains why Israeli officials would rather have Israeli hostages killed than to enter into negotiations with the PLO on freeing these hostages).

The Israelis have charged the PLO is a terrorist group and therefore cannot be negotiated with. Forgotten by this specious argument is the fact that Israel was created with the help of the frightful terrorism of the Stern Gang and the Irgun. Palestinians did not flee their homes during the Israeli War of Independence because of some migratory instinct but because of Zionist atrocities like the one at Dir-es-Sin when a whole Arab village was exterminated by the Zionists. The bombing of Arab civilians at Jerusalem's Jaffa gate is another example of how Zionists, who now condemn the PLO, practiced terrorism a quarter of a century ago.

Naturally it is difficult for Israel to recognize the Palestinian fact. But it was also difficult for the United States and South Vietnam to deal with the Vietcong and more difficult for the Portuguese government to negotiate with FRELIMO in Mozambique. But this difficulty must be overcome if peace is to be achieved in the Middle East.

The U.S.S.R. continued to voice its support for the PLO. Unlike the United States, Moscow, while seeking to maintain and strengthen its influence in the Mideast, was still reluctant to do anything which might set off a conflict in the area. Nevertheless, Soviet military power in the Indian Ocean and the Mediterranean was a factor which could not be ignored.

U. S. Influence. During 1974 Israel became more dependent upon the U.S., both militarily and politically. Since the Yom Kippur war Washington has poured billions into Israel in the form of miltary and economic aid. Congress, while tightfisted with other countries, is always willing to pass money bills for Israel. In spite of this aid, at times during 1974 it seemed as though Israel rather than Washington was calling the tune of American policy in the Mideast. This brought complaints from Senator William Fulbright and from General George Brown, chairman of the Pentagon's joint chiefs of staff, about Zionist influence in the United States.

President Ford rebuked General Brown. Ironically, Prime Minister Rabin came to Brown's defense by pointing out that the American general had done much for Israel during the Yom Kippur war and that there was too much talk in Israel about the power of the Zionist lobby in Washington.

Another Middle East War? Even without big power involvement, another Arab-Israeli war would perhaps be more destructive than any of the past wars. U. N. Secretary General Kurt Waldheim warned that a war was likely unless there was a settlement in 1975. King Hussein said nuclear weapons might be used. Since both sides possess missiles, Arab and Israeli cities could suffer terrible consequences. War would almost certainly mean another oil boycott, thus aggravating international economic problems.

In 1974 the world certainly realized the dangers of another Middle East war, but in spite of the shuttle diplomacy of Henry Kissinger, not enough was done to prevent such a conflict.

Mountaineering

MOUNT EVEREST looms above a base camp in Nepal. Twenty-one mountaineering teams, the most permitted to enter in one season since Nepal opened her peaks to foreigners in 1950, planned to climb the Himalayas in 1974. They included a Spanish expedition on Mount Everest and a team of Japanese women on Mount Manaslu, the first all-female group to climb higher than 26,250 feet. Barclays Bank International also financed an expedition up the southwest face of Mount Everest, a climb called "one of the last great challenges left to mankind."

The American Expedition to Dhaulagiri Studies in Physiology

by

I. DRUMMOND RENNIE, M.D.; M.R.C.P.

Associate Director, Section of Nephrology
Rush-Presbyterian — St. Luke's
Medical Center, Chicago. Ill.

Acute Mountain Sickness. Every year climbers, hikers, skiers, and tourists using cars, ski lifts, planes, and helicopters to ascend mountains, go too high, too fast, and are struck down by the miserable and occasionally fatal symptoms of acute mountain sickness. I have frequently had to treat sufferers, several of whom have become critically ill, even unconscious, and who would not have survived without energetic therapy and rapid evacuation to lower altitudes. The consequences of rapid ascent by lowlanders to high altitudes were perhaps most dramatically demonstrated in 1953 when the Chinese, previously acclimatized by a long sojourn on the high Tibetan plateau, were able to overrun with ease the Indian troops hastily sent up from the plains of the Ganges, who were completely incapacitated by the transition.

The Human Body at High Altitudes. Scientists have, for hundreds of years, been interested in what happens to the human body at high altitudes. When the great Swiss Horace Bénédict de Saussure offered a prize to the first man to climb Mont Blanc (at 15,781 feet the highest mountain in the Alps), it was widely believed that no one could live at that altitude, and de Saussure himself, who made the second ascent in 1787, made careful observations on himself and his companions at the summit and later (1788) at a high-altitude station which he set up and occupied for sixteen days on the Col du Géant.

It had been known for a century, since John Mayow (1674) had shown that the volume of air in a container diminished as a result of an animal's breathing, that there was something in the air necessary for life. This something was discovered by de Saussure's contemporary, Antoine Lavoisier (1743-1794) to be the element which he named oxygen in 1777. De Saussure, knowing that atmospheric pressure decreased with altitude, assumed that any effects upon the body were due to diminished oxygen pressure.

Simultaneously in 1783 ballooning began with the Montgolfier brothers who used hot air in their balloons and the physicist Jacques Alexandre Cesar Charles who used hydrogen. Throughout the nineteenth century large numbers of balloon and mountaineering ascents were made, most of them for strictly scientific purposes. The French physiologist Paul Bert published in 1877 a monumental work of over one thousand pages on the history and present status of high-altitude physiology entitled *Barometric Pressure*. In it he also recorded the results of work done in low pressure (hypobaric) chambers.

Beginning with the Italian physiologist Angelo Mosso's hut near the top of Monte Rosa (14,660 feet), in 1898, permanent high altitude stations were set up all over the world. The work done on Pikes Peak (14,300 feet) for example, by John Scott Haldane, C. J. Douglas, Yandell Henderson, and others has been fundamental to the understanding of how gases combine with blood and how respiration is regulated. The highest of these stations, and the one with which I have been most closely associated, is the Arctic Institute facility on the summit plateau (17,600 feet) of Mount Logan (19,850 feet) in the Canadian Yukon.

The Rationale for Research. Even though many climbers—and a few balloonists—have died because of too sudden exposure to high altitudes, the health and safety of mountain climbers has been the least important reason for these studies. The millions of patients in hospitals who have too little oxygen going to their tissues—whether, for example, due to severe lung diseases such as pneumonia, to heart defects or failure, or to anemia—provide the rationale for this research. The fact that the hypoxic patient at sea level frequently shows symptoms reminiscent of those seen in physically fit climbers who suddenly become ill at high altitude tends to emphasize to the investigator the importance of this research.

Acclimatization. One of the most striking phenomena to both layman and physiologist is the process of acclimatization. This can be very dramatic. An unacclimatized lowlander suddenly put at 28,000 feet would become unconscious in a few minutes even if he were completely at rest, yet E. F. Norton, on Everest (29,028 feet) in 1924, having spent weeks in a long and steady ascent, climbed to 28,100 feet without the use of additional oxygen. How often, high on Logan, soon after my arrival by small plane—wracked by breathlessness, nausea, and excruciating headaches—have I envied the climbers who have come there on foot and are capable of and enjoying prolonged physical exertion.

This process of acclimatization reaches its most complete form in the natives of the Andean Altiplano, many of whom have never been below 13,000-14,000 feet since birth. I have studied these people during several scientific expeditions to Peru. Understanding acclimatization is basic to an understanding of how the body uses oxygen and responds to lack of it, and of what happens to patients—for example those with congenital heart disease—who are chronically lacking in oxygen.

The American Expedition to Dhaulagiri. When I was invited to join the American expedition to Dhaulagiri (26,795 feet) in Nepal as a climber and physician, I recognized a tremendous opportunity to extend research at great heights using highly motivated human *guinea pigs* who would be going far higher and exerting themselves far harder for longer periods than I could expect any volunteers to do.

Dhaulagiri is the sixth highest mountain in the world and the highest in central Nepal. It was first attempted in

1950 and repulsed numerous determined assaults before the Swiss climbed it in 1960. An attempt by a small American expedition in 1969 to climb the unexplored southeast ridge met with disaster when seven members were killed in an avalanche at 17,000 feet. We were going to try this same southeast ridge.

The Design of the Experiment. Because of the tremendous physical and emotional demands on all of us, and because of the dangerous conditions and severe weather we would certainly meet on the mountain, whatever research I planned had to be safe, quick, and convenient. It could not involve complex collections of specimens, repeated sampling or any rigid schedules. None of these could possibly be kept up under the shifting and unpredictable conditions of the mountains.

On Logan, Dr. Regina Frayser, now professor of physiology at the Medical University of South Carolina, Charleston, S.C., had been investigating the tiny vessels supplying the retina, the light-sensitive membrane lining the back of the eye. Like the brain, the retina normally receives through the blood a great deal of oxygen in order to function properly.

Dr. Frayser took photographs of the backs of the eyes of volunteer young Canadian soldiers before and after they had been flown abruptly from an altitude of about 2,600 feet up to 17,600 feet on the Logan plateau. The photographs taken at high altitude showed changes that were extraordinary and, to a climber, a little frightening. First the blood vessels, the small arteries and veins, dilated and became tortuous as the blood flow increased. This adaptation presumably allowed oxygen to be delivered to the active retinal cells despite the decrease in the blood oxygen level. The most striking finding, however, was the appearance of hemorrhages in the retinas of some of the experimental subjects. These hemorrhages seemed to occur quite randomly and very rarely caused symptoms because the retina is almost entirely concerned with peripheral, shadowy vision. Why they occurred in some people and not others was thoroughly obscure, but they resembled very much the hemorrhages seen both in some types of anemia and in severe high blood pressure.

I wanted to extend the observations on Logan, at a much greater altitude, to include acclimatized people who would be exerting themselves exceedingly hard for long periods and who were apparently fit. The design of the experiment could not have been simpler: retinal photographs would be taken at sea level in New York before setting out, and again at base camp (19,400 feet) as each climber came down to base from the highest point he had reached. An ideally simple and noninterfering experiment, and so it proved to be, though actually taking the photographs was very much more awkward than I had reckoned.

First, the equipment had to be hauled up on the backs of porters (or my own back) to base camp—a three-week journey, during the last part of which we would be dangerously exposed to avalanches and crevasses. Then I had to set up my research tent on the snow, where huge drifts threatened to engulf it completely, so that it had repeatedly to be dug out. I would balance the camera, its base, and transformers on food boxes in this tiny windswept laboratory, kneeling on the uneven floor, breathless at the slightest exertion. While I was waiting for the eye drops to dilate the pupils of the experimental subject I would go out to crank up the tiny one-horse-power generator in its hole in the snow and try to coax it to produce enough power for the viewing light and flash on the camera.

Then I and my fellow-climber guinea

A SCIENTIST takes notes in Nepal. The nation plans to make Mount Everest into one of six national Himalayan parks to lure an expected 189,000 tourists by 1980.

pig would crawl into the tent and in these agonizingly cramped quarters, sweating under a black tarp when the sun was out or freezing up the camera with condensation when the afternoon clouds came up, I would take the pictures. Outside, the engine would cough and race, and I would twiddle knobs and swear as the flash failed or my subject moved.

The Results were perplexing. Five of the climbers had hemorrhages, in each case multiple. The other ten had none, nor did any of the high-altitude sherpas. All fifteen climbers had been to 23,700 feet or higher. The perplexing thing was that the five who developed hemorrhages could in no way be distinguished from the ten who did not when one took into consideration the highest point reached (for example, one of the summit trio had hemorrhages; two did not), the loads carried, the speed of ascent, the state of fitness, or the length of stay at altitude.

We know from this that climbers such as those we tested—all of whom were fit and able to work extremely hard, all of whom had been above 19,000 feet for more than six weeks and were well acclimatized and apparently free of symptoms—may develop just the same sort of hemorrhages that unacclimatized soldiers at rest in the Logan high camp get. But we still don't know what exactly brought on the hemorrhages nor why they occurred in only a third of the expedition. As with most research, I have found out a few more facts and merely illuminated further areas for investigation.

As for the expedition: a great success. The crest of the southeast ridge was reached after ten days of severe ice climbing, and though the ridge itself thereafter proved to be unclimbable, the summit was reached by three climbers on May 12, 1973, by the northeast spur, without the use of oxygen. More importantly, everyone got off the mountain alive.

Music

STEVIE WONDER, foreground, Mick Jagger, and Roberta Flack attend a party celebrating Wonder's U.S. tour in September. On March 2 the blind musician won four Grammy's, the musical equivalent of the Academy award, for the best pop male vocal performance for his "You Are the Sunshine of My Life," the album of the year *(Innervisions)*, best rhythm and blues song ("Superstition," which he wrote), and best rhythm and blues male vocal performance ("Superstition").

BOB DYLAN, after eight years absence from the concert circuit following a near-fatal motorcycle accident in 1966, made a twenty-one city, forty concert, successful comeback tour in 1974.

DUKE ELLINGTON

Edward Kennedy (Duke) Ellington, black master-musician, died on May 24 in a New York City hospital of pneumonia that followed treatment for cancer of both lungs. He was seventy-five years old. Funeral services in the Cathedral of St. John the Divine, where the Duke had presented one of his sacred concerts, were attended by ten thousand admirers. As a composer and performer the Duke had been a preeminent figure for forty years and had won international critical praise.

Born into a middle-class, Washington, D.C., family, Edward Kennedy Ellington was nicknamed Duke by a neighbor — a tribute to his undeniable "class." His first interest was painting, but in high school he turned down a scholarship to an art school and chose music as a career. Although he had very little musical training, by the time he was twenty he was playing the piano with a small band. Before long the group moved to New York City. After a four-year stretch at a night club on Broadway, Ellington's Washingtonians, as the band was called, became the big attraction at Harlem's Cotton Club. A nightly radio broadcast and recordings spread the band's fame. Before long the Duke was composing much of the music it played: music that had the freshness and vitality of improvisation. He enjoyed composing a piece one day and hearing it played the next. In the 1930s the band appeared in feature-length movies and also made an overseas trip that introduced American jazz to European audiences. During the Depression, and later when the popularity of bands declined, the Duke managed to keep his group of loyal and carefully-selected musicians together. He was always

more interested in making music than in making money.

During these years the Duke's compositions were expanding in length and complexity, many of them far removed from the jazz category. They included tone poems, songs, instrumental pieces, sacred music, and ballet music. The Duke found his inspiration everywhere — in the Bible, in Shakespeare, in Africa, in Tin Pan Alley, in the ghettos. Everything that he experienced served to stimulate his creative energies; more than anything he was moved by the half-joyous, half-melancholy moods of his people. He had the happy — and unusual — faculty of combining innocence and sophistication.

At the Newport Jazz Festival of 1956, the band played — to dancing-in-the-aisles response — a composition its leader had written twenty years before. In the 1960s and 70s, the Duke's honors piled up. He was awarded the French Legion of Honor, made a member of the Royal Swedish Academy of Music, given the U.S. Presidential Medal of Freedom and honorary degrees from twenty-two colleges and universities. Two African countries issued postage stamps bearing his picture. On a goodwill mission launched by the State Department, the band toured the world. On one trip that included the Middle East, the Far East, and the Soviet Union, forty-three countries were visited.

Among Ellington's well-remembered compositions are: "Mood Indigo," and "Do Nothing 'Til You Hear From Me." Mercer Ellington, the Duke's only child, who acted as road manager, assumed the leadership of the seventeen-piece band.

Nixon Administration

IN A FAREWELL SPEECH to his administration aides, President Richard Nixon gives a thumbs-up sign as his wife Pat and his daughter Tricia Nixon Cox watch.

by
GODFREY SPERLING, JR.
Chief, Washington News Bureau
The Christian Science Monitor

The Resignation. The year 1974 was marked by the end of Richard Nixon's remarkable, twenty-seven-year career in the political spotlight.

Nixon stepped down from the presidency when, in early August, it became clear to him that impeachment and ouster were imminent—all because of the Watergate scandal. Only a few days before his exit the president had indicated he intended to continue his fight to stay in office, despite the approval by the House Judiciary Committee of three articles of impeachment.

But then on August 5 Nixon startled the nation by releasing partial transcripts of three conversations with his former chief of staff, H. R. Haldeman. To most members of Congress these texts clearly showed presidential participation in the Watergate cover-up just six days after the break-in of the Democratic national headquarters on June 17, 1972—participation which Nixon for two years had persistently denied.

Soon Republican Senate leaders Hugh

Scott and Barry Goldwater were at Nixon's White House door, informing him that his support in Congress had now dissolved—that there was nothing that would now save him from being forced out of the White House.

General Alexander Haig, Nixon's chief of staff, had asked that Scott and Goldwater meet with the president to inform him of Congress's anti-Nixon mood.

General Haig, who had become convinced himself it would be better for the nation if Nixon resigned, counseled the two senators not to recommend such a course of action—lest they stiffen the back of the president to the degree that he would decide to "tough it out" to the bitter end.

Now faced with the prospect of inevitable removal, Nixon announced on August 8 that he would step down the next day.

This presidential resignation was without precedent. While much of the nation welcomed the move—and the bringing of a non-Watergate-involved Vice-President Gerald Ford to the nation's helm—there were many Americans who felt that Nixon should not have been allowed to thus skirt the Constitutionally prescribed impeachment process.

Further, many Americans believed that the Nixon resignation would probably mean that they now would never know the real facts of Watergate, the complicated affair which had its beginning in 1972 when five men were caught and two others were shortly thereafter found to be involved in the burglary of the Democratic headquarters in the Watergate apartment office in Washington.

These fears seemed to be confirmed when, shortly after taking office, President Ford pardoned Nixon.

This Ford pardon came as a complete surprise, since the president had indicated in his first press conference that he would let the legal processes run their course before considering the pardon of his predecessor.

But a few days later Ford suddenly called the press together for a Sunday pronouncement: he said that he had for reasons of mercy decided to pardon Nixon—that he had determined he would relieve the anxieties of Nixon and his family over a pardon which he now had decided would eventually be forthcoming.

Now that the former president could not be indicted and tried for possible involvement in the Watergate-related acts or in the cover-up, the question remained how directly could he be pulled into the trial of the other defendants as a witness?

The illness of Nixon, resulting from a worsening phlebitis condition, appeared to mean that his testimony would have to be confined to depositions.

Defenders of the Ford early-pardon decision, including Nelson Rockefeller, named by Ford to become vice-president, contended that Nixon had been fully punished by the disgrace of resignation. "He's been hanged," said Rockefeller. "Why should he be drawn and quartered?"

Nixon's Accomplishments. Nixon's final year was so overshadowed by Watergate that his accomplishments seem difficult to find.

Yet he and his far-ranging secretary of state, Henry Kissinger, did a masterful job of bringing about a troubled peace in the Mideast. And a presidential trip to Moscow, while resulting in no really significant pacts, did add to the appearance of a closer working relationship between Russia and the United States.

On the domestic side the president's achievements were few and far between. To begin with, Congress battled Nixon to his knees on the issue of impounding funds which had been allocated. Congress defeated the president on twenty-five of thirty impoundment-related issues that came to a vote during 1974.

Obviously, because of Watergate and Nixon's diminishing public approval (he finally dropped to a record-setting one-fifth approval rating in the polls), the Nixon clout with Congress had evaporated. Gone were the days when Nixon could point to his greater than 60 percent vote victory in 1972 and tell Congress that he had a mandate from the people to get certain things done.

Politically the president had, indeed, fallen on exceedingly bad days, long before he finally decided to step down. Even among the long-time Nixon loyalists who manned the Republican party leadership positions around the United States the support for the president had been fast ebbing for more than a year before the end came. From state chairmen and national committeemen across the nation came the plaint uttered in words like these: "Watergate is killing us. We would be much better off if Ford were president."

Also in Congress itself the Republican conservatives, led by Senator Goldwater, were becoming Nixon's most vocal critics on the Watergate issue.

Meanwhile, Nixon was having to take his mind off his Watergate troubles, whenever he could, to try to cope with a mounting crisis at home — an energy shortage, precipitated by an Arab cutoff of oil shipments, and an inflation that just would not come under control.

The Nixon call for voluntary conservation of energy usage drew a helpful response from the American people. Further, the Nixon diplomacy finally persuaded the Arabs to renew oil shipping to the United States.

But Nixon was unable to get a hold on soaring prices. Over the years he had flitted back and forth on how to control inflation, first being opposed to wage-price controls, then invoking them, and then moving away from them. Nothing he tried seemed to work.

Thus it was that Richard Nixon ended his career after a final year of complete frustration.

This was a man who had served his country for two terms as vice-president and for one and one-half terms as president. Before that he had been in both the House and Senate. And in 1960 he had come within a hair of being elected to the White House, having been nosed out by only a relatively few votes by John F. Kennedy.

The Verdict of History. What would history say of Richard Nixon? It was far too early to tell. It seemed certain that Watergate had damaged him irreparably. No longer was it likely that he would achieve his goal—of becoming one of the great presidents.

But Nixon would be remembered for his notable, even spectacular successes in the foreign field: his opening up of ties with Peking and his search for detente with Soviet Russia. Also, while his critics may say Nixon did not end the Vietnam war fast enough, there will be those who give him credit for winding down that war.

Nixon diplomacy in the Mideast will also likely be noted as one of his major achievements.

Nixon was now gone from the national leadership scene. One prediction seemed unchallengable: he would be the subject of books and other writings for years to come. Future biographers, historians, and even playwrights, would find this man and his times particularly fascinating. Before Watergate Nixon was often viewed as dull by those in both academic and artistic circles. With Watergate, whatever else may be said about him, Richard Nixon was no longer dull. One well-known author has said that Nixon now may become the most-written-about president of them all.

IRISH TEENAGERS in Londonderry build a street barricade in this World Press Photo Holland prizewinner by Christopher Henning. Children's war games are real in Northern Ireland.

by
THOMAS P. PEARDON, Ph.D.
Professor Emeritus of Political Science
Barnard College, Columbia University

Frustration. In Northern Ireland (Ulster), 1974 was a year of frustration. It saw the collapse of the first experiment in the sharing of power between the Protestant majority and the Roman Catholic minority and a revival of extremism among the Protestants. Great Britain showed signs of growing tired of its heavy and expensive responsibilities for the maintenance of law and order; there was talk of the withdrawal of British troops. The hope of active cooperation by the Irish Republic in the solution of the problems of the North was not realized. Violence continued at a high level and at the end of the year there was fear of outright civil war between the new increasingly polarized communities. Peace and stability seemed as far off as ever.

The Sequence of Events was more disappointing because the previous year had seen so many apparent gains for efforts to achieve unity between Protestants and Catholics. An assembly in which the majority favored compromise

NORTHERN IRELAND

had been chosen by proportional representation. Before the year ended this assembly had agreed (though with difficulty) on an executive containing representatives of both faiths. Agreement had also been reached in principle on a council of Ireland containing members from both Ulster and the republic to the south. If and when created it was supposed to discuss and perhaps act on matters concerning the whole island.

In January, however, the tide began to flow in an opposite direction when the council of the Protestant Unionist party voted down policies of power-sharing with the Catholics by a substantial majority (454-374). As a result, Brian Faulkner, head of the new executive, resigned as leader of the Unionist party. This reverse was soon followed by disappointing results in the general election of February 28.

The February Election. Although geographically a part of Ireland, Ulster is constitutionally joined with Great Britain in the United Kingdom of Great Britain and Northern Ireland. It sends twelve members to the Parliament at Westminster. In February the campaign and issues in Ulster were peculiar to Ireland. There were no candidates of the Conservatives, British Labor party, or Liberals; and the only questions that counted were power-sharing and the proposed council of Ireland. The Protestant hard-line leaders formed an alliance that won 51 percent of the popular vote, and carried eleven of the twelve seats. The moderate Catholic Social Democratic Labor party won the other. Even though the peculiar workings of the single member district system (which is familiar to Americans as that used in electing the House of Representatives) magnified the results of the election, the outcome showed a swing to the Protestant hardliners who had received only 35 percent of the popular vote when the Ulster assembly was chosen in 1973.

New Policies. As a result of the February election in Great Britain as a whole, Harold Wilson of the Labor party succeeded Edward Heath as prime minister. He selected Merlyn Rees, miner's son educated at Oxford, as secretary of state for Northern Ireland. New directions of policy soon emerged. It was announced that, no matter what happened, the number of British troops in Ulster would be reduced and responsibility for antiterrorist activities and the maintenance of security transferred from British to Ulster authorities. An all-party committee of the Northern Ireland Assembly was to assume control over police and courts. As a conciliatory gesture, it was promised that persons interned without trial would be released gradually on probation and that two illegal organizations, one Protestant and one mainly Catholic, would be recognized as legal. These steps to transfer responsibility for Northern Ireland back to the Northern Irish were immediately interpreted to mean that London was getting ready to withdraw. This widely held belief was not destroyed by strong denials.

Irish Responses. On the assumption that the British will was weakening, the Irish Republican Army (IRA) now stepped up its violence. But the response of the Protestant hardliners was more involved. In the first place, they demanded new elections on the ground that the results in February demonstrated that the coalition of Protestant and Roman Catholic moderates which controlled the Assembly no longer represented the will of the majority. Secondly, they insisted even more vehemently that plans for a council of Ireland, north and south, be abandoned. In fact, there was some reason to believe that the Protestant loyalists (as they called themselves) might become reconciled to the prospect of power-sharing in some form; but that they

NORTHERN IRELAND

would resist to the death any measures aiming at union between Ulster and the republic.

When the British government ignored these demands the Protestant loyalists turned to economic action.

The Protestant 'Workers' Strike. By May three categories of Protestant groups had emerged: political parties, paramilitary action groups trained in the use of arms and ready to employ force, and the Ulster Workers Council. This last organization went on strike to enforce demands for early elections and for the ending of plans for a council of Ireland. The British government refused to negotiate with the strikers and so the walkout spread. Factories were closed, essential services cut to emergency levels, barricades erected. Traffic stalled, industrial and commercial life came to a standstill. Troops removed the barricades (which the workers immediately put up again), but apart from this the army was not used against the strikers. The danger of a civil war was too great for that.

The Collapse of Power Sharing. The strike was the turning point of the year. By resorting to direct action the Ulster Workers Council had rallied most of the Protestants behind them; the hardliners had reasserted their claim to represent majority opinion. Recognizing this fact, and angry at the British refusal to negotiate, the Unionist moderates who had followed Brian Faulkner resigned from the coalition executive.

Uncertain what to do, the Wilson government then recessed the assembly for four months and resumed direct rule of the province. It had already been announced that implementation of the plan for an all-Ireland council should be postponed. British policy lay in ruins. The victorious strikers went back to work. In two weeks they had transformed the whole situation.

The deeper significance of the strike was best expressed by Merlyn Rees himself: "it liberated something that must be taken into account: Ulster nationalism." There was more talk henceforth about the possibility of independence of Northern Ireland; in Great Britain there were more voices calling for withdrawal.

The July White Paper. Now began what Rees called "the great reappraisal" of policy, culminating in a White Paper issued on July 4. New elections were to be held to choose a constitutional convention of seventy-eight members selected by proportional representation. They were to be given at least six months in which to draft a new government of Northern Ireland. Several conditions were laid down as to the nature of any new constitution; it must provide for the sharing of power between Protestants and Roman Catholics; it must be acceptable to the British Parliament as well as to the people of Ulster; and it must recognize in some way the special relationship between Ulster and the Republic of Ireland. Elections to the proposed convention were scheduled for early in 1975, but the worsening of the political situation during the rest of 1974 caused some doubt as to whether that schedule would be met.

The October Election. The resurgence of the Protestant hardliners continued through the second elections to the British Parliament on October 10. Both moderates and loyalists formed loose alliances for this contest. It is true that the latter (United Ulster Unionist Coalition) won only ten seats as compared with eleven in February but their share in the popular vote rose from 51 percent to 58 percent. All the moderates taken together attracted only 33 percent. The polarization of the religious communities was obvious.

Continued Violence. Nor was the drift to polarization a peaceful one. The toll

NORTHERN IRELAND

of deaths since the troubles began in 1969 passed 1,000 in April; it seemed likely to reach 1,200 before the people of Ulster would celebrate the Christmas season of peace and good will. The dead included more than 200 British soldiers.

Paradoxes. Yet opinion polls taken in the spring of the year showed that 96 percent of the population disapproved of the use of violence to attain political ends; only 2 percent were positively in favor of it. Seventy-four percent would accept power-sharing with the opposite community in the future government of the province, although a smaller percentage gave power-sharing as their first choice. Equally striking was the fact that only 16 percent of the Roman Catholics preferred the end of partition to other possible arrangements for the future.

Another paradox was the continuation of economic progress through all the political troubles. According to John Hume, Catholic Social Democratic and Labor Party (SDLP), minister of commerce in the now defunct Faulkner coalition, industrial output rose more than 28 percent, productivity per man hour more than 28 percent, between 1969 and 1974. This was a better record than Great Britain could show.

Uncertain Future. Faced by massive difficulties at home, the British government was trying to transfer to the shoulders of her own people responsibility for finding solutions to Ulster's problems. It was uncertain if this meant that the British will to stay was weakening. Prime Minister Wilson insisted on several occasions that this was not so—the British army, he said, would remain as long as it was needed to keep order. But in Great Britain itself letters and petitions were being sent to MPs expressing impatience at the continued drain in lives and money resulting from the British presence in Ulster. They were indifferent to the fact that withdrawal might endanger extensive British investments as well as give encouragement to extreme nationalists in Scotland and Wales. Could the United Kingdom itself survive, asked *The Economist,* if Northern Ireland were cut loose?

Those who dreamed of an independent Ulster (still only a minority among Protestant spokesmen) seemed to assume that Great Britain would continue to give economic assistance provided that in return the Catholics had some share in power and that their civil rights were fully guaranteed. The issue of continued economic aid would be of fundamental importance — approximately one-half of Northern Ireland's 1973-1974 expenditures ($2.1 billion) is provided by Great Britain in one form or another. Nor would agreement on the form of power-sharing be easy. As was said earlier, there is some indication that the idea itself has become less objectionable to the Protestants than it formerly was, but perhaps only as regards membership in the legislature, not the executive where the balance of power rests in modern governments. Protestant opposition to ending partition and joining the republic is, of course, as strong as ever.

Nor was there much hope that a constitutional convention could reach agreement. It was true that both communities felt outraged and deprived of their rights under direct rule. But they were also estranged from each other. Extremists on both sides were said to be expecting civil war. The IRA continued to be active, and the Protestants were recruiting and training a 20,000-man force—there was talk of 50,000— to defeat the IRA as the Home Guards had done in earlier campaigns. In spite of the fact that 96 percent of the total population deplored violence, ordinary people on both sides—either through loyalty or fear—gave at least passive support to their own men who employed it.

NORTHERN IRELAND

TWO NORTHERN IRISH CHILDREN look down at Belfast from the cave in Cave Hill. The Women Caring Trust, which has raised $50,000 for projects aimed at helping the Roman Catholic and Protestant children of Northern Ireland to know one another, sponsors "mixed outings," day trips for youngsters of both faiths to the Irish countryside.

The Irish Dimension. There is no doubt that the republican government at Dublin was sorry to see the experiment in power-sharing fail in 1974 or that it wants the British army to stay in Ulster. Yet it was alleged that Dublin had not done enough to help Brian Faulkner by taking stronger measures against the IRA in the south, by extraditing wanted men to the north, and by similar steps. In addition Dublin has consistently refused to change the Irish constitution to eliminate clauses that are offensive to Protestants. However, in practice, it has also abandoned any effort to advance the cause of unity at the present time, even by so small a step as working for the establishment of the council of Ireland. In fact Dublin has publicly recognized that Northern Ireland is *de facto* a part of the United Kingdom and likely to remain so for some time. Dublin knows that it could not possibly give the North anything like the economic aid or the social benefits that go along with British rule.

Panama

PANAMA CANAL LOCKS are 110 feet wide and 1,000 feet long. Nearly a thousand ships afloat or under construction are too wide for the locks. Another 1,200 squeeze through partially loaded; they cannot navigate the channel with a full cargo.

by
GEORGE BLANKSTEN, Ph.D.
Professor of Political Science
Northwestern University
Author of *Argentina and Chile* (1969)

The Panama Canal Zone Agreement. In 1974 the governments of the United States and Panama entered into a far-reaching agreement providing for the eventual termination of the sovereignty of the United States over the Panama Canal Zone. It thus appeared that a fundamental redefinition of U.S.-Panamanian relations, and the role of the canal in them, had been set in motion during the year.

Historical Background. In the years before 1903, the Isthmus of Panama had been a part of the Republic of Colombia. In the latter years of the nineteenth century interest grew in a number of quarters in the feasibility of digging across the isthmus a canal which would join the Atlantic and Pacific oceans at that point. The first attempt to undertake this imaginative and adventurous project was launched, late in the nineteenth century, by the de Lesseps Company, a French enterprise. The ill-starred de Lesseps venture was doomed to failure. Not only did the geological difficulties of the project turn out to be insurmountable for the French, but sanitary problems and financial complications also developed. Malaria and yellow fever came to be major problems, along with financial miscalculations. The project was at length abandoned by the de Lesseps organization, which left a controlling interest in the apparently defunct scheme in the hands of Philippe Bunau-Varilla, a French financier.

At the end of the nineteenth century, the Spanish-American War stirred interest in the United States in the desirability of completing the abandoned canal. The spectacle of the movement of U.S. military and naval units *through the Straits of Magellan* in order to travel from Cuba to the Philippines, the two major theaters of action in the war, convinced many in the United States that the completion of the canal across the Isthmus of Panama should be postponed no longer. In this climate of opinion, Bunau-Varilla met with U.S. President Theodore Roosevelt, an outspoken proponent of the canal project, to sell the remaining French interest in the projected waterway to the United States. Roosevelt enthusiastically accepted the transaction. As the isthmus still belonged to Colombia, early in 1903 the Hay-Herrán Treaty was negotiated by government representatives at Washington and Bogotá. This provided that the United States would pay $10 million outright, and $250,000 annually, to Colombia for the right to build and administer a canal across the Isthmus of Panama. The treaty was well received in the United States, but failed of ratification in the Colombian senate.

The subsequent developments did much to contribute to Theodore Roosevelt's image as the wielder of a "Big Stick" in the Caribbean and to a growing Latin-American view of the United States as a fundamentally imperialist power. Bunau-Varilla sought another interview with the U.S. president. "Roosevelt asked, 'What do you think is going to be the outcome of the present situation?' " Bunau-Varilla recorded in his autobiographical *From Panama to Verdun,* "It was then or never. I could by my answer know exactly what the president had in mind. I remained silent for a moment, and I pronounced the following four words in a slow, decided manner: 'Mr. President, a revolution!' " Shortly thereafter, Roosevelt wrote to Albert Shaw, editor of the *Review of Reviews,* "Privately I freely say to you that I would be delighted if Panama were an independent state, or if it made itself so at this moment; but for me to say so publicly would amount to an instigation of a revolt, and therefore I cannot say it." In November of 1903 a revolt on the isthmus, instigated by Bunau-Varilla and supported by the United States, resulted in the creation of the newly independent Republic of Panama, now separated from Colombia. The United States hastened to recognize the new state and to enter, near the end of 1903, into the Hay-Bunau-Varilla Treaty with Panama.

The Hay-Bunau-Varilla Treaty remained controlling in the U.S.-Panamanian relations for more than seventy years. Washington was to pay $10 million outright and $250,000 annually to Panama; in return, the United States was granted leasehold in perpetuity over the Panama Canal Zone, with the right to build and operate a canal there. In pursuance of this agreement, the United States completed the construction of the long-unfinished Panama Canal, which at length was opened for business in 1914.

A number of problems have beset the canal, especially in the years since World War II. For one thing, the events of World War II demonstrated the growing problem of the obsolescence of the canal's facilities, leading many to believe that either the canal should be widened or that a new, more modern waterway should be constructed in the area. Morever, the device of leasehold in perpetuity, a particularly unfortunately antiquated form of imperialism, came under attack with increased regularity. Panamanians frequently rioted and demonstrated against it, demanding some redefinition of the role of the canal in the relations between the United States and Panama.

The need for redefinition—and modernization—of the arrangement came to be accepted in the United States in the 1960s. The Subcommittee on American Republic Affairs, a unit of the U.S. Senate's Committee on Foreign Relations, accepted a report recommending that the administration of the Panama Canal be internationalized under the jurisdiction of the Organization of American States (OAS), the regional international organization in the Western Hemisphere. This recommendation was unpopular in Panama and in the United States, but was favorably received in some of the other countries in the OAS. In 1963, a commission headed by Dr. Milton Eisenhower, brother of U.S. President Dwight D. Eisenhower (1953-61), proposed that the canal be jointly administered by both the United States and Panama under an arrangement expected to result eventually in complete control of the waterway by the Panamanian government. Concerned by the obsolescence of the existing canal, the administration of U.S. President Lyndon B. Johnson (1963-69) entered into a commitment either to widen it or build a second, more modern, waterway.

Events of 1974. Turning his diplomatic talents to the Western Hemisphere, U.S. Secretary of State Henry Kissinger undertook the task of redefining and modernizing the place of the Panama Canal. A new U.S.-Panamanian agreement was reached in principle on January 10, and a month later Kissinger journeyed to Panama City to take part in ceremonies including the signing, with Panama's Foreign Minister Juan Antonio Tack, of a new treaty intended to replace the Hay-Bunau-Varilla Treaty of 1903. The 1974 pact specifically provided for the abrogation of the 1903 treaty and the termination of the concept of leasehold in perpetuity. Beyond that, the new arrangement would provide eventually for the extension of Panamanian, rather than U.S., sovereignty over the Canal Zone. Following some of the recommendations of the Eisenhower commission, the new agreement provided that the Panamanian government would receive a share of the Canal Zone's receipts and that the canal would be bilaterally administered and defended by the governments of both Panama and the United States. Honoring the commitment of the Johnson administration, the 1974 treaty provided also that in the future either the existing Panama Canal would be widened or a second, more modern canal would be built in the area.

As the year drew to a close, it seemed likely that the new treaty would encounter opposition when submitted to the U.S. Senate for ratification. Resistance against transfer of sovereignty over the Canal Zone appeared in Washington. On March 29, thirty-two U.S. senators, led by Strom Thurmond (R., S.C.) and John McClellan (D., Ark.), signed a resolution expressing opposition to the transfer of sovereignty envisaged in the new treaty. This opposition appeared to be formidable, as it crossed party lines in the United States. The eventual fate of the new treaty thus seemed uncertain as the year ended. Whatever the outcome, it nevertheless was clear that 1974 had seen the passing of a critical milestone in the changing role of the Panama Canal in the Americas.

Politics

PRESIDENT GERALD FORD in his Oval Office at the White House: politicians questioned whether he would run for president in 1976.

by

GODFREY SPERLING, JR.

Chief, Washington Bureau,
The Christian Science Monitor

The Election. After the midterm general election of 1974 a big question remained: Was the Democratic sweep a Republican loss rather than a Democratic victory?

The facts of the results were, of course, clear. The voters had bulged the Democratic membership of the House to two-thirds and given the Senate a near two-thirds Democratic coloration. Elsewhere, around the United States, eight of the ten big-population states (Florida, New York, Massachusetts, California, Pennsylvania, Texas, Illinois, and New Jersey) were now in the hands of Democratic governors. Only Michigan and Ohio, among the big states, elected Republicans to their chief-executive posts.

The Democrats' Position. All this meant that the Democrats had moved into a particularly advantageous position for winning the presidency in 1976.

History shows that such great midterm elections by the party out of presidential power are often followed by a presidential victory two years hence by that same party.

Further, the Democrats now held governorships in states that encompassed about 85 percent of the U.S. population.

Such a tremendous political stronghold of state chief executives obviously gives the Democrats powerful political leverage toward capturing the big-electoral-vote states in the presidential race two years hence.

Expression of Anger. But did the Democrats really win that impressively or was it simply that the Republicans were repudiated by the voters?

Postelection checks showed that many voters had taken out their ire over Watergate and the Nixon administration on the Republicans.

Many Republicans did it by staying away from the polls. Thus, while only 38 percent of the electorate voted, it has been estimated that a large majority of the nonvoters were Republicans.

And those who did vote (or many of them) cast their ballots for a Democrat to express their anger over Watergate and Nixon's presidency.

It was, it seems, in large part a punishment vote aimed at Richard Nixon.

But many who did not vote and many who voted, too, were fed up with government and government leaders at every level. And if they did get to the polls, they tended to show this alienation by marking their ballots for a Democrat.

Candidate Caliber. Often this voter inclination was supported by the caliber of candidates themselves, the Democrat more often than not having better or more attractive credentials.

SENATOR EDWARD KENNEDY announced at a press conference on September 23 that he would not be a candidate for president in 1976.

Because of Watergate, Republican slate-makers in every state had found it most difficult to persuade good people to seek office. Attractive, capable men and women were saying "no"; they did not want to get hurt by the Watergate political fallout.

Many top-flight Republican office holders, in Congress and in lesser jobs across the nation, decided that this was a good year to retire. And, again, good replacements were difficult to find.

The Presidential Sweepstakes. All this adds up to an election which may not presage a similar result in 1976.

It could very well be that this was the moment the voters got Watergate out of their system, once and for all.

Thus, the presidential sweepstakes may be something else again—with the candidates starting off afresh.

Ford's Chances. However, it must be said that if all things are somewhat equal by November, 1976, the likely Republican candidate, Gerald Ford, will have the advantage simply because he is the president.

By that time he will have had so much visibility that this identification factor alone will give him the edge over the Democrat who emerges as the presidential nominee.

Senator Edward Kennedy would be as well known as President Ford. But Senator Kennedy has bowed out early, giving family considerations as his reason for not seeking the presidency this time.

For the senator, who was the leading Democratic presidential possibility in the polls when he dropped out, there were other considerations, too: He knew that many people would feel he had had his own Watergate—the drowning incident at Chappaquiddick. And he was continuing to get assassination threats—a danger he knew would be compounded if he became a presidential candidate.

Ford's Campaign. Had the president been hurt politically by the devastating GOP defeat of 1974? Certainly Ford had injected himself fully into the campaign. For more than a month he stumped intensively, visiting some twenty states and imploring the voters to keep the Democrats from getting so many congressional seats that there would be an imbalance in the Congress.

Certainly, there was little evidence the president helped Republicans generally across the nation.

Yet there was little inclination on the part of the Democrats to say that the president had been repudiated by the results.

Indeed, the judgment among observers in Washington tended to put the president's impact as neutral. He had neither hurt nor helped, they concluded.

Because Ford had been in the presidency only three months, this judgment was expressed by the pundits: He really had nothing in the way of a record to put on the line. Therefore there was nothing for the voters to repudiate.

However, it may well be that the president did gain something, personally, from his extensive campaigning.

He certainly became better known.

Further, he may well have "set up" the Democrats for the presidential year. That is, if the Democratic Congress refuses to pass his programs, particularly those on the economy, he now is in a position to go back to the electorate in 1976 and say, "I warned you not to vote Democrats in. Now they are obstructing me." And he might, like Harry Truman, campaign against a "do-nothing" Congress.

The Democratic Majority. Of course, the large Democratic majority in Congress might result in the Democrats taking the responsibility for putting together and pushing through some strong programs for the nation.

But there was a question here: Did the new Democratic majority really constitute a unified force in Congress? The answer was not hard to arrive at. Obviously the conservative-liberal split among Democratic congressmen would seriously divide the Democrats on such important issues as wage-price controls, national health insurance, federal restrictions on individual use of energy, tax cuts or increases, what to do about the unemployed, conservation measures in general, and a number of other key issues.

Obviously, too, these Democratic congressmen did not agree among themselves on foreign affairs issues, including how best to deal with the Soviet Union, Israel, the Arabs, and the great oil problem.

There were other questions that related to the Democratic Congress's ability to take the initiative in providing constructive legislation: Did the Democrats have the leadership to move the nation forward? And, further, did they have the creativity necessary to come up with programs that would command national support? Most specifically, did the Democrats have good, alternative answers to the number one national problem—the economy?

Other Questions. The election left other questions. One came out of the Ford campaign. Several politicians who talked to the president came away with the impression that he would not be a candidate in 1976. However, longtime Washington friends of the president insist that he already is gearing up for the race. And top GOP leaders around the country say that Ford has no alternative—that he will be drafted if he does not volunteer. The president in early winter said he definitely would run in 1976. This may or may not be his last word on the subject.

A BURRO and a villager get water from the same fountain. The average Portuguese salary, at $180 a month, is the lowest in Europe.

by

GEORGE HILLS

Author of *Spain — A Survey of Politics, Economics, and Social Conditions* (1969) and *The Rock of Contention — A History of Gibraltar* (1972), Broadcaster and Lecturer on Portuguese Current Affairs.

Coup d'Etat. Early on April 25, 1973, a small body of troops seized key points throughout Portugal and surrounded Lisbon. They were in control of every important point in the capital save one by 7:30 A.M. In that one, the headquarters of the National Guard, the prime minister, Marcello Caetano, took refuge. He surrendered that evening to General Antonio de Spinola who was acting on behalf of a group of junior officers who called themselves the Armed Forces Movement. At midnight the movement named Spinola head of a "Junta of National Salvation," and he issued a policy statement. He promised a civilian government within three weeks, the dissolution of the whole apparatus of the Antonio de Oliveira Salazar state, the disbandment of the security police, freedom of speech and political association, amnesty for all political prisoners, negotiations to end the wars in Africa, and, within a year, free elections.

General Spinola was acclaimed wherever he appeared in public. He had a distinguished record of personal bravery and success against the guerrillas in Angola. As governor general and commander in chief in Guinea-Bissau he had contained within a limited area the activities of guerrillas when they appeared to be on the eve of final victory. He was currently deputy chief of staff of the armed forces. His name was on everyone's lips, for a mere four weeks earlier, on February 22, he had published a book, *Portugal and the Future*, challenging the most sacred tenet of Caetano's political faith: that it was Portugal's divine mission to mould several million Africans into Portuguese; that Portugal should not count the cost, since victory was certain in the end. General Spinola had argued from facts he knew personally, and concluded that there was "no military solution," that is, no likelihood of a Portuguese victory over the guerrillas in Angola, Guinea, or Mozambique. Portugal had to recognize the right of the peoples of those territories to determine their future and their ability to manage their own affairs. All that Portugal could strive for, he hoped successfully, was to persuade those peoples to become "a Lusitanian community" of equals, else Portugal would diminish into "a canton of Europe."

When the book first appeared Caetano had been urged by President Americo Thomaz to dismiss Spinola and his superior, the chief of staff General da Costa Gomes, who had endorsed him. Caetano had refused on the grounds that the views expressed were so outrageous that they could not appeal to more than a few malcontents, and that any action would give the impression that the government took them seriously.

It is probable that the book, by itself, would have been a mere seven-day talking point, had its publication not coincided with other events.

The Wars in Africa. In July, 1973, the *London Times* had published the allegations of Catholic missionaries that troops under Portuguese command had been guilty of massacres in Mozambique. From October, 1973, the hierarchy of Portugal had been expressing its grave disquiet over Portuguese policies in Africa. In January, one of the bishops of Mozambique had revealed that the stories published in the *Times* coincided in substance with evidence he himself had presented to the authorities in March, 1973. With that the official contention that the Portuguese troops were engaged in a "civilizing mission" in Africa had begun to fall on deaf ears.

Through the years from the outbreak of the rebellion in Angola in 1961, and in Guinea and Mozambique subsequently, Portugal had admitted to some losses, but claimed that the guerrillas had been contained within insignificant areas. That claim, weakened in September, 1973, when several countries had recognized the effectiveness of the guerrillas' control of the greater part of Guinea, received a death-blow when in January and February the news spread of FRELIMO (Mozambique Liberation Front) guerrilla operations in the central farming area between Beira and Rhodesia, 200 miles and more south of where they were supposed to be contained.

Discontent in Portugal. It was in January and February that the ordinary people of Portugal had begun, quite independently of Spinola's book, to wonder whether the African effort was worth the cost. The real costs—44 percent of the budget, and 8 percent of the Gross National Product—compounded with the rise in the world price of fuels and other commodities to cause a staggering and sudden fall in the standard of living of the Portuguese, reckoned already two years previously by international bodies to be the lowest in Western Europe. It was so low because over a million young men had emigrated during the previous ten years to avoid service in Africa for periods of two and frequently four years. The loss which resulted—though partly compensated by the remittances which the emigrés sent their families—had left

Portugal, a country of only 9 million inhabitants, without the manpower to maintain its industries, let alone develop them.

There was simultaneously discontent in the army.

The army as a profession had long appealed only to a few young men: pay was poor in comparison with possible earnings elsewhere. Drafted university graduates made good the shortage of junior officers in the expanded army made necessary by the wars in Africa; but there was now a shortage of majors, and promotion to that rank and above was limited to the professional. In mid-1973 the government had offered the drafted captains permanency in the army and promotion. The professionals felt themselves insulted: the "amateur" was being equated with them. The discontented formed a secret society, the Captains' Movement, and brought their grievances about pay and promotion to the notice of Spinola whose reaction was one of impotent sympathy. In January the pay scales were revised, but in the meantime, somehow, the aims of the movement had become more radical, its members believing with Spinola that Portugal could not win in Africa, but going much further. In a leaflet circulated early in March they stated that it was the duty of the army to save the nation from its government.

The Abortive Coup. The government could now no longer ignore the Captain's Movement, and on March 5 ordered the posting of four of its members away from the Lisbon area. Three nights later, the movement met at midnight to discuss resistance to the order. At 3:00 A.M. the government placed under house arrest 200 officers suspected of attending the meeting. The president instructed all senior officers to attend a rally on March 14, and there to reaffirm their loyalty to the regime. Generals Gomes and Spinola did not attend, and were dismissed.

The movement planned a nationwide army uprising for the night of March 15-16, but, it would appear, the signal for coordinated action miscarried, and at dawn March 16 only some companies of the Fifth Infantry Regiment left their barracks at Caldas da Rainha under their captains, and in armored cars and trucks made for Lisbon, fifty miles away. Eight miles from their objective a force of tanks, artillery, and National Republican Guards barred their way. The two forces faced each other all day without firing a shot. At 3:30 P.M. the rebels surrendered.

There were a few arrests and some minor changes in the cabinet, and by March 28 all appeared quiet in Portugal. Four weeks later the same troops were joined by a greater number in the second, and this time successful, coup. By that time, however, the Captain's had become the Armed Forces Movement, with a coordinating committee whose views on Portugal and its future, time was to show, were substantially different from those of the man whom they chose to be the first figurehead of their new Portugal.

Spinola's Presidency. The jubilation of the crowds at the overthrow of the old regime reached a climax on May 1 which Spinola declared a national holiday. The promise of a civilian government within three weeks was fulfilled when on May 15 General Spinola was formally declared president. On the following day, the president swore in a provisional government headed by a university professor of independent views, Adelino da Palma Carlos. Both the leader of the Socialist party, Dr. Mario Soares, and the secretary general of the Communist party, Alvaro Cunhal, had stressed, upon their return from exile at the end of April, that they would seek their political ends through democratic means, and they both ac-

PORTUGUESE FARM WOMEN wash their clothes in a meandering stream. The economy of Portugal, the most backward country in Europe, is dominated by agriculture, fishing, and forestry.

cepted ministerial posts in the cabinet, in which quite a wide diversity of views was represented.

By May 15, the whole apparatus of the Salazar state had been dissolved *de facto;* members of the state security police were occupying prison cells whose previous inmates had been men convicted or suspected of acts against the ousted regime; various Left-wing parties had surfaced, and liberal and centrist parties were being formed. The Salazar state-controlled labor organizations had been dissolved in theory, but in practice had been taken over by either the Communist or Socialist party, and it had by then become evident that one of the guerrilla leaders in Africa was prepared to collaborate with Spinola's plan to hold plebiscites in Angola, Guinea, and Mozambique.

Over the next eight weeks the Left-wing members of the Cabinet made it clear that they were prepared to accept the guerrilla leaders' demand that power should be handed over to them without any popular consultation. President and prime minister considered that undemocratic. Developments in Portugal itself worried them even more. The Communist minister of labor seemed unable or unwilling to restore order in industry where men were either on strike or had taken over private enterprises. Spinola urged the need for a presidential election to clarify his position and power, and for general elections sooner than April 1, 1975. The Left would have neither. Carlos resigned his premiership on July 9, and Spinola dismissed the rest of the cabinet.

It now became evident that the president was a mere figurehead. Indeed it was by no means clear who were now the rulers of Portugal, the Junta, a new council of state nominated by the Armed Forces Movement, or the secret coordinating committee of the Movement. Colonel Vasco Gonçalves, of known Left views, emerged on July 14 as the new premier. The Socialist and Communist parties acclaimed the appointment, and the two were more strongly represented in the new than in the outgoing cabinet.

Negotiations with Guinea, begun in May and interrupted in June, were resumed, and on September 10, Portugal formally recognized Guinea as an independent state.

FRELIMO continued active operations until the end of July, then consented to confer with Portuguese officals. On September 7, it became public knowledge that Portugal had agreed to June 25, 1975, as the formal date for the independence of Mozambique, and to the immediate transfer of all power there to a transitional government dominated by FRELIMO.

Whites in Lourenço Marques and Beira rose in revolt with the support of blacks to whom FRELIMO was a tribal rather than a Mozambican movement. The Portuguese government ordered its troops and police to collaborate with FRELIMO forces in the suppression of the revolt, and it collapsed after four days of fighting. Spinola then announced that he personally would conduct negotiations over Angola, where there was a greater proportion of Portuguese to African inhabitants, and three separate guerrilla movements had been operating against each other as much as against Portuguese forces.

Once again developments in Portugal itself were perturbing Spinola even more. The country's economy was now in a chaotic condition following the concession of wage increases of up to 100 percent. Political organizations and individuals to the right of the Marxist parties were complaining of harassment by the Left. On September 10 Spinola called upon "the silent majority" to "defend itself against totalitarianism." The Liberal leader, Jose de Almeida Araujo began to organize a mass rally of that "silent majority" for Saturday, September 28. The prime minister, Gonçalves, now a brigadier general, banned it as "fascist," but allowed marches and parades of Communists. On the 29th Spinola resigned the presidency, stating that it was impossible for him "to carry on as the faithful guarantor of the program of the Armed Forces Movement" in "the climate of anarchy reigning in the country," but that he still hoped that the Portuguese had not escaped from one tyranny only to fall under another.

Over the next three days, nearly 300 people were arrested, and on October 2 a government spokesman alleged that the Right had planned the assassination of Spinola and the restoration of the Salazar regime under cover of the planned rally. The news was received by the foreign press of Western Europe with cynical skepticism. General Costa Gomes took over the presidency, and General Gonçalves continued at the head of a cabinet now decidedly representative only of the Left.

Postage Stamps

New Fields. The U.S. Postal Service (USPS), $385 million in the red, branched out into the educational and stamp-collecting fields in 1974. In March USPS launched an educational program for elementary schools designed to provide pupils with a wide-ranging study of America's mail system. According to Postmaster General E. T. Klassen: "Effective mail service depends to a great extent on the customer's knowledge of how to use the mails effectively. The place to begin teaching that is in the schools, where our future customers are."

USPS also began a $5 million advertising campaign to get a larger slice of the stamp-collecting market by pushing the sale of albums, kits, and commemorative stamp issues.

Washington's stamp output is $7 billion worth a year, making it the world's number one stamp producer. The total philatelic market in the United States alone is estimated at over $500 million a year, and more than 16 million citizens save U.S. commemoratives fresh from the post office. A USPS survey indicated that, of all new commemoratives of the world purchased by U.S. collectors, its own stamps constitute some 50 percent. The USPS feels its share of the market could be pushed up to two-thirds through its stamp collecting promotion.

Philatelic Criticism. Some dealers criticize the big marketing program to whet collecting interest, saying collectors are being exploited by a flurry of U.S. issues. The eight jumbo designs linking classic paintings to the centenary of the Universal Postal Union was the third U.S. stamp series to be condemned by the American Philatelic Society (APS), the 31,000-member U.S. collector group. APS labeled the issue "overextended,"

COMMEMORATIVE STAMP SERIES honors the role of the chemical industry in China's development plan. From top, fertilizers, rubber, synthetic fibers, alkalies are illustrated. Until President Richard M. Nixon lifted trade barriers with China early in 1972, Chinese postage stamps fell under federal "trading with the enemy" restrictions. Both the 1973 Scott and Minkus stamp catalogs listed for the first time the approximately 1,200 stamps issued by the People's Republic of China since 1949.

placing it in the company of Arab sheikhdom stamps, most of which are not even accorded a place in the Scott catalog, the "bible" of U.S. collectors.

In response to philatelic criticism Canada conceded that it was putting out too many stamps and curtailed its 1974 program in March, a rare and perhaps unprecedented action in the stamp world. The nation reduced the number of its commemorative stamps to thirty-three from the forty-five originally planned.

Innovations. The USPS, which handles 90 billion pieces of mail a year, introduced in March its second rate increase in less than three years. Later USPS unveiled several innovations designed to improve service and cut operating costs. One was a new method for forwarding mail called the Centralized Mechanical Mark-Up System or "central mark-up," which relieves mailmen of readdressing the almost half million pieces of mail a day that are "undeliverable as addressed." The task was switched to clerks at post offices using mechanical mark-up aids.

Another was "centralized delivery" involving delivery of mail to customers at "cluster boxes" at the end of a street instead of at each home. The decision to install cluster boxes nationwide will await the results of public reaction in experimental areas. USPS estimated it could save about $15 per year per cluster-box customer.

In June the highway post office, a four-wheeled descendant of the Pony Express, followed its predecessor into oblivion. The system, in which 400 vans moved toward their destination as mailmen sorted letters, was cancelled after a thirty-three-year history.

In December the no-lick postage stamp with its pressure-sensitive adhesive made its appearance. The dove-of-peace Christmas issue also became the first precanceled stamp.

GERALD FORD repeats the oath of office as he becomes the thirty-eighth president of the United States. Warren Burger, chief justice of the U.S. Supreme Court, administers the oath as Mrs. Betty Ford watches.

by
ROBERT J. STEAMER
Dean, College II
University of Massachusetts, Boston

Separation of Powers. When the men of 1787 created the brilliant new-style American Constitution, a constitution, in John Marshall's phrase, "intended to endure for ages to come," they envisioned a system of government in which the fundamental operating principle would be the separation of powers. That is, the legislative, executive, and judicial branches would exercise powers independently of, although in cooperation with, the other two. Yet, under certain conditions each of the branches would act as a check on the others. When Congress consents to executive appointments and treaties, for example, it is acting in the domain of executive power; when the president vetoes a congressional enactment, he is exercising legislative power; and when the Supreme Court declares acts of the president or Congress unconstitutional, it is acting not as a judicial body but momentarily as executive or legislature. It is an incredibly complex and subtle arrangement, and many observers in 1787 predicted that it would not work. While the founding fathers were well aware of the difficulties inherent in this tripartite division of powers, they justified it on the ground that it was the only means of avoiding the kind of tyranny that had existed in governments since time immemorial, including the tyranny of George III, the erstwhile sovereign of the American colonies.

Presidential Powers. In spite of the

recurring crises in the American system, it has managed to survive and prosper while governments all around it, of nations large and small, have fallen, many violently. It has survived, first, because the separated powers scheme did just what the framers intended, and second, because it took on a slight imbalance by which one branch, the presidency, became the general focus of government, a sort of rallying point for all the political forces that make up the American nation. Reading the Constitution, one perceives a crucial distinction between Article I in which the powers of Congress are rather minutely detailed and Article II in which presidential powers are both few in number and couched in rather broad terms. In all probability it cannot be otherwise since the executive is in charge of the day-to-day running of the government and must be responsive to details that require immediate attention, and perhaps more significant, must be able to cope with emergencies. Neither a congress consisting of 535 voices, nor a court whose function is primarily judicial can react to a crisis swiftly and vigorously. And this points up a dilemma. The American people must trust the president, but it is also the better part of wisdom to believe in original sin and not trust him absolutely. He is, after all, human, like the rest of us.

Development of the Presidency. From the very moment that George Washington took the oath of office, the presidency became an amalgam of what the Constitution prescribes and what the individual incumbent contributes to the office. Throughout history some presidents have given the office great strength and dignity; others have contributed nothing, or even subtracted from or obscured presidential authority. Theodore Roosevelt divided holders of the office into "Buchanan presidents" and "Lincoln presidents," Roosevelt considering himself in the mold of the latter. Both James Buchanan and Abraham Lincoln were in office as the cauldron of civil war was at the boiling point, and one said, in effect, that he could do nothing to prevent the breakup of the Union; the other declared that he would use all the resources of his office to hold the Union together. Abraham Lincoln stretched the Constitution to the limit, in fact, and violated some of its strictures. He nevertheless retains the respect, which with time has turned to reverence, of the American people. He does so because at no time did Abraham Lincoln seek power for its own sake, for self-aggrandizement.

Other presidents besides Lincoln have expanded the authority and prestige of the office, but until the advent of Richard Nixon none sought to usurp power and corrupt the Constitution itself. Aside

"The Constitution provided that the President should negotiate treaties with the advice and consent of the Senate. Was the Senate's concurrence to be secured by distant communication or face to face? Washington tried the latter method by going to the Senate chamber to be present at the debate concerning a proposed treaty with the Creek Indians. So much time was wasted, despite the frowns that increasingly darkened Washington's face, by what he considered inconsequential bickering that, as he left the chamber, he was overheard to say that he would 'be damned if he ever went there again!' "

James Thomas Flexner, describing the first president's only personal appearance to testify before Congress, in **Washington: The Indispensable Man,** published by Little, Brown in 1974.

GEORGE WASHINGTON PORTRAIT by Charles Willson Peale depicts him in the blue and buff uniform of the American Revolution with the blue sash which marks him as commander in chief. It is prominently displayed in the West Parlor of Mount Vernon.

from George Washington who gave the office form and dignity, those who have contributed most to its effectiveness (and enlargement) were Andrew Jackson, who emphasized its popular role; Woodrow Wilson, who brought to it a party and legislative leadership akin to that of British-style prime ministers; and Franklin Roosevelt, who combined the contributions of the strong presidents of

ABRAHAM LINCOLN, one of the best-loved U.S. presidents, has often been depicted by folk artists. This polychromed wood statue, carved in Illinois in 1860, was part of "The Flowering of American Folk Art" exhibition at the Whitney Museum of American Art in New York City during the winter. It is from the collection of Howard A. Feldman.

the past to make the office a prime mover in social reform.

Presidential Controls. For presidents who overstep the bounds of constitutional authority there are two major institutional controls: the pronouncements of the Supreme Court and impeachment. The court has, on several occasions, directed presidents (or someone carrying out presidential policy) to alter or reverse their policies on the ground that they had transcended constitutional bounds, and presidents have always complied with the Supreme Court's directions. After the decision on the Cherokee Indian cases, Andrew Jackson was reputed to have said, "John Marshall made his decision; now let him enforce it," but it is not clear that Jackson ever uttered the phrase. More importantly, as events developed, the Indian question never reached the point of pitting President Jackson against the Supreme Court. The record of history indicates that presidents have had a healthy respect for Supreme Court decrees.

Impeachment is the ultimate authoritative measure for removing a president from office, a power of Congress not to be used lightly, but nevertheless to be used if a president engages in "treason, bribery, or other high crimes and misdemeanors." Thomas Jefferson thought impeachment a "mere scarecrow," and so it seemed to be until the House and Senate moved against Andrew Johnson in 1868. Prior to that time the only resolution of impeachment introduced in the Congress was against President John Tyler in 1843. But introduction was the first and last step, for the full House rejected the resolution.

The Johnson Impeachment grew out of the aftermath of the Civil War when a president, bent on healing the wounds of conflict, inherited a Congress determined to punish the southern rebels. After vetoing several punitive measures, only to see them overridden by an angry Congress, President Johnson went to the people, publicly denouncing his congressional antagonists. He declared that Congress was violating constitutional rights and exercising power which "would result in despotism or monarchy itself." One of the laws which the president had vetoed, later overridden by Congress, was the Tenure of Office Act which prohibited a president from removing any civil officer he had appointed with Senate consent without first obtaining Senate approval to the removal. Throwing down the gauntlet on a Friday (February 21, 1868) Johnson fired Secretary of War Edwin M. Stanton, a hostile opponent of Johnson's views on southern reconstruction. The following Monday the House voted to impeach by a straight party-line vote of 126 Republicans to 47 Democrats. Eleven articles of impeachment were then drawn to be placed before the Senate for the president's trial. Nine of the articles were based on the firing of Stanton; the tenth alleged that Johnson had brought the office of president into "contempt, ridicule and disgrace" (a high misdemeanor); the final article was essentially a summary of the first ten. After thirty-three days of old-fashioned oratory on both sides in the trial before the Senate, a vote was taken on May 16 on Article XI. The result was 35-19 for removal, just one vote shy of the two-thirds necessary to convict. The Senate voted immediately to adjourn until May 26 when it sat as a court once again and voted on Article II. The vote held at 35-19. Johnson's opposition gave up and the Senate adjourned. The first full-scale presidential impeachment trial had failed.

Historians differ in their views of the effect of the Johnson trial on the presidency, but the general consensus is that it strengthened executive power. Since the language of the Constitution leaves high crimes and misdemeanors undefined, honest men might differ over whether there was probable cause for impeachment. The weight of opinion,

THE PRESIDENT'S RESIDENCE, seen here from Lafayette Park, was first called the Presidential Palace. It was officially named the White House in 1902 at the suggestion of President Theodore Roosevelt.

however, is that the Johnson affair involved fundamentally a political disagreement, and that the framers did not intend Congress to depose presidents for such reasons. Had they so intended, it would have been easier to devise a system like that of the British cabinet in the first place.

Impeachment Resolutions Against Hoover. Predictions were that impeachment would never be used again. Only twice more prior to 1974 was an impeachment resolution introduced against a president — in 1932 and 1933 — both against Herbert Hoover. They came to naught. As late as 1956, Clinton Rossiter, an authority on the presidency, wrote: "I predict confidently that the next president to be impeached will have asked for the extreme medicine by committing a low personal rather than a high political crime — by shooting a senator, for example."

Nixon's Case. On February 6, 1974, after two years of what clearly was the most serious political scandal in American history, the House of Representatives, by a vote of 410-4, authorized its Committee on the Judiciary to conduct an impeachment inquiry. After six months of examining evidence the committee voted to recommend impeachment of the president for his conduct in the

Watergate affair and for implication in three other activities. Article I charged that Nixon, using the power of his office, engaged in a course of conduct designed to delay, impede, and obstruct the investigation of Watergate. Article II alleged that the president had repeatedly engaged in the conduct of violating the constitutional rights of citizens: wiretapping newsmen and government officials, breaking into private quarters, and using government agencies such as the Internal Revenue Service and the FBI to punish his enemies. Article III charged the president with willful disobedience of the committee's subpoena for tapes and documents. Two other articles, one dealing with the secret bombing of Cambodia and the other with Nixon's personal finances, were not approved. The impeachment charges never went before the full House, for Nixon resigned from office on August 9, 1974, apparently convinced that impeachment and removal from office were certain. The evidence of wrongdoing — already made public — was overwhelming.

Probably all men who have ever served as presidents craved power. However, none but President Nixon had crossed that blurred but visible line between acceptable and unacceptable conduct. None had clung so fervently to the hope that the rule of law could not reach him, and in the end Congress saw that it had but one course. It had to protect the Constitution of the United States, and it did so responsibly, calmly, and steadfastly, validating the wisdom of the separation-of-powers concept and demonstrating the toughness of the American Constitution.

Ford's Pardon. Before the shock waves of Watergate began to subside, the new president, Gerald Ford, precipitated a minor crisis by pardoning Nixon "for all offenses against the United States which he, Richard Nixon, has committed or may have committed or taken part in during the period from January 20, 1969, through August 9, 1974." President Ford, while asserting that he believed in equal justice for all Americans, nevertheless insisted that Nixon had suffered enough and that any long, drawn-out battle in the courts would polarize public opinion and cause all of the latent ugly passions to reemerge. Aside from the question of whether the pardon was a wise move, there is no doubt that under the Constitution the president was empowered to grant it. The pardoning power was placed in the Constitution in order to permit presidents to perform acts of mercy, and mercy is, after all, coextensive with compassion, grace or benevolence, and it may, as President Ford believed in this instance, take precedence over the punishment which strict justice demands.

A Healthy Institution. The presidency will not emerge unscarred from the trauma of Watergate, but it still appears to be a very healthy institution. Testifying to its survival potential is history itself: 185 years, 38 presidents, and still no scoundrel or despot determined to abolish the American Constitution has made the grade. Nixon was immoderate, resentful of his political enemies, and most of all, almost pathologically paranoiac, but his weaknesses were flaws in character and not malevolent impulses bent on destroying the system that nurtured his successful climb to the top. In 1974 we might echo English journalist Walter Bagehot's pronouncement after the impeachment trial of President Andrew Johnson. "Few nations," he wrote, "perhaps scarcely any nation, could have borne such a trial so easily and so perfectly." Presidential power, now as then, is here to stay, but it is likely to be a more restrained and responsible power after Watergate. And this is as it should be in a democracy.

Protestantism

by
THE REV. DONOVAN SMUCKER, Ph.D.

Professor of Social Sciences
Conrad Grebel College
University of Waterloo
Waterloo, Ontario

North American Protestantism is like a big river with many tributaries. In this network one part can slow down while another gains new force until the mainstream feels its effect.

Religious Events in the Capital. In one of the Washington, D.C., tributaries, Senator Harold Hughes pushed scandal off the front pages by announcing that he was dropping out of politics for a person-to-person religious ministry through the International Christian Leadership. Former presidential aide Charles Colson is one of the persons who found renewal of religious commitment in the small circle of political leaders who share the outlook of Senator Hughes. Colson said that since finding Christ he no longer believes in the need to win with an "anything goes" policy.

Before going to jail, Jeb Stuart Magruder released his book, *One Man's Road to Watergate,* in which he indicated that he had placed too much emphasis on materialistic success, underestimated the temptations involved in the world of politics, and, above all, discovered that he had a private morality but a wholly inadequate sense of public morality. Magruder hinted that he will devote much of his time in the future to religious study and expression.

In another part of Washington, author James Baldwin gave an address at the Episcopal Cathedral of St. John the Divine in which he reminded the congregation that he was a preacher and the son of a preacher.

Another Stream of Influence is the burgeoning charismatic movement at

YORK MINSTER is the largest cathedral in Great Britain. Shown here are the southwest towers and the great east window. In May Dr. Donald Coggan was appointed by Queen Elizabeth II to succeed Dr. Michael Ramsey as archbishop of Canterbury, the spiritual leader of the world's Anglican community of more than 45 million people. As 101st primate of all England Dr. Coggan will also be the spiritual leader of the 30 million Britons belonging to the Church of England.

work in both Catholic and Protestant groups whose numbers continue to swell. David Wilkerson, author of the multimillion-copy best seller, *The Cross and the Switchblade,* has a new book, *The Vision,* with the subtitle, "A Terrifying

Prophecy of Doomsday that is Starting to Happen Now." In his vision of the future, Wilkerson predicts that the first persecution of Christians in North America will be aimed at tongues-speaking Christians. Meanwhile, Canadian immigration officials deported eight members of the New Bethel Fire-Baptized church of Atlantic City who entered Canada illegally when a fourteen-year-old member of the Pentecostal sect said she had a vision in which God instructed her to flee from an impending tidal wave that would engulf Atlantic City and Philadelphia. Such misplaced fears over the centuries have made main-stream Protestants skeptical of doomsday prophets even in these days when despair is common.

Catholic-Protestant Relations. Nothing makes Protestants wince as much as the designation of the adversaries in Ireland as Catholic versus Protestant. An Anglican bishop in the Republic of Ireland has delivered a warning to those who see the Irish tragedy as "a straight Protestant-Catholic confrontation" because they are guilty of oversimplification. He cited many examples of Catholic-Protestant cooperation: "Less than 1 percent of the people are involved in violence; yet, in a complex urban situation, this small group can hold the whole country to ransom." Bishop McAdoo also said that only one person in ten of the violent people would have any real connection with the churches." In any case, the relationship between Catholic and Protestant in North America stands out in contrast as cooperation and goodwill increase year after year.

English Anglicanism. Nothing illustrates the differing relationship of the church and state in the United Kingdom better than the announcement that Harold Wilson, Congregationalist prime minister, had chosen Dr. Donald Coggan to succeed Dr. Michael Ramsey as archbishop of Canterbury, the highest office in the Church of England. To North Americans it is inconceivable that the head of the government would choose the key leader of the largest church. Now for the first time there are more Anglicans outside England (32.9 million) than in it (32.5 million).

Chinese Morality. Elsewhere in the world China is a place of fascination and challenge for thousands of plain Protestants who recall the good old days when the Protestant ethic nurtured thrifty, disciplined, bright people who accepted authority. It remained for a Catholic leader, Bishop Fulton J. Sheen, to say it: the "ascetic principle" which traditionally served North American society had passed to China. Their "natural morals" have eclipsed the morals of Americans. Documentaries and the occasional visiting troupe of Chinese dancers or athletes reveal an austere collectivism not even dreamed of in the Middle Ages.

The Bible. The one hundred national Bible societies met in New York this year, announcing that the worldwide distribution of 249,152,091 Bibles, testaments, and Scripture portions represented a 14 percent increase over last year. In the United States Kenneth M. Taylor of Moody Bible Institute has paraphrased the Bible into modern language. Much to his amazement his version, *Living Bible,* has sold 15 million copies. A university professor said that Kenneth Taylor understands why Norman Rockwell and Lawrence Welk influence a living American English more than King James or T. S. Eliot.

Protestant Colleges. Last year the College of Emporia, a ninety-two-year-old United Presbyterian school in Kansas, closed its doors despite the enrollment of 432 students and a long history of educational leadership in the Midwest. In November, 1973, the college could not meet its payroll, and a $125,000 matching-grant offer was lost. In 1969 the college had an enrollment of 1,000.

This is an ominous development for the other Protestant-related colleges. When thirteen out of seventy-two professors were fired at another Presbyterian college, Bloomfield of New Jersey, the president cited a study of 507 private colleges, predicting that 365 of those colleges could be forced to close by 1980. The American Association of University Professors has taken Bloomfield College to the courts because eleven out of thirteen professors removed from the faculty had tenure.

The Mormons. One church-related college not worried about the future is Brigham Young University (BYU) of Provo, Utah, the largest church college in North America with twenty-five thousand students. Along with its number one position in enrollment, BYU maintains strict dress standards which ban mini skirts, long hair, and bare feet. Under the sponsorship of the Church of Jesus Christ of Latter Day Saints (Mormons) the university is best known for its outstanding programs in the fine arts. Meanwhile, the Latter Day Saints Church Relief Society is waging a war on inflation by assisting the women of the church to make inexpensive clothing and to purchase food more wisely.

Trends in Canada. The recently completed census in Canada revealed trends similar to those in the United States in relation to organized religion: the mainline churches have four out of five members but are not growing as rapidly as the marginal churches. Church membership has not shown decline but church attendance is definitely downward. The proposed merger between the Anglicans and the United Church of Canada is almost dead. Dr. George Goth of the Metropolitan United Church of London, Ontario, observed: "If the United Church and Anglicans were united, both traditions would be smothered. The one hundred bishops to be set up according to the plan of Union would smother us in a tremendous bureaucracy."

The moderator of the United Church of Canada received wide publicity for his statement that it would be a good idea to tax the churches: "Taxes are one way in which caring hands are extended beyond the narrow circles of our private concerns. If our cities are to become neighborhoods, our country a community, and our earth a family home, it will be by raising and spending more public money."

The Caribbean Conference of Churches, the fifth such regional body in the World Council of Churches and the first in which the Roman Catholic church is a founding member, is now a reality, uniting sixteen denominations among thirty islands. The sermon at the founding conference was delivered by Dr. Philip A. Potter, a black West Indian Methodist who is now general secretary of the World Council. There are 8 million Christians in the Caribbean. Continued migration from the islands to Canada and United States has deepened the knowledge of these countries as something more than tourist areas.

Baptists. Arlene Westbrook of Charlotte, N.C., became the seventh woman to become an ordained minister of the Southern Baptist Convention. A Baptist magazine in Des Plaines, Ill., has attacked the Archie Bunker television program, "All in the Family," because it has the subtle effect of discouraging people from holding *any* strong convictions —lest they be classed as bigots.

Protestantism Is Holding Its Own. Protestants in North America are holding their own in the mainstream while observing some onrushing rapids in the tributaries. There are no floods and no dry streams.

AMERICAN FLAG GATE was part of "The Flowering of American Folk Art, 1776-1876," an exhibit celebrating the bicentennial which opened at the Whitney Museum of American Art in New York City on February 1. The gate, dated 1872, came from the Darby Farm, Jefferson County, New York.

Revolutionary War

1774—Eve of Revolution

by

E. B. LONG

Historian and Author
Associate Professor of
American Studies, University of Wyoming

". . . the inhabitants of the English Colonies in North America . . . are entitled to life, liberty, and property, and they have never ceded to any sovereign power whatever, a right to dispose of either without their consent . . . ." *(Declaration and Resolves of the First Continental Congress, October 14, 1974.)*

Aftereffects of a Tea Party. The flames kindled in 1773 by the monopoly on tea granted by the British Crown to the East India Company continued to mount in the British colonies of North America. The December, 1773, Tea Party in Boston and the destruction of tea elsewhere became a continuing *cause celèbre*, not only in North America but in parliament. There were more disorders in Annapolis, Md., in Boston and New York. Colonial leaders continued to use the uproar over tea to further their aims. Except in the minds of a very few, the flames had not yet reached the point where they might completely melt the British Crown in North America, but certainly the long-standing disputes, which had repeatedly flared up, were blazing now with a heat greater than ever.

Parliament Acts. An angry British parliament acted in the spring and summer of 1774. While Edmund Burke, Lord Chatham, and others tried to stem the demands for retaliation, in London and throughout Great Britain cries were many for the punishment of the uproarious colonies. Intransigence had been tolerated for too long.

The Lord North ministry definitely was willing to take a calculated risk and attempt to establish a firm hand over Massachusetts so that the other colonies would get into line. The ministry had received erroneous advice from Massachusetts on attitudes of the people. General Thomas Gage had reported, "These provinces must be first totally subdued before they will obey." The famous writer Dr. Samuel Johnson denied that the colonists possessed any inherent rights.

In March, parliament, with the blessing of the Crown, passed the first of the Coercive Acts. The Boston Port Bill cut off Boston from the world by prohibiting loading or unloading of ships except for military stores and shipments of food approved by customs officers. If Massachusetts were to compensate the East India Company for the losses of the infamous Tea Party, the king was authorized to reopen trade.

In May from parliament came the Administration of Justice Act which provided that any crown official indicted for a capital offense would be tried in Great Britain rather than in Massachusetts. In June the Massachusetts Government Act was passed, which, in effect, annulled the Massachusetts Charter. Members of the Colonial Council, previously elected by the Massachusetts House of Representatives, were to be named by the king and would hold office at royal pleasure. The attorney general, lower judges, sheriffs, and justices of the peace were to be appointed and removed by the governor. Juries were to be called by the sheriff rather than elected. And, lastly, except for the annual election, the governor had to give permission for that favorite New England institution, the town meeting, to be held.

Another in your year book's series of year-by-year research into the events leading to the American Revolution in preparation for the bicentennial anniversary in 1976.

These three acts, aimed primarily at Massachusetts, were dubbed the Coercive Acts, and were joined by two more which further riled the colonists.

Quebec and Quartering. In May came the Quebec Act. Its main purpose was to provide a permanent government for Canada. There was to be a centralized administration and a crown-appointed council. The Roman Catholic church was given a privileged position.

Parliament further ruled that Canada's southern boundaries extended clear to the Ohio River, thus apparently shutting off colonial settlement west of the Alleghenies. This aroused much consternation among land speculators and would-be emigrants, not only in Massachusetts, but in Connecticut and Virginia, which had major claims in the area now projected to be part of Canada.

In June parliament passed the Quartering Act which applied to all the thirteen colonies. Quartering, whereby British troops could be housed in public taverns and deserted buildings, had been legalized in 1765 and 1766. It had long been an object of protest, and now the new act legalized the quartering of troops in *occupied* dwellings.

While Massachusetts citizens in general had not been happy with Governor

Thomas Hutchinson, they were far from pleased when, on May 13, General Thomas Gage arrived in Boston as the new governor. More British troops were soon sent to the colonies.

Intolerable Acts. These five parliamentary measures soon became known in the colonies as the Intolerable Acts. Propagandist Sam Adams and his followers had found a new cause to heat up the fires of possible separation. While they might vary in the degree of their ardor, many new adherents now strengthened the colonial cause.

From Providence, R. I., on May 17 came a call for an intercolonial congress, echoed soon by Virginia, Pennsylvania, and New York. Massachusetts and others joined in, suggesting that a congress convene in Philadelphia in September. The Committee of Correspondence of Boston proposed a solemn league and covenant which would ban all business with Great Britain and consumption of British imports after the first of October. All the colonies but Georgia named delegations to the congress.

First Continental Congress. Fifty-six delegates from twelve colonies gathered in Carpenter's Hall in Philadelphia on September 5, 1774. While there had been other meetings of the colonies, this was the beginning of the historic Continental Congress which evolved in time into the Congress of the United States.

The leadership had forceful representatives of the more radical element, including John and Samuel Adams, Christopher Gadsden, Richard Henry Lee, and the more conservative element headed by Joseph Galloway, James Duane, and George Read. Peyton Randolph of Virginia was named president. Secrecy in deliberations was pledged and each colony had one vote.

By September 17 the Suffolk Resolves were endorsed by the congress. The work of Joseph Warren, these measures from Massachusetts declared the Coercive Acts unconstitutional and not to be obeyed. The people of Massachusetts were urged to form a government which would withhold tax monies from the royal government until the Coercive Acts were repealed. The people were advised to form their own armed militia. Stringent economic sanctions were recommended against Great Britain.

But the conservatives countered with a plan by delegate Galloway which proposed a plan of union between Great Britain and the colonies. Each colony would govern internally but there would be an overall colonial administration with a president-general named by the king. He would have a veto power over a grand council with representatives from each province. But this president and council would be inferior to and a distinct branch of parliament. The plan was defeated by a narrow six-to-five vote.

Delegate John Adams, in his notes, wrote that there was much "nibbling and quibbling in congress," but at the same time he was convinced that "America will support Massachusetts or perish with her . . ." Delegate George Washington of Virginia, not one of the acknowledged leaders of congress, wrote a friend, ". . . it is not the wish or interest of that government (Massachusetts) or any other upon this continent, separately or collectively, to set up for independency; but this you may at the same time rely on, that none of them will ever submit to the loss of those valuable rights and privileges which are essential to the happiness of every free state, and without which life, liberty and property are rendered totally insecure . . ."

Declaration and Resolves. On October 14 the First Continental Congress issued its conclusions. The Coercive Acts and the Quebec Act were condemned as unjust, cruel, and unconstitutional. Recent revenue measures were attacked, as

was the dissolving of colonial assemblies. The rights of the colonies and the colonists were put forth, including those of "life, liberty, and property." The local legislatures would have exclusive power in making laws for taxation and internal policy. These would be subject only to royal veto. Some thirteen acts of parliament passed since 1793 were declared in violation of colonial rights. Until these were repealed, economic sanctions were called for. Chief among these was the end of all exportation to Great Britain, Ireland, and the West Indies after September 10, 1775.

Congress prepared an address of protest to the king and people, drafted by John Jay, and adjourned October 26, agreeing to meet again in May of 1775 if needed.

Continental Association. Congressional delegates also formed the Continental Association patterned after such an organization in Virginia. This association pleaded the cessation of all importation from Great Britain by December 1 and total discontinuance of the slave trade.

Nonconsumption of British products was provided for as was an embargo of all exports to Great Britain, Ireland, and the West Indies. Committees in each town, county, and city were to be elected to enforce the rules. By April, 1775, there were such associations in twelve colonies, with Georgia having a modified plan.

The Power of the Pen. Political writings expressing many views had been burgeoning in the colonies for many

OLD IRONSIDES, the U.S. frigate *Constitution*, launched in 1797, is being rebuilt with a congressional appropriation of $45 million. The most famous ship to fly the American flag, it was expected to be rebuilt in time for the nation's bicentennial celebration.

years. People read and they listened to long, detailed discourses on their plight. Historians believe the delegates to the Continental Congress had been influenced by the 1774 views of James Wilson of Pennsylvania in his *Considerations on the Nature and Extent of the Legislative Authority of the British Parliament.* Wilson proposed that the colonies owed allegiance to the king alone and that parliament had no authority over them.

Thomas Jefferson in his *Summary View of the Rights of British America* called on George III to listen to the liberal thought being expressed. John Adams favored a dominion status for the colonies in his *Novanglus Letters*, published after congress adjourned. These answered the Tory or pro-British views of writer Daniel Leonard. Adams felt that the colonies were not part of Great Britain's realm and were in fact separate "realms" with the king as sovereign.

Military Beginnings. On the first day of September British troops went from Boston to nearby Charlestown and Cambridge and took over guns and powder owned by Massachusetts. The colonial militia gathered, but there was no fighting. General Gage began fortifying the Boston Neck. On the colonist side, John

Hancock was chosen by the Massachusetts House of Representatives to lead a Committee of Safety which would control the militia. A special group known as the Minute Men was organized to be ready instantly for duty.

To the north at Portsmouth, N. H., a group led by John Sullivan entered Fort William and Mary and seized arms and gunpowder after subduing a small British garrison. There were no casualties. Paul Revere of Boston had previously warned the colonists that the British were planning a larger garrison at the fort.

At Home in the Colonies. While all the events in Great Britain and the meeting of the first Continental Congress were the main topics of the year, other activities were going on in what was to become the United States. People were engaged in developing their lands and businesses; they were pushing into the west beyond the Alleghenies; and they were absorbed with their personal lives and problems.

The governor of Virginia, the Earl of Dunmore, John Murray, attempted to control land for Virginia in what was known as the Ohio Country. The Shawnee and Ottawa Indians opposed Dunmore's troops. The Indians were defeated at the Battle of Great Kanawha or Point Pleasant on October 10, in what is known as Lord Dunmore's War. The Indians gave Virginia hunting rights in Kentucky and agreed to white access to the Ohio River.

Clear across the continent, the Spanish, led by Captain Juan Bautista de Anza, Father Francisco T. H. Garcés, Juan Pérez, and others, were exploring the west coast overland.

On the border of Virginia and Tennessee the War of Logan followed the murder of the family of Logan, chief of the Mingoes. A frontiersman named Greathouse and his companions were accused of the crime. Indians retaliated against the settlers.

James Harrod of Virginia moved across the mountains to establish Harrodsburg in what was to become Kentucky. Although burned by Indians, this first permanent settlement in the future state was rebuilt in 1775. The westward movement maintained its momentum, for many other land purchase and settlement plans were under way.

Rhode Island and Connecticut prohibited importation of slaves. Ann Lee, known as Mother Lee, arrived in America from England with a small band of followers to found the Shaker community. Political writer Thomas Paine arrived in Philadelphia from England.

Portent. By the new year of 1775 the political temperature in the American colonies was rising rapidly. Could it be controlled this time as in the past? Complete independence from Great Britain was not yet urged, except by a few extreme hotheads. On the other hand, more and more colonists favored some sort of dominion status with the colonies remaining loyal to the Crown but out from under what they regarded as an arbitrary and unfeeling parliament.

A major step toward a loose organization for joint cooperation — even union — had been made by the convening of the Continental Congress, but the colonies still jealously guarded their separate sovereignties. The Tory opposition, favoring no drastic change, was coalescing. In Great Britain the government decided to act against the recalcitrants across the Atlantic.

Time and events were catching up with each other in the American colonies. The long, intermittent buildup of differences was finally to result in confrontation. Yet, at the end of the transitional year of 1774 few would predict real war or real independence from Great Britain.

NELSON ROCKEFELLER testifies during the hearings on his nomination.

Rockefeller Confirmed. The country had been without a vice-president for more than four months when, on December 19, Nelson Aldrich Rockefeller, sixty-six, was sworn in as the nation's forty-first vice-president. The Senate Rules Committee had conducted a lengthy, exhaustive, and somewhat repetitious investigation of the man selected by President Gerald Ford, finally voting unanimously to confirm. In the Senate itself, the vote was 90 to 7. After comparatively brief hearings, the House Judiciary Committee approved in a vote of 26 to 12. Assent from the whole chamber followed, with a vote of 287 to 128. The negative votes were cast by both liberals and conservatives. An hour or two later Rockefeller took the oath of office, a ceremony shown on national television.

The Hearings. The position of second place in the national government was one which Rockefeller had earlier scorned, but once he was nominated he did not conceal his eagerness to be confirmed. At the hearings he answered questions forthrightly, presenting his qualifications persuasively and meeting objections with vigor. Since there were few if any doubts as to his competence, the inquiry centered on his vast wealth and its possible misuse as an instrument of political power. The inquiry also covered the part he had played in the publication of a book attacking his gubernatorial opponent, Arthur J. Goldberg, and his role as governor during the Attica prison riots. He was, apparently, exonerated from responsibility in connection with this tragedy.

As the grandson of a U.S. senator and of America's first billionaire, oilman John D. Rockefeller, his inheritance, in all senses, was impressive. He testified to personal holdings, mostly in trusts, that

IN THE CAPITOL Vice-President Rockefeller will preside over the Senate as its president, but will vote only in case of a tie.

totaled $218 million, an average annual income over the past ten years of $4.6 million, and a personal net worth of $62.5 million. His charitable donations were proportionately huge. He admitted that monetary gifts and unsecured loans he had made to friends and associates had sometimes been ill-advised, and assured his hearers of future discretion in this regard.

A Creditable Record. Since Rockefeller occupied a number of appointive posts in government over the years, the material he submitted in a seventy-two-page biography was familiar. He was born in 1908, the third of the six children of John D. Rockefeller, Jr. He received a rigorous Protestant upbringing, with emphasis on moral and ethical values. After graduating from Dartmouth with an economics degree and a Phi Beta Kappa key, he spent some time acquainting himself with family business interests. Then, showing Democratic leanings, he served President Franklin Roosevelt as coordinator of inter-American affairs, helping to formulate the Good Neighbor policy. Under President Harry Truman he worked on the Point Four program for helping under-developed nations. A study he made for President Eisenhower led to the establishment of the Department of Health, Education, and Welfare, and his appointment as its under-secretary.

In Elective Office. In 1958 Rockefeller was elected governor of New York, and had nearly completed his fourth term in that office when in December, 1973, he resigned. While governor he backed an extensive antipollution program, the reform of divorce and abortion laws; state-sponsored housing units; and a very costly and elaborate development that involved redesigning Albany's governmental center, with new buildings and a spacious mall. During these years he made known his availability as a presidential candidate, but the Republican party failed to nominate him. He was criticized for not supporting Barry Goldwater and his support of Richard Nixon was not particularly enthusiastic.

The new vice-president is probably unique among politicians in his passion for art. His personal collection — mainly of modern works — is valued at $16 million. Six children were born of Rockefeller's first marriage, which ended in divorce. There are two children from his second marriage.

This man of substantial attainments and wide experience was expected to play an energetic role in the remaining two years of the Ford administration.

Sailing

***THE COURAGEOUS*, right, fights it out with the *Intrepid* during America's Cup trials off Newport, R. I.**

by
ART DUNN

Sunday Sports Editor
Chicago Tribune

America's Cup. The Australians came to Newport, R.I., buoyed with money and confidence for the twenty-second challenge to wrest Sir Thomas Lipton's "Ould Mugg" from the New York Yacht Club, where it has been bolted to a table for 123 years.

"It's harder to win that damn cup than it is to put a man on the moon," declared Bob Miller, who designed the aluminum *Southern Cross* for the Australian Spirit of West syndicate headed by Alan Bond of Perth. "Twelve-meter yachts are money down the drain," added boat-designer Miller. "I want to put the America's Cup out of its misery."

To that end, Bond supplied a reported $9 million to bring a forty-four-man colony to Newport with *Southern Cross* and trial horse *Gretel II,* which lost the last challenge in 1970.

Against the meticulously organized and lavishly financed Aussies, the United States posed a quartet of possible defenders headed by *Intrepid,* the wooden yacht which won the last two America's Cup series, and *Courageous,* a sleek aluminum ship also designed by Olin Stephens II. For the first time in America's Cup competition, aluminum hulls were permitted.

The trials to determine the challenger were no contest as Skipper Jim Hardy's *Southern Cross* whipped France in four straight. The American saildowns, though, generated the finest racing of the series.

Intrepid had a 6-4 edge in the July

SAMUEL (WHEELS) WAKEMAN, foreground, helps crank winches to trim the sails of the *Valiant* in the 1970 America's Cup race. The *Valiant* was eliminated in the 1974 America's Cup trials on August 20. Wakeman, thirty, was a foredeck crew member of the 1974 winner, the *Courageous*.

trials, but after eight races in the series to select a defender, each yacht had won four times. Prior to the ninth and final run, veteran helmsman Ted Hood took command of *Courageous* and the $1.5 million yacht triumphed by one minute, forty-seven seconds to earn the right to face *Southern Cross*.

Fog and uncertainty hung over the final best-of-seven series in September. Though the Australian craft was supposed to perform best in brisk winds, *Courageous* soundly thrashed the challenger by 4:54 in the opener. *Southern Cross* was guilty of several tactical errors, including delay in setting spinnakers, poor choice of sails, and overstanding her mark.

Coming off the start on the second day, *Southern Cross* waited too long to tack and trailed by thirty-four seconds on the first of six legs. She could never recover and lost by 1:11.

After fog and becalmed seas caused a postponement of the third race, *Southern Cross* installed a new rudder to increase speed. It did little good as *Courageous* romped to victory in 5:27 in a brisk nor'western wind. "It's a bloody disaster," said an Australian sympathizer accurately.

It was even worse the following day. In winds of seven knots, *Courageous* rolled past the start twenty seconds ahead and breezed home seven minutes, nineteen seconds in front to retain international sailing's oldest prize.

The accumulated margin of 18:51 was the largest in the 123-year history of the America's Cup. *Southern Cross* was faster on only three of twenty-four legs in the four races.

Elsewhere *Dora IV*, a sixty-four-foot Chicago yacht owned by Lynn Williams, scored a rare double in freshwater sailing by winning both the Port Huron to Mackinac Island and the Chicago to Mackinac races.

THE REMAINS OF A WALLED FORTRESS from the twelfth century are carefully preserved on the island of Gotland, Sweden, but in Stockholm a new architectural era was evolving with such speed that tourists seeing the bulldozed sites often ask if the city was very badly bombed in World War II.

by
ERIK J. FRIIS

Editor and Publisher, The Scandinavian-American Bulletin; General Editor of the book series The Library of Scandinavian Literature; The Library of Scandinavian Studies; and The Scandinavian Scene. Coeditor, Scandinavian Studies (1965)

Denmark. Inflation, high taxes, an unfavorable balance of payments, oil and gasoline shortages, and difficulties in balancing the budget were some of the major problems facing the Danish people in 1974. The 1974-75 budget was passed at the end of March after a lively debate in the parliament (Riksdag) and the submission of no less than 559 amendments. The new budget, as finally approved, was based on an increase in tax revenue of 22 percent, or 11.96 million Danish kroner. The expenditures were increased by 19 percent, or 11.9 billion Danish kroner, over the previous year. During and after the debate on the budget it was pointed out by various critics that consumption should be reduced, exports should be promoted, and the balance-of-payments deficit should be reduced.

The Danes went to the polls on March 5 to elect members of local rural and municipal councils. The Social Democrats, with 691,172 votes, finished in first place but ended up with almost 300,000 votes less than they had garnered in 1970. The other parties finished as follows: Liberals, 406,992; Conservatives, 271,424; Radicals, 227,331; Progressives, 170,179; Socialist People's party, 91,765; Communists, 77,207; Christian People's party, 71,500; Center Democrats, 47,614; Justice Union, 36,047; Left Socialists, 22,559; Others, 17,393. The turnout of voters was only 50 percent, the lowest figure in this century.

Taxes continued to take center stage throughout the summer and fall. In May the Hartling coalition government received the backing of some of the opposition parties and was thus able to introduce increases in consumer taxes and charges. Some of these were to be in effect for the duration of 1974 only, while others were to be permanent. Poul Hartling managed to effect a compromise on housing with the aid of the Social Democrats. Throughout the summer, however, rumors were rife that the government would resign or be forced to resign and would call a new election, and in September, during the debate on a taxation bill, it again looked as though this would occur. But by obtaining last-minute support from the Social Democrats, the Socialist People's party, and four members of the Progressive party, the government was able to put through its tax program and continue in office. The bill provided some tax relief for the average Dane, but higher welfare costs and food prices wiped out much of the gain. In November an unusual protest of no fewer than 75,000 people took place in Copenhagen, the object of their ire being a new tax on pleasure craft exceeding nine meters in length. The protesters also called for the resignation of the Hartling government.

An interesting development during 1974 was the fact that a majority of the Danish electorate now opposes membership in the European Economic Community (EEC). The referendum of October 2, 1972, led to the Danish application for membership in the EEC, but if the referendum were held at the present time 53 percent of the Danish voters would say no to EEC membership.

Queen Margrethe II and Prince Henrik, her French-born consort, bought a farm and chateau in France, in the district of Cahors. The so-called Chateau de Caix will be restored and will be used during the royal couple's holidays in France.

Finland. President Urho K. Kekkonen in February paid another of his many unofficial and what have proved to be very useful visits to the Soviet Union and had talks with President Nikolai Podgorny and Prime Minister Aleksei Kosygin. While hunting together, the leaders discussed Finland's oil debts to the Soviet Union, incurred during the recent energy crisis, as well as the European Security Conference, at that time meeting in Geneva but slated to continue in Helsinki.

On March 22 representatives of the Baltic Sea states — Finland, Denmark, the German Democratic Republic, the Federal Republic of Germany, Poland, Sweden, and the Soviet Union — signed in Helsinki a convention on the protection of the marine environment of the Baltic Sea. It has for years been evident that the shallow Baltic Sea has become very polluted, mainly due to the fact that all the countries bordering on it are heavily industrialized. The convention, the first of its kind, calls for the prevention and monitoring of pollution from land-based sources and also pollution caused by shipping. The convention also established a permanent body, the Baltic Sea Commission for the Protection of the Environment. Its secretariat will be located in Helsinki.

An indication of the instability of Finnish politics is the fact that the Kalevi Sorsa cabinet received many kudos upon reaching the age of two, having become one of the most long-lived cabinets in Finland since the establishment of the republic. The cabinet is supported by four parties, the Social Democrats, the Center Party Agrarians, the Swedish People's party, and the Finnish Liberals. Even the opposition parties agreed that Prime Minister Sorsa and his colleagues had done quite well, even in the face of a 17 percent inflation, wildcat strikes, and the general vicissitudes of Finnish politics. Many people thought the Sorsa cabinet might ride out many future storms and have a good chance of equaling or even surpassing the record of four years set by the T. M. Kivimäki cabinet in 1932-36.

Youth surges to the fore in Finland as in other countries. One example is Minister of Education Ulf Sundqvist (Social Democrat), who at twenty-eight is the youngest man ever to become a Finnish cabinet minister. His youth made him liable to serve in the military, and he spent three months of 1974 in the service. During his absence another politician took over his department, but on Sundqvist's return to his cabinet post in September, a case without parallels in Western history was happily concluded.

A number of cabinet changes took place in the fall. Jan-Magnus Jansson, of the Swedish People's party and minister of trade and industry, accepted the position of editor of *Hufvudstadsbladet,* the influential Swedish-language newspaper in Helsinki, and was succeeded by Kristian Gestrin, who had been minister of defense. To the post of minister of defense was appointed Carl-Olaf Homen, who at thirty-eight was another young man who got a chance to demonstrate his ability.

Dr. Ahti Karjalainen, minister of foreign affairs, paid official visits to the German Democratic Republic and the Federal Republic of Germany and signed almost identical agreements with the two Germanys in which they recognized the Finnish policy of neutrality and agreed to adhere to a policy of nonaggression toward Finland. Both Germanys, however, turned a deaf ear to Finnish claims to war reparations.

Iceland. During 1974 Iceland celebrated the 1,100th anniversary of its settlement with local festivals throughout the land. As part of the festivities a new road which enables motorists to drive all around the island was opened in the southeastern part of Iceland. The main celebration took place on July 28 at Thingvellir, the old meeting place of the Icelandic parliament (Althing). No fewer than 50,000 people, one-fourth of the population of the country, witnessed a special session of the Althing and heard the president of Iceland, Dr. Kristjan Eldjarn, and prominent speakers from the other Scandinavian countries and the United States. The American representative was Secretary of the Interior Rogers C. B. Morton. Coins, stamps, and medals were issued to mark the occasion, and the Icelandic Althing announced that the anniversary was to be permanently commemorated by the construction of a national archives building and the establishment of a museum of maritime history. The history of Iceland began in A.D. 874 when the Norwegian chieftain Ingolfur Arnason left Norway in order to escape the harsh rule of King Harald Fairhair. He became the first settler in Iceland, on the spot where the capital Reykjavik was to be established many years later. His example was followed by hundreds of Norwegian farmers and also by people of Norse and some Celtic stock from Ireland and the Western Islands. Iceland was Christianized in 930, became a part of the Norwegian realm in 1261, and was united to Denmark in 1387. The country became fully independent in 1944.

The Court of International Justice at the Hague decided against Iceland in the case brought before it by Great Britain and West Germany. The plaintiffs had maintained that Iceland could not unilaterally exclude British and West German trawlers from the area of the seas lying between twelve and fifty miles from her shores. Iceland, which had extended her fisheries zone to fifty miles in 1973, did not send any representatives to defend her case at The Hague, since the Icelanders contended that the court had no jurisdiction. The feeling in Iceland was that before long the government would extend the fisheries limits to 200 miles, and this would be supported by a majority of the nations that attended the U. N. Law of the Sea Conference at Caracas.

The Icelandic Althing was dissolved by Prime Minister Olafur Johannesson on May 9, after he had lost his majority in the legislative assembly, and June 30 was set as the date for new elections. The government's downfall was caused by the resignation of one of the ministers and by dissension as to how to combat inflation and bolster the deteriorating economic situation. The cabinet continued in office until after the elections and the selection of a new government. The parliamentary elections ended in a stalemate, since the three government parties and the opposition elected thirty representatives each. The makeup of the new Althing was as follows: Independence party, 25 seats; Progressive party, 17 seats: People's Alliance, 11 seats; Social Democrats, 5 seats; and Liberals and Leftists, 2 seats. Since the Independence

WELL-KEPT-UP BUILDINGS line the shore of Lille Lungegardsvatnet in Bergen, Norway. Oil funds have already eased Norway's burdensome income taxes, shortened the workweek, and lowered the pension age from seventy to sixty-seven years.

party had registered the greatest gains, President Kristjan Eldjarn asked Geir Hallgrimsson, the chairman of that party, to form a new government. His first efforts to form a coalition were to no avail, and the president asked the

caretaker prime minister, Olafur Johannesson, to form a cabinet. Not until August 27 was it announced that the Independence party and the Progressive party had reached an agreement to form a cabinet together. Geir Hallgrimsson became prime minister and Olafur Johannesson became minister of justice and trade.

Municipal elections took place on May 26, with the Independence party receiving 50.5 percent of the votes in the country as a whole, a gain of 7.7 percent since 1970. The second largest party, the Progressives, lost 1.1 percent, and ended up with 18.9 percent of the national vote.

The economic situation continued to give everyone cause for great concern. Inflation ran rampant, and in February a general strike completely paralyzed the economy for four days. A new wage agreement brought with it price increases, the Icelandic krona was devalued another 4 percent, and the fishing industry was hard hit by the increased oil prices. A bright note was introduced with the lowering of the graduated income tax, but the sales tax was increased from 13 to 17 percent.

Norway. The energy crisis hit Norway early in the year, as it did so many other countries. The government aimed at a reduction in the consumption of oil by 20 to 25 percent, and supplies of heating fuel were cut down by 25 percent. Rationing of gasoline began on January 25, but by February 7 all restrictions on the sale of gasoline were rescinded.

Oil continued in the spotlight throughout the year. The government in 1972 established the Norwegian State Oil Company (Statoil) which will serve as an independent operator and will have full control over all stages of oil production on Norway's sector in the North Sea. Present production averages 50,000 barrels a day and so far the oil has been brought to shore by ships. It is expected that Norway will be self-sufficient in oil by 1976, and that by 1981 the country will be among the ten largest oil exporters in the world. Increased public revenues from oil royalties are to be used to ease taxation and effect increased public investment. It is expected that some of the future income from oil operations will be used to pay for assistance to the developing countries. By 1978 1 percent of Norway's Gross National Product will, it is planned, be devoted to such assistance.

Aleksandr Solzhenitsyn, the Russian Nobel Prize-winner for literature in 1973, visited Norway in February with a view to settling there. He was welcomed by the Norwegian government and was a guest in novelist Sigrid Undset's old home at Lillehammer. But in the end he decided to make Switzerland his permanent home.

Since there was much dissatisfaction, throughout Europe especially, regarding Henry Kissinger's and Le Duc Tho's being awarded the Nobel Peace Prize by the Norwegian government, some people who wanted to do something about it organized the so-called People's Peace Prize. Money was collected in Norway, Sweden, Denmark, Finland, Belgium, the Netherlands, France, Italy, and Austria, and the committee decided to award the prize, amounting to 1.5 million kroner, to Archbishop Dom Helder Camara of Brazil. On February 10, Archbishop Camara was hailed at Oslo's City Hall, where in his speech he dwelled on the fact that two-thirds of the world's population suffers want and privation. He received one-half of his prize in Oslo, and then proceeded to West Germany where he received that part of the prize that had been collected there.

Prime Minister Trygve Bratteli made a six day official visit to Moscow in March and conferred with Premier Kosygin and Party Secretary Leonid Brezhnev. Among the material results of their talks were an agreement on shipping and the exchange of ratification documents on consular treaty. It was also agreed that negotiations should begin on a Norwegian-Soviet demarcation line dividing the continental shelf and its possible oil deposits in the Barents Sea. Discussions on the Barents Sea began on November 25. Although the Spitzbergen archipelago was not on the

THIS DANISH SHIPYARD was emptied of workers on May 16 when tens of thousands of Danes walked off their jobs to protest sales tax increases pushed through Parliament the night before. The taxes, which raised prices of some items from 5 to 25 percent, were designed to soak up buying power, curb imports, and slow the drain on Denmark's currency reserves.

agenda, there was much apprehension in Norway that the Russians would try to effect changes in the 1920 treaty, which gave sovereignty of the islands to Norway but allows other nations to explore its natural resources. There are about 2,000 Russians in Spitzbergen, which is also of great strategic import to the U.S.S.R.

In November it became known that Norway plans to extend its fishing limits, in three stages, to as much as 200 miles from shore. The first phase will involve a ban on foreign trawling in an area totaling 5,000 square miles, primarily along the northern coasts. A broad diplomatic effort was launched to make the European fishing nations agree to these plans.

Two changes took place in the Norwegian cabinet during the year. Tor Halvorsen, who had been minister of environment, became minister of social affairs upon the death of Sonja Ludvigsen. Gro Harlem Brundtland became the new minister of environment.

A new national park was established by government action in June. It is located in the Dovre Mountains and is called Dovrefjell National Park. Three areas were designated nature protection areas. The ninety-square-mile park consists of two separate areas, east and west of the valley of Drivdalen. The new park includes the peak Snöhetta and the valley of Stölaadalen, the home of many musk oxen.

Three Norwegian divers in September located the wreck of a Danish slave ship near Norway's south coast. The ship was known as the *Fredensborg,* was owned by the Danish East Asia Company, and went to the bottom in 1768. It was engaged in the so-called triangular trade, involving slaves and ivory from Africa, and mahogany and gold from America. The divers found the wreck to be in fairly good condition and salvaged fifteen precious elephants' tusks. At year's end the work of salvaging more of the cargo was proceeding apace.

Sweden. Fifteen months of diplomatic nonrelations between the United States and Sweden came to an end on March 21 when the two countries appointed new envoys to take charge of the embassies in Stockholm and Washington. Prime Minister Olof Palme announced the selection of Count Wilhelm Wachtmeister, a foreign ministry official, to be his country's new ambassador, and President Richard Nixon simultaneously announced that Robert Strausz-Hupe, a former professor of political science and at the time ambassador to Belgium, would represent the United States in Sweden.

The year 1974 saw the end of the oldest written constitution in Europe, dating back to 1810 and as amended in 1866. The new constitution was adopted by the parliament (Riksdag) on February 27, with 321 votes for and 19 against. Under the new constitution, to go into effect on January 1, 1975, the king becomes virtually powerless and is no longer commander-in-chief of the armed forces; the cabinet rules but is responsible to the Riksdag. The authority of the speaker of the Riksdag is greatly increased. The voting age is lowered to eighteen, and the number of representatives in the Riksdag is reduced by one to 349 (this to make certain that future elections will not end in a tie vote in the Riksdag, as was the case following the last election).

Princess Christina, a sister of King Carl XVI Gustaf, was married to a Swedish commoner, Tord Magnuson, in June. She remains Sweden's "First Lady" as long as the king is unmarried. She is now known officially as Princess Christina Mrs. Magnuson.

A working agreement on economic goals and the financing of impending social reforms over 1974-75 was concluded on May 22 between the governing Social Democratic party — which holds 156 of the 350 seats in the Riksdag — and the Liberal party which holds 34 seats. The agreement was preceded by round-table talks in which the Center, Conservative, and Communist parties also took part. The agreement emphasized the importance of fighting inflation. It also stated that if corporate profits remain high in 1975, there might be a case for special treatment of "boom" profits. The question of how wage earners should exercise influence and benefit from capital growth in companies also deserves a fair and reasonable solution, it was stated.

The Nordic Council, representing the five Scandinavian nations, held the first part of its 1974 session in Stockholm in February. Among the questions dealt with were uniform Scandinavian laws; and a Nordic convention on the environment was adopted. The second part of the session took place in Aalborg, Denmark, in the fall.

Three Swedes won Nobel prizes in 1974. The authors Eyvind Johnson and Harry Martinson shared the prize for literature, and the economist Gunnar Myrdal shared the Nobel Memorial Economics Prize with the Austrian Friedrich von Hayek.

Sea Mammals

SEALS communicate right down to their whiskers. According to research by Dr. Thomas C. Poulter of Fremont, Calif., sea mammals not only use echo ranging signals — the series of clicks, honks, barks, and screeches whose echoes determine the size, shape, and distance of fish — to find their way in the world's oceans but also employ their whiskers which have highly sensitive nerve endings. The whisker signals do not go to the same part of the brain as the hearing signals and this makes it almost impossible to jam the signals.

The Battle for Survival. Once 4 to 5 million whales roamed the oceans, but the 40-million-year-old sea mammal is now fighting a losing battle for survival against human predators. Whales have dwindled to a few hundred thousand in number.

Some specialists doubt that enough blue whales — the largest creature the world has ever known — still exist for isolated males and females to find each other and propagate the species. It was not until the late 1960s that total hunting bans were placed on the blue and humpback whales. In 1974 their numbers were estimated at 7,500 and 3,000

WHALING in the nineteenth century is depicted in this primitive painting from The Flowerng of American Folk Art show held during the winter at the Whitney Museum of American Art, New York City.

respectively. The gray, bowhead, and right whale populations are down so low that their hunting is now also banned. The United States outlawed all commercial whaling by Americans in 1972 and banned the importation of all whale products.

The IWC. In June the fifteen-nation International Whaling Commission voted 13-2 (the Russians and the Japanese opposing) to suspend the hunting of selected species of endangered whales. The last two nations whaling on a major scale are Japan and the Soviet Union. Together they account for 85 percent of the annual commercial whale catch. Both nations conduct pelagic or deep-sea whaling from factory ships, while the other IWC members practice coastal whaling from shore-based factories.

Scoffing at estimates that there are no more than 100,000 fin whales, the Japan Whaling Association contends there is no proof that whales face extinction. According to Japan the finbacks have a natural increase of 3,200 annually and are unharmed by the Japanese-Russian catch of 1,450 yearly. Influencing the Japanese point of view is the nation's $100 million whaling industry and the 50,000 fishermen and their families engaged in whaling. An important source of protein for Japan, whale constitutes 6 percent of all meat consumed in the country.

The problem facing the IWC is that it can only monitor, not enforce. New quotas on whale hunting were agreed to by Japan and Russia, but the overall number of animals to be killed was only slightly less than in 1973. The Soviet Union and Japan had ignored catch quotas imposed by the commission in 1973.

Mysteries of the Sea. Actually scientists know little more about the whale than Captain Ahab knew about Moby Dick. Information is lacking about where whales go and how many there are, about the workings of their bodies and how they breed.

The humpback whale was thought to be almost extinct in the northwest Atlantic, but late in the year a major mating and nursery ground was discovered in the West Indies. There appear to be twice as many humpbacks as originally thought, perhaps as many as 1,000 including calves.

Much that is known about whales has been learned from research on dead animals. One of the many mysteries of the sea is why some whales beach themselves and die. A new theory which is finding strong support among scientists is that tiny, wormlike parasites in the inner ears of whales interfere with the mammals' echo-location system by making them partly deaf and thus unable to find their way. The twenty-three pilot whales stranded on November 5, 1973, at Kiawah Island, S.C., were all found to have such infestations in the middle ear and sinuses.

Senior Citizens

The Cost Squeeze caused millions of elderly to suffer as they found themselves caught between static or slowly growing incomes and rapidly mounting prices for food, clothing, and housing. As a result of cost-of-living increases during the year many senior citizens did without new clothes, cut back or eliminated social activities, and reduced, often drastically, their spending for food. The Great Inflation, like the Great Depression, was leading to nutritionally unbalanced eating and postponement of medical care, two changes in lifestyle that began to take their toll on the health of the aged in 1974.

The WHO Study. Older people in the poorer countries are often better off than older people in the more affluent nations, according to a study by the World Health Organization (WHO), released in July. It found that elderly citizens of poorer lands still enjoy respect and a satisfying sense of status, privileges the aged have lost in industrialized nations. In poor lands, care of the old is a matter of family responsibility, while in rich countries the older person was found to be more often fully or partly dependent on the state for support.

EVERY DAY during 1974, four thousand more Americans reached the age of sixty-five.

Storage Bins. Since 1967, when Medicaid went into effect, growing numbers of Americans have placed their aged parents in nursing homes. More than a million of the U.S. elderly were in nursing homes in 1974. In these storage bins for the old and infirm, Medicaid costs were nearing $10,000 a patient often for neglectful care. According to one New York doctor, "the patients are not there because unscrupulous nursing homes are out soliciting, but because we as people are only too willing to relieve ourselves of any burden, be it mother, father, or uncle."

Shakers

AN OLD LAMPPOST frames two simple buildings at Shakertown, Pleasant Hill, Kentucky. Founded in 1806, the Pleasant Hill society was dissolved in 1910. Restoration of the commune was made possible by a $2 million federal loan.

A Made-In-America Sect. In 1774 Mother Ann Lee arrived in America with seven followers, having received a vision (called by the Shakers a "gift") that her church should be founded in the New World. After settling in Watervliet, N.Y., Shakers built their first colony in New Lebanon, N.Y., in 1787.

By 1824 there were 6,000 Shakers in nineteen communes in New York, New Hampshire, Massachusetts, Maine, Connecticut, Kentucky, Ohio, and Indiana.

After the Civil War Shaker communes began to fail. In 1957 a trust fund was established with the money realized from the sale of commune land, and its income was used in maintaining remaining societies. In 1973 the small colony at Canterbury, N.H., turned its assets over to a preservation foundation, leaving the village at Sabbathday Lake, Maine, as the last Shaker commune. When it closes, the fund becomes a charitable trust with assets devoted to the preservation of the Shaker heritage.

STRAW SUN BONNET was characteristic of Shaker feminine attire. Plain but functional, it was designed and produced within each community.

SHAKER TENETS

Do not be troubled because you have no great virtues. God made a million spears of grass where He made one tree.

Clean your room well, for good spirits will not live where there is dirt. There is no dirt in Heaven.

Shaker Life and Work. Although they referred to themselves as "Believers" (the proper name of their sect was the United Society of Believers in Christ's Second Appearing), "the world" (as they called nonmembers) dubbed them Shakers from the movements of their religious dancing rites, performed to shake sin from their bodies. The name was eventually accepted by the society.

Within a framework of rules governing daily life, each Believer received "the gift to be free to oneself and to be accepted as oneself." Neither dreamers nor mystics, the Shakers "lifted their hands to work and their hearts to God," for work was regarded as a part of worship.

They saw no virtue in hard labor when they could devise easier methods and used their ingenious inventions to increase the time available for meditation and study. The circular saw, flat broom, clothes pin, pea sheller, screw propeller, washing machine, and threshing machine were among the many Shaker inventions.

In furniture design Shakers were the original space-savers. Shaker furniture had lean, simple lines, timeless style, and the durability that comes with superb workmanship. Still a major creative force in the U.S. decorative arts heritage, Shaker has been called the only truly American style of furniture. Because many of the pieces are appropriate in today's smaller homes and blend well with either antique or modern styles,

WEARING AUTHENTIC DRESS, a Shakertown guide demonstrates weaving in the Sisters Shop at Pleasant Hill.

SIMPLE SHAKER STOVE seems remarkably modern in design.

Shaker furniture is being reinterpreted by such commercial firms as Drexel which brought out a line of Shaker-inspired designs during the year. Both Cohasset Colonials of Cohasset, Mass., and Shaker Workshops, Inc., of Concord, Mass. put out kits for do-it-yourself Shaker reproductions.

The Bicentennial. Among the celebrations of the Shaker bicentennial was a three-day meeting in August at the Sabbathday Lake colony which included the reading of papers on Shakerism's relationship to radical Christianity and to millenial and apocalyptic movements. In October Western Reserve University and the Shaker Historical Society of Shaker Heights held a bicentennial convention.

A half dozen Shaker museums were open to the public in New England, New York, and Kentucky in 1974. About thirty colleges and universities offered courses in Shaker history and religion.

Drawings by George Armstrong

HERBAL MEDICINES, made from Shaker-grown herbs, were one of the sect's principal sources of income. The famous herbal tea, *Life Everlasting*, is still sold at the Shaker Village at Sabbathday Lake, Maine.

Shopping Centers

WOODFIELD in Schaumburg, Ill., is the world's largest shopping center.

by
ROBERT K. LONG

Former Social Studies Editor, Scott, Foresman and Company, Free Lance Editor and Writer

The All-Malls. Shopping plazas have become major social as well as economic centers of life in America. The post-World War II migration of people from the city and the simultaneous development of a network of superhighways have switched buyers from downtown shopping areas to large, widely scattered regional shopping centers.

A typical shopping center may feature two or three department stores and a hundred or so smaller shops. Office buildings, hotels and motels, medical centers, and apartments rise within or near it. All are serviced by acres of asphalt that accommodate the thousands of cars that bring millions of customers.

There were 13,240 shopping centers in the United States in 1974, about 200 of them with more than 800,000 square feet of leasable space. Their annual sales added up to more than $100 billion a year, accounting for over 40 percent of the nation's retail gross.

Shopping Centers of the Past. Merchants throughout history have displayed their goods in concentrated spots. The Asians haggled over prices in bazaars. The Greeks had shops under the colonnades of their stoa. The Roman forum featured a two-storied mall lined with open-front shops. In medieval cities the market square acted as the social and commercial center. Later, as cities grew in size, so did the scope of their business enterprises. Large stores, small shops, hotels, museums, and theaters formed downtown areas of concentration. Cities also had neighborhood centers, as did smaller towns, where stores lined both sides of the street for a block or so. This same pattern of growth was followed in America, except that the village green rather than the cathedral square was the focal point of many towns.

As cars and roads became major factors in American life, shopping strips grew up along highways. A person could drive in, park near a store, get his goods, and whip out again. They were convenient but they were seldom objects of beauty, and there was no reason to stay around once a person's business had been transacted.

Modern Malls. These clusters of shops evolved into today's shopping centers—places planned to attract and hold customers. The modern mall may be traced to Seattle, Wash., where the first — two rows of stores with a broad sidewalk between them — opened in 1950. Minneapolis, Minn., claims the distinction of being the first place where two large department stores shared the same regional shopping center. Until 1956 it was felt rivals should be kept apart, but this experiment proved that both stores benefited because people could more easily do comparison shopping and find exactly what they wanted.

AT THE BAZAAR in Isfahan, Iran, shoppers are protected from the hot desert sun in cool arcades.

THE PONTE VECCHIO is an early shopping center built atop a bridge over the River Arno in Florence, Italy. It is still lined with jewelry shops and silversmiths as it was during the Renaissance.

Developing a Shopping Center. There are firms which specialize in developing shopping centers. They search for suitable sites where major roads meet, because easy access is vital. They study population growth predictions and determine the median income of families within a few miles' radius so they can know what kinds of tenants to attract. They persuade large department stores to open branches. And they purchase enough land so they can control the immediate environs.

Some locate near existing attractions, for the mutual benefit of both, while others create the attraction that may awaken a neighborhood. Many have been set up in rural areas which eventually turned into new suburbs because of them. A few have even been built in cities to help these cities survive and prosper.

Famous U.S. Malls. The Galleria in Houston has a rooftop athletic club with indoor tennis courts and a jogging track. It also features ice skating in an enclosed mall 630 feet long modeled after the Victor Emmanuel Galleria in Milan, Italy. Woodfield in Schaumburg, Ill., is the world's largest shopping center with 2 million square feet of leasable space. Among other features it boasts a baby-sitting service and day-care center.

There also are many smaller, specialized shopping centers that draw tourists as well as shoppers. They have been formed by converting older buildings to preserve the past and give a special flavor to the present. Among them are converted trolley barns, county courthouses, and theaters. Two of the best-known are Ghirardelli Square and The Cannery, both in San Francisco.

Community Focal Point. But it is not commerce alone that attracts people to these mini-cities. It also is their handsome design and their social and cultural attractions. Many are collections of beautiful buildings with gardens, pools, fountains, sculptures, and tree-lined walks. Others are completely enclosed under one immense roof; proper ventilation and lighting give them a springlike climate all year.

Many have fine restaurants, snack shops, banks, and branch libraries. There are community meeting halls for various civic and church groups. Special events draw thousands of spectators to shopping centers, many of whom shop on the same trip. Such events include art fairs and concerts by symphony orchestras, bands, and pop stars. Automobile, boat, fashion, and garden shows attract shoppers. Political candidates hold rallies.

In winter, senior citizens can come to enclosed shopping malls and walk with no fear of falling on ice. Teenagers and others with time on their hands meet to shop and visit. Shopping centers are places where individuals can go, mingle with the crowd, and overcome feelings of loneliness. Singles, couples, and families stroll around shopping centers in the evening and on weekends.

As gathering places and community focal points shopping centers are replacing the corner drugstore and the local tavern. According to some sociologists, the mall is giving a needed cohesion to suburban sprawl.

A New American Lifestyle? Although there were still vestiges of social pressure for people to marry and live two by two, tolerance seemed to be growing in 1974 for a new American, the single.

Fed by the maturation of those born during the postwar baby boom, the U.S. single population jumped by 2 million a year throughout the 1960s. By 1974 the vast unwed minority over the age of seventeen approached 49 million. Nearly 18 million of these were from twenty to forty-four years of age.

Helping to swell the singles ranks was a slowing of the marriage rate (the 1973 increase was the smallest since 1959) and a divorce boom (a 90 percent jump in the past ten years). Those divorced were also waiting longer to remarry or just not remarrying at all.

The sharp rise in the single population could indicate either the development of a radically different lifestyle or merely a shift in the timing of marriage.

Singles

THE REAL PROBLEM in being single is how to adjust to a society based on couples. A single person just isn't invited places.

RIDING is one of the sports unmarrieds participate in to meet new friends. Singles bars are often called demeaning as dating centers.

The Singles Industry. Whatever the reason, business and advertising quickly zeroed in on what was considered a new and lucrative consumer target. Singles were believed to have more disposable income and were seen as using their purchasing power directly, unaffected by the decisions of other people, making them manageable impulse buyers.

SINGLES resent being categorized according to marital status. Twenty-one million of the nation's single people were "formerly married" (divorced, separated, or widowed).

The singles industry includes bars, apartment complexes, travel and social clubs, dating services, and even the packaging of single servings of food. *Singles*, a new national magazine beamed to the special singles segment of the population, began publication during the year.

The Solitary Sin, in fact the only sin left among swinging singles, is loneliness. Loneliness is an affliction singles would rather not recognize and they rarely refer to it by name. Instead, they call it being bored or alienated. Most singles brag that they are never lonely and take as an insult any implication of loneliness. The loneliness of singles has little to do with sex, which seems to be readily available anywhere, any time, but rather is concerned with the need for affection, for the enduring human concern of one person for another.

SKIING

Professional. Europeans continued to dominate the Grand Prix as they captured the top three spots in the November-through-April competition. Hugo Nindl, a thirty-one-year-old Austrian National team veteran, became the first pro skier to win more than $90,000 in a season. Nindl had twice been runner-up in money earnings on the circuit.

Renzo Zandegiacomo of Italy trailed Nindl by $33,000 with $60,200 for second place. Alain Penz of France was third. Americans Hank Kashiwa of Bellingham, Wash., and Californian Spider Sabich completed the top five.

Amateur: Gustavo Thoeni, twenty-three-year-old Italian customs guard, successfully defended his World Series of Skiing title in 1973-74. The best U. S. male finishers were Bob Cochran of Richmond, Vt., fifth; and Geoff Bruce, Corning, N. Y., sixth.

Annemarie Moser-Proell of Austria took the women's title, but was defeated in January, providing the U. S. team with its finest hour as nineteen-year-old Cindy Nelson became the first American skier to win a World Cup downhill event. The U.S. National champ from Lutsen, Minn., outdueled Mrs. Moser January 13 in Grindelwald, Switzerland, but finished fourth overall in the downhill and fifteenth in all events.

Moser-Proell, twenty-one, who lost fifteen pounds and gained a husband since she failed to win any Olympic gold in Japan, received her fourth World Cup crown on the strength of three gold medals. Her performance paced Austria to the team title. Italy was second, West Germany third, and the United States fourth.

EAGER SKIERS await their turn to be carried to the summit. In 1974 there were more than 2,000 mechanical ski lifts in the United States, ranging from the T-bar to the tramway.

Skiing

by

ART DUNN, Editor

Sunday Sports Section
Chicago Tribune

Soccer

by

ART DUNN

Editor, Sunday Sports Section
Chicago Tribune

BRAZILIAN SOCCER FANS watch a night game in Rio's Marcana, the largest stadium in the world. It was built when Brazil was the host country for the World Cup Soccer Championship in 1970.

The World Cup. Considered by millions as the most coveted and prestigious sports award, soccer's World Cup quadrennial extravaganza was staged for the sixteen finalists in nine German cities. The finals in Munich resulted in a mild upset as the host nation defeated Holland 2-1 before 80,000 onlookers and an estimated world television audience of 600 million.

Under tightened security to prevent a recurrence of the 1972 Munich Olympic killings, the favored Dutch struck early when their star Johan Cruyff was tripped near the goal and Johan Neeskens converted the penalty kick in the first minute.

West Germany, which advanced to the finals by edging Poland 1-0 on Gerhard Muller's goal, achieved a tie on a penalty kick by Paul Breitner. Then in the final minute of the first half, Muller booted in the eventual winner, his twenty-first goal in international competition.

Holland employed an advanced style of soccer, called "the dutch whirl," with no fixed positions and a more intricate strategy than the conventional game. The Dutch gained the finals past defending champion Brazil 2-0 in a penalty-filled game.

Brazil had won three of the last four cups, including the last two, but retiring Pele chose not to play this time, although he was in Germany as a television commentator. The South Americans could not even salvage third place as Poland nipped them 1-0 on Grezgorz Lato's seventh goal of the three-week tournament.

Victory in the World Cup gives West Germany possession of the three top trophies in soccer. Earlier in the year the nation's finest club team—Bayern München—defeated Madrid to capture the European Champions Cup. Two years ago, Germany won the European Nations Cup.

West Germany suffered only one setback in its march to soccer supremacy. In a first-round World Cup game played after both teams were assured of advancing, East Germany scored a 1-0 victory over its free world countrymen, the first soccer game ever between the two Germanys.

U.S. Soccer received a boost when Dettmar Cramer, forty-eight, a renowned developer of soccer in Europe, signed a four-year contract as head of U.S. Olympic and World Cup teams.

James P. McGuire, president of the U.S. Soccer Federation, termed it "the most significant development in soccer in this country."

The North American Soccer League (NASL) continued to attract increased attention and crowds. In the league championship at Miami's Orange Bowl, the Los Angeles Aztecs, an expansion team, beat the Miami Toros 4-3.

NASL Rookie of the Year, Doug McMillan, tied the game at three with 2:08 left in regulation. In the overtime series of penalty kicks, Los Angeles's Tony Douglas scored the decisive goal.

Pele, the first player to score more than one thousand goals, retired from professional soccer after leading Brazil to three World Cups and banking an estimated $10 million. The thirty-three-year-old Edson Arantes do Nascimento joined the Santos team as a skinny fifteen-year-old and in the ensuing eighteen years dominated the game. He was declared a national asset by Brazil's president in 1961.

WEST GERMAN SOCCER PLAYER UWE SEELER, left, displays the new gold World Cup trophy, while Pele, Brazilian soccer star, holds aloft the Jules Rimet Cup, which Brazil was allowed to keep after its third cup victory in 1970. They participated in opening ceremonies of the 1974 World Cup Soccer Championship at Frankfurt, West Germany.

Southeast Asia

VICTORIA HARBOR, Hong Kong, is ablaze with lights at night. Although the colony has only just over 400 square miles of land, its population was estimated at 4,219,300 in 1974. More than 90 percent of the residents live in less than 10 percent of its limited space — giving a staggering population density of about 100,000 people per square mile.

by
KENNETH P. LANDON, Ph.D.

Professor of Southeast Asian Studies,
American University
Contributor, The Politics of Opium (1974) and
The Sino-American Detente
and its Implications (1974)

The Political Center of Gravity in Southeast Asia slipped southward from the mainland states toward the Malacca Straits and the nations of Indonesia, Malaysia, Singapore, and the Philippines, bolstered by Australia to their south. These are the states adjacent to the Indian Ocean which is of increasing significance because of such developments as: the Arab-Israeli problem and the involvement of Arab states in support of Muslim insurgency in the southern Philippines, the energy crisis, the rising interest of the Soviet Union in India, the increasing visibility of Soviet naval vessels in the Indian Ocean since the 1967 Arab-Israeli war, Japanese concern that their oil lifeline from the Middle East through the Indian Ocean which carries over 90 percent of Japan's oil requirements might be threatened, and U.S. development of a naval station at the island of Diego Garcia.

ASEAN. For the first time in history Australia and the states forming the Association of Southeast Asian Nations (ASEAN) are concerned about their security on the Indian Ocean side. Australia protested U.S. development of Diego Garcia as a naval station fearing that this would trigger an arms race with the Soviet Union. Indonesia felt so strongly that high-ranking representatives of the two superpowers visited Djakarta in March to explain their positions in the Indian Ocean area. The Soviet deputy foreign minister, Nicolai Firyubin, and U.S. Deputy Secretary of State Kenneth Rush were told by the Indonesians that they did not want the ocean to become the scene of an arms race, preferring a zone of peace as advocated by ASEAN in November, 1971.

Thailand is the only ASEAN state in the mainland, and its concern was reflected in a request on July 13 that the United States should fly no more military aircraft from Thai air bases for operations over the Indian Ocean. Such aircraft had begun reconnaissance flights in November, 1973, from Utapao air base.

Japan's Economic Interests were also moving southward in Southeast Asia. On January 5, Japan and China signed a full-scale international trade agreement, the first pact between the two Asian powers since they normalized their relations some fifteen months previously. The trade pact activated Japanese Prime Minister Kakuei Tanaka to set out on a trade mission to the ASEAN states.

On January 8 in Manila Tanaka said that his government would add a new cabinet minister to provide "administrative guidance" (equivalent to law in Japan) to Japanese businessmen in the Philippines and other Southeast Asian states to harmonize them with the needs and ways of their host nations. He acknowledged that allegations that Japanese are ruthless, self-serving, and domineering in the way they do business are well known. Tanaka sought assurances that the Philippines would continue to supply Japan with lumber, copper ore, and food.

The climate for new Japanese-Philippine deals was enhanced by President Ferdinand Marcos's sudden ratification on December 27, 1973, of the treaty of amity, commerce, and navigation that had been negotiated between the two countries in 1960. In a joint statement Marcos and Tanaka called the ratification "a historic milestone." A new $17 million Japanese loan agreement was also signed.

A YOUNG INDONESIAN GIRL poses with one of her sisters. In Indonesia, 12 percent of the children die before becoming one year old.

Tanaka went on from Manila to Singapore and Kuala Lumpur and engaged in essentially routine diplomatic-trade mission discussions. But when he arrived in Bangkok on January 10 he was confronted by student demonstrators bearing "Jap go home" placards. After meeting with Thai Prime Minister Sanya Dharmasakti and other officials, Tanaka received a delegation of thirteen students led by Sombat Thamrongthanyawongse, secretary-general of the National Student Center which had played such a vital role in the overthrow of the military government October 14, 1973.

The Thai students demanded that Tanaka give assurances that Japanese trade and investment would benefit the Thai as well as the Japanese and that the some 7,500 Japanese businessmen would cease exploiting Thai labor and begin training Thais for managerial posts.

This student confrontation was a mild preview of the riots which occurred when Tanaka arrived in Djakarta on January 15. The Indonesian students were uneasy about their government's economic development programs which seemed to benefit the elite and not the general population. A student activist, Hariman Siregar, decried such evils as expropriation of land for government programs; forced sales of rice to the government; the growth of nightclubs, massage parlors, and golf courses; but above all the selling of Indonesia's resources to foreigners and especially to the Japanese who were engaged in the economic exploitation of Indonesia to the detriment of the Indonesian people. The students demanded the dissolving of the four ASPRI (advisers to Suharto) who were fostering the development plans, an end to corruption, the lowering of taxes, and more control over Japanese business interests.

As October drew to a close Tanaka was back in the region again for a twelve-day tour, this time focusing on Australia and New Zealand south of the ASEAN states, and making a side trip to Burma to look into the possibilities of oil development. In Australia on November 2, Tanaka concluded plans to build a joint uranium-processing plant in northern Australia at a cost of between $1.3 and $2.6 billion. Tanaka was also after more of Australia's coal and other raw materials, and he remarked that "without the prosperity of Australia, Japan cannot grow. Without the well-being of Japan, Australia cannot improve its growth."

Relations with China. The last week of May, Prime Minister Abdul Razak of Malaysia was in Peking reaching agreement to establish full diplomatic relations with China, the first of the ASEAN states to do so. The Philippines began to open the way to diplomatic recognition by the visit of Imelda R. Marcos, the first lady of the Philippines, in September when she was received more attentively than most visiting heads of state. Technically Indonesia has diplomatic relations with China, but they have been suspended since the 1965 abortive Communist coup effort which was supported by China.

When Prime Minister Razak returned from Peking he said that China's leaders had assured him that the issue of pro-Peking rebels in Malaysia was an internal problem "for us to deal with as we think best." He said that if they continued to fight "we will have to wipe them out," but would prefer to welcome them back into Malaysian society. He said that during his six days in China it was agreed that the 4 million Chinese who form 40 percent of Malaysia's population would not have dual nationality. Those who retained Chinese nationality were enjoined to "abide by the law of the government of Malaysia, respect the customs and habits of the people there, and live in amity with them."

Islamic Relations. Having established good relations with China, Razak turned to the Muslim world and became host to the Islamic Foreign Ministers Conference held in Kuala Lumpur for five days in late June. The meeting brought together some of the political leaders of the Arab world. The hottest subject was the Moro insurgency against the Marcos government in the southern Philippines. The fighting during the year had been intense and had led to the destruction of the city of Jolo, a particular target of Muslim criticism. Muslim representatives from southern Thailand and the southern Philippines attended the conference and stated their complaints against their respective governments.

Razak attempted to dampen the discussion but a report critical of the Marcos government was made by Saudi Arabian Foreign Minister Omar Sakaff and Libyan Foreign Minister Abdel Ati al Obeidi. The Libyan acknowledged that Libya was aiding the Muslim rebels in the southern Philippines with arms and ammunition. He urged that President Marcos should reach a political settlement with the Moro National Liberation Front.

Razak moved swiftly to defuse the jihad (holy war) atmosphere and was joined in this effort by Indonesian Foreign Minister Adam Malik who supported a resolution that urged the Philippine government "to find a political and peaceful solution through negotiation with Moro Muslim leaders . . . within the framework of the national sovereignty and territorial integrity of the Philippines."

Malaysian Elections. With credit spilling over from both Islamic and Chinese communities Razak moved toward general elections on August 24. Since becoming prime minister in 1970 Razak

AT AN INDONESIAN MARKET a stall displays hot peppers and small cloves of garlic. Garlic, in great demand as a spice, is the country's biggest money crop, vying with rice and corn in a three-crop economy.

SOUTHEAST ASIA

had broadened his government to include parties that made gains in the 1969 elections. His new National Front coalition brought together nine parties, and on August 24 he won a landslide victory.

Sabah. The pebble in Razak's political shoe, causing national and international concern, was the autocratic leader of Malaysia's Sabah state, one of the thirteen composing the nation. Chief Minister Tun Datu Haji Mustapha bin Datu Harun, or simply Tun Mustapha, was providing the staging area for Arab aid to Muslim Moros in the southern Philippines. Razak invited Mustapha to join his cabinet as minister of defense, hoping to draw him out of Sabah. Mustapha responded by sending his own assistant to become deputy minister of defense.

When it joined the federation in 1963, Sabah retained autonomy over immigration and internal security as did Sarawak, which makes control of Sabah by the Kuala Lumpur government difficult. Mustapha also heads the Sabah Foundation which controls 3,300 square miles of timber. Mustapha's power lies in his promotion of ambitious development schemes and in what he dubs cash dividends from the "nonprofit" foundation. Thus in June 260,309 people, or about 90 percent of the adult population of Sabah, received a cash grant of $26. Mustapha is politically untouchable.

Cambodia. For Cambodia the year was one of national and international stalemate. Reports from Cambodia read: "Cambodian capital hit again;" "Cambodia blocks enemy forces aimed at capital;" "Rebel effort to topple Lon Nol fails." The war reeled on through the year in Cambodia with some 300 Cambodians killed or wounded daily. During the five years of war, one-tenth of the population has been killed or wounded with a casualty figure of 600,000. Battles which decide nothing churn through the countryside, with government forces on one side and the Khmer Rouge on the other, supported by North Vietnamese advisers and some troops. President Lon Nol didn't leave his palace for two months until the siege atmosphere shifted from Phnom Penh to the ancient capital of Oudong which was taken first by one side and then the other.

The contest for Cambodia shifted toward the end of the year to the U.N. General Assembly where in 1973 the Khmer Rouge, headed by Prince Norodom Sihanouk, failed by only two votes to unseat the Lon Nol government's representative. The contest in 1974 has become one of resolution and counter-resolution as each side recruits votes and attempts to frustrate the other. As of November stalemate continued at the United Nations for both Cambodian sides.

Laos coasted through the year without much violence and succeeded in bringing about a negotiated settlement between the two sides representing the Lao government and the Communist Pathet Lao to form a coalition government. Several factors were at work: the United States, U.S.S.R., and China favored a coalition government; both Lao sides respected the king and required no major changes in government structure; both sides were tired of fighting each other in behalf of outsiders; and even with a coalition government each side would remain essentially in control of its own region which was differentiated geographically, racially, and economically.

On April 4, the two royal princes, Souvanna Phouma and Souphanouvong, led the members of the coalition cabinet and the National Political Council to an audience with King Savang Vatthana. The king signed a decree declaring the coalition official. Within sixty days all foreign troops were supposed to leave Laos. The Thais and Americans were out by June 4, but some 40,000 to 60,000

FISHING JUNKS often bring illegal Chinese immigrants into Hong Kong, but most of them swim from the mainland, staying in the shark-infested water from four to twelve hours until they reach land under British jurisdiction. The police estimate about 41,000 "illegals" entered Hong Kong in 1974, up by 35 percent from 1973.

North Vietnamese troops remained although it was claimed they weren't there.

There were differences within the Lao coalition over the existence of the old National Assembly which brought on a heart attack for Souvanna Phouma. But by November he was in charge again and was pleased to note that the coalition had avoided controversial subjects and carried on routine administration.

Thailand used the year to work with the United States in winding down the American presence and its own role in the Vietnam war. By the end of the year two air bases had been closed at Ubon and Takhli, and the number of American military was down to about 25,000. The general atmosphere among the Americans was one of boredom. Air America, the airline that served U.S. activities in the area, ceased operations the end of April, and its maintenance contracts were taken over by Thai Airways Aircraft Maintenance Co., Ltd.

On October 5, Thailand's interim National Assembly approved a new constitution with a 280-6 vote in spite of student objections. The constitution provides for elections within 120 days or about February 1, 1975. On October 7 King Bhumibol Adulyadej promulgated Thailand's ninth constitution.

A political party explosion of sorts occurred during the year as Thais prepared for general elections. At least twelve parties were identifiable with prominent individuals reflecting the personal quality of politics in Thailand.

Burma. As for Burma, a new constitution was promulgated in January to provide for a single-chamber assembly of 451. Elections were held in February, and on March 2 President U Ne Win announced that exactly twelve years after he seized power on March 2, 1962, he was dissolving the Revolutionary Council and returning power to the people. He and other military civil officials accordingly exchanged their uniforms for civilian clothes.

SIBERIAN FIELDS produce good crops, but the greatest domestic challenge facing the Soviet Union is how to attract millions of new settlers to Siberia — and keep them there. Life in Siberia is hard, cold, and expensive. The brave pioneers who go there must pay about 40 percent more than the average U.S.S.R. citizen for extra food in winter, padded clothing, and thousands of miles of air trips back to the West for visits and holidays.

Soviet Union

by

AARON R. EINFRANK

(Mr. Einfrank formerly lived and worked in Moscow as a foreign correspondent. He now specializes in Soviet affairs.)

Concessions. Confronted by enormous problems at home, the Soviet leadership showed in 1974 that it would make concessions to international public opinion in return for economic assistance to the lagging Soviet economy.

The most startling development was the Kremlin's promise to U.S. Secretary of State Henry Kissinger that restrictions on Jewish emigration would be eased. In return, the United States agreed to give the Soviets most-favored-nation (MFN) trade status, thus opening the way for further development of U.S.-Soviet trade and the granting of American financial credits to Moscow. Under the terms of the behind-the-scenes agreement, Senator Henry Jackson would drop his amendment to the U.S. Trade Bill which had blocked the granting of MFN status to the Soviets for more than a year.

The Kremlin bowed to international pressure when they deported writer Aleksandr Solzhenitsyn after he had published in the West his searing indictment of Stalinist concentration camps, *Gulag Archipelago*. Other dissidents who were allowed or asked to leave included the novelist Vladimir Maximov; the writer and critic Andrei Sinyavsky, who had been imprisoned for publishing "anti-Soviet" works; the dancers Valery and Galina Panov; cellist Mstislav Rostropovich and his singer wife Galina Vishnevskaya; poet-songwriter Alexander Glaich; and civil rights activist, Pavel Litvinov, the grandson of one of Stalin's foreign ministers.

Also allowed to leave was Simas Kudirka, the Lithuanian seaman who was returned to the Soviets by the captain of a U.S. Coast Guard cutter after Kudirka fled from a Soviet fishing vessel in 1970. (Kudirka was able to claim U.S. citizenship by virtue of his mother's having been born in Brooklyn.)

Those who were permitted to emigrate would have been executed during the period Josef Stalin ruled.

Another gesture to world opinion was the release of the civil rights leader, former general Pyotr Grigorenko who had been confined to a mental asylum because he dared to criticize Soviet authorities.

Thanks to international pressure, Moscow had one of its few exhibitions of noncomformist art since the early days of revolution. The first attempt in September to stage the exhibition was broken up with characteristic Communist brutality by Soviet police using bulldozers and water cannons. Two weeks later, after an international uproar, the nonconformist artists were allowed to stage their exhibition in a Moscow park, much to the delight of thousands of Muscovites. However, Soviet president Nikolai Podgorny in November warned that deviation from the norms of "socialist realism" was "inadmissible" in Soviet art.

The Kremlin also showed itself flexible on the Berlin issue, thanks to the prospect of West German technical and economic cooperation. The Soviets wanted the West Germans to build a nuclear power plant on Soviet soil, especially because the Soviet nuclear power program is lagging far behind the West.

At the European security conference in Geneva and at the Central European troop reduction talks in Vienna, the U.S.S.R. showed itself slightly more flexible as the Soviet leadership stressed that it was earnest about detente.

A Mixed Blessing. But developments in 1974 were not all of a positive nature, and even positive phenomena could in some instances be viewed as a mixed blessing.

The Jackson amendment did not primarily serve humanitarian purposes—it was designed to satisfy the Zionists who want Soviet Jews to settle in Israel, thus strengthening the military, economic,

 SOVIET UNION

GUM, the largest department store in Moscow, holds a sale. Unknown in the Soviet Union a few years ago, sales are now a regular feature in stores, apparently demonstrating that many Russians are refusing to pay high prices for some items, which then are marked down.

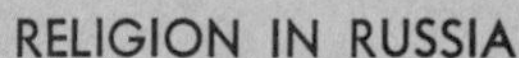

RELIGION IN RUSSIA

THIS GILDED, ONION-DOMED CHURCH is one of four within the Kremlin that have served through much of Russian history as ecclesiastical guardians of the national spirit. Millions of rubles have been spent in tourist cities like Moscow and Leningrad to restore cathedrals to their former glory, prompting Communist propagandists to complain that people were "idealizing the life of the Church."

Freedom of religion is guaranteed under the Soviet Constitution, but state atheism places tight controls on religious life. Worship is restricted to registered communities, and in the new industrial cities of Siberia and elsewhere in the country the authorities do not permit church construction. Laws strictly forbid religious instruction for children, especially Sunday schools. Churches are hemmed in by bureaucratic restrictions, while antireligious propaganda tries to convince the population of the scientific truth embodied in atheism.

Yet in this land of official atheism, religion is alive and growing. In the seventy-four dioceses of the Russian Orthodox church, there are an estimated 30 million followers, more than twice the number of Communist party members. The three Russian Orthodox seminaries in Zagorsk, Leningrad, and Odessa have long waiting lists of applicants. The Roman Catholic and Lutheran churches of the Baltic republics have 5 million members and authorized Baptists about a million. There are also sizable numbers of followers of Islam and Judaism and smaller groups of Jehovah's Witnesses, dissident Baptists, and Buddhists.

Officially the large majorities of church-going people are described as aged, mostly superstitious grandmothers. The propagandists claim only the uneducated and backward are attracted by religion, but Communist concern over a growing religious revival among the young has surfaced in press comments on "the vitality and tenacity" of religion. **Pravda,** the Communist party newspaper, has warned that "the dying off of religion under socialism is not an automatic process," and that it requires increasingly sophisticated antireligious vigilance. That the propaganda has backfired, however, is indicated by the many seminary applicants who, when asked how they acquired their faith, reply that they started on the path by reading the atheist magazine **Natural Science and Religion.**

The notable increase in religious interest among young men and women could be no more than curiosity about a long-forbidden realm, and it is true that the young are drawn to the Russian Orthodox church out of admiration for its art, music, and architecture, as well as belief. Pageantry has power in a country where civil ceremonies are dull and drab. The surge of interest may merely be nostalgia

THE CATHEDRAL OF THE ASSUMPTION is at Zagorsk, the spiritual center of the Russian Orthodox church, to which Russian peasants, foreign churchmen, and thousands of tourists make their pilgrimage each year.

A PORTRAIT OF ST. SERGIUS (1314?-1392?), a saint of the Eastern Orthodox church popular in Russia, hangs over the entrance to the small chapel housing the so-called Miraculous Fountain in the 634-year-old Trinity-St. Sergius Monastery in Zagorsk. It is one of a dozen monasteries maintained by the Russian Orthodox church.

for the Russian past or an attempt to find a cultural identity and recover a cultural heritage, but it is this link between religion and the Russian past that most troubles Soviet Communist ideologists.

PRAYER
by
Aleksandr Solzhenitsyn

O Lord it is easy to dwell with You!
So easy for me to believe in You!
When Spirit clouds over and I, crushed, am made dumb
When even the smartest people know not what tomorrow will bring
You bestow the clear assuredness of being
Vigilantly keeping the channels of Goodness unclogged.
Surpassing thus the summit of earthly glory I behold the Way,
which alone I never could have found
Wondrous Way, opposite to despair,
Whence myself shall become the reflection of Your world.
What need have I to speak what You alone shall reveal to me, and if I find not the time to carry it through
It means You've chosen others for the task.

A number of intellectuals, disillusioned with what they regarded as fruitless protest in the late 1960s, turned to the church in the early 1970s. The most prominent dissident and believer is Aleksandr Solzhenitsyn, the exiled novelist whose final manifesto sent to Soviet leaders urged that the Russian Orthodox church be permitted to operate without official harassment and that it be restored as the leading source of moral values in place of Communism. This prayer by Solzhenitsyn, translated from the Croatian by Hilda Prpic, was first published in February.

and social viability of the Jewish state.

During a November meeting in Moscow, Soviet physicist and civil rights spokesman Andrei Sakharov told New York senator James Buckley that emigration should be open to all Soviet citizens as well as to people of Jewish extraction.

Dissident Soviet historian Roy Medvedev, who is Jewish, issued a statement in Moscow saying that Western demands on emigration might play into the hands of the Kremlin hardliners. Roy's exiled brother, Zhores Medvedev, told a Congressional committee in Washington that the Soviet leadership was using emigration to get rid of the very people who might reform and democratize Soviet society.

Even from a Zionist standpoint, the Jackson amendment was not all it was cracked up to be. Many Soviet Jews, once out of the U.S.S.R., decided to settle in Europe, the United States, and Canada rather than in Israel. In some cases Jewish emigrants posed a problem in the West. In Brussels, several hundred Soviet Jews had to be assisted by Catholic organizations; Jewish organizations would not help them because they did not want to go to Israel. The U.S. government had to allocate funds for the settlement of Soviet Jews in the United States even though these emigrants had left the U.S.S.R. under the pretense of wanting to live in Israel.

The dissident movement in the U.S.S.R. showed that it was not united. Andrei Sakharov took issue with a statement by Solzhenitsyn who had urged the Kremlin leaders to forget about catching up with the West and to concentrate on problems at home. Sakharov felt that this view might contribute to making the U.S.S.R. an even more closed, inward-looking society.

Proof that emigration is still not free in the U.S.S.R. was the defection of Mikhail Baryshnikov of the Kirov Ballet, considered by many to be the best Soviet male dancer. Baryshnikov thus joined other famous Kirov defectors, Rudolf Nureyev and Natalya Makarova, who are now performing successfully in the West.

Aging Leadership. This was the fifty-seventh anniversary of the Soviet revolution and the tenth anniversary of Nikita Khrushchev's ouster which brought the present leadership to power. And after ten years the Soviet leaders seemed to be showing their age.

Party leader Leonid Brezhnev, who is sixty-eight and has the reputation of being a hard drinker, was forced to cancel public appearances because of indisposition. Premier Aleksei Kosygin is seventy and President Podgorny seventy-one. Perhaps an indication of the advancing age of the leaders was their cancellation of the traditional Moscow civilian parade on the November 7 anniversary. The short military parade was held in Red Square as usual, but thousands of civilian marchers were told to go home because of bad weather. This permitted the leaders to leave the reviewing stand several hours earlier than normal. Moscow residents could not remember a similar instance when November 7 marchers, after waiting for hours in the cold, were told their services were not needed.

In spite of any problems caused by age, the Kremlin leaders—and particularly Brezhnev who is first among equals—worked hard at trying to convince the world that the U.S.S.R. is sincere about its desire for international detente.

U.S. Relations. With the Watergate scandal hanging over his head, President Richard Nixon was allowed to make a summer visit to Moscow where he was royally feted and had talks with Brezhnev. The visit resulted in the signing of a number of U.S.-Soviet agreements, but the key question—that of strategic

SOVIET TEENAGERS dance to the music of a combo in a Moscow café. Commenting on whether the guitar was a bad influence in the U.S.S.R., Moscow's *Krasnaya Zvezda* wrote, "Yes, the guitar is a bad influence. People like to sing banal songs to its accompaniment, songs without ideological content . . . As long as detestable characters sit in dark corners, performing pale imitations of Western songs, the guitar must be regarded with suspicion."

arms limitation was left unresolved.

The biggest Watergate cover-up actually took place in the U.S.S.R. It was only in the last hours of the Nixon Administration that the Soviet news media told Soviet citizens of Nixon's problems. Until then Watergate was considered by the Kremlin as a nonstory and a plot against detente.

Moscow expressed pleasure with President Gerald Ford's statement that the new administration in Washington would continue the Nixon policy of detente with the U.S.S.R. Soviet eagerness to have Brezhnev meet Ford in November at Vladivostok was another indication that the Russians are serious about detente.

Following the Vladivostok summit talks between Ford and Brezhnev, both leaders expressed optimism about working out a comprehensive strategic arms limitation agreement which would expand the accord reached by Brezhnev and Nixon in 1972. Kissinger went even further than the official communique on the talks when the secretary of state told newsmen that the summit represented a "breakthrough" in the difficult strategic arms limitation negotiations. If such an agreement were reached, it could be signed in Washington in 1975 during Brezhnev's scheduled visit to the United States.

Military Might. Detente to the contrary, the U.S.S.R. continued to build up its military might during 1974. The Soviet navy is now in a position to challenge U.S. control of the world's vital sea-lanes. The Soviets have a numerical superiority in intercontinental missiles, and have the largest armed forces in the world, 3 million men. American defense policy is based on the alleged qualitative superiority of U.S. weaponry, particularly multiwarhead missiles. But Soviet missile tests in the Pacific during the year showed the U.S.S.R. was catching up in the quality race. There were indications that the growing power of the Soviet military domestically gave the Soviet defense ministry a veto over Brezhnev's efforts to work out arms control agreements with the Americans.

Trade. The U.S.S.R. continued in 1974 to import vast quantities of goods from the West. Two-way trade with the United States was expected to exceed $1 billion. And the Russians wanted even more.

President Ford had to cancel Soviet grain-purchase contracts because of the possibility that these purchases might increase food prices in the United States as was the case in 1972 and 1973 when Soviet wheat purchases depleted American stocks. Washington eventually allowed the Soviets to purchase 2 million tons of grain, about a million less than what Moscow wanted. A U.S. Agriculture Department delegation left the U.S.S.R. in a huff because of Soviet refusal to allow the U.S. experts to get a good look at the Soviet harvest.

The Harvest. As the Soviet grain purchases in the United States and other countries showed, the U.S.S.R. did have agricultural problems during 1974. But this was still a good year, second only to the fabulous 1973 harvest. However, a Brezhnev speech revealed that there had been big losses in the 1973 harvest due to bad management, lack of equipment, and inadequate storage facilities. Estimates of the 1973 loss were generally about a quarter of the 220 million-ton grain crop.

Industry. Industrially, 1974 was also not particularly bad, at least according to Soviet statistics. Automobile production in the first nine months was up 23 percent, reaching a phenomenal figure—by Soviet standards—of 839,000 cars. But grain-harvesting machine production fell by 7 percent. The five-year plan for 1971-75 is running far behind the original goals. This explains why the Russians asked the West Germans to build a huge steel plant at Kursk and why Moscow ordered 9,000 trucks from West Germany.

Rather than make internal reforms in the economy—which means also political reforms — the Soviet leadership sought to import technology and goods which the party-ridden Soviet economy is incapable of producing.

Soviet factories continued to turn out shoddy, unwanted goods. *Pravda* reported the story of a brick plant that kept producing bricks nobody wanted—5 million bricks went from the plant direct to the garbage dump.

Inflation. Officially Soviet citizens did not suffer from inflation because of price controls. Yet prices do have a way of creeping up in the U.S.S.R. A pound of chicken could cost $1.60 or more. Pepsi-Cola became popular thanks to the building of a Pepsi plant in the Soviet Union—a bottle cost 53 cents. A small Soviet-made Fiat auto cost 7,500 rubles in a country where the average wage is between 130 and 140 rubles per month. (At the official exchange rate the ruble is worth slightly over $1.30, but the black market rate is much lower.)

Fortunately for the Kremlin, the rising price of oil and gold, both of which the U.S.S.R. exports, allowed the country to earn the foreign currency necessary for massive purchases abroad. While the Soviet government publicly supported the Arab oil boycott, Soviet oil flowed to Western markets, including the United States.

Siberia. Faced by Chinese claims to large areas of Soviet Asia, Moscow made great efforts to attract American, West German, and Japanese investment to help the development of sparsely populated Siberia. However, Siberia requires such massive investment that foreign investors were wary of overcommitting themselves. The U.S.S.R. started a 2,000-mile railroad from Lake Baikal to the Amur region in the Pacific coast area. The rail line will help tap Siberian resources and provide a partial alternative to the Trans-Siberian railroad which is close to the Sino-Soviet border. An indication of the military strategic nature of the new line is that China expressed concern about any Japanese participation in rail-building schemes in Soviet Asia.

TOURISTS in Moscow have their picture taken in Red Square with the Lenin Mausoleum in the background. In 1974 more than 2 million foreign visitors came to the Soviet Union, 90,000 of them from the United States.

The Sino-Soviet Rift continued as Peking and Moscow exchanged verbal blasts throughout the year, especially in U. N. forums. No violence was reported, but Peking refused to hand over the three-man crew of a Soviet helicopter which landed on Chinese soil. Peking charged the crew with spying. Surprisingly, China at the end of the year offered Moscow a nonaggression treaty. But the Russians were not delighted with the offer because China wants a mutual troop withdrawal on the border, something which the Soviets feel might substantiate Chinese claims to Soviet territory.

Moscow and the Communist World. In East Europe there were reports of Soviet pressure on maverick Rumania as well as speculation about a possible Soviet intervention in Yugoslavia once President Tito dies. Moscow's relations with its East European satellites were complicated by the Russian desire to sell Soviet natural resources to the West for higher prices than the satellites could afford. Over the years Moscow has forced East Europe to become dependent on Soviet oil and other raw materials, and now that policy has backfired for all parties concerned.

The Kremlin kept up its campaign for a convening of a conference of European Communist parties and of world parties. Rumania and Yugoslavia, which boycotted the last European parties conference in 1968, tentatively agreed to attend a European conference in 1975 provided no party was criticized. This means that Belgrade and Bucharest do not want to have anything to do with a Moscow-staged "excommunication" of the Chinese from the Communist movement. The Moscow proposal for a world parties conference remained in limbo. The last world meeting, held in Moscow in 1969, saw the Kremlin defeated in its attempt to get the meeting to condemn the Chinese.

Other Foreign Relations. Moscow moved to strengthen its position in the Arab world. Relations with Egypt improved. Moscow's support for the Palestine Liberation Organization was more pronounced. Soviet arms flowed to the Arabs at a profit to Moscow because these arms shipments were often paid for with oil dollars.

In the Indian Ocean the U.S.S.R. increased its naval presence, thus threatening a vital sea-lane of the West.

The Kremlin expressed pleasure at events in Portugal and Greece. The Cyprus crisis was a benefit to the Kremlin because Greece withdrew from the North Atlantic Treaty Organization (NATO) military structure. However, Moscow refrained from fishing too eagerly in troubled waters because of the danger this might have to detente.

The Soviet Space Program. In the early part of the year the Soviet probes to Mars failed. Then there was a success with the *Salyut* 3 orbiting space station. In August, a mishap occurred when a *Soyuz 15* space ship could not dock with *Salyut* 3 because of a failure in the docking mechanism. In November the unmanned *Luna*-23 was damaged in landing on the moon and could not collect moon soil samples. On December 2 the U.S.S.R. launched a two-man *Soyuz 16* as part of a dress rehearsal for the Russian-U.S. joint space link-up in July, 1975.

The Civil Rights Movement remained miniscule, weakened even further by emigration. It was estimated that there were 10,000 political prisoners in Soviet prisons, concentration camps, and asylums. Among those still incarcerated were the dissident Vladimir Bukovsky and the Ukrainian historian Valentin Moroz.

Religion. Westerners in the U.S.S.R. noted an upsurge in religious feeling among the Soviet population, including, amazingly enough, young people. The regime promptly took countermeasures as *Pravda* ordered a stepped-up anti-religion campaign. In the Ukraine a Catholic priest, Father Bernard Miskevich, was convicted for giving First Communion instruction to children. In Moscow a Russian Orthodox priest, Father Dmitry Dudko, was expelled from his parish because the authorities did not like his popular sermons which referred to Soviet reality. Baptists and other religious groups were also persecuted. The Jackson amendment was not concerned with these people.

SOVIET UNION

Soviet Life. Despite the influx of western goods and technology, Soviet society remained much the same. The elite could have cars, *dachas* (country houses), and even the privilege of traveling abroad—all denied to the masses. Highly nutritious food was scarce, especially meat, but the Kremlin provided bread, thus preventing the starvation that occurred during the Stalinist era.

Fears continued to be expressed in official circles about the low Russian birth rate as compared to the high birth rates of nonwhite Soviet minorities in the eastern part of the country. Nationalism in the Baltic, in Georgia, and in the Ukraine brought crackdowns from the Russian-dominated government in Moscow.

Crime was a subject of public discussion as never before. Narcotics and gun control laws were tightened. The volunteer police force—the Druzhinniki—was increased in an effort to control violence and pillage of public property even though these volunteers sometimes act as vigilantes who terrorize the people they are supposed to protect.

The rumor mill in Moscow worked overtime in the fall when there were reports of a Jack-the-Ripper killer on the loose in the Soviet capital. There were also reports of escaped convicts terrorizing the capital. Rumors about crime find fertile ground in the U.S.S.R., because most crime incidents are not publicized. Finally, the Moscow police had to admit that there was a wave of muggings, and that two women had indeed been murdered. The battle against alcoholism continued, and as in the past vodka remained "the curse of Russia."

Education. The Kremlin ordered a streamlining of Soviet higher education, but it was uncertain how far the reforms would go. Bribes to get young people into institutions of higher learning were common. There were reports of the buying and selling of degrees, including the degree of doctor of medicine. A survey by a Moscow magazine showed that out of 3,000 young people polled only thirty individuals were willing to work in a factory or on a farm—this in a country which supposedly does everything for the working class.

A LADY LION TAMER performs with the Moscow Circus, the best-known troupe in a nationalized Soviet circus network that employs 12,500 people. In 1974 box office admissions (at a top ticket price of $1.60) reached 61 million at performances in the U.S.S.R.'s fifty-eight permanent circus buildings, in its fifteen tents, and at one-night stands by its fifty traveling circus road shows in the countryside.

The year was marked by the deaths of prominent Soviet citizens, including the famous Jewish violinist David Oistrakh, sixty-five; World War II Marshal Georgi Zhukov, seventy-seven; and Culture Minister Ekaterina Furtseva, sixty-three. (Prior to her death, Furtseva lost her seat in the one-party parliament, the Supreme Soviet, in the wake of allegations that she had used public funds to build a dacha.)

The Big Question in 1975 is how long the aging Kremlin leadership can last. Brezhnev has said detente must be made "irreversible." But his successor—or successors—may not think the same way.

Space

by

ERIK BERGAUST

Internationally Syndicated Science Writer. Author of *Reaching for the Stars* (the biography of Dr. Wernher von Braun); *The Nuclear Encyclopedia* (1971); *The Next Fifty Years on the Moon* (1973); *Rescue in Space* (1974); and *Cities in the Sea* (1975). Founder and first president, The National Space Club; former director, Aviation and Space Writers Association; director, Environmental Writers Association of America.

Space Benefits. The space age began on October 4, 1957, with a beeping, short-lived, and uncontrollable orbital chunk of metal called *Sputnik I*. A mere seventeen years later, by the year 1974, all of mankind was beginning to reap the harvest and enjoy the "down-to-earth" benefits of an unbelievable myriad of space accomplishments. Telephone and television communications via satellite reached a peak. Improvement of satellite world weather forecasting, plane and ship navigation, and scientific surveys definitely and measurably was under way. Earth resources satellites had become a reality for the energy-starved and food-hungry world. Application of space satellite technology became a blessing for people in Appalachia, the Rocky Mountain remote areas, and the villages in Alaska—where education via satellite and television was given a boost, and where health service and health care were also aided.

Private industries progressed impressively in the field of marketing of commercial satellite services. Foreign countries looked to the United States for a new export product — orbiting devices that would help them improve their living standards.

News from the Moon. As we now

TRACKS from the *Apollo 14* astronauts' handcart, used to gather samples of lunar material, extend, gleaming white, from the Antares landing craft on the surface of the moon.

SPACE

THIS ACCELERATOR, below, powers a million-volt electron microscope at U.S. Steel's research center near Pittsburgh, Pa., used to study the moon rocks. The microscope, the largest in the Western Hemisphere, is so powerful it can resolve features eight-billionths of an inch apart and helps metallurgists and chemists probe the moon samples almost atom by atom.

MOON ROCK brought back by *Apollo 12.*

LUNAR SAMPLE under polarized light.

look back on the six Apollo landings, we are infinitely richer in facts concerning the Moon. Some of these facts and observations have already been tentatively assembled in models that are leading to a much fuller understanding of lunar history. Although it is extremely difficult to account for the remaining facts with a consistent explanation, major areas of understanding can be briefly outlined.

Age. It has been established with some confidence that the filling of the mare basins largely took place between 3.2 and 3.8 billion years ago. This has been demonstrated from analysis of the mare basalts obtained from the *Apollo 11, 12, 15,* and *17* missions and *Luna 16*. Because these mare fillings represent a major feature on the lunar surface, it has been inferred that the time of formation of more than 90 percent of the cratering on the Moon was 4 billion years ago or earlier. In comparison, the ocean basins of the Earth are younger than 300 million years. (Earth rocks older than 3 billion years are almost unknown.)

The analysis of the highland material collected on the *Apollo 14, 15, 16,* and *17* missions and *Luna 20* has shown the widespread occurrence of breccias with an apparent age of 3.8 to 4.1 billion years.

There is strong circumstantial evidence that rocks dating back to 4.5 to 4.6 billion years ago must exist within the Moon, although very few of the Apollo rocks have crystallization dates lying between 4.0 and 4.6 billion years. It now appears that heat from the intense bombardment of the lunar surface by projectiles, ranging in size from microscopic to tens of kilometers in diameter, was effective in resetting most of the clocks used to determine the absolute age of the rocks.

Volcanic Activity. There seems to be almost unanimous agreement that exten-

"I'LL MISS all those Apollo chaps."

sive lava flows underlie dark mare regions, as shown both by rocks returned by the *Apollo 11, 12, 15,* and *17* missions and *Luna 16* and by the high-resolution photographs that give convincing pictures of features comparable to lava flows on Earth. Almost all craters appear to be caused by impacting projectiles, thus leaving the questions of volcanic rocks in the terra regions unanswered. With the conclusion of *Apollo 17,* it has been suggested that volcanic activity in the highland region during the last 3 billion years may be highly restricted or virtually nonexistent.

Quakes. Apollo experiments investigating whether the Moon is "alive" or "dead" indicate that, compared to Earth, the Moon is seismically quiet. However, there are many very small quakes, possibly triggered by tides, at approximately 800 km below the lunar surface.

Below 1,000 km, the Moon is partially molten. A quiet Moon is consistent with the conclusion that vulcanism and other types of tectonic activity have been rare or absent from the lunar surface for the last 2 to 3 billion years. Lunar seismology reveals that the Moon has a crust more than 60 km thick. Both the precise origin of this crust and the compositions causing the discontinuity in seismic velocity are still subjects of debate. From the Apollo program we can conclude that the Moon, at one time, was very much alive and now is very quiet.

The Overall Magnetic Field of the Moon has been found to be negligible, as was thought before the Apollo missions. However, the magnetometers placed on the lunar surface reveal surprisingly strong local fields, variable both in direction and in intensity. Studies have also determined that mare lava flows crystallized in a magnetic field that was much stronger than that of the present Moon. These discoveries raise the possibility that, during its early history, the Moon either was exposed to a relatively strong interplanetary magnetic field or had a magnetic field of its own that has since disappeared.

The Thermal History of the Moon was investigated on the *Apollo 15* and *17* missions through measurements of the heat escaping from the Moon.

These measurements indicate that the rate of energy flow escaping from the Moon is approximately half that of the Earth. This is surprisingly high, considering the relative size of the two planets. If these measurements prove to be characteristic of the Moon, perhaps the explanation is that the Moon is richer than the Earth and that these elements are strongly concentrated in the upper parts of the Moon.

Lunar Evolution. Two current theories of lunar evolution have resulted from information concerning (1) the concentration and location of radioactive materials, (2) the inferred volcanic history of the Moon, and (3) the inferred upper limits of internal temperature. The first is that the Moon was chemically layered during its formation. The low initial temperature of the lunar interior (below 500 km) gradually increased, perhaps reaching the melting point during the last billion years, while the initial hot temperature of the lunar exterior gradually decreased. The other theory is that much of the Moon was molten at its origin. Of course, both of these theories will undergo discussion and revision in the coming years.

Lunar Surface Data. The most extensive and diverse data obtained on the lunar surface are concerned with the chemistry and mineralogy of the surface materials.

Chemical Characteristics. The study of samples from the six Apollo sites and the two Luna sites reveals a number of chemical characteristics. Although it is very early to generalize from these relatively few samples of the whole lunar surfaces, two orbital experiments provide excellent data regarding the regional distribution of various rock types. These experiments are the X-ray fluorescence experiment and the gamma ray experiment.

The X-ray fluorescence experiment defined the prime difference between the chemistry of the mare and highland regions. The mare regions have aluminum concentrations two to three times lower than those of the terra or highland regions and magnesium concentrations one and one-half to two times greater than those of the terra regions. These differences in the chemical concentrations throughout the equatorial region of the Moon are consistent with the chemical analysis of the returned samples. All mare basalts have been found to be unusually rich in iron and sometimes rich in titanium.

Mineralogy. The orbital gamma ray experiment results show that the region north and south of the crater Copernicus is remarkably rich in radioactive elements. A band going from north of the Fra Mauro site to west of the *Apollo 15* site contains soil twenty times richer in uranium and thorium than either mare or terra in other parts of the Moon. The existence of a rock rich in these elements was also inferred from samples from the *Apollo 12, 14,* and *15* missions. The differences between lunar rocks and terrestrial rocks are so marked that the Moon must be chemically different from the Earth.

The Moon appears to be much richer in elements that form refractory compounds at temperatures of approximately 1600 to 1800 K. Many scientists are now coming to the conclusion that the chemistry of the lunar surface reveals that some separation of solid material and gas in the lunar dust cloud took place at temperatures in excess of 1600 K. The strong depletion of elements that are volatile at high temperatures in the outer portion of the Moon is consistent with the enrichment of refractory elements.

Origin Theories. None of the three theories regarding the origin of the Moon—separation from the Earth, capture from a circumsolar orbit, or formation from a dust cloud surrounding the Earth—can be absolutely eliminated by the present data. However, the chemical differences between the Earth and the Moon, the depletion of volatile elements, and the enrichment of refractory elements in lunar samples make it unlikely that the Moon was torn out of the Earth.

In Summary, the age of the Moon is well determined, and the Moon has a crust (the chemical composition of which is fairly well understood), a mantle, and a partially molten deep interior. The understanding of the mascons is well underway. Facts substantiating the early theories of the atmosphere have been obtained. Basic questions that were asked five years ago—whether the Moon is hot or cold, alive or dead, or has craters formed by vulcanism or impact—are no longer asked. Apollo data have changed the types of questions asked. Post-Apollo questions are more detailed, more specific, and more sophisticated. Yet, despite the great strides taken in knowledge about the Moon, its origin and formation are still unknown.

A Storehouse of resources has been returned from the Moon: almost 385 kg of lunar materials (obtained from six different landing sites on the near side of the Moon), thirty-seven drive tubes, and twenty drill stems. To date, only 10 percent of this lunar material has been examined in detail. Approximately 33,000 lunar photographs and 20,000 reels of tapes of geophysical data have been collected. Thus, in four years of lunar exploration, knowledge of lunar characteristics has been substantially increased, and vast resources of scientific data have been collected that will lead to a decade of data analysis.

The Apollo Program has led to a revolution in providing the first deep understanding of a planet other than the Earth through the development of new techniques of exploration, investigation, and analysis, and through the integration of the scientific knowledge gained in interdisciplinary fields. Apollo lessons may force a reconsideration of many of the techniques and models that are currently used in understanding the early history of the Earth.

Interplanetary Knowledge. Yet, the most spectacular space accomplishments during 1974 probably were the scientific probings of interplanetary space in our quest for more knowledge about our neighbor planets. Scientifically, this is where mankind gained the most new ground, but the ramifications and benefits of the exploration of space may not be measured for perhaps many decades. One of these ventures was initiated with the Pioneer spacecraft.

Pioneer Spacecraft. Speed records have toppled like tenpins since *Pioneer 10* was launched March 2, 1972. That spacecraft shattered all previous land, air, space, and sea speed records. It roared away from Earth at more than 51,200 kilometers an hour (32,000 mph), arriving at Jupiter December 5, 1973. As it streaked within 129,600 kilometers (81,000 miles) of the planet's boiling clouds, it reached a speed of 131,200 kilometers an hour (82,000 mph).

On December 3, 1974, a sister spacecraft, *Pioneer 11,* burst through that speed as it approached the giant planet. As the newest interplanetary voyager brushed by Jupiter at an altitude of 42,560 kilometers (26,613 miles), it attained more than 169,000 kilometers an hour (106,000 mph).

Pioneer 11 is the first spacecraft to kick itself from one outer planet to another. A 992 million-kilometer (620 million-mile) trip to Jupiter isn't enough: *Pioneer 11* will come all the way back past the Sun, then head out again to twice the distance of Jupiter. In September, 1979, after a billion-mile trip, *Pioneer 11* will send men their first close-up pictures of the rings of Saturn.

Mileage records are falling, too. A good U.S. auto will get about 15 to 20 miles per gallon of gasoline. Not the Pioneer spacecraft. When *Pioneer 10* reached Jupiter in 1973, it had traveled about 992 million kilometers (620 million miles) on its 41,000 gallons of rocket fuel. That's about 15,000 miles per gallon, or 1,000 times better mileage than the typical auto gets.

Astronomers have studied Jupiter through telescopes since 1610 when Galileo Galilei took his first look. But no one had seen Jupiter at close range until the Pioneer spacecraft flashed past and took several hundred pictures. Even today, no one has looked at Jupiter's polar regions. *Pioneer 11* will give us the first view, and scientists are betting they'll be surprised at what they see.

Jupiter itself is a record-setter. The dominant planet in the solar system, it could swallow 1,000 planets the size of Earth. Jupiter is so huge that its gravity is staggering. A 67.5-kilogram (150-pound) man would weigh 178 kilograms (396 pounds) at Jupiter's cloud tops.

The big planet also has more satellites than any other. Astronomers thought they had done well to find twelve. But recently Dr. Charles Kowall, an astronomer at California Institute of Technology, found a thirteenth satellite in a picture he took with one of the telescopes atop Mount Palomar.

Information returned by the Pioneer spacecraft seems to support preexisting theories about the planet. In other cases, the findings contradict previous theories. In both instances, however, *Pioneer 10's* visit to the planet has provided the first firm ideas of what Jupiter is like, says Dr. John Wolfe, Pioneer project scientist. All previous Jupiter measurements had been made from Earth, a half billion miles away.

Jupiter's Interior. Jupiter is almost certainly a liquid planet, for it is too hot to solidify, even with its enormous internal pressures of millions of atmospheres.

Both temperature and pressure rise as one goes deeper. At the zone of transition to liquid, 1,000 kilometers (600 miles) below the top of the atmosphere, the temperature is calculated to be 2,000°C. (3,600°F.). At 3,000 kilometers (1,800 miles) down, temperature is 5,500°C. (10,000°F.) and pressure is 90,000 Earth atmospheres. At this point, the weight of the Jovian atmosphere has compressed the hydrogen gradually into the form of a liquid about one quarter as dense as water. At 25,000 kilometers (15,000 miles) down, the temperature reaches 11,000°C. (20,000°F.) and the pressure is 3 million atmospheres. At this level, liquid hydrogen turns to liquid metallic hydrogen.

The gravity-sensing measurements so

far show that, unlike Earth, Jupiter has no concentration of mass, such as a rigid crust or other solid areas. The measurements show that the planet is in "hydrostatic equilibrium" or is largely liquid. At Jupiter's center, theoreticians believe, there may be a small rocky core, perhaps containing some iron. The gravity analysis, not yet complete, may well show this small core.

Pioneer measurements indicate that Jupiter radiates two to three times more heat than it receives from the Sun. This means that Jupiter is losing heat at a tremendously rapid rate.

Jupiter's Atmosphere. Jupiter's atmosphere, the planet's 1,000-kilometers (600-miles) deep outer layer, consists primarily of hydrogen and helium gas with very small amounts of the other elements.

Pioneer found that the atmosphere accounts for about 1 percent of Jupiter's total mass.

Calculations based on *Pioneer 10* findings put the ratio of elements in Jupiter's upper atmosphere close to 80 percent hydrogen to 20 percent helium, with less than 1 percent for all the other elements. This is similar to the ratio of elements found in the Sun.

Clouds and Heat Balance. Jupiter's cloud layers form in the planet's predominantly hydrogen-helium atmosphere. They are believed by theoretical astronomers to make up a kind of four-decker sandwich.

Ammonia "ice" crystals, measured from Earth, are believed to form the top of Jupiter's clouds. Below this are red-brown clouds, probably of ammonia hydrosulfide crystals, and below that, water ice-crystals. Still lower, liquid water droplets containing ammonia in solution may be present. (Water has never been observed.)

Just what the "weather" is in these lower cloud layers is unknown, aside from the up-down circulation of the atmosphere.

There may be lightning, storm activity, and other phenomena, because Jupiter has a large amount of energy and violently circulating atmosphere.

Jupiter's seventeen relatively permanent belts and zones appear to be comparable to the continent-spanning cyclones and anticyclones which produce most of the weather in the Earth's temperate zones. On both planets, these phenomena are huge regions of rising or falling atmosphere gas, powered by the Sun (and in Jupiter's case also by its internal heat source).

On Earth, huge masses of warm, light gas rise to high altitudes, cool off, get heavier, and then roll down the sides of new rising columns of gas. General direction of this atmospheric heat flow on Earth is from the tropics toward the poles.

Coriolis forces, (produced by planetary rotation) cause the descending gas, which would normally move north or south, to flow around the planet west to east. However, on Earth, unstable flow converts this west-east motion into the enormous spirals known as cyclones and anticyclones.

With Jupiter's high-speed, 22,000-mph rotation, these round-the-planet coriolis forces are very strong.

Because of instabilities like those on Earth, flow should be in even more violent spirals than Earth's. But several factors appear to have a "calming effect," so that the motion is mostly linear. These factors include Jupiter's internal heat source and heat circulation, lack of a solid surface, and liquid character.

As a result, the combination of convection (due to the Sun's heat plus internal heat) and Coriolis (due to Jupiter's rapid rotation) stretches the planet's large permanent weather features completely around the planet,

JUPITER'S RED SPOT is quite prominent in this photograph of the planet taken by *Pioneer 11* on December 2 from a distance of about 660,000 miles. Although features of its south pole are not clear, the image shows details in that area never seen before.

forming the belts and zones.

The Great Red Spot. While the Pioneer spacecraft have not completely explained the Great Red Spot, it appears to be a centuries-old, 40,000-kilometer (25,000-mile-wide) vortex of a violent storm, as first proposed by the late Dr. Gerard P. Kuiper. The spot is calculated to rise some eight kilometers (five miles) above the surrounding cloud deck. This is shown by the fact that the clouds at the top of the spot have less atmosphere above them and are cooler (and hence higher) than surrounding clouds.

Pioneer 10 pictures show that the spot's internal structure appears to be a pinwheellike vortex and that its rapid circulation pattern makes it rigid enough to displace the clouds of the south tropical zone strongly northward.

A second "red spot," about one-third the size of the Great Red Spot, can be seen in the Pioneer pictures. This is located in the northern counterpart of the southern hemisphere zone containing the Great Red Spot. The little red spot also is cooler than its surrounding clouds, and is believed to rise as high as the Great Red Spot. This second spot lends support to the idea that "red spots" are occasional meteorological phenomena on Jupiter, found in the middle of the planet's bright zones where the atmosphere is rising, says Dr. Andrew Ingersoll, California Institute of Technology.

Ionosphere. Jupiter's ionosphere rises 300 kilometers (1800 miles) above the 1/10 millibar level. It is ten times thicker and five times hotter than had been predicted. Average temperature of the ionosphere is about 1,000°C. (1,800°F.) It has at least three sharply defined layers of differing density, and its unexpected depth is due to the diffusion of its ionized gas by high temperatures. High temperature of the ionosphere is believed due to impacts of high-energy particles, and to hydromagnetic waves from Jupiter's magnetosphere.

Jupiter's Moons. Going out from the planet, Jupiter's four planet-sized moons show a progression of densities. The closest moon, Io, is 3.5 times the density of water; Europa, 3.14 times; Ganymede, 1.94 times; and Callisto, 1.62 times.

Thus, the two inner moons, having a density a little more and a little less respectively than that of the Earth's Moon, must be primarily rocky. The outer two probably consist largely of water-ice, as indicated both by their density and by Jupiter's heat characteristics.

Pioneer measurements have shown that the masses of the moons are as follows: Io, 1.22 Earth-Moon masses; Europa, .67 lunar masses; Ganymede, 2.02 lunar masses; and Callisto, 1.44 lunar masses. Ganymede is definitely larger than the planet Mercury; Callisto, about the same size; and Io and Europa, somewhat smaller. The four large moons have an average surface temperature on the sunlit side of −145 degrees C. (−230 degrees F.).

Io, the closest large moon, which turns out to be 23 percent heavier than previously thought, has a tenuous atmosphere. This makes it the smallest known celestial body with an atmosphere. Io also has an extended ionosphere almost as dense as that of Venus, reaching to about 700 kilometers (420 miles) on the day side. This dense ionosphere may mean an unusual gas mixture; an ionosphere with these characteristics may indicate the presence of elements such as sodium, hydrogen, and nitrogen on Io. Earth measurements show the presence of sodium on Io, and Pioneer measurements indicate the presence of hydrogen.

Magnetic Field. *Pioneer 10* found that the strength of Jupiter's magnetic field at the planet's cloud tops is more than ten times the strength of the Earth's field at the Earth's surface. Total energy in the Jovian field is 400 million times that of Earth's.

Radiation Belts. As on Earth, the high-energy particles which form Jupiter's inner radiation belt are trapped within the planet's inner magnetic field. In the weak outer magnetic field, particles bounce around, but eventually make their way to the field's outer edge. There they are spun off into space by the high-speed rotation of the planet and by the radiation belts themselves. Particles also escape in other ways.

Voyage to Mercury. Other big space events in 1974 include the feats of *Mariner 10*, the first spacecraft to explore Mercury. It reached that planet in February/March, passing Mercury on the dark side about 620 miles (1,000 km) above the surface, and passing the planet again in September.

Mariner 10 was launched November 3, 1973, on the first dual-planet mission to Venus and Mercury, and the first mission designed to use the gravitational attraction of one planet to reach another. It reached Venus on February 5, returning a full complement of scientific data, including more than 4,000 photographs. The gravitational attraction of Venus altered the spacecraft's flight path, aiming it toward the orbit of Mercury. A trajectory correction performed on March 16 refined the flight path from a miss-distance of about 4,400 miles (7,000 km) on the sunlit side of Mercury.

Photography of Mercury began on March 23, at a range of 3.3 million miles (5.28 million km), with transmission of the early calibration photographs to Earth scheduled during that day. A total of 2,000 photographs of Mercury were transmitted to Earth.

The incoming photography was designed for three basic objectives. The first objective was to obtain 90 percent coverage of the visible, sunlit portion of the disc at an approximate resolution of 1.5 miles (2.5 km). The second photographic series had the objective of attaining high resolution, 0.8 miles (1.3 km) of 30 percent of the visible disc. The third series would seek a resolution from 0.5 miles (0.8 km) down to about 900 feet (300 meters). This third series of pictures was expected to permit good geological interpretation of the planet Mercury.

On March 29, as the spacecraft flew past the dark side of Mercury, its scientific experiments began to search for an atmosphere, temperature ranges on the surface, and Sun and Earth occulations, and to observe the interaction of the solar wind with the planet. The flight path past the dark side was chosen to allow the occulations, to observe the solar wind interactions, and to measure

SPACE

temperature changes from the night into the day side.

Mercury is a small, dense planet close to the Sun, with essentially no atmosphere, and surface temperatures varying from extremely hot to very cold. It has an eccentric orbit, and a very slow rate of rotation.

This innermost planet is very difficult to observe from Earth because of its orbital position close to the sun, its small size, and its relatively low reflectivity. As a consequence, pending the flyby mission of *Mariner 10,* remarkably little is known about Mercury, although recent improvements in Mercury knowledge, based partly on new ground-based radio techniques, have been striking. The general expectation of many observers is that this planet tends to resemble the Moon more than any other known body. However, Mercury is not the Moon, and the lack of knowledge about it has permitted many speculations.

Mercury's diameter is half again as large as the Earth's Moon. Its mass, however, is believed to be about five times as great. Densities from about four to six have been asserted in recent decades, attesting to the difficulty of obtaining precise data from Earth-based observations. Mercury's surface, like the Moon's, has a low visual albedo. Radar reflectivity, microwave, infrared, and photometric characteristics are approximately those of the Moon's.

Motion and Rotation. Mercury's orbit is rather eccentric, with the solar distance varying from about 29 million to over 43 million miles. As a consequence, the amount of sunlight and heat falling on the planet varies by more than a factor of two.

The planet's rotation period is locked to its orbital period in a ratio of 2:3. This ratio produces a solar day for Mercury which is equal to 176 Earth days, or two Mercury years, long. Until 1965, it was believed that this ratio was 1:1, that is, it was believed that Mercury always turned the same face to the Sun, as the Moon does to Earth. Radar measurements since 1965 have confirmed and defined the 2:3 relationship.

Atmosphere. One reason temperatures are believed to be so extreme on Mercury is that it does not appear to have any significant amount of atmosphere. Early visual observations of possible clouds, and later optical instrument readings of polarization and spectral bands associated with CO_2 have suggested that Mercury's atmosphere, if any, is extremely tenuous. Many planetologists believe that the atmosphere can be no more than a few millionths as dense as ours. The high temperature on and around Mercury would tend to cause any atmosphere to escape, even though the surface gravity is slightly more than that of Mars, and more than twice the Moon's.

Inert gases, such as neon, argon, and krypton may be present in a Mercury atmosphere, but are not easily detectable by Earth-based methods. *Mariner 10's* two highly sensitive ultraviolet spectrometers were designed to search for these and other gases at very low abundances.

Surface Characteristics and Features. Under the difficult conditions of observing from Earth, Mercury seems to be a smaller, darker, less-distinct version of Mars, yellowish instead of reddish. At best, Mercury in the telescope does not present as good an image as the Moon offers to the naked eye.

Recent radar investigations of part of Mercury's surface reveal altitude differences as great as 1 to 1½ miles (1.5 to 2.5 km), over distances of 100 to 200 miles (160 to 320 km). They also show many detectable surface features—some possibly circular like the lunar craters. Many planetologists expect to find lunar-type craters on Mercury.

Photometric and infrared measure-

SOVIET COSMONAUTS Anatoly Filipchenko and Nikolai Rukavishnikov completed ninety-six orbits of the earth in the Russian spacecraft, *Soyuz 16*, on December 8. The six-day mission was a successful dress rehearsal of the planned July, 1975, linkup in space with American Apollo astronauts.

ments also suggest that the surface texture of Mercury resembles the Moon's: a mixture of unconsolidated material of various particle sizes and relatively high porosity. The light and dark areas may correspond to geological features, as do the lunar highlands and maria.

Since so very little is known about the surface of Mercury, it is obvious that television pictures and other *Mariner 10* scientific experiments will produce a very large improvement in this area of knowledge. Space scientists are currently hard at work studying and analyzing the *Mariner 10* findings. Such data are likely to be revealed and released during 1975.

Mercury's Interior and Magnetism. Mercury is dense enough to have iron as an important chemical constituent. If it were fully differentiated, the iron core would extend roughly two-thirds of the way up from the center. With silicate rock on top, however, the planet is so small that the interior is unlikely to be hot enough for its materials to settle out and separate. In this respect, too, it may resemble the Moon.

SPAIN'S INDUSTRIAL ACTIVITY dropped off in the fall after years of spectacular expansion. SEAT automobile works, which is to Spain what General Motors is to the United States, announced a 10 percent reduction in production in November.

by
GEORGE HILLS

Author of *Spain — A Survey of Politics, Economics, and Social Conditions* (1969) and *The Rock of Contention — A History of Gibraltar* (1972), Broadcaster and Lecturer on Iberian Current Affairs.

The New Government. General Francisco Franco insisted that nothing untoward should follow the assassination of Prime Minister Carrero Blanco. There was no declaration of a State of Exception. The police issued a list of six members of the "commando" of the Marxist-Leninist branch of the ETA (the self-styled Basque Liberation Movement) which they believed to have been the active perpetrators of the deed, but no mass roundup of possible accomplices occurred then, nor when, from the safety of France, four of the six confirmed the suspicions of the police. The director general of the paramilitary Civil Guard, the Right-wing Lieutenant General Carlos Iniesta Cano called upon the twelve captains general of the military districts, that is, Spain's most senior serving army officers, to support him in strong action against all Spaniards suspected of Left-wing views. They refused; they were under orders from the liberal-minded chief of staff, General Manuel Diez-Alegría to stand by against the possibility that extremist groups of either the Left or Right might take advantage of the political upset. Iniesta was severely reprimanded and denied any extension of service beyond May when he reached the normal age for retirement.

Everything was to be done according to the law. Vice-Premier Torcuato Fernández Miranda was sworn in as temporary premier. The Council of the Realm submitted the three names from which the head of state had to choose the new premier. Franco chose quickly. The new prime minister was to be Carrero Blanco's minister for internal affairs, Carlos Arias Navarro, one time mayor of Madrid, earlier director general of national security, and professionally a lawyer.

Arias chose eleven fellow lawyers for his cabinet, the first in nineteen years without a single member of *Opus Dei.* Indeed, none of his nineteen ministers was likely to be inhibited by political ideology or religious beliefs; they were all pragmatists. On being sworn in as premier on January 4, Arias announced that the cornerstone of his policy would be the maintenance of public order. To that end, however, he considered necessary "a development of the people's participation in political life." He expanded that statement before the Cortes on February 12: they were to have placed before them bills to reform local authorities on a more democratic basis, and to legalize political associations.

In the opinion of die-hard Falangists, Arias's proposals were contrary to the principles of the *Movimiento* which he had sworn to uphold, and they took full advantage of the relaxation of censorship by the new government to say so in print and public gatherings. The government was jeopardizing the unity of the nation, the very basis of its independence and greatness; the assassination of Carrero, they argued, was an indication of the anarchy that could be expected if the government persisted with its policy of allowing free discussion even to Marxists. Left-of-center journalists, of course, took the view that the proposals were not radical enough, and that the exasperation of terrorists was the product of the lack of freedom.

The government was perturbed not so much by the frequency of acts of terror-

FRANCISCO FRANCO celebrated his eighty-second birthday on December 4. According to *Arriba*, a Right-wing newspaper, "the full resumption of his intense activity as a statesman after the summer illness (made) this anniversary happier and more emotional."

ism in the country — a frequency not much higher than in France and lower than in the United Kingdom — as by the fact that the organization most responsible, the ETA, was proving a veritable hydra. Around the date of Arias's speech, in the period of February 8-21, the police discovered evidence that the ETA had more than made good the losses in militant activists and explosives that it had suffered in 1973 and previous years.

The criticisms from Left or Right in a dozen or so journals each representing a different political point of view were, however, of little consequence. None could be said to have influence over more than minuscule percentages of the population, and in the divisions of its critics there was strength for the government. The government felt it could not exercise the same tolerance toward the one organization whose influence was still substantial—the Roman Catholic church.

The Clash with the Church. As the texts of the Lenten pastorals of bishops came into government hands, the government became apprehensive. As before, they contained severe criticisms of the regime's social policies as inadequate in justice, and pointed to irreconcilable differences between the law and Catholic doctrines on the rights of man. On Friday, February 22, they read the text of a homily — one of a series — which the bishop of Bilbao, Antonio Añoveros Ataun wished his pastors to read the following Sunday. It was brief, mostly quotations from papal pronouncements on the rights of workers and of cultural minorities. The bishop mentioned the difficulties imposed by the authorities on the culture of the Basques. He referred to the Basque *pueblo,* people. That, the government decided, was the attribution to the Basques of the right to form a separate state, and therefore "a grave attack on the unity of the Spanish nation" and as such a crime. They called on the Papal Nuncio to veto the homily. He replied that he had no authority to do so. The bishop insisted that the official interpretation was untenable.

The homily was read in virtually every church in the diocese. Falangists organized disturbances in three. The following Wednesday the Bilbao chief of police informed the bishop that he would be "kept to his house for his own protection" against the alleged anger of the people, and on the following Sunday an aircraft would be standing by to take him out of the country. The bishop said that he would leave only under orders from the pope, or if overpowered by force; and he warned Catholics that the canonical penalty for the use of force against a bishop was excommunication.

Falangists and other ultranationalist journalists were given full rein to attack the bishop and the church generally, while the government-controlled television and radio publicized only the official point of view. There was talk during the next week even of breaking off diplomatic relations with the Vatican; but during that same week the government was left in no doubt that Bishop Añoveros had the full support of the clergy and laity of his diocese, of the body of the Spanish hierarchy, and of the Vatican whose radio commentator praised the bishop's "high pastoral qualities." Any action against Bishop Añoveros therefore would be action against the whole church and too dangerous for any Spanish government, so talk of severity and excommunication subsided thereafter into the restatement on all sides that the existing Concordat was useless as a guide to church-state relations in 1974.

Once the dust of the Añoveros battle had settled, bishops throughout the country returned individually to the themes of social injustice and offenses against human rights. In September

SPAIN

there was yet another collective document on those points. This time the government did not intervene. In June and again in July there had been meetings in Madrid and the Vatican to discuss once more the text of a new concordat, and a new confrontation could prejudice further talks scheduled for the autumn.

Opposition to Arias. The Añoveros episode over, the Ultra-Falangists reverted to propaganda against the February proposals. When, in May, Arias put his bill for local government reform before the National Council of the Movement (constitutionally, in effect, the Senate) and before the Cortes, it quickly became evident that the Falangists in both would fight its every clause. The heart of the matter was its stipulation to open all the offices of aldermen (councillors) to independent candidates, and to make them elective by direct universal suffrage. That innovation could be seen as the legal precedent for the introduction of similar rules subsequently in the labor organizations and in the Cortes. The known unpopularity of undiluted Falangism made it unlikely that with free elections the Ultras would retain even their current limited influence in government.

The slow progress of the bill held up the introduction of the second controversial bill—that to legalize political associations. The delay seriously perturbed those who saw in the Portuguese revolution a warning to Spain that in the event of a sudden end to the regime, power could easily pass into the hands of those who alone had managed to maintain nationwide political organizations clandestinely—the Marxist Left. The secretary general of the Communist party, Santiago Carrillo, poured scorn on Arias's proposals as vehemently from exile as the Ultras did within the country.

Thus the extremists helped each other wittingly or not. The Ultras, smarting under the fact that their most prominent military supporter, General Iniesta, was being retired, were delighted when Carrillo claimed that General Diez-Alegría had been in touch with *him* just after the Carrero assassination. It was a statement which, true or false, could lead only to Diez-Alegría's dismissal, especially as foreign press correspondents had

PRINCE JUAN CARLOS was officially Spain's head of state for forty-four days, from July 19 to August 31.

A SPANISH BUTCHER complains as a consumer watchdog questions him on meat weighing. Revelations of fraud, from simple cheating on weight in butcher shops to the watering of milk by dairy companies, are noted daily in Spanish newspapers as the once impoverished country moves to the point where consumerism has become big business.

frequently referred to him as a possible Spanish Spinola. The official excuse was that he was two years over age for the post.

Throughout June and into July, Arias kept on saying that his government was "determined on the process of political development." The Ultras intensified their opposition, while all others exhorted Arias to get on with the task. A long-feared and yet sudden event was to make it more difficult.

On July 9, Franco developed thrombophlebitis to an extent which made necessary his transfer to hospital.

Franco's Illness. Though the public was reassured on television and by official announcements that Franco's illness was not serious, his doctors could not guarantee his survival from one day to another. That posed a problem for Arias and Prince Juan Carlos, chosen by Franco as his successor. Any measure of liberalization carried through while Franco was still head of state could not be attacked thereafter as contrary to the principles of the *Movimiento,* for Franco, as their author, was the best interpreter of their vague wording. On the other hand, the Ultras were known to be plotting to oust the prince who was now known to favor democratization. His position would be stronger if he was acting head of state at the moment when Franco died.

On July 19 Franco suffered a severe hemorrhage, and was not expected to survive the day. Arias thereupon persuaded Franco to hand over the headship of the state temporarily, and the prince to accept it.

The transfer of power grievously displeased two groups of people. It had long been known that Franco's immediate family had harbored hopes that they might persuade him to rescind his choice of Juan Carlos as his successor in favor of Prince Alfonso, since the marriage of the latter to Franco's granddaughter Carmen. Her father, the marquis of Villaverde was seen to react violently to Arias's success in obtaining Franco's assent to the transfer. The other group were the Ultras. The day following the transfer General Iniesta spent a longer time at the hospital than any other nonfamily visitor but one: José Antonio Girón, the most prominent Ultra-Falangist in Franco's governments of the period 1940-57, and—since April, 1974, after years of silence—a frequent public speaker and writer against liberalization. The Ultras were antimonarchist, but given no other choice, preferred Alfonso to Juan Carlos. Their alliance with the family constantly at Franco's bedside, however, produced no immediate results.

Prince Juan Carlos was allowed to fill the post of head of state until Franco was declared fully recovered, August 31, a period of forty-four days. Most of the period coincided with the summer holidays, and he was called upon to exercise his powers only to a limited extent. He put his signature to seven decrees prepared by the government—one of them lifting wage controls put into effect the previous November—and he chaired two cabinet meetings. His major act was his first—ratification on July 19 of the U.S.-Spanish Declaration of Principles signed by Secretary of State Henry Kissinger and Foreign Minister Pedro Cortina Mauri the very day that Franco entered hospital.

The declaration, of itself, merely verbally reinforced Spain's existing role in western defense; but on the occasion of its initialing, Foreign Minister Cortina revealed publicly that the United States had exhorted its NATO allies to consider Spain's membership. Into the phrase of the declaration that both countries recognized their respective "territorial integrity," Spain could read a U.S. undertaking to support Spain's claim to Gibraltar, whose recovery from Great Britain became during the year once more Spain's major foreign policy effort. In its turn Spain was subjected to pressure by Morocco to surrender phosphate-rich Sahara. Spain promised no more than to hold a referendum in 1975 among its 80,000 inhabitants. Events in Portugal were declared to affect in no way Spain's relations with its neighbor, but there was tension with France over French unwillingness to take action against Spanish members of ETA who were mounting hit-and-run attacks from French hideouts.

Franco's Recovery. Franco's immediate family saw in the favorable non-Falangist press reaction to Prince Juan Carlos as temporary head of state the recession of their hopes for Alfonso. They presented Franco with selected press cuttings to persuade him to resume the headship, and replaced with other medical advisors those who cautioned against it. Thus it was that Franco was declared fit to take back his position. Arias said he looked forward with confidence, in the light of experience, to Prince Juan Carlos's becoming king of Spain. At a dinner in Barcelona the marquis of Villaverde proposed a toast to his son-in-law as "the future king of Spain, Alfonso XIV." Iniesta and other Right-wing generals remained in constant attendance on the family. Arias reaffirmed his determination to get his local government reform bill on the statute book before the end of the year, and by then also to have the text of his political associations bill before the Cortes. Opposition to them increased, as the Ultras were joined by some of the Carlists. A bomb in a Madrid café which killed twelve persons and injured upwards of seventy, and the discovery of the hiding places of an extremist Marxist group which the police labelled Communist, gave the Ultras just what they needed to raise the specter of an international plot to set up a Communist regime in Spain.

More than politics was now involved. The press was openly hinting at cases of serious financial malpractice by the leaders of the Ultras. They feared that any move toward democracy would endanger the fortunes involved. Working on the fact that Franco was reacting as would any normal eighty-year-old man, they showed him clippings of the publicity which the press had given Carrillo since February, reminding Franco of the troubles which the Communists had caused in his youth, as well as somewhat erotic advertisements for films. With those they prevailed upon Franco to dismiss Minister of Information Pio Cabanillas. Arias still pressed on with his bill for political associations, which in effect would have made legal all political parties except the Communist. Franco would not have it put before Cortes and presented Arias with a statute which became law by decree on December 23 but which allowed no associations except of the Right. Spain's major problem was now Franco's longevity.

Sri Lanka

by
MICHAEL COPE
Internationally Syndicated Columnist

THE BEAUTY OF SRI LANKA SCENERY, such as this beach near Colombo, is being promoted by the country to boost tourism and earn scarce foreign exchange. Several Westerners, mostly from the United States and Western Europe, have taken advantage of Sri Lanka's new five-year "permanent" tourist scheme which is open to those with proven incomes of over $175 a month if they deposit $3,500 as a "safeguard".

Caught in the Maelstrom. For Sri Lanka, perhaps better known as the 25,323-square-mile island of Ceylon lying twenty-two miles off the southern tip of the Indian subcontinent, 1974 was a year of economic disaster compounded by political bitterness and dissent. The young nation, which acquired independence from Great Britain twenty-seven years ago, was a chronic victim of inflation, and caught also in the maelstrom of the bitter ideological differences between Communist China and the Soviet Union.

Too Much Welfare. Behind the country's difficulties was an overly generous social welfare program of education, free medical treatment, and long-standing food handouts which the Left-wing coalition government of the world's first woman prime minister, Mrs. Sirimavo Bandaranaike (India's Indira Gandhi and Israel's Golda Meir won office after Mrs. Bandaranaike's first term in 1960) can no longer afford. One leading economist defined the worsening situation: "We are now operating on a week-to-week basis. We check how much comes in and how much goes out. We don't think in terms of beyond a week. We can't."

Effect of Oil Prices. As in so many other underdeveloped nations, the catastrophe was due largely to the massive rises in oil prices, although increases in rice, sugar, and other foods, as well as machinery, pushed Sri Lanka's overall imports bill up by 200 percent in two years. Offset against this is the country's wobbly tripod of exports—tea, rubber, and coconut — commodities for which prices on world markets lagged far behind in the overall inflationary upswing. By year's end Sri Lanka was more than

$2 billion in debt to other countries and was compelled to spend two-thirds of its $450 million foreign exchange earnings to buy rice and wheat on inflated world markets. It was during the May Day celebrations in Colombo, the capital, that Prime Minister Bandaranaike warned the 13 million Sri Lankans: "The economic crisis has almost squeezed the breath out of us—we are literally fighting to survive now."

At this point Communist China came in with an emergency gift shipment of 40,000 tons of rice; Russia, the United States, Canada, Australia, Pakistan, and even India which has its own desperate food shortages, also agreed to send food. The fact that Sri Lanka's population had doubled in the past twenty-five years imposed an enormous strain on the massive subsidies which the government has always put on wheat, sugar, and flour imports, as well as the free rice ration. By summer the ration of these basic foods had been cut to three pounds a week, while the free rice ration on which the present United Front coalition government landslid to victory in 1970, was cut from four to one and one-half pounds.

Analysts studying Sri Lanka's rapidly deteriorating situation were hard put to see a solution. Besides the desperate economic situation and widespread food shortages, there were nearly 1 million unemployed, about three-quarters of

A RICE FARMER tills a paddy in up-country Sri Lanka. The floundering economy of the country is still based on agriculture.

SRI LANKA

them educated to high school level.

Ideological Differences within the United Front government were viewed by some as so acute as to deny it the conviction it needed within itself. The cabinet included members of Mrs. Bandaranaike's own Sri Lanka Freedom party which she describes as "democratic socialist," the Trotskyite Lanka Sama Samaja party which is extreme Left-wing, and the pro-Moscow Communist party.

With this mixed cabinet, it was the prime minister's delicate task to maintain something of a balance between the big powers—juggling for control of the Indian Ocean which, in the context of world politics has assumed increasing significance lately—and Sri Lanka itself, where the former big British naval base at Trincomalee on its northeast coast assumed strategic importance. Against this background Mrs. Bandaranaike's government, conscious of the Moscow-Delhi-Dacca alliance, sought to establish a good relationship with Peking as some sort of counterbalance to the Soviet naval build-up in the Indian Ocean. But it was the Russians who responded first and positively when in 1971 the Colombo government was threatened by an insurrection of extremist guerrillas — students and unemployed university graduates — by dispatching a squadron of MIG jet fighters to the island "thus painlessly and legally consolidating the Soviet presence in the Indian Ocean that everyone had been so excited about hitherto," noted one British observer.

But despite the divisiveness within her cabinet and the defiance of the Right-leaning opposition, the United National party (UNP) led by J. R. Jayawardene, Mrs. Bandaranaike maintained a firm and authoritarian hold, not only on the 157-seat legislature, but on the country as a whole. In May, a civil disobedience campaign launched by the UNP was countered by a twenty-eight-hour nationwide curfew, a banning of all UNP rallies, the closure of all newspapers sympathetic to the UNP, and the threat of widespread confiscation of property belonging to those convicted of violating the emergency regulations. But violated they were by the outraged UNP; Jinadasa Nivathapala, a UNP front bench member, told a packed illegal rally in Colombo: "The ban is unconstitutional, illegal, and undemocratic . . . we are defying the government and we don't care. There is not enough bread, there is not enough rice, and there is not enough food or cloth. We will protest and continue to protest."

A Family Affair. Of particular interest to Western observers watching the swaying checks and balances in this sensitive region was the growing influence in Sri Lanka of Sunethra Rupasinghe, the prime minister's daughter, and her husband Kumar, a restless, long-haired radical who edits the leftist weekly newspaper *Janavegaya* in which he frequently quotes the philosophy of China's Communist mentor, Chairman Mao Tse-tung, and the late Cuban revolutionary guerrilla, Che Guevara. Kumar also leads a powerful militant organization, also called Janavegaya which means "People's Force." Sunethra wields considerable power and respect within Mrs. Bandaranaike's cabinet as coordinating secretary. Kumar frequently advises the prime minister on policy and controls most of the government supporters in Parliament. He is generally believed to have been responsible for the closure of opposition newspapers in May, and is known to wield powerful influence in the Sri Lankan foreign service.

As one disillusioned dissident was quoted: "It's pure feudalism here. Everyone is either a cousin or a nephew or an uncle. There is one family and they are all sitting on the throne."

Streaking

A MASKED STREAKER startled spectators at the Gallende ski jumping contest in Missoula, Mont., on March 11.

by
PAUL BOHANNAN, Ph.D.

Professor of Anthropology
Northwestern University

Nothing to Hide. During the early spring of 1974, when "cover-up" was the political issue of the day, the fact that the common men and women of the land had nothing to hide was given dramatic — and often hilarious — testimony in a craze that was called streaking. The dictionaries told us that "to streak" was "to cancel by drawing a line or lines across; to mark with lines of a different color, substance or texture." It had long been an American slang word meaning "to move very fast." By the middle of March, however, the entire nation knew that streaking also meant to strip off all one's clothes (though some streakers wore tennis shoes and ski masks) and run as fast as possible through a public place.

The Best of Streaking. The streaker who got the most coverage, as it were, was the one who streaked through the

Oscar-presentation ceremonies of the Academy of Motion Picture Arts and Sciences; when the program was rerun for television, he was cut off at the waist. The one with the most noble message was probably the one who streaked through the presentation ceremonies of the National Book Awards yelling "Read books! Read books!" And the one who got the best laugh was probably the young hair stylist from San Francisco who streaked through the lower chamber of the Hawaii state legislature. When he was arrested for open lewdness, he tried to explain, "I am the streaker of the house."

Sober-Sided Analyses. Streaking called forth almost as many sober-sided analyses as it did streakers: Marshall McLuhan, who told us a few years ago that the medium was the message, seems to have forgotten that point when he explained to the press this time that "Streaking is a put-on, a form of assault . . . It's an art form, of course. All entertainment has elements of malice and power in it. Streaking has a political point, too. It's a form of activism." Laurel Richardsen Walum wrote to the *New York Times:* "As a political sociologist, I would like to shed some light on the recent and puzzling phenomenon of 'streaking.' Obviously, it is a very subtle and sophisticated anti-Nixon campaign, and its ingenuity is a welcome harbinger of political spring. Clearly, the streakers are carrying the following messages: full disclosure, no cover-up. Streaking belies any belief that students have withdrawn or copped out of political involvement."

Some letter columns in the newspapers were full of indignation: "If young people are taught they are animals long enough through the theory of evolution they'll soon begin to act like them," one Tennessee woman declared. A fundamentalist chaplain intoned: "Streaking is a deliberate effort to flout an older society's different view of nudity."

The psychiatrists had a field day. Dr. David Abrahamsen, a Manhattan psychoanalyst, was quoted in the *New York Times* as saying that the streakers "were trying to liberate themselves" after a "long winter without sexual outlets." He went on to explain that young people could not get the gasoline to drive their cars to shady lanes and that the resulting sexual frustration had led to streaking. Dr. Robert Michaels of the New York Psychiatric Institute said that streaking was a "defiance of accepted cultural norms—more naughty than sexual." He claimed it was both disturbing and silly, then added that if it had a political point it was that "social customs and norms are based on arbitrary rules."

Student Reaction. Most college students—but certainly not all—said that streaking was merely fun. They were almost as amused by the comments as by the streakers. Most campuses found it a funny frolic—and most were streaked across, sometimes by several dozen participants in a "streak-in."

Streaking's Place in History. Streaking has been compared to goldfish swallowing, the fad of the 1930s, to telephone-booth stuffing of the 1940s, and to pantyraids on the campuses before World War II. Many observers noted that streaking was "better" than trashing the offices of R.O.T.C. (Reserve Officers Training Corps) departments or sitting in college administration buildings, occurrences of the late 1960s and 1970 when America was most deeply involved in the Vietnam war.

All of these fads can be seen as a sort of mirror image of the moral mood of the country—and all but the desperate movements of the late 1960s have taken the form of farce or satire. It is no accident that the fad of streaking—for baring all and running fast—occurred in the spring of 1974.

Supreme Court

JUSTICE WILLIAM O. DOUGLAS and his wife Cathy talk to newsmen in his Supreme Court office. The justice broke the court service record set by Justice Stephen J. Field in 1897 by having served thirty-four years and 196 days on October 30, 1973. The seventy-six-year-old Douglas was hospitalized with a stroke on December 31.

by

ROBERT J. STEAMER

Dean College II (Arts and Sciences)
University of Massachusetts
Author of *The Supreme Court in Crisis* (1971)

A Historical Opinion. It appears to be a law of history that during an annual term the Supreme Court will hand down at least one opinion of lasting historical significance, an opinion that will take its place among the monuments created by such giants as John Marshall, Charles Evans Hughes, and Earl Warren. It was toward the end of the 1973-74 term that the court kept its appointment with destiny when, on July 25, Chief Justice Warren Burger, speaking for a unanimous bench in the case of *United States* v. *Nixon,* directed the president to surrender the tapes of sixty-four White House conversations by date, time, and participants to the grand jury investigating the Watergate cover-up.

President Richard Nixon's lawyers had contended that the taped conversations could not be subpoenaed since such an order would make public confidential conversations between the president and his close advisors, a move that would be inconsistent with the public interest. Technically, the president argued: (1) that the separation of powers precludes judicial review of a president's claim of privilege; and (2) if the chief executive could not be sustained on that ground, the Supreme Court should hold as a matter of constitutional law that executive privilege prevails over a court-issued subpoena. In a carefully reasoned opinion the chief justice rejected both the president's contentions. While conceding that "great deference" must be shown by the courts to the "president's need for complete candor and objectivity from his advisors" in running the government, Burger maintained, nevertheless, that "this presumptive privilege must be considered in light of our historic commitment to the rule of law." While thus recognizing a legitimate area of "executive privilege," the opinion insisted that the courts must have final authority in determining its scope and that "privilege" must yield to the demands of criminal justice. In respectful but firm language the justices offered Nixon the choice of obeying the court or risking certain impeachment and removal from office. Furthermore, they put all future presidents on notice that they are subject to the law like everyone else and that the principle of official confidentiality cannot serve as a cloak to hide evidence relating to a crime. Although for several months President Nixon seemed to be heading inexorably toward a personal and public demise, it was the Supreme Court with its clear and unequivocal logic that terminated his presidency and firmly affixed to the American Constitution the standard that presidents, like all citizens, are subject to the rule of law. It was clear to even the most casual observers that the American system, under conditions of extreme duress, was amazingly stable. The decision also emphasized the principle that Supreme Court justices responsibly maintain a clear loyalty to the Constitution which transcends any obligation to the president who appoints them. The opinion was unanimous, and four of the eight participating justices, including the chief, had been appointed by Nixon. (Justice William H. Rehnquist had disqualified himself in this case because of his service in the Department of Justice during Nixon's presidency.)

Freedom of Speech. While the executive privilege case dramatically pinpointed the Supreme Court's indispensable role as the balance wheel in a complex system based on written rules that apply to those who govern, most of the court's work, while dealing with matters of less vital public concern, continued in general to validate the same principle. In three separate cases involving city and state ordinances dealing with disorderly conduct and abusive language, the court upheld the individual's claim under the First Amendment. In *Lewis* v. *New Orleans* Mollie Lewis had been arrested and convicted for violating a New Orleans ordinance making it unlawful to curse or use obscene language toward a policeman who was performing his official duties. A majority of the court, in an opinion by Justice Brennan, reversed Mrs. Lewis's conviction, declaring that the ordinance as construed by the Louisiana courts was susceptible of application to protected speech and was, therefore, overbroad and unconstitutional under the First and Fourteenth Amendments.

Another case involved Edward Norwell who protested verbally when a policeman questioned his presence on a Cincinnati street at night and arrested him for being "loud and boisterous" and for "annoying" the officer. Norwell was convicted of violating the city's disorderly conduct ordinance, but the Supreme Court unanimously overturned his conviction, maintaining that Norwell's constitutionally protected right of free speech had been abridged since he had been arrested for verbally protesting the officer's treatment of him. *(Norwell* v. *Cincinnati.)* In a third case, *Hess* v. *Indiana*, the court reversed the conviction of Gregory Hess who was jailed for disorderly conduct, based on his statement during an antiwar demonstration on the Indiana University campus. While standing at the side of a street being cleared by the sheriff, Hess said: "We'll take to the (obscenity deleted) street later." A majority of the court held that Hess's words could not be punished as being "obscene," as "fighting words," as a public nuisance, or even as words likely to produce violence. They were at best, said the court, counsel for moderation, and at worst, nothing more than advocacy of illegal action at some indefinite future time.

Freedom of Religion. An interesting case was decided under the freedom-of-religion clause of the First Amendment in *Johnson* v. *Robison.* William Robison, a conscientious objector who had completed two years of alternative civilian service, was denied educational benefits under the Veterans Readjustment Act of 1966. Rejecting Robison's claim that the law denied him his right of free exercise of religion, the court argued that the withholding of educational benefits was at most an incidental burden on Robison's religious freedom and that conscientious objectors were excluded not because of any legislative intent to interfere with religious freedom but because inclusion of such conscientious objectors would not rationally promote the law's purpose, namely, to aid servicemen in readjusting to civilian life.

Criminal Procedure. Dealing with appeals of persons accused of a crime continued to occupy a large part of the court's time during the term. In two cases involving the right to counsel, the court was willing to extend an old doctrine in one, but was ready to call a halt in the other. In *Berry* v. *Cincinnati* the court held unanimously that persons convicted of misdemeanors without a lawyer prior to a decision in 1972, when the right to a counsel had been extended to lesser crimes, were entitled to have their convictions reversed. At the same time the court refused to extend the rule of *Douglas* v. *California* (1963) which requires the appointment of counsel for indigent defendants for the first appeal from a conviction. In *Ross* v. *Moffit* Justice Rehnquist for a majority of six declared that a state need not appoint counsel for a discretionary appeal to the state's highest court nor to the U.S. Supreme Court. The dissenters, led by Justice William O. Douglas, maintained that the poor should have precisely the same access to appeals as the rich, but the majority replied that the Fourteenth Amendment does not demand absolute equality or precisely equal advantages and does not require the state to equalize economic conditions. In three cases in which unreasonable searches and seizures were alleged, a majority of the court upheld the police. In *United States* v. *Edwards* the defendant was lawfully arrested and jailed late one evening. His clothing, which was removed and searched the next day, revealed paint chips that matched those on the window sill of a U.S. post office where Edwards had allegedly attempted illegal entry Edwards contended that his clothing could not have been searched without a warrant. Not so, said Justice Byron White, for warrantless searches may be made incidental to arrest, and the fact that the clothing was not searched at the moment of Edward's arrest was a technicality without substance.

In *United States* v. *Matlock* law enforcement officers arrested a bank robbery suspect in front of the house in which he lived, and then obtained consent to search the house from a woman who said she shared the same bedroom with the suspect. The officers found $4,995 in cash which was used as evidence to indict Matlock for bank robbery. Over his protest that a search warrant should have been obtained, the court held that a search is permissible when voluntary consent is given either by the defendant or by a third party who possesses common authority over, or sufficient relationship to, the premises or effects sought to be inspected.

In this day of widespread drug abuse, it was inevitable that the court deal with the search of persons who were initially arrested for traffic violations but were then found to possess narcotics. It did so in the companion cases of *United States* v. *Robinson* and *Gustafson* v. *Florida.* In both instances a majority of the court held that a full search of a person who has been lawfully arrested is "reasonable" under the Fourth Amendment even though the arresting officer has no suspicion that the arrestee is armed or dangerous. One suspects that as recently as five years ago these cases might have been decided the other way. Whether this is due to a change only in personnel or a change in the times will be debated for years to come.

Indicative of the decline in social standards even in courtroom demeanor is the case of *Eaton* v. *Tulsa* in which Terry Eaton was convicted on a charge of criminal contempt for referring to his alleged assailant during cross examination as "chicken shit." In a *per curiam* opinion the court held that since the expletive was not directed at the judge, it could not validly support a conviction for criminal contempt. Justice Lewis F. Powell, in a concurrence, observed that "language likely to offend the sensibilities of some listeners is now fairly commonplace in many social gatherings as well as in public performances."

Prisoners' Rights. As more and more inmates of penal institutions have been given a greater degree of freedom, the court has faced the necessity of determining the nature of prisoners' rights. Four such cases appeared on the docket during the past year. In one, *Procunier* v. *Martinez,* the court decided that prisoners' personal mail might not be censored unless the regulation furthered a substantial governmental interest unrelated to the suppression of expression. In this instance a California law was held to be too vague and therefore invalid. In a second part to the case the court struck down a prison regulation which prohibited law students and legal paraprofessionals from conducting attorney-client interviews on the ground that it was an unjustifiable restriction on the prisoners' rights of access to the courts. At the same time in *Pell* v. *Procunier and Sable* v. *Washington Post,* the court upheld regulations banning face-to-face interviews between news media representatives and individual inmates on the premise that neither party suffered a loss of freedom of speech. And in *Richardson* v. *Ramirez* the court upheld a California law which denied the right to vote to convicted felons who had completed their sentences. Speaking through Justice Rehnquist, the majority of six maintained that the language of the Fourteenth Amendment which reduced a state's representation in Congress for denying its citizens the right to vote "except for participation in rebellion or other crime" clearly permits states to disenfranchise persons who have committed crimes, the "equal protection" clause being inapplicable to those stated exceptions.

Equal Protection of the Laws. For some fifteen years after the *Brown* decision in 1954 the bulk of cases alleging a denial of equal protection under the Fourteenth Amendment arose as a result of alleged racial discrimination, but for the past five years only peripheral questions relating to the race issue have reached the court. The latest controversy—busing to achieve racial integration—was decided by the court on the final day (July 25) before adjourning for the term. In *Milliken* v. *Bradley* the Supreme Court struck down Detroit's city-to-suburb school busing plan in a 5-4 decision. The majority held that city school busing must be confined to its own geographical boundary unless suburban communities are found to have practiced segregated education. The Detroit busing plan, which would have merged the central city with fifty-three school districts over a 700-square-mile area involving busing 300,000 children, was rejected on the narrow ground that no judicial finding had been made of segregation violations by the outlying communities. Such being the case they need not be forced into a cross-busing plan. In dissent Justice Thurgood Marshall observed that the nation will be "ill-served by the court's refusal to remedy separate and unequal education, for unless our children begin to learn together, there is little hope that our people will ever learn to live together."

In a significant nonracial equal protection case, the court ruled in favor of the individual. In *Memorial Hospital* v. *Maricopa County* the court declared unconstitutional an Arizona law requiring a year's residence in an Arizona county as a condition to an indigent's receiving medical care at the county's expense. As phrased by Justice Marshall the requirement operates to penalize indigents and is in violation of "equal protection of the laws" since it creates an "invidious classification" that impinges on interstate travel by denying newcomers "basic necessities of life."

Probably the most publicized "equal protection" case was *DeFunis* v. *Odegaard* which challenged the concept of preferential treatment for applicants to law school from minority groups. The litigation ended in a whimper as the court dismissed the case without reaching the merits. DeFunis, although denied admission by the University of Washington Law School, had been admitted under a lower court order, and by the time the issue had reached the Supreme Court he was about to graduate. The court thus held the case to be moot (no issue to be resolved). But others in DeFunis's predicament were already standing in the court's anteroom. The issue will most certainly be on the court's docket again.

Two additional decisions of permanent significance were those handed down in *Cleveland Board of Education* v. *LaFleur and Cohn* v. *Chesterfield County School Board*. In both cases pregnant school teachers brought actions challenging the constitutionality of mandatory maternity-leave rules of Cleveland, Ohio, which required pregnant teachers to take unpaid maternity leave five months before the expected childbirth. Eligibility to return to work was not accorded until the child had reached the age of three months. Both rules were held to deny due process in that the law creates an arbitrary presumption that every teacher who is five months pregnant is incapable of returning to school and that every mother is not fit to resume work until three months have elapsed following childbirth.

The Court and Democracy. There is little doubt that the Supreme Court continues to be inseparably linked to the fate of our democratic system of representative government. As Justice Robert Houghwout Jackson once said: "Judicial functions, as we have evolved them, can be discharged only in that kind of society which is willing to submit its conflicts to adjudication and to subordinate power to reason." With all the confusion and disharmony in the nation, the court continues to exercise an authoritative and stabilizing function as it brings reason to bear on society's most pressing emotional challenges.

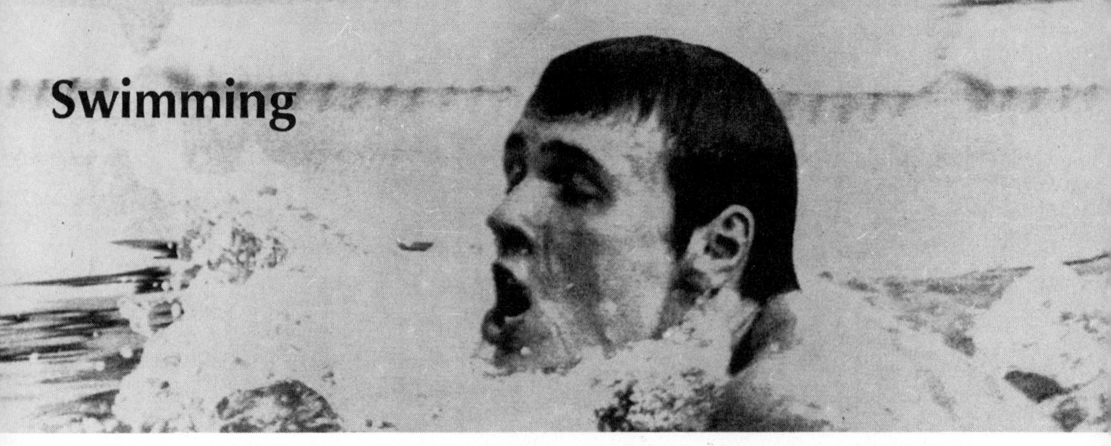

HUNGARY'S ANDRAS HARGITAY sets a new world record by winning the 400-meter individual medley in 4:28.89 at the European swimming championships in Vienna, Austria, on August 20.

by
ART DUNN

Editor, Sunday Sports Section
Chicago Tribune

U.S.-East German Meet. The confrontation between the sport's two major powers over the Labor Day weekend in Concord, Calif., created the biggest splash of 1974.

The visitors were coming off an impressive victory in the European Championships but the American team, paced by John Naber, Tim Shaw, and Shirley Babashoff, dunked the East Germans 198-145. In a record-shattering two-day meet, seven world standards were broken (four by U.S. swimmers) and two more were tied.

The Men's Competition produced four world records, five American records, one East German, and one European record.

Shaw and Naber — both Californians —were the stars for the U.S. men, who won all fifteen events for a 119-61 triumph. Shaw, just sixteen years old, from Long Beach, Calif., set three world freestyle records a week earlier in the National AAU Long Course Championships.

He could not eclipse those marks against the Germans, but did swim well enough to win his specialties—the 200-, 400-, and 1500-meter freestyles.

Naber, eighteen, bested world recordholder Roland Matthes twice in backstroke events and once in the 400 medley relay. Naber did not take away any of Matthes's world records, but he handed the twenty-five-year-old European his first losses in seven years.

The first came in the 200-meter, which Naber led throughout and won impressively 2:02.8 to 2:05.3, good enough for an American record. The next day he caught the six foot, four, Matthes at the finish to win the 100-meter backstroke by less than a quarter of a second.

The Girls authored even more records than their male counterparts, breaking four world marks and equaling another. The East Germans won ten of the fourteen events to edge the Americans 84-79.

Miss Babashoff, a tall, seventeen-year-old blonde from Mission Viejo, Calif., won the 200- (tying her own world record), 400-, and 800-meter freestyles and swam the winning leg of the 400-meter freestyle relay in world record time.

The top performer for the East German girls was Ulrike Tauber, who accounted for fourteen points with two wins, a second place, and a fourth. She set no world records, though she already had two to her credit.

The Americans also won the diving portion of the meet, 24-20.

Television and Radio

Parent Pressure. Definite improvement in television programing for children is the result of pressure brought on the networks by parent groups. Chief among these is Action for Children's Television (ACT) which has worked zealously for years in this cause. The time devoted to commercials — once nearly a quarter of every hour of entertainment — has been reduced this year from twelve to ten minutes an hour, without, it is reported, any decrease in profits for the advertisers. Qualitatively also there have been gains: fewer episodes of violence; replacement of animated figures and cartoons to some extent by live actors; and some quite good Saturday morning features to compete with the pace-setting Public Broadcasting programs. ACT continues its campaign against advertisements for expensive and unsafe toys, sweets, nonnutritious snacks, vitamins, and drugs.

Congress has alerted the FCC to the need to protect children from violence and obscenity on television. The agency cannot enforce standards or censor, but it can withhold licenses. A program-rating system similar to that adopted by the motion-picture industry has been suggested. Such a system would warn parents of programs unsuitable for the young, as Public Broadcasting now does.

Another generation of children reared by television is reaching young adulthood, a generation inclined to cynicism not only about commercials but other material as well.

Tired of the Tube? Television did not hold audiences spellbound in 1974, as it did in 1973, in spite of events of great national import. Watergate was still there in the form of reports of legal actions, interviews with persons involved, and rumors, but the public was weary of bad news. It was also disinclined to listen to the daily fragments of bad news that came from overseas, and foreign news coverage became sketchier. Talk shows continued to soothe people into the notion that problems could and would be solved.

Luring Them Back. One successful attempt to lure people back to radio, at least for fifty-two minutes every night, was made by CBS with its Radio Mystery Theater, "Adventures in the Macabre," a show which often features talented actors. It is now in its second year. Designed for young adults, its Gothic tales, Edgar Allan Poe stories, and old-time melodrama are punctuated by chilling screams and even more mind-blasting sounds. Other channels were offering science and space thrillers and drama.

Religious Radio. Most of the religious stations — 400 or 500 out of the nation's 8,000 — are in the South and mid-South. On the commercial stations the Gospel messages, exhortations, and hymns are interspersed with advertisements. The noncommercial stations must depend on listeners for support. With too many rock-and-roll stations competing for listeners, one of them in New Jersey has switched to religion and finds the change profitable.

The Lutheran Laymen's League has long been known for high-quality programs, rated as cultural rather than specifically religious. "The Lutheran Hour" is broadcast by 1,100 stations, many of which carry it as a public service.

100 Years Ago: Lawn tennis was introduced to the United States by Mary Ewing Outerbridge who set up the first court on Staten Island, New York.

Else Garnett (Dandy Nicholls), the cowlike wife of Britain's Alf Garnett (Warren Mitchell), is called a "silly old moo" by her husband instead of a "dingbat," the term used by America's Archie.

ARCHIE BUNKER (Carroll O'Connor) demands help in a hurry from the nurse when Edith (Jean Stapleton) and his son-in-law Mike (Bob Reiner) convince him he may have eaten a poisonous mushroom. Like her English counterpart, Else, Edith exhibits flashes of blinding logic and deep reasoning. The son-in-law in all three versions suffers a record amount of insult.

ARCHIE BUNKER:
Bigot and Hero

Not an Everyman, but an Everyslob, he embodies all the most odious prejudices of his nation. Yet he has become the most popular television character in broadcast history. In the United States, as Archie Bunker, a loading platform worker, he is the hero of "All in the Family," a situation comedy in its fifth season that has been solidly integrated into the Saturday-night lifestyle of America. In Great Britain, as the arch-reactionary dustman (garbage collector) Alf Garnett in "Till Death Us Do Part," he is eagerly watched by two out of every three viewers in the United Kingdom. In West Germany, he is Alf Tetzlaff in "One Heart and One Soul," a program which premiered on December 31, 1973, with 14 million viewers and quickly won 35 percent of the country's television audience.

The British script writer Johnny Speight created Alf Garnett, the first of the bigot heroes, in 1964. Producers Norman Lear and Bud Yorkin bought the U.S. rights to "Till Death Us Do Part" in 1970 and gave birth to the all-American bigot Archie Bunker. Wolfgang Menge, creator of the West German version, found that his Alfred Tetzlaff was even debated in the Bundestag and was supposed to have "lost the Social Democratic party so astonishingly many votes" in a 1974 election.

All the shows have certain elements in common: the bigot hero is a radical rightwinger who is against all forms of change. He is set against a daughter and son-in-law representing the younger generation who act as the needle which goads him into outrageous statements and behavior. The situations of each episode are usually ordinary and everyday.

Some critics point out that the Archie Bunker programs preach tolerance by ridiculing intolerance. Research findings released in the fall by Dr. Neil Vidmar of Western Ontario University and Dr. Milton Rokeach of Washington State University indicated, however, that frequent viewers of "All in the Family" were prone to admire and condone Archie Bunker's behavior, and that the program encouraged bigotry by permitting the viewer to defend and legitimize his own prejudices. But the real reason for Bunker's popularity may be that he injects an authentic note in the clichéd world of unreal television.

THE BUNKER FAMILY, German style: left to right, daughter Rita (Hildegard Krekel), wife Else (Elisabeth Wiedemann), son-in-law Michael (Diether Krebs), and father Alfred (Heinz Schubert). The creator of the West German version, Wolfgang Menge, states "whatever Archie Bunker represents in the United States is always taken to be only a strongly conservative minority of Americans, but Alfred is taken to symbolize the German national character, as if he were a fossil from the Hitler era."

BILLIE JEAN KING holds the U.S. Open trophy after defeating Australia's Evonne Goolagong in the finals of the women's singles at Forest Hills, N.Y., on September 9.

Tennis

by
STEVE NIDETZ

Sports Department
Chicago Tribune

The Lovebird Pair. While the lovebird pair of Jimmy Connors and Chris Evert dominated the playing fields, it was politics as usual in the tennis clubhouses of the world.

Connors, the brash twenty-one-year-old lefty from Belleville, Ill., and his fiancée Evert, two years younger, from Fort Lauderdale, Fla., won nearly every major tennis title during the year.

Connors started out by slamming his way to the Australian Open title, while Evonne Goolagong continued her mastery of Evert on grass courts by taking the women's title.

With tennis growing in popularity, after the tournament two companies offered prices of at least $100,000 to the man or woman winning the Grand Slam (Australian, British, French, and U.S. Open titles).

Unlike Evert, Connors had signed a contract to join the fledgling World Team Tennis (WTT), which started in May with all the fanfare of P. T. Barnum in sixteen cities in the United States and Canada.

The league began with much flourish and large contracts, such as those signed by Connors, Billie Jean King, John Newcombe, and Goolagong. But fans found the format confusing and began staying away in droves.

The league, which had been sanctioned by the International Lawn Tennis Federation, also ran into problems when players like Connors and Goolagong tried to play in European tournaments before Wimbledon.

Banned by both the Italian and French Opens (which later led to a $1 million law suit by Connors), both Jimmy and Evonne were deprived of a shot at winning the Grand Slam.

The ban eventually had little effect on Goolagong, since she lost to Kerry Melville in the quarterfinals at the All-England Club (Wimbledon).

But Connors slashed to the finals in the rain-soaked fortnight, meeting Ken Rosewell of Australia in a one-sided final. The thirty-nine-year-old Australian, who had come from behind to upset American Stan Smith in five sets in the semifinals, was no match for Connors and lost 6-1, 6-1, 6-4 in just ninety-three minutes.

Evert added her crown by demolishing Russian Olga Morozova 6-0, 6-4 in less than an hour, and that night, at the Wimbledon Ball, the champions danced the first dance to "The Girl That I Marry."

With most of the other top women stars playing team tennis (King, Goolagong, Rosemary Casals), Evert had the tournament circuit nearly to herself, winning the French, Italian, and U.S. Clay Courts titles on her way to an incredible fifty-six straight match winning streak.

That streak came to an end at Forest Hills, when the pony-tailed beauty found Goolagong too much to handle on grass again, losing 6-0, 6-7, 6-3 in a match which extended over three days due to heavy rains.

Billie Jean. That left the door open for King, labeled "Mother Freedom" for her role as player-coach of the WTT Philadelphia Freedoms.

It had been a difficult year for Billie Jean. She had been upset by Morozova at Wimbledon, and her Freedoms, despite posting a 39-5 record, lost the WTT playoffs to the Denver Broncos in two straight matches.

But all that was forgotten as King played the best match of the U.S. Open before 15,303 fans packed into the stadium at West Side Tennis Club.

King defeated Goolagong 3-6, 6-3, 7-5 in a match filled with breathtaking rallies.

Connors, however, had little trouble dispatching Rosewall again in the men's finals, winning 6-1, 6-0, 6-1 in the most one-sided men's final at Forest Hills in its eighty-three-year history.

That left Connors with three-fourths of a Grand Slam, missing only the French title, denied him by politics. When asked if winning the U.S. title gave him the feeling of being a Grand Slammer, Connors said no. But then he challenged Rod Laver, the Australian who won Grand Slams in 1962 and 1969 and has never met Connors, to a $100,000 winner-take-all match in 1975.

The only major tournament Connors didn't win was the World Championship of Tennis (WCT) in Dallas. But that also was pure politics because Connors and his manager, Bill Riordan, refused to join Lamar Hunt's winter tour and held one of their own under the auspices of the U.S. Lawn Tennis Association.

John Newcombe won the WCT title with a 4-6, 6-3, 6-3, 6-2 win over Swedish teenager Bjorn Borg.

Team Tennis. As for team tennis, while all sixteen teams finished the season, none made money, several announced they were for sale, and the outlook for 1975 was bleak.

Davis Cup. In Davis Cup action, the United States lost its first 1974 match to Colombia when most American stars decided it was more lucrative to stay at home than play for the cup.

The 1974 cup went to South Africa by default when India refused to play the white-supremacist nation. It was a governmental decision.

The U.S. cup prospects for 1975 brightened, however, when several pros decided to make time to play and then went out to defeat Commonwealth Caribbean 5-0 in the first round.

EMILE PUTTEMANS of Belgium sets a new world indoor record of 13:24.6 for the 5,000-meter run in Paris on March 17.

Track and Field

by

ART DUNN

Editor, Sunday Sports Section
Chicago Tribune

Ivory Crockett. "There were so many gathered at 9.1 that even the record was getting crowded. I fixed that."

The speaker was Ivory Crockett moments after he affixed his name to the track and field world record book by running 100 yards in 9 seconds May 11 at Knoxville, Tenn.

Crockett, a twenty-five-year-old computer marketing salesman from Peoria, Ill., averaged 22.73 miles per hour to lower the standard by a tenth of a tick. Seven sprinters had recorded 9.1 clockings, the first being Bob Hayes—now a flanker with the Dallas Cowboys football team — in 1963.

Other Champions. Crockett, rated only number ten sprinter in the world in 1973, was not a factor in this year's National Amateur Athletic Union (AAU) Track and Field Championships. San Diego State's Steve Williams won the 100-meter dash in 9.9 to equal the world record. Crockett was seventh in 10.2.

The sprint star of the U.S.-U.S.S.R. dual meet in Durham, N.C., was Jones. He won the 100 and 200 meters and anchored the 400-meter relay team, as the U.S. men beat the Soviets, 117-102. But Russia's women's team defeated the United States, 90-67, to give the U.S.S.R. its ninth victory against two defeats and a tie in the series.

The second year of the professional International Track Association was dominated by Ben Jipcho of Kenya, thirty-one-year-old middle distance star and 1973's top amateur track performer.

Other World Records. In all, seventeen world records were established in 1974. Rick Wohlhuter of Chicago authored two by running a 1:44.1 over 880 yards and 2:13.9 in the 1,000-meter run. Poland's Irena Szewinska also broke two records — in the 200- and 400-meter dashes.

Jim Ryun's long-standing 1,500-meter record was finally eclipsed by Filbert Bayi of Tanzania, who covered the metric mile in 3:32.2. Two other Americans set world marks—Californian Jim Bolding in the 440-yard hurdles and Julie Brown of Billings, Mont., in the three-mile run.

Boston Marathon. Ireland's Neil Cusack, a twenty-two-year-old East Tennessee State student, ran the third fastest time in the seventy-eight-year history of the event. Running in his second Boston Marathon, Cusack covered the 26-mile, 385-yard course in two hours, 13 minutes, and 39 seconds. The Irishman finished 46 seconds in front of Tom Fleming of the New York Athletic Club.

United Nations

by
JEFF ENDRST
U. N. Reporter for Radio Free Europe and Religious News Service

ABDELAZIZ BOUTEFLIKA, thirty-seven, is the youngest person ever elected president of the U.N. General Assembly. Algeria's foreign minister for the past eleven years, he presides over the twenty-ninth annual session, which has the longest agenda in U.N. history.

A Different Direction. By any past standard, the 1974 debates in the United Nations were quite different in tone, direction, and substance. By the year's end,

UNITED NATIONS

the United States and some West European countries issued thinly veiled warnings that the forebearance of their public and money-appropriating legislatures was not limitless. They complained of "the tyranny of the mechanical majority."

The aggressive tone was set by repercussions of the oil crisis. They hit the General Assembly in April when at a special session the oil-rich countries led a palace revolution in which the "have" nations, still reeling under the impact of quadrupled oil prices, were told that they must also provide billions in emergency funds with which the United Nations would bail out several dozen countries already penniless and suffering from massive starvation.

Led by militant Algeria, the nonaligned bloc received political support from the Communist countries, and the special assembly ended with a Plan of Action seeking to remedy centuries-old economic inequities in a hurry.

The industrialized West said that the "have-nots" would not be helped by cutting off the hands which were supposed to feed them. But the nonaligned Communist coalition held firm, despite the fact that many nervous economic victims of the strategy could only guess at who would come to their aid and when.

Law of the Sea. Later, in Caracas, Venezuela, the U.N. Law of the Sea conference spent ten weeks trying to reconcile the needs of traditional maritime powers with the economic hopes and needs of developing countries. Although the results were inconclusive, it appeared that the big naval and merchant marine powers, in order to secure their right to ply all international waters, grudgingly conceded to the developing countries the principle of a 200-mile economic sea zone if the latter agree to a twelve-mile territorial sea principle.

At this conference, the Communist countries, except China, turned up on the side of the West.

World Population Conference. In Bucharest, Rumania, the first political World Population Conference under U.N. auspices led to another compromise. While it had been called to deal with the prospect that the present population may double by the end of this century, the majority—again dominated by the nonaligned, many of whom suffer the most from overpopulation—forced a decision which in effect said that it is a question not of numbers, but of a just international division of resources and labor.

The Vatican was the only participant which expressly excluded itself from the "consensus" of the conference, although many others said they were not happy with the result. China, which by U.N. accounts has the most people and also the most drastic and effective birth control program, fully sided with the Vatican, saying that given the proper tools, man is "invincible."

The General Assembly Session. This then was the setting for the twenty-ninth regular General Assembly session in New York in September which increased its ranks to 138 by admitting Bangladesh, Grenada, and Guinea-Bissau, and attracted 9 presidents or prime ministers and 108 foreign ministers to offer their views on the state of the world.

President Gerald Ford, in his first major foreign policy statement, came to the Assembly "just for a little straight talk among friends," but promptly invited the oil-producing countries to think about food when they are talking about oil and other natural resources they hope to monopolize.

Secretary of State Henry Kissinger dropped the other shoe in Rome in November at the World Food Conference, organized at his initiative. Speaking in stark terms, he said "the answer is not yet clear" whether interdependence would spur joint progress or common disaster to humanity.

The Soviet Union and its Communist allies argued that this was a matter of social systems, saying that theirs was not responsible for the past and was unaffected by the present.

For the Soviet Union, the key argument was détente and how to extend it to military and economic fields. Foreign Minister Andrei Gromyko, who used to send collective shivers down the spine of the world diplomatic community in past years by his dire warnings of impending doom unless others conformed to the Marxist-Leninist vision of the world, this time delivered a speech full of hope and political sunshine filtered through Moscow's rosy interpretation of an East-West détente.

China quickly labeled détente as "a kind of quack medicine hawked by the Soviet social imperialists." It never deviated from its stated conviction that instead of a balance of power between Washington and Moscow, "each side is desperately trying to out-trick and overwhelm the other, and the wildest arms race is on."

There were intermittent calls for a dialog on the oil crisis, but there was no evidence that the continuing confrontation between those who have oil and those who desperately need it at prices they can afford would ease quickly or considerably.

Feeding the Hungry. U. N. Secretary General Kurt Waldheim issued several urgent appeals to the "industrialized and other donor countries" to come up with the money the special Assembly in April said was urgently needed to prevent disaster in the Indian subcontinent, West Africa, and other regions.

But the projected $5 billion in voluntary contributions was coming in slowly and sometimes in forms which could not feed the hungry. Some of the oil-rich countries pledged relatively modest funds to the U.N. fund, but others preferred to take care of their regional friends first, on a bilateral basis. The Communist countries refused to contribute anything to the United Nations, and refused to tell the United Nations what, if anything, they were doing "over and above" their normal bilateral foreign aid transactions.

The European Economic Community pledged $500 million on condition that others in a position to contribute would do so.

The United States pledged $1 billion —some in food, some in money, some in write-offs of past debts—pending congressional approval.

Thus, in December, a situation developed when U.N. experts concluded that the world's emergency need for 1975 was 7.5 million tons of cereals, and that the food was available. What was lacking was cash translated from political pledges or conditional stipulations.

South Africa. There were several unprecedented developments in the United Nations in 1974. The Assembly first refused to recognize the credentials of the South African delegation which, ironically, for the first time had black representatives in it. It then voted to deny South Africa the right to speak and vote, and recommended expulsion. Only an unprecedented triple veto by France, Britain, and the United States prevented the first ouster of a founding member from the organization.

The Palestine Question. For the first time, the Assembly debated "the question of Palestine" instead of merely Palestine refugees in the Middle East. Against strong opposition from Israel, the United States, and some Western countries, the majority then invited the Palestine Liberation Organization (PLO) to take part in the debate.

The emotional highlight of this event

was the appearance of PLO's leader, Yasir Arafat. Assembly President Abdelaziz Bouteflika of Algeria took it upon himself to accord the man whom Israel blames for countless murders the kind of treatment until then reserved only for heads of state. The bulk of the Assembly, which in the past often criticized international terrorism for which the PLO took credit as "military actions," then gave Arafat a standing ovation.

The Palestinean revolutionary, minus his beard and sunglasses, but with a gun holster—and many swore that there was a gun in it—said he had come with an olive branch in one hand and a gun in the other. He called for a Palestine as it existed in 1947, and promised equality to all Jews now in Israel in a "secular" state governed by political majority.

Israel saw Arafat's remarks as a PLO reaffirmation of its alleged goal to liquidate the Jewish state.

Security around Arafat was the name of the game. It took 1,000 local, state, and federal officers to guard Arafat and his delegation, at a cost of $750,000 to New York taxpayers. Arafat spent a night at the Waldorf-Astoria Hotel. Before he was spirited out of town to pay a visit to Fidel Castro in Havana, the Arabs threw a lavish reception for him at the United Nations at which guests stood up to forty-five minutes in a receiving line to shake Arafat's hand or be kissed by him, Arab style.

Cambodian Representation. Another dramatic highlight was provided by the Assembly's debate on who should represent Cambodia in the United Nations. By a two-vote margin, the Assembly upheld the Lon Nol government in Phnom Penh against the aspirations of Prince Norodom Sihanouk who heads a rebel government from exile in Peking. This time, the nonaligned bloc unity fell apart, perhaps because many of its members have hostile minorities or "liberation movements" of their own.

On Korea, the United States and its allies did not object to an alternative arrangement to the U.N. Command which came into being with the 1950 war, provided a change would not impair the stability on the Korean peninsula. No change was in sight, but some movement from the existing status quo was discernible.

Disarmament. The Soviet Union still did not get its wish to have the U.N. call a world disarmament conference, but some new and startling language crept into the debate for the first time. The Soviets spoke of "fire storms" to affect the ozone layer in the atmosphere so as to create "windows" to allow increased penetration of hard ultraviolet radiation "killing all forms of life and turning land into a dead desert."

The Soviets also mentioned "infrasound" to create acoustic fields on the sea to combat individual ships or whole flotillas. In addition, they said nuclear devices could be used in the Arctic and Antarctic to creat tidal waves, wiping out whole areas.

The United States did not dispute these arguments. Senator Stuart Symington (D., Mo.), who served on the U.S. delegation this year, commended the Soviet warnings for wide coverage and study.

U. N. Buffer Zones. The Cyprus situation found the U.N. peacekeeping force on this Mediterranean island precariously sandwiched between warring Greek and Turkish Cypriots, but despite the Turkish invasion, and President Makarios's temporary exile, the U.N. presence undoubtedly provided calming and moderating influence.

The same was true in the Middle East where U.N. buffer zones separated Israeli troops from the Syrians in the Golan Heights, and from the Egyptians in the Sinai. But Waldheim and the

Arabs warned that political progress must come soon lest there is another Middle East war sometime in 1975.

Portugal became the political darling of the United Nations by voluntarily and with surprising speed and apparent eagerness submitting a decolonization timetable for Mozambique and Angola. There was no mention of Macao, since China feels that this tiny Portuguese colony on the mainland is none of the United Nations' business.

Human Rights. The Assembly continued to be preoccupied with the reported human rights violations in Chile. It also made an appeal for clemency for those in Ethiopia not yet executed but still in trouble with the new military government.

Other Actions. After intermittent efforts which started in the 1930s in the League of Nations, the Assembly came up with a definition of aggression, in the hope that this might give potential violators of international law a pause.

There were continuing but inconclusive efforts to revise the U.N. Charter to give a better break to countries which had had nothing to do with its language in 1945 when U.N. membership stood at fifty-one. Resistance came mainly from the veto-vested nuclear powers, except China, who argued that the charter was all right, but its implementation was deficient on the part of many.

Australia started a movement which would institutionalize the Latin American tradition of granting free passage out of a country once a foreign embassy in that country grants political asylum to a local dissident.

China carried its anti-Nationalist fight in the United Nations to a successful conclusion by prevailing upon Waldheim to remove from an Assembly hall a marble slab with Confucian quotations. Peking then sent a huge "Great Wall' tapestry and an ivory carving, symbolizing the ancient and the new in China. The legal status and future ownership of the Confucian plaque, under the "one-China" U.N. formula, remains undecided.

YASIR ARAFAT, head of the Palestine Liberation Organization (PLO), speaks to the U.N. General Assembly on November 13.

U Thant. Finally, the third U.N. secretary general, U Thant of Burma, died of cancer in New York retirement and became the first to lie in state on the U.N. grounds before his remains were flown to Burma for a burial which was as controversial as his ten-year stewardship of the world organization in the turbulent waters of international politics.

A FISHERMAN casts his net in the Mekong Delta of South Vietnam, a rice-rich area that has been the main target for land ownership reform by the South Vietnamese government. Over 2.5 million acres have been given to farmers since 1970 in a program financed mainly by U.S. aid, but plantation overlords began to reclaim their former holdings in secure areas in 1974.

by
KENNETH P. LANDON, Ph.D.

Professor of Southeast Asian Studies, American University
Contributor, *The Politics of Opium* (1974) and *The Sino-American Detente and its Implications* (1974)

Conflict. The atmosphere in South Vietnam throughout 1974 was one of conflict. President Nguyen Van Thieu called on his troops on January 4 to attack the Vietcong in their own territory because "The Vietnam war had begun again." President Thieu was recognizing the high capability of Communist forces to mount major drives even though minor engagements were the usual pattern of conflict.

January 27 marked the first anniversary of the agreement that "A cease-fire shall be observed throughout South Vietnam as of 2400 hours Greenwich mean time (GMT) on January 27, 1973 . . . The parties undertake to maintain the cease-fire and to ensure a lasting and stable peace." During the year the two sides continued relentlessly to pursue their strategies for victory, gnawing away at one another in every phase of the life process. The two sides charged one another with more than 335,000 cease-fire violations.

Statistics. The potential for large-scale military conflict was reflected in the statistics, unreliable except for general magnitudes, of the two sides. The Vietcong or Provisional Revolutionary Government (PRG) was supposed to have about 40,000 political cadres working with their fighting force of 38,000 guerrillas. Their major strength lay in the 170,000 North Vietnamese combat forces supported by 70,000 logistics personnel composing seventeen North Vietnamese infantry divisions located in four military regions.

Opposing them were the Saigon armed forces with thirteen divisions; forty Ranger battalions; some 18,000 aircraft, of which 480 were fighter-bombers; plus a navy. If full-scale conflict erupted it was probable that the Communists could dominate regions in the North and in the highlands while Saigon could control the heavily populated areas around Saigon and in the delta. It was a standoff which did not encourage a major move by either side. The casualties mounted, nevertheless, and by December Saigon listed 13,700 troops killed in action during the year. This did not include civilian casualties.

U. S. Aid. President Thieu used the atmosphere of conflict to put pressure on the United States to increase the magnitudes of economic and military aid. As early as January 6 the Nixon administration asked Congress for increased arms aid for the fiscal year ending June 30. Disputes over the magnitudes of aid simmered throughout the year with considerable acrimony surfacing when Ambassador Graham Martin crossed wires with Senator Edward Kennedy. Eventually on December 5 an aid package was approved by the Senate amounting to $2.7 billion of which $1.27 billion was earmarked for South Vietnam for all forms of aid. In the context of Indochina, Cambodia was granted $377 million and Laos $70 million. These magnitudes were about half of the amounts requested.

People Control. The social aspect of the conflict was reflected by the movement of refugees back into areas previously devastated by war. Thus in January an additional 150,000 peasants were encouraged to return to the Quantri area, a fifteen-mile-wide strip between the mountains and the sea controlled by government forces. The area was scarred and empty after the 1972 Communist spring offensive. During late 1973 about 80,000 had already drifted back.

The conflict for control of people was more vital than the conflict for land. The North Vietnamese and PRG controlled the hinterlands while Saigon controlled the lowlands and most of the people. The PRG estimated that it controlled about 12 percent of the population out of a total of about 19.6 million, or about 2.3 million. The PRG had serious manpower problems which caused great difficulty in developing the economy and which made it hard to attract people to its zones of influence. The North sent down as many as 40,000 new settlers to help fill in the central highlands and the areas near the Cambodian border. An additional problem for the PRG was that it had no identifiable capital to which it could attract foreign diplomats from those states that recognized it.

In the rice-rich Mekong delta area Thieu's land reform program which had begun in 1970 as a political effort to woo peasants from the Communists continued to be generally successful. Some 2.5 mil-

THE CEASE-FIRE WAR keeps South Vietnamese troops on the move. From April through August the South Vietnamese government reported an average of 1,313 soldiers killed each month. This photograph by Paul J. Harrington won the features first prize in the Military Pictures of the Year competition.

lion acres had been transferred in ownership from landlords to peasants, relieving the peasants of onerous rents that had amounted to a third of their crop.

Thieu never lost sight of his own political fortunes and had his supporters in the National Assembly submit a draft amendment to the constitution on January 15 that would enable him to run for a third term and would extend the length of the term from four years to five. On January 19 when the amendment came to a vote the legislature erupted in chair-throwing chaos. Four opposition leaders shaved their heads in protest. Both Catholic and Buddhist opposition elements were poorly organized, and the amendment was approved by a two-thirds majority.

Paracel and Spratly Islands. The year also opened with conflict with China over the Paracel and Spratly islands. On January 11 the People's Republic of China charged that South Vietnam in "a brazen announcement" had put "more than ten islands of China's Nansha Islands" under its administration, Nansha being the Chinese name for the Spratly Islands lying about 350 miles southeast of Saigon. Peking claimed that these and the Hsisha or Paracel Islands "have always been China's territory."

Perhaps the oil potential of these islands triggered the dispute, as the Saigon government had an arrangement with Exxon, Shell, Mobil, and others to search offshore for oil. If the oil companies were successful then Thieu would have won the double prize of oil revenues and another and firm basis for continuing American involvement in his affairs.

Saigon accused Peking of violating South Vietnamese sovereignty by landing Chinese nationals on three of the Paracel islands about 200 miles east of Saigon and about 175 miles from China. Vietnam's claim stemmed from a landing on the islands in 1802 when Emperor Gia Long sent an expedition in search of guano and swallow's nests to make soup. France administered the islands from 1881 until 1939 when the Japanese took them over. The islands were recognized as China's territory in the 1951 peace treaty signed with Japan at San Francisco. But the South Vietnamese claimed that Vietnam had recovered the sovereignty of the islands after Japan surrendered.

By January 18 Saigon had eleven naval vessels in the Paracel area and a landing party tore down the Chinese flag. Chinese gunboats then engaged the Vietnamese and sank one vessel. During a meeting of the Joint Saigon/PRG Military Commission, the Saigon officials proposed that the PRG and Hanoi join in a stand against Chinese occupation of the Paracels. The PRG and Hanoi deferred taking a position on the issue. By the end of the year China had dug in on the Paracels and an archaeological team had unearthed ninety-five pieces of ancient Chinese porcelain, a half ton of copper coins, and four stone tablets, the artifacts dating back to the Tang and Sung dynasties of the tenth to thirteenth centuries.

North Vietnam's Strategy for the year was delineated by the first meeting in fourteen years of the Lao-Dong (Workers) party in February which adopted economic plans for 1974 and 1975 and drafted a five-year plan for 1976-1980. It was considered imperative that North Vietnam develop industry and agriculture to provide the needs of the state. In the spirit of this economic strategy the North Vietnamese trade union federation opened its third congress with twenty-two foreign delegations, including one from the World Federation of Trade Unions and two from India. Other non-Communist states attending included Egypt, France, Italy, Iraq, Japan, Morocco, Syria, and a Palestinian delegation. Curiously, China did not attend, although Albania did. China was displeased that Hanoi had not supported her in the Paracel Islands dispute with Saigon.

Le Duan, head of the Lao-Dong party, told the delegates that there must be "priority national development of heavy industry on the basis of the development of light industry and agriculture."

South Vietnam Reaction. Thieu seemed to react to the new Hanoi strategy by renovating his cabinet in a sweep that exceeded any reorganization since 1969, ousting many officials accused of corruption. He then asserted that South Vietnam's most urgent problem was economic development.

The Political Settlement Meetings. The weekly meetings outside Paris between representatives of the South Vietnamese government and the PRG in an effort to work out a political settlement had been a dialog of the deaf for forty-five sessions. Then on March 22 the PRG handed the Saigon representative a six-point plan that proposed a new cease-fire, the immediate creation of a council of national reconciliation and concord, and the holding of general elections. Saigon dubbed the proposal another item in endless propaganda and ironically proposed April 19 as the deadline for the establishment of the council and July 20 as general election day, *but* there must first be a discussion of specific matters relating to an overall political and military arrangement.

At that point the North seized a South Vietnam ranger base at Tong Le Chan, and the South Vietnamese representative in Paris broke off further discussions. Thieu also ended the diplomatic privileges of the PRG military representatives located near Saigon, stopped their press conferences, and cut their telephone lines.

Elections. President Thieu made another move in political warfare by holding nationwide provincial and city council elections on July 14. At stake were some 478 seats in local consultative councils in forty-four provinces and eleven autonomous cities. Thieu supporters won 315 of the 478 contested seats enabling him to dispose of dubious military and civilian persons in his Dan Chu (Democratic) political party and so strengthen his own base against his critics.

THE BABYSITTER **by Michael S. Tomczyk won first prize for portrait/personality in the Military Pictures of the Year. The United States allotted $7.2 million in fiscal 1974 to help Vietnamese children orphaned, abandoned, or made destitute by the Vietnam war.**

Nixon's Resignation. The resignation of President Richard Nixon on August 9 made the political and military atmosphere in South Vietnam murky, causing Thieu and his supporters to grope for new guidelines and providing new opportunity for Thieu's critics to act under cover of the gloom. Thieu was uncertain what he could anticipate from President Gerald Ford. President Ford reassured Thieu on September 12 when he appealed personally to congressional leaders to restore the millions of dollars cut from the foreign aid request.

Opposition Movements in South Vietnam. The major problem for Thieu became the increasing boldness of his non-Communist opponents. They sensed that Thieu dared not use violence or imprison them because of the possible adverse reaction of the American press and Congress. The various groups began cautiously in September to demonstrate against Thieu; they accused his administration of corruption, of not dealing with urgent economic problems, and of not carrying out the political provisions of the Paris Agreements looking toward a national council of reconciliation and general elections.

There was more talk about a third force which was provided for in Article 12A of the Paris Agreements: "Immediately after the cease-fire, the two South Vietnamese parties shall hold consultations in a spirit of national reconciliation and concord, mutual respect, and mutual nonelimination to set up a national council of national reconciliation and concord of three equal segments."

Three opposition movements emerged which were reminiscent of the rising surge of 1963 against President Ngo Dinh Diem. The most powerful was the National Reconciliation Force (NRF) backed by the An Quang militant Buddhist church in which some of the same personalities surfaced who had opposed Diem. This movement was triggered by the Catholic Anti-Corruption and Peace Building Committee which was followed by the forming of the Committee for Freedom of the Press.

Both Buddhist and Catholic militants gravitated toward retired General Duong Van Minh ("Big Minh") who had been active in the overthrow of Diem in 1963. On September 20 the opposition groups marched through the streets of Saigon in their first joint public action. The police stood by and did not interfere under orders from Thieu. Other demonstrations followed with rising tempo.

On October 1 Thieu answered his critics in a two-hour television address in which he promised to ease restrictions on the press, to liberalize the requirements for forming political parties, and to resign if "the entire people and army no longer have confidence in me."

The eleven members of the ruling council of An Quang Buddhists continued to escalate their pressure against Thieu, urging him to make significant steps toward peace or resign. Said the venerable Quang Do, one of the eleven leaders, "We have publicly asked General Thieu to resign voluntarily if he feels he is standing in the way of peace and national reconciliation. If he is not willing to go, then he will be pulled down." The problem for the opposition, however, was that they supported no person of prominence to replace Thieu.

Appeasement Moves. Thieu attempted to appease his critics by forcing ten cabinet ministers to resign, by sacking 377 middle-ranking military officers, and by shifting three of the four regional military corps commanders to lesser posts, all having been accused of graft and corruption. On November 1, National Day, Thieu made a plea for support of his newly sanitized administration. But the opposition was not mollified and so, after the U. S. Senate had approved the American aid level at $1.27 billion for the coming year, Thieu ordered his police onto the streets. The shouts of the opposition diminished to mutters for the time being. Thieu could not appease his opposition by any move less than a declaration that he would not run for a third term in office.

JUDGE JOHN SIRICA charges the jury, upper left, in the Watergate cover-up case on December 30. Listening to the judge, lower left, are the five defendants: front row, John Mitchell, Robert Mardian, and John Ehrlichman; rear row, Kenneth Parkinson and H. R. Haldeman.

Watergate

by
ROBERT J. STEAMER

Dean, College II
University of Massachusetts

The Fatal Error. At noon on August 9, Richard Milhous Nixon, the thirty-seventh president of the United States, resigned from the nation's highest office, the first president to do so in the two-century history of the republic. The inexorable march of events that eventually toppled the chief executive began on June 17, 1972, when a private security guard in Washington's Watergate apartment hotel noticed a door with its lock taped open and called the police. They caught and arrested five men who were burglarizing the headquarters of the Democratic National Committee. Reporting the story the next day, the *Washington Post* noted that there was no apparent reason why the suspects had broken into offices of the Democratic National Committee, nor had there been any indication that they were working for anyone else. But even as the president's press secretary, Ronald L. Ziegler, described the affair as a "third rate burglary," the president, and those closest to him, knew all too well the meaning of the Watergate complex burglary.

Ironically Richard Nixon on June 17, 1972, had never been more successful politically. He had made a historic visit to China; he had met with the top Soviet leaders in Moscow and had returned home with the possibility of a permanent thaw in the cold war; he was bringing to a close the most divisive war in the nation's history. The Democratic convention was to open in less than a month, and pressures were building for the nomination of Senator George McGovern of South Dakota, a man considered by most professionals to be the weakest of all possible Nixon opponents. The pollsters were indicating with some consistency that Nixon was a certainty for a second term, standing no less than 19 percentage points ahead of all announced candidates. On November 7, 1972, Richard Nixon defeated Senator McGovern in an unprecedented landslide, carrying every state in the union but Massachusetts; and Watergate seemed destined for historical oblivion, to receive at most an insignificant footnote as future historians chronicled Nixon's record of successful presidential leadership. But that scenario was not to be, for Nixon committed a fatal error, an unforgivable sin. He publicly lied to the American people about his involvement in a criminal act. Such a defect in character in the nation's highest official was intolerable. Other presidents and their administrations had not been untouched by corruption, but no previous president had been personally involved in criminal activity nor had any, to Nixon's extent, assumed that the president was above the law and essentially untouchable by legal processes.

Origins. Watergate had its origins in January, 1972, when Attorney General John Mitchell, presidential counsel John Dean, and acting director of the Committee for the Reelection of the President (CRP) Jeb Stuart Magruder listened to G. Gordon Liddy, general counsel to the CRP, propose a million-dollar intelligence plan to help defeat the Democrats; a plan which included, in addition to electronic surveillance, such bizarre proposals as abduction of radical leaders, muggings, and the use of call girls to elicit information from leading Democrats. Although rejecting this plan, Mitchell, at a subsequent meeting, according to Magruder, set into motion a $250,000 intelligence-gathering operation. Checks amounting to $89,000, obtained from illegal corporate contributions to Nixon's campaign, were "laundered" through a Mexican bank, sent to one Bernard L. Barker who deposited them in a bank in Miami along with another $25,000 check given to the CRP by Kenneth Dahlberg, Republican finance chairman in the Midwest. It was Barker, fellow Cuban refugees Eugenio Martinez and Virgilio Gonzales, and Frank Sturgis, who, along with James McCord, security chief for CRP, were caught on June 17.

The operation had been engineered by G. Gordon Liddy, former White House aide and one time Federal Bureau of Investigation (FBI) agent, and by previous Central Intelligence Agency (CIA) operative, E. Howard Hunt, Jr. As it turned out, the Democratic National Committee headquarters had been broken into by the same group on May 27 when McCord had placed wire taps on the telephones of Democratic party officials Lawrence O'Brien and R. Spencer Oliver, Jr. Transcripts of telephone conversations were passed to Magruder and to Mitchell, the latter—according to Magruder's testimony—having then ordered Liddy to get better information.

The official cover-up of the affair appears to have begun on June 20 when John Dean, White House counsel, perused the documents in Hunt's safe and discovered files detailing the activities of the White House "plumbers," a unit established in mid-1971 to stop security leaks and to investigate sensitive security matters. Among other things Dean found that the office of Dr. Lewis Fielding, Daniel Ellsberg's psychiatrist, had been burglarized on September 13, 1971, in an attempt to get confidential data for use against Ellsberg, the chief defendant in the Pentagon papers case. Later Jeb Magruder declared that the cover-up was "immediate and automatic," and that no one had ever considered that "there would not be a cover-up."

Nixon, however, maintained that he knew nothing about the break-in. On August 29, almost two months after the burglary, he told a news conference: "I can say categorically . . . that no one on the White House staff, no one in this administration presently employed, was involved in this very bizarre incident."

1973. During 1973 three significant events occurred which, when pieced together, sealed the president's doom. First, during the trial of the original seven Watergate conspirators (Liddy, Hunt, Barker, Martinez, Gonzales, Sturgis, and McCord) which began in January, Federal District Court Judge John J. Sirica revealed that McCord had written him a letter charging that the break-in defendants were under political pressure to plead guilty and remain silent, that perjury had been committed, and that high officials in the administration were involved. It later became known that during the period immediately following the break-in the president had held several meetings with White House assistants John Dean, H. R. Haldeman, John Ehrlichman, and former Attorney General John Mitchell, in which Watergate was under continuous discussion. On April 6, John Dean began talking with Watergate prosecutors about his role in the cover-up. Although asked to resign by the president, he refused to leave unless Haldeman and Ehrlichman also resigned. Dean made his point, and on April 30 the president in a nationally televised address announced the resignations of all three—as well as that of Attorney General Richard Kleindienst.

A second crucial event was the investigation of Watergate by a select Senate committee chaired by Senator Sam J. Ervin, Jr., of North Carolina. From the initial hearing on May 7 the committee listened for several months to a parade of administration officials, high and low, including John Dean, testify in exhaustive detail. Dean not only confessed to his own participation in the cover-up, but accused Nixon, Mitchell, Haldeman, and Ehrlichman of knowing involvement. All denied the charges. Probably the most damaging testimony, made in an almost inadvertent, offhand way, was that of former White House aide Alexander Butterfield, who revealed that President Nixon secretly taped his own conversations. Almost immediately Senator Ervin requested the president to make key tapes available to the committee, and Archibald Cox, whom Nixon had appointed as special prosecutor for the Watergate affair, similarly asked that the recorded conversations be turned over to the grand jury inquiring into the matter.

This led to the third event, the firing of the special prosecutor. The president rejected demands for taped conversations on the ground of executive privilege, but Cox and Ervin issued subpoenas which resulted in an order of Judge Sirica, confirmed by the court of appeals, that Nixon turn over the tapes of several conversations subpoenaed by Cox. The president then attempted to effect a compromise in which he would summarize the taped conversations, but Cox refused, thus setting the stage for the "Saturday-Night Massacre."

On Saturday, October 20, Mr. Nixon ordered Attorney General Elliot Richardson to fire Cox and abolish the office of special prosecutor. Rather than obey that order, Richardson, along with Deputy Attorney General William D. Ruckelshaus, resigned. Solicitor General Robert H. Bork was made acting attorney general and carried out the president's wishes. Sustained protest followed these events, including demands from such diverse journals as *Time* and *The National Review,* as well as from the *New York Times,* that the president resign. Before the year was out, Nixon attempted to mend his fences by appointing a new attorney general, William Saxbe of Ohio, and a new special Watergate prosecutor, Leon Jaworski, a prominent Houston attorney. He also agreed to yield certain tapes and documents to Judge Sirica; but, even then, evasiveness and duplicity rather than candor characterized the president's moves. He maintained that two of the subpoenaed tapes did not exist, and one of those which he had turned over to Sirica contained an eighteen-and-a-half-minute buzz obliterating a crucial discussion between Haldeman and the president. Electronics experts reported that the gap was the result of at least five separate erasures. Meanwhile, criminal proceedings were under way against former White House officials John Dean, Egil Krogh, Jr., Dwight Chapin, and Nixon campaign coordinator Jeb Stuart Magruder.

SENATOR SAM ERVIN of North Carolina listens to Watergate testimony.

1974. Simultaneously, the Congress and the nation's courts moved toward the climax of Watergate, a drama that had been playing to a national audience for more than two years. As 1974 opened, Nixon named a Boston trial lawyer, James D. St. Clair, to head his legal defense, a move which emphasized the president's awareness of his deteriorating position. In February the House of Representatives, with only four dissenting votes, authorized the Judiciary Committee to inquire into the possibility of recommending the president's removal from office. In another office in Washington, Special Prosecutor Jaworski was arguing that the president had not turned over to him all the taped conversations he had requested, and moved to subpoena some sixty-four presidential talks with Dean, Ehrlichman, and Haldeman. Nixon's reaction was to announce that he would make public edited transcripts of his recorded conversations, and he released a 1,308-page document comprising the edited tapes. Jaworski, however, was not satisfied and persuaded Judge Sirica to issue an order requiring that additional tapes and records be issued to the grand jury investigating Watergate. This order created a major confrontation between the president and the Supreme Court as Nixon claimed that executive privilege prevailed over the subpoena. On July 24 the Supreme Court ruled that the president must acquiesce and produce controversial tapes and documents.

Concurrently the House Judiciary Committee, consisting of twenty-one Democrats and seventeen Republicans, voted to approve three articles of impeachment accusing the president of (1) pursuing a course of conduct designed to obstruct justice in the Watergate investigation; (2) abusing presidential powers (using the Internal Revenue Service to pressure and harass political opponents, wiretapping phones of newsmen, interfering in antitrust suits, and failing to take action against known perjury); and (3) subverting constitutional government through defiance of congressional subpoenas. With impeachment in the House of Representatives a certainty and with virtually no chance of acquittal, the president resigned, convicted of wrongdoing, in part, by his own conversations.

As the record unfolded, it became clear that the president was the man behind the web of Watergate, that he had taken the irreversible step on June 23, 1972, (six days after the break-in) of ordering his aides to ensure that the FBI not learn about the network of wrongdoing—wiretapping, burglaries, cover-ups, lies, laundering of money, secret funds, enemies lists, dirty tricks, "plumbers," forgeries, Internal Revenue Service audits — authorized by the White House.

But why? Perhaps *Washington Post* reporters Carl Bernstein and Bob Woodward, both of whom were assigned full-time to follow Watergate from the time of the break-in on June 17, 1972, have the answer. Nixon, they argue, "totally failed to perceive the goodwill extended to any president by the people, the bureaucracy, the military, the press, his political party, the Congress, and the institutions of justice. Instead of using them as allies—in the tradition of his predecessors—he perceived them as enemies and in the process he eroded their ability to help him." In the end he not only disgraced himself but demeaned the presidency, an office that embodies the hopes, aspirations, and very soul of the American people. But the nightmare of Watergate ended in a bright dawn as the American system survived intact, displaying a healthy resilience and staying power rarely, if ever, matched in the history of great peoples.

Aftermath. Since the conviction of the original seven Watergate burglars, forty-nine criminal cases have reached the courts, involving thirty-six men and thirteen corporations, and President Nixon has been named as an unindicted coconspirator in the Watergate cover-up by a grand jury that believed sufficient evidence existed to indict him. Yet the trial of the century, that in which H. R. Haldeman, John Ehrlichman, and John Mitchell were charged with conspiracy to obstruct justice, seemed to be anticlimactic.

On December 30 the jurors began their deliberations after a warning from Judge Sirica to ignore the pardon of President Nixon and to concentrate on the evidence. The trial had been in progress for sixty-one days during which time the jury had heard more than eighty witnesses and thirty tape recordings (twenty-eight made by Nixon). The court reporter's transcript of the proceedings ran to 12,348 pages. The jury of nine women and three men deliberated for fifteen hours on three days. Three men who under Nixon had been among the most powerful officials in the United States — Haldeman, Ehrlichman, and Mitchell — were convicted of all charges leveled against them. Robert Mardian, a former assistant attorney general and official of the Nixon reelection campaign, was found guilty of the only charge he faced, a single count of conspiracy. Kenneth Parkinson, Nixon reelection committee lawyer hired after the break-in, was acquitted.

But the public had become tired of the endless repetition of events, for most certainly, regardless of present litigation and that to come, Watergate ended when Nixon resigned from office.

GERMAN FINANCE MINISTER Helmut Schmidt visits Secretary of State Henry Kissinger at the State Department in March. Schmidt gave his recipe for dealing with the news media: "Here is what I always do when about to meet the press — first brush my teeth and then sharpen my tongue."

West Germany

by

WOLFE W. SCHMOKEL, Ph.D.

Director of Graduate Studies
Department of History
University of Vermont

The Public Mood. As 1974 began, the public mood in West Germany seemed dispirited, the future outlook dim. Under a government which had lost its original energy and reforming optimism and seemed to be miring down in factional disputes, the country's economy, the pride of its national achievement, appeared to be faltering from the blows of the energy crisis and worldwide inflation. Relations with the Communist countries of Eastern Europe, whose improvement had been the prime foreign policy goal of Chancellor Willy Brandt's government since 1969, remained beset by difficulties; the European Economic Community (EEC), the other cornerstone of West German foreign policy, not only failed to progress toward greater political unity, but was retreating from the degree of economic integration achieved in the 1960s. Some perceived dangers to the social and political stability of the country as the darkening economic outlook gave encouragement to radical factions, whom the government seemed unwilling to confront.

Toward the end of the year, these problems had not been overcome, but there was progress toward their solution, and the mood of the country had become perceptibly more confident. West Germans were not as optimistic about the state of their nation as some foreign observers, who talked of a "second economic miracle," and saw the Federal Republic as an oasis of stability in a crisis-torn Europe; nevertheless they recognized that their country had come through a very difficult period in better shape than most of their neighbors, and that they might hope to manage equally successfully in the future.

Unexpected Changes. To a large extent this new mood was due to the unexpected change which occurred in Bonn's political leadership in May, 1974. Prior to that time the coalition government of Social Democrats (SPD) and Free Democrats (FDP) led by Chancellor Brandt was widely criticized for failing to deliver on its far-ranging program of domestic social reform or to provide energetic leadership in a critical economic situation. Tensions between the coalition partners, and among the leadership of Brandt's own Social Democrats were highlighted by prolonged cabinet wrangling over a major bill, designed to provide for worker participation in corporation management. The Social Democrats' powerful floor leader, Herbert Wehner, and Finance Minister Helmut Schmidt had publicly criticized the chancellor's hesitant, detached leadership style.

A series of state and local elections, in Hamburg, Schleswig-Holstein, and the Rhineland, demonstrated a dramatic decline in voter confidence in the government parties, with the Social Democrats suffering more than their FDP coalition partners. Public distrust of the Social Democrats was sometimes heightened by revolutionary Marxist pronouncements from the leaders of the party's youth wing, the Young Socialists, who actively supported demonstrations and strikes directed against government policy and the economic stability of the country. The SPD seemed to be unwilling to make a drastic break with the leaders of the Young Socialists. In February, the government's capitulation to a strike by the Public Service Employees' Union, whose wage demands the chancellor had previously described as unacceptably inflationary, strengthened the impression that the government was unable to control sections among its own supporters.

Political jockeying and tension between the government parties was intensified last winter by the announcement that Gustav Heinemann, the Federal Republic's president since 1969, would not seek a second five-year term. Walter Scheel, then foreign minister and leader of the Free Democrats, decided to seek the prestigious ceremonial post, thus opening up the prospect of a redistribution of cabinet seats.

Into the midst of these developments exploded the announcement that Günther Guillaume, a close personal associate of Chancellor Brandt, had been unmasked as a spy and officer of the East German intelligence service. Guillaume, who had come to West Germany as a "refugee" in 1954 and had worked his way into the inner circle of the chancellor's office via the SPD machinery, had accompanied Brandt on many of his trips as a personal aide, and had had access to the highest level of classified documents. Despite a general warning from one of the federal counterintelligence services that his East German background might make him a security risk, he had been employed in his sensitive position without a thorough security clearing. After Guillaume's arrest, West German newspapers widely reported that

WALTER SCHEEL, who became West Germany's president in June, was elected "Knight of the Order Against Deadly Earnestness" by the Aachen carnival committee. Although the Aachen presentation included this line: "One day Scheel will be on everyone's lips — as a postage stamp, glued at the back," the new president's first decision was his refusal to let the West German post office print his likeness on stamps.

the agent threatened to reveal derogatory information about the chancellor's private life unless he was released in exchange for West German intelligence operatives held in the German Democratic Republic.

After several days' hesitation and heightening speculation, Chancellor Willy Brandt submitted on May 7 a tersely worded letter of resignation, in which he accepted personal responsibility for the affair. (Brandt retained, however, the chairmanship of the SPD, perhaps to demonstrate continuity in leadership. This arrangement has already created some friction with Helmut Schmidt, his successor as chancellor—especially with the publication this fall of Brandt's memoirs, which contain pointed criticisms of some government leaders—and it is widely expected that Brandt's chairmanship of the party will be temporary.)

The most widespread reaction to the chancellor's resignation among the German public and press was sympathy for the chancellor, whose accomplishments, especially in contributing to detente by establishing improved relations between the Federal Republic and Eastern Europe, had gained worldwide recognition. Respect was expressed for his frank and courageous assumption of responsibility. Regret, however, was tinged with a certain amount of hopeful anticipation of more energetic leadership from a new term.

Helmut Schmidt. On May 16 West Germany's parliament, the Bundestag, formally elected Helmut Schmidt as the fifth Federal chancellor. Born in 1918 and a World War II veteran, Schmidt had been politically active in the Social Democratic Party since 1946. He gained national prominence in 1962 when, as Hamburg's senator for interior, he acted with exceptional energy and success in organizing relief measures after a major flood catastrophe. In 1966 he joined the "Kiesinger-Brandt Grand Coalition" government as minister of defense. In 1969, upon the resignation of Karl Schiller from the cabinet, he became finance minister and was widely regarded as the number two man in the Social Democratic leadership and heir-apparent to the chancellorship.

Schmidt's style and image differ dramatically from his predecessor's: action-oriented, austere, direct and bluff in manner, he fits the average German's image of a typical native of Hamburg. Generally regarded as a representative of the SPD's right wing, he is an essentially nonideological leader who has

WEST GERMANY

been known to express open contempt for "dreamers." He is a technician of politics, a man who concentrates on getting things done. As minister of defense, then of finance, he had ample opportunity to become acquainted with government leaders, especially those of the Western alliance; he established a particularly close relationship with Giscard d'Estaing, France's new president. In his foreign policy views, he has been an outspoken supporter of an "Atlantic" orientation, champion of the North Atlantic Treaty Organization (NATO) and of continued close relationship with the United States.

Genscher. Schmidt's number two man in the new government is Hans-Dietrich Genscher. Minister of the interior under Brandt, he moved to the foreign office and assumed the leadership of the Free Democratic Party when Walter Scheel, his predecessor in both positions, was elected to the presidency of the Federal Republic in May. Other cabinet changes left the political balance between SPD and FDP ministers undisturbed, but introduced a number of new faces, mainly from the ranks of Bonn's ministerial bureaucracy.

The New Era. The new chancellor's policy statement, delivered before the Bundestag on May 17, clearly set the tone for a new era in West Germany. By far the greatest portion of the statement was devoted to economic affairs, with an emphasis on the limits of governmental action and resources. Promises were few, and limited to the pledge to carry out some of the Brandt cabinet's major uncompleted reforms. Thus, the government would press for enactment of worker participation in management by 1975, and a related plan for the industrial profit-sharing would be presented to the Bundestag before the end of its term in 1976. A watered-down tax reform, cutting taxation of lower-bracket incomes, would be carried through.

Little was said about foreign policy, aside from a rather perfunctory endorsement of Brandt's policies toward Eastern Europe, a general pledge of continuity, and a reiterated commitment to the European Community (coupled, characteristically, with a warning that any German economic assistance to EEC partners was "justifiable only if the recipient country makes resolute efforts of its own to ensure the effectiveness of such aid"). In all, the policy statement and the actions of the government since then justify the comment of a major German newspaper that "the flights of fancy of the Brandt-Scheel governments of 1969 and 1972 have been followed by a rather lean opening balance presented by the Schmidt-Genscher cabinet. The great dream is over."

The New Budget, too, presented to the Bundestag in October, stressed limitations on government spending, cutting staff, and the shelving of expensive programs, rather than new social reforms and extension of the welfare state, which had been the themes of the Brandt years. Schmidt has given proverbially short shrift to cabinet ministers who have sought to expand their budgets. The July resignation of Minister of Economic Cooperation Erhard Eppler was brought on by Schmidt's insistence on foreign aid cuts. In the same vein, the chancellor has made it clear to other Common Market countries that there is a limit to his government's willingness to subsidize the community's programs unilaterally—especially in the agricultural sector and in developing economically backward areas, particularly in Great Britain, Ireland, and Italy. The expectations of some Eastern European countries, for example, Poland, that Bonn would pay for normalized political relations with large amounts of low-term credits have likewise been disappointed.

THE ROMAN-GERMANIC MUSEUM, constructed on the southern flank of the Cologne Cathedral over the famous Dionysus mosaic excavated there, opened on March 4.

Dissidents. Schmidt has been equally direct and forceful in dealing with left-wing dissidents in his own party, who had been voicing opposition to his stability-oriented, basically conservative economic policies. Some of the most clearly antidemocratic leaders of the Young Socialists were expelled from the SPD, and Schmidt warned others that their class struggle speeches alienated moderate voters and that open opposition to party policies would not be tolerated.

Favorable Public Reaction to the new leadership style, emphasizing efficiency, performance, and a degree of austerity, was reflected in the Lower Saxony state elections last June, which showed less than the expected gains for the Christian Democratic opposition, and in the steadily rising approval rate for the chancellor in public opinion polls published since then. The performance of West Germany's economy has of course contributed to this positive image.

The Economy. Belying pessimistic projections made last winter, the Federal Republic weathered the effects of the Arab oil production cutback and of increased energy prices rather easily. A temporary ban on Sunday driving and general speed limits (a novelty on West German highways) were imposed last winter, and the price of gasoline increased by more than 10 percent, to approximately $1.40 a gallon. However, no general shortages developed. Despite the increased cost of imported fuel, upon which West Germany is far more heavily dependent than, for example, the United States, the general inflation rate stabilized at slightly over 7 percent, well below original official projections for the year. The anti-inflation measures enacted last year, emphasizing restrictions on public spending, credit, and investment; additional taxation of certain profits; and high interest rates appear to have successfully checked inflation without creating a recession. Unemployment remained minimal, at just over 2 percent with over 2 million foreign workers still employed in the Federal Republic.

One reason for this success is clearly the Federal Republic's position as the proverbial one-eyed man in the country of the blind: while 7 percent inflation was too much for most Germans, it was considerably less than that of other countries. German exports thus remained attractive despite increasing costs and the rising value of the German mark in relation to other currencies. Thus, while Germans cut back their borrowing and spending at a dramatic rate, export orders continued to increase, and the country's industrial production was thus maintained at a high level.

Trouble Spots. To be sure, there were some trouble spots in the economy: rising fuel prices cut back on automobile production, with Volkswagen, the country's largest producer, experiencing the hardest year in its history. The construction industry was in marked decline, with cutbacks in government construction projects coming at a time when it seemed that the West Germans' longstanding housing gap had at last been closed.

The export boom also creates its own problems. West German export surpluses, which may reach a new record of $17 billion for the year, spell corresponding deficits for others. West German economists and government leaders expressed concern about the strains these one-sided trade balances have imposed on the economies of Bonn's trading partners, especially the members of the Common Market. The granting of a $2 billion credit to stave off the virtual collapse of the Italian economy was a result of this growing concern.

The general state of the European Community continued to alarm West Germany's leaders and public. In a number of cases, member countries have had to abandon the Common Market's commitment to mutual free trade and common economic policies to deal with their critical trade deficits. Thus, France abandoned the agreement calling for fixed exchange rates between major European currencies, and unilaterally devalued the franc. Italy and Denmark were forced to restrict imports from other EEC countries. Great Britain's government threatened to leave the community entirely. It can be expected that West Germany will do everything in her power to maintain the Common Market. It seems to be recognized by her present leaders, however, that this is not the time to expect major advances toward greater political and economic unity.

Ostpolitik ceased to be a headlinemaker. The exchange of diplomatic "permanent representatives" between the Federal Republic and the (East) German Democratic Republic (GDR) and the ratification of a treaty with Czechoslovakia merely completed a process of normalizing relations, begun in 1969. The Guillaume affair, attempts by the GDR to impose restrictive conditions on access to West Berlin, and difficulties created by Poland and the Soviet Union over permitting emigration of people of German origin were some of the indications that detente was far from bearing full fruit.

The Soccer Victory. On a lighter note, West Germans were able to celebrate a major sports victory. The home team emerged as the champions in the quadrennial World Cup soccer playoffs, hosted by the Federal Republic this summer. The finals, held in Munich's Olympic Stadium, saw a 2-1 West German victory over Holland.

Wolves

WOLVES, like American Indians, have lived at peace with nature for thousands of years. Both have been hunters, but neither would over-kill or hunt for sport; both have been an integral part of the ecosystem.

DANGEROUS ANIMALS OR ANIMALS IN DANGER?

by
R. MARLIN PERKINS

Host, "Wild Kingdom" television series
Director, Wild Canid Survival and Research Center

Wolf Myths. For ages myths and legends about wolves have struck terror into the hearts of men ignorant of the ways of the wilderness. The werewolf — half man, half wolf — was a fiend who committed murder and rape in the dark of the night. As proof of the bloodthirsty habits of wolves, a Russian painting — showing a wolf pack chasing a sleigh with a

mother throwing a dog to the rapacious wolves in a desperate effort to protect her child — was reprinted all over the world.

Yet there is no proven record anywhere of a wolf killing a human being unprovoked. The facts about the wolf, now being painstakingly assembled by biologists, offer no reason for its persecution. Despite the prevailing myth, the wolf is *not* dangerous to man: indeed, it is very shy of humans and tends to avoid them whenever possible. The old stories of the half wolf-half man undoubtedly were derived from the practice of families hiding their imbeciles and malformed children in cellars and attics and letting them out only at night for air and exercise. An unsuspecting person walking home in the dark and coming upon one of these bearded, half-crazed unfortunates may well have mistaken him for a wolf monster. His anguished cries might also have been construed as "wolf howls." And so the terror of the werewolves began and grew.

The Poisoning of the West. Because wolves have always been somewhat in competition with herdsmen, sheep- and cattle-raisers have always feared that wolves would destroy their livestock. However, in only a few cases — where the wolves' natural habitat has been completely taken over by ranches and their natural food supply threatened — has this ever been proven true.

Real trouble for wolves began in earnest in the United States in 1944 when a new poison called 1080 was perfected. Odorless and tasteless and slow to deteriorate, 1080 does not break down in the body of the victim and is extraordinarily deadly. The poisoned animal dies a horrible death and then becomes poison bait for every form of life that feeds on dead animals, including our national symbol, the eagle. When snow and heavy rains come, the 1080 is washed into the rivers and streams and into underground water tables, spreading its deadly poison in an ever-widening circle to include man himself.

Another poison device is the "coyote getter," a stick with a cyanide cap baited with meat. When an animal bites the meat the cap explodes and he dies a cruel death by cyanide poisoning. This device has been responsible for killing innumerable wolves and coyotes in the Southwest and almost completely exterminating kit foxes, grizzly bear cubs, and raccoons in that area. Cyanide "coyote getters" and 1080 are indiscriminate killers.

The Case for the Wolf. Although a few scientists decried it, the terrible slaughter of wolves went unnoticed by a public which grew up reading *Little Red Riding Hood* and *The Three Little Pigs.*

The tide began to turn in June, 1965, when *Never Cry Wolf* by Farley Mowat was published. Now in its fifteenth printing, the book made readers aware of wolves, their family life, their intelligent ways, and their loyalty to one another, in the same way that *Born Free* taught the public about lions.

On October 18, 1969, the National Broadcasting Company televised a film called *The Wolf Men.* A documentary about the dedicated people working to save wolves, it showed Richard Grossenheider, Dr. Michael Fox, Dr. John Fentress, Lois Crisler, Dr. Durward Allen, Dr. David Mech, and Mary Fine doing research on wolves in northern Minnesota, Isle Royale, Mich., and Alaska, and at a private wolf sanctuary in St. Louis, Mo.

For the first time the public was alerted to studies at Isle Royale that proved that wolves do *not* destroy the moose population but live in the stabilized harmony typical of nature's true balance when man does not interfere.

The final scene of *The Wolf Men* showed hunters shooting down wolves from aircraft. This unnecessary bloodshed was so appalling to people who had never realized the terror of the animals killed in this manner and the uselessness of this so-called "sport" that Congress was flooded with mail. Public sentiment forced the introduction of two bills — one in the House of Representatives and one in the Senate — which provided penalties of $5,000 and/or imprisonment for shooting animals from aircraft.

In the last five years more than five thousand wolves have been killed in Alaska for bounty. Over $250,000 was paid out, at $50 a wolf, an amount which does not even pay for the expense of shooting the wolf; it is all just part of the "fun."

In 1970 a group of people deeply concerned about wolves and their rapid disappearance formed the Wild Canid Survival and Research Center in St. Louis, Mo. The organization began a data bank, which already is becoming an international clearing house for information on all of the captive wolf stock of the world. This will be a significant factor in helping those with captive stock to reduce inbreeding.

In 1973 a beautiful true story of wolves caled *Cry of the Wild,* filmed in Canada by Bill Mason, was shown as a feature film in theaters throughout the United States. In the same year a book for young people fourteen years old and over, *Julie of the Wolves* by Jean Craighead George, won the Newbery Award for Children's Literature. It told of the author's experiences with wolves in Point Barrow, Alaska.

An Ambassador for Wolves. For several years Mr. and Mrs. John Harris of Hayward, Calif., have been quietly saving orphaned and unwanted wolves that had been mistakenly taken as pets and could not be kept by their original owners. Wolves, being totally independent and undomesticated wild animals, are unsuitable as pets. Under special conditions wolves will allow people to live with them by wolf rules; wolves cannot live with man by man's rules.

One of the wolves raised by Harris was Jethro, who grew up to become a very special wolf. Harris traveled from coast to coast with this completely gentle and trustworthy wolf, visiting schools so that children could meet a real wolf and learn for themselves that wolves are not bloodthirsty beasts. The greatest ambassador for wolves that ever lived, Jethro went to Congress and appeared on several national television programs. He often traveled with his great friend Clem, a wolf who belonged to an American Indian. In August, 1973, the two wolves were locked for the night in their specially equipped van parked in front of an apartment house where Harris was sleeping. The next day the wolves were scheduled to appear at a Boy Scout jamboree. During the night someone broke into the van and fed the two trusting and unsuspecting wolves chicken poisoned with strychnine. They were dead when John Harris found them early the next morning.

The Tragedy of the Wolf is that of predators in general and well embodies our national attitude toward nature, a fossil of the fears and superstitions of our ancestors.

The wolf has been killed out of most of its original range in the world. Canada and Alaska still have some survivors. In the United States there are about 15 wolves protected on Isle Royale, Mich., about 90 in the the southern tip of Texas, perhaps 300 left in northern Minnesota. A few have recently been sighted in Yellowstone National Park. The others have all been hunted, trapped, or poisoned to virtual extinction. Time has almost run out for wolves. They cannot gather together to protest, but the Wild Canid Survival and Research Center organized an international conference in June at Washington, D.C., to discuss the present status of the greatly endangered animals of North America.

And so the struggle to save a species of life goes on. More and more people are concerned with helping to save the wolf as more and more people learn the truth, at last, about one of the most social, intelligent, and magnificent of all the wild animals alive today, the wolf.

THE WAYS OF THE WOLF

by
MICHAEL FOX, Ph.D.

Associate Professor of Psychology
Washington University, St. Louis, Mo.

Hunting. Wolves will hunt alone, seeking small prey, rodents, and rabbits, and picking up what carrion they can. It takes two or more wolves to bring down larger prey, and by cooperating as a pack they can overcome prey many times their own size. A healthy moose could kill a wolf with its front hooves, and a caribou easily outruns any wolf. The wolf pack "tests" the prey to see if

WOLVES have to be superintelligent to survive. Hunting and trapping by man have ensured that only the quickest to learn and the wisest would survive.

A WOLF PACK begins a hunt.

LOW-RANKING WOLF in this pack has tail between his legs, at far right.

WOLFJOY

Joy is the feasting, not killing,
And sharing with cubs.

Joy for the cubs
Is the pack coming home
And wild games after supper.

Joy is wallowing in fresh-fallen snow
Or strange-smelling things
And biting a river
That always escapes.

The joy of the pack
Is the chorus at dusk;
Singing together,
To celebrate life.

it is sick or injured since they have little chance of catching it if it is healthy. Wolves use strategy while hunting, notably driving into ambush or distracting the prey so that one wolf can rush in safely and get a firm hold.

Deer fawns and moose and caribou calves fall prey to wolves. This seems cruel, but usually there is a surplus of fawns and calves each spring (an evolutionary adaptation to anticipated disease and predation), so the population can withstand this and also benefit from the "pruning." Since the calves are all born about the same time and mature quickly, the period when they are vulnerable is very short anyway.

In contrast to the wolf, man the hunter, if he has a choice, will not kill the sick and injured, but shoots the prime or trophy animals instead. This has a very different effect on the herd and could be detrimental. The wolf has little choice — he must take what he can get — and this is invariably not detrimental to the prey species, but is, in fact, beneficial. If it were detrimental, there would be no deer, caribou, or moose left since wolves have been hunting them for hundreds of thousands of years!

FRIENDLY GRIN (ears up).

Pack Social Organization. A wolf pack is essentially an extended family consisting of the offspring of a mated pair, one or more juveniles from the previous year, and other nonbreeding adults which are often related to the mated pair and assist them in caring for the young.

Within the pack there is a dominance hierarchy or pack order which changes as wolves mature, age, and die. There is an alpha or number one female who dominates the other females and a number one male who not only rules over the males but is the leader of the pack. He is the decision-maker. Other wolves, even older ones, respond to him submissively and affectionately as cubs to parents. Allegiance to the leader helps keep the pack together and this, together with avoidance of strange wolves, and defense of their range against intruders, keeps wolf packs apart. Each pack has its own territory which is marked out by urinal "scent posts." Occupancy is perhaps advertised by howling.

Body Language. Wolves have a rich vocabulary of visual signals which communicate social rank, mood, and intentions. Subtle changes in tail and ear positions and of body and head angle and height, making and breaking eye contact, and various facial expressions convey this information. Two emotions of varying intensity, such as fear and submission, or submission and defensive threat, can even be signalled at the same time. Although these displays are instinctive, a wolf learns who is who in the

DOMINANT WOLF gives threat stare to subordinate who displays submissive grin (ears back).

INTENSE THREAT is displayed by a female defending her young.

pack and what to expect in certain social situations. He is aware of the various roles he and other wolves play in different contexts. This awareness is termed "metacommunication"—"he knows that you know that he knows." Because of this, the frequency and complexity of communication signalling can be reduced. A mere glance or slight flick of the ears suffices.

Aggression. Since each wolf knows its place in the rank order, conflicts are reduced. Once a stable dominance hier-

A WHINING WOLF is jaw-wrestled to the ground by his leader. The muzzle bite is well-controlled and inhibited. There is no bloodshed.

A DOMINANT WOLF settles a dispute in a ritualized fight. Note wolves in submissive stances at right.

WOLVES

archy is established, peace reigns in the pack. Any disagreements are settled by *ritualized fighting* or "jaw wrestling," and sometimes just by a threat display without any physical contact at all. The alpha wolves may "police" others, subordinating an upstart with a direct stare, and breaking up squabbles between two lower-ranking wolves.

What seems to be very aggressive is the pinning of whining subordinates to the ground by a growling leader. Subordinates often solicit this. Such behavior is not aggressive but is a ritual display of rank between pack members, serving to reaffirm the unity of the pack and allegiance to the leader.

More severe fighting does occasionally break out during the breeding season and leadership roles may change. A pack may split up at this time. Severe injuries are rare. As soon as a wolf gives a surrender signal and shows submission toward the other contestant, the latter will immediately stop fighting. Wolves do show chivalry!

Sex. The bonds that keep a wolf pack together are social, not sexual. A mature female is sexually receptive for only about two weeks in the year. Usually only the alpha female mates. If a low-ranking female attempts to mate with a male, she will usually be blocked by the alpha female. Similarly, a low-ranking male will be inhibited by a male of higher rank. The pack order serves then as a social form of birth control.

Parental Behavior. Unlike most canids which reach sexual maturity at

THE SHORT COURTSHIP PERIOD is a time of happiness for wolves. Note the open-mouth play expression of female wolf on the left.

one year of age, the wolf is not mature until at least two years. This *may* be adaptive in order to keep the pack together so that yearlings stay with the parents an additional year and help in hunts and in raising young.

Much of the social life of the pack revolves around the care and rearing of young. Father brings food to the mother while the cubs are nursing. He carries it in his stomach and regurgitates it at the entrance to the den. When the cubs are older, both parents and other pack members feed them in this way. When parents go off hunting, another adult will baby-sit. Adults play for hours with the cubs and are extremely tolerant and affectionate, but not overpermissive.

Cubs soon learn their places within the pack. Little is known about how the older wolves teach cubs to hunt, but much is probably picked up by observation and imitation alone.

CUBS wait as mother crushes marrow bones for them.

Socialization and Group Rituals. As the cubs play and interact with each other and with adults, they become socialized or emotionally bonded at an early age. This bonding period wanes at about four months, and cubs begin to

MOTHER stands while cubs nurse.

THE PACK HOWL, a celebration of togetherness.

shy away from strangers.

Older cubs persist in mobbing the leader, licking his face, whining and tail-wagging in the same way they once did in order to solicit food from their parents. The food-soliciting and mobbing greeting toward parents becomes the collective "love-in" display of affection and allegiance shown by subordinate adults to the leader. Such ritual ceremonies are performed especially when they wake up, before they split up to hunt, and when the pack is reunited after a hunt.

Another ritual follows this, namely the pack howl or chorus. The sound of a wolf pack in full song perhaps best exemplifies the highly evolved sociability of the wolf. It sparks fear in the trapper who does not understand. But in those who do, it touches a deeper essence and reaffirms an archetypal link between man and animal. We are all brothers; the wilderness is not ours, but we are a part of it. All is one.

Women's Liberation

COAL MINING, one of the last all-male fields, hired women as equal rights went underground in 1974.

by
ROBERT STEAMER

Dean, College II
University of Massachusetts

Moving Forward. While faltering here and there, the movement to elevate the status of women vis-a-vis men in the various aspects of society's organized life generally retained its forward momentum during 1974.

ERA. In 1973 the legislatures of Maine, Montana, and Ohio had considered the Equal Rights Amendment (ERA) but failed to adopt it. In 1974, however, all three reconsidered and voted to ratify, bringing the total ratifying states to thirty-three, just five short of the requisite thirty-eight. At the same time the amendment failed to obtain approval in Georgia, where one legislator said that the measure would "lower our ladies down to the level of men," and Tennessee became the second state (Nebraska being the first) to attempt to rescind its original approval. Although the legality of rescission has not been clarified, if the Tennessee and Nebraska actions are deemed lawful, the proposed amendment will have had a net gain of only one in 1974 for a total of thirty-one instead of thirty-three.

Court Actions. In the courts women

WOMEN'S LIBERATION

have been the winners in some suits, the losers in others. Probably the most important victory for sexual equality was the Supreme Court's ruling that the Equal Pay Act did not permit traditional pay differentials. The Corning Glass Works had paid male night-shift inspectors more than female day-shift inspectors, and although it had opened its night-shift jobs to women, the court decided that this did not "cure" the violation of the law. What Corning, and all other employers, must now do is to pay all workers at the same base rate, regardless of sex or shift worked. Female workers sustained a loss, however, when the Supreme Court ruled that California's job disability insurance program did not unconstitutionally discriminate against women by not including benefits for pregnancies. Justice Stewart, for the majority, noted that nothing in the Constitution requires a state "to create a more comprehensive social insurance program than it already has" and that it may decide against insuring particular employment disability risks. In dissent three justices maintained that California had created a double standard by "singling out for less favorable treatment a gender-linked disability peculiar to women." The court declined to hear several cases involving male-female parity, an action which favored the women's liberation movement only in some instances. The justices refused to disturb lower court holdings permitting: (1) more restrictive college dormitory regulations for women than men; (2) alimony awards which allegedly discriminate against men; and (3) the granting of custody of children to the mother in divorce cases. The court also let stand a lower court ruling denying an injunction to a father (of an illegitimate unborn child) which would have prevented the mother from obtaining an abortion. In other decisions local judges ruled that prostitution laws discriminated against women since punishment was not provided for men, nor were male customers arrested. Suits are now in progress in New Jersey and Connecticut in which women are charging sex discrimination by insurance companies who deny coverage allegedly because single women are living with men without benefit of wedlock. Although women (fifteen) joined the men at the Merchant Marine Academy this year for the first time, a U.S. district court in Washington ruled in June that since law and custom forbid women's participation in combat roles, women might properly be excluded from the Air Force and Naval Academies.

Employment. Neutral observers considered the judicial settlement in San Francisco by the Bank of America a major breakthrough in women's rights. Rather than simply agreeing to retroactive pay to compensate for past acts of discrimination, the bank agreed to pay $3.75 million over a period of five years to a trust fund which gives special incentives to female employees to advance to top managerial positions. Under the terms of the agreement the proportion of women officers would be increased from the current 31 percent to 40 percent by the end of the year. On April 15 nine major steel companies signed agreements with the federal government under which back pay and expanded job opportunities would be provided for women. A timetable called for women in 20 percent of production and maintenance vacancies and for the selection of women and minorities in 25 percent of the vacancies in supervisory positions. In spite of impressive gains for women in business and industry, the Census Bureau reported in July that the income of a typical full-time, year-round, working woman was $6,485—57 percent of the income of a full-time male employee who earned $11,468.

WOMEN'S LIBERATION

Religion. Considerable controversy continued to be the norm as churches began to face the demands for greater female participation in clerical management. Women of the Episcopal church had won the right to be deacons, the lowest order in the general ministry, at the 1970 triennial general convention, but they were denied ordination as priests. However, on July 29 in a ceremony at the Church of the Advocate in North Philadelphia four bishops and eleven female deacons defied church law as the bishops ordained the women to the priesthood. Some fifty priests joined the bishops in a symbolic laying-on-of-hands, but two days later two of the new priests were suspended by their diocesan bishops. In mid-August the House of Bishops met in emergency session in Chicago and resolved overwhelmingly that the ordination of the eleven women was invalid, a move that had the effect of demoting the new female priests to deacons. At the same time the bishops urged the 1976 general convention to reconsider the question of female ordination. Meanwhile the Southern Baptist Convention rejected a resolution on June 12 that would have enforced a 20 percent quota for women on church governing bodies. While tabling another resolution calling for a woman's right to ordination and equal pay for equal work, the convention approved of abortion in cases of rape, incest, fetal deformity, or possible harm to the health of the mother. Pope Paul VI personally authored a pro-feminist passage in a 30,000-word "apostolic exhortation" entitled *Marian Devotion.* While urging increased devotion to the Virgin Mary, the pope characterized her as a "new woman" who "was far from being a timidly submissive woman or one whose piety was repellent to others." The pope appeared to emphasize a parallel between Mary and modern feminists, calling her an activist who supported the liberating energies in the world.

REPRESENTATIVE ELLA T. GRASSO (D., Conn.) was elected governor of Connecticut, the first woman elected governor without succeeding her husband.

Abortion. The controversy over a woman's right to abortion continued unabated. A Senate judiciary subcommittee held hearings on March 6 and 7 on two proposed Constitutional amendments which would overturn the Supreme Court's ruling that a woman has a right to decide whether or not to have an abortion. One of the amendments would guarantee, with no exceptions, the right to life at the instant of conception. The

WOMEN'S LIBERATION

other would permit an abortion only when a reasonable medical certainty existed that the mother's life would be endangered with a continued pregnancy. John Cardinal Krol, archbishop of Philadelphia, testified: "The right to life is not an invention of the Catholic church or any other church. It is a basic human right which must undergird any civilized society." Presenting the committee with the opposite view was Colgate University professor Barbara McNeal who asked: "Should a male-dominated (Catholic) religious hierarchy determine the moral posture and legal status of the opposite sex when the woman in question is caught up in a dilemma no man can understand?" At the very moment that the Senate committee hearing was in progress, a federal panel of judges in Philadelphia ruled unconstitutional the Pennsylvania medical assistance program for welfare recipients which required concurrence of two doctors before a state welfare recipient could receive reimbursement for abortion. In the court's view the law discriminated against recipients who chose to have abortions.

The International Scene. In February, 120 women members of U.N. delegations held a forum under the leadership of U.N. Assistant Secretary General Helvi Sipila. The purpose of the meeting was to formulate ideas which would help women to contribute to population control and economic development. In its report the forum stressed the need to break the "vicious circle" created by the relationship between the low education and inferior employment status of women and high fertility. Any alteration of the cycle, the report concluded, required greater sharing of the world's resources. In Lisbon last May three authors known as the "Three Marias" (Maria Velho de Costa, Maria Teresa Horta and Maria Isabel Barreno) were acquitted of charges that they had offended public morals in a book in which they had attacked suppression of women's rights in Portugal. Upon being set free, all three announced they would start a women's liberation movement with legalized abortion as its first order of business.

Hungary, following action previously taken by Rumania and Bulgaria, repealed the "abortion on demand" law and restricted abortions to women: (1) over forty; (2) who had three or more children; (3) who had become pregnant through rape; (4) who were single or had been separated from their husbands for six months. In a fifth category are couples with no home of their own. France, on the other hand, decided to permit abortion up to the tenth week of pregnancy.

French president Giscard d'Estaing appointed Françoise Giroud, the prominent feminist editor of the weekly news magazine *L'Express*, to a cabinet post as secretary of state for the status of women. And in the Western Hemisphere Prime Minister Pierre Elliott Trudeau appointed the first woman to a viceregal post in Canada when he named Pauline McGibbon lieutenant-governor of Ontario. Later in the year Maria Estela Martínez de Perón became the first woman chief of state in the Americas when she assumed the presidency of Argentina upon the death of Juan Perón on July 1.

Footnote. On May 7 the fifty-four-year-old League of Women Voters of the United States agreed to admit men to full membership but deferred a name change to 1976. How seriously politicians would take an organization called the League of Voters or League of Men and Women Voters caused concern among many league members who saw the change as devitalizing what had been the most effective vehicle for women's participation in politics in the history of the republic.

UNCONSCIOUS RACISM HURTS BLACK STUDENTS

by

S. I. HAYAKAWA

Former president, San Francisco State College

The Great Awakening. One of the great awakenings in American universities in the 1960s was their realization that they had so few black students. Struck suddenly by this fact, many schools embarked on special admissions programs to bring more black students to their campuses.

The results were often gratifying. At San Francisco State we are graduating this June a number of students who never expected to go to college, but, given the chance, joyfully took advantage of it. Sometimes, however, the results were disastrous.

Black Special Admissions Programs. Usually universities recruit the most promising students they can find. But in the case of black special admissions programs, many universities worked by a different set of rules.

White administrators made the curious assumption that a middle-class Negro is, in a sense, not a Negro at all, but one who has "lost his true identity." Hence they sought out the "real" or "authentic" black, of the kind "too steeped in his own culture to score well on white, culturally biased tests."

Thomas Sowell started out as a Harlem youth to become an economist of distinction and a professor at the University of California at Los Angeles. In *Black Education: Myths and Tragedies* (McKay), he tells an incredible story of a black girl with College Board scores in the top 1 percent, who was denied admission by Cornell University with the following reasoning:

"Her cultural and educational background does not indicate deprivation to the extent necessary for qualification as a disadvantaged . . . student. In spite of the fact that both her parents are laundry workers, she has been adequately motivated by them to a point where she has achieved academic success and some degree of cultural sophistication."

One would think that the daughter of laundry workers would be just the kind of student a special admissions program is for, but no, she had the tough luck to be a brilliant student. Cornell wanted "real blacks" — those burdened with enough cultural deficiencies to be least likely to succeed, but believed to have "special qualities not shown by conventional academic indices."

Universities were not alone, says Sowell, in giving special preference to the underqualified student. Guidelines for the distribution of federal scholarship funds and foundation grants were almost unanimous in "leaving the better qualified black students out of their programs and often out of luck as far as going to college was concerned."

The Fate of Underqualified Blacks. What happened to these poorly qualified black students at Cornell, Brandeis, and many other universities is now a familiar story. Doing badly in their courses, fearful of competition with their better-prepared white classmates, they formed into defiant, separatist, revolutionary cliques. They demanded relevant [easier] courses — for example, black studies — in which they could determine the subject matter and hire their own faculty.

Black leaders of the kind that Sowell calls "hustling messiahs" discovered that guilt-ridden ["socially conscious"] liberal administrators could be frightened into granting unreasonable demands for money or power.

The Antioch Story. Antioch is a famous liberal arts college in Yellow Springs,

Ohio. Nearby is the city of Xenia, which was a station of the Underground Railroad of pre-Civil War days. Hence in Yellow Springs there is a long-established Negro community, mostly working people with steady jobs.

Eager to prove itself progressive, Antioch established a special admissions program for blacks in the late 1960s. The children of local Negro families were not recruited, since they were "middle class" and had presumably "lost their black identity." Students who could meet Antioch's high admission standards were excluded by the costs of going there — over $4,000 a year. As Sowell tells the story:

"Meanwhile, Antioch was out scouring the slums of Chicago, Pittsburgh, and other distant cities to find the appropriate kind of Negro students from the ghetto, who were brought with full financial support . . . This did not work out. Friction and animosity developed between these students and the traditional, white Antioch students from vastly different backgrounds.

"Friction developed between the ghetto kids and the black community of Yellow Springs. Indeed, friction developed among the black Antioch students themselves, some of whom were intimidated and assaulted by others." Kenneth B. Clark, distinguished Negro psychologist who was on the board of directors of Antioch, resigned in protest against the administration's policies.

All this was five years ago. Antioch College has been torn with strife ever since. As of this writing, the college has been closed for almost two months — and the end of the turmoil is not in sight.

Reprinted from Dr. Hayakawa's syndicated column courtesy The Register and Tribune Syndicate.

100 Years Ago: Winston Churchill, British statesman, was born.

NOSTALGIA

Looking Backward became recognized as a national obsession in 1974. Nostalgia, the sentimental remembrance of things past, was virtually the mainstream of activity.

The celebration of the youth culture, as evidenced in plays like *Hair,* disappeared. The young were requesting Glenn Miller and other big-band sounds from amazed disk jockeys and buying the "best of" records of Nat "King" Cole and the Mills Brothers. "Touch dancing" became the rage, as youth rediscovered dancing together.

Films went from *The Summer of '42* to the Depression of '33 *(Paper Moon)* and back farther into a spate of 1920s pictures *(The Great Gatsby),* disproving the old theory that each period tends to look back just about thirty years with fond memories. Fans eagerly tuned in reruns of "The Shadow" and "The Green Hornet" on the radio. The four most successful musicals on Broadway were set in the past. *Lorelei* was a new version of the 1950s musical *Gentlemen Prefer Blondes,* which in turn was made from a popular 1920s novel. *Irene* was a restaging of a 1920s hit. *Over Here* brought back the Andrews Sisters in a glorification of the wartime 1940s. *Grease,* New York's longest-running musical, recalled the rock and roll high school scene of the 1950s. There was even a Nostalgia Book Club.

The Good Old Days. Every one knew that the warm feeling for yesterday was an illusion. In the good old days it did not snow more, the girls were not prettier, life was not better, and everyone was not happier. Anyone who had lived through the Depression knew the reality of hard times. Nostalgia was an edited or idealized version of the past, attractive

 OPINION

LITTLE ORPHAN ANNIE was a national heroine in the 1930s as she singlehandedly fought the Depression and a series of dastardly villains. This strip from 1936 began a reissue of Harold Gray's "vintage" Annie in newspapers on April 22, fitting perfectly the current mood of nostalgia for the good things of the past.

THE ROARING TWENTIES were chronicled in *The Great Gatsby* which premiered in March starring Mia Farrow and Robert Redford. It was the roaring seventies for 1920s author F. Scott Fitzgerald whose books sold nearly a million copies in the United States alone in 1974. Film rights to this third motion picture version of Fitzgerald's 1925 novel cost $350,000.

A VOICE OUT OF THE PAST: Radios of the 1920s and 1930s, complete with crackling static and music that sounds as if it is being played through a megaphone, are now popular collectors' items. Among the collectors are the 800 members of the Antique Wireless Association, and shrewd second-hand dealers are hiking prices on such hot sets as the Atwater Kent Model Five. Above, a period picture from the Farm Security Administration Collection in the Library of Congress shows a couple enjoying their prized radio during the Depression.

only in contrast to a depressed picture of the present.

The truth seemed to be that people were fatigued with the pressures of contemporary living — the divisiveness, the fragmentation, the increasingly fast changes that made human connections transitory. Nostalgia was a safety valve, a way of getting perspective.

THE CALM AND QUIET pervading William Churchill's *Leisure* was newly appreciated as sentimental painting of the nineteenth and twentieth centuries rode the nostalgia wave back into favor. The picture was included in the Whitney Museum of American Art exhibition "The Painters' America: Rural and Urban Life, 1810-1910" in the fall.

Quotations of the Year

January

"Through the exploitation of cheap oil, you had your affluent society and then the permissive society in which almost everything was free and freedom was abused . . . the era of cheap oil is past."

—The Shah of Iran.

February

"I do not expect to be impeached."

—President Richard Nixon.

March

"I propose an extraordinary act of statesmanship and courage — an act at once noble and heartbreaking, at once serving the greater interests of the nation, the institution of the presidency, and the stated goals for which he so successfully campaigned. That act is Richard Nixon's own voluntary resignation as president of the United States."

—Senator James L. Buckley, conservative Republican of New York.

April

"When I hit the next one I'll probably run around the bases backwards."

—Henry Aaron, after hitting his 714th home run to tie Babe Ruth's record.

May

"It is nothing to get excited about. We are firmly committed only to the peaceful uses of atomic energy."

—Prime Minister Indira Gandhi, commenting on India's nuclear test.

"Somewhere between my ambition and my ideals I lost my ethical compass. I found myself on a path that had not been intended for me by my parents or my principles or by my own ethical instincts. It has led me to this courtroom."

—Jeb Stuart Magruder, before being sentenced for his role in the Watergate conspiracy.

June

"I do not believe it is possible to conduct the foreign policy of the United States under these circumstances when the character and credibility of the secretary of state is at issue. And if it is not cleared up, I will resign."

—Secretary of State Henry Kissinger.

July

"To read the powers of the president as providing an absolute privilege as against a subpoena essential to enforcement of criminal statutes on no more than a generalized claim of the public interest in confidentiality of nonmilitary and nondiplomatic discussions would upset the constitutional balance of a 'workable government' and gravely impair the role of the courts."

—The Supreme Court.

August

"I am acutely aware that you have not elected me as your president by your ballots. So I ask you to confirm me as your president with your prayers."

—President Gerald Ford at his swearing-in.

September

"Let us not delude ourselves. Failure to cooperate on oil and food and inflation could spell disaster for every nation represented in this room."

—President Gerald Ford, addressing the U.N. General Assembly.

October

"There is only one point on which all advisers have agreed: We must whip inflation right now."

—President Gerald Ford in his message to Congress.

"There is no war, nuclear or conventional, by which the so-called winner, assuming there was one, could conceivably win back by war the resources used and destroyed in waging it."

—Prime Minister Gough Whitlam of Australia, addressing the United Nations.

November

"It is inadmissible that those who have control of the wealth and resources of mankind should try to resolve the problems of hunger by forbidding the poor to be born."

—Pope Paul VI, addressing delegates to the World Food Conference.

"I have come bearing an olive branch and a freedom fighter's gun. Do not let the olive branch fall from my hand."

—Yasir Arafat, addressing the U.N. General Assembly.

December

"I feel as though this was the most thorough examination that has ever been made of any citizen in this country."

—Vice-President-designate Nelson Rockefeller, after hearings on his nomination ended.

Calendar of 1975 Events

"GOOD GRIEF . . . We're outta gas." This cartoon by Jeff MacNelly of the *Richmond* (Va.) *News Leader* won first prize in the editorial cartoon "Dragonslayer" contest sponsored by the U.S. Industrial Council.

			1	2	3	4
5	6	7	8	9	10	11
12	13	14	15	16	17	18
19	20	21	22	23	24	25
26	27	28	29	30	31	

JANUARY . . .

1. New Year's Day. Legal holiday in all states and territories.

Rose Bowl Football Game. Pasadena, Calif.

4. Hula Bowl Game. Annual football classic. Honolulu, Hawaii.

6. Twelfth Day or Epiphany. Known also as Christmas Day and Twelfth-tide.

9. Richard Milhous Nixon's Birthday. Thirty-seventh president of the United States. Born in 1913.

11. Senior Bowl All-Star Football Game.

15. Martin Luther King's Birthday. Born in 1929. Died April 4, 1968.

16. National Nothing Day. Purpose: To provide Americans with one national day when they can just sit without celebrating, observing, or honoring anything.

30. Franklin D. Roosevelt's Birthday. Thirty-second president of the United States, born in 1882. Died April 12, 1945.

						1
2	3	4	5	6	7	8
9	10	11	12	13	14	15
16	17	18	19	20	21	22
23	24	25	26	27	28	

FEBRUARY . . .

1. American Heart Month. By presidential proclamation.

National Freedom Day. By presidential proclamation.

2. Groundhog Day.

3. Abraham Lincoln's Birthday. Observed on this day in Delaware and Oregon.

8. Boy Scouts of America Sixty-Fifth Birthday Anniversary.

9. National Crime Prevention Week.

11. Mardi Gras. New Orleans, La. Last feast before Lent.

Shrove Tuesday. Always the day before Ash Wednesday. Sometimes called Pancake Tuesday.

12. Abraham Lincoln's Birthday Observed on this

1975 CALENDAR

"THE NAME of the game is 'nostalgia'."

day in most states. Sixteenth president of United States. Born in 1809. Died April 15, 1865.

Ash Wednesday. Lent begins.

14. St. Valentine's Day.

17. George Washington's Birthday. Legal holiday applicable to federal employees and to the District of Columbia.

22. George Washington's Birthday. First president of United States. Born in 1732. Died Dec. 14, 1799.

23. Daylight Saving Time begins at 2:00 A.M. (except where state legislatures provide exemption).

						1
2	3	4	5	6	7	8
9	10	11	12	13	14	15
16	17	18	19	20	21	22
23	24	25	26	27	28	29
30	31					

MARCH . . .

1. Red Cross Month. By presidential proclamation.

2. Save Your Vision Week. By presidential proclamation.

9. Girl Scout Week.

16. National Boys' Club Week.

National Poison Prevention Week. By presidential proclamation.

17. St. Patrick's Day.

19. Swallows Return to San Juan Capistrano. Traditional date since 1776 for swallows to return to old mission of San Juan Capistrano, Calif.

23. Holy Week. The week before Easter, beginning on Palm Sunday and ending with Easter Eve. Memorializes the suffering of Christ.

Palm Sunday.

27. Pesach or Passover, First Day. Jewish Holy Day, also observed following day. Begins eight-day celebration of delivery of Jews from slavery in Egypt.

28. Good Friday. Observed

1975 CALENDAR

in commemoration of the crucifixion. Oldest Christian celebration.

30. Easter Sunday. Most joyous festival of Christian year.

		1	2	3	4	5
6	7	8	9	10	11	12
13	14	15	16	17	18	19
20	21	22	23	24	25	26
27	28	29	30			

APRIL . . .

1. April Fools' or All Fools' Day.

Cancer Control Month. By presidential proclamation.

5. National Cherry Blossom Festival. To celebrate the blossoming of Japanese cherry trees in Washington, D.C., and herald the opening of the spring season in the nation's capital.

8. National Panic Week. To inject a little humor into any situation which seems to create unnecessary panic.

13. Pan American Week. By presidential proclamation.

15. I Gave Day. (Income tax deadline) To inflame taxpayers at the thought their taxes are even higher because of tax exemptions of contribution-beggars.

23. Secretaries' Day.

				1	2	3
4	5	6	7	8	9	10
11	12	13	14	15	16	17
18	19	20	21	22	23	24
25	26	27	28	29	30	31

MAY . . .

1. Law Day. By presidential proclamation.

Loyalty Day. By presidential proclamation.

May Day. Celebrated by many peoples for many reasons since remote times. Now a holiday celebrated throughout much of world commemorating the international solidarity of workingmen. Recognized as a labor holiday since the agitation by labor organizations in the United States in 1886 for the establishment of the eight-hour day.

3. Kentucky Derby. Churchill Downs, Louisville, Ky.

8. Ascension Day. Forty days after Easter Sunday. Commemorates Christ's ascension into Heaven. Observed since A.D. 68.

"DO you realize that while we sleep, inflation doesn't?"

1975 CALENDAR

End of World War II in Europe.

Harry S. Truman's Birthday. Thirty-third president of the United States. Born in 1884. Died Dec. 26, 1972.

11. Mother's Day. By presidential proclamation.

Police Week. By presidential proclamation.

17. Armed Forces Day. By presidential proclamation.

24. Total Eclipse of the Moon. Visible in all but northwestern part of North America.

T.U.R.T.L.E.S. DAY (TAKE UR TIME; LET's EVERYONE SLOW-DOWN!) To underscore the need for conservation of energy.

26. Prayer for Peace, Memorial Day. By presidential proclamation.

29. John F. Kennedy's Birthday. Thirty-fifth president of the United States. Born in 1917. Died Nov. 22, 1963.

1	2	3	4	5	6	7
8	9	10	11	12	13	14
15	16	17	18	19	20	21
22	23	24	25	26	27	28
29	30					

JUNE . . .

6. D-Day Anniversary. Allied Expeditionary Force landed in Normandy on this date in 1944.

8. National Flag Week. By presidential proclamation.

9. National Little League Baseball Week. By presidential proclamation.

14. Flag Day. By presidential proclamation.

15. Father's Day.

21. Summer Begins. 7:27 P.M., EST.

29. National Safe Boating Week. By presidential proclamation.

		1	2	3	4	5
6	7	8	9	10	11	12
13	14	15	16	17	18	19
20	21	22	23	24	25	26
27	28	29	30	31		

JULY . . .

4. Fourth of July or Inde-

"I TRIED to beat them for seventy bucks . . . How about you?" Paul Szep's editorial cartoon for the *Boston Globe* was one of several that won him the Pulitzer prize for cartooning in May.

pendence Day.

8. Nelson Aldrich Rockefeller's Birthday. Forty-first vice-president of United States. Born in 1908.

14. Gerald Rudolph Ford's Birthday. Thirty-eighth president of United States. Born in 1913.

15. St. Swithin's Day. Rain for forty days hereafter when it falls on this day, according to old English belief.

17. Tish'Ah B'Ab or Fast of Ab. Jewish holy day.

20. Moon Day. Anniversary of man's first landing on moon.

25. National Farm Safety Week. By presidential proclamation.

					1	2
3	4	5	6	7	8	9
10	11	12	13	14	15	16
17	18	19	20	21	22	23
24	25	26	27	28	29	30
31						

AUGUST . . .

3. National Smile Week. To encourage everyone to look at the bright side of things and put on a happy face.

14. Victory Day or V.J. Day. (End of World War II in Japan.)

19. National Aviation Day. By presidential proclamation.

27. Lyndon B. Johnson's Birthday. Thirty-sixth president of United States. Born in 1908. Died Jan. 22, 1973.

	1	2	3	4	5	6
7	8	9	10	11	12	13
14	15	16	17	18	19	20
21	22	23	24	25	26	27
28	29	30				

SEPTEMBER . . .

1. Labor Day. Legal public holiday.

6. Rosh Hashanah or Jewish New Year. Jewish holy day.

15. Yom Kippur or Day of Atonement. Holiest Jewish observance.

17. Citizenship Day. By presidential proclamation.

Constitution Week. By presidential proclamation.

23. Autumn begins at 10:55 A.M., EST.

28. Gold Star Mothers' Day. By presidential proclamation.

			1	2	3	4
5	6	7	8	9	10	11
12	13	14	15	16	17	18
19	20	21	22	23	24	25
26	27	28	29	30	31	

OCTOBER . . .

5. Fire Prevention Week. By presidential proclamation.

National Employ the Physically Handicapped Week. By presidential proclamation.

13. Columbus Day. By presidential proclamation.

14. Dwight D. Eisenhower's Birthday. Thirty-fourth president of United States. Born in 1890. Died March 28, 1969.

15. National Day of Prayer. By presidential proclamation. (Set by the president annually on a day other than Sunday.)

White Cane Safety Day. By presidential proclamation.

18. Sweetest Day.

23. Swallows depart from San Juan Capistrano.

24. United Nations Day. By presidential proclamation.

26. American Education Week. By presidential proclamation.

Standard Time begins at 2:00 A.M.

27. Veterans' Day. Legal public holiday.

31. National UNICEF Day. By presidential proclamation.

Trick or Treat or **Beggar's Night.**

						1
2	3	4	5	6	7	8
9	10	11	12	13	14	15
16	17	18	19	20	21	22
23	24	25	26	27	28	29
30						

NOVEMBER . . .

1. All Saints Day.

2. All Souls Day. Commemorates the faithful departed. Catholic observance.

11. Armistice Day. Also recognized in some places as Remembrance Day, Veterans Day, Victory Day, and World War I Memorial Day.

18. Total Eclipse of the Moon. Partially visible in North America.

27. Thanksgiving Day. By presidential proclamation.

	1	2	3	4	5	6
7	8	9	10	11	12	13
14	15	16	17	18	19	20
21	22	23	24	25	26	27
28	29	30	31			

DECEMBER . . .

2. Pan American Health Day. By presidential proclamation.

7. Pearl Harbor Day.

10. Nobel Peace Prize. Presentation of world renowned Nobel Peace Prize in Oslo by the Nobel Committee of Norwegian Parliament.

22. Winter begins at 6:46 A.M., EST.

25. Christmas Day. Celebrated throughout the United States, its territories, and the rest of the Christian world.

31. New Year's Eve.

Sugar Bowl Football Classic. New Orleans, La., Superdome.

1975 Index . . .

B

C

D

E

F

G

H

I

J

K

1975 INDEX

T

U

V

1975 INDEX

PHOTOGRAPHIC CREDITS: 1-3, Joseph Fire, *Modern Maturity Magazine;* 6-7, © 1974, Science Research Associates, Inc., reproduced by permission of the publisher; 8-9, courtesy Rockwell International; 11, Rohn Engh, *Modern Maturity Magazine;* 12, courtesy *The Orange Disc,* Gulf Oil Corporation; 12, 14, John Keller, *The Texaco Star;* 13, *Farm Journal;* 15, Fruehauf Corporation; 16, Joseph Brignolo, *The Texaco Star;* 21, Ethiopian Airlines; 22, 27, Wendy Watriss, courtesy *Signature Magazine;* 25, *ZooNooz,* San Diego Zoo; 28, photo by William B. Potter, courtesy *PPG Products;* 30, 32, courtesy *PPG Products Magazine,* PPG Industries, Inc.; 31, Standard Oil Company of California; 33, British Information Services; 33, British Press Service; 34, Smithsonian Institution; 36, The Detroit Institute of Arts, gift of The Kresge Foundation and Mrs. Edsel B. Ford; 36, National Gallery of Art, Washington, Ailsa Mellon Bruce Fund; 41, Official U.S. Navy Photograph; 63, Farrar, Strauss and Giroux; 65, 87, 92, *Life,* © Time, Inc.; 67, 68, 71, John Keller, *The Texaco Star;* 68, Canadian National Railways, reprinted from *International Nickel Magazine* 1970/2, published by the International Nickel Company, Inc.; 69, Confederation Life Collection; 73, *Pontiac Safari Magazine;* 75, *The Texaco Star;* 77, National Park Service, courtesy *Friends Magazine;* 78-79, Geigy Pharmaceuticals; 81, 83, photos by Ed Aber, *Soldiers;* 84-85, photo by Joseph Brignolo, *The Texaco Star;* 90-91, 92, 93, 95, photo, Arthur W. Galston, *Natural History;* 94, 95, 96, reprinted from May, 1974, *Psychology Today Magazine,* © 1974 Ziff-Davis Publishing Company, all rights reserved; 109, 110, Michael Cope; 111, P. and A. Photo; 125, United Nations; 126, United Nations/T. Chen; 129, International Nickel Co., Inc.; 130, *The Texaco Star;* 131, *Commerce Magazine;* 132-133, John Vachon, *Signature Magazine;* 134-135, Howard Sochurek, *Signature Magazine;* 138-139, Czech Government Committee for Tourism, *Travel Magazine;* 142, The Sheffield Tube Corporation, New London, Conn.; 143, *Friends Magazine;* 144-145, Western Electric Co.; 147, The United States Fidelity and Guaranty Company; 148, 153, Prudential Insurance Company of America; 150-151, permission granted by City Art Museum of St. Louis, National Historical Society, *American History Magazine;* 155, *PPG Magazine;* 159, Joseph Brignolo, *The Texaco Star;* 160, Harry M. Caudill, *American Forests Magazine;* 163, Bucyrus-Erie Co.; 165, Warner Bros.; 171, Hunton, USDA; 172, Sugar Research Foundation; 173, Bob Taylor; 195, CBS; 199, Levitt and Sons, Inc.; 212, British Travel Association; 225, photo by Ernst A. Jahn, *Americas;* 226, photo by Hubert Pryor, *Modern Maturity;* 229, 231, 248, Standard Oil Co.; 230, *Sierra Club Bulletin;* 233, Josef Muench, courtesy *Arizona Highways;* 234, Harvey Caplin photo; 226, Montana State Highway Commission; 237, 240, 241, 242-243, 245, 246, Joseph Brignolo, *The Texaco Star;* 238, *The Texaco Star;* 240, 241, Robert Isear, courtesy *The Lamp,* Standard Oil Company of New Jersey; 252, Robert Stahman, *Signature Magazine;* 252, 252-253, *Farm Journal;* 255, Sperry Univac, Division of Sperry Rand Corporation; 259, Radovan, The Hebrew University of Jerusalem; 263, Ideal Toy Corporation; 273, Toronto Star Syndicate; 276, UNICEF; 278, Queens Borough Public Library; 292, 296, 299, United Nations; 309, British Travel Association; 310, United Fruit Company; 316, 319, Europa Press; 321, photo by John H. Whitehead, Oxford Paper; 322, *Chemical and Engineering News;* 325, SSG David Hinkle, *Army Digest;* 326, Howard A. Feldman, Carte Blanche Corp.; 327, 338, Elaine Powell, *American Forests Magazine;* 329, reprinted from *International Nickel Magazine* 1970/4, published by The International Nickel Company, Inc.; 332, Museum of American Folk Art, Carte Blanche Corp.; 335, Michael Philip Manheim, courtesy *Dodge News Magazine;* 340, George Silk, *Life,* © Time, Inc.; 341, Scandinavian Airlines; 344-345, *The Orange Disc,* Gulf Oil Corporation; 347, *The Texaco Star;* 349, *ZooNooz Magazine,* Zoological Society of San Diego, San Diego Zoo; 350, Carte Blanche Corp., courtesy Museum of Fine Arts, Boston, M. and M. Karolik Collection; 351, Eli Lilly and Company; 352, 354, Victor Hagen, *Travel Magazine;* 353, 355, George Armstrong; 356, *Commerce Magazine;* 357, 359, 373, 374, 375, 379, 381, courtesy *The Orange Disc,* Gulf Oil Corporation; 358, Joseph Brignolo, *The Texaco Star;* 359, Ed Aber, *Soldiers Magazine;* 360, courtesy *PPG Products Magazine,* PPG Industries, Inc.; 361, *Steelways Magazine;* 362, 364, 369, *The Texaco Star;* 366, 367, reprinted from *International Nickel Magazine* 1970/1, published by the International Nickel Company, Inc.; 370-371, 377, *Life Magazine* © 1966; 382, 383, NASA, *Life* © Time, Inc.; 384, U.S. Steel; 385, drawing by Ed Fisher; © 1973 *The New Yorker Magazine,* Inc.; 390, NASA; 394, 398, Europa Press; 397, BP Singer Features; 400, BOAC; 401, Ed Lark; 412, BBC Copyright Photograph; 412, CBS; 413, Alexander von Mokos; 417, 421, United Nations/T. Chen; 422, James B. Bladen, Military Pictures of the Year; 436, Rheinisches Bildarchiv; UPI, 17, 40, 42, 49, 52, 103, 104, 113, 116, 119, 120, 123, 124, 125, 127, 128, 170, 178, 180, 184, 185, 186, 187, 188, 192, 207, 227, 228, 229, 261, 262, 263, 264, 267, 301, 314, 323, 363, 393, 405, 410, 427, 430, 432, 434, 449, 451; Wide World, 46, 47, 105, 108, 115, 117, 122, 127, 170, 176, 177, 184, 185, 187, 188, 189, 208, 221, 223, 263, 264, 275, 280, 300, 302, 313, 337, 339, 395, 403, 414, 416, 455.

Our Family's History

For the Year

"The Man of the Year"

The family's favorite picture of Father goes here.

Name ________________________________

"The Woman of the Year"

The family's favorite picture of Mother goes here.

Name ________________________________

OUR FAMILY TREE

Our Children's

SPECIAL ACHIEVEMENTS

Name__________

Achievement No. 1__________

Achievement No. 2__________

Achievement No. 3__________

Name__________

Achievement No. 1__________

Achievement No. 2__________

Achievement No. 3__________

Name__________

Achievement No. 1__________

Achievement No. 2__________

Achievement No. 3__________

Name__________

Achievement No. 1__________

Achievement No. 2__________

Achievement No. 3__________

Name__________

Achievement No. 1__________

Achievement No. 2__________

Achievement No. 3

Name____

Celebrated____________birthday on____________________

at______________________with__________________guests.

Remarks____

____

Name____

Celebrated____________birthday on____________________

at______________________with__________________guests.

Remarks____

____

Name____

Celebrated____________birthday on____________________

at______________________with__________________guests.

Remarks____

____

Name____

Celebrated____________birthday on____________________

at______________________with__________________guests.

Remarks____

____

Name____

Celebrated____________birthday on____________________

at______________________with__________________guests.

Remarks____

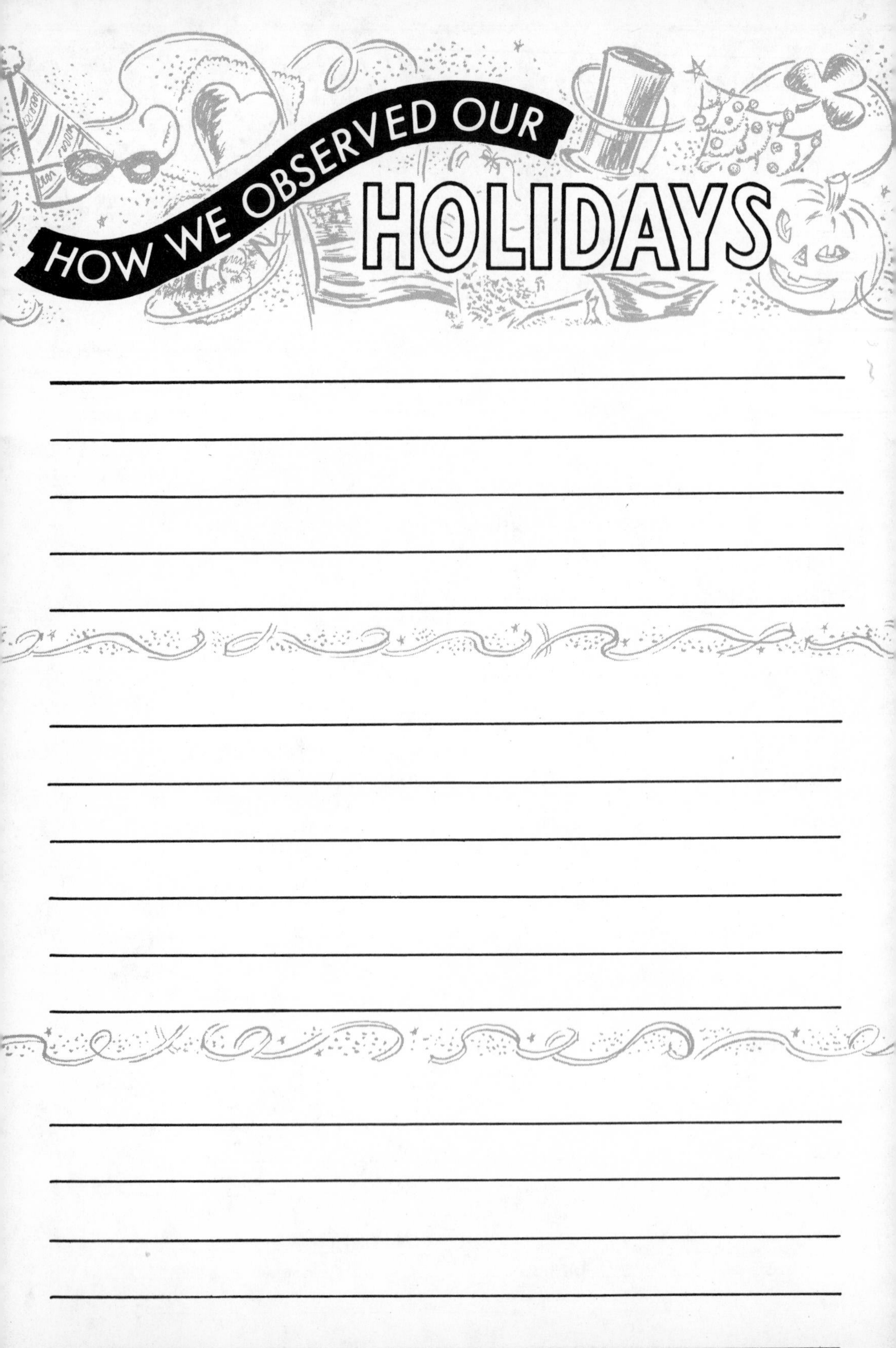
HOW WE OBSERVED OUR
HOLIDAYS

MEMORABLE FAMILY EVENTS

Weddings

Baby's First Word

Promotions

Baby's First Footstep

New Home

Births

Anniversaries

Event ____________________

Date ____________ Remarks ____________________

____

Event ____________________

Date ____________ Remarks ____________________

____

Event ____________________

Date ____________ Remarks ____________________

____

Event ____________________

Date ____________ Remarks ____________________

____

Event ____________________

Date ____________ Remarks ____________________

OUR VACATION

WHERE WE WENT ____________________

HOW ____________________

WHEN ____________________

The biggest thrill of our vacation was ____________________

VACATION HIGHLIGHTS

IN STORY OR PICTURES OR BOTH

FAMILY HEALTH RECORD

	June	December
NAME		
WEIGHT		
HEIGHT		
NAME		
WEIGHT		
HEIGHT		
NAME		
WEIGHT		
HEIGHT		
NAME		
WEIGHT		
HEIGHT		

Inoculations:

EDUCATIONAL HONORS

Name______________________________ Level______________
(Grade or Year)

Honor____

Name______________________________ Level______________
(Grade or Year)

Honor____

Name______________________________ Level______________
(Grade or Year)

Honor____

Name______________________________ Level______________
(Grade or Year)

Honor____

GRADUATIONS

Name____________________ Graduated from____________________

______________________________ Date____________________

Name____________________ Graduated from____________________

______________________________ Date____________________

Cumulative Index . . . 1971-1974

This index covers past year books from 1971 through 1974. The index for this year's book begins on page 464.

The year in which an article or reference occurred is given first; the page numbers follow the colon (for example, **Buddhism**, 1972:176, 177). When an entry appears in more than one year book, the references are given in chronological order. Obit. stands for obituary.

INDEX FOR 1975 YEAR BOOK BEGINS ON PAGE 464.

INDEX FOR 1975 YEAR BOOK BEGINS ON PAGE 464.

B

INDEX FOR 1975 YEAR BOOK BEGINS ON PAGE 464.

INDEX FOR 1975 YEAR BOOK BEGINS ON PAGE 464.

INDEX FOR 1975 YEAR BOOK BEGINS ON PAGE 464.

INDEX FOR 1975 YEAR BOOK BEGINS ON PAGE 464.

INDEX FOR 1975 YEAR BOOK BEGINS ON PAGE 464.

D

INDEX FOR 1975 YEAR BOOK BEGINS ON PAGE 464.

INDEX FOR 1975 YEAR BOOK BEGINS ON PAGE 464.

INDEX FOR 1975 YEAR BOOK BEGINS ON PAGE 464.

G

INDEX FOR 1975 YEAR BOOK BEGINS ON PAGE 464.

INDEX FOR 1975 YEAR BOOK BEGINS ON PAGE 464.

I

INDEX FOR 1975 YEAR BOOK BEGINS ON PAGE 464.

INDEX FOR 1975 YEAR BOOK BEGINS ON PAGE 464.

INDEX FOR 1975 YEAR BOOK BEGINS ON PAGE 464.

M

INDEX FOR 1975 YEAR BOOK BEGINS ON PAGE 464.

INDEX FOR 1975 YEAR BOOK BEGINS ON PAGE 464.

INDEX FOR 1975 YEAR BOOK BEGINS ON PAGE 464.

INDEX FOR 1975 YEAR BOOK BEGINS ON PAGE 464.

O

INDEX FOR 1975 YEAR BOOK BEGINS ON PAGE 464.

P

INDEX FOR 1975 YEAR BOOK BEGINS ON PAGE 464.

Q

INDEX FOR 1975 YEAR BOOK BEGINS ON PAGE 464.

INDEX FOR 1975 YEAR BOOK BEGINS ON PAGE 464.

INDEX FOR 1975 YEAR BOOK BEGINS ON PAGE 464.

INDEX FOR 1975 YEAR BOOK BEGINS ON PAGE 464.

INDEX FOR 1975 YEAR BOOK BEGINS ON PAGE 464.

INDEX FOR 1975 YEAR BOOK BEGINS ON PAGE 464.

INDEX FOR 1975 YEAR BOOK BEGINS ON PAGE 464.

INDEX FOR 1975 YEAR BOOK BEGINS ON PAGE 464.

INDEX FOR 1975 YEAR BOOK BEGINS ON PAGE 464.